INSIDERS' GUIDE®

INSIDERS' GUIDE® SERIES

INSIDERS' GUIDE® TO

THE GREAT SMOKY MOUNTAINS

FOURTH EDITION

DICK McHUGH AND MITCH MOORE

INSIDERS' GUIDE®

GUILFORD, CONNECTICUT

AN IMPRINT OF THE GLOBE PEQUOT PRESS

The prices and rates in this guidebook were confirmed at press time. We recommend, however, that you call establishments before traveling to obtain current information.

INSIDERS' GUIDE®

Text design by LeAnna Weller Smith
Map design by XNR Production, Inc. © The Globe Pequot Press

ISSN 1542-5193
ISBN 0-7627-3504-X

Manufactured in the United States of America
Fourth Edition/First Printing

Great Smoky Mountains. CITY OF GATLINBURG DEPT OF TOURISM & CONVENTION CENTER

[Top] *Mountain overview.* CITY OF GATLINBURG DEPT OF TOURISM & CONVENTION CENTER
[Bottom] *Cades Cove.* CITY OF GATLINBURG DEPT OF TOURISM & CONVENTION CENTER

Roan Mountain. CITY OF GATLINBURG DEPT OF TOURISM & CONVENTION CENTER

Daredevil Falls. DOLLYWOOD

[Top] *Dolly Parton.* DOLLYWOOD
[Bottom] *Bumper boats at an amusement center in Pigeon Forge.* DICK McHUGH

75-year-old taffy machine at the Old Mill Candy Kitchen. MITCH MOORE

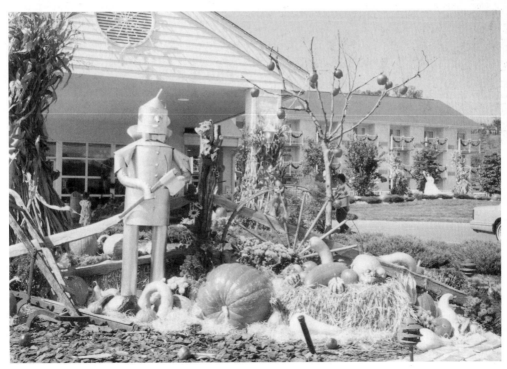

[Top] *1870s church on Bird's Creek Road between Pigeon Forge and Gatlinburg.* DICK McHUGH
[Bottom] *Comfort Inn Apple Valley decorates for the Harvest Festival.* MITCH MOORE

[Top] *Locomotive in Townsend.* MITCH MOORE
[Bottom] *Covered bridge crossing the Little Pigeon River in Pittman Center.* DICK MCHUGH

The Biltmore Estate is one of the area's top destinations. BILTMORE ESTATE

Sunset in the Great Smoky Mountains. CITY OF GATLINBURG DEPT OF TOURISM & CONVENTION CENTER

The Village, Gatlinburg, a charming slice of the Old World. CITY OF GATLINBURG DEPT OF TOURISM & CONVENTION CENTER

Shopping in downtown Gatlinburg. CITY OF GATLINBURG DEPT OF TOURISM & CONVENTION CENTER

Skyview of the City of Gatlinburg. CITY OF GATLINBURG DEPT OF TOURISM & CONVENTION CENTER

CONTENTS

CONTENTS

Directory of Maps

Smokies Overview

to I-40

to Douglas Dam Park

WINFIELD DUNN SCENIC PKWY.

66

Douglas Dam Rd. 338

411 441

SEVIER ST.

Middle Prong

NICHOLS ST.

MAIN ST.

■ **Courthouse**

DOLLY PARTON PKWY.

411

BRUCE ST.

CEDAR ST.

PRINCE ST.

■ **Community Center and Civic Center**

66

Little Pigeon River

Winfield Dunn Scenic Pkwy.

West Prong

FORKS OF THE RIVER PKWY.

COURT AVE.

PARKWAY

GARY WADE BLVD.

McMAHAN AVE.

HENDERSON AVE.

PARK RD.

441

EASTGATE RD.

Area of Inset

Main St. 411 441 35

to Knoxville

Middle Prong Little Pigeon River

W. Prong Little Pigeon River

Sevier County High School
■ Dolly Parton Pkwy.

to Newport

35

411

E. Fork

Pittman Center Rd.

Middle Prong

Industrial Park Rd.

416

Hospital Ⓗ

Middle Creek Rd.

Parkway

Park Rd.

441

Entrance to Governor's Crossing

Collier Dr.

71

Governor's Crossing ■

to Pittman Center Rd.

Apple Valley Rd.

🚦1A

Music Rd.

Jayell Rd.

Ridge Rd.

Middle Creek Rd.

321 321

73

441

71

to Pigeon Forge

to Dollywood

🚦1A Numbered traffic lights

N

0   1   2 km
0   1   2 mi.

Sevierville, Tennessee

Pigeon Forge, Tennessee

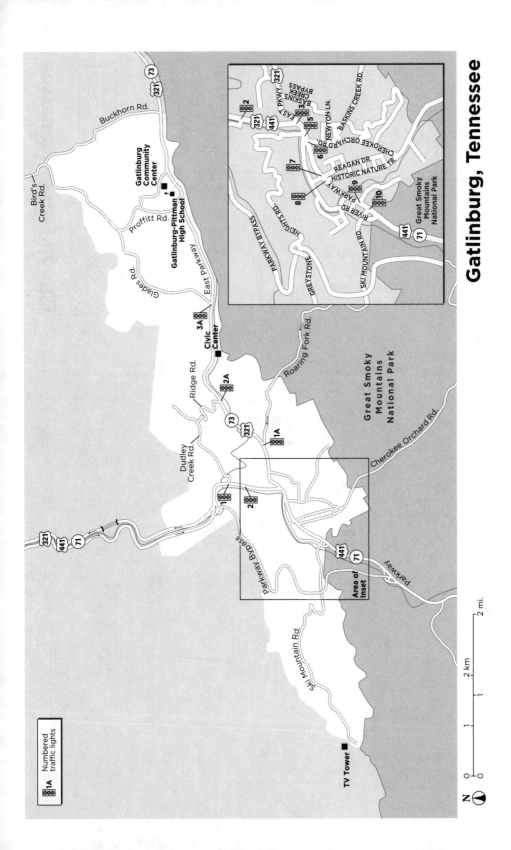

Gatlinburg, Tennessee

Numbered
traffic lights

Buckhorn Rd.
Bird's Creek Rd.
321
73
Gatlinburg Community Center
Gatlinburg-Pittman High School
Proffitt Rd.
Glades Rd.
East Parkway
Ridge Rd.
Dudley Creek Rd.
3A
Civic Center
2A
73
321
1A
Roaring Fork Rd.
Parkway Bypass
Ski Mountain Rd.
Area of Inset
Parkway
321
441
71
441
71
TV Tower
Great Smoky Mountains National Park
Cherokee Orchard Rd.

321
73
2
321
441
EAST PKWY.
BASKINS CREEK BYPASS
321
5
NEWTON LN.
BASKINS CREEK RD.
CHEROKEE ORCHARD RD.
6
7
REAGAN DR.
HISTORIC NATURE TR.
8
9
HEIGHTS RD.
PARKWAY BYPASS
GREYSTONE
RIVER RD.
PARKWAY
SKI MOUNTAIN RD.
10
441
71
Great Smoky Mountains National Park

N

0   1   2 mi.
0   1   2 km

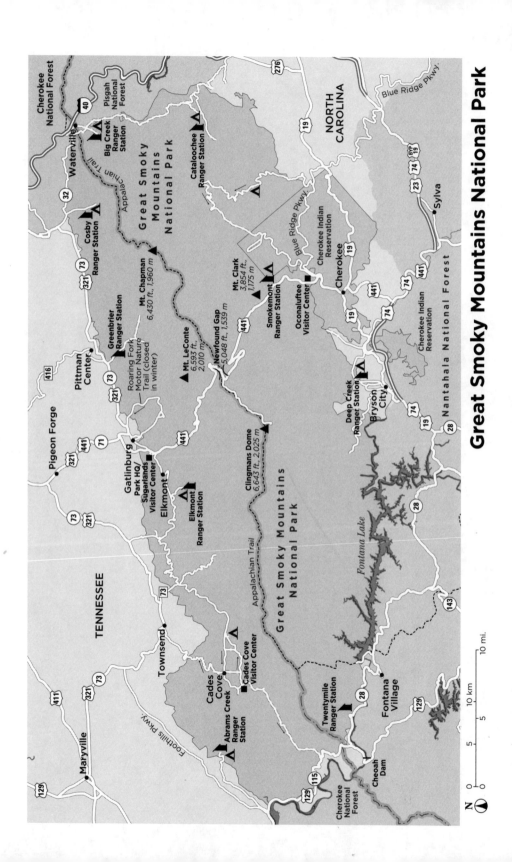

Great Smoky Mountains National Park

ACKNOWLEDGMENTS

I'm fortunate to have discovered this area a few years before most of the rest of the world, and to have adopted it as my home on its merits as a place in which to live and raise children. Because I got here when Gatlinburg was a small town and Sevier County was an insular community, I am privileged to know a few more people than those who followed me, and to share the belief that it's still a tight society if you want it to be. To that end, the best way to express my gratitude on a personal level would be to refer the reader to the 1976 Sevier County telephone book, where most of us have friends and family on every one of its 37 pages.

In the case of this book, I'm particularly grateful to a large group of friends and acquaintances who came forward with information when they learned about the project. That saved a lot of wear and tear on the little fat guy. Specifically, and with full and apologetic knowledge that somebody's going to be left out, I particularly thank two groups: On the professional side, thanks to my good friend and frequent co-conspirator Gordon Brugman, whose photographic skills saved me a lot of footwork, and whose outrageous sense of humor keeps me on as even a keel as I can maintain; to Jan Brugman, the all-American girl who shares Gordon's life and his love of photography; to Betty Webb, my long-time friend at Gatlinburg's splendid Anna Porter Library, for her untiring patience in helping me find a lot of really obscure information, and her encyclopedic memory that filled in a lot of gaps; and to Kay Powell, Pigeon Forge's indefatigable tourism director, who actually knows what's going on in that amazing city from day to day. Personally, and here's where I'm probably going to drop more balls than I catch, I'm grateful to my Saturday night poker gang—Mac and Susie Macdonell, Marilyn and sometimes Bob Gosse, Betty and Cecil Posey, and Harry Maloney, for passing along every tidbit of information and gossip so that I knew what was happening locally; to Connie and Arne Walker, Barry and Karen Jinks, Lori Tierney, and a bunch of others who never lost faith that someday I'd finish this job; very importantly, to my partner and friend Mitch Moore, whose marvelous talent for putting words on paper is combined with a finely tuned sense of the absurd that allowed him to work with the likes of me. And especially to you, dear reader, thanks for buying this book; I hope the lessons you learn from it are worth the cost; and, finally, to Joan, my life partner of 40-plus years, who brought me to this enchanted place, and who has rightfully maintained that we couldn't find a better place to grow old together.

—Dick McHugh

I presume that one of the reasons I was selected for this project was that I already knew quite a bit about this area. Having lived here for seven years at that point, I also had the advantage of a unique perspective—that of both newcomer and entrenched local. Regardless, I'm sure there are those around these parts who would balk at the notion of ever calling me a true "insider." After all, there is the school of thought that if you're not born and raised in the Smokies, you're not a local and you never will earn that status. Despite what any naysayers might claim, I think I've been here long enough to know what's what about a few things. But in the process of researching this book, I discovered there was still a whole lot I didn't know about this area. To those who helped me with those gaps in my Smokies education, I express my sincere thanks.

ACKNOWLEDGMENTS

I would like to single out the various departments of tourism and chambers of commerce in our cities of Sevierville, Pigeon Forge, and Gatlinburg whose assistance was valuable to me on a number of chapters; and every hotel, motel, restaurant, wedding chapel, go-kart track, attraction, real estate company, music theater, and retail shop that I peppered with my relentless questions.

I would like to thank Insiders' Guides, not only for giving me a regular writing gig for the better part of six years, but for the opportunity to get out there and really explore my home in the Smokies. I would also like to thank Colonial Real Estate for their invaluable assistance in updating the real estate chapter. Finally, I must extend my most sincere sentiments of gratitude to my coauthor and partner in crime, Dick McHugh. We had never met before teaming up for this book, and along the way we discovered that our respective areas of expertise complemented each other nicely—he being a Gatlinburg resident, knowledgeable of that end of the county, and I being the Seviervillian, quite familiar with that territory. Between the two of us, we hopefully did some justice to Pigeon Forge. Every step of the way it seemed that when one of us was lacking in one area, the other was able to take up the slack. The fact that we also share similar writing styles and a mutual admiration of the semicolon (much to the dismay of our editor) hopefully has made for a smooth, informative, entertaining read.

And thanks to you who have purchased this fourth edition of the *Insiders' Guide to the Great Smoky Mountains*. My wish is that through it, you'll be able to discover a quite unique little corner of America, just as some of us have managed to rediscover it.

—Mitch Moore

PREFACE

So you've got the Smokies on your mind. Good thinking! With upwards of 10 million people coming to visit this enchanted place every year, and more than a thousand of them deciding to stay in the area, you're in good company. If you're among the one-third of our visitors who come here at least once every three years, you've probably noticed that changes are afoot everywhere you look lately. And change is not something most of you come here to see. Take heart—what you came here for is still here. It's just that attitudes and appetites are changing, and a place that depends on tourism for its own survival has to make adjustments.

The difference between evolution and revolution is time. Evolution is an ongoing process that occurs naturally enough that no real change is noticed when things go along at their normal pace. Our mountains are a product of evolution; among the most ancient on Earth, the Great Smokies were once as tall as the Swiss Alps and rockier than the Rockies themselves. They were also at the bottom of a vast ocean.

As the rest of the planet changed to what it is today, so did the Smokies. Shaped and molded by nature's awesome hand for eons, the Smokies have been rounded into a beautiful, peaceful, accessible wilderness paradise that's yours to explore and fall in love with in a different way every time you enter it. The foothills at the northern edge of the Smokies are another story: Unprotected from the whims of capitalism and the entrepreneurial talents of the most progressive society in the history of the planet, what's going on in east Tennessee is anything but evolution. It isn't really a revolution, either; it's more of an explosion.

If you remember the Smokies of the 1970s and before, when people dropped in for a few days of rest beside a river, treat the memory like a child grown up: Cherish it . . . and let it go. You can still come to the Smokies and relax beside a river for a few days, but what you have to go through to get to that river has changed in ways you probably never imagined. The gentle folk of east Tennessee's Great Smoky Mountains, once a bastion of tranquility, have made some major concessions to the fact that today's American vacationer is looking for more than rippling water and breathtaking scenery. The biggest product of those concessions is that the big, open spaces you used to see on your way into Gatlinburg and Pigeon Forge are now filled with attractions and accommodations that make it possible for you to enjoy a week or more of your vacation time without getting within 10 miles of the mountains that used to be the primary attraction.

The mountains haven't changed. Great Smoky Mountains National Park is still at the end of the trail leading into the area, and so are those cool rippling streams in those friendly mountains that seem to want to enfold you in their warmth. The natives are still the same folks you can't quite forget when your stay ends. And the new residents, who used to be visitors like you, are still doing their best to emulate the friendliness of the natives.

East Tennessee's Smokies are a growing, happening place. Sevierville is awakening to the tourism market in ways that change for the better every day; Pigeon Forge is firmly established as a first-rate family destination; and Gatlinburg's world-famous craftspeople abound in greater numbers than ever before. And Great Smoky Mountains National Park is still the nation's most visited. What used to be, still is; there's just a whole lot of what's new in front of it, and more to come. You have a choice: Come to the new Smokies that are alive and throbbing to the beat of a new millennium, or come back to the Smokies that have always made you feel welcome and comfortable and sent you back home rested and at peace.

And if that Smoky Mountain smoke gets in your eyes, as the old song says, welcome back again. You'll love being here for the rest of your lives, and we'll see what we can do to help make your transition as smooth and easy as your decision to stay.

HOW TO USE THIS BOOK

The Great Smoky Mountains and their environs have been one of America's most popular tourist destinations for more than half a century, and it suddenly looks like the whole world has discovered the place all at once. The growth that's taken place in the Gatlinburg–Pigeon Forge–Sevierville area in the last several years is so rapid and so widespread that even the residents are losing track of it. There's so much to see and do in the Smokies that you can blow half your vacation trying to figure out what to do while you're here, and you probably didn't come to this peaceful place to get stressed out trying to cram all the enjoyment the place has to offer in the short time you've got. That's why we wrote this book.

Don't be intimidated by the size of this volume. A place that has as much going for it as the Smokies area takes a lot of explaining. Remember, this is a guide. You should carry it with you in your travels to help bring the kaleidoscope of things to do in the Smokies into focus. If you need help finding anything, look in the index under the subject heading that fits your question, then go to that chapter and you'll find the subject arranged from north to south, always starting with Sevierville and going southward through Pigeon Forge and Gatlinburg. And if you want to feel more like a local than a tourist, pay special attention to the Insiders' Tips, (marked with a ℹ️) and Close-ups in each chapter. Both will take you a little deeper into area lore, history and customs.

We've also included a chapter on Cherokee and the area in North Carolina immediately south of the national park. (For much more information on beautiful western North Carolina, we encourage you to pick up a copy of the *Insiders' Guide to North Carolina's Mountains*.)

The Great Smoky Mountains National Park is pretty well covered in its own chapter, but things that are as common to the park as they are to the cities, like campgrounds and annual events, will also be mentioned in the appropriate chapters. If you're looking for a specific place or business, flip to our comprehensive index to see where it's mentioned in the book.

We'd also like to point out rather proudly that the maps in this book are the most up-to-date available. Road construction is one of the biggest growth industries in the Smokies right now, and the changes are happening almost faster than the map producers can keep up with. What our maps show is current as of January 1, 2004. The chapters on Getting Here, Getting Around; Accommodations; and Attractions should be particularly helpful in showing frequent visitors what's new each year—if you haven't been here since 1996 or so, there are a few new places that'll blow you away!

Even if you live here or come often enough to qualify as a part-time resident, it's tough to stay abreast of the changes taking place along the northern half of the Smokies Corridor, from Interstate 40 to Pigeon Forge's northern city limits. We're taking special pains to document those changes as they occur.

As you travel through the Smokies Corridor, we hope you'll be impressed by the efforts of the municipal and park managers to provide directional signage. Sometimes it almost seems like overkill, but the prevailing attitude that too much is better than too little is characteristic of the local knowledge that tourism is the lifeblood of this area. The folks who built this industry did that on purpose, and they have a personal stake in seeing that you enjoy your stay, come back often, and tell your friends. This book is another link in the chain of information that supports the local efforts, and it's the only one we know of that encompasses the entire area as exhaustively. As the area continues to grow, we'll update this Insiders' Guide to stay abreast as best we can.

Your help will be appreciated—if you see something in the Smokies that we've omitted, or something we might have done a little better, let us know. Write to us at the *Insiders' Guide to the Great Smoky Mountains,* P.O. Box 480, Guilford, CT 06437-0480, or access our Web site at www.InsidersGuide.com with your comments (good or bad—we can take it), and your input will be part of our update efforts.

AREA OVERVIEW

Sevier County, Tennessee, home of Great Smoky Mountains National Park, is whatever the visitor or the prospective resident wants it to be. As the host area for the most-used entrance to America's most-visited national park, Sevier County (say "severe") has become a center for tourism, with all the advantages and disadvantages that attend such status. As a mostly rural county in some of east Tennessee's most beautiful and fertile countryside, it's a place where the family values generated by an agricultural lifestyle are still practiced and considered socially important. And as an area leader in light industry, Sevier County is undergoing significant change to attract new industrial business and new people to run it.

What it really boils down to is that Sevier County, Tennessee, originally occupied by white settlers around 1781 and established in 1784 as a part of Greene County in the ill-fated state of Franklin (see our History chapter), is a combination rarely found east of the Mississippi anymore. It's a settled area with a rich history that's world-famous for what it is today, and is just beginning to realize and develop its own potential. And for all that the Smokies Corridor is that makes it attractive to upwards of 10 million visitors annually, the future would be scary if it weren't planted in such a solid past.

At 660 square miles, Sevier County is among the largest in Tennessee, but the settled area this book deals with takes up less than 10 percent of that space. There is also the little matter of about 240 square miles of wilderness at the southern end of the county that's not available for any kind of development, and hopefully never will be—it comprises about 30 percent of Great Smoky Mountains National Park. It's as much a matter of topography as any other consideration that the corridor itself—defined by Winfield Dunn Parkway

(Tennessee Highway 66) south from exit 407 on Interstate 40 to its merge with U.S. Highway 441 in Sevierville, and then south through Pigeon Forge and Gatlinburg to the national park entrance—bisects the county from top to bottom. The Smokies Corridor does, however, encompass all four of the incorporated cities in Sevier County and includes about two-thirds of its 75,000-plus permanent population.

Sevier County is politically divided into four cities and a whole lot of unincorporated communities. The unincorporated areas, spelled out in our Neighborhoods and Real Estate chapter, depend on the county for educational services (see the Education chapter), police protection by the county sheriff, fire control by volunteer departments, ambulance service, and electric service. An elected commission of representatives from 15 civil districts oversees the operation of those facilities and departments necessary to govern any county; day-to-day operations are supervised by an elected county mayor. Although the influx of new population is bringing profound change to the political and economic face of the Smokies Corridor, it's still not a very good idea for anybody but a Republican to seek elected office in Sevier County.

The cities take care of their own police and fire/emergency services within their city limits, and each city also provides public works services at various levels. The cities deliver their refuse to a county-owned facility for disposal, and unincorporated areas have convenience stations where residents and businesses take their trash. The lone airport is jointly owned and operated by the cities of Gatlinburg and Pigeon Forge and is located within the city limits of Sevierville.

The three principal cities that make up the corridor (the fourth is a very special

Vital Statistics

Mayors: Sevierville—Bryan Atchley; Pigeon Forge—Ralph Chance; Gatlinburg—Jerry Hays; Pittman Center—Glen Cardwell

Governor: Phil Bredesen

Capital: Nashville

Major cities (in East Tennessee): Knoxville, Chattanooga

Outlying counties (surrounding Sevier): Knox, Blount, Cocke, Jefferson; Haywood (North Carolina)

Permanent population: Sevierville—12,000; Pigeon Forge—4,500; Gatlinburg—4,000; Pittman Center—600; Sevier County—75,503 (2002 Census); Tennessee—5,483,535 (2000 Census)

Area (Sevier County): 592 square miles (one-third of that lies in Great Smoky Mountains National Park)

Nickname: The Volunteer State

Motto: Agriculture and commerce (Authors' note: We know that's a terrible motto, but we verified it with multiple sources.)

Average temperatures:
    July (High/Low): 89/67
    January (High/Low): 42/25

State/cities founded: Tennessee—1796; Sevierville—1795; Pigeon Forge—1841; Gatlinburg—1807

Major universities: University of Tennessee, Carson Newman College

Important dates in history:

1781—First permanent white settlers in what are now Sevierville and Pigeon Forge

1785—Treaty of Dumplin Creek acquires Cherokee land for homesteading

1785—First formation of Sevier County

1796—Tennessee achieves statehood

1830—The Old Mill established in Pigeon Forge

1863—Battle of Gatlinburg

1864—Battle of Fairgarden

1896—Current county courthouse built

1901—Sevierville incorporated

1921—Pi Beta Phi settlement school established in Gatlinburg

1940—Dedication of Great Smoky Mountains National Park

1942—Gatlinburg incorporated

1943—TVA completes construction of Douglas Dam on French Broad River

1946—Pigeon Forge Pottery opens

1961—Pigeon Forge incorporated

1962—Ober Gatlinburg opens

1978—Gatlinburg's Great Smoky Arts & Crafts Community incorporated

1982—Pigeon Forge tourism snowballs thanks to Knoxville World's Fair

1983—Area's first outlet mall opens in Pigeon Forge

1986—Dollywood opens

2000—Ripley's Aquarium of the Smokies opens

2001—Dolly's Splash Country opens

2004—Bass ProShops Inc. breaks ground for sales/entertainment complex

Major area employers: Dollywood, TRW, Ober Gatlinburg, Ft. Sanders Sevier Medical Center

Famous native: Dolly Parton

Major airport: McGhee Tyson Airport, Alcoa

Major interstates: Interstates 40, 75, and 81

Public transportation: Municipal trolley systems in Pigeon Forge and Gatlinburg

Military bases: None

Driving laws: Seat belts, juvenile car seats, speed limits, wipers/headlights, HOV lanes, etc.

Alcohol laws: Age, DUI limit, buy on Sundays, buy in supermarkets

Daily newspapers: *The Mountain Press*, *Knoxville News Sentinel*

State sales tax: 7%

Municipal sales taxes: Gatlinburg and Pigeon Forge—2½%; Sevierville—2¾%

Hotel/motel surtax: Gatlinburg and Pigeon Forge—3½%

Restaurant surtax: Gatlinburg and Pigeon Forge—3%

Chamber of commerce/visitor center addresses and phone numbers:

Sevierville Chamber of Commerce
110 Gary Wade Boulevard
(800) 255-6411
(865) 453-6411

Gatlinburg Chamber of Commerce
811 East Parkway
(800) 568-4748
(865) 436-4178

Pigeon Forge Department of Tourism
1950 Parkway
(800) 251-9100
(865) 453-8574

Gatlinburg Visitors & Convention Bureau
234 Historic Nature Trail
(800) 343-1475
(865) 436-2392

Time/temperature phone number: (865) 453-6171

case that we'll deal with shortly) are still controlled primarily by the descendants of the original settlers of the area. Each is uniquely different from the others because of what it took to tame the land in the late 18th and early 19th centuries. The chapter on the county's history will cover in greater detail their individual development, but the differences in the roles the cities of Sevierville, Pigeon Forge, and Gatlinburg played in the evolution of the county are central to an understanding of how Sevier County operates. As usual, we'll start with Sevierville and proceed south, with one significant exception from the norm: This chapter will include the town of Pittman Center, an incorporated area east of Gatlinburg on U.S. Highway 321. Pittman Center is one of Tennessee's newest cities, incorporated in 1974, and so dedicated to the preservation of its mountain heritage that it officially discourages commercial development.

The definitive visitor to Sevier County is a tourist family. Mom, Dad, and the kids are here to have a good time in the middle of enough variety to satisfy everybody, and Tennessee's Great Smoky Mountains are going to see that enough satisfaction is delivered to keep the family coming back for generations to come. And if that tourist family happens to include a cleverly disguised industrial scout, we'll convince him that Sevier County has everything necessary to bring his business in: good roads, plenty of land to build a business and new homes, and a place to raise a family with strong roots.

SEVIERVILLE

Compared to its neighboring cities, the most unusual thing about Sevierville is its normality. Although Pigeon Forge and Gatlinburg are hopelessly synonymous with the tourism industry, Sevierville has

As you travel through Sevier County, particularly in the Sevierville area, you might notice a number of establishments that claim to be the "official" tourist information centers. Be aware that they are usually operated by vacation rental developers whose jobs are to give you some sort of sales pitch. Visitors are certainly under no obligation to participate, but sticking with the city-operated and -sanctioned information centers will ensure that you're not hit with the hard sell when all you're really interested in is learning about what there is to do in the Smokies.

managed to retain much of the virginal character of Small Town U.S.A. In fact, the local chamber of commerce bills it as "Your Hometown in the Smokies," and there's a lot of truth to that. If it were plucked out of the county and placed in another part of the state, Sevierville would likely sustain itself as it has for more than two centuries—with farming and industry as well as small businesses that are locally owned and cater to the townsfolk.

To be sure, Sevierville has begun to reap the economic benefits of tourism, as Pigeon Forge did in the 1980s and Gatlinburg before that. Accommodations, restaurants, shopping centers, and even music theaters have gradually become familiar fixtures on the Sevierville landscape. But even today, the town has its own distinct personality that, rather than being defined by tourism, has merely been complemented by it. Economically, the town is viable, not so much because of the influx of dollars from the Johnny-come-latelies, but because it has always been so (see the History chapter).

Much of Sevierville's flavor has as much to do with politics as it does economics. When the city was chosen to be the county seat in 1795, the stage was set for it to become a hub of governmental and commercial activity. Today, the network of offices and agencies that has grown and spread from Sevier County's first rudimentary government not only employs hundreds of residents but also naturally draws to it the rest of the county's citizens that receive its services. From court appearances to license plate renewals, Sevierville is the place you have to go.

Geographically, the town is laid out like many of its size and background. The historic downtown area is wedged between the east and west forks of the Little Pigeon River. Just a few blocks from downtown, you'll find most of the city's schools, the police station, the city's community center, and a former movie theater turned civic center. From its central core, the town has expanded in all four directions with balanced concentrations of residential, commercial, and municipal growth. Although the Smoky Mountains dominate Sevierville's southern horizon, much of the city is actually characterized by relatively flat terrain, with the occasional undulation or foothill dropped in for character.

Radiating from downtown, Forks of the River Parkway, then the Parkway (US 441; it's just named "Parkway") lead south to Pigeon Forge and feature much of the city's commercial and tourist-oriented development. Traveling north on Winfield Dunn Parkway (TN 66), you'll also find rapid growth in residential areas as well as accommodations, shops, restaurants, and attractions geared toward the vacationer.

Chapman Highway (US 411 and 441 concurrently) leads west toward Seymour and Knoxville; its surrounding areas primarily remain a mixture of residential neighborhoods and undeveloped farmland. As Dolly Parton Parkway (aka US 411) takes you east, away from downtown, you'll notice that much of the old and new growth alike have a more local flavor to them. Fast-food restaurants, retail stores, and service-oriented businesses have seemingly sprung up overnight in an effort to serve the growing numbers of Seviervillians who have moved eastward to escape entanglements with heavy tourist traffic.

One only has to take a drive through the county's three main towns to see how Sevierville is "mundanely unique" to Sevier County. It's the only city in the county that has a movie theater, new car dealerships, a hospital, factories, an airport, and a good ol' small-town main street. Churches, schools, and banks are in abundance, and although Wal-Mart has taken a healthy bite out of the retail pie, mom-and-pop businesses generally hold their own.

As mentioned earlier, tourism has been both directly and indirectly responsible for much of Sevierville's recent growth—a growth that is unmistakable. Of the roughly 1,600 businesses that call Sevierville home, about 50 percent of them are in some way linked to the tourist trade. These include hotels, outlet centers, restaurants, music

According to one marketing survey conducted on behalf of the Sevierville Chamber of Commerce, the average visitor to that city is between the ages of 45 and 64, earns between $35,000 and $60,000 per year, and has had at least some college education. The number one reason cited for visiting Sevierville was "vacation." Tied for second were "shopping," "scenery," and "entertainment/theaters."

theaters, and attractions. Looking at the statistics provides a fairly reliable litmus test of this contention. For example, the number of available hotel and motel rooms has increased more than 300 percent since 1988. As of March 2004, nearly 2,000 rooms were in existence, compared with only 443 15 years ago (see our Hotels and Motels chapter for details). Between 1991 and 2003, city hotel-motel tax revenues increased from less than $100,000 to more than $500,000.

Local manufacturing is another good barometer of Sevierville's economic health. Another substantial chunk—about 20 percent—of the city's economy is accounted for by local industry. Along sections of Dolly Parton Parkway, you'll find three industrial parks that are home to more than a dozen national and local manufacturers. These thriving companies turn out products such as textiles and high-tech electronics as well as lights, magnets, and valves that wind up in automobile assembly. One of the most fundamental indicators of Sevierville's growth is its increase in population. The current estimated population is more than 12,000 year-round residents. Compare that with only 4,556 back in 1980. Projected estimates for the year 2010 place the city's population at more than 17,000.

As Sevierville continues to feel its oats, it regularly faces issues that naturally accompany growth. One issue is the city's liquor laws. Be aware (or should we say "beware"?) that there are no liquor stores in Sevierville. The only alcohol sold over the counter is beer, which can be found in most local supermarkets and convenience stores. Until just a few years ago, no alcohol of any kind was sold by the drink, ostensibly to preserve the town's "family atmosphere." Changes in city law now allow for beer to be sold by the drink in restaurants that have a seating capacity of at least 150 and where at least 50 percent of sales are from food. Also, beer can be sold at city golf courses, special events, and at the minor league baseball stadium. Right now there are more than 10 "wet" restaurants, and that number is growing in an ongoing effort by restaurateurs to please the tourists. Oh, the times they are a-changin'!

PIGEON FORGE

For more than 100 years, Pigeon Forge was a sleeping giant, a rural farm community nuzzled peacefully against the Smoky Mountains' majesty. Unlike its northern neighbor, Sevierville, which had developed sturdy economic legs of its own from day one, and its southern neighbor, Gatlinburg, which began to prosper in the '40s and '50s because of the national park and mountain crafts, Pigeon Forge suffered from an identity crisis until about 25 years ago. Until then, Pigeon Forge was nothing more than rolling farmland dotted by the occasional restaurant or hotel that lined the Parkway in the hopes of sporadically snagging vacationers on their way to and from the mountains (see our History chapter).

During the '80s, Pigeon Forge reaped benefits from the Knoxville World's Fair and the opening of Dollywood Entertainment Park. Then, the benevolent giant awoke and today stands as tall (in a figurative sense) as the mountain peaks that serve as its backdrop. Since then, Pigeon Forge has made up for lost time, generating gross sales tax revenues surpassing those of Gatlinburg (nearly $6.5 million in 2001) and even surpassing that town in

permanent residents (it's right at 5,083). In the summer, the town's daily population swells to more than 40,000.

Today, Pigeon Forge is almost Las Vegas–like in appearance, with a "main drag" that's packed full of hotels and motels, restaurants, attractions, music theaters, and shopping outlets. Sign after neon sign pulses brightly in the night, promising more fun, more entertainment, and more value than the guy next door. One interesting aspect to all of this (a frightening aspect to some) is that the benevolent giant is still growing!

Unless you are a local, familiar with the residential areas and side roads (see our Real Estate chapter), the axiom "what you see is what you get" stands as a fair assessment of the city's geography. Pigeon Forge is laid out pretty much along the steady course of the Parkway (US 441), running for approximately 4 miles from the abrupt cutoff of Sevierville's city limits near Apple Valley Drive to The Spur, which leads to Gatlinburg. The Parkway is frequently intersected, either by small side streets with finite lengths or by roads leading into the more rural sections of the county. Along these paths is where you'll find most of the city's residences as well as many of its churches, small businesses, and government offices.

Needless to say, the distilled essence of today's Pigeon Forge is largely a product of tourism, an industry in which serving the visitor is a priority in all sectors. The indisputable facts are that the town as a whole has grown and prospered, experienced low seasonal unemployment rates, and has generated a half-billion dollars or more in gross business receipts in recent years. That figure for 2003 was $659,854,551.

Now, the different spins you can apply to these facts vary, according to whom you ask. City administrators and promoters, as well as business owners and upper-level managers, are, no doubt, thrilled with the state of affairs. Those who work on tourism's front lines often present a different picture. Although jobs are plentiful in season, the market tapers off from late fall through early spring, and layoffs are a standard operating practice. Also, a great number of the jobs available are service-oriented positions (hotel and motel housekeeping, food service, retail, etc.), which pay at or slightly above minimum wage and offer few benefits.

By the way, "union" is a dirty word in Sevier County. Past efforts to rally hotel and motel workers have failed; today, most employees realize that business owners can readily draw replacements for them from a large and eager pool. Although some may go so far as to demonize the economic powers that be, most local citizens are willing to live with the negatives of seasonal employment and moderate wages for the sake of working in a vibrant economy in a beautiful mountain setting.

In defense of this situation, we can say that things used to be worse. There was a time when "seasonal employment" meant working the summer months only; these days, the off-season grows shorter and shorter each year. Also, you'll find that, as in larger cities, many waiters, bartenders, and the like are aspiring performers, looking to get a foot in the door of area music and variety theaters. As a case in point, one of the hosts of Dixie Stampede's show started out as a server at that particular Pigeon Forge attraction before working his way up to the show's front man position (see the Music Theaters and Nightlife chapter).

There's also no denying that Dollywood has been an unqualified boon to the city of Pigeon Forge. Much of Pigeon Forge's early success in tourism came from absorbing some of Gatlinburg's spillover with its hotels and restaurants. Soon, entrepreneurs realized that there was a market for developing attractions in Pigeon Forge that would draw people there for its own sake. Enter Dollywood, which was built on a site that had previously been a Silver Dollar City theme park. Since 1986, thanks to the name recognition of and promotion by Dolly Parton,

Dollywood has consistently expanded. It is now the state's single most visited theme park, accommodating more than two million visitors annually, and its parent company, Dollywood Entertainment, is Sevier County's largest single seasonal employer. (See our Dollywood chapter for a more in-depth look at the park.)

Dollywood Entertainment is also responsible, in large part, for the explosion in the Smokies' music theater business. Several theaters had existed in Pigeon Forge, going back as far as 1984, and Dollywood Entertainment itself had started Dixie Stampede in 1988. But with the company's opening of Music Mansion in 1994 and the city's creation of an infrastructure for a multitheater development known as Music Road, the era of an outright "theater community" in Pigeon Forge was ushered in. Suddenly, visions of the town nipping at the heels of Branson, Missouri, were dancing through the heads of local developers and promoters.

If you're a shopaholic or a music fan, Pigeon Forge is definitely the place for you. With 7 outlet malls and 10 music theaters in the space of just a few miles, you'll have no shortage of places to go for fun in the Smokies.

Although there are times that growth in Pigeon Forge appears to be unbridled, city planners will tell you that they don't want their city to become another Branson, with too much stuff packed into too little space. So far, the city appears to have stuck to its guns. The Parkway's six wide lanes generally allow for smooth travel through town (except during the town's frequent custom auto shows), and Sevierville's widening of the Parkway up to Pigeon Forge city limits has undoubtedly helped with traffic flow. Considering that the average traffic flow on Pigeon Forge's section of the Parkway ranges between 58,000 and 75,000 cars per day, cautious city planning is probably a wise option.

One subject on which the city has refused to budge is alcohol sales. Like Sevierville, there are no liquor stores here, and only beer can be purchased in supermarkets and convenience stores. However, alcohol can't be served by the drink within city limits. One notable exception to this rule is the Pigeon Forge landmark, Alf's restaurant, which was "grandfathered" in when local alcohol ordinances prohibited by-the-drink sales; yes, you can still get a cold beer at Alf's (see our Restaurants chapter). Another exception is Mountain Valley Vineyards, where, thanks to state agricultural laws, wine can be purchased by the bottle (see our Attractions chapter).

GATLINBURG

There has always been a certain charm about downtown Gatlinburg, probably because of the intimacy of the city itself. Despite the fact that any day or night can find upwards of 20,000 people browsing the shops and attractions crammed into a half-mile on a couple of streets, there's a relaxed atmosphere that makes Gatlinburg a pleasant place to spend some time. The Parkway strip from the area of traffic light #3 (the traffic lights in both Pigeon Forge and Gatlinburg are numbered—see our Getting Here, Getting Around chapter) to the park entrance is full of enough variety shops and amusements to use up whatever part of a day you want to give it, and there's enough variety sprinkled in to keep the kids amused as well.

Gatlinburg today is a city of about 4,000 souls that takes care of a visitor population averaging 35,000 a day. The only way to accomplish this feat is to pretend you're a city of 35,000 that has a single main street less than a mile long. All services provided by any city are provided in Gatlinburg on that basis. That's why the downtown is always sparkling clean and heavily planted with seasonal flowers, and it's also why this so-called small town seems to be crowded with police officers on walking beats, bicycles, motorcycles, and in patrol cars.

Gatlinburg is, in fact, one of the safest places you'll ever visit. With the proper warnings and precautions, young children can be left to their own devices in the downtown area in the same manner you'd let them go their own way in a theme park. In the history of the town, there's no record of a child ever being harmed in downtown Gatlinburg. Ever.

It's also probably one of a very few cities its size that has three fully operational fire halls, a 150,000-square-foot convention center, and a 50,000-plus square-foot community recreation center (when you read about it in our Parks and Recreation chapter, you probably won't believe it). A mass transit system consisting of several trolleys on six different routes serves locals going to and from work, and visitors using it for its convenience.

We'd do well to remember at this point that the downtown business district is a very small part of the corporate package—the city limits of Gatlinburg extend about a mile north of downtown and stretch about 4½ miles out the East Parkway. The Great Smoky Arts & Crafts Community, a few miles east of downtown, in an area locally known as the Glades is almost entirely within the city limits and is more than 10 times larger in area. There are also four residential areas ringing the downtown area that dwarf it in size. Gatlinburg has a lot of vacant land; it just isn't real adaptable to construction. The only property with true development potential is along the East Parkway to the city limits, and it's going fast.

The city government consists of five city commissioners elected entirely at

Gatlinburg is the only city in Sevier County where the sale of liquor in any form is legal. Most restaurants offer liquor by the drink, and the city has six package liquor stores; they're listed in the Yellow Pages under "Liquor Stores."

large. Commissioners serve four-year terms, which are staggered so that elections take place every two years. The commissioners elect a mayor from their body every year. The day-to-day operation of the city is directed by a city manager, who is hired by and responsible to the commissioners. Gatlinburg has 355 permanent employees on the rolls today. Citizen participation in local government is unusually high. There are more than a dozen advisory boards serving the city's community development and recreation departments, involving volunteer participation of close to 100 citizens.

Because it's the only city in Sevier County where it's legal to sell liquor, and because state law mandates that all taxes collected on the sale of liquor be used for education, Gatlinburg has its own board of education, which disburses these funds to the city's two schools. Additional teaching positions and equipment purchases provided for by liquor tax monies were prime considerations in a 1998 poll conducted by the *Wall Street Journal*, which recognized Gatlinburg-Pittman High School as the best high school in the South. The 180 graduates of the class of 2002 at GPHS reaped more than a million dollars in scholarship money, including 10 National Merit Award scholarships.

Gatlinburg has come a long way in a short time as a center for tourism and as a host city to people looking for temporary gratification. It's also done an admirable job of standing still long enough to attract a growing population of people from all walks of life who become willing participants in the city's ongoing drive to continually reinvent itself without losing touch with its pioneer heritage. Content at this point to concede that its only industry is making people happy, and willing to do what's necessary to reach that goal without compromising its singular brand of integrity, Gatlinburg moves forward still believing that all stories that start with "Once upon a time" must inevitably end with "and they all lived happily ever after."

If you see armed men in camouflage uniforms walking the streets of Gatlinburg in late September or mid-October, try not to show any fear. It's bear season, and a strange quirk in state law makes it legal to hunt within city limits, regardless of whether the city has laws forbidding the open display of weapons (Gatlinburg does). You probably won't actually see hunters on the Parkway, but there are usually a lot of them cruising the roads in the Ski Mountain area.

PITTMAN CENTER

This is an unusual case, and to keep it in perspective we've compressed history and overview into a single statement. Pittman Center is an incorporated city east of Gatlinburg that has no business district, no post office (it's served by Gatlinburg), practically no commerce, and no desire to ever have any of the above. It probably wouldn't even be a city if one of its citizens hadn't gotten crosswise with the Gatlinburg building inspector back in 1974, but we're getting ahead of ourselves.

The community of Pittman Center was established when the Elmira District of the Central New York Conference of the Methodist Episcopal Church founded a missionary school in the mountains east of Gatlinburg and named it for their own superintendent, Dr. Eli Pittman. The school was operated by the United Methodist Church until 1955, when the Sevier County Board of Education bought the three-story building for $20,000 and assumed responsibility for the education of the fewer than 100 students. The Methodist Church then donated the 650 acres it had originally purchased to the community. A new school was built next to the original building in the early '60s, and the high school grades were transferred to the new Gatlinburg-Pittman High School when it was built in 1964.

The little mountain community, never wanting anything more than to be left alone, then languished into the 1970s while Gatlinburg continued to grow to the east, slowly annexing land and extending its influence into unincorporated land by enforcing a nebulous "development district" statute that gave it legal control of development within 5 miles of its own expanding city limits. Things came to a head in 1974, when an unnamed Pittman Center man was stopped from building a house on his own land by a zealous Gatlinburg building inspector trying to protect Gatlinburg's "development status" by enforcing Gatlinburg's building codes.

Into the fray jumped the venerable Conley Huskey (1907–1994), a Pittman Center native and longtime political giant in the area. Knowing that the only way to stop Gatlinburg from exercising its influence in Pittman Center, and eventually annexing it, was to incorporate the area into a city of its own, Conley Huskey drew up and circulated a petition practically overnight to incorporate a new city. He waited two weeks to file the petition so the two pregnant women in the area could deliver their babies and bring the population to the 365 heads the state laws of the time required. The vote to incorporate was 128 for, 24 against, and Pittman Center became a city in 1974. And Conley Huskey's unnamed friend built his house.

Conley Huskey, a longtime Sevier County commissioner, paid most of the costs of incorporation out of his own pocket (he recalled once that he'd have been $10,000 better off if he'd kept his mouth shut) and was rewarded by being elected Pittman Center's first mayor, an office he held until 1990. The old school building had fallen into disrepair by this time, but it was renovated and is now Pittman Center's city hall. At three stories, it's also the most imposing structure in the city. Pittman Center has gone on record as being dedicated to the preservation of its mountain heritage and, as such, has resisted any sort of commercial growth.

The city's biggest asset at the time of incorporation was Cobbly Nob golf course (now Sunterra Resort), a privately operated facility on municipal land. Pittman Center sold the golf course to a private developer in 1978 and used the proceeds from the sale to pave every road in the city. Pittman Center today is just about what it wants to be: a protected mountain community of less than 10 square miles and a population of about 600. The city is governed by a mayor and board of three aldermen, elected at large every two years. The day-to-day affairs of the city are overseen by a part-time administrator who directs the activities of the city's five full-time employees: a recorder, two policemen, and two maintenance men. The operating budget for fiscal year 2005 is $788,000, generated mostly by a property tax rate of 77 cents per $100 assessed valuation and a 3 percent hotel-motel tax. Fire service is provided by a well-equipped volunteer department.

Gatlinburg's bicycle-riding policemen have become an attraction all by themselves. Tourists are continually stopping the cycle cops to ask for information. The most frequently asked question is, "Why are you riding that bike?" The answer is that the bicycles let the police move rapidly through traffic, increasing their effectiveness at responding to emergency situations.

GETTING HERE, GETTING AROUND

The area we refer to as "the Smok- ies" is a large chunk of east Ten- nessee and a smaller portion of western North Carolina with an irregular and totally arbitrary border. To keep it as simple as possible, we're primarily talking about the corridor that is described by Tennessee Highway 66 and U.S. Highway 441 along a path of about 30 miles from exit 407 off Interstate 40 to the Great Smoky Mountains National Park entrance at the southern city limit of Gatlinburg. Keep going, and you'll eventually wind through the park and into North Carolina.

We'll start this chapter with a small section on getting here, then concentrate on telling you how to get around once you're here. It can be a challenge, and sometimes we have a little traffic, but trust us to get you where you want to go.

GETTING HERE

By Air

Gatlinburg–Pigeon Forge Airport
1255 Airport Road, Sevierville
(865) 453-8393
Let's start off with one vital piece of infor- mation. When you land at this airport, you won't be in either Gatlinburg or Pigeon Forge—you'll be in Sevierville. Don't ask us to explain this one. It's probably the same logic responsible for locating the Gatlin- burg Municipal Golf Course in Pigeon Forge.

The airport itself is a full-service, fixed base operator. Its 5,500-foot runway can accommodate aircraft ranging from small, single-engine planes to corporate jets. Although no commercial airlines fly in here, it does frequently receive aircraft

chartered by individuals or companies. There are no landing fees, but there is an aircraft parking fee of $5.00 per night.

Amenities available on-site include a maintenance crew, jet fuel, and gas for piston-driven planes. The airport does not operate a shuttle service, but there is a rental car office on the premises that can be reached at (865) 453-8918. The service is provided by the local Ford dealership, and a limited number of cars are kept on hand at the airport itself. Of course, you can also leave by taxi, if you wish. See the "Getting Around" section for information on rental cars and local cab companies.

McGhee Tyson Airport
Alcoa Highway, Alcoa
(865) 342-3000
www.tys.org
This airport is in the community of Alcoa, approximately 15 miles south of Knoxville on U.S. Highway 129 (Alcoa Highway). The airport accommodates 14 airlines provid- ing nonstop flights to 18 major cities including Atlanta, Dallas–Fort Worth, St. Louis, Chicago, and Washington, D.C. Among the more familiar carriers that fly in and out of Knoxville are Northwest, United, U.S. Airways, and Delta, the latter accounting for roughly 35 percent of the airport's traffic.

In 2000, McGhee Tyson wrapped up the final phase of a major terminal renova- tion, an expansion spurred by the airport's

---

Piloting your own plane to the Smokies? You'll need to know that the FAA desig- nation for Gatlinburg–Pigeon Forge Air- port is GKT, and the runway headings are 10 and 23 for eastbound and west- bound approaches, respectively.

Even though Knoxville's McGhee Tyson Airport is classified as only a medium-size facility, it has still felt the impact of September 11, 2001. You can expect your car trunk to be inspected before entering the parking garage and for lines to move a little slower at the baggage check-in counters and at the security checkpoint. Also, nonticketed friends and family dropping you off or picking you up at the airport cannot accompany you past the security gate.

Alamo: (800) 327-9633 or (865) 342-3210

Avis: (800) 331-1212 or (865) 342-3220

Budget: (800) 527-0700 or (865) 342-3225

Enterprise: (800) 736-8222 or (865) 342-1650

Hertz: (800) 654-3131 or (865) 342-3232

National: (800) 227-7368 or (865) 342-3240

Thrifty: (800) 367-2277 or (865) 342-3250

recent growth in popularity. The $53 million face-lift included increased ticket counter space, a single security checkpoint, an expanded baggage handling area, and more waiting areas. The renovation added 140,000 additional square feet to the building and also increased the number of passenger gates, concession areas, flight information displays, and escalators.

Both short- and long-term parking sites are available. In both cases, the first 30 minutes are free, and then you're charged in hourly increments. Maximum per-day rates are $8.00 for long-term parking and $12.00 for short-term.

Entering the main terminal, you'll find the baggage claim areas and a number of rental car agencies on the lower street level. The upper level includes the gates and ticketing areas as well as some typical airport facilities and amenities—restaurants, snack bars, and gift shop.

Transportation from McGhee Tyson Airport

For transportation from McGhee Tyson Airport to the Smokies, there are a number of options available. The following national car rental agencies maintain fleets at the airport. We've listed toll-free numbers as well as local numbers that provide direct access to each company's airport rental office:

If you're driving to the Smokies from the airport, there are two basic ways you can go. Traveling north on US 129 (Alcoa Highway) will take you directly to I-40 near downtown Knoxville. Head east on I-40 to exit 407 and you'll be at the north end of the Smokies Corridor. An alternate, not to mention more scenic, path would be to take US 129 south from the airport for about 2 miles and bear left, following the signs to Maryville and Alcoa. Tennessee Highway 35 will take you east through those two communities. Once you're in Maryville, follow the signs for US 411 North. That highway will take you north to Seymour and then east, directly into Sevierville. Depending on traffic, both routes to Sevierville are about a 45-minute to one-hour drive.

Several taxicab companies provide transportation from McGhee Tyson Airport. The following taxi services will usually either have cars waiting outside the terminal at street level or be at the terminal within about five minutes:

AAA Taxi: (865) 531-1930

ABC Taxi: (865) 970-4545

Benchmark Taxi: (865) 567-0035

Sunshine Taxi: (865) 310-7047

Tennessee Taxi Service: (865) 984-8555

All of the companies that service the airport operate on a fixed fare schedule. A one-way trip to Sevierville costs $40; one-way to Pigeon Forge is $45; one-way to Gatlinburg is $50. Prices are based on a one-passenger fare; additional passengers cost $3.00 each.

Another option is to contact Sassafras Transportation at (865) 971–4075. This company makes trips to Sevierville for $11.50 per person, Pigeon Forge for $12.80 per person, and Gatlinburg for $14.10 per person. Fifteen percent discounts are offered for senior citizens and students. Children younger than five ride free.

Sassafras Transportation utilizes a 15-passenger van to take riders directly to their hotel or motel in each of the three cities. The company's main drawback is its limited Sevier County schedule. June through August, they make one trip per day, at 12:30 P.M., Monday through Saturday. The rest of the year, trips run Monday through Friday.

By Ground

Greyhound Bus Terminal
100 Magnolia Avenue NE, Knoxville
(865) 522–5144

Unfortunately, if you plan to get to the Smokies by bus, Knoxville is about as close as you're going to get, because there are no major bus routes that run into Sevier County. Knoxville's Greyhound terminal receives approximately 35 to 40 arrivals daily. Because there are no rental car agencies located at the bus station, your best bet for getting to the Smokies is to contact Sassafras Transportation at (865) 971–4075 (see above). Sassafras Transportation's one-way, per person rates from the bus terminal are $5.00 to Sevierville, $6.30 to Pigeon Forge, and $7.60 to Gatlinburg. They make two Sevier County runs per day, at 8:30 A.M. and 1:10 P.M.

GETTING AROUND

There is no more beautiful or peaceful place on the planet than the Smokies. There is a serenity here that's simply not available anywhere else, and it comes from a combination of several agreeable factors that come together quite nicely here.

You might want to repeat this mantra to yourself a few thousand times if you're sitting in the parking lot that the Smokies Corridor is wont to become without notice on any given summer day. Traffic is a problem in any place where upwards of 75,000 people are all trying to go anywhere at the same time. And when 50,000 of them are on the same street at the same time, it doesn't matter how long the street is—you've gotten yourself into a traffic jam that only time will resolve, and you're on your time, and it probably didn't come cheap. So let's see what we can do to save a little time and a lot of frazzled nerves. And let's maybe even see if we can make your arrival a little easier.

Handy Hint #1: The roads we discuss are all paved and wide enough for trailers or RVs to pass. Other routes are used by the locals and some of our more knowledgeable visitors, and they'll be glad to share them with you, but we're going to stick with the routes that don't require special handling.

Handy Hint #2: If you're bumper-to-bumper in Great Smoky Mountains National Park, you're stuck—we can't help you. Take whatever comfort you can from the beauty of your surroundings and pray that your gas and your composure hold out until you break free.

First, let's tell you about negotiating the Smokies Corridor. Here's how the corridor lays out: exit 407 on I-40 is TN 66, also known and labeled as the Winfield Dunn Scenic Parkway. Unless you're coming into the area from the southeast via U.S. Highway 321 into Gatlinburg, or have chosen to forgo the interstate system at a point west of exit 407, chances are you'll enter the area at exit 407. It's the way most travel services recommend for travelers coming from the north, south, or west. People coming from the east (the Carolinas and those folks from Georgia and Florida who don't use Interstate 75) usually get off I-40 at the Foothills Parkway (exit 445) and come in to Gatlinburg on US 321—a route that's discussed later.

A word of caution: There are very few places in the area where roads have only one name or only one state or federal route number. Every road name we use is the one that observation has proven correct. In cases where one road is identified by maps and highway signs as having several route numbers, our maps will show only the numbers that are used by the local gentry. For example, the Parkway, our main stem and primary reference point, can have up to seven different identifications from Sevierville to the Park entrance. We'll use only "Parkway" and "US 441," and our maps are marked accordingly. In the section on bypasses and back roads, we'll address the name changes more specifically.

Eight miles south of exit 407, TN 66 intersects Dolly Parton Parkway (US 411N/441S—see why we try to use simpler terms?) in Sevierville. You'll probably see the golden dome of the courthouse as you approach Dolly Parton Parkway. More than a century old, the Sevier (pronounced "severe") County courthouse is one of Tennessee's oldest and one of the prettiest in America (see our Attractions chapter for more). After crossing Dolly Parton Parkway, another mile brings you to the end of TN 66 at US 441 south. Turn-

ing right toward Pigeon Forge, you're now on what is locally known as the Parkway, and if you've managed to avoid bumper-to-bumper traffic so far, the honeymoon is about to end.

Remember the intersection where you turned onto the Parkway—it will come up later for visits to a few places. For now, though, you're closing in on your first destination: your home away from home for the duration of your visit (if you're staying in or near Pigeon Forge or Gatlinburg. If you're staying in Sevierville, you've probably already checked in by now).

Proceeding south along the Parkway, you'll notice that the first few miles are crowded with motels, convenience stores, and local services, with a few gift/craft shops and restaurants thrown in. You're still in Sevierville, the county seat, which is just beginning to tap into the tourism market (more on this in our Area Overview chapter).

Keep your eyes peeled for the Wal-Mart megastore on the right and Governor's Crossing resort complex on the left. When you pass these places, you're approaching Pigeon Forge, and the landscape will change dramatically. The first building that's actually in Pigeon Forge is the Pigeon Forge Department of Tourism, and if you still thirst for literature and/or more information, it's a good place to stop and get your bearings. Then, welcome to action-packed Pigeon Forge! You actually left Sevierville and entered Pigeon Forge when you crossed the river, but the sign's hard to see.

The next 3 miles are a steady stream of motels, restaurants, amusements, and shops strung out shoulder-to-shoulder along both sides of the Parkway. If you're staying in Pigeon Forge, start looking for your lodging place as soon as you cross Apple Valley Road. In average conditions you'll have sufficient time to look because you're probably going to be in really slow-moving traffic. If you know which side of the road you're staying on, get in the lane you'll be turning out of, and resist every temptation to get out of it. If you're going

---

When you make your hotel reservations, ask the clerk if the hotel provides a shuttle service that can pick you up at either the Gatlinburg–Pigeon Forge Airport or the McGhee Tyson Airport, south of Knoxville.

---

on to Gatlinburg, stay in one of the two center lanes all the way through Pigeon Forge.

Pigeon Forge used to have only one traffic light. The city's unbelievable explosion into tourism in the late 1980s changed that forever, and now it seems like a traffic light is some kind of status symbol. They may be necessary to help regulate traffic, but it sure seems like there are a lot of them on a straight stretch of highway. Pigeon Forge has numbered its traffic lights on the Parkway. Right now there are 10 traffic lights and 11 numbers, including one with a number and an alphabetic suffix. Here's how they lay out, running north to south:

0. The entrance to the parking lots for Music Mansion, the Louise Mandrell Theater, and the Alabama Grill, this intersection will become increasingly popular as the road is developed to wrap around the west side of the Parkway and become Music Row. Several music theaters are in planning and early construction phases along this road.

1. Henderson's Chapel Road boasts several new motels already, with more expected as Music Row is built and developed.

2. Teaster Lane goes off to the left, leading to a spate of music theaters and the largest concentration of outlet malls. Teaster Lane is also the southern bypass around the Parkway, leading to Lower Middle Creek Road and Dollywood Lane.

2B. Community Center Drive leads into Pigeon Forge's educational campus, city park complex, and the Pigeon Forge community center described in our Parks and Recreation chapter.

3. Wears Valley Road (US 321S/Tennessee Highway 73W) is no longer the northern terminus of the Forge, but it's where you turn left (east) to go to the largest selection of outlet malls—if that's where you're heading and you missed Teaster Lane at light #2. In the other direction, Wears Valley Road is being developed so fast it's hard to stay abreast, but the Pigeon Forge educational complex

Tennessee has a very tough drunk driving (DUI) law, and your status as a visitor will not let you off the hook. What it boils down to is this: If you are stopped for suspicion of DUI and fail a field sobriety test, you will then be asked to submit to a breath analysis. If that test indicates a blood alcohol level of 0.08 percent or higher, you are subject to arrest and incarceration for a minimum of 48 hours. You could also lose your driver's license for a year. Don't test this law! You can't win unless you're cold sober, and even then it's not a pleasant experience.

of three schools is about a half-mile down on the right. Several campgrounds are on Wears Valley Road and are described in our Campgrounds and RV Parks chapter.

Wears Valley Road is also an excellent alternative route to Cades Cove at the extreme western edge of the national park and to the resort community of Townsend in Blount County.

4. Approaching the center of the downtown area on the Parkway, traffic light #4 is a regulator that prevents unbelievable traffic snarls at the entrance to the Pigeon Forge Factory Outlet and Z Buda Outlet malls (see our Outlet Shopping chapter).

5. Jake Thomas Road goes off to the left (north), leading to Teaster Lane.

6. Pine Mountain Road goes south (right), leading to the Pigeon Forge city offices and U.S. post office.

7. In what was the center of Pigeon Forge before the boom, the lighted intersection at Old Mill Avenue provides access to the Old Mill shopping area and Patriot Park. This is the original traffic signal in the city, and Old Mill Avenue leads to Middle Creek Road, which is handy to know about as a convenient bypass.

8. The "Dollywood" light is so named because it's where most traffic turns to go to the area's biggest single attraction. Note: This is Dollywood Lane where it

Pedestrians in Gatlinburg have the right-of-way in crosswalks. This means that if they step off the curb, you have to stop for them. In the heart of downtown, some of our visitors think the entire Parkway is a crosswalk. Be very wary; hitting a pedestrian in Gatlinburg would be a capital crime if the locals had their way.

leaves the Parkway, but when it passes the Dollywood entrance about a mile out of town it becomes Upper Middle Creek Road, confusing even to lifelong locals, and it leads out of town and runs alongside the Gatlinburg Golf Club. Upper Middle Creek is a major "back road" and will be described in-depth later on. The traffic light that appears just as you see the golf course is Middle Creek.

9. There is currently no traffic light #9.

10. You'll know when you're out of Pigeon Forge by the sudden disappearance of businesses and the equally sudden appearance of wilderness when you pass through the southernmost traffic light. Be aware that the right-hand lane ends at this light. Unless you're planning to go up Conner Heights Road at the intersection, get out of the right lane.

The next 4 miles pass through federal property, on what's referred to locally as The Spur. With mountains rising from the right shoulder and the lovely Little Pigeon River on the left, this short respite from the hodgepodge of commercialism behind and before you is a preview of the Great Smoky Mountains National Park. This is a flat, twisty road. When you leave Pigeon Forge and when you enter Gatlinburg 4 miles later, you're traveling almost due south. In between, you'll go west, north, and east before heading south again.

Handy hint: This illustrates one of the local phenomena that make visiting here such a hoot sometimes. When you get a general direction from a local, like, "Go east for 3 miles," do what you're told. In

the 3 miles you travel, you might think you're going every direction but east, but you'll get where you wanted to go.

As you approach Gatlinburg you'll notice on the right the Gatlinburg/Great Smoky Mountains National Park welcome center. This is another handy place to pick up literature and information, including a lot of park literature that's difficult to get through the mail. Continuing past the welcome center, a broad sweep in the road takes you past the park bypass and into downtown Gatlinburg. It may also bring you to a screeching crawl as the traffic begins reacting to traffic lights you can't quite see yet. Hello, Gatlinburg!

Gatlinburg usually doesn't have as much traffic as Pigeon Forge, but it seems like more sometimes, because Gatlinburg doesn't have as much Parkway as Pigeon Forge, either. Two miles long and never more than four lanes wide, the Parkway in Gatlinburg provides exactly zero opportunities to pull over to the side and take stock. There's no "to the side"—the buildings come right to the sidewalk, which comes right to the curb. It's helpful to know where you're going at all times in Gatlinburg. If you plan to park, plan ahead. It's so essential that there's a section devoted to parking lots later in this chapter. For now, let's finish the Parkway portion of the Smokies Corridor.

From the end of The Spur at the north (upper) end of town to the Great Smoky Mountains National Park entrance 2 miles later, Gatlinburg, like Pigeon Forge, is punctuated by 10 numbered traffic lights. They are, in order:

1. The Dudley Creek bypass to US 321N. Details will be explained later.

2. A blinker 200 yards south of #1. If you have any reason to cross the river on the north end of the Parkway (there's a motel there, and some cabins on Laurel Street), this is your only chance.

3. (A Biggie)—US 321 comes in from the left and the Parkway swings right. US 321 is the only road out of Gatlinburg to the east, and it leads immediately to a string of motels. Further east are a scat-

tering of businesses, the U.S. post office, Gatlinburg's city hall complex, and the Great Smoky Arts & Crafts Community. *Note:* This piece of road has gone through several name changes in the last decade. At various times it has been TN 73, East Main, US 321 (its current federal designation), and its current local handle, East Parkway. The locals (except for postal workers and firemen) have given up trying to keep current and will refer to it as either "73" or "321." This guide will use the latter, along with East Parkway.

4. There is no traffic light #4—nobody knows why.

5. River Road goes off diagonally to the right. It travels roughly parallel to the Parkway for less than a mile, past several motels, restaurants, and attractions, and rejoins the Parkway outside of town, near the Great Smoky Mountains National Park entrance sign.

6. Just a block from #5, Cherokee Orchard Road goes off to the left, leading to another large group of motels and condos in the Baskins Creek area. Cherokee Orchard rises as it continues east and south to its intersection with Historic Nature Trail (formerly Airport Road). If you meant to turn onto River Road and missed it, you can recover here by turning right.

7. A flashing light (yellow if you're on the Parkway) at Reagan Drive—handy if Reagan Drive has any importance to you (a few motels, a couple of churches, the downtown fire hall, and the Gatlinburg branch of the Sevier County Court Clerk's office are on Reagan Drive). You can also get to River Road by turning right, but when you get to River Road at the bottom of the hill, you'll be on Maples Lane.

8. Historic Nature Trail (formerly Airport Road) goes off and up to the left. The Gatlinburg Convention Center, a few attractions, several motels, and most of the downtown churches are on Historic Nature Trail. From the intersection at Cherokee Orchard Road, Historic Nature Trail passes Mynatt Park and a residential area on the right and enters the Great

Smoky Mountains National Park. We'll deal with it again in this "Getting Around" chapter.

9. Another blinker at the aerial tramway terminal is forgettable unless you're staying in a motel on the other side of the river.

10. The last light, at Ski Mountain Road. A right turn will take you through the River Road intersection and up Ski Mountain. Mostly chalets and condos, Ski Mountain Road is the only way a visitor would want to go into the Chalet Village area.

Some hardy souls also think it's the only route to Ober Gatlinburg ski resort. Wrong. The only sensible way to get to Ober Gatlinburg is to park in town and ride the aerial tramway. Think about this: Ski Mountain Road goes straight up from town and straight down from the ski lodge, except for that nifty little double hairpin in the middle, and when it's covered with snow and ice it still goes straight up and straight down. It's a narrow two-lane road with no shoulder for most of its length. Ride the tram to the ski lodge. There's more detail on this in the Attractions chapter.

If you go through traffic light #10 heading out of town, you're in the woods as quickly as you were when you left Pigeon Forge. The big difference this time is that you're now in 50 miles of woods, interrupted only by the Pigeon Forge/Sevierville bypass a mile or so ahead, and the Sugarlands Visitor Center another mile up the road.

That's the Smokies Corridor for everybody that used exit 407 to get here. For those rugged individualists who came a little more overland, here's where you are:

If you came out of Knoxville on US 441, or onto 441 from US 411 in Seymour (a popular route for knowledgeable Georgians), continue east about 12 miles to the traffic light at TN 66 (it's well posted) and hang a right. You're now in the Smokies Corridor, and you'll be on the Parkway in a mile.

If you came through the park from Townsend on Little River Road (TN 73E), turn left at the Sugarlands Visitor Center. You're now on US 441 going north, and if you don't take the bypass to Pigeon Forge, you'll be at traffic light #10 in Gatlinburg in about as much time as it takes you to read this paragraph.

If you came into Gatlinburg from the east on US 321S (a favorite route for people coming out of the Carolinas), you will enter downtown Gatlinburg at traffic light #3.

Finally, if you came into Sevierville from the east on US 411S from Cocke or Jefferson County, turn left at the traffic light at US 441S (if you turn right, you'll be in a supermarket parking lot). If you miss the intersection, you've got two more chances in the next 2 blocks. Take either one and stay on it. Both roads end at the Parkway.

If you got truly crazy and came out of Townsend on Wears Valley Road (US 321/TN 73E), turn right at the traffic light after you pass the giant Kroger store. You'll be on the Parkway in Pigeon Forge.

Now that everybody's in the corridor and settled, the rest is remarkably easy. Every direction in the rest of this book will use one of the landmarks previously mentioned (e.g., "from traffic light #7 in Pigeon Forge" or "from the Sugarlands Visitor Center") to get you started. Using this chapter as your guide, go from wherever you are to that starting place, and then enjoy your time in the Smokies. The important thing to note here is that the alphabet soup that makes up the road system in the Smokies Corridor consists of only one north-south road (US 441 in all its descriptions) and four major east-west roads (I-40, US 411/441 [Dolly Parton Parkway] in Sevierville, Wears Valley Road in Pigeon Forge, and U.S. 321 [East Parkway] in Gatlinburg). You'll get used to the various descriptions sooner than you think, but remember these simple pointers to make moving around as simple as possible:

Regardless of what city you're in, the terms "Parkway" and "Main Street" will always refer to US 441. In Sevierville a short portion of US 441 west of the downtown area is actually named Main Street.

US 411 (note the difference) is Dolly Parton Parkway in Sevierville—it's also Main Street and Chapman Highway on the western end (toward Knoxville), and Newport Highway east of Sevierville.

What you may hear called "73" in Gatlinburg is actually US 321N, and it goes east out of town at traffic light #3.

SHORTCUTS AND BACK ROADS

Now that we've scared you to death with all this talk of traffic, we should let you know that there are ways to get around in the area without using the Parkway. They are known and used by the local population, and the folks who live here are not averse to sharing the knowledge with our visitors—we know where our bread is buttered. The problem is that most of our visitors don't ask about these byways until they've been burned by the traffic, and then they tend to get specific about where they want to avoid. Herewith, a list of handy little back routes on paved, generally level roads.

For openers, let's go back to your introduction to the area coming off exit 407 from I-40. If you've spent the last 10 minutes or so enjoying the view of the courthouse dome from the Winfield Dunn Scenic Parkway (TN 66) and you haven't seen a traffic light yet, take heart. A light is just around the bend you're creeping up on, but you're probably in a traffic situation that's not going to ease off until you get to Gatlinburg, some 20 miles down the road.

At our daytime average speed of 10 to 20 miles per hour, we're talking an hour or so to Pigeon Forge, and God knows what it'll take to get to Gatlinburg. Here comes a small slice of salvation that can get you to those two towns much quicker. What you want to do is turn left at the traffic signal, so get over as soon as you can.

The traffic light you're approaching is at Dolly Parton Parkway (US 411/441), the main east-west thoroughfare in Sevierville. We're going to take a detour by turning left on Dolly Parton and putting all that traffic in the rearview mirror. Warning: This gambit is for people staying in Pigeon Forge or Gatlinburg. If you're staying in Sevierville, this shortcut isn't much help—you've got to get back into the traffic jam. Do it by turning right at the second traffic light you come to on Dolly Parton Parkway. That puts you back on the Parkway (US 441). This intersection is where US 411 and 441 part company; US 411 continues east toward our first bypass road, and US 441 drops southward toward Pigeon Forge and Gatlinburg.

Back to our escapees: If your goal is Pigeon Forge, your target is Middle Creek Road, about a mile from where you fled TN 66. It's clearly labeled and there's a traffic light at the intersection. Also note that Middle Creek goes off only to the right—it's not a cross street yet (long-range planning projects a new road that will run east off TN 66 south of the French Broad River and will drop south to meet Middle Creek). Hang a right onto Middle Creek Road.

For the first mile, you'll be in an area of local businesses and professional buildings. After you pass Fort Sanders/Sevier Medical Center, the county's only hospital, you'll pass through 4 or 5 miles of farmland. When you see the entrance to Dollywood's parking lot on your left, you're approaching Pigeon Forge. If you stay on Middle Creek, you'll merge with Dollywood Lane near the center of Pigeon Forge and renew your acquaintance with the Parkway at traffic light #8. This side trip has cost you about 3 miles and probably saved you an hour.

If you're headed for Gatlinburg, stay on Dolly Parton Parkway and go through the light at Middle Creek. Less than a mile up the road, you'll pass an industrial park on the right and Sevier County High School on the left. A mile or so later, you'll reach a traffic signal where your only option is to turn right; take it, and you'll be on Pittman Center Road (Tennessee Highway 416).

Settle back and enjoy the scenery for a while. You've begun a journey of some 8 to 12 miles, depending on precisely where you're going, and you're on a road through some real pretty farmland. The road itself will change its name two or three times; pay no attention.

Five miles in from your turning point, Pittman Center Road turns left. Keep going straight, and you're now on Bird's Creek Road. The road coming in from the right is Upper Middle Creek, which comes out of Pigeon Forge as Dollywood Lane. We'll get back to it shortly.

Continuing on Bird's Creek, you'll enjoy more rural scenery for the next 4 miles until you come to a stop sign. You're now in the Great Smoky Arts & Crafts Community, which means you're closing in on Gatlinburg. You're also within a mile of the end of Bird's Creek Road.

As you approach the intersection at Glades Road (again, right turn only), notice that Bird's Creek seems to flow onto Glades. If you're headed for downtown Gatlinburg, go with the flow. Glades Road ends at US 321, 2 miles (turn right) from traffic light #3 in downtown Gatlinburg. If your destination is a lodging place more than 5 miles east of Gatlinburg on US 321, skip the turn at Glades Road, and bear just slightly left. Now you're on Buckhorn Road.

(These name changes occur a lot around here, and most of them came about when old roads were rerouted in years past to intersect other roads. When the roads came together, nobody could see a good reason to change the name of one of them just because the intersection formed a straight line instead of a corner.)

Sometimes the lure of the roads leading away from the main thoroughfares is just too attractive to resist, and you find yourself on a winding mountain or country road with no earthly idea of where you are. The solution is simple: Every back road in the county is paved and leads eventually to a highway. When you come to a highway, don't cross it. Turn onto the highway and stay on it until you get to something that looks familiar. It shouldn't take long.

From the time you enter the Parkway in Sevierville, think of it as a giant funnel. It starts out as a six-lane road in Sevierville, continues that way through Pigeon Forge (although the outside lanes there are virtually at a standstill during the summer), and narrows down to four lanes on The Spur and through Gatlinburg. At the Sugarlands Visitor Center, the four lanes become two regardless of which way you're going.

Buckhorn Road continues south about 2 more miles to US 321, a little more than 5 miles east of downtown Gatlinburg. A left turn here will take you toward Pittman Center and the condo communities of Cobbly Nob, Brandywine, and Bent Creek.

The two bypass routes described above are the longest alternate routes in the area, but they will cut out long waits in Parkway traffic. Used in reverse, they're handy for getting back to I-40 when you leave the Smokies.

Let's go back to Upper Middle Creek Road for a minute. Remember, this is the one that leaves Pigeon Forge as Dollywood Lane at traffic light #8 and runs past the Gatlinburg Golf Club. Upper Middle Creek intersects Bird's Creek Road (near Pittman Center Road) about midway between Pigeon Forge and the Great Smoky Arts & Crafts Community. If you're out that way and want to get to Pigeon Forge without going back through Gatlinburg, it's the best route. Upper Middle Creek goes left off Bird's Creek just past Caton's Chapel School.

That takes care of the really big shortcuts. Now let's tackle the little ones that make in-town travel a little more palatable, starting in Pigeon Forge. There really aren't any shortcuts in Sevierville to speak of because the city's laid out in a very compact fashion. To keep things in perspective, we're saying the Parkway runs north and south through town:

Skirting Pigeon Forge to the East

Teaster Lane is a bypass around the Parkway on the east side of Pigeon Forge that runs from traffic light #2 just north of Wears Valley Road to Dollywood Lane/ Upper Middle Creek. Coming south on the Parkway (from Sevierville), turn left at traffic light #2 and follow the road as far as you want to go. The traffic light near the southern end is Middle Creek Road; a left turn will take you to the back entrance to Dollywood and, eventually, back to Sevierville.

You can get to Teaster Lane from the Parkway at Jake Thomas Road (traffic light #5) about halfway between Middle Creek and Wears Valley Roads. Teaster Lane includes most of Pigeon Forge's outlet malls.

The Western Side of Pigeon Forge

These directions take you from north to south; if you're traveling north, use Teaster Lane. Florence Street runs off Wears Valley Road a block west of the Parkway (Mel's Diner is on the corner). Running parallel to the Parkway for about half its length, the street goes through a very nice middle-class neighborhood and a kaleidoscope of name changes. You can get back to the Parkway just about anywhere along the way.

When it passes the Pigeon Forge Civic Center and its name becomes Rena, take the next left. If you don't, you'll wind up out in the countryside and the only way to get back is to backtrack. Pigeon Forge is planning a western bypass using Florence/Rena as a base, which will run from Wears Valley Road to Conner Heights Road at the southern end of the city. When complete (no real firm date exists), you'll be able to go around Pigeon Forge from Wears Valley Road to the Parkway Spur.

Let's go on to Gatlinburg. As mentioned earlier, the only safe "back way" from Pigeon Forge to Gatlinburg is the Dollywood Lane/Upper Middle Creek–Bird's Creek–Glades route. However, you can take the Parkway Spur south and bypass Gatlinburg on either side before getting into the downtown gridlock.

The park bypass runs off the Spur just past the Gatlinburg Welcome Center and is highly recommended if the Great Smoky Mountains National Park is where you're going. Two roadside turnoffs provide spectacular views of Gatlinburg on the way over. You'll come off the bypass inside the park boundary, and the Sugarlands Visitor Center (a must-stop for first-time visitors) is about a mile ahead. The bypass is clearly marked on your return.

In Gatlinburg the Dudley Creek bypass (turn left at traffic light #1 and follow the signs) will put you on US 321 about a mile and a half east of downtown. If you're heading toward Gatlinburg (west) on US 321, look for the Ace Hardware and NAPA Auto Parts stores on the right. Turn right at the traffic light and you'll be headed back to the Spur.

Caution: This route is steep and narrow in some places. Large vehicles and towed loads should think twice.

We come finally to Gatlinburg's in-town bypasses, the Baskins Creek/Newton Lane Bypass and Cherokee Orchard Road. These are convenient anytime you're on the east end of town and want to get around the Parkway in the heart of the business district.

First, the Baskins Creek/Newton Lane Bypass: This one requires alertness at both ends. It's clearly marked, but if you miss it on the east end (US 321), there's no turning back, and a whiff on the Cherokee Orchard end could drop you into the busiest intersection in town.

Coming west toward downtown on US 321, the street sign says "Baskins Creek Bypass." It's on the left, about halfway around a sweeping curve, and there's a large earthen breastwork at the corner. If you miss it, the only way to get back is to make an illegal U-turn on a hill in heavy traffic. Just go on down to the Parkway at traffic light #3, turn left to traffic light #6, and turn left again. Now you're on Cherokee Orchard Road, 2 blocks from where you would have come out if you hadn't missed the turn.

Cherokee Orchard climbs rapidly as it goes away from downtown and curves around to intersect Historic Nature Trail (formerly Airport Road) at the equivalent of about 8 city blocks from the Parkway. A right turn on Historic Nature Trail will take you back toward downtown; a left leads out of town.

If you're hurtling down Cherokee Orchard toward town, you'll see two side streets very close together right at the bottom of the hill. The second one is marked as the NEWTON LANE BY-PASS. Take it to the right and you'll go around town to US 321. You might note the Anna Porter Public Library at the corner of Cherokee Orchard and Newton Lane, and the municipal parking lot beside it. Both can be valuable resources if used properly.

Finally, River Road in Gatlinburg is a viable bypass to get to Ski Mountain Road and the Great Smoky Mountains National Park. Bear right at traffic light #5. Because River Road is populated primarily by motels and restaurants, pedestrian congestion is lighter.

The alternate routes described in this chapter can be invaluable in terms of saving time and tempers. Remember that there are even more alternate roads available, but they're not really intended for heavy traffic or unfamiliar drivers. For the most part, the real "back roads" are not really safe to drive on unless you know what to expect in the way of sudden turns, rapid elevation changes, livestock and wild animals in the road, and other obstacles too numerous to mention. Bring this guide with you and use it frequently; it should help you realize the joy you came here seeking.

PARKING IN GATLINBURG

If you must drive into town, there is some parking available. Several private lots on Historic Nature Trail (formerly Airport Road), adjacent to and across the street from the convention center, operate on a sliding rate scale depending on what's going on in town at the time. They usually work on an hourly basis and sometimes offer an all-day or maximum rate. There are a few private lots scattered along the Parkway behind the storefronts, but they fill up early. During the summer when school is not in session, the Pi Beta Phi elementary school PTA operates the school's parking lot as a fund-raiser. The school is on Cherokee Orchard Road, 1 block from the Parkway at traffic light #6.

The City of Gatlinburg operates five parking lots and two multistory decks in and around town. Rates are variable, depending on location, and long-term permits are available at City Hall on East Parkway. Two of the seven lots offer free parking.

1. The Welcome Center Park and Ride lot on the Parkway Spur coming from Pigeon Forge (96 spaces). Parking is free, and the purple route trolley will take you into the center of town for a quarter a head. The lot is unattended.

2. The north Parkway lot, next to Hillbilly Golf before traffic light #3 (34 spaces). Parking is metered (honor system), and the lot has public rest rooms. Convenient to businesses and attractions north of the main business district, it's a hike into town and back if you've got kids to consider. A monthly permit is available at City Hall for $35. The lot is unattended.

3. The Fred McMahan Downtown Parking Garage (398 spaces). Gatlinburg's newest parking structure is at the intersection of the Parkway and East Parkway (US 321N), south of traffic light #3. Hourly rates are $1.75 (minimum) for the first hour and $1.00 per additional hour, with a maximum charge of $6.00 per day. A long-term parking permit is available for $35 a month. The deck is operated by an attendant.

4. Aquarium Parking Garage (400 spaces). Directly behind the Ripley's Aquarium, this structure has the same short-term rate schedules as the Fred McMahan Downtown Garage; the monthly permit here is $60. It is also attended.

5. Anna Porter Library (72 spaces). Turn left at Cherokee Orchard Road (traffic light #6), go 2 blocks to Newton Lane, and turn left again. Entrance is just past the library. Coming in from US 321, turn left at the Baskins Creek Bypass. Lot entrance is on the right just after the road levels out. It's a short walk to downtown, and the lot has a flat rate of $3.00. An attendant operates the lot.

6. Reagan Drive (189 spaces). Reagan Drive intersects the Parkway at traffic light #7—look for Ripley's Believe It or Not! museum. The lot is 2 blocks up on the left, next to the fire hall. It's a moderate downhill walk into town and a strenuous uphill walk back.

Payment is honor system with meters; a monthly permit costs $15. No attendant is present.

7. City Hall park-and-ride (84 spaces). Located on US 321, 2 miles east of downtown, between City Hall and the post office. Parking is free; ride the blue route trolley into town. The lot is unattended.

Car Rentals

In addition to the Knoxville-based companies mentioned in the "Getting Here" section of this chapter, there are several car rental agencies in Sevier County. Local companies are good for those traveling in larger recreational vehicles who may want a more manageable form of getting around town. They may also be an attractive option for those who experience car trouble and have to put their personal vehicle in the shop for a day or so.

In Sevierville you can contact Enterprise Rent-A-Car at (865) 908–3044 or McNelly-Whaley Motor Company at (865) 453–2833. McNelly-Whaley is the local Ford dealership that also maintains a satellite office at Gatlinburg–Pigeon Forge Airport in Sevierville. In Gatlinburg call Southland Car & Jeep Rentals at (865) 436–9811.

These rental agencies maintain fleets with as few as 7 cars or as many as 50. Fleet sizes will vary from season to season, but you might find it harder to find cars during the peak tourist months. Except for the one Ford dealership, most of the companies keep a variety of makes and models on-site, including vans. Most will also deliver their cars to you.

We found that prices range from as low as $28 per day for subcompact models to $80 per day for luxury and sport models. Although credit cards are the standard form of payment, most of the companies will accept cash. In these cases, a more substantial up-front deposit is required. If you live outside Tennessee and wish to pay with cash, you may want to call ahead to verify if a particular company will accept your cash deposit.

Taxis

You will also find a number of cab operators located throughout the county. Don't expect to see the traditional yellow checkered cab pull up to your door, however. Some of these companies, especially the newer ones, utilize late-model minivans that accommodate more passengers. Most of the businesses we've included service the entire Sevier County area (and, in some cases, transportation to the airport and bus station in Knoxville). In Sevierville contact Donald Newman Taxi at (865) 453–6551, and in Pigeon Forge you'll find All Right Taxi at (865) 429–3531. In Gatlinburg call All Park Taxi and Tour at (865) 908–0911 or C & O Taxi Service at (865) 436–5893.

Jeep, Motorcycle, ATV, and Scooter Rentals

Jeeps, motorcycles, ATVs, and scooters provide alternative means of transportation that are more than just another way

of getting from point A to point B. On a beautiful day in the mountains, there's nothing like traveling with the wind in your hair and the sun in your face—just for the fun of it. It's also a great way to see the sights.

Two area businesses rent these types of vehicles on an hourly or daily basis: Lee's Scooter and Jeep Rentals, (865) 436–3060; and Southland Car & Jeep Rentals, (865) 436–9811. As is the case with regular automobile rentals, these rental fleets are frequently in use during the peak season months, so availabilities are limited. Rental terms will vary from company to company, but in general you can expect to pay an up-front deposit and must be able to show a driver's license and proof of insurance. Some companies will also have minimum age requirements for certain types of vehicles.

Trolleys

Short of having the use of a car while visiting the Smokies, your next best bet is to utilize the trolley systems of Pigeon Forge and Gatlinburg. The trolleys are a dependable, inexpensive way to get around that will take you most anywhere you might want to go. Their combined service routes run from the north border of Pigeon Forge all the way into the national park as well as the Great Smoky Arts & Crafts Community. And if you've been on your feet all day, nothing beats just plunking

Although the trolleys in Pigeon Forge and Gatlinburg don't accommodate wheelchairs, both cities provide special vans that are wheelchair accessible. You can reach the Pigeon Forge Fun Time Trolley at (865) 453-6444 or the Gatlinburg Trolley at (865) 436-3897. Both trolley systems require 24-hour advance notice.

down your quarter (or more, in some cases), sitting back, and taking in the sights while someone else does the driving.

Although Sevierville currently doesn't have a trolley system, city officials have been studying the possibility of implementing one in the near future with routes running throughout the city and possibly to Dollywood.

Pigeon Forge Fun Time Trolley
(865) 453-6444

The main office and the fleet for this trolley service are on Old Mill Avenue, at the Patriot Park site, behind the Old Mill. Five trolley routes cover more than 100 stopping points throughout the city of Pigeon Forge.

The largest route, the Main Street Trolley, runs the length of Pigeon Forge's Parkway, making turnaround loops at the north and south ends. Another long route sticks less to the straight and narrow, meandering along many of the secondary roads that parallel and bisect the Parkway. This Wears Valley Trolley travels to the Pigeon Forge Community Center via Teaster Lane before heading out to the city limits on Wears Valley Road. It returns on Wears Valley Road, heading back to the trolley office via a network of back roads that runs behind Pigeon Forge Factory Outlet Mall.

Two more trolley routes service Dollywood's main entrance and Dolly's Splash Country, respectively, and a fifth route takes riders to the Gatlinburg Welcome Center on the Spur, near the north entrance to that town.

There are two transfer points, one at Belz Mall and the other at the trolley office. At the Belz Mall location, you can switch from the Wears Valley Road/Teaster Lane trolley to the Parkway trolley. At the main office you connect to both of these routes as well as the Gatlinburg route and the two Dollywood routes.

The Pigeon Forge Fun Time Trolley runs from 8:30 A.M. to midnight, April through October. In November and December trolleys run from 10:00 A.M. to

10:00 P.M., except for Thanksgiving Day, Christmas Eve, and Christmas Day. Trolley fare is 25 cents each time you board. Both coins and tokens are accepted. You can purchase individual tokens for 25 cents each at the trolley office or the Pigeon Forge Department of Tourism.

Although the regular trolley system is basically shut down from early January through March, you can still view the city's holiday decorations on its Winterfest Trolley Tours of Light, which run November through February (see our Festivals and Annual Events chapter). Tours depart from the trolley office Monday through Friday evenings, beginning at 6:30 P.M., from mid-November through New Year's Day. In January the tours run Monday, Wednesday, and Friday only at 6:30 P.M. Heated buses and informed hosts will guide you through the history of all the light displays. The cost of each trolley ride is $3.00 per person.

Gatlinburg Trolley
(865) 436-3897

This system services more than 100 locations in Gatlinburg. Its base of operations is the new Mass Transit Center located downtown, between Ripley's Aquarium of the Smokies and the parking garage located behind the attraction.

The trolleys themselves are green and orange, but don't confuse these colors with the different color-coded routes that traverse the city. Each trolley has a sign posted on its front and sides indicating which route it follows.

Red Route—This trolley originates from the Mass Transit Center, travels up River Road, up the south end of the Parkway, up Historic Nature Trail (formerly Airport Road), and through the Baskins Creek neighborhood before circling back to base. This route operates from 8:00 A.M. to midnight daily, early April through October. From November through early April, only one trolley runs the route, Sunday through Thursday from 10:00 A.M. to 6:00 P.M. and Friday and Saturday from 10:00 A.M. to 10:00 P.M. The fare is 25 cents.

Purple Route—The trolley runs from the Mass Transit Center downtown, along the Parkway to the Welcome Center and Park-n-Ride lot located on the Spur (US 441) at the north end of the city. Like the Red Route, this route operates from 8:00 A.M. to midnight daily, early April through October. From November through early April, only one trolley runs the route, Sunday through Thursday from 10:00 A.M. to 6:00 P.M. and Friday and Saturday from 10:00 A.M. to 10:00 P.M. The fare is 25 cents.

Blue Route—This route runs from the Mass Transit Center, up US 321, all the way out to the Gatlinburg Community Center. It also serves the free Park-n-Ride lot located next to City Hall. The schedule is identical to that of the two routes previously outlined. The fare is 25 cents.

Yellow Route—These minitrolleys run along US 321, from downtown Gatlinburg out to the Great Smoky Arts & Crafts Community, making a loop around Glades Road and Buckhorn Road through the community itself. The normal operating schedule is from 8:00 A.M. to midnight, early April through October. In November and December, these trolleys run daily from 10:00 A.M. to 6:00 P.M.; January through March, they run Saturday only from 10:00 A.M. to 6:00 P.M. The cost is $1.00.

Tan Route—This circuit runs from the Mass Transit Center, down River Road and the Parkway to Sugarlands Visitor Center in Great Smoky Mountains National Park. From there, it continues further into the park, to the Laurel Falls parking area and Elkmont campground, eventually returning to downtown. The round-trip travel time is 1½ hours. This route runs June through October only, and the fare is $2.00.

Pink Route—This trolley departs from the Mass Transit Center and takes passengers to the Pigeon Forge trolley office at Patriot Park and, of course, Dollywood. In season, daily trolleys depart approximately every hour. In November and December, these trolleys run only on weekends and holidays. The fare is 75 cents.

Beginning in November, you can enjoy the city's Winterfest Trolley Rides of Light. Not to be confused with any of the trolleys' winter schedules, these special sightseeing trolleys offer spectacular views of Gatlinburg's Winterfest lighting displays. Tours depart from the visitor information center at traffic light #3 and cost $4.00 per person for ages 12 and older. In November and December, they run nightly at 6:30, 7:30, and 8:30 P.M. In January they run Saturday only, on the same schedule. However, since tours don't run on Thanksgiving, Christmas, and a few other selected days, the city advises calling (865) 436-3897 to verify specific times and dates. See our Festivals and Annual Events chapter for more information about these trolley tours.

HISTORY 🏛

AND THEN THERE WERE MOUNTAINS

It all started with one drawn-out event, a geological cataclysm that created our very landscape. The Great Smoky Mountains were formed around 200 million years ago during a collision of continental land masses, which geologists refer to as the Appalachian orogeny. As layer upon layer of rock strata and ocean sediment were slowly folded and forced skyward, the face of the earth became permanently changed, and the stage was set for a chain of events that continues to unfold today. After all, history is always being made.

Along with its towering fortresses of stone, nature was busy at work in other areas long ago, carving valleys, leveling pastures, and causing rivers and streams to spring forth with water. As was the case with the native inhabitants and early settlers of other uncharted lands, geography played a crucial role in primeval mountain life. Mountain settlements were valued as much for their protection as they were for their beauty. And locating near a river was imperative. Running waters were the source of life for drinking, washing, fishing, and in later centuries, grinding corn and generating electricity.

It's a given that the many places and things that make up our communities are named after the people who influenced their time. But the legacies of mountain and river are readily apparent in today's Smoky Mountain communities. An old settlement and an existing highway share the name Boyd's Creek. Sevierville was originally known as Forks of Little Pigeon, and today's city of Pigeon Forge takes its name from that same water source. Upper and Lower Middle Creek Roads are important thoroughfares through the county, and the names of countless businesses and streets contain the "M" word, the word that never finds its way far from the local vocabulary—"mountain."

THE FIRST INHABITANTS

Despite their strong association with Cherokee Indians, the Smoky Mountains were first home to various prehistoric Indians that preceded the Cherokee by as many as 20,000 years, according to some scientists. The earliest documented Native American existence in the area points to the Archaic Period Indians, who lived here as far back as 10,000 years ago and as recently as 900 B.C. They lived in small nomadic groups of 25 to 30 people and survived primarily off the hunting of animals.

The Eastern Woodland Indians made their homes in the mountains between 900 B.C. and A.D. 900. Artifacts like arrowheads, pieces of pottery, and crude tools have been recovered from different sites around the county and suggest that the Woodland Period Indians enjoyed a more agrarian, less nomadic lifestyle. This time also marked the advent of the burial mound, the means through which many modern discoveries of Indian relics have been made.

Following the Woodland People were the Indians of the Mississippian Period (A.D. 900 to 1600). This period saw increases in both tribal populations and the complexity of political organization, and is generally regarded as the peak of prehistoric Indian culture. Existence of their lifestyle has been revealed through several notable local digs: on McCroskey Island in the French Broad River, a site in Pigeon Forge, and at the McMahon Indian Mound located along the east bank of West Fork of the Little Pigeon River in the heart of Sevierville. Today, a hotel and a historical marker stand on the McMahon site (see our Hotels and Motels chapter for more).

The Cherokee were descendants of these early Indian civilizations. They primarily made their homes in present-day North Carolina and used East Tennessee lands as hunting grounds. As white visitors and settlers made their way into Cherokee territory, years of alternating peace and conflict were the backdrop for Indian existence. The tribe maintained a strong presence in the Smokies until they were marched en masse to the Oklahoma territory in the 1840s on the infamous Trail of Tears. Today, however, a fairly strong Cherokee population still makes its home in western North Carolina (see our Cherokee, North Carolina, chapter).

EARLY VISITORS

One of the Cherokees' earliest recorded experiences with outsiders was friendly enough, according to historical accounts. Hernando de Soto journeyed into the area in 1540, likely during a gold expedition, and received a warm greeting from the natives. However, as the years passed, more and more traders, usually white men, infiltrated the region and didn't always receive such warm receptions. In fact, many were killed by the Cherokee, including two Virginia traders named Boyd and Daggett. In 1775 these two men were slaughtered, and their bodies were thrown into a creek. Incidentally, this was the origin of the name Boyd's Creek, a site that would later play an important role in the development of Sevier County.

In 1776 large numbers of white men were introduced to the area as colonial armies clashed with the British and their allies, the Cherokee. That year, Colonel William Christian from Virginia led 1,800 infantry in a punitive expedition against a number of Cherokee Overhill towns located along the Indian War Path, the area's only travel route of the time, which extended from Pennsylvania to Georgia. Many of the soldiers who passed through

When visiting downtown Sevierville, take an hour or so to visit the Sevier County Heritage Museum on Bruce Street. The self-guided tour is interesting, informative, and free. See the Attractions chapter for a more detailed description of what the Heritage Museum has to offer.

this area remembered its beauty and resources and returned here to settle in the years following the Revolutionary War.

Two particular battles from that war relate to local history. Colonel John Sevier led a group of men from Washington County, North Carolina (as Tennessee was known at the time), against the British at the Battle of King's Mountain on October 7, 1780. Although the British were defeated in that clash, what was of more local significance was the subsequent Battle of Boyd's Creek two months later. As Sevier and his men returned from King's Mountain, they discovered that their settlements had been attacked by Cherokee Indians during their absence. At Boyd's Creek on December 16, Sevier led 100 men to victory against the Cherokee in what was to be the first of 35 Indian battles in which the colonel would engage over the years.

SETTLEMENT AND EARLY GOVERNMENT

At war's end, a number of those who fought for the Continental Armies received land grants in recognition of their service. Many made homes along Dumplin' Creek, just north of the French Broad River, and later along Boyd's Creek and the Little Pigeon River. One of the earliest known of these settlers was Isaac Thomas, a former Indian trader who had been a guide for William Christian in 1776 and was a scout and a guide for John Sevier at Boyd's Creek. He was given 1,000 acres west of West Fork of the Little Pigeon

River around 1781 or 1782, making him one of Sevierville's first permanent white residents. He even gave Sevierville its first name, Forks of Little Pigeon.

Over the next couple of years, other notable local fathers made their way toward the Smokies. In 1782 Major Hugh Henry built a homestead at Dumplin' Creek near the present-day community of Kodak. Henry's Station, or Henry's Crossroads as it was known, was typical of the small blockhouses used by settlers in those days; these "forts" were not only used as dwellings but as protection against Indian attack.

In 1783 Captain Samuel Newell settled near what is now the unincorporated town of Seymour in west Sevier County. Newell was a veteran of battles with both the British and the Cherokee; he was to be prominent in the political structure of the area, from its formative years all the way through Tennessee statehood. His home, Newell's Station, would later be the first "county seat" of an infant Sevier County.

Also in 1783, another prominent figure of early Sevierville, James McMahon, settled on 400 acres between the east and west forks of Little Pigeon River, present-day site of Sevierville's downtown district. It was on this land that the McMahon Indian Mound was first excavated in 1881.

During the early 1780s, pioneers were faced not only with the hardships presented by a rugged wilderness existence but also by the political goings-on of the day. Although North Carolina had passed an act in 1783 reserving much of what we now know as East Tennessee for the Cherokee, it was also issuing land grants and selling land to white settlers in that same territory. Needless to say, this only exacerbated tensions between the whites and the Indians, leading to frequent conflict.

By 1784 the North Carolina treasury was severely drained by the war. It no longer had the resources or the inclination to support and protect its outposts to the west. The settlers of Washington County and the recently formed Greene County had become frustrated with North Carolina's neglect and inability to protect their settlements from Indian attack. In November of that year, the settlers met in Greeneville and organized their own government for a territory they named the State of Franklin, a moniker that they hoped would ingratiate them with the national government in their efforts to achieve statehood. Despite a noble attempt, however, Franklin fell short of its goal, coming within six votes of becoming the 14th state.

Although it failed in those efforts, Franklin did manage to come to more peaceful terms with the Cherokee. In 1785 a delegation from Franklin, led by its governor, John Sevier, met with Cherokee leaders and warriors at Henry's Station near Dumplin' Creek. With the signing of the Treaty of Dumplin' Creek, much of today's East Tennessee was officially opened up for homesteading. Although the Cherokee were well compensated in exchange, not everyone in that nation was in agreement with the peace accord, and numerous massacres were still led against the white settlers.

THE BIRTH, REBIRTH, AND REBIRTH OF A COUNTY

Sevier County was first formed on March 31, 1785, when the Franklin legislature divided existing Greene County into three smaller counties, one of which was named for Franklin governor John Sevier. The first county court was held at Newell's Station.

Legend has it that Timothy Reagan, the man employed to build Sevier County's first prisoners' stocks in 1795, persuaded the county sheriff to allow himself to be locked in them in order to test them out. Reportedly, the sheriff was left locked in the stocks for a considerable amount of time, much to the amusement of the local residents.

In 1788, however, the state of Franklin collapsed due to dissension among its citizens as well as North Carolina's failure to recognize it as a sovereign entity. The following year, a brief attempt at reorganization was made with the formation of the state of Lesser Franklin, but when John Sevier and other leaders swore allegiance to North Carolina, Franklin ceased to exist once and for all.

Sevier County went through a second incarnation when the former State of Franklin was ceded to the federal government and became part of the Territory of the United States South of the River Ohio. William Blount was appointed its governor, and by 1794 Sevier County was reformed, with its first court being held at the home of Isaac Thomas on November 8. Samuel Newell remained active in this new government, becoming one of the Sevier County court officials, as did Samuel Wear and Mordecai Lewis, both of whom will be discussed in our history of Pigeon Forge.

Finally, in 1796 Sevier County as we know it today came into existence when Tennessee achieved statehood. The new state name was derived from Tenasi, the name for Cherokee villages along the Little Tennessee River. Its first court was held on July Fourth in the county's first courthouse, which was located in the heart of Sevierville. Several county notables had represented their home district at Tennessee's constitutional convention, including Samuel Wear, Samuel Newell, and Sevierville resident Spencer Clack. Clack had moved to Sevierville around 1788 and settled on 400 acres on the north side of East Prong of Little Pigeon River. He was an active force in local government, education, and religion.

Sevierville

Although the legislative act that had reestablished Sevier County in 1794 also called for a commission to locate a county seat, it wasn't until 1795 that the commission finally chose a site at Forks of Little Pigeon; Isaac Thomas suggested the name Sevierville in honor of John Sevier. The commission acquired a 25-acre tract of land from James McMahon, whose centrally located homestead made the property a good prospect. There, a primitive courthouse along with a prison and stocks were constructed. Also, the rectangular piece of land was parceled off into 50 half-acre lots that were sold to the highest bidders for home construction. The establishment of Sevierville made it the seventh-oldest town in Tennessee, and following the planting of those early roots, the fledgling community blossomed into the center of the county's economic and governmental activity.

Sevier County's first three courthouses, all of which were believed to have been destroyed by fire, were located in a section of downtown where Sevierville's two main thoroughfares, Cross Street (now Court Avenue) and Main Street, intersected. When a fourth brick courthouse was erected on the site in 1856, this one-acre tract came to be known as Public Square; in addition to having a courthouse and a jail, the site also evolved into the commercial and social hub of Sevier County.

Such was the situation until 1896, when the current courthouse was built on a new site 1 block away. Shortly after World War I, a major fire devastated several key Public Square businesses, and in 1948, U.S. Highways 441 and 411 (running concurrently) were widened. These events helped usher in a period of general decline during which existing Public Square businesses were either replaced by new ones or eliminated altogether. Today, this section of downtown is unremarkable from a commercial standpoint. Nevertheless, the area is liberally festooned with historical markers and other placards, which remind today's citizens of Public Square's once-strong pulse.

Sevierville was typical of most 19th-century Sevier County communities in

One of the early city ordinances enacted by Sevierville's first city council in 1901 is of peculiar interest. The act was intended to "prevent the teasing, worrying, or annoying of persons of unsound mind, imbeciles, idiots, lunatics, and fools within the corporate limits of the Town of Sevierville." No one can say that Seviervillians aren't a compassionate bunch!

that education was a priority among its residents. By 1923 as many as 99 different schools were reported to be in operation throughout the county, most of them small, one-teacher schools. In 1806 Nancy Academy was founded in Sevierville, one of the city's first wobbly steps in the pursuit of public education. Offering a curriculum based on "the three Rs," Nancy Academy thrived for almost a century until internal conflict, a fire, and a theft contributed to the school's demise in 1892.

In 1890 Nancy Academy was succeeded by another secondary school, Murphy College. Although the school was administered under the auspices of the Methodist Episcopal Church, its curriculum was "free from sectarian teachings," according to its catalog. The school folded in 1935 due to the hardships of the Great Depression as well as the county's expanding public school system. The original Murphy College building was renovated and today houses the administrative offices of the county's school system. The larger, multibuilding facility that was later used by the college is now home to the Church of God Home for Children, a local orphanage.

Sevierville experienced another period of heavy population growth in the early 1800s. Following the War of 1812, veterans were given land grants in the area, just as they had been following the Revolutionary War. Many of Sevierville's early fathers who had fought for our nation's independence also saw action in the War of 1812, including Spencer Clack and Isaac

Thomas. By the way, it was the massive enlistment of area residents in that war that helped earn Tennessee the nickname "The Volunteer State."

Although the Civil War touched the town and the county as a whole, neither was as directly affected as some other regions of the South. One reason was that few slaves were found in the area—because of the hilly terrain, farms tended to be smaller and didn't generate the income necessary for the land owners to purchase large numbers of slaves. There were a few plantations in the county, nonetheless, including Wheatlands, near Boyd's Creek, and Rose Glen, located on today's Pittman Center Road.

Officially, Tennessee was a Confederate state, but most of East Tennessee sympathized with the Union. As such, many who wanted to fight for the Union Army had to make their way across the state line to neighboring Kentucky to enlist. Some even dressed up as women to be able to cross the tightly regulated borders. The only major Civil War battle to take place in the county was the Battle of Fairgarden, about 7 miles east of Sevierville. In 1864, a division of Union soldiers attacked a stronghold of Confederate troops and forced them back several miles. Reportedly 65 Confederate soldiers were killed and more than 100 were taken captive. Outside of this engagement, the county only saw a few minor skirmishes, and it was used by both armies as a source of food and supplies.

The turn of the 20th century was an eventful period in Sevierville. One of the darker but still more colorful chapters of local history (literally and figuratively speaking) was the White Cap era of the 1890s. Not to be confused with the racially motivated Ku Klux Klan, the White Caps were a group that practiced what could best be described as vigilante justice, often stepping in to weed out "lewd" and "immoral" people from the county. Those targeted were first given written notice to leave the county; those who failed to do so were severely whipped by

White Caps. At their peak of influence, around 1894, whippings of men and women were almost nightly occurrences.

After several years, however, the White Caps were gradually infiltrated by a more serious criminal element who knew that their crimes would go unpunished as long as they operated within the White Cap ranks. As the vigilantes lost favor with the public, another group, the Blue Bills, were formed to confront them and try to head off their attacks. The Blue Bills were composed largely of local professionals and businessmen who clashed frequently with the White Caps, often with serious consequences.

Tensions finally came to a head when two White Cap members murdered Sevierville residents William and Laura Whaley. The two culprits were convicted and hanged in Sevierville's Public Square in the late 1890s, making them the last to be publicly executed in the city. In the years that followed, legislation and a tough stance by local law enforcement soon turned Sevier County into one of the most peaceful, law-abiding counties in the state. Fortunately, that trend has continued to this day.

The turn of the century also brought a couple of politically relevant changes to Sevierville. The county's fifth courthouse, which is still in operation, was completed in 1896 (see our Attractions chapter), and on April 11, 1901, Sevierville finally became an incorporated town. Several previous attempts to do so had been shot down because the town was divided over the issue of alcohol sales (some things never change!). With the incorporation of 1901, Sevierville became a dry town, and until just a few years ago, alcohol still was not sold by the drink (see Area Overview).

Sevierville continued to thrive in the first half of the 20th century. Its population was still fairly small, but for its size, it was a healthy, self-sufficient community. Over the next 50 years, however, a number of significant events slowly but surely connected it to the rest of the globe. Two world wars were responsible for hundreds

of local men either enlisting or being drafted to serve their country. As was the case in many other parts of the nation, young men's lives were changed permanently when they left the safety of their farms to engage in battle halfway around the world. Dozens never returned to their hometown in the Smokies.

In 1909 Sevierville's commercial links with outside markets were expanded with the completion of the Knoxville, Sevierville, and Eastern Railroad, the first incarnation of what would be generally known as the Smoky Mountain Railroad. Unfortunately, the railroad languished under several owners until its ultimate demise in 1961; the increased popularity of the automobile limited its success. The railroad did enjoy a brief period of profitability in the 1940s during the construction of Douglas Dam, but today, no vestiges of its existence remain in the city (except for a street named Railroad Street).

Douglas Dam itself brought massive amounts of inexpensive public electricity to the Smokies for the first time. Built on the French Broad River between 1942 and 1943 by the Tennessee Valley Authority (TVA), the dam flooded a lot of good, level farmland, but it helped light up an area that, until then, had either gone without electricity or had relied on small, private companies for power. The TVA was to lay its hands on Sevierville again in the 1960s when it literally rerouted the course of the Little Pigeon River near downtown to help prevent more of the major, destructive flooding that had plagued the city for decades.

It wasn't until the post–World War II era, however, that the rest of the world would finally start to make its impact on Sevierville. After the war the interstate highway system and America's intensified love affair with the car brought more and more visitors to the Smoky Mountains. For decades, most of these travelers simply saw Sevierville as a place through which to pass on their way to Gatlinburg and the mountains. When Knoxville hosted the

1982 World's Fair, all of the county's communities prospered from the spillover, including Sevierville. Throughout the 1990s and into the new millennium, the city has continued to develop into a tourist destination in its own right (see Area Overview).

Pigeon Forge

By the late 1700s, Pigeon Forge had followed a similar course to that of Sevierville, serving as a place of settlement for soldiers after the war for America's independence. At least this was so until Sevierville became the county seat; from that point on, the two communities followed different paths. Sevierville expanded in every sense while Pigeon Forge remained a small, sleepy mountain village until tourism began to really take root and flourish in the 1970s and 1980s.

In 1781 Samuel Wear became the first permanent white settler in what is now Pigeon Forge. Wear was a Revolutionary War colonel who had been a longtime friend of John Sevier and had served as a captain under Sevier at the Battle of King's Mountain. He was given a land grant of 500 acres and built his homestead near the mouth of Walden's Creek, a tributary of the Little Pigeon River. Wear was a key figure in the formation of the state of Franklin and served as Sevier County court clerk for 27 years, starting with the first county court at Newell's Station in 1785.

During this same period, other settlers who were to play major roles in the development of Pigeon Forge put down roots, including Floyd Nichols, Barefoot Runyan, and Mordecai Lewis. It is believed that Lewis probably operated a mill back in those days; it is known that his land occupied the present-day site of the Old Mill (see our Attractions chapter) on the banks of the Little Pigeon River. His land also adjoined that of Isaac Runyan, a son of Barefoot and his wife, Margaret Rambo.

Most of these early Pigeon Forge settlements were located along the river, where two primary types of businesses developed: mills and ironworks, or forges. Isaac Love, another significant figure of early Pigeon Forge, married a daughter of Mordecai Lewis and inherited the Lewis family mill. By 1820 Love was operating an ironworks on the same site, and 10 years later Isaac's son, William, built the present-day Old Mill there. Still in operation, the Old Mill may be the oldest existing mill in Tennessee. On May 29, 1841, a post office was established under the name Pigeon Forge, and William Love was appointed postmaster. In those days, this post office was located on the same site as the Love's mill and forge, making it the center of the town's activity.

The name Pigeon Forge was derived from the existing iron works as well as the Little Pigeon River. The river itself had gotten its name from the huge flocks of migratory passenger pigeons that had frequently stopped there throughout the 1700s and early 1800s to feed on the abundance of beech trees. Unlike the town that bears its name today, the passenger pigeon dwindled into extinction. The last one died in captivity at the Cincinnati Zoo in 1914.

In the 1840s the ironworks gradually failed due to the lack of transportation in and out of the area. The Sevier County Turnpike Company had built a "road" that extended into Sevierville, but this was nothing more than a glorified trail. Another factor that led to the decline of the forges was the low iron content of the existing ore veins. And when a blast furnace at the Love's ironworks exploded,

---

i

The parkway that runs through Pigeon Forge was built after World War II. Before then, people going from Sevierville to Gatlinburg traveled down Pittman Center Road to Glades Road, and into Gatlinburg on Tennessee Highway 73, a distance of about 20 miles on dirt roads.

---

the family moved to Missouri, selling their business to John Sevier Trotter, a local miller who later revived the ironworks.

When the Civil War broke out, Pigeon Forge was used as a northern stronghold; 30 townsmen joined the Union forces. Although there were no battles or skirmishes in the town, hard times befell those who stayed behind to mind the home front. Schools were abandoned, roads deteriorated, and the flow of supplies from the outside dried up.

At the turn of the century, progress slowly crept into this rural Sevier County community. It wasn't until 1890 that the town's second store opened for business, and in 1898 Pigeon Forge's first telephone was finally connected. By 1907 the town's population was still only 154, but the following 30 years brought steady growth—stores, churches, and schools would spring up in greater numbers.

In August 1916 the Pigeon Forge Railroad Company extended the Knoxville, Sevierville, and Eastern Railroad line, bridging the Little Pigeon River in Sevierville and then running southeast into Pigeon Forge. Completed in 1920, this extension contributed to KS & E's revenues and aided with the flow of timber and lumber traffic out of the area. However, the growing popularity of large trucks as a means of transportation contributed to the abandonment of the Pigeon Forge rail extension in 1929.

The establishment of Great Smoky Mountains National Park in 1934 was ultimately to affect the lives of Forge residents in an irreversible manner. The birth of the park naturally led to larger numbers of visitors passing through Pigeon Forge on their way to Gatlinburg and the Smoky Mountains. In 1946, however, the Pigeon Forge tourism industry began in its own right with the city's first sale of a parcel of land smaller than a farm. The tobacco barn that stood on the land eventually became Pigeon Forge Pottery, which did a thriving business across the street from the Old Mill until 2000. That's when longtime owners the Ferguson fam-

On November 11, 1925, a monument to Colonel Samuel Wear was dedicated in Pigeon Forge. General W. T. Kennedy of Knoxville, who spoke at the dedication ceremony, made a prediction before the assembled group. He foresaw the creation of a national park in the Great Smoky Mountains as well as a "broad concrete highway" that would run from Knoxville through Sevierville, Pigeon Forge, and Gatlinburg all the way to North Carolina via the national park. This speech was made 10 years before Great Smoky Mountains National Park was established and decades before today's multilane parkway ever became a reality.

ily sold the shop—perhaps fittingly—to owners of the Old Mill.

As more businesses and accommodations grew to serve the growing tourist traffic, Pigeon Forge found itself being transformed from a sleepy, rural town composed primarily of farmland into a viable economic community. In response to this metamorphosis, residents voted (by a narrow margin) to incorporate the town in 1961. From there, the snowball effect took over in changing both the character and the physical landscape of Pigeon Forge. Tourist-oriented businesses multiplied exponentially, particularly during the '70s and '80s. The 1982 World's Fair in Knoxville and the opening of Dollywood in 1986 both contributed to making Pigeon Forge an actual tourist destination, rather than a mere stopover.

Today, the large expanses of cornfields have been replaced by restaurants, hotels, attractions, and shopping malls which host over 40,000 visitors per day (see Area Overview). Regardless, the legacies of the Pigeon Forge of old live on in the descendants of the founding fathers who still reside there. Pigeon Forge's permanent population of around 4,500 doesn't have to look too far beyond the gift shops and go-kart tracks to see the green, wooded hillsides that still roll away toward the horizon and remind them of the way things once were.

Gatlinburg

Imagine, if you please, that it's any hour of daylight on a summer day of anytime between 1810 and 1910, and you're vacationing in Gatlinburg, Tennessee, soon to become a prominent national resort. To make it a little easier to visualize, let's say you're standing at the foot of the space needle, the city's tallest street-level landmark, looking back along the Parkway to the Ferris wheel at Fun Mountain. What do you see?

First, you don't see the space needle or Fun Mountain. In fact, you're probably not even standing on or near a road; you're in a field, probably corn, belonging to either a Reagan, a Maples, or an Ogle, depending on the time. Also, depending on the time, you may be at the edge of White Oak Flats. And one more certainty: You can count on your fingers the number of people you see. If you see any people at all.

Like most cities in most everywhere else, Gatlinburg got its start as a farming community when non-nomadic American Indians (the Cherokee in this case) settled here somewhere around 500 years ago and established farms in the fertile bottomland. The biggest mistake these noble citizens made was to invite certain white men to share the bounty of their fields and forests. By the beginning of the 19th century, the land belonged to the white men through various treaties and the granting of Tennessee's statehood in 1796.

Among the white men who had hunted and fished this particular area as a guest of the Cherokee was a South Carolinian named William "Old Billy" Ogle, whose wife was part Indian. He staked a claim on a choice piece of land (very close to the Arrowmont School campus today) and cut and hewed enough logs to build a cabin. He then returned to South Carolina to grow a crop of food large enough to

feed his family for the year he figured it would take to move to Tennessee and establish a home. He never made it back.

When Billy Ogle left his Tennessee property and returned to South Carolina, he walked into a malarial flu epidemic that took his life. His widow, Martha Jane, approaching 50 and still tending to seven grown children (and some of their children), left South Carolina and the flu for an "extended" visit with her brother Peter Huskey in Virginia. From there the brood migrated to Tennessee, stopping briefly at Wears Fort on Waldens Creek (west of Pigeon Forge), and then made their way into White Oak Flats, probably through Wears Valley and Elkmont (history is a little vague on this point, but no other roads existed at the time). Martha Jane's oldest son, Isaac, built the cabin his father had left the provisions for (there's also some historical disagreement on this point— some historians insist Isaac bought 50 acres of land, but from whom is a mystery), and a new community began its existence. The year was 1805.

It's significant to understand that Martha Jane Huskey Ogle and her family were by no means entering an untamed wilderness. They knew exactly where they were going and what they were going to find. The immediate area they inhabited was mountainous and previously unsettled by white people, but the region was not. Sevierville was an established city before 1800, and so was Knoxville. And, despite the fact that Big Orange football was almost a century up the road, the University of Tennessee had been in operation for more than a decade when the Ogle family established the White Oak Flats community.

The arrival of Martha Jane Huskey Ogle and her young in this valley established the area known then as White Oak Flats and, in a naturally expanded form, known today as Gatlinburg. The change of names occurred in the 1850s when a decidedly unpleasant man named Radford Gatlin arrived and opened a general store. In addition to the rumored possession of a slave (not a social asset in East Tennessee), Radford Gatlin brought with him a sulfurous wife, no children, an attitude that didn't sit well with the locals, and enough government contacts to secure a postal commission, which he used to name the community in his own honor in 1856. By 1859 Gatlin had succeeded in alienating enough of the townsfolk that he was invited to seek his fortunes elsewhere. He agreed to go peacefully if the name "Gatlinburg" would be retained, and the locals bought the deal.

Gatlin disappeared into an uncertain history, but it is known that he worked for the Confederacy during the Civil War. The city was occupied briefly by Confederate troops during the Civil War while saltpeter for gunpowder production was being mined in the mountains. Union forces came in around Christmas in 1863, took over the town without firing a shot, and Gatlinburg's involvement in the war ended. It was significant only in that the Battle of Gatlinburg was the last known "conflict" in which Native Americans were engaged. They were camp followers of the Confederate troops, and their actual status has never been clearly defined.

From its founding as White Oak Flats and the noneventful involvement in the Civil War, the town remained frozen in time for almost a century. The establishment of the post office in 1856, and the accompanying adoption of the name Gatlinburg, were the only significant changes in the town's basic operation from around 1825 until 1912, when a curious twist of fate occurred that was to change the face of Gatlinburg forever.

Pi Beta Phi Women's Fraternity is a national organization dedicated to education and health care. In the latter 19th and early 20th centuries, the good ladies of Pi Beta Phi worked as American missionaries, bringing the blessings of formal education and basic hygiene to isolated communities. In 1912 Pi Beta Phi considered two locations in East Tennessee as sites for a settlement school; neither site was in Sevier County, but their selection

committee chose Sevierville as a central location to meet and discuss the alternatives. During their meeting, someone suggested that they add Gatlinburg to their list of possible sites, and because it was handy, they decided to have a look. They must have liked what they saw, because Gatlinburg is where they established their school.

Gatlinburg's native craftspeople still include several artisans who learned their crafts from O. J. Mattil and Winogene Redding. The current "older" generation of native craftspeople are the children of the Redding/Mattil generation.

The Pi Phis brought an ambitious agenda with them. Their primary goal was to provide formal education to the mountain children, which in turn provided alternatives to subsistence farming as a lifestyle. Beyond that, they also brought consistent medical care and hygiene training to the community at large. They didn't really plan to set the town up in an industry, but not too long after their arrival the Pi Phis found that Gatlinburg had something the nation was crying out for. The handcrafts that had virtually disappeared from America during the industrial revolution that Gatlinburg had apparently slept through were not only still being practiced here, they were still being used for everyday life.

Enter O. J. Mattil and Winogene Redding. Mattil was brought to Gatlinburg as a vocational instructor in 1922. After indoctrinating the locals in the latest farming techniques, he set up classes for the boys in woodworking, basketry, and carpentry. Until he was able to afford a generating plant and woodworking machinery (Gatlinburg didn't have electricity at the time), Mattil's classes worked with hand tools. While all this was going on in Mattil's workshop, the other members of the Pi Phi staff were finding examples of Gatlinburg's native craftsmanship in most of the homes they visited. Knowing the marketability of the items they saw just about everywhere, the Pi Phis started recruiting the local craftspeople to both teach the youngsters their crafts and to produce their goods for sale. In 1926 Pi Beta Phi opened the Arrowcraft shop as a local outlet and started shipping the crafts of Gatlinburg to other Pi Phi outlets across the country. Winogene Redding organized and managed the whole program. It wasn't long before the crafts of Gatlinburg were in demand all over the United States. In less than five years, Gatlinburg had gone from an isolated farming community to the craft capital of America, and Pi Beta Phi was the driving force that made it happen.

It is possible that Gatlinburg's crafts would have become nationally known without the intervention of Pi Beta Phi. Forces were already at work to create the Great Smoky Mountains National Park in Gatlinburg's backyard, and the natural influx of tourism could have given the city its craft market a decade or so later. It's also possible that by the time the park and its visitors arrived, handcrafts would have disappeared from Gatlinburg like they had in most of the country.

The arrival of the Pi Phis brought about a change in the fortunes of Gatlinburg that is still paying generous dividends. For as long as craftspeople are able to make a living in this industry in this place, the names of Pi Beta Phi, O. J. Mattil, and Winogene Redding should be spoken only in capital letters. Winogene Redding stayed on with Pi Phi through the transfer of the school to the county educational system, and she worked as a weaving instructor and author at the Arrowmont School until her retirement in the early 1960s. She died in Nashville in 1981, having made a profound impact on the weaving industry and those she taught to practice and to love it.

In 1928 O. J. Mattil broadened his horizons and those of several thousand craftspeople in nine southeastern states as a prime mover in the formation of the Southern Highlands Handicraft Guild. He remained a dominant figure in that organization until his death 50 years later. In 1945, long after the school they had established in Gatlinburg had become part of the county educational system, Pi Beta Phi and the University of Tennessee established the Arrowmont School of Arts & Crafts on the land it occupies today in downtown Gatlinburg. The Arrowmont School is considered one of the preeminent institutions of its kind in the world. It's given the attention it deserves in our Education and Child Care chapter. The Arrowcraft Shop stands today in its original location at the intersection of the Parkway and Cherokee Orchard Road in downtown Gatlinburg. Pi Beta Phi sold the shop to the Southern Highlands Handicraft Guild in 1993.

As the older of the sister cities that play host to more than 10 million visitors each year, Gatlinburg finds itself torn between its gentle past and an uncertain future that promises to be anything but gentle. By the mid-1980s, Gatlinburg had pretty much settled into a routine of busy summers and idle winters with an economy fueled mainly by prosperous, middle-aged tourists, when a couple of strange things happened: The face of tourism changed dramatically, and Pigeon Forge reacted quickly and positively to the change. As suddenly as if it had been swallowed by an unseen and unknown force, the conservative Gatlinburg tourist base was engulfed by a tidal wave of younger, livelier people, married and single, who were looking for a good time and had the money to pay for it. And they brought their kids with them. And poor old Gatlinburg, blindsided by a change it never saw coming and hemmed in on three sides by the Great Smoky Mountains National Park, is struggling mightily to accommodate a whole new population in an area that really wasn't big enough for the old one.

Because new development space downtown is unavailable, any new idea means the city must first decide if existing structures are compatible. If so, fine; if not, the first tool used in new construction is the wrecking ball. Faced with the reality that the new tourist population is not as laid-back as the previous generations, Gatlinburg is reinventing itself annually to meet the demand of its new clientele and is methodically and regretfully destroying its own history to do it. Still an international center for handcrafted merchandise and fine art, Gatlinburg strives to maintain those industries as the primary link to its past while it continues to come up with new ways and new places to accommodate the best guesses it can make for the shape its future will take.

THAT WAS THEN

The tiny portion of Sevier County that constitutes the Smokies Corridor would be a textbook example of niche development if textbooks were updated monthly.

The explosive growth of the Smokies Corridor is a direct result of the establishment of Great Smoky Mountains National Park, and the area's identity has been developed by the folks who originally came to the area to enjoy the scenery and the hospitality of the local residents. It's regrettable to some local purists that a lot of people come to the Smokies for a variety of reasons totally separate from the "old days," but the fact that they come in larger numbers each year speaks well for the future. Although almost 90 percent of Sevier County's land is still farmland and wilderness, about the same percentage of the population, including a lot of folks from surrounding counties, is involved in the tourism industry. When historians of the future consider the emergence of the Smokies Corridor as a principal tourist destination, it will be interesting to see if they're able to figure out why all those people first chose to come to this place.

HOTELS AND MOTELS

Once upon a time, Gatlinburg had exclusive bragging rights when it came to hotels and motels in Sevier County. For decades, its proximity to Great Smoky Mountains National Park made it the area's dominant visitor destination. Accommodations in Pigeon Forge were built initially just to catch the tourist overflow from Gatlinburg, and lodgings in Sevierville could practically be counted on one hand.

The climate began to change in the 1980s. When Knoxville hosted the World's Fair in 1982, all of the local communities prospered from the spillover, and when Dollywood Theme Park opened in 1986, Pigeon Forge picked up steam as a tourist destination in its own right. These days, the number of hotels and motels in Sevierville is growing rapidly as well, evidence of the entire region's phenomenal expansion.

It's difficult to keep up with the statistics when it comes to charting the growth of the hotel/motel industry in the Smoky Mountains. Seemingly, as soon as city and county officials get an accurate tabulation of the number of lodging facilities and rooms to be found in the area, another foundation is poured at another construction site. To put things in ballpark terms, however, there are approximately 200 hotels and motels representing nearly 17,000 individual rooms in Sevier County alone. That's a lot of guest soap. But then again, the supply of rooms usually fights to keep up with demand, and in the Smokies the demand is high and the supply is both eclectic and broad-reaching.

Of course, the properties you'll encounter occupy a wide berth when it comes to factors such as price, amenities, and location. What's unique, though, is that when it comes to the types of establishments to be found, there is a distinct pattern in the makeup of each community as you travel south from Interstate 40. The accommodations on the northern outskirts of the county and in Sevierville itself tend to be well-known franchises that are newer and offer a long slate of amenities tailored to the traveler. The trade-off is that they're often farther away from the bulk of the action in the Smokies. Conversely, the big franchises are less prevalent as you travel through Pigeon Forge and draw nearer to Gatlinburg. That is where you'll encounter more independently owned lodgings, many that have been family-run for generations. Although they are closer to the heart of area activities, the range of available amenities can sometimes be narrower. In either case there are certainly advantages, trade-offs, and exceptions to the rules, all of which will be explored in more depth in each city's respective section.

Rules of Thumb

A number of policies, services, and amenities are common to the vast majority of the hotels and motels in Tennessee's Great Smoky Mountains. We'll outline them here and leave you to make the assumption that these conditions exist unless otherwise stated. For example, it's safe to presume that most of the rooms provide cable television. Most, but not all, of the TVs are accompanied by remote controls and receive at least one free movie channel. However, call ahead to confirm this when making reservations. Other safe bets are that the properties are open all year, are carpeted and air-conditioned, provide both smoking and nonsmoking rooms, accept most major credit cards, have at least one swimming pool, and don't allow pets. Again, exceptions to these rules will be noted in the individual write-ups.

In most of the descriptions in this chapter, you won't find too much detail about room aesthetics unless something noteworthy or distinctive warrants its mention. We found that the layouts and decor of most of the standard rooms and suites are fairly consistent from one property to the next.

Whether the hotel was brand-new or an older facility that had been recently remodeled, we almost always found clean, well-maintained, pleasantly decorated interiors.

We also discovered that first impressions of hotel exteriors could be deceiving. In many cases, we came across older motels at which one might ordinarily just give a cursory glance when driving by. However, stopping to look inside the rooms often revealed deceptively plush surroundings. Generally, variances in rates are reflections of a property's location and the number and types of amenities offered, not necessarily the cleanliness of its rooms.

As we take you on our guided tour of hotels and motels in the Smokies, we will start at I-40's exit 407 and head south on Tennessee Highway 66. The facilities we've included are more or less presented in the order in which you'll encounter them, and we'll stick to that plan until we've traveled all the way through Sevierville, Pigeon Forge, and Gatlinburg to the entrance of Great Smoky Mountains National Park. In Gatlinburg, we will take detours to check out lodgings on secondary roads and parallel streets, but otherwise, we will remain faithful to our north-south course.

Most of the hotels and motels listed in this chapter have Web sites you can visit to get information on amenities or to book rooms online. Note that some of the Internet addresses we've included will take you directly to the properties mentioned in the write-ups while some lead you to the Web sites of the parent companies. In those cases, you might have to poke around until you find a link to the specific Smokies property you're interested in.

Any Reservations?

One question that inevitably crosses the mind of the prospective Smoky Mountains visitor is "How far ahead should I make reservations?" That mainly depends on the time of year you plan to travel. If your agenda has you staying here during an unusually busy time, like the Fourth of July holiday, you'll want to hit the phones as much as six months ahead of your intended arrival. For the most part, the proprietors with whom we spoke recommended making reservations anywhere from two to six weeks prior to a visit during peak season. During the off-season, it's a buyer's market where you can often arrive in town with no reservations and pick your room (although we never advise doing that!). Major credit cards are generally the most accepted form of deposit when making reservations. Cancellation policies vary from one hotel to another. A few require as much as 72 hours advance notice of cancellation, but the typical time is 24 hours. When it comes to specific reservation information as well as cancellation procedures and fees, we recommend getting the particulars from each of the lodgings that you contact.

PRICE CODE

Our pricing guide is based on two adults staying in a standard room on a weekend night during the peak season (traditionally the summer vacation months and October, when the autumn leaves turn). Although many of the places we've included allow children to stay at no additional cost, there was some variance among the ages at which one was considered to be a "child." Where applicable, we've mentioned these specific cutoff ages, but in general they range from 12 to 19 years old. The room rates at many of the hotels and motels we encountered were simply flat fees. In these cases, the customer purchases a room at a single price, no matter how many people occupy it. Keep in mind, though, that many establishments place limits on the number of people allowed in each room and will charge extra for additional adult guests.

$	Less than $70
$$	$70–$90
$$$	$91–$110
$$$$	$111–$130
$$$$$	$131 and more

One exception to our price guide is worth noting. Although some of the more expensive hotels and motels might be out of your budget during the summer, those same properties can have substantially lower rates during the off-season. It was not uncommon for us to find hotels that charge more than $100 per night in October charging $30 or $40 per night for the same room in April or May. Again, the laws of supply and demand keep things in check.

SEVIERVILLE

As mentioned previously, each of the three primary communities in our area has its own particular character as it relates to the bigger accommodations picture. Even in the region that we are designating as "Sevierville," a number of factors might influence your selection.

The first six establishments we've included are all on or near Winfield Dunn Parkway (TN 66), the main route that runs from I-40 to downtown Sevierville (some are officially located in the small, unincorporated community of Kodak). They are almost exclusively franchises of national chains, most of which have been constructed within the past ten years. Although they are somewhat removed from the lion's share of the area's most visited spots (Pigeon Forge is 8 to 15 miles away; Gatlinburg is 15 to 20 miles), there are advantages to choosing them.

If you've made a long journey to get to the Smokies, the last thing you want to do is sit in bumper-to-bumper traffic trying to reach your hotel. The Winfield Dunn Parkway accommodations tend to be heavy on comfort and amenities, and they can make for a welcome end to what might be a long and tiring drive. Also, these hotels and motels are ideally situated for a vacation that may include outlying areas in addition to the Smokies. Those who have Knoxville or Asheville, North Carolina, on their itineraries will greatly benefit from the uncongested and centrally located TN 66 lodgings. See our Day Trips chapter to get some suggestions for such excursions.

The remainder of the Sevierville section includes many hotels that are similar in age and atmosphere to those that were just mentioned but have the added advantage of being within a few minutes' drive of an abundance of shopping, dining, and entertainment options. But we'll get there soon enough. In the meantime, buckle up!

Ramada Limited $$
3385 Winfield Dunn Parkway, Kodak
(865) 933-7378, (800) 348-4652
www.ramada.com
Conveniently located just off I-40 at exit 407, this hotel is one of the first you'll encounter on the Smokies Corridor, and it offers a pleasant night's stay for the traveler who's eager to get off the road. In operation since 1992, Ramada Limited is a good pick if you're looking for an attractive room at a price that won't break your pocketbook. The inn's 65 standard rooms and 15 suites are accessible from interior corridors on all three floors. All rooms have two queen-size beds. Some feature whirlpool tubs and balconies as well. For fun in the water year-round, take a dip in the indoor swimming pool. Children stay free at this hotel, and discounts are available for AARP and AAA members.

Holiday Inn Express $$$$
2863 Winfield Dunn Parkway, Kodak
(865) 933-9448, (800) 939-9448
www.4lodging.com
Typical of the new breed of hotels found

along the road to Sevierville, this franchise exudes comfort and was voted 1998's "Newcomer of the Year" by its parent corporation. Access to rooms is inside, and room keys are required to enter the hotel through doors other than those in the lobby. The hotel's 73 standard rooms feature private balconies and porches as well as computer modems for the traveler who can't leave work at home. Fifteen suites offer a broader amenities package, including sleeper sofas, refrigerators, microwaves, fireplaces, coffeemakers, and whirlpool tubs.

The property boasts a breakfast bar, guest laundry room, indoor pool, and whirlpool. This Holiday Inn Express is totally smoke-free and presents a light, pleasing decor with accompanying views of the surrounding countryside. Children younger than 19 stay at no cost; AARP and AAA discounts are extended as well. Although the hotel is still several miles out of Sevierville, it's convenient to shops, restaurants, and two golf courses.

Clarion Inn Willow River $$$$
1990 Winfield Dunn Parkway, Sevierville
(865) 429-7600, (800) 610-0565
www.innofthesouth.com

Old Southern charm abounds at this Clarion Inn that opened its doors in 1997. Pulling into the parking lot, you're greeted by fastidiously manicured landscaping and a three-story structure with large, stately columns and an exterior facade awash in white. Inside, the antebellum decor remains consistent. The lobby blends elegance and 19th-century simplicity, featuring accents of ornate lighting fixtures and intricately carved stair railings. Rocking chairs are prominent, and several pieces of *Gone With the Wind* memorabilia adorn the walls and tables.

This Clarion's 89 rooms have either two queen beds or one king bed and a sleeper sofa. Refrigerators, coffeemakers, and private balconies with porches are standard for these units. Those who desire fireplaces and whirlpools in their rooms can opt for one of 16 deluxe suites. Clarion Inn

Although the number of visitors to the Smoky Mountains drops off dramatically at the end of summer, there is always a heavy influx of vacationers who come to see the stunning fall foliage in October, which peaks around the second and third weeks of the month. We recommend making reservations for this time of the year many months in advance.

Willow River sets out a generous morning feast in its continental breakfast area and has both laundry facilities and meeting rooms at the disposal of its guests. An indoor pool and hot tub are accessible 24 hours a day. The outside pool area is unique in itself with a white gazebo and elevated deck overlooking the water. The entire scene is surrounded by the "Lazy River," a man-made channel, similar to those in water parks. All you have to do is grab one of the small inner tubes provided and shove off with the current.

Those making excursions away from the hotel will find themselves only a few miles from Sevierville and Eagles Landing Golf Course. Golf and honeymoon packages are both offered here. The rates at Clarion Inn Willow River are on a per-room basis and allow occupancy of up to six people, depending on the size and number of beds in the room. They honor AAA and AARP discounts and have both group and corporate rates.

Super 8 Motel $$$
1410 Winfield Dunn Parkway, Sevierville
(865) 429-0887, (800) 800-8000
www.super8.com

In keeping with the tradition of Super 8 Motels, this one is an overall good value. Children younger than 12 stay free, and discounts are available to seniors. Sixty rooms make up this property, each with a unique split-bedroom layout. The sleeping areas contain either queen- or king-size beds and are separated by a common bathroom. All rooms are tastefully decorated and furnished and open onto a private porch or balcony overlooking a scenic, tree-lined stretch of the Little Pigeon River. Each of this Super 8's three floors has a common area—there's a whirlpool spa on the first floor, a porch with rocking chairs on the second floor, and an exercise room on the third floor. The motel's location provides handy access to nearby Douglas Lake and Eagles Landing Golf Course. Open since 1995, it is family-owned and has received superior quality assurance ratings from its parent company.

Comfort Inn Mountain View Suites $$$
860 Winfield Dunn Parkway, Sevierville
(865) 428-5519, (800) 441-0311
www.choicehotels.com
If the comfort and privacy of a suite is what you're looking for, this Comfort Inn is a good selection. Open since 1988, this three-story facility provides exterior entry to most of its 95 two-room suites. Several are accessible from the inside and face the indoor pool and spa area. From others, you'll enjoy pleasant views of the Great Smoky Mountains from your private balcony. The suites can sleep up to six people and offer various combinations of amenities, including in-room whirlpool spas, woodburning fireplaces, minibars, microwaves, coffeemakers, and refrigerators. Each suite is well furnished and has two televisions, one in the bedroom and one in the sitting room.

During your stay you might take in the free continental breakfast in the morning or perhaps unwind at either of the two swimming pools. There is an indoor pool and one outside, complete with waterfalls and whirlpool spa. Comfort Inn Mountain View Suites has meeting facilities and golf packages available on request. AAA and senior discounts are honored, and children younger than 16 stay at no additional cost. Comfort Inn Mountain View Suites has won several beautification awards from the city for its neatly landscaped and often festively decorated grounds.

Hampton Inn $$$$
681 Winfield Dunn Parkway, Sevierville
(865) 429-2005, (877) 807-6132
www.hamptoninn.com
This Hampton Inn's four interior, security-controlled floors and 42 rooms and suites are housed in a compact, stucco-look structure located just on the outskirts of Sevierville proper. The 32 standard rooms each contain two queen beds and are of elegant and tasteful decor. The 10 suites are spacious and open, featuring king beds and either a recliner or sofa. Fireplaces, refrigerators, microwaves, coffeemakers, and whirlpool tubs complete the king suite package. For the hearing impaired, there is even a system available in some rooms that allows for outside communication via keyboard.

Their complimentary breakfast buffet includes a healthy selection of fresh fruit. The health-conscious will also want to take advantage of the exercise room, and kids can give their thumbs and fingers a good workout in the game room. Constructed in 1994, the hotel provides guest laundry facilities, fax services, and a meeting room that accommodates 100 people. A variety of discounts are offered for those seeking extra value. Children younger than 18 stay free, and seniors can ask about Hampton Inn's Lifestyle 50 discounts, which allow up to three additional guests to share a room at no extra charge.

Landmark Inn $$$
401 Forks of the River Parkway
Sevierville
(865) 453-0318, (800) 548-9038
www.landmarkinnthesmokies.com
This long-established, independently owned motel extends comfort, convenience, and value in the heart of Sevierville. Its 80 standard rooms are pleasing to the eye and have balconies and porches with direct views of the Great Smoky Mountains and the Little Pigeon River. Landmark Inn's 20 specialty rooms contain amenity combinations that may include

refrigerators, kitchenettes, coffeemakers, fireplaces, and in-room whirlpool tubs. The motel's proximity to the river makes a number of fun activities immediately available to guests. Kids will enjoy feeding the ducks, and anglers can drop their lines in the water in search of the big one. For peaceful and scenic strolls, check out the city's Memorial River Trail Greenway, a paved walking/jogging trail that flanks the Little Pigeon River and passes directly in front of Landmark Inn.

The Mize Motel $$
804 Parkway, Sevierville
(865) 453-4684, (800) 239-9117
Offering a clean and comfortable room at a great rate, the Mize Motel has been a fixture on Sevierville's Parkway since the days when motels in the city were sparse. Its gray stone exterior is typical of the older mom-and-pop motels, but the interiors of its 42 standard rooms and four efficiency apartments have been nicely remodeled in recent years. The kids will enjoy romping in the shaded lawn in front of the motel or splashing in its heated pool. Although the rooms aren't heavy on amenities, this is a good choice for the vacationer who simply wants decent accommodations in a location convenient to planned destinations. The Mize Motel is closed December through March. They offer AAA and senior discounts, and children stay free.

Sleep Inn $$$
1020 Parkway, Sevierville
(865) 429-0484, (888) 429-0484
www.choicehotels.com
This three-story hotel, built in 1996, contains 70 interior-access rooms, each imbued with what could almost be described as an art deco motif. The units are filled with plenty of curves and stylish furnishings; the glass doors in the showers add to the character. Rooms also include coffeemakers and are laid out with either two double beds or one king-size bed.

Free continental breakfast, an outdoor pool, and meeting/banquet facilities round out Sleep Inn's offerings. This hotel's location puts guests within 1 mile of the Governor's Crossing development, a multifaceted collective of shops, restaurants, and attractions.

Green Valley Motel North $$
1544 Parkway, Sevierville
(865) 453-4066, (800) 426-4066
Green Valley Motel's 52 rooms are split between two buildings, and the rooms are entered from the outside. The original, older structure houses approximately 22 units; the remainder of the rooms are in a three-story addition. The decor of all the rooms is consistent, however, from one building to the other, and the layout offers a choice of either two double beds or one king bed. The newer rooms feature private balconies, and some come outfitted with whirlpool tubs and refrigerators. Green Valley Motel extends discounts to seniors, and children younger than 13 stay free. The motel is closed January through March but offers handy access to the Governor's Crossing complex as well as Tanger Outlet Center at Five Oaks.

Cultivate the friendship of your desk clerk—he or she is a fountain of information and can save you many hours of frustration.

Oak Tree Lodge $$$
1620 Parkway, Pigeon Forge
(865) 428-7500, (800) 637-7002
www.oaktennlodging.com
Although it's in a rapidly developing area between Sevierville and Pigeon Forge, Oak Tree Lodge benefits from its placement among open, green fields bordered by white fences. This pastoral setting, combined with charming, antebellum architecture, makes for a vacation or business stay

replete with Southern atmosphere. The three-story structure accommodates 64 standard rooms and 36 suites in a combination of both interior and exterior access. All rooms feature either a double queen bed or single king bed setup, refrigerator, and coffeemaker, as well as private balconies and porches. In suites, you'll discover fireplaces and whirlpool tubs.

Built in 1990, Oak Tree Lodge boasts both indoor and outdoor pools, an exercise room, continental breakfast, and private catering, and they can even help you arrange for babysitting services. In-room VCRs are available for rental if you or your gang are in the mood for a flick. The hotel lies within a short distance (walking distance, in some cases) of outlet shopping malls and restaurants. Other sites of interest that are either on or near the property include tennis courts, hiking trails, a horseback riding stable (see Parks and Recreation), and an on-site meeting facility that can seat up to 100. Oak Tree Lodge recommends making reservations six months in advance.

Comfort Inn Apple Valley $$$$
1850 Parkway, Sevierville
(865) 428-1069, (800) 233-3443
www.comfortinnapplevalley.com

This Comfort Inn has racked up its share of accolades in recent years, having been named International Comfort Inn of the Year in 1995 and having taken awards from the city of Sevierville for Winterfest and Harvest Festival decorations. Inside, the quality continues throughout the hotel's 100 extra-large standard rooms and 10 suites. All rooms are located within three interior-access floors and have either two queen beds or one king-size bed. Standard rooms feature private balconies, refrigerators, and in-room coffeemakers. Suites are available with whirlpool tubs and in-room fireplaces.

Comfort Inn Apple Valley offers its guests both indoor and outdoor pools as well as an indoor whirlpool spa. Groups can take advantage of the conference room facilities, and all guests will enjoy the convenient continental breakfast served each morning. This hotel is situated in a handy section of Pigeon Forge. The Apple Valley farms complex is a short walk away, and the majority of Pigeon Forge's music theaters and outlet shopping malls can be accessed with a brief trolley ride. Seniors receive a 10 percent discount.

PIGEON FORGE

During the last 15 years, the section of northern Pigeon Forge and southern Sevierville have fused into one continuous band of businesses geared to the vacationer. As such, most people driving south on the Parkway aren't aware when they've crossed from one city to the next. But one particular characteristic of Pigeon Forge's identity is noticeable, if you're aware of it—a heavier concentration of independently owned accommodations. From smaller, mom-and-pop motels to multistoried luxury hotels, fewer of the easily recognized franchise names are represented in this mix. As such, this section will help acquaint you with a healthy dose of unfamiliar names and place less emphasis on the franchises. Because there are so many properties in Pigeon Forge from which to choose, we've presented only a sampling (albeit a large one) of what we feel are the better picks.

Keep in mind another premise when perusing these listings. In Pigeon Forge, especially south of traffic light #3, almost every hotel or motel is within easy walking distance of restaurants, entertainment, attractions, and shopping. In some cases, where we feel a particular lodging is extremely convenient to a local point of interest, such a reference is made. Otherwise, assume that most anything you want is just outside your door. Also keep in mind that Pigeon Forge has a trolley system with numerous stopping points that can take you inexpensively up and down the Parkway. See our Getting Here, Getting Around chapter for more specifics.

Mountain Melodies Inn $$$
1949 Parkway, Pigeon Forge
(865) 453-2250, (800) 838-9777

This facility is well placed for those with music and variety shows on their agenda. Directly across the Parkway from the Louise Mandrell Theater, it's within a short walk of several other Pigeon Forge music theaters as well. Open since 1995, Mountain Melodies Inn has 60 standard rooms and 25 suites offering queen and king beds. All rooms include private balconies and refrigerators. Fireplaces and whirlpool tubs are available in suites. Their in-room television system provides the latest movie hits on a pay-per-view basis. The hotel is a five-story building that provides interior access to all rooms, and there's plenty of room for the family car in the two-level parking area.

Microtel Suites Pigeon Forge
Music Road $$$
2045 Parkway, Pigeon Forge
(865) 453-1116, (800) 234-1412
www.microtelinn.com

If you're looking for comfortable accommodations for the family at a great value, consider this five-year-old Microtel property in the heart of Pigeon Forge's theater community; showplaces like the Louise Mandrell Theater, Ole Smoky Hoedown, and Memories Theatre are within easy walking distance.

All of this Microtel's 71 units are suites with a queen bed and queen sleeper sofa. Amenities in all standard suites include telephone with dataport and in-room safe as well as kitchenettes with coffeemaker, refrigerator, and microwave. Each of the hotel's four floors has one deluxe-size suite offering more living space. The wheelchair-accessible suites include accessible showers.

Guests have access to a number of common amenities, such as a self-service laundry room, meeting room, outdoor pool, and a breakfast room that serves free continental breakfast each morning. Pets are welcome for a $15 fee. For travel

Booking a reservation for a weekend during the peak season? Here are a couple of caveats: a) Rates may be even higher than we've indicated if your city of destination is hosting a major special event, and b) many hotels require two- and sometimes even three-night minimums during high-traffic weekends.

convenience, the Pigeon Forge trolley makes a stop at the hotel's Parkway entrance.

Ramada Limited $$$$
2193 Parkway, Pigeon Forge
(865) 428-0668, (800) 269-1222
www.pigeonforgeramada.com

This Ramada Limited successfully puts forth a pleasant country decor without slipping into tackiness. The many wooden fixtures and the stacked-stone fireplace in the lobby are just some of the elements that help create a cozy, rustic ambience. When it comes to amenities, however, this property is certainly not primitive. Guests can take advantage of a spacious indoor pool and whirlpool partially surrounded by large and numerous windows. An exercise room, game room, and breakfast room are also on hand for traveling convenience. All of the 126 standard rooms in this three-story, interior-access hotel feature two queen beds, a refrigerator, and a microwave. There are also nine suites on the premises that include coffeemakers, fireplaces, and in-room whirlpool tubs. Overall, the furnishings and trappings combine both elegance and simple country charm. All rooms are also equipped with VCRs, and a movie rental center is located in the lobby. This Ramada Limited is in a location central to the Pigeon Forge music theater community (many are within walking distance) as well as an abundance of restaurants and outlet shopping opportunities. They honor both AAA and senior discounts.

Music Road Hotel $$$$$
303 Henderson Chapel Road
Pigeon Forge
(865) 429-7700, (800) 429-7700
www.musicroadhotel.com

Just 1 block off the Parkway, this hotel goes all out to provide a total vacation experience on a large scale and at a competitive price, considering all that's available. The beige, seven-story structure towers above lush, colorful landscaping and the peaceful waters of the Little Pigeon River. As a matter of fact, guests can relax in rocking chairs along the lobby-level observation deck that runs the entire riverside length of the building. The river isn't the only water to be enjoyed here, however. The outside pool area is like a mini water park, complete with pool, waterfall, fountain, spiral slide, and Lazy River ride. Kids will also appreciate the nearby arcade and snack bar. The indoor pool is open 24 hours a day and includes a whirlpool area as well.

The 90 standard rooms and 73 suites also reflect Music Road Hotel's overall attention to detail. All rooms are accessed from inside the hotel, and 80 percent of them are smoke-free. The standard rooms are substantially larger than the average hotel room. Each comes with two queen beds and a roster of amenities including a refrigerator, a microwave, a private balcony, and an iron and ironing board. The bathrooms are conveniently equipped with two sinks, a linen closet, a hair dryer, and a telephone. The suites are similarly outfitted but also offer fireplaces, in-room whirlpools, and king-size beds.

When you first step into the Music Road Hotel, you're drawn into the large, open lobby by its elegant furnishings, wood floors, and huge stacked-stone fireplace. Just off the lobby is a generous continental breakfast area, which includes muffins, pastries, cereals, bagels, and of course, coffee. Also found on the first floor are a number of meeting rooms for groups and businesses as well as another arcade. Music Road Hotel offers senior discounts and group rates.

National Parks Resort Lodge $$$$
2385 Parkway, Pigeon Forge
(865) 453-4106, (800) 843-6686
www.nprlodge.com

Formerly known as the Heartlander Country Star Resort, this hotel's central proximity to both outlet shopping malls and music theaters makes it a strategic choice for the vacationer. The multisize conference and meeting facilities offered make it a logical option for the business traveler.

One hundred sixty standard rooms and eight suites each contain either two double beds or a king bed as well as private balconies for enjoying Smoky Mountain views. This property is five stories tall, provides interior room access, has a large game room with pool table, and boasts a shop where guests can pick up gifts and sundries. An outdoor pool, indoor pool, and whirlpool spa round out this hotel's guest package. Pets are allowed, but owners are required to pay a one-time, non-refundable fee of $20. AAA and senior discounts are honored, and children younger than 12 stay free.

Radisson Inn & Suites
Pigeon Forge $$$$
2423 Teaster Lane, Pigeon Forge
(865) 429-3700, (800) 333-3333
www.radisson.com

At this Radisson property, comfort, convenience, and inspiring views make for a winning Smokies vacation combination. The seven-story, coral-hued building is located a short distance off the Parkway on a quiet hilltop, peacefully removed from the bustle of traffic. This site provides a direct "back road" route to Belz Factory Outlet World and Tanger Outlet Mall, both just down the street.

Inside, a number of services and amenities are found, including a game room, meeting rooms, an expanded continental breakfast, laundry facility, and exercise room with sauna. There are two swimming pools, both indoor and outdoor; the interior site has a whirlpool. In-room accommodations are consistent among this Radisson's 70 interior units. Each provides a refrigerator, microwave oven, coffee-maker, and a private balcony that opens your room to memorable mountain views. Rooms come with either a double queen bed setup or a single king-size bed and sleeper sofa. Five spacious suites provide guests with the added luxuries of hair dryers, irons and ironing boards, fireplaces, and whirlpool tubs. Built in 1995, Radisson Inn & Suites Pigeon Forge offers discounts for AAA members and seniors. Children younger than 18 stay for free.

Econo Lodge Riverside   **$$$$**
2440 Parkway, Pigeon Forge
(865) 428-1231, (800) 632-6104
www.econolodge-pigeonforge.com
In 2000 this motel underwent a complete face-lift; in fact, the new owners did everything but completely tear it down and rebuild it. As a result, rates are a bit higher than what previous guests may remember, but the cosmetic overhaul of the rooms and the addition of on-site amenities make up for the price hike.

With about 180 units on the premises, Econo Lodge Riverside provides clean and spacious rooms in a pleasant setting near the Little Pigeon River. If your intent is to dive into the music theaters and shopping opportunities in Pigeon Forge, you'll find this motel to be handily situated. Belz Factory Outlet World and Tanger Outlet Mall are a short distance away, as is Ogle's Water Park. When you're not out on the town, you'll find relaxation at the picnic spot down by the river, where you're welcome to feed the resident duck population.

For sleeping arrangements, you may select one of 160 standard rooms with either double queen beds or one king bed. You may also choose from the 15 rooms with Jacuzzi tubs and two family suites with bunk beds and fold-out sofas. All rooms come with microwaves, refrigerators, and coffeemakers.

Econo Lodge's lobby is warm and welcoming with its thick wood rafters and stone fireplace. They've also added an indoor heated pool with accompanying

hot tub and kiddie pool. Guests will also enjoy the motel's complimentary continental breakfast.

Mountain Trace Inn   **$$$$**
130 Wears Valley Road West
Pigeon Forge
(865) 453-6785, (800) 453-6785
www.mountaintraceinn.com
This is, perhaps, one of the best-placed accommodations in Pigeon Forge. Ogle's Water Park, two outlet malls, a supermarket, and a coin-operated laundry are all within easy walking distance. It is just off the Parkway on Wears Valley Road, one of the routes to the scenic and historic communities of Wears Valley and Townsend. The building itself consists of four floors and 89 exterior-access rooms. All rooms have two queen beds and refrigerators. There are also three family suites and 10 honeymoon suites that are enhanced by amenities such as whirlpool tubs, fireplaces, and kitchenettes. The main part of the motel was constructed in 1992, with 42 units added in 1995. Another recent addition was the indoor pool and whirlpool facility that conveniently features changing rooms. Other services that guests might consider a boon include a free continental breakfast and nondenominational worship services held each Sunday morning. Mountain Trace Inn has AAA and senior discounts. Their rates are flat, per-room fees that allow up to five people per room.

Timbers Log Motel   **$$$**
134 Wears Valley Road East
Pigeon Forge
(865) 428-5216, (800) 445-1803
www.timberslogmotel.com
Shopping fanatics, this is the place you want to be! Timbers Log Motel can be found directly across Teaster Lane from Belz Factory Outlet World, Tanger Outlet Mall, and other retail finds like Old Time Pottery (housewares galore). While you're shopping, the kids can go nuts themselves across the street at the Track, an amusement center featuring go-karts,

miniature golf, bungee jumping, and video games (see our Attractions and Kidstuff chapters).

The motel itself, however, offers plenty of its own charms. With an exterior constructed of hewn logs and mortar, this lodging conveys the feel of a mountain cabin but does so in the heart of Pigeon Forge activities. There are 22 standard rooms that have either two queen beds or one king bed and also reflect this same rustic approach. Some of the rooms, but not all, include a refrigerator or coffeemaker. There are also 20 suites steeped in woodsiness and set up in a variety of configurations, including a two-level layout. Some are tailored to families, with kitchenettes and multibed arrangements that can sleep up to six. Some are more suitable for honeymooners, with fireplaces and whirlpool tubs. Timbers Log Motel was built in 1989 and provides three floors of exterior-access rooms. Pets are allowed with a one-time $10 fee, and discounts are available for seniors. The rates charged are on a flat, per-room basis.

Valley Forge Inn $$$
2795 Parkway, Pigeon Forge
(865) 453-7770, (800) 544-8740
www.valleyforgeinn.net
Developed in three phases beginning in 1988, Valley Forge Inn supplies a mixed bag of room layouts and amenities. The inn's 150 standard rooms and 21 suites are divided among three buildings, the tallest of which is four stories; rooms are accessible from the outside as well as interior hallways. In the original structure you'll find that the typical room has two queen beds and a well-remodeled package of furnishings and decor. The second and third buildings, which went up in the early and mid-1990s, contain both standard rooms and suites. Some of the perks to be found in many of these include refrigerators, microwave ovens, coffeemakers, fireplaces, whirlpool tubs, and private balconies. Some of the newer suites are big enough to sleep six in a single king and two-queen bed combination. On the

top level of the newest building, there are even 10 two-level town houses with two bathrooms in each. Valley Forge Inn is near the Little Pigeon River and extends free continental breakfast, a coin-operated laundry, indoor and outdoor pools, and in-room satellite television. Seniors can look for 5 percent discounts on rates.

Park Tower Inn $$$
201 Sharon Drive, Pigeon Forge
(865) 453-8605, (800) 453-8605
www.parktowerinn.com
Standing just 1 block west of the Parkway, Park Tower Inn is one of the best overall values in this area. There are 113 rooms and 9 suites on the property, all of which are entered from interior corridors and are spacious and colorfully decorated. Refrigerators, two queen-size beds, and large, open balconies are the norm for standard rooms. Suites and rooms with kitchenettes offer an expanded range of amenities such as whirlpool tubs, fireplaces, and coffeemakers. On-site conveniences abound at this hotel, which was built in 1994. Three elevators provide easy access to all six floors, and microwave ovens are centrally located at each level. In addition to the outdoor pool, there is a massive indoor aquatic facility, complete with pool, two whirlpool tubs, and a Lazy River ride for inner-tube relaxation. Vacationers and business travelers alike will appreciate Park Tower Inn's free continental breakfast, guest laundry, game room, and exercise facilities. They can also add an excellent security-monitoring system and meeting facilities to their roster of pluses. AAA and senior discounts are available, and quoted rates are good for up to four people per room.

Maples Motor Inn $$
2959 Parkway, Pigeon Forge
(865) 453-8883, (888) 453-8883
www.maplesmotorinn.com
Found on the Parkway, a short hop from Pigeon Forge Factory Outlet Mall, this family-owned inn is a nice place to bring your own family. Providing agreeable

rooms at an equally agreeable price, Maples Motor Inn has 57 units in its original building, all of which have refrigerators. Another section was built in 1996, in which a selection of large, feature-filled suites can be found. These suites provide whirlpools, fireplaces, and kitchenettes in a spacious, well-furnished floor plan. Outside, a large pool is flanked by a smaller kiddie pool. Vacationers with children in tow will also benefit from the picnic area and toddler playground found on the grassy lawn. Maples Motor Inn is closed during January and February and takes all major credit cards except American Express. Children younger than three stay at no additional charge.

Mountain Breeze Motel $$-$$$
2926 Parkway, Pigeon Forge
(865) 453-2659, (888) 453-2659
This remodeled, two-story motel in the heart of Pigeon Forge's "main drag" treats guests to a number of in-room comforts at a hard-to-beat price. Rates for two people vary, depending on the number and size of beds required. The rates are lowest for rooms with one queen bed, higher for one king bed, and higher still for setups with two queen beds. Efficiencies and suites are available as well. All rooms provide guests with a refrigerator and coffeemaker while some have microwaves. There is a heated outdoor pool as well as a kiddie pool and hot tub on the premises. Mountain Breeze Motel gives AAA and senior discounts and honors Visa and Discover cards only.

Willow Brook Lodge $$$$
3035 Parkway, Pigeon Forge
(865) 453-5334, (800) 765-1380
www.willowbrooklodge.com
When you first arrive at this motel, your attention is soon drawn to immaculate landscaping, a homey architectural style, and an exterior color scheme that's very easy on the eyes. Sixty-one rooms and 17 suites offer different floor plans, amenities, and sleeping arrangements that have been arranged into six different accom-

modations packages. Guest rooms have either two queen-size beds or one king-size bed and sleeper sofa. All have refrigerators, and some have balcony views of the Little Pigeon River. Four suite combinations offer a variety of configurations of queen and king beds, sleeper sofas, whirlpool tubs, fireplaces, microwaves, coffeemakers, and refrigerators. Some have private balconies and separate living and dining areas. Constructed in 1991, Willow Brook Lodge provides exterior access to all three floors. Coffee and donuts are provided each morning, and discounts are extended to AAA members and seniors. Children younger than 12 stay at no extra cost.

Holiday Inn Pigeon Forge
Resort Hotel $$$$$
3230 Parkway, Pigeon Forge
(865) 428-2700, (800) 555-2650
www.4lodging.com
Well-equipped rooms, along with extensive on-site amenities, make this a great headquarters for a vacation or business stay. Approximately 200 rooms and 10 suites are housed in this Holiday Inn's five interior-accessible floors. The typical unit has two extra-long double beds, while a few have king-size beds. All rooms provide a hair dryer, an iron and ironing board, and in-room coffeemaker for guest convenience. Some rooms come with refrigerators, and microwave ovens are included in the suites.

Although the rooms are certainly comfort intensive, there are plenty of other treasures to be found on the premises, making a stay at this Holiday Inn Resort virtually a vacation in itself. The lobby is open and features a sitting area next to a large stone fireplace. Further exploration reveals an open arcade area that's reminiscent of a carnival midway. Kids will love the video games and other coin-operated attractions found there. Beyond the arcade lies a large atrium section featuring an indoor pool and whirlpool tub. The pool is flanked by lush greenery and a waterfall that cascades from a high stone wall. A laundry facility and an exercise room are available to guests. Meeting and conference rooms of all sizes are also located on the premises, able to accommodate almost any group with the services and the facilities they need.

This Holiday Inn Resort is one of the few lodgings in the area that boasts a restaurant in the hotel itself. Louie's Restaurant and Grill delivers a well-rounded menu and serves breakfast, lunch, and dinner. One of their acclaimed specialties is their all-you-can-eat steak dinner, which gives guests the option of selecting and cooking their own cuts over Louie's large, open grill. The restaurant also provides room service during its business hours and is available to cater banquets in the meeting facilities.

Attention to service is a priority at this particular property, which was a 1997 recipient of Holiday Inn's Torchbearer Award, designating it as one of the top 25 Holiday Inn hotels in the world. Some pets are allowed, and babysitting services can be arranged provided that the hotel is given advance notification in both cases (preferably at the time reservations are made). AAA and senior discounts are honored. Although room prices are charged as a flat, per-room rate, rollaway beds can be provided for an additional $6.50 fee.

River Lodge South $$$
3251 Parkway, Pigeon Forge
(865) 453-0783, (800) 233-7581

Although the lobby, office, and a handful of rooms are located on the Parkway, the bulk of River Lodge South's 71 rooms and six suites are situated 1 block to the east, overlooking the Little Pigeon River. Ground-floor rooms open in the rear onto a grassy riverside embankment where picnic tables and barbecue grills allow guests the benefits of cooking out near the water. You can also feed the ducks with food purchased from small coin-operated machines located nearby. Units on the second and third floors of the motel have private balconies. Inside the rooms, two

queen beds and refrigerators are standard. Several suite options are presented, including various combinations of kitchenettes, fireplaces, and in-room whirlpool tubs. Family units are available with split-bedroom floor plans. The outdoor pool is heated, and a limited continental breakfast is served in the mornings. Be sure to ask about AAA and senior discounts.

Vacation Lodge $$-$$$$
3450 Parkway, Pigeon Forge
(865) 453-2640, (800) 468-1998

When Pigeon Forge's business district consisted of a couple of gift shops, a general store, and a motel all clustered around the city's only traffic light, the Vacation Lodge was the motel. Like the city, the Vacation Lodge grew in all directions during the 1980s to its present size of more than 90 rooms in a variety of configurations. Ample parking and central location make the Vacation Lodge a favorite of people planning to park their cars where they're staying and enjoy Pigeon Forge on foot or by using the Fun Time Trolley. The Old Mill area, one of the city's oldest shopping centers and still the place where most of the handcrafts and truly unique gifts are available, is across the Parkway and a block back on Old Mill Street.

Riverside Tower $$$
3455 Parkway, Pigeon Forge
(865) 453-5500, (800) 453-5500
www.riversidemotels.com

There are three Riverside properties listed in this book, and they're all owned and operated by the same old-line area "motel family." Riverside Tower is the first in line and is an imposing six-story structure that provides panoramic views in luxurious settings on all four sides. The spacious suites all have balconies for private people-watching, and the indoor pool is comfortable year-round. Queen beds and fireplaces with gas logs make every room cozy, and gas grills on the balconies make eating in an adventure. Riverside Tower has meeting facilities to accommodate up to 100 people. Pigeon Forge's historic Old

Mill shopping area and Patriot Park are a short walk up River Road, which forms the back boundary of the hotel.

Riverside Motor Lodge $$$-$$$$
3575 Parkway, Pigeon Forge
(865) 453-5555, (800) 242-8366
www.riversidemotels.com
Situated between the Little Pigeon River and the Parkway in central Pigeon Forge, the Riverside Motor Lodge offers all amenities necessary to fill your vacation with happy memories. Your choice of two-bedroom family suites or intimate honeymoon suites provides all the comforts of home. Every room has its own kitchenette and Jacuzzi, and gas fireplaces add a cozy touch. The solarium setting gives the indoor swimming pool an outdoor feel without the noise and wind of the traffic. Suites on all five floors are easily accessible by elevators at both ends and in the middle of the property.

River Chase Motel $$$$
3709 Parkway, Pigeon Forge
(865) 428-1299, (888) 754-3316
Built in 1982, the River Chase has constantly upgraded itself to the 105-unit facility that sits at the corner of Dollywood Lane today. The four-story structure has a variety of upscale rooms and an enviable return rate to attest to its gracious treatment of its guests. From double rooms to super suites with private balconies, refrigerators, and microwave ovens, the River Chase offers a high degree of comfort and convenience, and one of the most exciting attractions around for the kids: The inside and outside swimming pools each have their own water slide! The inside slide is more than 100 feet long.

Briarstone Inn $$$
3626 Parkway, Pigeon Forge
(865) 453-3050, (800) 523-3919
www.smokymountainresorts.com
Convenient to most of Pigeon Forge's amusements and restaurants, the Briarstone Inn is operated by another one of the city's oldest and most experienced host families. Comfortable rooms with queen beds, in-room coffee, pay-per-view TV, and available Jacuzzi and fireplace suites provide a wide range of choices for any size group from honeymooners to families. AARP and senior citizen discounts are offered, as well as special discounts at local restaurants.

Bilmar Motor Inn $$-$$$
3786 Parkway, Pigeon Forge
(865) 453-5593, (800) 343-5610
Another of Pigeon Forge's more established motels, the Bilmar was built in 1976 on what was then the southern edge of town. It's closer to the center now, but the 76 rooms at the Bilmar are still as comfortable and welcoming as the folks who have greeted their guests for more than 20 years. A large open area in front of the heated swimming pool makes the Bilmar a favorite spot for watching the parade of hot rods and vintage cars that invades Pigeon Forge most weekends of the summer. And since a good number of the car owners stay at the Bilmar, up close and personal views that you wouldn't normally get are right at your door.

Norma Dan Motel $$$
3864 Parkway, Pigeon Forge
(865) 453-2403, (800) 582-7866
www.normadanmotel.com
Celebrating its 45th season under single-family ownership, the Norma Dan has kept pace with the growth of Pigeon Forge. From its small beginnings as a 12-room motel in 1958, the Norma Dan has expanded to the beautiful 85-room multi-story structure it is today, with one of Pigeon Forge's biggest swimming pools. Because of its popularity with tour groups, the Norma Dan also has one of the biggest and best-protected off-street parking lots in the city. Some of the Norma Dan's earliest couples, who spent their honeymoons in the mountains, are still coming back, and now they take advantage of the AARP discount program and bring their grandchildren.

Conner Hill Motor Lodge $$
3921 Parkway, Pigeon Forge
(865) 428-0287, (800) 447-9534

Conner Hill is another one of the city's older motels, but it's kept so sparkling clean that it looks new to the first-time visitor. They still get a few first-timers every year, but most of Conner Hill's business is repeaters who found them in the '70s and early '80s when motels were few and far between in Pigeon Forge. The 65-unit structure is reminiscent of the older buildings, with a lot of wrought iron and wood in its spacious design, but the rooms are as new as tomorrow. Your choice of queen-size or water beds is about as complicated as it gets in choosing your accommodations. Shopping and amusements are within easy walking distance to Conner Hill, and Dollywood and the Gatlinburg Country Club are a drive of five minutes or less.

Even if you're visiting the Smokies during the dead of winter, don't rule out packing a bathing suit or pair of trunks. Many area hotels have heated indoor pools for year-round swimming fun.

River's Landing Resort $$$-$$$$
4025 Parkway, Pigeon Forge
(865) 453-9081, (800) 345-6799
www.riverslandingontheparkway.com

River's Landing was a landmark when it stood practically alone on the south end of Pigeon Forge back in 1969, but now it's closer to the center of town. One hundred thirty-one rooms with easy access to the on-site restaurant and the biggest indoor swimming pool in the Smokies have made the River's Landing popular with two and three generations of families who come back year after year. A playground for the little ones and the large poolside arcade for the bigger kids will keep everyone occupied while Mom and Dad kick back for a while in the hot tub. Guest laundry service is available as an added convenience.

Green Valley Motel $-$$$
4109 Parkway, Pigeon Forge
(865) 453-9091, (800) 892-1627

The Green Valley Motel was built mainly to lodge families, and its 70 percent rate of repeat visitors indicates it was done right. Ground-floor access to most of the 50 rooms and convenient restaurants and gift shops within easy walking distance have made the Green Valley a popular lodging place for generations of visitors to the Smokies. The same family that built it all operates the outlet store adjacent to the Green Valley, and most of the veteran guests do a lot of their shopping without ever leaving the property.

River's Landing $$$$
3929 South River Road, Pigeon Forge
(865) 453-4444, (888) 345-6799
www.smokymountainresorts.com

No, it's not a misprint or a repeat: River's Landing has opened a 50-room motel on the Little Pigeon River, just a short distance from its original place on the Parkway. Private balconies overlooking the river and fireplaces in every room make the River's Landing on the river a cozy place to enjoy an evening without any outside distractions. The public hot tubs beside the pool and the same friendly service that made the original River's Landing a big favorite are all present in the new edition. We expect the newer River's Landing to enjoy the same lofty level of popularity as its nearby senior sibling.

Creekstone Inn $$$
4034 South River Road, Pigeon Forge
(865) 453-3557, (800) 523-3919
www.smokymountainresorts.com

A new standard in gracious living, the Creekstone is a 172-room high-rise hotel on the Little Pigeon River, with a full slate of amenities to please the family, the honeymooner, or the most discriminating guest. Spacious rooms and suites with fireplaces, refrigerators, in-room coffee-makers, and Jacuzzis make staying in your room a pleasure when the pressure of enjoying your vacation starts to wear a little bit. Convenient parking on the ground level, with elevators to the rooms above, takes the hassle out of getting to your car or your room. The private balconies that grace each room provide a great place to watch and feed the resident flock of ducks, and the river running along the back edge is an inviting place to just sit and watch or go down and cool your tired feet.

GATLINBURG

As the progenitor of the tourism industry in the Smokies, Gatlinburg is still a favorite lodging place for veteran visitors. In fact, Gatlinburg's more than 100 hotels and motels, boasting a total of nearly 7,000 rooms, depend heavily on repeat business. The lodging scene in Gatlinburg runs through the full spectrum of accommodations, from old-fashioned tourist cabins in settled neighborhoods to luxury high-rise hotels in the heart of downtown. The list that follows is a representative sample of the broad variety of hotels and motels in Gatlinburg, most of which are within walking distance of the downtown business district. Those that require more than a 10-minute walk to the Parkway are all within 100 yards of a trolley stop. All of Gatlinburg's hotels and motels provide wheelchair accessibility with ground-floor entrances to rooms that are specifically designated for smoking or nonsmoking use. Most of the multistory facilities have elevators, and all have ramps between levels. Most offer AARP and senior citizen discounts; call ahead to be sure.

The facilities listed will be in order as follows, and please remember this is a sampling, not a complete list. First, we'll deal with the entire length of the Parkway, from the entrance to town at the Highland Motor Inn to the Clarion, which is within 100 yards of the Great Smoky Mountains National Park entrance ("On the Parkway"). Next, we'll go back to traffic light #6 and turn left (east) onto Cherokee Orchard Road to look at the idyllic Bask-ins Creek section. Then, from traffic light #5, we'll travel south and west along River Road and into the Ski Mountain neighborhood west of the Parkway. Our next grouping is on Historic Nature Trail (formerly Airport Road) (traffic light #8—the Space Needle corner) and includes a mixture of large convention-oriented and small family-owned motels. Finally, we'll travel east out U.S. Highway 321N from traffic light #3, where most of the smaller independent facilities and Gatlinburg's biggest independently owned motel are found.

On the Parkway

Highland Motor Inn $$$
131 Parkway, Gatlinburg
(865) 436-4110, (800) 635-8874
The Highland is easy to find: It's the first building you'll see on the right as you enter Gatlinburg on The Spur. Opened in 1962, the Highland has the Parkway at its front door and the Little Pigeon River and Herbert Holt Park behind it. Pets are welcome at the Highland (limit two, nominal fee). There are several amusements and shops in the immediate area, and the trolley stops at the Highland's front door.

Stony Brook Motel $
167 Parkway, Gatlinburg
(865) 436-5652, (800) 633-5652
Away from the center of town but conveniently near it on the purple trolley route, the Stony Brook Motel has 40 rooms with fireplaces and refrigerators. Several amusements and stores are in sight without going into the downtown area.

Fairfield Inn & Suites-
North Gatlinburg $$-$$$
168 Parkway, Gatlinburg
(865) 430-3659, (866) 430-3659
www.marriott.com
The first lodging establishment on the left as you enter Gatlinburg, the Fairfield Inn has 101 rooms that run the full gamut of

accommodations, with most of them containing two queen beds and all providing a coffeemaker. The three-story back portion features wooded views. The continental breakfast is on the house. The Fairfield has two heated pools, one with a spiral water slide. The purple route trolley stops at the front door if you need it; with a restaurant, a package liquor store, and a wedding chapel on the property and a miniature golf course next door, you can meet most of your needs without leaving the property.

Comfort Inn on the River $$$
293 Parkway, Gatlinburg
(865) 436-5047

Three floors of private balconies directly over the Little Pigeon River (you can fish from your balcony!) make you forget there's bumper-to-bumper traffic right outside the door. From standard two-bedrooms to luxury suites with fireplaces and Jacuzzis, the Comfort Inn's spectacular view of the river and the mountains in the background make you forget you're in a city at all. Built before the tourist boom of the 1970s, this establishment is a classic reminder of what the Smokies are really all about.

Rocky Waters Motor Inn $$$-$$$$
333 Parkway, Gatlinburg
(865) 436-7861, (800) 824-1111
www.rockywaters.com

When Ralph Lawson first built the Rocky Waters in the late 1930s, the road ran down the other side of the river. When the new road was built, the Rocky Waters's owners built a bridge and a new building on the new Parkway, and now it's the only motel in town with units on both sides of the river. A hundred rooms and three cabins provide a broad variety of accommodations, all with private balconies on the Little Pigeon River. The on-site launderette is a step-saver for Mom and Dad after the kids have enjoyed an afternoon in one of the two pools or after a relaxing dip in one of the spas.

Terrace Motel $-$$
396 Parkway, Gatlinburg
(865) 436-4965

This is a lot like stepping back in time. Its current owners built the Terrace in 1959 along the banks of Roaring Fork Creek. They've kept the place immaculate ever since, without losing the rustic appeal of a mountain retreat. Twenty luxury rooms and a series of cabins run away from the Parkway to provide seclusion and a rippling stream right at your doorstep. Bright, modern furnishings in the rooms contrast with the original pine paneling in the cabin units to give you an enchanting choice of old and new, both featuring the hospitality that makes the Smokies a vacation favorite.

Best Western Zoder's Inn $$$$
402 Parkway, Gatlinburg
(865) 436-5681, (800) 528-1234
www.zoders.com

Wallace Zoder came to the Smokies in 1934 to work as an engineer in the developing national park. Seeing the early potential of the area, Wallace built his motel beside the Parkway (it was called Main Street then) to house the summer guests who were beginning to trickle in. The old building is gone now, replaced over the years by the ultramodern 90-room structure that pampers today's travelers, but Wallace and Dot Zoder's traditions of service and comfortable, courteous accommodation are being carried on by their children and grandchildren. World-class luxury at surprisingly reasonable rates are the norm at Zoder's. Not content with the continental breakfast you can get most anywhere, the Zoders have added a sumptuous wine-and-cheese reception from 5:00 to 7:00 P.M. every evening and a great cookies-and-milk bedtime snack from 8:00 to 10:00 P.M., all served in the refreshment bar next to the guest lobby. And as if that's not enough to satisfy anybody, a walk along the creek to the back of the six-acre woodland will wash a whole day's cares away.

Best Western Twin Islands　　$$$
539 Parkway, Gatlinburg
(865) 436-5121, (800) 223-9299
www.oglesproperties.com

How about an island right in the middle of downtown Gatlinburg? Well, there are two, and the Luther Ogle family built a superb motel that uses up both of them. One hundred nine rooms, all with river views and some with private balconies, surround a central courtyard that makes you feel like you're in a private resort. All of downtown Gatlinburg is just outside the front driveway. Like the rest of the old-line family properties, Twin Islands furnishes the rooms like living rooms instead of bedrooms, with fireplaces and Jacuzzis available in several suites. If you're looking for complete privacy, the Honeymoon Island suites provide isolation without taking you away from the bright lights.

Greystone Lodge at the Aquarium　　$$$
559 Parkway, Gatlinburg
(865) 436-5621, (800) 451-9202
www.greystonelodgetn.com

If you're in the part of the Greystone that's near the Parkway, you're looking at one of Gatlinburg's most exciting recent additions: Ripley's Aquarium in the Smokies is described in detail in our Attractions chapter. If you're at the other end of the Greystone, you're looking at the west prong of the Little Pigeon River. This is a big complex—260 rooms in all, in several structures that reach as high as five stories along the river and stretch out for more than a quarter of a mile. Continental breakfast is served every morning from 7:00 to 10:00 in the refreshment bar beside the lobby. Several room configurations vary from two double beds to queen and king rooms, some with hot tubs and fireplaces.

Riverside Motor Lodge　　$$$
715 Parkway, Gatlinburg
(865) 436-4194, (800) 887-2323
www.riversidemotels.com

The original Riverside Motor Lodge was built in 1925 by local entrepreneur Steve Whaley, who insisted to his amused friends that "Some day a half-million people a year will visit Gatlinburg!" A commemorative plaque on the front wall identifies the Riverside as Gatlinburg's oldest continuously operated lodging establishment. Steve Whaley lived to see his prediction realized and much more. The Riverside has undergone a lot of changes in the ensuing 70-plus years, including the establishment of Gatlinburg's first shopping mall as an attachment to the front of the building.

Today's Riverside is a combination of old and new, with enough repeat business to make reservations hard to come by in the summer, especially on weekends, when the place is taken over by square-dance groups from all over the country. Now in the center of the downtown business district that grew up around it, the Riverside hearkens back to a gentler time with its paneled and carpeted hallways leading to comfortable rooms. Originally built on ground that led to the banks of the Little Pigeon River, the Riverside now has River Road at its back door, where a separate lobby welcomes the traveler. By clinging stubbornly to the spirit in which it was built, the Riverside Motor Lodge has established itself as a living example of how Gatlinburg's original innkeepers felt they should treat their guests.

Ramada Inn Four Seasons　　$$$-$$$$
756 Parkway, Gatlinburg
(865) 436-7881, (800) 933-8678
www.reaganresorts.com

The Ramada is as close to the middle of everything as you're likely to find, but its unique layout shelters its guests from street noise. With 148 luxurious units, plus 2 cabins, the Ramada offers a variety of accommodations that's hard to match. The indoor swimming pool is elegant, and the on-site convention facility has three good-size meeting rooms, a full stage, and its own kitchen. The Gatlinburg Convention Center is just a block away, and you'll also find several restaurants and many attractions nearby.

Gatlinburg Inn

You may be familiar with the feeling: You're walking along the busy main drag of a tourist mecca, trying to take in all of the sights and sounds around you, and suddenly something is very much out of synch. It's not something wrong, it's just suddenly . . . different. It's like a rock group has started playing Brahms.

What's happened here? Well, if you're on the Parkway in Gatlinburg, you've probably come to one of the truly rare sights in town: a section of street that doesn't have a building hovering over the sidewalk. And then you see it, set back from the low stone wall that protects its parking area from the sidewalk. Announced by an unpretentious wood sign, the Gatlinburg Inn appears to have been built at the wrong end of the property.

If you're moved to look beyond the parking lot into this strange place that seems so serene among the bright lights and carnival sounds, you cross the parking lot, return the greeting of the security guard who seems to have materialized from thin air, and walk up the stairs, across the wide front porch, and through the automatic door that seems out of place until you remember this is a place of public accommodation. The door was installed in the '50s, long before any laws concerning such things were written.

Inside the lobby, you're back in the time warp. The reception desk is at the back, and the smiling people tending it obviously know you're there, but they haven't spoken yet because you're not close enough for their modulated tones to reach you comfortably. The lobby is like an old movie set but obviously very real. The hand-blocked wallpaper and matching curtains cover what little of the walls are not taken up with the huge wood-framed windows that look out to the world you just left, and wrought-iron plant stands loaded down with various flora in pots of every description seem to circle the room.

Fringed area rugs cover the parts of the slate floor that contain overstuffed couches and chairs surrounding tables that hold various magazines. If you happen not to see it, the Westminster chimes on the grandfather clock will announce its presence every 15 minutes. And a row of rocking chairs invites you to sit and regard the scene outside. If you're very lucky, you learn that the gracious lady sitting in one of the rocking chairs is Mrs. Wilma Maples, the manager. And if you sit quietly and pay attention (this part's easy—for all her old-world charm, she's a commanding presence), Wilma Maples will tell you about the inn from before its beginnings and about the remarkable, Bunyanesque man who built it as part of his life-long quest to bring a better standard of living to the people of Gatlinburg.

Rellie L. (Rel) Maples (1905–1985) was a Gatlinburg native who was raised to the notion that service was nobler than self and that monuments were built on a foundation of trust. After graduating from high school at Lincoln Memorial University and attending the University of Tennessee, Rel Maples came home to a city affected by the Great Depression but not ruined by it. He worked as a cook in the CCC camp while the Great Smoky Mountains National Park was being built, and then built his own cafe on the Parkway in town on land owned by his grand-

Located in the heart of downtown, the Gatlinburg Inn was established in 1937 by Rel and Wilma Maples (inset) as an oasis of civility in a busy tourist mecca. REL AND WILMA MAPLES

father Ephraim Ogle. When the log restaurant burned, Rel Maples started making blocks the next day to rebuild it with more fireproof material. The Village shopping mall stands on the site today.

Rel's parents had a patch of land a little way up the Parkway from the Log Cabin cafe. In 1937 he harvested the corn and potatoes on it and started clearing the land with a mule-drawn scoop to build a hotel that would house the growing number of tourists coming to visit the mountains. The Gatlinburg Inn opened its doors in 1937, in very much the fashion it appears today.

Although its appearance hints that it was built for the gentry of the time, the Gatlinburg Inn was in fact built for the average tourist. It was a coincidence that most of the tourists in the years before and immediately following World War II were well-heeled and traveled with

entourages and had certain expectations about amenities. Rel Maples understood these things and made certain that the Gatlinburg Inn met the standards of its clientele. The 67 rooms and 7 suites were designed and furnished for comfort without compromise, and most of the original furniture is still in use. The chairs and sofas have been reupholstered several times (old will do—shabby won't), but the quality built into the inn endures, and so does its absolute refusal to surrender to any cookie-cutter trends in the lodging industry today. Also in keeping with the fashion of the time, separate quarters in the lower level housed the chauffeurs and domestic staffs of the inn's visitors.

The dining room of the Gatlinburg Inn was a masterpiece of propriety. The supplier of the hand-painted china, sterling silver finger bowls, and crystal used in the dining room joked that the dining room furnishings cost as much as the rest of the hotel, and he probably was close to right. Wilma Maples remembers the dining room fondly, particularly the Tuesday night dinners when the guests would gather for dinner and then retire to the tennis courts for square dancing. As the nature of tourism changed with the times following the war, the "new" tourists objected to the idea of dressing for dinner, so Rel and Wilma regretfully closed the dining room in 1972 rather than lower their own standards.

Wilma Miller Maples is not a Gatlinburg native. Born to a large family in Union County, Wilma came to Gatlinburg in 1943 as secretary to the chief ranger in the park. She worked summers at the Gatlinburg Inn from 1946 to 1950, when she moved to Oak Ridge to work for a research engineer. That job lasted until 1953 when she received a letter from Rel proposing marriage and a return to Gatlinburg. "It came out of the clear blue sky," she recalls, "and I really didn't know what to make of it at first." Wilma returned to Gatlinburg and became Mrs. Rel Maples in 1954 for "the best 31 years of my life."

The Gatlinburg Inn is as important to Gatlinburg's growth as the man who built it. In 1950 Rel Maples persuaded Bill Mills to join him in the establishment of the First National Bank of Gatlinburg, ending the necessity for the city's residents to travel 14 miles to Sevierville whenever they needed change. The inn hosted the first city offices prior to the construction of the original city hall, and the city's first large-press newspaper was printed in the basement.

Wilma recalls almost wistfully the days when the inn hosted the cream of American society, from captains of industry to an A-list of entertainment people. Igor Sikorsky, the inventor of the helicopter, was a guest there, and so was Melville Bell Grosvenor, son of the founder of the National Geographic Society. J. C. Penney, who changed America's shopping habits, stayed at the inn when he visited the area, and so did the parents of Stanley Marcus, who took Penney's concept to a level of luxury still unmatched in this

McKay's Inn Downtown $$-$$$
903 Parkway, Gatlinburg
(865) 436-5102, (800) 625-2971
www.mckaysinn.com
With more than 50 years of lodging visitors under their belts, McKay's Inn Downtown has a pretty good handle on what the tourist is looking for in the Smokies. Seventy-four rooms and suites provide enough variety to satisfy any taste, and McKay's location directly across from the Gatlinburg Convention Center makes it a natural for convention and tour groups.

McKay's is affiliated with several major travel clubs, including Encore, and supports several motor coach associations. A set of large rooms with a balcony directly overlooking the Parkway provides one of Gatlinburg's favorite gathering places for parade watchers.

**Quality Inn at the
Convention Center** $$$-$$$$
938 Parkway, Gatlinburg
(865) 436-5607, (800) 933-8674
www.reaganresorts.com

country. Tennessee Ernie Ford brought his parents. Liberace and Frank Fontaine were satisfied guests, as was "Pistol Pete" Maravich, the late basketball superstar. Wilma remembers with particular fondness the frequent visits of Boudleaux and Felice Bryant, the hall-of-fame songwriting team, who stayed in room 388 almost every winter for more than 20 years. The Bryants were so much like family that they were given keys to the front door, in case they stayed out past the inn's closing hour. During their stay in 1967, the Bryants wrote "Rocky Top." The list could go on for a long time, but you get the idea: The Gatlinburg Inn is a haven for travelers who enjoy being sheltered in an air of total civility, regardless of their background or social position.

If the Gatlinburg Inn seems a little out of step today it's only because it has refused to change its pace with the rest of the world. The inn remains open from April through October, and 95 percent of its clientele are repeat guests who first came as children and are now bringing their own children and grandchildren for

a graphic demonstration of how they grew up. And they're greeted by employees who've been there for as long as the guests can remember, especially the redoubtable head housekeeper, Grace Bales Barker, who, according to Wilma Maples, "God sent to me in 1969 after Rel's heart attack." And because the inn is particularly resolute about record-keeping, the older guests can look back at the old registers and find the dates and rooms they stayed in on every visit.

Wilma Maples continues to operate the Gatlinburg Inn as Rel intended it be run, and she laments the passing of the time when the operation was business as usual. And although she also regrets the passing of Gatlinburg from the friendly little mountain town it was, she understands with crystal clarity what's going on and why. Notwithstanding that, this iron-willed lady will go on as long as she can, operating her hostelry in the gentler fashion of her heart while her feet are planted firmly in the present.

To inquire about staying at the Gatlinburg Inn, call (865) 436–5133.

If the wall between the two buildings ever falls down, it'll be the Quality Inn *in* the convention center. This beautifully designed motel is literally the convention center's next-door neighbor—both facilities are built right on the property line that separates them. Convenience is only part of the story here. The unique topography of this motel provides a spectacular view of the mountains out the back and arm's length availability of more than two dozen attractions and restaurants out the front. Most of the rooms are unusually large and

well appointed, with comfortable furniture in addition to home-style amenities that tell you this is more than the usual "chain" property.

Bon-Air Lodge $$$
950 Parkway, Gatlinburg
(865) 436–4857, (800) 848–4857
www.smokymountainresorts.com
Tucked into a hillside just off the Parkway, the Bon-Air has a stairway leading down to the backyard of the Gatlinburg Convention Center. Recently renovated from top

to bottom, the Bon-Air features 74 over-size rooms with a choice of bed configurations, fireplaces, and Jacuzzis. The view of the mountains from the balconies on the back building is spectacular, and the popular veranda on the front building overlooks the Parkway. If you can tear yourself away, downtown Gatlinburg is at your doorstep and the Great Smoky Mountains National Park entrance is just a couple of blocks up the Parkway.

Clarion Inn & Suites $$$$$
1100 Parkway, Gatlinburg
(865) 436-5656, (800) 933-0777
www.clariongatlinburg.com

Luxury is the minimum standard at the Clarion—every one of the 131 rooms, from king and queen bed double units to the penthouse suites with their own elevators, is richly appointed to pamper the most demanding guest. Private balconies in every room provide great views, and the only rooftop meeting and banquet facilities in Gatlinburg give a special flavor to large gatherings. And speaking of flavor, the Clarion's deluxe continental breakfast is renowned as one of the best in a town famous for that sort of thing. Several unique gift and sundry shops are located in the building, and the aerial tramway to Ober Gatlinburg is just across the street. The Clarion is just 100 yards from the entrance to the Great Smoky Mountains National Park, and four of Gatlinburg's finest restaurants are in that space, along with the interesting Calhoun's Village, one of the city's many shopping malls.

Baskins Creek Neighborhood

Jack Huff's Motor Lodge $$
204 Cherokee Orchard Road, Gatlinburg
(865) 436-5171, (800) 322-1817
www.jackhuffs.com

Nobody alive in Gatlinburg can remember when the Huff family didn't operate several lodging facilities, and Jack Huff's is one of the oldest. Located a block off the Parkway and directly across the street from Pi Beta Phi elementary school, Jack Huff's Motor Lodge is another of the many independent motels in the city that reminds us of a different time. Sixty clean, comfortable rooms are maintained in a style that makes the guests feel at home, and it must be working—more than 75 percent of Huff's business is made up of people who've stayed there before. The morning coffeepot in the lobby is a gathering spot for what seems to be an ongoing reunion. Downtown Gatlinburg is just outside the door at the rear entrance to the Village, one of Gatlinburg's most popular shopping malls.

Bales Town & Country Motel $$
221 Bishop Lane, Gatlinburg
(865) 436-4773, (800) 458-8249
www.balesmotel.com

Bill Bales's grandfather built the original motel in 1955, and now Bill III (Bill's son) and his wife, Marsha, welcome old and new guests. In addition to standard guest rooms where comfort is the keynote, the Bales Motel also has a couple of town houses and a cottage on the grounds for larger parties. Long-term rentals are available, and guests paying for six nights will get their seventh night free. Two blocks from downtown Gatlinburg in the secluded Baskins Creek neighborhood, Bales Town & Country offers a glimpse of how the local families live.

Bradley's Court $
111 Woliss Lane, Gatlinburg
(865) 436-4884

Another time-warp property, Bradley's Court was built in the '50s and '60s by current operator Chuck Bradley's parents. Twenty units that are long on comfort and history are built into a mountainside at the end of the street, giving the guest a feeling of total privacy within walking distance of downtown. Chuck hasn't forgotten how to take care of families: Rollaway beds are available at a nominal charge for more heads than the standard room can rest, and most rooms have a sleeper sofa. The swimming pool has an attached baby pool, and a large grassy area is just right for lying around.

Jerry Lee Motel $$-$$$
208 Woliss Lane, Gatlinburg
(865) 436-5198
www.gatlinburg.com/jerryleemotel

You can sit on your balcony at the Jerry Lee Motel and get as good a view of the mountains as you're likely to find anywhere. Stroll a couple of blocks through a quiet neighborhood in the other direction and you're in the heart of the downtown business district. The kids won't be bored while you're gazing at the scenery, either—the Jerry Lee has its own arcade right next to the on-site grocery store and swimming pool. Opened in the 1960s, this is another of Gatlinburg's old-line, family-owned and -operated accommodations.

Johnson's Inn $$$
242 Bishop Lane, Gatlinburg
(865) 436-4881, (800) 842-1930
www.johnsonsinn.com

Originally built in 1946 and constantly improved to keep pace with the times, Johnson's Inn sits within sight of downtown but not within hearing distance. The four-story tower that contains most of the motel's 48 rooms has an elevator and gently sloped ramps for total wheelchair accessibility. Johnson's customer loyalty is so high and so important to the owners that they publish their own newsletter to keep their guests up-to-date with what's going on in their home away from home. Jacuzzi suites and fireplaces in selected rooms provide for pleasurable evenings away from the maddening crowds.

Kingwood Inn $$-$$$$
117 Bishop Lane, Gatlinburg
(865) 436-4509, (800) 637-3143
www.kingwoodinn.com

Tucked into a mountainside at the end of the road, the Kingwood offers seclusion from the hubbub of the business district 3 blocks away. Seven cottages on the grounds provide additional privacy for larger groups, and the Kingwood has a launderette for the convenience of its guests. The popularity of the Kingwood as a home away from home is attested to by the fact that 80 percent of their guests have returned annually since their 1964 opening.

River Road & Ski Mountain

River Terrace Resort & Convention Center $$$-$$$$$
240 River Road, Gatlinburg
(865) 436-5161, (800) 521-3523,
(800) 251-2040
www.riverterrace.com

For a place as close to town as it is, the River Terrace offers guests in its 205 rooms an awful lot of good reasons not to leave the grounds. One of the city's favorite restaurants is right in the center, two heated outdoor pools and the spa are convenient, and there's a lounge for the nightlife lover. Toss in the on-site health-food store with its own lunch menu and yoga, aerobics, and martial arts sessions, and you might not have time to go anywhere else. The River Terrace's 20,000-square-foot convention center is large enough to attract good-size convention groups or huge family reunions. Advance notice is requested and a deposit is required if you plan to bring your pets.

Riverhouse Motorlodge $$$-$$$$$
610 River Road, Gatlinburg
(865) 436-7821
www.riverhousemotels.com

The Riverhouse believes in pampering its guests. Spacious rooms with a choice of beds and fireplaces (choose wood or gas logs—after Labor Day) have private balconies overlooking the Little Pigeon River. It's hard to stand on the balcony and believe you're only a block from downtown Gatlinburg. And, maybe best of all, the staff at the Riverhouse will deliver a continental breakfast tray to your room every morning! Long, easy-grade ramps make the second-floor rooms easily accessible to wheelchairs.

Fairfield Inn $$$$
680 River Road, Gatlinburg
(865) 430-7200, (800) 228-2800
www.smoky-mtns.com
Laid out in a parklike setting along the Little Pigeon River, the Fairfield's 54 rooms all have fireplaces and private balconies overlooking the water. The hot-tub suites and extra-large king suites heighten the relaxed atmosphere. The quiet setting on River Road is just far enough away from downtown to shield the bright lights and noise but close enough to walk in less than five minutes. Ober Gatlinburg's aerial tramway mall is less than a block away and so are several excellent family restaurants.

Best Western Fabulous Chalet Inn $$$$
310 Cottage Drive, Gatlinburg
(865) 436-5607, (800) 933-8675
www.reaganresorts.com
Just across the river from River Road (turn at the traffic light by the Ober Gatlinburg tramway mall), the Fabulous Chalet has a combination of river views and mountain views. Regardless of whether your room has a single king bed or a suite with a hot tub and fireplace, the view is breathtaking. Set back in one of Gatlinburg's nicer residential areas, the Fab Chalet (local parlance) is a short stroll from a couple of truly outstanding restaurants and the Ober Gatlinburg tramway mall, and about 2 blocks from the entrance to the Great Smoky Mountains National Park. Downtown Gatlinburg is about 3 blocks in the other direction.

Bearskin Lodge on the River $$$
840 River Road, Gatlinburg
(865) 430-4330
www.bearskinlodgeontheriver.com
This entry in the lodging business was opened in late summer 2000 by Gatlinburg's oldest family. An imposing log-and-

stone structure, Bearskin Lodge is built partially on the property where the late Hattie Ogle McGiffin, Gatlinburg's matriarch for more than half of the 20th century, was born. The Lodge has 96 rooms in its five stories, and smoking is permitted only in rooms on the fourth floor. Eight distinctive room configurations are spread throughout the building, ranging from a single queen bed to luxury suites with everything your heart desires. Most rooms have private balconies over the river, gas fireplaces, and whirlpool baths. In keeping with the reputation for hospitality, the Ogles have built for almost two centuries, Bearskin Lodge on the River is designed to make anybody's stay in Gatlinburg a memory for life.

Riverhouse at the Park $$$$$
205 Ski Mountain Road, Gatlinburg
(865) 436-2070
www.riverhousemotels.com
At the southwest intersection of River Road and Ski Mountain Road, Riverhouse at the Park is conveniently situated for a short walk into downtown Gatlinburg or a short hike into the Great Smoky Mountains National Park. There's a trail just across the river that's a great favorite with local exercise walkers at all hours of the day and night. Forty-eight rooms at three levels of accommodation, ranging from merely wonderful to "I don't deserve this," offer spectacular views of the Little Pigeon River and the mountains. Creature comforts from whirlpool baths to wet bars and fireplaces abound, and the Riverhouse staff brings your breakfast to your room every morning. The level of pampering at the Riverhouse would make anybody feel guilty that wasn't totally convinced they deserve it.

Grand Prix Motel $-$$$
235 Ski Mountain Road, Gatlinburg
(865) 436-4561, (800) 732-2802
www.grandprixmotel.com
With the park for its backyard, the Grand Prix offers special low-cost lodging for hikers among its 30 rooms. Two kitchen

units will accommodate up to eight people each, and honeymoon suites are also available. An on-site Laundromat provides real convenience for the family. Pets are always welcome at the Grand Prix.

Watson's Motel $$
426 Ski Mountain Road, Gatlinburg
(865) 436-4747, (800) 621-8249
Herbert and Georgia Watson built their original motel in 1948. Daughter Alana Tinker has kept the property under family control and improved it to its present 67-room status, plus a family-size guest cottage. Kitchens are available in almost half of the rooms, and the motel has its own after-hours attraction that's kept a lot of their visitors coming back year after year: Bears and deer come out of the park wilderness across the street almost every night to eat at Watson's. If you brought your pets with you, keep them in your room during the side show.

Historic Nature Trail

Historic Nature Trail (formerly called Airport Road) runs uphill from the Parkway at traffic light #8, which is the corner where the Space Needle rises from the street. An eclectic combination of lodging places runs from small (20 rooms and fewer) family-owned motels to two of the city's largest franchise establishments. The Gatlinburg Convention Center and churches representing most Christian denominations are all convenient to the Historic Nature Trail motels.

Gillette Motel $$$
235 Historic Nature Trail, Gatlinburg
(865) 436-5601, (865) 436-5376,
(800) 437-0815
www.gillettemotel.com
A block up Historic Nature Trail from the Parkway, the Gillette Motel is directly across the street from the Gatlinburg Convention Center. The 80 rooms in an imposing three-story structure are usually

filled during the summer by repeat visitors and conventiongoers, but the location makes the Gillette worth a look. During the Christmas season the Gillette is a consistent prize-winner for its spectacular lighting efforts.

Bearland Lodge & General Store $$$
305 Historic Nature Trail, Gatlinburg
(865) 436-4565, (800) 654-8827 (in Tenn.), (800) 654-9593 (out of state)
www.bearlandlodge.com
Location is only part of the story here. The Bearland is right across the street from the Gatlinburg Convention Center and a long enough block from the Parkway to feel secluded. The 30 rooms have enough variations to satisfy any taste and most family sizes, and the Bearland General Store is one of the most popular shopping places in the neighborhood. Fireplace units are stocked with unlimited wood in season, and a new fire is laid each morning by the housekeeping staff. Six downtown churches are within a 3-block walk.

Rocky Top Village Inn $$$
311 Historic Nature Trail, Gatlinburg
(865) 436-7826, (800) 553-7738
Named for Tennessee's state song, the Rocky Top is owned by the tune's co-writer, Felice Bryant. Eighty-nine luxurious rooms in several configurations appeal to most tastes, and a guest loyalty rate of more than 75 percent attests to the Rocky Top's hospitable treatment. Bring your pets, too—they're welcome at the Rocky Top (advance notification appreciated).

Alto Motel $$
404 Historic Nature Trail, Gatlinburg
(865) 436-5175, (800) 456-4336
www.ismoky.com/mountains/lodging
An intimate 21-unit facility, the Alto specializes in quiet accommodation. Three blocks from downtown and within walking distance of five churches, the Alto maintains an atmosphere of peace and quiet that reflects the mountains. Because 70

> If you're staying in a Gatlinburg motel and you want to go downtown, take the trolley. It's cheap, dependable transportation, and everybody on the trolley seems to be having fun. It's cheaper by a long shot than parking downtown and a lot easier to find.

percent of its guests are annual repeaters, the Alto suggests all reservations be made in advance.

Gazebo Inn $$$
417 Historic Nature Trail, Gatlinburg
(865) 436-2222
www.allstays.com

A lovely front lawn surrounded by flowers greets you at the Gazebo Inn, establishing an air of serenity that carries right through the comfortable 60-room structure. Guests are pampered in the Bavarian ambience that fits the Smokies perfectly. Connecting rooms, fireplaces, nonsmoking rooms, balconies, and patios all combine to make the Gazebo a relaxing place when the pressures of travel are at their most pressing.

Glenstone Lodge $$$
504 Historic Nature Trail, Gatlinburg
(865) 436-9361, (800) 362-9522
www.glenstonelodge.com

If this place leaves a light on for you in every room, they'll illuminate a fair stretch of Historic Nature Trail, and that only covers about a quarter of what's available. More than 200 comfortable rooms with king, queen, or double beds (you choose) and 8 deluxe and executive-type suites surround a central atrium that's totally isolated from the street. Full banquet and catering facilities complement the award-winning restaurant and on-premise meeting rooms. The Gatlinburg Convention Center is close enough to reach in less than a five-minute walk.

Holiday Inn Sunspree Resort $$$$
520 Historic Nature Trail, Gatlinburg
(865) 436-9201, (800) 435-9201,
Groups (888) 562-2946
www.4lodging.com

You won't have any trouble finding the Sunspree—just put your shades on and look for the sign that almost renders them useless. It wouldn't be totally fair to call the big pink Sunspree sign garish (it's a nice shade), but it sure is bright.

The Sunspree itself is brilliant. Forget the name "Holiday Inn"—if this place could float, it'd be the greatest luxury cruise ship you could imagine. The Holidome, the central part of the complex where you check in and out, has a full-service restaurant, a lounge with planned family and adult activities, a market/deli, a pizza counter, a pool with extra seating space to eat while you watch the swimmers, and the activities desk, where you can plan a day or a week for the kids or the whole family, including picking up tickets to most of the local attractions. The eight-story tower adjoining the Holidome has interior guest rooms, a 4,800-plus square-foot ballroom, and a pool and spa on the fourth floor big enough to entertain large groups. Lest we forget that it's a lodging facility, the majority of the 400 rooms and suites are in the terrace area at the back of the property, where three multistory buildings feature views of the mountains in the (near) distance and LeConte Creek practically at your feet. Mynatt Park, one of Gatlinburg's real jewels (see our Parks and Recreation chapter), is right next to the terrace section. The Gatlinburg Convention Center and downtown are a couple blocks the other way. We could go on and on, but you've probably gotten the picture: If you want to go to a resort right in the middle of everything that has everything to offer, the place with the most visible sign in the Smokies is probably what you seek.

Ledwell Motel $$
615 Historic Nature Trail, Gatlinburg
(865) 436-5304

Near the top of Historic Nature Trail, about 4 blocks from downtown, the Ledwell is across the street from Mynatt Park, Gatlinburg's largest municipal playground. The Motor Nature Trail in the Great Smoky Mountains National Park is a short drive up the road, and the red trolley route stops at the Ledwell's front door for the convenience of the guests. Forty-five rooms offer all the amenities you'd expect, and free coffee is served in the lobby every morning.

Sidney James Mountain Lodge $$$
610 Historic Nature Trail, Gatlinburg
(865) 436-7851, (800) 578-7878
www.gatlinburgtravelodge.com

Right at the top of Historic Nature Trail, the Sidney James offers luxurious accommodations in what appears to be the middle of the woods. Gatlinburg's beautiful Mynatt Park is right next door, and one of the most popular sections of the Great Smoky Mountains National Park is just up the road. More than 130 attractively decorated rooms, with beds you really hate to get out of, look out on LeConte Creek and the mountains, and the indoor pool is considered one of the most beautiful in the Smokies. Conventions of up to 500 can be accommodated in the conference section, and the Sidney James prints its own travel guide with discount coupons for lots of local attractions and restaurants. The on-site cafe is a great place to start the day or enjoy a midday snack. Ski packages are available in season.

East Parkway

Following East Parkway (US 321N) east of town from traffic light #3, a succession of smaller, family-owned and -operated lodging places is within a few blocks. These are mostly places that were built on farmland in the 1950s and '60s and vary in size from intimate to huge. With a few exceptions, these are comfortably furnished, moderately priced accommodations that boast extremely high return percentages, where you'll be treated more like a visiting family member than a guest tenant. This strip of road is served by the orange trolley route, and the trolley will stop at, or within 50 feet of, the door to every motel listed.

Laurelwood Motel $
115 Willow Lane, Gatlinburg
(865) 436-4155

The Laurelwood was built in 1950 by the Luther family, and they still run it. One block from traffic light #3, this friendly old 14-unit facility sits parallel to East Parkway and below it far enough to mask out the sound of traffic. Comfortable, pine-paneled rooms look out on a parklike front yard with shuffleboard courts, picnic tables with charcoal grills, and lots of green space. A residential neighborhood at the back preserves the quiet atmosphere the Laurelwood was built in back before the town grew up.

Creekside Inn $$$
239 Sycamore Lane, Gatlinburg
(865) 436-5977, (888) 219-3301
www.creeksideinngatlinburg.com

One block south of East Parkway, the Creekside Inn features four stories of rooms with private balconies on beautiful Roaring Fork Creek. Fireplaces, Jacuzzis, and kitchen facilities are available, and every room's telephone can be dialed directly. Wildlife sightings are common across the creek, and downtown Gatlinburg is a pleasant 3-block stroll from the Creekside's front door.

East Side Motel $$
315 East Parkway, Gatlinburg
(865) 436-7569

Tom and Marlene Trentham built the East Side in 1971 on land that was part of her grandfather's farm. Four-fifths of the East Side's guests come back, most of them annually, and Marlene says running the motel is a lot like having a great big house and a great big family to fill it. The East Side is convenient to both ends of downtown at the same time—traffic light #3 is a short walk or trolley ride from the front door, and the Bishop Lane bypass is just across the street.

Sleep Inn $$$
177 East Parkway, Gatlinburg
(865) 436–9945, (866) 753–3717
www.gatlinburgsleepinn.com
Opened in 2001, this facility has 70 rooms on three floors, each with a private balcony overlooking the East Parkway—an excellent vantage point for viewing any of Gatlinburg's several seasonal parades. A complimentary continental breakfast helps jump-start your day, and a lazy river and hot tub in the indoor pool site provide a chance to relax at the end of the day from whatever rigors you've subjected yourself to. Most of the rooms are two-bed size, and Sleep Inn provides an exercise room and laundry facilities. The attached parking deck is a time and labor saver when going to and from your vehicle.

Brookside Resort $$$–$$$$
463 East Parkway, Gatlinburg
(865) 436–5611, (800) 251–9597
www.brooksideresort.com
The only word to describe the Brookside is huge—six multistory buildings containing 230 rooms in every imaginable configuration stretch along 3 blocks of the East Parkway, with Roaring Fork Creek at the back. The Brookside's front lawn, featuring the black bear statue that's a favorite landmark, is bigger than most of the lodging properties in town. With the blue trolley stopping at the front door and Winery Square shopping center right across the street, the Brookside has unmatched convenience. Add the on-site basketball, volleyball, and wallyball courts, and the available riverside pavilion with its own kitchen facility, and you can park your car at the Brookside and not get back into it until you leave.

Virgil's Motel $$
959 East Parkway, Gatlinburg
(865) 436–4838, (865) 436–5516
www.virgilsmotel.com
Mattie Belle and the late Virgil Trentham opened their motel in 1948 in what was "way out of town" at the time. Now their daughter Claudette Kendig and her husband, Bob, keep the place fresh and new-looking for new and established guests (one guest has rented the same room every year since the '60s). Virgil Trentham was a legend among fly fishermen in the area, and Mattie Belle's related to everybody, and she still drops by frequently, so a stay at Virgil's is one of the best history lessons you can get in Gatlinburg.

BED-AND-BREAKFASTS AND COUNTRY INNS 🛏️🍴

Changes in America's social mores since the social revolutions of the 1970s led the lodging industry to adopt new standards in tolerance toward the marital status (or the lack thereof) of its visitors. In the Great Smoky Mountains, this liberal attitude is best reflected in the growth of a new niche entry: the bed-and-breakfast inn.

Other tourist areas accommodated the bed-and-breakfast crowd by converting big old homes and boarding houses to increase the intimacy of their accommodations and adding a meal or two to hang on to their guests a little longer. That approach didn't fly in the Smokies. First, the few big old homes left in the area are in many cases still in use by succeeding generations of their builders. Secondly, the hotel/motel industry had just about wiped out the very few boarding homes in the area with the ongoing explosion of construction that began in the late '70s and continues to this day.

The result of all this is that the bed-and-breakfast industry in the Great Smoky Mountains is driven by a growing number of great, new, old-looking structures that were mostly built in the last decade. Regardless of their location (and some of them are going to give you a whole new appreciation of the term "remote"), the bed-and-breakfast inns of the Smokies are in the vanguard of a vibrant, growing addition to the established lodging industry. Designed and built with the specific market in mind, the Smokies' bed-and-breakfast inns are intended to satisfy the demands of a clientele that consists almost exclusively of couples. Children are not actively discouraged, but most of the inns limit the number of occupants in a single room, and the limit is usually three.

Several have "couples only" policies, and they'll be mentioned in the individual descriptions.

Being of recent construction, the inns have many of the amenities you'd find at any upscale lodging place: Expect cable or satellite television with one or more premium channels, central heating and air-conditioning, and some form of hot tub or whirlpool. Telephones are commonplace, and stereo systems are standard fare in most places. The shared bathrooms that always made boarding homes such an adventure are not in evidence in the Smokies. With only a few exceptions that compromise scenery for convenience, the views of the mountains from private or semiprivate balconies and full-width porches are absolutely spectacular—every inn can state with some justification that their view is "the tallest," "the widest," "the highest," ad infinitum.

The "breakfast" part of the equation is usually what you'd expect to find in a place like Tennessee, where bacon and sausage are considered vegetables. The three basic Southern food groups (meat, flour, and grease) are served in copious amounts, with some surprising gourmet touches added. Enough fruit, cereal, and whole-grain baked goods are usually available to satisfy the health-conscious, and afternoon and pre-bedtime snacks are commonly offered. Some of the inns will serve lunch and dinner to large groups with sufficient advance notice. Pets are a universal no-no, and please don't ask for any exceptions—the guests that killed off the pet question brought a pot-bellied pig with them.

The unique nature of this segment of the lodging industry makes it almost imperative that reservations be made well in advance. It's more like you're visiting in a very solicitous house than staying in a motel, and the hosts need as much planning time as they can get. Everybody we talked to said they welcome walk-in traffic on the rare occasion when they have vacancies, but "rare" is the operative word here. Conversely, because of the individual planning necessary to take care of guests on a practically individual basis, cancellations usually require about 10 days advance notice for full refunds—specific differences will be individually noted. Check-in times are all midafternoon (around 3:00 P.M.), and the earliest checkout is 11:00 A.M. Smoking is without exception restricted to outdoor areas.

A word of warning as we begin our journey. Except for a few places convenient to downtown Pigeon Forge and Gatlinburg, the inns described herein (and it's not a complete list—there were some places we simply couldn't send an unsuspecting visitor) are in areas of the county where the average tourist probably wouldn't go for any other reason. We've extended ourselves to provide clear directions to every one, and they're all accessible on paved roads. As usual, we'll begin in Sevierville and move south—please note that all accommodations are south of Dolly Parton Parkway (U.S. Highway 411/441).

PRICE CODE

Our pricing key indicates the average cost of a room for two adults, exclusive of taxes, during the tourist season (April through October). Where two codes are present, the higher code usually applies to guest cottages. Most places accept credit cards—we've noted the ones that don't.

$	Less than $100
$$	$100–$130
$$$	$131–$160
$$$$	$161–$200
$$$$$	Over $200

SEVIERVILLE—EAST

Blue Mountain Mist Country $$–$$$
Inn & Cottages
1811 Pullen Road, Sevierville
(865) 428-2335, (800) 497-2335
www.bluemountainmist.com
Set peacefully among several prosperous farms, Blue Mountain Mist is a haven of country charm and style. The inn is on a 60-acre farm owned by the Ball family, surrounded by mountains on three sides. The 17 rooms include nine with queen beds, three suites with queen beds and additional bedding for family members, and five cottages. A hearty country breakfast is served family-style in the sun-drenched dining room, and coffee and desserts are offered each evening.

The immaculate grounds invite the visitor to kick back and enjoy a respite from the pressures of the day, or to stroll through the gardens and maybe throw a few rounds of horseshoes. The hammock on the corner of the full-width front porch is almost irresistible on a warm summer afternoon. Nestled in the woods behind the inn, five quaint cottages offer privacy with style. Each cottage has a kitchenette and grill and a private yard with a picnic table. Bedside Jacuzzi tubs and fireplaces grace each cottage, and breakfast in the inn is included with cottage reservations.

Traveling east out of Sevierville on Dolly Parton Parkway (US 411N), Middle Creek Road is a lighted intersection about 2 miles from downtown. Turn right on Middle Creek and go south past the hospital and several professional buildings about 3.9 miles to Jay Ell Road on the left. Turn left about 1½ miles to Pullen Road. Blue Mountain Mist is the huge, turreted farmhouse-style structure on the corner.

SEVIERVILLE—PARKWAY

Calico Inn $
757 Ranch Way, Sevierville
(865) 428-3833, (800) 235-1054
www.calico-inn.com

An intimate establishment with three guest rooms, Calico Inn welcomes school-age children, with a limit of three people per room. The attitude and the surroundings are laid-back, with a panoramic view of the mountains forming a backdrop for the nearby woods and fields. After the country breakfast has filled you to the brim, you can relax on the front porch and watch squirrels and rabbits at play or head for the wonders that await you in America's favorite vacation spot. Whatever your choice, the comfort of Calico Inn awaits you at the close of your day. Convenient to all the attractions on the Parkway, Calico Inn is a rustic structure 2 miles off the Parkway on New Era Road, just south of the Wal-Mart center.

WEARS VALLEY

The three inns on and adjacent to Wears Valley Road have addresses in both Pigeon Forge and Sevierville. Political boundaries aside, they're described here in the order you would come upon them if you turned westbound on Wears Valley Road (U.S. Highway 321) from the Parkway in Pigeon Forge.

Hilton's Bluff Bed & Breakfast Inn $$
2654 Valley Heights Drive, Pigeon Forge
(865) 428-9765, (800) 441-4188
www.hiltonsbluff.com
Close enough to the Parkway that you could hear traffic if the woods didn't get in the way, Hilton's Bluff is a 10-room inn with a variety of bed configurations and plenty of space for corporate meetings, church retreats, weddings, and rehearsal dinners. Bright and airy rooms and game facilities make Hilton's Bluff an ideal place to relax without ever leaving the property. Three honeymoon-style suites have heart-shaped two-person Jacuzzis. The day begins with a full country breakfast and ends with delicious surprise snacks and refreshments. There's always something to do at Hilton's Bluff: The selection of parlor games is outstanding, the library has sev-

It would be nice to say that the level of service you get at the bed-and-breakfast establishments is typical of the rest of the area, but it isn't—it's much better. Don't be afraid to ask for anything that seems reasonable to you.

eral interesting fiction and nonfiction books, and there's enough woods just outside to make for a leisurely stroll. The Pigeon Forge trolley stops at the corner just below the inn. Valley Heights is just half a mile from the Parkway—it's the second street off the Parkway to the left.

Von Bryan Mountaintop Inn $$
2402 Hatcher Mountain Road, Sevierville
(865) 453-9832, (800) 633-1459
www.vonbryan.com
Von Bryan Inn is a palatial structure that commands an unparalleled vista of beautiful Wears Valley, with the Smokies rising behind it. Seven rooms with private baths and a choice of king or queen beds enjoy this view, and the swimming pool and picnic area behind the inn are dominated by Bluff Mountain rising in the distance. The log chalet in front of the inn has two queen beds, two twin beds, two bathrooms, a whirlpool bath, and a wraparound deck that provides both of the spectacular views. Hatcher Mountain Road is 7 miles from the Parkway on Wears Valley Road. Von Bryan Mountaintop Inn is 2½ miles up Hatcher Mountain Road. The run up Hatcher Mountain seems a lot longer the first time, but it's paved and worth the trip.

Little Greenbrier Lodge $-$$
3685 Lyon Springs Road, Sevierville
(865) 429-2500, (800) 277-8100
www.littlegreenbrierlodge.com
One of the oldest lodging structures in the area, Little Greenbrier has had a checkered history since it opened in 1939 as a hotel for businessmen and visitors to the national park. When the demise of the railroad to Elkmont took away its clientele,

A True Work of Art

It is generally agreed that artists are not like the rest of us. Most artists, it's usually conceded, are just enough off-center that they see things differently, and if they don't get real offensive about it, we're willing to cut them a little slack. As long as they return the favor by enriching our lives with their art, we'll put up with the fact that they might not have both feet planted on the same piece of ground.

And then there's Vern Hippensteal. Here is an artist who sees things with such clarity that he's able to record them on canvas as accurately as if he'd used a camera, but no camera can breathe life into a scene like Vern can. Maybe that's because Vern Hippensteal is a scientist by education (he's got a degree in physics), a printer by heritage (it's one of the family businesses), and, in his own terms, an artist by the grace of God. The difference between Vern Hippensteal and other truly gifted artists is that Vern lives in a disciplined world, with both feet firmly planted in his native soil. And when Vern and his wife, Lisa, decided to build and operate their own inn, the first thing they did was design it themselves, to reflect the peace and beauty of their birthplace.

Vern's artistic and mathematical talents came in real handy for the concept and the structural details. Lisa's experience growing up in the famed Mountain View hotel in Gatlinburg, managed for several years by her father, provided the nuts-and-bolts details that separate a classic lodging place from a merely outstanding one. Impeccable taste didn't hurt either, and this couple brims with that. The result is Hippensteal's Mountain View Inn, a monument to good taste and sensibility

that elevated itself to practically legendary status in less than a decade.

Even the location is an exercise in serendipity—Vern was stalling for time to find the right location when a piece of hilltop property came on the market—for about 15 minutes. Acting as their own general contractor and decorator, Vern and Lisa built, decorated, and opened their inn in 1990 in a manner so seamless that it seems now as if it's always been there. Even the location has a gentle irony—the easiest way to get there is to drive through the Great Smoky Arts & Crafts Community, which is a nice way to prepare you for what's coming. The driveway is a little more than half a mile long and is straight out of central casting: One minute you're on a gently climbing mountain road, then there you are. As you come around the last turn the inn appears in its entirety, looming over a landscape that most people can only imagine.

A quick look around tells you that this place is going to take a lot of exploring. It starts with a walk up the stairs, across the full-width front porch (try to ignore the rocking chairs—there'll be time for that later), and into the impossibly bright lobby where the dominant white of the wicker furniture and imposing limestone fireplace is complemented by the alternating black marble floor tile and walls covered with artwork. Everything about the lobby says, "Sit here and enjoy the rest of your life," and you really want to, but there's so much more that you press on. Follow the guide that has materialized beside you (if it's a tall guy with a beard, his name is Vern) up the stairs to the lodging area. At the top of the stairs is

Hippensteal's Mountain View Inn, from the only vantage point higher than itself.
VERN HIPPENSTEAL

the library. Some guests have been known to get past this point only to sleep and eat. The walls are lined with bookcases, and the selection is as eclectic as you'll find anywhere: Stephen King and Mark Twain share shelf space with Norman Vincent Peale, and a stack of jigsaw puzzles on the table invites you to stay. The room at the back is Vern's studio—if he's not your guide, he might be in there doing whatever artists do.

The rest of the second floor consists of nine elegantly furnished rooms, each named for the painting that the room is planned around. Queen beds and comfortable furniture grace each room with enough comfort that leaving isn't easy (notice a pattern here?), but there's still a lot to see. If at this point you're led to the other building, where two guest suites take up the second story, the nice couple on the porch there are probably Tom and Jane Woods, Lisa's parents, who live on the first floor. They're excellent company.

Back in the lobby, the dining room is at the end closest to the stairs. White wicker chairs and glass-topped pedestal tables make the room seem to float like a mirage, but the food served at the morning breakfast is very real, very solid, and very good. And once again, the natural ability of East Tennessee's natives to serve and nourish you is enhanced by the soul of the artist: Vern and Lisa see to it that your meal is served with the flair that their specialty dishes deserve.

The food prepares you for whatever your day in the Smokies entails. Vern and Lisa are inveterate hikers and will encourage you to go into the mountains and see why people can't get enough of this place. You may have plans of your own, but if you want to hang around, that's okay, too. There are games to be played and magazines to be read in the lobby, or the library may be softly calling to you. And there are still those rocking chairs on the porch, where the view of the Smokies range exceeds 200 degrees in width, stretching from Greenbrier pinnacle to the east across Mount LeConte to Mount Harrison. Vern talks about extending the porch completely around the inn, which would make Douglas Lake visible to the north. Just sitting and drinking in the constantly changing scenery is a pleasant way to pass a day.

To stretch the legs and further calm the soul, a stroll around the seven manicured acres of grass and woodlands will bring new discoveries as you find the gardens and flower beds, and an occasional sighting of the resident animal population is always a delight. If you get hungry or thirsty during the day, you're welcome to go into the kitchen and help yourself to whatever's available. Like always, someone will appear from thin air to help you if you need it; you'll never get used to it, but that's the way they do things here.

It's been lamented here that the face of tourism is changing—that people are in too much of a hurry these days, and they don't stop and smell the roses as often as they might. Some of that attitude has pervaded the Smokies, and the natives have mixed emotions about it. The money the modern tourist leaves here is good, and the increased security is comforting, but there's still room for people coming here who want to leave the outside world outside for a while and recharge their emotional batteries. Hippensteal's Mountain View Inn was built for those people by a couple who share their concerns and who have had the good sense never to leave the place so many others want to visit.

To get to Hippensteal's from traffic light #3 in Gatlinburg, drive 2 miles east on East Parkway (US 321) to Glades Road through the Arts & Crafts Community about 2.3 miles to its terminus at Bird's Creek Road. Turn left again, and less than half a mile later you'll come to the first of two forks; take the right one up and over the hill to the second fork, which you also take to the right for about another half mile to the inn's driveway (Taten Marr Way) on the left. For reservations at the inn ($$$), call (865) 436-5761 or (800) 527-8110, or visit their Web site at www.hippensteal.com.

the building went through several changes and several years of vacancy before being renovated and opened in its present form in 1993. Sufficient hardwood and wicker furniture was salvaged to retain the Victorian flavor of the original hotel. The lodge today has 10 rooms, eight of which have private baths. Private balconies and porches are available on both floors of the Victorian structure, with views of both the mountains and Wears Valley. Lyon Springs Road is 9 miles from the Parkway on Wears Valley Road, and Little Greenbrier Lodge is 1½ miles east (left) off Wears Valley Road. Lyon Springs continues into the Great Smoky Mountains National Park through Little Greenbrier Cove, coming out to the Little River Road at Metcalf Bottoms picnic area. At this point Gatlinburg is just 9 miles to the east.

GATLINBURG

The route through Gatlinburg will be the same one we've used throughout the book: We'll start on the Parkway and head through town. Then we'll go east out US 321 (East Parkway). The eastern side establishments are spread over an area of about 35 square miles, and all directions to them will begin at traffic light #3.

Eight Gables Inn $$
219 North Mountain Trail, Gatlinburg
(865) 430-3344, (800) 279-5716
www.eightgables.com
Twelve spacious rooms are furnished with a decidedly feminine touch, each with its own private bath and great view through large windows. The covered porch and grounds provide a relaxed atmosphere, as do the sitting areas inside the inn. The Magnolia Tea Room is the setting for the gourmet country breakfast (you'll love the potato pie au gratin) and is open for lunch Tuesday through Friday. Groups of up to 30 can be accommodated for luncheon meetings. The evening dessert bar for guests only is a big hit with the kids. Eight Gables is situated right between Gatlinburg and Pigeon Forge, and the trolley stop at the Gatlinburg Welcome Center provides service to both cities. Before you even get into Gatlinburg on the Parkway spur, Eight Gables Inn is across the road from the Gatlinburg Welcome Center.

Olde English Tudor Inn $-$$
135 West Holly Ridge Road, Gatlinburg
(865) 436-7760, (800) 541-3798
www.oldeenglishtudorinn.com
Right in the center of downtown Gatlinburg, the Olde English Tudor Inn is an oasis of comfort and serenity. The innkeepers live in the building, so you won't ever be isolated from the kind of service you like to expect. Eight comfortable guest rooms range in accommodation from double beds to king, all with views of the mountains or downtown. The rear patio and flower garden are a welcome break from the downtown hubbub,

The bed-and-breakfast industry in the Smokies probably offers the most intimate experience you'll have with the local population. Don't be surprised if you get emotionally involved with your hosts.

and the community room is a great place to meet new and old friends. To get to the inn, turn left at traffic light #7 (Reagan Drive), left again at Reagan Lane (the first street), and left one more time at Holly Ridge—the inn is the first place on the right.

Red Oak Lodge $$$$
436 East Parkway, Gatlinburg
(865) 430-3228, (800) 445-0167
www.redoaklodge.com
Just 2 blocks from downtown, Red Oak Lodge is the perfect choice for large groups—it can sleep up to 60 people in dormitory-type rooms and has two luxury suites for the group leaders. Individual showers in the dorms make getting ready for a big day go quickly, and catering service is available if your group wants to eat in.

GATLINBURG—EAST

The establishments east of Gatlinburg are spread out in an area accessible by roads running north off US 321, from 2 to 15 miles from traffic light #3 in Gatlinburg.

Timber Rose English Lodge $$
1106 Tanrac Trail, Gatlinburg
(865) 436-5852
www.timberrose.com
Built in the style of a true English lodge, Timber Rose offers lavish accommodations, only for couples, in five large suites. Each suite has its own private entrance and nearly every amenity you could wish for: a spacious living room, dining room, full kitchen, romantic bedroom, woodburning fireplace, and a hot tub on the

private porch. Opulent furnishings appear throughout the inn, featuring Corinthian statuary and stained-glass windows everywhere. The view of the Smokies is almost 100 miles wide, and the feeling is that you'll never want to return to civilization. In fact, it's hard to believe civilization is only a mile or so away.

Fresh-baked pastries and fruits are delivered to the suites every morning, and you'll know the daily chambermaid service has been there when you see yesterday's empty champagne bottle replaced by a full one in a silver cooler. The innkeepers at Timber Rose pride themselves on their ability to pamper their guests in an aura of total civility surrounded by a wilderness that will astonish you. Timber Rose is on the northern edge of Gatlinburg's world-famous Great Smoky Arts & Crafts Community, described at length in our Mountain Crafts chapter. To get there, go east 2 miles out East Parkway (US 321) from traffic light #3 to the traffic light at Glades Road. Turn left on Glades and go about 2 more miles to the blinking light at Powdermill Road, where another left turn will lead about 2 blocks to a fork in the road. Take the left fork (John's Branch Road) about 1¼ miles to Tanrac Trail, and turn right. Follow the road up about ⅓ mile.

Buckhorn Inn $$
2140 Tudor Mountain Road, Gatlinburg
(865) 436-4668
www.buckhorninn.com
The only establishment in the Smokies Corridor that is considered a true country inn, the Buckhorn Inn has been in business since 1938. Set on 35 acres of woodland in a secluded area 6 miles east of Gatlinburg, the inn has its own walking trails and lake for the enjoyment of its guests. Breakfast is included in the lodging fee, and lunch and dinner are available to guests by reservation only. The inn is located within the boundaries of the Great Smoky Arts & Crafts Community, providing a unique shopping experience. Special maps prepared by the inn's staff describe nearby

hiking trails in the Great Smoky Mountains National Park and throw in a few secret locations known even to very few locals. The main building contains six guest rooms with private baths, and four guest cottages on the property lend additional privacy in a sylvan setting. The Buckhorn Inn personnel are all specially trained to provide whatever information you want to plan your own day, and they can usually throw in a few hints to make a good time better. From traffic light #3 in Gatlinburg, take East Parkway (US 321) about 4½ miles east to Buckhorn Road and turn left. Tudor Mountain Road is about a mile in on the right.

FINALLY, SOMETHING REALLY SPECIAL

Our intent in this book is to keep you close to the Smokies Corridor, but once in a while something comes along that warrants a deviation from that standard. We found a bed-and-breakfast inn in Newport, about 25 miles east of Sevierville and Gatlinburg, that's so exceptional we decided to suspend the rules. If you go there, you'll thank us.

Christopher Place $$$$$
1500 Pinnacles Way, Newport
(865) 623-6555, (800) 595-9441
www.christopherplace.com
The drive from our main coverage area to Christopher's (see directions below) may have tested your patience a bit, but that will be forgotten before you get out of your car. And you just know you're going to love the person who greets you in the parking lot.

The main house at the inn is a Federal-style mansion with nothing to indicate you're in a lodging place. The three-story vestibule reveals a selection of inviting rooms in almost every direction. To the left, past a peek at the dining room and kitchen, the living room features a grand piano and a selection of comfortable furniture perfect for enjoying the wildflowers outside the picture window. Across the hall the library has books, puzzles, periodicals, and more comfortable places to sit with another attractive scene outside. If you continue through the vestibule and out the front door, you'll be on the full-width front porch. You can stand and gape at the view across the front yard (a lot of the mountains you're looking at are in North Carolina), or you can sit in one of the rocking chairs and just bask in the atmosphere of elegance you've entered. If you're like most everybody who's stayed at Christopher Place, you're already in love with it, and you probably haven't even seen your room yet.

And it doesn't really matter which of the seven suites you're staying in; the room is smashing. Whether it's Mountain Sunrise, the cheery corner room with the brass queen bed and the garden outside, or Camelot, the regal suite with the hand-carved mahogany king bed and the breathtaking mountain view, your room is going to be among the best you've ever spent a night in. And if your choice is the fabulous Roman Holiday suite, you'll dance on the edge of decadence for your entire stay—if you get out of the double whirlpool long enough to dance at all. But don't take our word for it—read the guest diary in your room. And add your thoughts to share with the next occupant. Every room has a private bath, a coffeemaker, stereo system with compact disc and cassette players, a hair dryer, and snuggly terry robes.

If you decide to come out for breakfast, do it at your leisure: Breakfast is served when you're ready to eat, and the hearty country fare will be supplemented with the personal choices you described when you made your reservation. If it's a birthday or anniversary, a special surprise will be added. And all of the food is hand-picked and brought in fresh by the staff every day—nobody around will make the trip up the mountain to deliver groceries.

When you've finished breakfast and feel like doing something, or nothing, you'll find you're in the right place for that,

too. The three acres of mountainside you're on contains enough to keep you busy if you want to stick around—the swimming pool and tennis court are real handy behind the gym, where a fully equipped weight room is available for a workout with free weights or exercise machines. The tanning bed, double shower, and sauna are all beside the gym, and a kitchenette with soft drinks will help keep you cool. If something more energetic than a stroll of the grounds is your preference, a hiking trail takes off from the back of the property and goes up the side of English Mountain. The trail will get you closer to nature at whatever level of challenge you want, and local wildlife sightings usually include wild turkey, red fox, gray squirrels, and raccoons. If you choose to seek other pleasures, Gatlinburg is about 45 minutes away to the south and east, and Interstate 40 will take you back to Sevierville and Pigeon Forge in about the same time. The Cosby entrance to the Great Smoky Mountains National Park is 15 miles south on Tennessee Highway 32, the same road that leads to Gatlinburg.

And if you're wondering who's there to take care of you, just wish out loud for something. The entire staff are past masters at the art of domestic invisibility. They are there when you need them; otherwise, they're not around—at least not where you can see them. These are the cream of the crop of East Tennessee natives who have an instinctive feel for service. They love to take care of people, and it shows mostly in the fact that they only show up when you want something they're trained to provide. They're also a great source of local information and can make arrangements for some unusual trips—ask them about a llama trek. And, no, you can't take the staff home with you.

Christopher Place has won nearly every award available to a bed-and-breakfast and carries the highest designations offered by every rating service that has seen it. The elegance of the accommodations and the effortless grace of the staff are hallmarks of hospitality anywhere at any level, and achieving their goal of providing you with an unforgettable vacation experience is as satisfying to them as it is rewarding for you.

Christopher Place can be tough to find. The key is to get to English Mountain Road on TN 32, and there are three approaches to that point:

From I-40 East (like from Knoxville or Interstate 81S): Take exit 435 in Newport and turn south (right) 3 miles; English Mountain Road is on the right.

From I-40 West (from North Carolina): Take exit 440 (US 321—Wilton Springs Road) 2 miles west to TN 32; turn right 3 ½ miles to English Mountain Road on the left.

From Gatlinburg: Take US 321 (East Parkway) to its terminus at TN 32 (about 17 miles from traffic light #3 in Gatlinburg). Turn left (north) on TN 32 about 10.3 miles to English Mountain Road on the left. Christopher Place tries to keep a directional sign at the intersection of TN 32 and English Mountain Road, but their efforts so far have failed. (It's been suggested that a less attractive sign might not get stolen as frequently. An alternative would be to just give a sign to everyone in the county named Christopher.) However, once you're on English Mountain Road, follow it 2 miles (it'll seem longer) through the rolling countryside of rural Cocke County until the pavement ends. The next right turn is Pinnacles Way, and it winds a mile up the face of English Mountain to Christopher Place.

VACATION RENTALS

For tens of thousands of Smoky Mountain vacationers each year, there's simply no substitute for the comfort and atmosphere offered by overnight and short-term accommodations rentals. Chalet, cabin, and condominium rentals are ideally suited for a variety of different vacation scenarios such as family vacations, honeymoons and romantic getaways, company retreats, church outings, or other group celebrations.

In a sense, it all boils down to what one wants out of a Smokies experience. One of the primary reasons people cite for coming here is the enjoyment of the mountains and all their natural surroundings. In that respect, vacation rentals are often your best option when it comes to accessing the beauty and the splendor of the environment while at the same time being able to relax in a virtual home away from home. Campgrounds certainly put you in touch with nature, and hotels and motels offer plenty of convenience and amenities, but overnight rentals are generally able to provide the best of both worlds and more.

There is a seemingly countless number of choices when it comes to selecting a rental property. The number of cabins, chalets, and condo units here totals in the thousands and grows larger all the time. In fact, the prospect of narrowing down your vacation lodging site could be a little overwhelming. Don't worry—that's what this chapter is for. We'll present you with a basic overview of what kinds of properties and amenities are out there and where they're located. We'll also provide you with a starting point in terms of prices as well as reservation and payment methods. From there, we'll point you in the direction of a number of rental companies and resorts in the area. Collectively, they'll give you access to just about any type of rental property in whichever area of the Smokies you desire.

What to Choose

Although there are infinite variations when it comes to the styles of Smoky Mountain vacation rental properties, they can loosely be classified under three basic types, which are primarily distinguishable by their architectural differences: chalet, cabin, and condominium.

The term "chalet" generally refers to the style of home reminiscent of those in mountainous European villages. The classic chalet's most distinguishing characteristic is its A-frame construction. Typically, you'll also find large and numerous windows for mountain viewing as well as ample outdoor deck space. In Sevier County, the largest concentration of chalets is found nestled in the hilly slopes surrounding Gatlinburg.

When you hear the word "cabin," images of a sturdy, rustic, log dwelling probably spring to mind. Although there is surely an abundance of log structures for rent throughout the Smokies, you might be surprised to find that many of them are anything but rustic. Developers have found log homes to be a popular lodging option with visitors, so it's not unusual to see new ones springing up everywhere. And despite their bucolic image, today's log rentals offer plenty of modern conveniences.

Cabins probably offer the widest berth in terms of architectural range. You'll find

The state of Tennessee requires that any company in the overnight rental business operate with a vacation lodging license obtained through the Tennessee Real Estate Commission. To be on the safe side, make sure that any overnight rental company you deal with is properly licensed.

everything from smaller one-bedroom cabins to sprawling ranch-style structures to multistory log homes with heavy-duty square footage. Many incorporate some of the popular exterior features common to chalets, such as large picture windows and porches. Cabins are found throughout the Sevier County area, but you're more likely to find them in the middle to northern sections where the terrain is generally less steep and more conducive to cabin construction.

Condominiums are the easiest type of rental to separate from the group. Put simply, they most often resemble apartment complexes and are noted for housing a large number of units in a centralized building or set of buildings. They range from multiple groupings of ground-level flats and townhomes to interior-access, high-rise structures. Condominiums are most prevalent in and around Pigeon Forge and Gatlinburg, but they can be found in Sevierville and outlying areas as well.

You'll notice in the listings of rental companies later in the chapter that some companies market themselves as "resorts." This means that the company's rental properties are centralized and offer common on-site amenities like swimming pools, tennis courts, or golf courses. Most resorts are made up of either condominiums or cabins.

One type of resort that isn't addressed in this book is the time-share. These are vacation rentals that are jointly owned by multiple owners, each of whom gets to stay in the unit a specified number of weeks each year. Since this touches on the concept of ownership rather than renting, we've avoided the subject for the purposes of this chapter.

Selecting a Location

Although overnight rentals are more heavily concentrated in Gatlinburg and Pigeon Forge, they can be found virtually any-

where in the county—and beyond. With that in mind, it's up to you to decide what your vacation priorities are when considering where you want to stay. If scenic mountain views are high on your list, you might want to be closer to Gatlinburg. If you want quick access to shopping and music theaters, consider Pigeon Forge. Basing yourself out of Sevierville will help you avoid a lot of the heavier traffic and also allow handier access to surrounding markets like Knoxville or Asheville, North Carolina.

There are a few specific sections of the Smokies that are noted for their abundance of rental choices. When dealing with overnight rental companies (see section below), you'll likely hear some of the following names in addition to the county's three main cities: Walden's Creek, a few miles off Wears Valley Road, outside Pigeon Forge; Wears Valley, about 10 miles southwest of Pigeon Forge; Ski Mountain, the generic name given to the concentration of chalet homes located a couple of miles from downtown Gatlinburg on Mount Harrison (see our Neighborhoods and Real Estate chapter); and Cobbly Nob, a resort area about 12 minutes from Gatlinburg on U.S. Highway 321.

Amenities

Along with type of structure and location, amenities are always a major factor when choosing a vacation rental. To the good fortune of the overnight renter, Smoky Mountain properties are usually rife with the luxuries and the "little things" that can make an overnight accommodation seem like home.

As a caution, however, we'll tell you that just because a particular property is laden with amenities doesn't mean that the cabin, chalet, or condo unit itself is necessarily attractive or offers good views. It may just be a dump that happens to have a lot of bells and whistles. There are just so many different properties out there, the only way to be sure is to ask your rental agent to e-mail or "snail mail" current photographs to you along with the property's other marketing materials. This type of information is also usually accessible on a rental company's Web site.

Although there are specific cabins, condos, and chalets that are exceptions to this list, most vacation rentals will include furnished linens and towels; kitchens equipped with dishes, silverware, cooking utensils, and appliances like refrigerator, stove, and microwave oven (you're responsible for the food!); hot tubs/whirlpool baths; fireplaces; washers and dryers (either in the unit or a laundry room); and cable or satellite television. Some places, especially the resorts, have access to other exterior amenities like swimming pools, tennis courts, and golf courses.

Money Matters

How much can you expect to pay for an overnight rental? The main determining factor is the size of the unit needed. A small, one-bedroom condo will obviously not be as expensive as a seven-bedroom cabin. You'll be hard-pressed to find a price lower than $65 to $85 per night for two people. Prices can go as high as several hundred dollars per night for a multiple bedroom unit.

In most cases, prices are based on occupancy per unit. For example, a one-bedroom condo might be considered to have a capacity of four people (one bed and a sleeper sofa), and a three-bedroom cabin may have a capacity of eight (three beds and a sleeper sofa). Because prices are structured according to a unit's capacity—larger accommodations will cost more because it's presumed that more people will be staying in them. You will also likely be charged extra for additional occupants beyond the unit's limit. Based on information from many of the companies with

which we spoke, an average figure is $10 per night per person for anyone over 12 years of age.

Although individual policies vary from one rental company or resort to another, there are some general guidelines and procedures that you'll encounter with just about all of them. These will especially be useful if you've never rented these types of overnight accommodations. It's strongly recommended, however, to confirm any particular company's specific policies when shopping around.

It's advisable to make reservations months in advance, especially for holiday or peak season periods. If you haven't already encountered this information in our other accommodations chapters, peak visitation times are during the summer months, October, and holidays like Fourth of July, Memorial Day, Labor Day, and, of course, Thanksgiving and Christmas. Six months out, you'll probably be safe, but many repeat vacation renters will book their regular unit for the following year on departure. It's typical for most companies to have reservations on their books for one and sometimes even two years in advance.

Most places require that you reserve a minimum number of nights. Two nights is an average minimum, especially when you're dealing with weekends. If you're booking for holidays or peak season periods, you're looking more at a three- or four-night minimum.

You will usually have to post a deposit within a certain time period after making your reservation in order to hold it. The amount can range anywhere from the amount of the first night's rental to 50 percent of the total cost of the stay, depending on your rental agency. Although credit cards are universally accepted, double-check with the booking agent to confirm which specific cards are accepted. Some companies also accept cash and even personal checks (if they receive your check well enough in advance). The balance of the total is expected on arrival.

If you are from out of town and interested in booking a vacation rental property in the Smokies, the Internet is an excellent research tool. Just about every rental company's Web site contains photos of all the individual properties along with detailed descriptions of amenities and, sometimes, virtual tours. In most cases, you can even handle your reservation requests and bookings online.

Cancellation policies also vary from one place to another, but two weeks seems to be a standard cutoff point to safely cancel your reservation (we spoke with companies that allow as few as 72 hours and some that require a month's notice). If you cancel before that cutoff time, you'll probably have a choice of either rescheduling your reservation or receiving a refund. Some places give a full refund, while some keep a nominal administrative fee.

Cancellation within the cutoff period usually results in full forfeiture of the deposit. The same goes for early departure during the time of stay. Most of the agents with whom we spoke, however, did mention that exceptions can sometimes be made if the customer can document a family emergency like death or serious illness.

Overnight Rental Companies

There are some helpful distinctions we'll point out that may deflect confusion when sifting through this section. Earlier in the chapter we made a reference to companies that call themselves "resorts," which are noted for their centralized accommodations and amenities. For the purposes of distinction, resort companies are somewhat unique when compared to the rental company whose inventory comprises separate properties located all over the county. In both cases, however, it's common for the individual units to be

owned by absentee investors.

Condominiums present their own peculiarities. Some condo units are marketed through rental companies. It's very common to see individual unit listings within a single condominium complex handled by different overnight rental businesses. On the other hand, the management of that same condominium development may also personally handle the marketing and property management for other units in the development. The choice of who manages a particular unit is usually up to the discretion of that unit's owner.

Some of the companies we've included below deal exclusively in rentals, but many are also full-service real estate businesses through which you can invest in rental property as well. Refer to our Neighborhoods and Real Estate chapter for information on other area companies through which you can buy, sell, and manage vacation rentals.

The addresses below are for each company's business office. This is usually where you go to check in, pay the balance of your rental, and get your keys. You might also receive specific instructions on how to get to your rental, if it's located at a separate site. We've included Web site addresses because they usually include photos of specific properties and pricing information. In most cases, you can even make your reservations from a company's Web page.

SEVIERVILLE

Oak Haven Resort
1947 Old Knoxville Highway, Sevierville
(865) 428-2009, (800) 652-2611
www.oakhavenresort.com
Oak Haven is easily accessible from Interstate 40 and Tennessee 66 (less than 8 miles from the interstate), but it still offers its guests a fair amount of seclusion with decent mountain views. On the property are 63 one- to four-bedroom log cabins, each of which is equipped with a hot tub, whirlpool bath, fully equipped kitchen, gas grill, and a TV/VCR/stereo

combination. An outdoor pool and a picnic pavilion with barbecue grills are available to all guests.

For those who wish to venture away from the resort, Douglas Lake is only 5 miles away, and Eagles Landing Golf Course is located next door (see our chapters on Parks and Recreation and Golf for more details about both). Several golfing packages are available. The resort is also within easy striking distance of Pigeon Forge and Gatlinburg.

Echota Resort
110 Echota Way, Sevierville
(865) 428-5151, (800) 766-5437
www.echotaresort.com
More than 60 fairly new but rustic log cabins and a central amenities area make up this resort just a few miles from downtown Sevierville. The one- to four-bedroom cabins feature vaulted ceilings, private hot tubs, kitchens with dishwashers and microwaves, washers and dryers, satellite TV, and gas grills. On-site amenities include a multipurpose clubhouse, swimming pool, and lighted tennis courts. Eagles Landing Golf Course and Douglas Lake are each a short drive away from the resort.

If you're thinking of getting hitched in the Smokies, you should know that Echota is also a wedding provider (see our Weddings chapter). Wedding packages are available to guests, and services can be performed in the clubhouse or even in guest cabins.

Hidden Mountain Resort
475 Apple Valley Road, Sevierville
(865) 453-9850, (800) 452-5992
www.hiddenmountain.com
More than 300 cabins, cottages, and villas make up this sprawling resort community that gives quick access to Sevierville and Pigeon Forge. Hidden Mountain is divided into two main areas. The west section is made up exclusively of cabins, while Hidden Mountain East comprises cabins, Music Mountain Villas, and Old Home Place Cottages. In-unit amenities vary from property to property.

There are swimming pools at both the east and west locations, and a clubhouse and exercise room are available to guests at Hidden Mountain East. Hidden Mountain Resort offers a number of dining and entertainment packages (priced separately from the accommodations), ranging from $40 to $375.

PIGEON FORGE AND WEARS VALLEY

Cove Mountain Realty
3174 Wears Valley Road, Sevierville
(865) 429-5577, (800) 245-2683
www.covemountain.com
Note that although this company has a Sevierville address, it's actually located in Wears Valley, about 10 miles southwest of Pigeon Forge.

Cove Mountain offers more than 125 rental cabins and chalets situated in and around the beautiful Wears Valley community. Guests are afforded wonderful views of mountain, forest, or river settings. The properties are a few miles away from the hustle and bustle of Pigeon Forge, offering access to Townsend, Cades Cove, and a back entrance to the national park. The cabins and chalets have anywhere from one to five bedrooms, each featuring a hot tub, gas grill, washer and dryer, cable or satellite TV, and a VCR.

If you're thinking of buying rental property in Sevier County while maintaining your primary residence outside the county, you might want to double-check your local voting rights. In Sevierville, Pigeon Forge, and Gatlinburg, you may vote on local issues as long as your primary residence remains in Tennessee. If you're from out of state, the laws vary from town to town. In Pittman Center, however, vacation homeowners may vote no matter where they're from. Outside city limits, owners of second homes generally don't have voting privileges.

Eagles Ridge Resort and Cabin Rentals
2740 Florence Drive, Pigeon Forge
(865) 453-2220, (800) 807-4343
www.eaglesridge.com
Another of the newer resorts to spring up in the Smokies in recent years, Eagles Ridge is a centralized village consisting of approximately 150 log cabins and chalets just 1 mile off the Parkway in Pigeon Forge. The accommodations range from one- to eight-bedroom units featuring kitchens, fireplaces, hot tubs, whirlpool baths, and outdoor grills. Common amenities include a swimming pool and clubhouse. Eagles Ridge offers golf and honeymoon packages and can coordinate catering services with area restaurants.

Kimble Real Estate and Rentals
3346 Parkway, Pigeon Forge
(865) 429-0090, (800) 447-0911
www.kimblerentals.com
Take your pick of nearly 100 properties found predominantly in the Pigeon Forge area, including cabins, chalets, condominiums, and one- and two-bedroom suites. The units are within ½ mile to 12 miles of Pigeon Forge. Those that aren't located in or near the city itself are generally situated east of Pigeon Forge in the direction of Pittman Center. Among the amenities found in Kimble's rental units are hot tubs, fireplaces, satellite and cable TV, VCRs, full kitchens, and barbecue grills. Some units have access to a swimming pool.

Laurel Crest Resort
636 Wears Valley Road, Pigeon Forge
(865) 428-5707, (888) 850-1415
www.bluegreen-corp.com
Villas and townhomes with flexible layouts and lots of amenities make up this Pigeon Forge resort located just a couple of miles from the Parkway off Wears Valley Road. The villas are one-bedroom units featuring well-equipped kitchens and entertainment centers. The deluxe units have whirlpool tubs and fireplaces as well. All units have sleeper sofas that bring the sleeping capacity to four people. You can also combine one-bedroom and one-bedroom deluxe layouts to create a two-bedroom configuration that would sleep eight.

The one-bedroom townhomes sleep up to four and have basically the same amenities as the villas, except washers and dryers are included as well. The two-bedroom town homes feature an upstairs master bedroom suite and can accommodate up to six guests. Both can be combined into a three-bedroom unit that sleeps up to 10 people.

Clubhouse amenities at Laurel Crest include heated indoor and outdoor pools, whirlpool hot tubs, an exercise facility, sauna, game room, and reading lounge. Staff coordinators also plan activity programs for children and teens.

GATLINBURG

Gatlinburg Real Estate and Rental Company
211 Parkway, Gatlinburg
(865) 436-5104, (800) 359-1661
www.gatlinburgchalets.com
The company's rental office has the advantage of being one of the first you encounter as you enter the heart of Gatlinburg from the north on U.S. Highway 441. Their inventory of rental property includes more than 80 chalets and cabins located within 4 miles of downtown. Amenities vary, but include saunas, hot tubs, whirlpool baths, fireplaces, and fully equipped kitchens. Units have from one to six bedrooms.

Stony Brook Chalets
1663 East Parkway, Gatlinburg
(865) 436-7428, (800) 633-5652
www.stonybrooklodging.com
Stony Brook manages about 40 cabins and chalets located throughout the Gatlinburg area—ranging from the Ski Mountain area to US 321 between Gatlinburg and Cosby. Accommodations are as small as one-bedroom units that sleep two and as large as seven-bedroom homes that can handle up to 20. Amenities and scenery vary from site to site.

The Highlands Condominium Rentals
855 Campbell Lead Road, Gatlinburg
(865) 436-3547, (800) 233-3947
www.highlandscondos.com
The Highlands' location gives it the illusion of being cut off from everything, but it's actually just off the Gatlinburg Bypass, and it's convenient to the national park and downtown. Guests can choose from 77 one-, two-, and three-bedroom condominium units, all of which are managed by the Highlands' on their five-acre site.

Each unit comes with a fireplace, whirlpool bath, kitchen, and private balcony. On-site amenities include two swimming pools, sundeck, sauna, indoor and outdoor hot tubs, and an exercise room. The views from the Highlands are great. You can see many of the vacation homes on Mount Harrison in the valley below and other mountains in the near distance. From time to time, the aerial tramway to Ober Gatlinburg passes by in the foreground.

Ski Mountain Chalets and Condos
416 Ski Mountain Road, Gatlinburg
(865) 436-7846, (800) 824-4077
www.skimtnchalets.com
You'll find this rental company as you start driving up Mount Harrison on Ski Mountain Road. About 100 one- to six-bedroom properties are on its rental program. All properties are located within 4 miles of downtown on Mount Harrison. The units come with fully furnished kitchens, TVs and VCRs, and barbecue grills. Some have hot tubs, whirlpools, washers and dryers, game areas, and stereos.

Mountain Laurel Chalets
440 Ski Mountain Road, Gatlinburg
(865) 436-5277, (800) 315-4965
www.mtnlaurelchalets.com
This real estate and rental company offers nearly 150 chalets and cabins that are primarily located on Mount Harrison and are anywhere from ½ mile to 4 miles from the main office. Depending on the unit, the views can be memorable. Because Ski Mountain Road meets downtown Gatlinburg at the south end of the city, many of

Mountain Laurel's properties provide fairly quick access to the national park. You can rent units with as few as 1 or as many as 11 bedrooms. Amenities vary from property to property.

Century 21 Four Seasons Realty
1441 Wiley Oakley Drive, Gatlinburg
(865) 436-6800, (800) 262-7684
www.chaletvillage.com
Perched along the east face of Mount Harrison (about halfway to the top), the Chalet Village section of Gatlinburg is where you'll find some of the most memorable views in town. The village itself is a collection of chalets and condominiums built mostly on steep, wooded sites. They're connected by Ski Mountain Road, the main thoroughfare to the top of Mount Harrison, and a mind-boggling network of hilly, curvy side roads. All but the most adroit of navigators will need a map to find their way among the maze, but the views make the trip well worth the effort.

More than 140 units in the Chalet Village area are on Century 21's rental program. Well-equipped kitchens, whirlpool tubs, cable TV, charcoal grills, fireplaces, balconies, decks, and porches are among the properties' features. Units have anywhere from one to eight bedrooms. Be aware that guests planning to stay from December through March are advised to use a four-wheel-drive vehicle or have snow chains available for travel up the mountain. In recent years, however, snowfall has been less than average, and driving up Ski Mountain Road has not been a hazardous venture.

Mountain Loft Resort
110 Mountainloft Drive, Gatlinburg
(865) 436-4367, (800) 991-0002
www.bluegreen-corp.com
This resort lies just off US 321, only a couple of miles from downtown Gatlinburg. It's owned by the same corporation that runs Laurel Crest Resort in Pigeon Forge and offers similar configurations of one- and two-bedroom villas and one-, two-, and three-bedroom townhomes. Refer to the

Most rental companies require that you book a minimum of two nights, but if you've got your sights set on a one-night stay, check to see if your rental office has an odd night that they need to fill between other reservations. Believe us, they won't pass up the chance to book it if you're otherwise dead-set against a longer stay.

Laurel Crest write-up in the Pigeon Forge section of this chapter for detailed descriptions of the various layouts and amenities available. Mountain Loft, however, also has two-bedroom chalets with lofts that sleep up to six. The chalets have amenities similar to those in the villas and townhomes.

At the clubhouse you'll find indoor and outdoor pools, hot tubs, an exercise room, sauna, and game room. Hiking trails are located nearby, and the resort provides 24-hour security service. Guests might also be interested in Mountain Loft's Courtesy Vacation Planning, whereby staff members help plan activities like golfing, fishing and rafting trips, horseback riding, and ski trips. Activities are also planned for children and teens.

Greenbrier Valley Resorts
3629 East Parkway, Gatlinburg
(865) 436-2015, (800) 546-1144
www.cobblynob.com
You'll have to travel a little out of your way to get there, but the properties you'll find through Greenbrier Valley Resorts offer quality accommodations in a peaceful, secluded notch of the county, well removed from all the hurly-burly of Gatlinburg and Pigeon Forge. This company is approximately 11 miles from downtown Gatlinburg on US 321 and has approximately 65 properties from which to choose, including log cabins, chalets, and condominiums.

Units have from one to eight bedrooms and amenities that include fireplaces, hot tubs, TVs and VCRs, stereos, washers and dryers, barbecue grills, and well-outfitted kitchens. Guests have full use of recreational facilities at the Village of Cobbly Nob, the residential community in which Greenbrier's properties are located. Facilities include three swimming pools, tennis courts, and 24-hour security. Most of Greenbrier's properties offer views of the Smokies or Bent Creek Golf Course, which is adjacent to Cobbly Nob (see our Golf chapter).

Deer Ridge Resort
3710 Weber Road, Gatlinburg
(865) 436-2325, (877) 333-7743
www.deerridge.com
If views are your thing, this scenic vacation resort won't disappoint. Located 12 miles from downtown Gatlinburg, just off US 321, Deer Ridge sits high atop a foothill peak with views of mountains that are so close they take your attention hostage. A little more than 80 one-, two-, and three-bedroom condominium units are available on-site, all having sleeper sofas and some having lofts. Each unit comes with a wood-burning fireplace, TV, VCR, two phones with dataports, and a kitchen with plenty of appliances, silverware, and dishes.

Clubhouse amenities include indoor and outdoor pools, sundeck, hot tub, sauna, steam room, lighted tennis court, game room, and video rentals. The resort's playground area features a children's playhouse, swings, half-size basketball court, volleyball area, picnic tables, grills, and covered pavilion. Bent Creek Golf Course is located less than 2 miles from Deer Ridge at the bottom of the hill. The resort offers its guests golf packages as well as discount tickets for Dollywood.

CAMPGROUNDS AND RV PARKS

There's something about mountains that makes people who wouldn't normally consider the possibility want to camp. The pioneer spirit embedded in most Americans makes the idea of going to sleep under the stars and waking to a fresh dewy morning, with maybe a babbling brook thrown in, stir the blood. And there's no better place for starry nights, dewy mornings, and babbling brooks than the Great Smoky Mountains.

In keeping with our promise of orderly presentation, we'll lay out most of the more than 40 campgrounds and RV parks along the Smokies Corridor in a north-to-south progression, starting at exit 407 on Interstate 40. Diversions will run away from the Parkway in whatever direction they occur. As usual, geography is on our side—very few of the roads that meet the Parkway actually cross it for any distance, so most turns off the Parkway are in a single direction without doubling back.

From this point forward, we'll use the term "campground" to denote any commercial or government-operated facility that rents space for a temporary shelter that you bring with you. Several of the campgrounds will actually rent you a trailer, and they'll be handled individually.

Naturally, the Great Smoky Mountains National Park proper is a camper's paradise, and four of its campgrounds that are contiguous to the Smokies Corridor will be dealt with in detail as the last section of this chapter.

Rules of Thumb

The commercial campgrounds tend to provide creature comforts that hook up to your portable home. Unless otherwise stated, you can expect 30- to 50-amp electrical service at all permanent sites, and most have cable TV. Water and sewer hookups are common, and those that are more than 5 miles from a downtown area usually have well-stocked stores and well-maintained on-site recreational facilities. Swimming pools are as commonplace at campgrounds as they are at hotels, and laundry facilities are usually available. Public bathrooms with showers are pretty standard, particularly in those facilities that feature separate tenting areas.

One of the true advantages of RV-type travel is the ability to bring your pets along. Unless specified otherwise, all of the campgrounds in the area permit pets on leashes.

Because facilities and prices vary based on several factors (convenience to the bright lights is foremost), we'll provide a price breakdown for each campground, based on a single camping space for two people in a single camping unit. (A separate fee averaging less than $5.00 is charged for vehicles in tow.) Unless stated, all prices quoted are plus tax. Additional-person charges run between $2.00 and $3.00 for everyone over five years old. The practice of including a seventh night free when a six-night stay is reserved and paid for in advance is so prevalent that we'll treat it as normal—if you're planning a weeklong stay, check out the possibility of getting your last night free. It's also safe to assume that major credit cards are accepted unless specifically stated otherwise.

Most of the campgrounds are affiliated with national associations or publications, and every one we visited took pride in showing us their high rating certificates.

The competition is fierce, and you are the beneficiary. Expect immaculate surroundings, except in places that cater to the more seasoned "primitive" camper, and don't be afraid to mention problems or shortcomings to the management.

On Reservations

Like any other lodging facilities in the Smokies, campgrounds are at their peak from early April through October, and reservations couldn't hurt. If you plan to be in the area at peak times like July, August, or October, reservations are highly recommended. If you're a seasoned trailer traveler, you know when your fellow RVers are on the road. Cancellations are normally accepted with seven days' notice required for a full refund of deposits, and we'll note exceptions.

SEVIERVILLE

Our sampling of six campgrounds that use the county seat as their mailing address falls into two categories—three are lined up along the corridor and three are in the vicinity of Douglas Dam Park, a TVA facility about 5 miles east of Tennessee Highway 66. (See our Parks and Recreation chapter for more on Douglas Dam Park.) We'll deal first with the ones on the corridor and come back to the Douglas Dam facilities.

Knoxville East KOA
194 Foretravel Drive, Kodak
(865) 933-8312, (800) 864-2267
Among the largest in the area, this KOA

Off-season rates for park model trailers and cabins can sometimes be negotiated to a figure low enough to make it worthwhile for you to leave your trailer home and still come to the Smokies and live in the style you're accustomed to enjoying.

facility is in view of I-40 for a lot of its frontage, though most of its campsites are buried in wilderness. Foretravel Road is the first turn left (east) after leaving I-40 from either direction—it's less than 100 yards from the freeway. Stretching back into the woods from the spacious office building are 200 level trailer/RV sites with full hookups and 100 tent sites with a choice of services. The large banquet hall seats 500, making this park a favorite for reunion groups and travel clubs. A stage and public address system are included. Knoxville East KOA is open year-round. A trailer space with full hookup is $18 a night; tent sites with water and electric are $15 per night, and a primitive tent site (no hookups) is $12. A large RV dealership with complete parts and service facilities is adjacent to the campground.

Ripplin' Waters Campground and Rental Cabins
1930 Winfield Dunn Parkway, Sevierville
(865) 453-4169, (888) 747-7546
www.gocampingamerica.com
Right on the highway about midway between I-40 and downtown Sevierville, Ripplin' Waters is convenient to just about everything and a short walk from a couple of antiques malls and amusements. In five years it'll probably be in the middle of everything you come to the Smokies to enjoy.

Ripplin' Waters is on a level plain with the Little Pigeon River at its back. One hundred fifty-five RV sites have full hookups, and you can fish directly from the riverside sites. A full hookup site is $20 per night ($21 riverside), and two furnished cabins are available at $62 to $75 per night, depending on how many are in your party. Ripplin' Waters is open March 1 through December 15 and offers monthly rental rates.

River Plantation RV Park
1004 Parkway, Sevierville
(865) 429-5267, (800) 758-5267
www.riverplantationrv.com
Just south of downtown Sevierville, River

Towing Services

When the best of plans go awry and you find yourself in need of a towing service, here are a few that have specially equipped wreckers and trained drivers to handle RVs and other large loads. All of the services listed accept major credit cards, and most of them have affiliations with major road service clubs and RV associations.

Sevierville
Baker's Wrecker Service, (865) 453-9203
Bradley's Wrecker Service, (865) 453-5005
Travis Towing and Recovery, (865) 932-0094

Pigeon Forge
Carr's Auto Service, (865) 453-3152
McCarter Garage & Wrecker Service, (865) 453-8238

Gatlinburg and the National Park
Anthony's Wrecker Service, (865) 436-2178
Cap's Towing Service, (865) 436-9773
Skyline Wrecker & Service, (865) 436-4653

Plantation has more than 250 total sites, with 200 full hookups. Tent sites are available, as are four cabins. A quiet walking trail along the Little Pigeon River provides a nice view of the mountains in the distance. Full hookup sites range from $24 to $28 in season, while water and electric-only sites are $21. Cabins with kitchen and bathroom are $62 per night in season, and primitive tent sites are $15. River Plantation has special monthly rates and year-round storage available. Special consideration is given for groups to provide adjacent sites around the pavilion.

Douglas Dam

When the Tennessee Valley Authority dammed up East Tennessee's rivers to provide electric power, they also created a bunch of pretty cool lakes that became vacation spots in their own right. One such is Douglas Dam in northeast Sevier County, where the TVA improved the situation by building a park around the dam. Two diverse privately owned campgrounds and two government-operated facilities resulted from these projects.

First, a word of warning: There are two roads named Douglas Dam Road. Both go east off TN 66 (about 4 miles apart), and they merge in Douglas Dam Park. The northern version is Tennessee Highway 139, and it enters the park below Douglas Dam. The southern road, Tennessee Highway 338, is about 2 miles outside of Sevierville, and it's the one we'll use to get you to all three of the campgrounds in this section. TN 338 stays above the dam until it crosses the French Broad River right in front of the dam and merges with TN 139.

Douglas Lake Marina & Campground
1590 Dyke Road, Sevierville
(865) 453-3506

The only commercial campground actually on Douglas Lake, this campground is adjacent to a full-service marina and has about 50 full hookup sites at $15 a night and 25 water/electric sites for $10. Sites can be used for vehicles or tents, with a limit of one unit per site. The campground is within easy walking distance of a public park and has its own boat launch. Well-placed signage guides you into the campground from Douglas Dam Road, a little more than 5 miles from TN 66.

The campground is open from April through October. A "no refund" policy is in effect.

Douglas Lake Campgrounds
Douglas Dam Park, Sevierville
(865) 397-2998 (weekdays)

This listing is actually for two separate campgrounds in the park that operate under identical rules.

The headwater campground is on the lakeshore right at the dam and has 54 sites, while the tailwater camp on the French Broad River directly under the dam has 68 sites. The Douglas Lake Canteen, the only commercial enterprise in the park, is at the entrance to the tailwater camp. Public restrooms are adjacent to both campgrounds.

To establish a campsite at either spot, campers are instructed at the entrances (by signage) to find a campsite; fill out the form provided at the entrance; and drop the completed form, with payment, in the deposit vault at the entrance within 30 minutes of arrival. Campsites are $20 a night; most have electrical hookups. Holders of Golden Age or Golden Access passports are entitled to a 50 percent discount on rates. No credit cards are accepted for payment, but personal checks are OK. The campsites are patrolled by TVA rangers, who also monitor the deposit vaults.

PIGEON FORGE

The campgrounds in Pigeon Forge are set in clustered groups at both ends of the city, with a couple of exceptions. The first group is spread along 2 miles of Wears Valley Road (Tennessee Highway 321)—turn right at traffic light #3. The Wears Valley Road campgrounds are all on the south (left) side going away from the Parkway, and all have camping sites and picnic facilities on Walden's Creek, which forms the back boundary of all of them. The rest are at the southern end of town, and all but one are within sight of or a short walk from the Parkway.

Clabough's Campground
405 Wears Valley Road, Pigeon Forge
(865) 453-0729, (800) 965-8524
www.smokiesusa.com/rvcamping.php

A ½ mile from the Parkway, Clabough's is actually two campgrounds bisected by a city street. One hundred seventy full-hookup sites include 15 along Walden's Creek. All sites are $23 a night except in October (peak foliage season), when the going rate is $25.

The campground is situated far enough off the road to provide seclusion from the traffic, and the on-site grocery store/gas station/deli is open 16 hours a day. The Pigeon Forge Fun Time trolley stops at the entrance to Clabough's.

King's Holly Haven RV Park
647 Wears Valley Road, Pigeon Forge
(865) 453-5352, (888) 204-0247
www.hollyhavenrvpark.com

More like a city of temporary shelters than anything else, King's has been a family-owned operation since the 11-acre park was part of a farm purchased by the family in 1928. King's is open year-round, with special activities during the summer season. The Friday night gospel sing in the pavilion is a local tradition. Full-hookup rates vary from $20 in January and February to $30 June through October. Tent sites with water and electric service are $15 to $20, respectively, for the same periods. Monthly rates are available on request.

Eagle's Nest Campground
1111 Wears Valley Road, Pigeon Forge
(865) 428-5841, (865) 428-8699,
(800) 892-2714

Eagle's Nest is open year-round and features extra-wide spaces for units with slide-out rooms or awnings. A total of more than 200 spaces covers the spectrum of services, and nine cabins provide rustic comfort. Eagle's Nest also offers trailer storage through the winter and has a computer connector in the office for those who can't leave cyberspace behind. Seasonal rates are $24 for full hookup, $23 for limited service, and $20 for tent spaces. Off-season rates are $1.00 lower across the board. Cabin rates are available on request.

Pigeon Forge KOA Campground
2849 Middle Creek Road
Pigeon Forge
(865) 453-7903, (800) 367-7903
www.pigeonforgekoa.com

Opened in what was really an out-of-the-way location in the 1960s, KOA is now the campground nearest to downtown Pigeon Forge. Nearly 200 trailer/tent sites and 15 "Kamping Kabins" are arranged near and along the west prong of the Little Pigeon River, with the business district on the other side. KOA is open April through November, with rates varying from $25 for a primitive site to $38 for a full hookup. The cabins are $45 for a single room unit and $58 for a two-roomer. The central location and KOA's long history make advance reservations highly recommended.

The following three campgrounds are all west (turn right) of the Parkway at traffic light #10. When we finish with these, we'll come back to the Parkway and pick up a sizable group on the east side.

Coming back and would just as soon leave your trailer here? Check with the campground operator for storage rates. Campgrounds that don't offer storage can usually put you in touch with places that do.

Shady Oaks Campground
210 Conner Heights Road, Pigeon Forge
(865) 453-3276
www.shadyoakscampgroundpigeon
forge.com

About ½ mile up Conner Heights Road, Shady Oaks is one of Pigeon Forge's older camping facilities. It was built by the Graham family in 1969, and the shade trees that have grown up around the 107 sites make it seem like you're in the wilderness. The on-site fishing facility deepens the impression. Proximity to downtown Pigeon Forge is enhanced by the appearance of the trolley every 20 minutes or so. The year-round campground offers 87 full-hookup sites and 23 large tent sites for $24.50 a night.

Mill Creek Resort Club
449 West Mill Creek Road, Pigeon Forge
(865) 428-3498, (800) 962-4799
www.mcresort.com

The Mill Creek Resort is a sprawling layout with easy access to 85 paved, pull-through sites, available year-round for $22.95 per night. Eighteen park model trailers and five log cabins, each designed for four to six people, rent for $80 a night when you can get them—there's usually a waiting list in midsummer and October. The mountain view is to die for, and the "back road" access to Pigeon Forge is a real asset in the peak season.

Mill Creek Road departs Conner Heights Road to the right about ½ mile west of the Parkway. It also runs off the Parkway a little north of Conner Heights, but it's in a confusing area. You can get familiar with it when staying at Mill Creek

Resort by turning right when leaving the resort and making careful notes when you hit the Parkway.

Lil' Ponderosa Campground and RV Park
909 Little Cove Road, Pigeon Forge
(865) 453-5278

Lil' Ponderosa is a perfect example of what 2 miles can do in terms of civilization in the Smokies. For openers, don't worry about finding Little Cove Road—just turn onto Conner Heights at traffic light #10 on the Parkway and keep going. The road changes names about ½ mile in, and Lil' Ponderosa has a lot of signage to keep you apprised of the mileage yet to go. It seems like more than 2 miles the first time you drive it, but the distance is deceiving. Once you get there, you know you're in the boondocks when you see various livestock grazing in the fields. Look at these animals carefully—sometimes they're not all domestic or farm animals. In keeping with the rustic setting, Lil' Ponderosa has a choice of posh to primitive in the way of accommodations: 40 full-hook-up trailer/RV sites rent for $22 a night, and 32 tent sites, all with electric service, are available for $18. Two primitive cabins sleep four to six at $45. The campground is open year-round, and Lil' Ponderosa has added a riding stable, described in our Parks and Recreation chapter.

Most of the campgrounds that have campfire facilities also have or provide firewood. Check with your operator before foraging for something to burn.

Returning to the Parkway for the last leg of Pigeon Forge campgrounds, the final four are jammed together at the southern extremity of the city in a fashion that could convince the unsuspecting traveler they're in one really huge campground. Despite the different addresses, it is actually possible to drive from the Creekstone Resort through the middle of Riveredge RV Park and into Foothills Campground without going on another street. Alpine RV Park is at the southern end of the line and is set back off the Parkway.

Creekstone Outdoor Resort
304 Day Springs Road, Pigeon Forge
(865) 453-8181, (800) 848-9097
www.creekstonecamping.com

Creekstone has an interesting choice of 120 sites, equally divided among the riverside, the woods, and the center of the park. Creekstone is open year-round, with rates ranging from $23 for center sites to $27 for riverside sites during the peak season. All sites are $15 a night December through March and range from $15 to $20, depending on location, in April, May, and November.

If you're southbound on the Parkway in Pigeon Forge, the best way to get directly into Creekstone Resort is off South River Road, a block east of the Parkway, before you get to traffic light #10. If you're northbound, go through the traffic light and take Jehu, the first street to the right. This will keep you from driving through another campground to find your spot.

Riveredge RV Park & Log Cabin Rentals
4220 Huskey Street, Pigeon Road
(865) 453-5813, (800) 477-1205
www.stayriveredge.com

The entrance to Riveredge is right at traffic light #10 on the Parkway. The resort itself is separated from the Parkway by the Little Pigeon River and a whole lot of trees.

Landscaped campsites in the woods and along the river—175 of them—belie the convenience to all of Pigeon Forge's attractions, and the on-site arcade is an attraction in its own right. Complete hookups are $25.00 a night April through December and $19.50 during the winter months. Twenty-one cozy camping cabins with full-size beds and bunk beds are $34.50 for two people during the season ($4.00 per additional person over four years old). For the ultimate in "roughing it," Riveredge offers seven one- and two-bedroom cabins with all the amenities, including gas fireplaces and Jacuzzis. These cabins rent for $115 per night, with a $12 charge per additional guest over 13 years old.

Foothills Campground & Cabins
4235 Huskey Street, Pigeon Forge
(865) 428–3818, (888) 428–3818
www.foothillsrvpark.com
A quiet, comfortable, family atmosphere prevails at Foothills Campground, tucked in the woods less than 100 yards from the Parkway. Its 42 full-hookup sites on shady level ground are complemented by 10 A-frame cottages and seven log cabins with great views of the mountains. Foothills is open April through November, with RV/tent sites renting for $22 a night. The one-room cabins have two double beds, central heating and air-conditioning, and cable TV for $48 a night for two people. The log cabins have a single spacious room with two double beds and a kitchen area with microwave and refrigerator. The cabins also have outdoor charcoal grills and picnic tables, along with covered porches with rocking chairs. Log cabin rental is $79 a night for two people. Additional people over six years old are $5.00 a head in A-frames and log cabins. Downtown Pigeon Forge is less than a mile up the Parkway, and the trolley stops at the campground office.

Alpine RV Park and Campground
251 Spring Valley Road, Pigeon Forge
(865) 428–3285
www.mypigeonforge.com
Just off the Parkway at the extreme southern end of Pigeon Forge, Alpine has a full spectrum of camping possibilities and is one of the few campgrounds in the area that have RV parts and service on-site. Built in the 1960s and constantly improved, Alpine has 76 full-hookup RV sites, 10 camping cabins, two park model trailers, a pair of two-bedroom cottages, and three primitive tent sites, all in a

secluded setting 400 feet east of the Parkway. Alpine is open mid-April through October. Full-hookup trailer sites are $21 a night, while tent sites with water and electric service are $19. Park model trailers are furnished with one queen and one sofa bed (bring your own linens) at $60, and the fully furnished two-bedroom cottages can sleep up to eight people for $100 ($90 if you bring your own linens). Additional people in the park model trailers and cottages are $5.00 each. The four camping cabins each have a double bed and two twin beds and will sleep four people comfortably. Air-conditioning and cable TV are included, but linens aren't. Nightly rental is $29.50 for two adults, with $4.00 apiece charged for additional people.

GATLINBURG

Again, we're looking at the old-versus-new situation that's so common here: The older, more established lodging places in the Gatlinburg area are generally more independent than you'll find in Pigeon Forge and Sevierville. In fact, every campground that's actually within the city limits is independently owned, and one is still operated by the family that built it. As we move east out of town on East Parkway/US 321N (the only direction in which commercial campgrounds are found), some larger campgrounds with franchise affiliations pop up. The last campground in this section is actually in Cosby, which is in Cocke County. We've included it in the Gatlinburg section because it's on the same road as every property east of the city. The Great Smoky Mountains National Park also has a campground at Cosby, and it's covered in the Park section of this chapter.

Twin Creek RV Resort
114 Low Gap Road, Gatlinburg
(865) 436–7081, (800) 252–8077
www.twincreekrvresort.com
Tucked into the foothills just off East Park-

way, Twin Creek is, by its own description, upscale.

The park is open from April through October and allows no tents on its large 72-space property. Every RV site is paved, with its own deck and fire ring. The resort is heavily wooded and beautifully landscaped, and features an arcade for the kids and a Sunday morning worship service open to all guests. Site rental ranges from $30 to $35 based on location (all sites are $35 in October). It's hard to believe downtown Gatlinburg is just a mile away, and the blue trolley comes into the campground for fun, convenient tranportation. A delightful old stone cottage on the grounds has been completely renovated inside for luxurious living in a rustic setting. It sleeps four people and is available on a restricted basis.

Gatlinburg RV Park
1640 East Parkway, Gatlinburg
(865) 430-3594

Opened in 1966 on a flat space alongside Little Dudley Creek that's not quite as secluded as it used to be, Gatlinburg RV Park still provides a lot of privacy; 64 full-service sites are convenient to the highway and Little Dudley Creek if you're into fishing and riverside picnics. The blue trolley stops right in front of the campground. Gatlinburg is less than 3 miles to the left, the biggest golf community in the county is about 10 miles to the right, and Gatlinburg RV Park is within the boundaries of the world-famous Great Smoky Arts & Crafts Community. Open April through November, Gatlinburg's sites rent for $22.50 per night.

LeConte Vista Campground Resort
1739 East Parkway, Gatlinburg
(865) 436-5437
www.travelingusa.com/leconte

A spectacular panoramic view of the Smokies is the beginning of the good things the Conner family has been offering since they opened LeConte Vista in 1968. A total of 75 shaded, drive-through spaces feature grassy tent sites and con-

crete pads for RVs. LeConte Vista offers a full slate of on-site activities, including a day camp for the children during the summer. Evening trips into Gatlinburg are simple: The blue trolley stops at the campground office. Picnic tables and fire rings spread liberally throughout the park provide excellent places for socializing and looking at that wonderful view. The 10:00 P.M. quiet hour is positively enforced. Full hookups for RVs and trailers are $29 per night; tents and vans are $20. Two one-room camping cabins are available for $35 a night.

Greenbrier Island Campground
2353 East Parkway, Gatlinburg
(865) 436-4243

Greenbrier Island is exactly what it says it is: an island campground in the pristine middle prong of the Little Pigeon River. Greenbrier Island isn't being immodest when it claims to be the "best campground in town"—it's the only one in the town of Pittman Center. Six miles from traffic light #3 in Gatlinburg, Greenbrier Island takes a lot of wrinkles out of "roughing it" by offering a variety of accommodations. In addition to 46 full-hookup RV spaces available at $19 a night, you can choose from 36 water/electric spaces, 24 improved campsites, or six primitive campsites at $15 each, all prices tax included. "Flint rock," the swimming hole at the north end of the campground, has been a favorite of locals for generations. The entrance to Greenbrier Island is a short distance off East Parkway on Pittman Center Road (Tennessee Highway 416). Greenbrier is open April through October.

Outdoor Resorts of America
4229 East Parkway, Gatlinburg
(865) 436-5861, (800) 677-5861
www.gocampingamerica.com/
orgatlinburg

The largest facility in the southern section of Sevier County, Outdoor Resorts is a "condo" campground (for lack of a better description), offering permanent sites for members' trailers and RVs, overnight sites for public rental, and public rental of furnished trailers. Sites with and without trailers are also available for sale to interested campers. A total of 376 sites includes more than 100 along the banks of Webb's Creek and 32 around the lake in the center of the resort. Two swimming pools complement the full spectrum of recreational facilities for all ages. A non-denominational church service is offered Sunday mornings at 11:00 May through October. A trailer space rents for $30.00 a night for a family of four during the season, $27.50 November through April. Rental trailers run from $65.00 to $80.00 per night, and some restrictions and deposit requirements apply.

Crazy Horse Campground & RV Resort
4609 East Parkway, Gatlinburg
(865) 436–4434, (800) 528–9003
www.crazyhorsecampground.com

Centrally located for both east- and west-flowing traffic, Crazy Horse is 12 miles from downtown Gatlinburg and 15 miles from the Wilton Springs exit 440 on I–40. The Foothills Parkway exit (443) is closer yet, but not recommended for towed loads. Crazy Horse has 212 camping sites about evenly divided between full hookup and water/electric, six rental trailers, and several cabins in various configurations. To accommodate a usually high population, Crazy Horse has three laundries, three bathhouses, a private lake, and the longest water slide in the Smokies—500 feet of twisting and turning fun. The Jack Tales Theater, at the back of the park, is a long-standing local favorite and will give campers and their families a chance to act in a series of plays adapted from fairy tales and local legends. Crazy Horse is open from April through October. Peak season is June through August and October. Full-hookup sites are $32.50 per night, and water/electric sites are $27.00 (add $5.00 for streamside sites). Camping cabins with electricity, small refrigerator, and heater sleep six at $50.95. Rental trailers and one-room cabins sleep four

and are $81.00 a night. The one-bedroom cabin with all the amenities for up to four occupants is $100.00.

Arrow Creek Campground
4721 East Parkway, Gatlinburg
(865) 430–7433, (888) 382–7769
www.arrowcreek.com

Nestled in a heavily wooded area, Arrow Creek is a secluded campground with the convenience of a major highway at its entrance. Sixty graveled and level sites accommodate all types of camping with whatever level of convenience is desired. Each site has its own picnic table and fire ring. The recreation hall, playground, and horseshoe pits will keep everybody occupied in a peaceful setting. Arrow Creek is open April through October, with peak-season rates in effect from mid-June to mid-August and throughout October. Full hookups are $20.95 in peak season, $18.95 nonpeak. Water/electric trailer sites are $18.95 and $16.95, respectively, as are tent sites with water and electric; primitive tent sites are $19.95 in season and $17.95 nonpeak. A cabin built in 2000 sleeps five for $49.00 a night.

Huc A Bee Campground & RV Park
4857 East Parkway, Gatlinburg
(865) 430–2680, (888) 866–5424

The newest of the area's campgrounds, Huc A Bee is set on a large knoll 15 miles east of Gatlinburg. Forty-nine good-size drive-through sites surround a recreation complex that includes a public hot tub and a social hall. A good selection of arcade games is available in the game room adjacent to the office. Rental car and jeep service is available, and the owner-operators live on-site to provide 24-hour security. Huc A Bee opens on

---

If you're towing a trailer or driving a large vehicle, avoid the Dudley Creek and Bishop Lane bypasses in Gatlinburg. Both are steep and curvy, with long downhill approaches to a usually busy US 321.

Easter weekend and stays open through December. RV/camper sites are $25 and tent/van sites are $20 a night.

Yogi Bear's Great Smoky Jellystone Park Camp
4946 Hooper Highway, Cosby
(P.O. Box 282, Gatlinburg 37738)
(423) 487-5534, (800) 210-2119
www.campjellystone.com

Don't let the name fool you: This isn't an amusement park. It's a campground for families who enjoy a place where there's always something going on. Jellystone's backyard is the Great Smoky Mountains National Park, with the popular Maddron Bald hiking trail jumping off right out of the campground. The Maddron Bald trail is a pleasant 1-mile walk back to a lovely picnic grove. In-season day camp sessions feature a Yogi breakfast and cartoons and a full slate of children's activities. Bingo, live entertainment, ice cream socials, and wagon rides keep everybody on the go if they don't want to just kick back beside one of the mountain streams running through the park. Jellystone is open from mid-March through October, with 70 trailer/RV sites, one rental trailer, three fully furnished and one camping (Bear Bones—get it?) cabin, and 22 tent sites. Most of the trailer sites are on an island surrounded by the stream. Streamside full hookup is $32 per night, water/electric hookup is $27 to $30. Off-stream full hookup is $25, and off-stream water/electric hookup is $21. Tent sites with water and electric service are $24, and primitive tent sites are $21. Rental trailers are $70 for up to four people. The three full cabins sleep six at $90 a night, and the Bear Bones cabin will accommodate six for $54.

GREAT SMOKY MOUNTAINS NATIONAL PARK

As you might expect, the Great Smoky Mountains National Park has a lot of opportunities for camping. The park service maintains 10 developed campgrounds with more than 800 total sites, all of which are charitably described as primitive. They're all accessible by RV or towed trailer, but there are no hookups or shower facilities. This section will list 4 of the 10, including 1 in North Carolina; the remaining 6 are all at some distance from the Smokies Corridor (4 are in North Carolina) and will be described in detail in the chapter devoted to the national park.

All park campgrounds are open from mid-May through October, weather permitting, and space usage is restricted to six people per site. Two tents or one RV and one tent are allowed per site, with exceptions granted only on-site in the case of immediate family members exceeding the limit. Stays in all national park campgrounds are subject to a seven-day maximum. Reservations are accepted up to three months in advance at Cades Cove, Elkmont, and Smokemont campgrounds by calling the National Park Reservation Service at (800) 365-2267; all other campgrounds are operated on a first-come–first-served basis. Information on other campgrounds is available by calling (865) 436-1266 for Tennessee campgrounds, and (828) 497-1930 for North Carolina. The park's Web site, www.gsmnp.gov, has a complete list of campgrounds.

Keep in mind that these campgrounds are in otherwise unsettled areas, and the only amenity you'll find is a flat place to park. Regulations vary from place to place, and you can expect to be informed of them in excruciating detail by the rangers in attendance. The following is a list of the four campgrounds in the national park that are contiguous enough to be considered part of the Smokies Corridor, starting with the easternmost and moving west, then south. Telephone numbers provided with campground listings are for ranger stations—not all campgrounds have phones. Check out our chapter on the park for detailed information on some of the recreational opportunities available in the national park. There's also information available at www.gsmnp.com.

Cosby Campground
Tennessee Highway 32

Set on the northeast edge of the park, Cosby campground is just off East Parkway (US 321N) about 20 miles east of Gatlinburg. The campground is accessible to several hiking and scenic trails and is a good jumping-off point for a hike to Hen Wallow Falls and old-growth forest. Cosby campground is open April through October with 175 campsites. Site rental is $14, and RV length is restricted to 25 feet.

Elkmont
Little River Road
(865) 436-1271

Situated 9 miles southwest of Gatlinburg and 5 miles from the Sugarlands Visitor Center, Elkmont is one of the original campgrounds in the park. Once a thriving settlement, the Elkmont area is being reclaimed by nature in accordance with the Park Service's philosophy of limited development. The surroundings are as wild as you'll find in an area as convenient to a paved highway. Elkmont is open April through November and has 220 single sites at $14, and group sites (maximum 15 people) by reservation only at $20 apiece.

Cades Cove
Townsend, TN
(865) 448-2472

One of the most popular day trip locations in the park, Cades Cove is also a camping favorite. The cove, with its preserved pioneer farmstead and open graz-

The idea of time-share trailers is catching on with some operators. If you're interested in earning some money with your trailer, some campgrounds will be glad to park it and rent it out for a percentage of the proceeds.

ing for a variety of wildlife, is 27 miles from Gatlinburg on Little River Road. The outdoor amphitheater and pavilion make Cades Cove a favorite for large groups. The campground is open year-round. One hundred fifty-seven sites for trailer, tent, and family camping each rent for $14. Group sites for eight to 20 campers are $36; up to 30, $50; and up to 30 with reserved pavilion, $66. Church group usage is very high in the summer, so you'll want to make reservations as early as possible.

Smokemont Campground
U.S. Highway 441, NC
(828) 497-9270

Just about the time Newfound Gap Road (US 441) levels off in its descent from the gap into North Carolina, the Smokemont campground comes into view on the north side of the road (left if you're going south out of Tennessee). Smokemont has an RV-only section with 43 sites and close to 100 tent sites. Due to its convenience to Cherokee (6 miles south), the campground is open year-round. RV sites are $14 a night. Group campsites are $25 for groups up to 20 and $36 for groups of 21 to 30.

RESTAURANTS

Millions of people visit the Great Smokies every year, and every one of them must eventually answer that nagging daily question of where to eat. Fortunately, you never have to go too far to find sustenance in these mountains. It takes little more than a casual stroll down the Parkway in any of our cities to come face-to-face with enough dining options to cover your mealtime decisions for an entire week and more. From massive portions of down-home Southern cooking to ethnic flavors from around the world, Smoky Mountain restaurateurs aim to please.

The restaurant business in these parts is fortunate in that it seems to be less vulnerable to seasonal influences than other tourism-based industries like shopping, attractions, and accommodations. Rare is the local restaurant that closes down in the off-season. After all, even when visitors aren't in town, Sevier County's 75,000-plus residents need places to go for the "power lunch" or the relaxed dinner out on the town.

Naturally, you'll find an abundance of national chains—not just the fast-food giants like McDonald's and Taco Bell, but also familiar "sit-down" restaurants like Shoney's, T.G.I. Friday's, and Applebee's. As a matter of fact, newer corporate-owned eateries are well represented and seem to spring up daily. This chapter, however, will take you in a different direction. With a few exceptions, we've culled the establishments that aren't necessarily household names (but perhaps may be someday). Some are less expensive, hole-in-the-wall cafes while others offer more pricey, upscale dining. Some are favorite local haunts while others are tourist "musts." What they all have in common, though, is that they offer the patron an enjoyable Smoky Mountain dining experience.

One of the best things about eating out around here is that the words "dress code" aren't a part of the local vernacular. No matter how elegant the setting or refined the cuisine, dressing for dinner usually means putting on jeans instead of shorts. Not one of the restaurants we're presenting requires a jacket or tie (although we'll assume that you will wear a shirt and shoes in accordance with state law!). As for reservations, they're usually not accepted because most restaurants receive heavy walk-in traffic; this is especially the case in peak season. What you'll usually have to do is just show up and put your name on a waiting list if necessary. In our write-ups, we will point out the places where you do need to make advance reservations.

The subject of parking must necessarily hinge on the city you're planning to visit. If you're dining in Sevierville or Pigeon Forge, you can count on finding plenty of free parking no matter where you go unless we tell you otherwise. In Gatlinburg you'll be more dependent on public transportation or lots and garages where you'll have to pay to park. Most restaurants along Gatlinburg's Parkway have limited parking, if any at all. We'll cover parking options within each restaurant's write-up in the Gatlinburg section of the chapter.

When evaluating a restaurant's prices according to our code, bear in mind that most places have a less expensive lunch menu as well as a reasonably priced children's menu (the cutoff age is usually between 10 and 12 years old). You can assume that most places serve lunch and dinner, but if a particular restaurant serves breakfast, for example, or is closed for lunch or dinner, we'll mention it. You can also work under the assumption that a restaurant accepts most major credit cards unless we specify otherwise. Traveler's checks aren't a problem, but don't even bother trying to pay with a personal check drawn on an out-of-town bank.

PRICE CODE

The following code is based on the price of two entrees from the dinner menu, not including appetizers, desserts, beverages (alcoholic or otherwise), taxes, or gratuities.

$	Less than $16
$$	$16–$25
$$$	$26–$35
$$$$	$36 and more

We close with a word about alcohol sales. Outside the city limits of Sevierville, Pigeon Forge, and Gatlinburg, restaurants can serve only beer by the drink. Each city, however, has its own different alcohol ordinances, ranging from "anything goes" to "nothing doing." Because we're covering Smoky Mountains restaurants geographically, we'll address each city's laws as we come to them.

SEVIERVILLE

Until just a few years ago, restaurants in Sevierville weren't allowed to serve alcohol of any kind. The city's current beer ordinance, however, allows a restaurant to serve beer if it has a seating capacity of at least 150 people and if at least 50 percent of its sales come from food. In the relatively short time since this law was passed, the number of beer-serving restaurants in Sevierville has grown from 0 to more than 10.

Double Play Cafe $
3450 Line Drive, Kodak
Here's a case where we're recommending a restaurant more for its location than its food. Sure, the food is fine; the menu consists primarily of appetizers and sandwiches with a few hot entrees dropped into the mix. But more important is the fact that Double Play Cafe is actually

inside the Tennessee Smokies baseball stadium, located on Interstate 40 at exit 407. The company that operates the restaurant also runs the stadium's concession stands, but in Double Play Cafe they've provided an opportunity to enjoy a wider range of menu items and sit-down service to boot in a light and airy atmosphere. Both the inside and patio dining areas directly overlook the third base side of the field, right on the main concourse. (You'll find more information about the Smokies and the stadium itself in our Attractions chapter.)

The prices are reasonable, and a meal for two that includes beverages will get you in and out for less than $20. Double Play Cafe is open daily for lunch and dinner. They also serve a variety of beers, both on tap and in the bottle.

Villa Mexico $
127 Forks of the River Parkway
Sevierville
(865) 453-3858
Villa Mexico has been one of the few Mexican restaurants in the county with any staying power. It has a limited amount of interior seating, and the decor is fairly nondescript as far as ethnic dining establishments go, but the cuisine is authentic and a refreshing break from Mexican fast food. Villa Mexico is open seven days a week for lunch and dinner, and it's located at the end of a strip plaza anchored by Kmart.

The menu offers everything that you'd expect from south of the border—tacos, burritos, enchiladas, and various combinations of the three. You'll also find more adventurous entrees like chilis rellenos, and chalupas. The house *especialidades* include popular sellers like the chimichanga and the fajitas (beef, shrimp, or chicken). If you're not a meat eater, you might select one of the vegetarian platters. Most dinners are served with rice and refried beans. For dessert, you'll enjoy traditional Mexican treats like flan, sopapillas, and fried ice cream. They also carry a small selection of domestic and imported beers.

Lotus Garden $
131 Forks of the River Parkway
Sevierville
(865) 453-3891

In a way, it's rather interesting that this Chinese restaurant is located next door to a Mexican restaurant (see Villa Mexico entry). But then again, it all makes perfect sense when you learn that both restaurants have the same owner (they also share the same restrooms)! Yes, there is apparently an advantage to diversification in the restaurant business.

For more than a decade, Lotus Garden has served delicious Chinese dishes made from beef, pork, chicken, and seafood. The shrimp with snow peas and water chestnuts is a house specialty as are the kung pao chicken, General Tso's chicken, and tangerine beef. The buffet offers all-you-care-to-eat portions of menu favorites like sesame chicken and roast pork, as well as soups, egg rolls, desserts, and more.

Lotus Garden's atmosphere is subtly Oriental. The main dining room is adequately spacious and reflects a minimalist approach to the Chinese decor. It's open for lunch and dinner seven days a week.

Virgil's '50s Restaurant $
109 East Bruce Street, Sevierville
(865) 453-2782

When you're sitting in a booth at Virgil's you almost expect Richie, Potsy, and the Fonz to walk through the doors at any moment. Everything about this downtown restaurant screams "1950s," from the black-and-white checkered floor tile to the pastel-colored stools at the counter to the 45-rpm records and other pieces of '50s music memorabilia hanging on the walls and from the ceilings.

Although you may be initially drawn to Virgil's because of the look, you'll definitely go back for the food. Breakfast and lunch are served Monday through Friday, featuring typical American fare and lots of home country cooking (breakfast is also served all day). Although most of the meals on the menu are priced around $6.00 each, there are a few entrees in the $7.00 to $10.00 range.

Like any good '50s theme restaurant, burgers and sandwiches are fixtures on the menu, but the real highlights are the homemade foods prepared by the owner's mother. She serves up a number of beef, chicken, and fish lunches with her country vegetables on the side. Interestingly, the beef liver and grilled onions is a frequently requested item.

From time to time, "Mom" is also known to prepare several specials that aren't on the menu, such as chicken and dumplings, meat loaf, and chicken pot pie, all of which are homemade. That attention to freshness and made-from-scratch philosophy carries through to the desserts too. You'll rave over the coconut, lemon, and butterscotch pies. And getting back to the '50s theme, you'll really make the scene when you belly up to the counter and order a banana split or shake from Virgil's soda fountain.

The facility has been a restaurant of one kind or another since 1929, when it was a place you could get a beer and swap a few tall tales. It was known as Newman's Restaurant for about 34 years until Virgil Carr purchased it and reopened it as a '50s restaurant in 1990. As with its predecessors, Virgil's has become a downtown institution and is popular with those who work nearby. They even deliver within the immediate downtown area.

Since beer sales became legal in Sevierville restaurants, many of the city's newer dining establishments have taken advantage of that ordinance. In addition to some of the "wet" restaurants mentioned in this chapter, there are several others belonging to regional and national chains that can also serve you a cold one. They include T.G.I. Friday's, Fuddrucker's, and Texas Roadhouse (all at Governor's Crossing), as well as Damon's in Sevierville.

The Old Town Cafe & Deli $
152 East Bruce Street, Sevierville
(865) 429-8628

You'll find this little cafe tucked away among the many shops of downtown Sevierville. It has operated as a restaurant under various ownerships for the better part of 50 years, and as the Old Town Cafe & Deli since 1991. Serving lunch only Monday through Friday, it caters especially to Sevierville's downtown workforce.

The menu is dominated by sandwiches and subs. One of the house specialties is the Steak Bomb sub, made of tender steak topped with cheese, onion, mushroom, and green peppers. Patrons also rave about the homemade soups and desserts. You can fight off a winter chill with the beef barley or potato soups, or cap off a meal with scrumptious desserts like key lime, strawberry rhubarb, and pumpkin pies, cheesecake, or several flavors of pudding. Diners will also find daily specials that aren't on the menu, more entree-style offerings such as meat loaf, chicken, and pot roast.

The Old Town Cafe & Deli isn't huge. Let's call it cozy and quaint with its bright, clean decor and country accents. If you decide to eat in, you'll have to vie for one of eight small tables or one of the few seats at the counter. Otherwise, they'll be happy to prepare your meal for carryout. If they have enough help on hand, they'll even deliver within the downtown area. No credit cards.

Walters State Culinary Institute $
Pittman Center Road, Sevierville
(865) 774-5800

If you've ever wanted to serve as a guinea pig for aspiring young chefs, this is your chance. If not, try it anyway. When you put yourself at the mercy of the students of this community college culinary arts program, you actually get a wonderful four-course meal and great service to boot, all at a remarkably low price. Located at the Walters State Community College campus in Sevierville, the institute serves lunch to the public Monday through Thursday (dinners are scheduled occasionally, too) throughout the academic year.

The menu changes daily, depending on the whim of the "chef of the day," one of the program's 60-plus students who supervises every aspect of the meal, from menu selection to assignment of cook and waitstaff personnel. A typical meal might feature a lineup of potato skins, Caesar salad, chicken breast Parmesan, pork loin, rice pilaf, and vegetables. Also, there are the occasional "international weeks" during which cuisine from various ethnic cultures is served buffet-style.

All guests are required to make reservations. Because menus are planned weeks in advance and distributed to those on the institute's mailing list, available spots usually fill up within days. To snag a spot, call the Culinary Institute and put yourself on their mailing list. When the menus are announced each semester, you will be contacted by e-mail and given the opportunity to make your reservations.

Walters State's culinary program has been in operation since 1998, and the school originally used an old restaurant facility in downtown Sevierville as its "campus." The school, which now takes up an entire wing of the college's $6.5-million building, boasts three state-of-the-art kitchens where food is prepared for 75 to 100 guests per meal. The cost of each meal is $9.00 per person (tax included), and any tips left behind help cover the culinary arts program's scholarship fund and operational expenses. Plenty of free parking is available at the Walters State campus.

Chiang House $$-$$$
624 Parkway, Sevierville
(865) 428-5977

Let's say you're in the mood for an Asian meal, but you can't make up your mind about what you're hungry for. You could go to a Chinese restaurant, a Japanese steak house, or a sushi bar. If you're the indecisive type, just go to Chiang House and make up your mind when you get there! This versatile house of Far East cuisine offers traditional Chinese dishes as well as those prepared Japanese hibachi-style; and yes, there's even a separate sushi bar. It's only been in business since 1997, but this place is the only sushi and hibachi game in town, making it a big draw among locals and tourists both.

We'll start with the Chinese menu. You can select from more than 60 entrees, including poultry, beef, pork, seafood, and vegetarian dishes. If you're undecided, the owners recommend General Tso's seafood, house scallops, and shrimp or two house delicacies (shrimp and chicken). Dinner and lunch entrees are both served with rice.

Add the element of entertainment to your Chiang House experience with their Japanese teppanyaki meals, where the food is prepared at your table hibachi-style. Kids and adults both absolutely love watching the highly trained chefs as they juggle, twirl, and spin their cutlery like masters. "Oohs," "ahhs," and lots of applause from the diners are almost guaranteed. The cooking of the meal is a true show and as much fun as actually eating it. Teppanyaki dinners include a shrimp appetizer, Japanese soup, and salad, and the entrees are served with rice and vegetables. The shrimp and scallop dinner is mouthwatering, and the filet mignon is one of the more popular dishes.

If you've ever wanted to sample exotic tastes from the sea like squid, octopus, or eel, you'll have your chance at Chiang House's sushi bar. If you're not that daring, try the tuna, shrimp, or salmon. The bar serves more than 15 types of sushi and sashimi, as well as sushi rolls and larger combination platters that will give you a representative sampling from the sushi menu.

For those who want to try a little bit of everything, you can dive into the lunch or dinner buffet, featuring soups and entrees from the Chinese menu and even sushi rolls. At Chiang House you can also order a beer with your meal; they carry a good selection of domestic brands in addition to several imported Japanese labels. The restaurant is open seven days a week for lunch and dinner. Reservations aren't required, but they are accepted.

Rocky River Brewery & Grille $$$
1444 Hurley Drive, Sevierville
(865) 908-3686

This restaurant and microbrewery was one of the premiere tenants of Sevierville's Governor's Crossing development when it opened in 1998. Located just off the Parkway, along the banks of the Little Pigeon River, Rocky River Brewery & Grille serves up hearty American fare along with an award-winning slate of microbrewed lagers and ales. You can dine there for lunch and dinner seven days a week.

Among the restaurant's biggest food sellers are the chicken fingers from the appetizer menu, black angus steaks (rib-eye and prime rib), and pizzas baked before your eyes in Rocky River's own wood oven. You'll enjoy your meal in one of several dining areas accented by stacked-stone walls and lots of warm color. The lofty, wooden ceilings add to the open feel of the restaurant. When weather permits, they also open the ample outdoor terrace for riverside drinking and dining.

The brewery is a large, glass-enclosed room that makes up the hub of the restaurant. Patrons can watch as brewmeisters oversee production of as many as 10 different labels. If their schedule allows, they'll even give you a guided tour of the facility, which is marked by many shiny, silver, 1,420-gallon fermenting vats. At any given time there are at least six different beers being brewed and served, mostly of German and English varieties. Among the more popular labels are the Ten Point (similar to a light beer) and the Golden Eagle, a bare bottom stout that won a gold medal at the Great American Brewing Festival in Denver.

Rocky River Brewery & Grille is also home to a sports bar that we discuss in more depth in our Music Theaters and Nightlife chapter.

NASCAR Cafe $$$
1425 Hurley Drive, Sevierville
(865) 428-7223
www.nascarcafe.com

Although our general rule of thumb is to focus on nonfranchise properties, we're making an exception in this case since the Smokies are a popular vacation destination among the NASCAR faithful. Debuting at Governor's Crossing in 1999, this restaurant is the fourth NASCAR Cafe to spring up in the Southeast. It helps racing fans kill many birds with one stone, offering not only food but also entertainment and shopping, all trimmed with a racing edge. We'll start off with the restaurant itself, which serves lunch and dinner seven days a week.

The entrees encompass something for most tastes. Chicken, steaks, ribs, pasta, and seafood appear with thematic names like Collision Chicken and Rockingham Ribeye. Club and barbecue sandwiches and burgers fill out the sandwich section. A familiar lineup of deep-fried appetizers and big salads round out the menu. The desserts are impressive, particularly the Chocolate Fudge Tire—a chocolate bar cake served under vanilla ice cream and chocolate fudge sauce—and the Banana Split the Field is a huge version of this dessert favorite.

If you're into NASCAR, however, the decor alone is worth the trip. Monitors showing racing events are stationed around the room, and championship banners hang from the high ceiling. But the most eye-catching aspect of your time at the cafe is the steeply banked, curved section of racetrack installed at ceiling level, dominating half the room. On this track are mounted eight life-size stock car replicas. At 45-minute intervals, the cars' wheels begin to spin, smoke bellows from the track as the tires "burn rubber," and the roar of gunning engines and squealing tires adds to the effect as another "race" gets under way. You might just as well be eating on the infield at Bristol!

Found just off the foyer is the Fuel Center, a bar serving a decent selection of

imported and domestic beers on tap and in bottles as well as wine coolers. The lounge has happy-hour specials during the week and, when demand warrants, live entertainment on specified nights.

The rest of the NASCAR Cafe facility is dripping with pure racing ambience. There's a large, well-stocked gift shop full of NASCAR clothing, souvenirs, and collectibles. Throughout different areas of the restaurant, you'll find lots of glassed-in NASCAR memorabilia, including photos, helmets, trophies, and plenty of other speed demon stuff. Outside the restaurant, stock cars (both real and replicated) are placed strategically throughout the parking lot. And if all this isn't enough, there's a fun center inside that features 25 racing-oriented video games and a driving simulator.

The Chop House $$$
1649 Parkway, Sevierville
(865) 774-1991
www.thechophouse.com

This Chop House is one link in a very small chain of similar restaurants found in the Southeast and Midwest. Located in the heart of Tanger Outlet Center at Five Oaks, it has quickly become a favorite place to eat for both out-of-towners taking a shopping-spree break and locals getting together for a business lunch. Since it opened in 1999, patrons have discovered that the Chop House offers a winning combination of great food and atmosphere.

Yes, you can get chops at the Chop House, both of the pork and lamb variety. Red meats are also quite popular; the menu offers a diverse selection of steaks, including prime rib, New York strip, and medallions Anthony (grilled tenderloin served with a rich Bordeaux sauce, Burgundy mushrooms, and a béarnaise sauce—a deceptively small but filling portion). There are also a number of chicken dishes as well as seafood entrees like North Atlantic salmon, baked scrod, and seafood pasta. Entrees include a choice of soup or salad and a choice of potato. You can add a half or full skewer of char-grilled shrimp to any entree for $6.00 or $11.00, respectively.

Appetizers, sandwiches, burgers, and salads round out the menu options at the Chop House. Choices include an Oriental chicken salad, lunch chops, and a porto-bello veggie burger. You can also create your own lunch combo or order the chef's lunch of the day. By the way, lunch items are available throughout the day.

The restaurant's atmosphere is one of warmth combined with simple but tasteful elegance. Dark woods, fireplaces, and shelves full of interesting knickknacks are utilized to maximum effect. Chop House guests may also choose to dine in the bar area, located just off the foyer. Guests can choose from foreign and domestic beers and wine coolers, or they can bring their own alcoholic beverages in with them. Reservations are not accepted, but you can call ahead for seating before your arrival.

Connor's
1641 Parkway, Sevierville
(865) 428-1991
www.thechophouse.com
You wouldn't think that two restaurants, run by the same owners and located practically adjacent to each other, would both be worthy of strong recommendation. But such is the case with Connor's, sister restaurant to the Chop House (see previous write-up). Standing just a stone's throw away from its predecessor, Connor's is also a favorite with both locals and the shopping crowd at Tanger Outlet Center at Five Oaks in Sevierville.

The menu is similar to the one at the Chop House in that the chefs who created

it have drawn from deep wells of culinary experience, used plenty of imagination, and taken no shortcuts when it comes to food preparation. Desserts, soups, biscuits, sauces, dressings, and other side items are prepared daily from scratch. The meals that arrive at your table are so good you'll want to pound the table with your fists.

But the owners have made the effort to ensure that the two menus aren't carbon copies of each other. Open for lunch and dinner daily, Connor's serves items like tasty cilantro lime-grilled shrimp and soy mustard-glazed grilled salmon. The shrimp and Cajun sausage with cheese grits and the sautéed pork tenderloin are required eating. Lunchers can get fat, juicy burgers and one of the few authentically prepared Reubens we've found in the area; even the soups and salads excel beyond the run-of-the-mill. And no self-respecting visitor in the South should pass up the opportunity to try Connor's fried green tomatoes appetizer. Served with cheese grits, tasso, and white gravy for dipping, these 'maters will make you think you've died and gone to the Whistle Stop Cafe.

For dessert, we recommend the caramel fudge cheesecake, the key lime pie, or the bananas Foster served with a cup of their home-ground Colombian coffee. By the way, if a beer would hit the spot, you can order from a wide selection of domestic and imported labels.

Applewood Farmhouse Restaurant $$$
240 Apple Valley Road, Sevierville
(865) 428-1222

1151 Parkway, Gatlinburg
(865) 436-4669
www.applewoodfarmhouserestaurant.com
We should probably preface this write-up with a short primer on Apple Valley Farms, an operational apple farm in Sevierville that has grown into an immensely popular tourist stop. Besides sporting two full-service restaurants, it's also home to the Apple Barn General Store and Cider Mill, the Apple Butter

Kitchen, the Candy Apple and Chocolate Factory, the Creamery, and the Apple Barn Winery. Read about this "delicious" Sevierville stopover in the Close-up of our Shopping chapter.

There are actually two restaurants that are part of the Apple Valley Farms complex—Applewood Farmhouse Restaurant and the newer Applewood Farmhouse Grill. Since their menus are very similar, we'll focus on the original Farmhouse Restaurant and include a few distinguishing facts about the newer Farmhouse Grill in parting.

As would be expected, the apple reigns supreme at Applewood Farmhouse Restaurant. You can get breakfast, lunch, and dinner there along with plenty of apple-licious side dishes. Mornings start out with all the traditional breakfast favorites like omelets, pancakes, eggs, and biscuits. Big appetites might be interested in the Farmhouse Special Breakfast, featuring your choice of eight different main items ranging from bacon to country ham hash and even rainbow trout. Each main dish comes with an Applewood Julep, applesauce muffins, apple fritters, homemade apple butter, biscuits, fried apples, grits and sausage gravy, home-fried potatoes, and two eggs cooked to order. Don't forget to ask for a doggy bag!

Lunches and dinners are also loaded with extras but include a few different side dishes, like homemade vegetable soup, mashed potatoes, and a vegetable. As for the entrees, some of the "Farmhouse Favorites" include Farmhouse Southern fried chicken, Farmhouse old-fashioned chicken & dumplings, chicken pot pie, and applewood pork loin. The last is a tender, boneless pork loin smoked over applewood and served with homemade apple relish.

The Applewood Farmhouse Restaurant in Sevierville is located in what was once an actual farmhouse, built in 1921. It was refurbished and opened in 1987 as a restaurant. As it exists today, the building has retained much of what was surely its original charm. A friendly, whitewashed exterior welcomes you into a world of country simplicity. The floors are wood and the wallpaper is highlighted by strips of apple designs along the ceiling molding. There are few accent pieces, but this maintains consistency with the restaurant's overall minimalist look. One of the rear dining rooms is surrounded by windows and offers views of the rest of the Apple Valley complex and the lazy Little Pigeon River just beyond.

Applewood Farmhouse Grill was opened on the Apple Valley Farms site in 1995. Although the construction is newer, it was designed to resemble its older sister. The breakfast and lunch menus are very similar to those of the original restaurant, but side salads and desserts are not included in the price of the dinners as they are at Applewood Farmhouse Restaurant. Overall, however, the prices on the dinner menu are a little less expensive. Both restaurants have a reasonably priced children's menu with kids' favorites like grilled cheese sandwiches, burgers, and fried chicken.

The Gatlinburg restaurant is the last building on the Parkway before you enter the national park. It's a cozy place, built more like a home than a commercial establishment.

PIGEON FORGE

Restaurants in Pigeon Forge are not allowed to sell alcohol of any kind by the drink. There is one exception, Alf's.

Alf's $
1965 Parkway, Pigeon Forge
No phone

When it opened in 1976, this restaurant was outside Pigeon Forge city limits. As such, it was able to sell beer by the drink. Years later, when it was annexed by the city, it was "grandfathered in" and allowed to continue serving. Until just a few years ago, it was the only place in the county north of Gatlinburg that served any kind of alcohol, so it became a favorite among locals who wanted to go out for a beer

How 'bout a Fried Bologna Sandwich?

Surrounding the grandeur of the Smokies and the glitter created by the cities that host their visitors, Sevier County still lives in a kind of time warp that's disappearing fast. While it holds on, the rural atmosphere that exists just outside the Smokies Corridor hides a lot of treasures that a lot of people thought gone from the American scene forever: the mom-and-pop general store.

This is a place few will remember, where locals, mostly farmers and other close-to-the-earth laborers, stop by daily for a loaf of bread or a dozen fresh eggs and, as often as not, stick around for a sandwich and a soft drink while they're at it. If you're here for the "whole hog," your meal will probably include:

- a fried bologna sandwich (self-explanatory).
- a MoonPie—a purely Southern concoction made in Nashville for close to a century. A MoonPie is a chocolate cookie about 4 inches across, covered with marshmallow cream and dipped in chocolate . . . yummmm!
- a big dope—a carbonated beverage, typically a 12-ounce Coke, Pepsi, or, if you're really Southern, RC Cola.

These places aren't real long on ambience, and sometimes they don't have a place to sit, but they do have a short menu of honest-to-God food that'll stick to your ribs and drive a nutritionist to the brink of madness. And it won't cost you an arm and a leg to eat. No self-respecting tour guide would be caught dead in these places, and don't look for a four-star rating or a maitre d'. The cook may be an old man, an older woman, or a kid that stands on a milk crate to reach the grill. They may

or may not write down your order, and you'll usually pay for whatever you tell the person at the cash register you had to eat. You'll usually get away with a cholesterol-laden fried sandwich or other simple fare, french fried potatoes or onion rings, and a soft drink you picked out of the cooler for less than a five-dollar bill.

Most of these establishments are small grocery stores with a grill and a lunch counter, and most serve breakfast and lunch. They usually open around 7:00 A.M. and serve through midafternoon. With a few noted exceptions, these businesses are on roads that ring the Smokies Corridor, and you'll find them on your way to some attraction or accommodation mentioned elsewhere in this book.

The places on this list had to meet three simple criteria to be mentioned: 1) They have to sell some other commodity (usually gas and/or groceries) besides food; 2) everything they serve must be cooked before your eyes; and 3) their menu must offer either a fried bologna sandwich or home-baked biscuits (most have both).

Throw away your diet for a while and enjoy a sample of what the locals really eat in the places where they really eat it. This section won't include a price code, but we'll throw in the price of a fried bologna sandwich ("FBS" before the street address) to give an indication; like we said earlier, a five-dollar bill will probably return a little change for each person eating. A note on locations: All of the places listed are in Sevierville or Gatlinburg. They are all on perimeter roads and are either within the city limits or in unincorporated areas. There are none in

Pigeon Forge proper, but a few are in areas of the county very close to that city.

SEVIERVILLE

Starting on Dolly Parton Parkway (U.S. Highway 411E), we'll work our way south on Middle Creek and Pittman Center Roads. The first listing is the oldest known business of this type in continuous operation by a single family.

Stanley Creswell Grocery
FBS: $1.75
1366 Dolly Parton Parkway
Sevierville
(865) 453-2402

The late Stanley Creswell opened his first grocery near this site before World War II. His children continue to operate the grocery and grill today. The current location, built in the early '70s, is less than a mile east of Sevier County High School. The grocery can seat about 30, and tables are distributed throughout the store wherever room is available. The grill is open Monday through Saturday, 5:00 A.M. to 2:30 P.M.

Middle Creek Market & Deli
FBS: $1.65
1319 Middle Creek Road
Sevierville
(865) 453-6224

One of two markets owned by the Chance family (Ralph is frequently the mayor of Pigeon Forge), Middle Creek Market's grill is open from 5:00 A.M. to 7:00 P.M. Monday through Saturday and from 7:00 A.M. to 4:00 P.M. on Sunday. Both of the Chance family's markets (see below) are renowned for two-fisted hamburgers and generous servings. A single order of fries or potato wedges is ample for two adults.

Chance's Market
FBS: $1.65
2060 Pittman Center Road
Sevierville
(865) 453-8817

The other Chance family enterprise; this one seats about 30 at tables and stools, with a menu that's virtually identical to the Middle Creek store. More Chance family members seem to work in this location, and one of them will gladly deliver your order to your table if things aren't too crowded. The grill is open from 6:00 A.M. to 7:00 P.M. Monday through Saturday, and 7:00 A.M. to 6:00 P.M. Sunday.

Dunn's Market and Grill
FBS: $1.35
2650 Upper Middle Creek Road
Sevierville
(865) 429-5804

Seven tables are scattered through Dunn's Market, with seating for as many as you can fit around them. The grill is open Monday through Saturday from 6:00 A.M. to 9:00 P.M., and Sunday from 6:00 A.M. to 6:00 P.M. Get here early for biscuits; Dunn's are considered by a highly prejudiced clientele to be the best thing on the menu.

GATLINBURG

McKinney's Market
FBS: $1.35
819 East Parkway
Gatlinburg
(865) 436-2272

There's no seating at Faye and Dale's (local terminology), but there is a drive-up window for your second visit and those that succeed it. Locally favored for its deli sandwich menu, McKinney's is a favorite stop for a cup of coffee and a biscuit sandwich on a chilly morning. Most of the morning clientele are firemen and construction workers on their way to work. McKinney's is a handy place to know—in addition to the deli-grocery and gas pumps, there's a family-owned auto parts and repair shop on the property. They're also open 24 hours during the season.

McCarter's Market
FBS: $1.75
103 Mills Park Road
Gatlinburg
(865) 436–4951
Don't let the address fool you—this place is on East Parkway, about 4½ miles east of downtown Gatlinburg. The mailbox is on Mills Park Road. A local landmark for more years than anyone recalls, McCarter's serves breakfast starting at 7:00 A.M., and if you want biscuits, you'd better be there before 9:00. A full slate of sandwiches for lunch is complemented by a lunch special Monday through Friday, until they run out of it. The house special is "Ron & Giff's Burger," a patty melt on special bread. McCarter's soup beans are locally famous. One of the larger places, McCarter's has seating for about 10 at the counter and several tables. The grill is open until 3:00 P.M. daily except Sunday. The market's open from 7:00 A.M. to 8:00 P.M. every day.

Lunchtime at McCarter's Market is a local tradition. DICK McHUGH

but just didn't feel like driving to Gatlinburg or Knoxville. As a result, it's a bit of an institution.

Alf's is easy to find. It's located on the Parkway directly across from the Louise Mandrell Theater. The signboard in front of the restaurant has remained unchanged over the years as far as anyone can recall: GOOD FOOD, COLD BEER. The relatively short dinner menu features steaks, ham, chicken, chops, and a few varieties of seafood, and most of what shows up on your plate is fried. Although dinners average around $7.00 each, the lunches are more reasonably priced at around $3.00. Burgers and other types of sandwiches are standard for lunch.

Admittedly, Alf's isn't going to win any culinary awards, but sometimes there's more to a restaurant than the food. You can shimmy into a booth and order a domestic beer by the bottle or the pitcher. For entertainment, there's a juke box, and you can look at the collection of license plates from all over the country that adorn Alf's walls. Or you can listen in on the conversations of some of Pigeon Forge's more colorful locals. Any way you view it, Alf's is proof that sometimes the simple things in life are often the most memorable. No credit cards.

Alabama Grill $$$
2050 Parkway, Pigeon Forge
(865) 908-8777

This celebrity-themed restaurant is located next door to the Louise Mandrell Theater. It's named after the country group Alabama and is almost as much a museum of country music as it is a restaurant. Between the music, the videos, and the 750-plus pieces of country memorabilia found throughout, Alabama Grill pays tribute to dozens of country music artists, including the restaurant's namesake.

The Alabama Grill experience begins before you even enter the restaurant. Outside, you'll find a limousine formerly used by the band as well as one of their custom tour buses. You can peek into the windows of the limo or take a self-guided tour through the bus.

When you enter the lobby, you'll come face to face with what could best be described as a sort of Alabama shrine. A large painted mural of the band dominates one wall, and below it are glass cases containing personal items donated by each of its members. The far right wall of the lobby is covered with many of the band's gold records. To the left is a newly expanded gift shop where you'll find all

sorts of Alabama merchandise like T-shirts, CDs, and cassettes.

Inside the main room of the restaurant is a large dining area flanked by several smaller dining alcoves. A giant neon guitar hangs over the center section, and all of the walls are packed to capacity with memorabilia. Most of the pieces are either costumes, gold records, musical instruments, or photographs of country stars ranging from Dolly Parton to Clint Black. You'll see one of Elvis Presley's guitars and a red jumpsuit that the King wore on stage. Complementing the artifacts, several television monitors play hits by country stars old and new.

At the far end of the dining room is a small stage backed by another mural of the band, this one made of stained glass. Once each hour, the restaurant's large video screen drops down to the stage and shows the band playing a 10-minute musical tribute to other country artists. During the tribute, the Alabama Grill server staff gets on stage for a line dancing performance. Audience members are welcome to join in and try out some boot scootin' steps.

No, we haven't forgotten that this is a restaurant, so on to the food! Alabama Grill serves lunch and dinner all week long. Many of the menu inclusions like the soups, desserts, and bread are all freshly made on-site; altogether, there are some 60 different items available. Those interested in a sandwich will find burgers in half-pound portions and a club sandwich that's loaded from top to bottom. From the dessert menu, there's an interesting cheesecake with an Alabama twist—a swirl of sweet potato.

Entree specialties include Alabama's "World Famous" Ribs and the Big Texan, a 16-ounce, country-fried steak served with gravy and mashed potatoes. Also keep your mouth open for homemade meat loaf and fried catfish. There are both fried and grilled dishes from the kitchen, and all entrees are served with freshly baked bread.

Mel's Diner $
119 Wears Valley Road, Pigeon Forge
(865) 429-2184

Although it was constructed in 1993, Mel's is a classic diner in the architectural sense with its shiny, silver railroad car appearance. You'll find it just 1 block off the Parkway on Wears Valley Road in Pigeon Forge. Inside, take a nostalgic journey back to the 1950s in the restaurant's cozy, sleek interior among the retro color scheme and rows of booth seating.

One of the neat things about Mel's is that it's one of the few dining establishments in the Smokies that's open 24 hours a day, seven days a week. For breakfast, they serve traditional morning fare like eggs and omelets, pancakes and waffles, and biscuits with gravy (don't forget, you're still in the South!). The rest of the menu consists primarily of American staples like burger and sandwich baskets and dinner platters, available between 11:00 A.M. and 10:00 P.M. Platter entrees include hefty portions of pork chops, ham, meat loaf, country-fried steak, and much more. They come with bread and a choice of two side vegetables.

Be sure to allow room for dessert at Mel's. The cakes, pies, and sundaes are out of this world, and the shakes come in flavors like butterscotch and pineapple as well as in interesting taste combinations like Chanana (chocolate-banana) and Strawnana (strawberry-banana). And if you don't feel like going out to eat, that's okay. You can call Mel's takeout express line, (865) 429-8562, for delivery within a limited area.

Chef Jock's Tastebuds Cafe $$$
1198 Wears Valley Road, Pigeon Forge
(865) 428-9781

Tastebuds Cafe is the baby of local chef Giaccomo Lijoi (Chef Jock, as he's better known). The cuisine here is a blend of French, Italian, and American and definitely not typical of what you'll find in most area restaurants. For example, as an appetizer you might try the shiitake & spinach fromage in French pastry or the artichoke & smoked jarlsberg dip. After trying these, potato skins tend to pale in comparison. Pasta, poultry, seafood, beef, and pork entrees are prepared with only the freshest ingredients and with a European touch. Among the menu favorites is the Chicken Jean Pierre, a plump breast sautéed in butter, garlic, shallots, mushrooms, parsley, provolone, chardonnay, and cream. The Veal Chef Jock is another house specialty similarly prepared. For the more health-conscious, some pasta and chicken dishes are prepared without oil. From time to time, the chef will also present customers with nightly specials such as rack of lamb or ostrich. The desserts are made fresh and change from day to day.

The restaurant is a little off the main drag, 2 miles off the Parkway on Wears Valley Road in Pigeon Forge. The atmosphere is relaxed and elegant without being ostentatious. The dining room is very intimate—okay, it's small. In fact, the seating capacity is 52, and they're almost always full for lunch and dinner. As a result, reservations are highly recommended here, especially for a Friday or Saturday night. Calling a day or two ahead will usually get you a table. But don't let any of this intimidate you. As at most restaurants in the Smokies, you can "come as you are," and casual attire is entirely welcome. By the way, Chef Jock's doesn't serve alcohol, but you can bring your own with you.

Tastebuds Cafe is open for dinner Tuesday through Saturday. The restaurant is closed on Sunday and Monday.

Bennett's Pit Bar-B-Que $$-$$$
2910 Parkway, Pigeon Forge
(865) 429-2200

714 River Road, Gatlinburg
(865) 436-2400
www.bennetts-bbq.com

Just because you're surrounded by Eastern mountains doesn't mean you can't dig in to the hearty, zesty flavors of the Southwest. Both Sevier County Bennett's serve satisfying portions of pork, beef, chicken, and ribs prepared just the way barbecue aficionados like them. The lunch and dinner menus present a broad selection of hickory-smoked and mesquite-grilled entrees, a 40-item, all-you-can-eat soup and salad bar, barbecue sandwiches, and much more.

Separately, or in various combinations, Bennett's offers five basic meats from its hickory smoker: chopped pork, sliced beef brisket, sliced sausage, chicken, and pork spareribs. Other entrees like steaks, shrimp, and chicken breasts are flamed over the mesquite grill. Interestingly, Bennett's serves breakfast as well. That menu contains morning favorites like pancakes, omelets, biscuits, and more but also features a number of breakfast specials like hickory-smoked portions of ham, bacon, pork chops, and even a 10-ounce strip.

The cooking methods used at Bennett's are true to good Texas form and result in foods that are moist, tender, and packed with flavor. The meats start with a generous basting in Bennett's special-recipe barbecue sauce. They're then smoldered over hickory wood and smoked for up to 14 hours. Then it's on to the open-pit hickory fire where selections are grilled to order.

Bennett's is a Denver-based chain with about 20 franchises nationwide. The Pigeon Forge Bennett's opened in 1991, and about a year later, the second one appeared on River Road in Gatlinburg. The Gatlinburg location also has a full-service cocktail lounge where you can relax with a game of pool, darts, video games, or televised sports. Both restaurants are open year-round.

Santo's Italian Restaurant $$$
3270 Parkway, Pigeon Forge
(865) 428-5840
www.santositalianrestaurant.com
Owner Santo Baiamonte brought his experience as a head chef in some of the area's finer restaurants to his own dining venture, which opened in 1991. His well-rounded Italian menu offers a host of tra-

In 2003 the Old Mill expanded its shopping/dining empire with the debut of the Old Mill Bakery Cafe. Located in a renovated home near the original mill, the cafe features a "fast casual" menu, served in either the dining room or the courtyard. You can also picnic in the shade of the giant oak tree on the front lawn.

ditional native dishes, including chicken, veal, seafood, and pasta creations. It's one of those menus where everything sounds so good, making the narrowing-down process a laborious one. The chicken parmigiana, veal parmigiana, and five varieties of spaghetti are all customer favorites. Other items to weigh are fettuccine with snow crab, vegetarian lasagna, and the fried ravioli. All entrees come with a choice of salad or minestrone soup in addition to fresh, hot garlic bread. Chefs prepare all sauces, soups, desserts, and entrees fresh daily.

Santo's serves dinner only, beginning at 3:00 P.M. If you dine in between 3:00 and 5:00 P.M., you can take advantage of the "early bird" specials, several moderately priced entrees that change weekly. If you make your visit after dark, however, you'll get the most out of the restaurant's ambience. The subdued lighting and background accompaniment of the house pianist help create a relaxed dining experience. Although the atmosphere comes across as elegant, Santo's is very family-friendly. Children and casual attire are both quite welcome.

The Old Mill Restaurant $$$
2944 Old Mill Avenue, Pigeon Forge
(865) 429-3463
www.old-mill.com
This restaurant stands next door to one of Pigeon Forge's most famous historical sites, the Old Mill. (See our Attractions chapter for more on this working mill.) The Old Mill Restaurant, however, is a veritable newcomer, having opened in 1993. From an architectural standpoint, these

two neighbors on the banks of the Little Pigeon River blend together well. The restaurant is a sprawling timber-look building that has gone a long way toward matching the exterior ambience of the mill. Inside the restaurant, wood floors, rafters, and simple country furnishings add consistency to the motif. The main dining room is split between two levels, allowing most diners pleasant views through large picture windows overlooking the Little Pigeon River below.

Three meals a day are served, all rife with flavors of the South. The Old Mill country breakfast is based on pancakes with grits, eggs, coffee, juice, muffins, and biscuits. You can then add morning extras like bacon, ham, or sausage. Both the lunch and dinner menus feature quite a few Old Mill Southern-style specialties like country-fried steak, sugar-cured ham, and chicken pot pie for lunch, or pork loin, chicken and dumplings, and pot roast and gravy for dinner. The dinner menu also has a large selection of both fried and grilled entrees, including beef liver, catfish, and ribeye steak. Most dinner entrees come with the Old Mill's trademark corn chowder and homemade fritters plus salad, vegetables, and dessert. For lighter dining, there are several salad, fruit, and vegetable plates from which to choose.

Duff's Famous Smorgasbord $
3985 Parkway, Pigeon Forge
(865) 453-6443
Many of you may recognize the Duff's name. For years these buffet-style family restaurants were fixtures throughout Middle America. Slowly, the chain dwindled away, and today only one Duff's still stands—this one in Pigeon Forge. It's open from mid-February through December, serving lunch and dinner only in the off-season months and adding a breakfast smorgasbord from May through October.

Actually, don't go to Duff's expecting to order from a menu, period. The restaurant specializes in its huge food bars. For one price, you have your choice of at least 6 hot entrees (fried chicken is always

there), 6 vegetables, 9 salads, and 10 desserts plus beverages. Carving stations with roast beef and ham are open after 3:30 P.M. on weekdays and all day on Saturday and Sunday. Duff's signature dessert is the Hurricane Cake, a spice cake topped with a gooey, buttery, brown sugar topping. Repeat visitors ask for it by name.

GATLINBURG

Back in 1981, when Gatlinburg was *the* destination in the Smokies, the city fathers foresaw great economic potential in the upcoming 1982 World's Fair being planned in Knoxville. Among the many changes they brought about to milk that potential was a liberalized alcohol code that permitted the sale of liquor by the drink in restaurants. Surprisingly, the city has maintained its insistence that spirits could only be sold with meals, thus preventing the descent into Hades that a lot of the locals predicted.

Gatlinburg's move into liquor sales has proved a boon to the local schools (taxes on liquor sales must, by state law, be used only for education) and has caused the neighboring cities to examine their own policies toward alcohol. In the following list, mixed drinks, beer, and wine are available with your meals unless otherwise stated. Also, as promised earlier, we'll tell you what the parking situation is on an individual basis.

The age factor also contributes to a phenomenon you probably wouldn't notice unless we brought it up. Atmosphere is not nearly as pronounced a factor in Gatlinburg restaurants as it is in the area to the north, because Gatlinburg's are generally older and don't feel obligated to compete for business by doing much other than offering good food and good service at reasonable prices. Accordingly, our descriptions of Gatlinburg's restaurants will omit all but the most obvious architectural and "ambience oriented" details and will concentrate on the menus. We're also stretching the envelope slightly to include some regional chains that merit inclusion because they've gone to extra effort to fit into the local picture.

Our usual route prevails; we'll work the Parkway from end to end, and then go east out East Parkway to pick up a few places outside the downtown business district. One final disclaimer: Each restaurant mentioned here, and it's not a complete list, is a free-standing structure devoted to food service. None of the places are in or associated with hotels, motels, or attractions, and only three are in shopping malls.

Down the Parkway

Smoky Mountain Trout House   **$$$**
410 Parkway, Gatlinburg
(865) 436-5416
www.zoders.com/trouthouse
They're a little vague about how long the Trout House has been in business, but Trout Eisenhower, the establishment's signature dinner, was so named during Ike's administration (1952–1960). While the usual restaurant fare is available and cooked as well as anyone around can do it, the pièce de résistance here is the local king of the game fish, caught fresh daily and offered in a dozen different presentations, some of which you'd never associate with a fish. You've probably heard of trout almondine, but how about trout dipped in sauce, coated with provolone cheese, and cooked in peanut oil? The Trout House is one of those "urban myth" places you hear about from time to time, a place that looks as unpretentious as a "greasy spoon" but leaves you knowing you've encountered culinary greatness. Just outside of the bustle of downtown, the Trout House opens at 5:00 P.M. for dinner and is kind of intimate—reservations are recommended for groups larger than six. Municipal parking facilities are within easy walking distance of the restaurant in both directions, and the purple route trolley stops at their door.

Atrium Restaurant   **$**
432 Parkway, Gatlinburg
(865) 430-3684
One of Gatlinburg's favorite local spots, the Atrium is open from 7:00 A.M. to 2:30 P.M. for a full meal or a quick breakfast or luncheon sandwich. Seating for 100-plus provides outstanding people-watching locations (a plate glass window is the only thing between the diner and the street), and the Atrium has its own four-story waterfall as a backdrop. The light and airy setting is enhanced by a profusion of plant life in hanging baskets and wall planters. The Atrium offers 25 varieties of pancakes for breakfast and a wide selection of soups, sandwiches, and entrees for lunch, with free parking at the front door. No alcohol is served.

Hard Rock Cafe   **$$-$$$**
515 Parkway, Gatlinburg
(865) 430-7625
www.hardrock.com
As one of the world's biggest full-service restaurant chains (more than 100 worldwide, nearly 40 in the United States), Hard Rock wouldn't normally rate a specific write-up in an Insiders' Guide. The difference here is that when Hard Rock moves into a new city, it does so with the intent to become a member of the community. The Ambassador's Club, an organization of Hard Rock employees, gets deeply involved in community affairs from the day they open their doors.

Night owls don't have many choices for 'round-the-clock dining in the Smokies. But if you've got a late-night craving, you can visit Mel's Diner on Wears Valley Road in Pigeon Forge or either of two Huddle House locations, one on Dolly Parton Parkway in Sevierville and the other on the Parkway in Pigeon Forge.

Local beneficiaries of this establishment include Friends of the Great Smoky Mountains and several environmental groups. The restaurant itself is a comfortable, 221-seat facility offering a menu heavy on barbecue and smoked meat entrees, with a broad selection of steak and pasta dishes and, of course, the burger selection that triggered the whole Hard Rock concept in London in 1971, when the Tennessee-born originator of the franchise couldn't find a decent hamburger.

Another unique feature of this restaurant is their own wedding chapel. A private dining room seats up to 165 for special events. On your way out, the distinctive logo merchandise is available at the cash register. The restaurant opens for lunch at 11:30 A.M. and closes at 10:00 P.M. weekdays and midnight on weekends. The merchandise store opens at 10:00 A.M. and stays open until the last customer has left. The closest parking is at the Parkway municipal structure, about a block away.

No Way Jose's $
555 Parkway, Gatlinburg
(865) 430-5673

The appearance of No Way Jose's may take authenticity to an extreme—the place looks like an urban renewal program somebody forgot about, say 10 years ago. Don't be fooled: When you get past the cluttered exterior and into the dimly lit dining room that really doesn't look like it seats 160, you're in for a treat. Daily deliveries of the best fresh meat and vegetables are cooked in authentic Mexican style and served in generous portions that leave you wishing you had room for more. Margaritas and Mexican beers complement the meals, and the menu includes enough "gringo" dishes to satisfy the less-adventurous palates in your group. Free parking is available at the front door, and the downtown aquarium parking deck is just across the street. No Way Jose's opens at 11:00 A.M. to catch the lunch crowd and closes around 10:00 P.M.

North China Chinese Restaurant $
Parkway, Gatlinburg
(865) 436-6572

Situated at the back of Charlie's Alley shopping mall, North China is also approachable from River Road, where there's a handy commercial parking lot. Opened in 1979, North China is a Gatlinburg mainstay with about 50 seats and a menu that's anything but "one from column A, one from column B." Every dish on the menu (and there's a bunch to choose from) is prepared in the regional style of the area it represents, and it's cooked and served by people who've been there. The large Hsieh family keeps bringing help over when they need it. And be prepared to eat Chinese—all 60 of the main menu selections and the dozen or so soups and appetizers are ethnic. The only concession to Occidental tastes is the drink selection, which includes American soft drinks and beer in addition to Oolong tea. Family-style dinners are available, where each person selects an entree that's served in enough quantity that everybody in the group can sample everything on the table. North China is open daily from 11:00 A.M. to 10:00 P.M.

Pancake Pantry $
628 Parkway, Gatlinburg
(865) 436-4724
www.pancakepantry.com

Arguably the favorite visitors' breakfast spot in the downtown area, the Pancake Pantry doesn't really need parking—it's within 3 blocks of more than a thousand motel rooms in the downtown and Baskins Creek areas. Open for breakfast and lunch, the Pancake Pantry's breakfast menu includes more ways to fix a pancake than you'd ever believe possible, and the soup-and-sandwich luncheon menu fills you up nicely without stuffing you. Opened in the early '70s, the Pancake Pantry's outstanding architecture and quick, friendly service have made it a landmark in downtown Gatlinburg. No credit cards.

Lineberger's Seafood Co. $$
903 Parkway, Gatlinburg
(865) 436-9284
www.linebergersseafood.com

A refugee from the low country of South Carolina, Lineberger's features one of the most complete lines of fresh Atlantic seafood in the area. The restaurant is strongly reminiscent of the seafood houses that line Murrell's Inlet, just south of Myrtle Beach, which is exactly what the Lineberger family had in mind when they opened in Gatlinburg over 40 years ago. The window views afforded from most seats make Lineberger's a great place for people-watching as you await and enjoy the extensive variety of seafood dishes and platters cooked to your order. Land-lubber offerings like steaks, chicken, and chops will suit the aquatically challenged, but a visit to Lineberger's shouldn't really be for that type of eating.

Lineberger's opens at 4:00 P.M. Monday through Friday, and noon on weekends.

Best Italian Cafe and Pizzeria $-$$
968 Parkway, Gatlinburg
(865) 430-4090
www.bestitalian.com

The name may seem a little arrogant at first, but nobody who's ever eaten at the Best walks away complaining. Opened in 1975 in half the space it currently occupies at the back of Elk's Plaza, this is as authentic an ethnic restaurant as a native of New York City can make it. Atmosphere? "Fuggedaboudit!" People come here to eat. Again and again. If it's Italian, they make it; if not, see the quote above. "The Best" made its local reputation in the '70s when it was the only pizza place in town (it's still the overwhelming favorite of locals) and grew from that start to a full-fledged eatery. From antipasto and garlic rolls that defy description as appetizers through absolutely authentic entrees with those great names that roll so trippingly off the tongue (fettuccine, manicotti, parmigiana) to the sinful desserts you struggle to eat, "the Best" justifies its name. And as you go back to

the real world singing softly to yourself, you won't even remember what the place looked like, but you'll remember where it is. The Best Italian Cafe is open seven days a week from 11:00 A.M. to 11:00 P.M. Sunday through Thursday, and until midnight on Friday and Saturday. Parking is convenient in the small Elk's Plaza lot adjacent to the restaurant and the commercial parking deck across the Parkway.

Howard's Restaurant $$
976 Parkway, Gatlinburg
(865) 436-3600
www.howards-gatlinburg.com

For more than 50 years, Howard's was that memorable place in the middle of downtown where people sat right out in the open along the Parkway. Now closer to the south end, it's still the same people serving the same great food in a bigger setting. As close to an old-fashioned eatery as you'll find anywhere, Howard's features a full line of hearty steaks and gourmet burgers, skillet-cooked trout, and baby back ribs cooked just the way you like 'em, on both the grown-up and children's menus. Long famous for home-made french fries, desserts, and salad dressings, Howard's new location includes a spacious upstairs lounge where you can relax until it's time to get serious about eating. The lounge has live entertainment Wednesday through Saturday evenings. Open year-round for lunch and dinner, Howard's is convenient to the Elk's Plaza parking lot.

The Park Grill $$$
1110 Parkway, Gatlinburg
(865) 436-2300
www.parkgrillgatlinburg.com

One of the city's architectural wonders, the Park Grill is built almost entirely of huge spruce logs. The main beams in the restaurant are 2 feet in diameter. The bright, airy feeling conveyed by the massive structure is complemented by the extensive use of leaves as a primary decorating motif and the park ranger uniforms on the staff. All of it is a reminder that the

Park Grill is one of the area's larger bene-factors of Great Smoky Mountains National Park. It wouldn't be a tragedy if the food took a backseat to the surround-ings, but that's not the way it is. The menu is eclectic and outstanding, with some-thing to satisfy any taste in grand fashion. The pork tenderloin is a local legend, and so are the homemade desserts made fresh daily by the resident pastry chef. The Park Grill is an adventure in fine dining in amazing surroundings. Parking is available behind the restaurant, which opens every day at 4:00 P.M.

The Peddler Restaurant $$$
820 River Road, Gatlinburg
(865) 436-8735
www.peddlergatlinburg.com

Just off the Parkway, the Peddler is located in one of Gatlinburg's most his-toric buildings: The center of the structure is the log cabin that was the homeplace of the late Hattie Ogle McGiffin, the city's acknowledged matriarch. The Peddler is part of a small regional chain that oper-ates like an independent restaurant. The local management is deeply involved in civic and national park affairs.

Custom-cut steaks (they bring the loin to your table and you tell them how big a steak you want) and fresh seafood dishes make the Peddler a "special occasion" favorite for families and couples looking for one really sumptuous meal to put an exclamation point on their trip to the Smokies. The Peddler's salad bar is con-sidered one of the best in the area; you have to be careful not to load up on salad items so much that you can't eat the entree. The Peddler has its own parking lot in front of the building—if the lot's full, figure you're going to wait the better part of an hour to get seated. Open daily at 5:00 P.M., the Peddler stays open until everybody's served.

Out East Parkway from Traffic Light #3

Greenbrier Restaurant $$$
370 Newman Road, Gatlinburg
(865) 436-6318
www.greenbrierrestaurant.com

Convenient but well removed from any other distractions, the Greenbrier is located on a mountaintop just 1½ miles from traffic light #3. Take East Parkway out to the traffic light at Newman Road (Virgil's Motel is on the opposite corner), turn right, and drive up into the parking lot where the road ends. Some member of the Hadden family will probably be wait-ing to show you to a table either over-looking the highway you just came off or set in an intimate room where your group has the place to itself.

Although beef dishes are the staple here (prime rib lovers will think they've gone to heaven), the Greenbrier also has an extensive seafood menu, and they do more things with chicken than anyone else in the area. To ensure fairness, the Greenbrier refuses to take reservations, but if they know you're on the way, they'll try to have your table waiting when you arrive. Because of the size of their several dining rooms, the Greenbrier can accom-modate groups of up to 30 people. The barroom is a local favorite when there's football on television. The Greenbrier's advertising says they're open from 5:00 to 9:30 or 10:00 P.M., depending on the day of the week, but nobody's ever been accused of running a guest out because the clock said it was time to close.

Mountain Lodge Restaurant $
913 East Parkway, Gatlinburg
(865) 436-2547

There's seating for about 125 people in the deceptively large Mountain Lodge, which means you probably won't have to wait long to get seated for breakfast or lunch. Open daily (except Tuesday) from 7:00 A.M. to 3:00 P.M., the Mountain Lodge is a huge local favorite for its extremely Southern breakfast menu and its large selection of lunch goodies. The daily special is on a blackboard at the entrance; the way the staff (which usually includes several of the Smith family that owns the place) treats you will make you think you're the most special thing that's happened to them all day. Ample parking is available on both sides of the building.

If you're dining as a group, be prepared to have a gratuity automatically added to the tab. Some places add the tip for parties with as few as 6 people, while others draw the line at 10 or 12 guests. In any instance, remember that restaurants require their servers to claim a percentage of their sales as tip income, regardless of whether the tips were actually made. The automatic gratuity, therefore, is often a measure to ensure that servers don't have to pay income tax on money they didn't make!

The Great Smoky Arts & Crafts Community

It wasn't that long ago that a day in the Great Smoky Arts & Crafts Community meant a leisurely drive of a few hours and visiting a couple dozen shops where handcrafts and art were produced and sold. Today, with upwards of 100 shops and galleries, a day gets you halfway through the if you hurry. It's fortunate that the increase in the number of businesses in the Glades has been accompanied by the establishment of four excellent eateries spread throughout the community. One is themed, two offer beer and wine on their menus, and all have plenty of convenient parking. Most of them are also near enough to craft shops of every description that you can shop before and after eating without having to get in your car. Most of them have abbreviated hours because they're operated by families who also have lives.

Garden Gallery Cafe $
337 Glades Road, Gatlinburg
(865) 436-4120
Set beside a riotous garden of wild and cultured flowers, the Garden Gallery Cafe offers a continental-style breakfast menu and then gets serious for lunch. An impressive array of hot and cold sandwiches is complemented by homemade soups that are locally adored and a salad menu that will please any palate. The dessert menu is subject to whatever Dawn and John can whip up on any given day, and the soda fountain–style drink menu includes malts and shakes, ice cream, and lemonade that's to die for.

Ma's Kitchen $
690 Glades Road, Gatlinburg
(865) 430-7799
This may be the most appropriately named restaurant in the area; it's a small converted house that has just one room, and that room is a kitchen. There's no doubt that everything you're served at Ma's is cooked right there; you're right there watching it happen. Donna and Sue (and frequently their kids) will take your order from a basic Southern menu, and then they'll pitch in to help Jamie cook your order and serve it. Nothing real fancy on the menu, and the rest of the place is every bit as unpretentious—they serve good, honest, salt-of-the-earth food in generous enough amounts that you won't go away hungry. Weather

permitting, you can eat in the front yard's parklike setting. Ma's Kitchen is open Monday through Saturday from 7:00 A.M. to 2:00 P.M., and on Friday they reopen from 5:00 until 8:00 P.M., but you'd best get there early for the Friday evening meal; the local football crowd shows up in great numbers around 6:00 P.M.—whether or not it's football season.

The Fox & Parrot Tavern— A British Pub $$
1065 Glades Road, Gatlinburg
(865) 435-0677

About as "ethnic" a place as you'll find in Gatlinburg, the Fox & Parrot is based on the design of any English pub built since man began walking upright. The naturally comfortable log interior is festooned with the national flags of every country in the British Isles and their patron saints. The menu is right out of old Blighty itself, including such delicacies as bangers and mash, toad in the hole, Cornish pasties, scones, Eccles cakes, and some sandwich combinations you may actually have heard of. Although the food is more than enough reason to warrant a visit, the awesome part of the Fox & Parrot is the beer

menu: They've got more than 60 brands of foreign and domestic beers and ales available bottled or on tap. Because of a strong local following, including the Thursday night darts league, the Fox & Parrot has evening hours. They're open Monday through Thursday from 11:00 A.M. to 8:00 P.M., Friday and Saturday until 10:00 P.M., and Sunday from noon to 5:00 P.M.

The Wild Plum Tea Room $$
555 Buckhorn Road, Gatlinburg
(865) 436-3808

The oldest of the craft community's eating establishments, the Wild Plum Tea Room is a great favorite with several local ladies' social and service clubs. The menu begins with a soup du jour that's usually worth the trip and is followed by an equally delicious salad-and-sandwich menu. All entrees in-clude a serving of the restaurant's signature wild plum muffins (you'll defnitely want to take some home). The beverage list includes a selection of beers and wines, and if you liked the muffins, you'll probably love the wild plum tea. The Wild Plum Tea Room is open Monday through Saturday from 11:00 A.M. to 3:00 P.M.

MUSIC THEATERS AND NIGHTLIFE ⑨

No one disputes the fact that the Smoky Mountains are this area's top tourist drawing card. But let's face it, after dark, the national park isn't that fun—unless you're camping out! So what does everyone do in the Smokies after the sun retreats for the day? Plenty. Sure, you can go to a restaurant, but after that you might decide that the night is still young.

We have many nighttime entertainment suggestions for you, separated into two categories. Most Smoky Mountains nightlife comes courtesy of the area's many music and variety theaters, all of which are profiled in the first part of the chapter. These are all family-friendly shows in which the entertainment is wholesome, and alcoholic beverages are not served. But we also know there are those of you who like to dance, make fools of yourselves on a karaoke machine, or sit back and relax with a locally brewed beer. The Nightlife section of this chapter will detail some places where you can find that particular sort of live or interactive entertainment.

MUSIC AND VARIETY THEATERS

The transformation of the entertainment scene in the Smokies over the past 10 years or so has been nothing short of phenomenal. Prior to 1994, there were only three or four smaller music halls in Pigeon Forge and one theater in Gatlinburg. That was the extent of the area's music theater "community." What took place in the years following was a strong and steady push by local governments and developers to turn Sevier County into a virtual musical mecca, with the hope

that vacationers would make pilgrimages here as much for the entertainment as for the mountains and other tourist drawing cards. Some even hoped that Sevier County would reach the levels that Branson, Missouri, had in terms of numbers of theaters, visitors, etc.

That's not quite the case yet, but there are still some 15 music and variety theaters in the county, most of which are located in Pigeon Forge, but some of which reflect the efforts by Sevierville and Gatlinburg to keep a leg up in the market.

Most of the shows you will find are music-oriented, with an emphasis on country music. However, if your tastes reside elsewhere, you won't feel left out. Some area shows tip their hats to other musical genres such as rock 'n' roll, Broadway, gospel, and bluegrass. Then there are the theaters that have their focus more on comedy and variety. The result is a menu of diverse entertainment choices that growing numbers of tourists are getting hooked on.

All of the area's music and variety theaters are wheelchair accessible, nonsmoking facilities. They also have adequate free parking, except in one case (noted later) where you'll have to pay. Each is equipped with concession stands and, in most cases, souvenir shops full of everything from coffee mugs to T-shirts to tapes and CDs by the theater's artists. The theaters tend to be very audience-friendly. You can take your drinks and snacks into the auditorium with you, and although video- and audiotaping are prohibited, most venues allow flash photography during performances. All theaters sell reserved seats, so it pays to buy early if you know which shows you want to see, so you'll have a better chance at a good seat.

Note that the ticket prices quoted in our write-ups include tax, and that most theaters have discounted prices for groups. Although the ticket prices we've quoted were confirmed for the 2004 season, be sure to verify any theater's ticket prices when making reservations. And it's always highly advisable to make advance reservations, especially during peak season. If you do so by phone, a credit card number is required. If you purchase your tickets ahead of time at the theater's box office, both cash and credit cards are accepted; personal checks are not. Finally, although you'll find that we've given you a general sketch of each theater's seasonal schedule, we recommend calling each theater to get specific dates for any particular time period.

Pigeon Forge

Louise Mandrell Theater
2046 Parkway, Pigeon Forge
(865) 453-6263, (800) 768-1170
www.louisemandrell.com
Join the multitalented star, Louise Mandrell, at her "home" in the Smoky Mountains. Opened in 1997, this 1,400-seat auditorium is part of Pigeon Forge's Music Road development and the place where Mandrell shines approximately 250 dates each year. There are usually four to six shows each week, beginning at 7:30 P.M.

In addition to the evening performances, there are a few 2:30 P.M. matinees sprinkled into the schedule during peak season and the holidays. In October Mandrell does two or three matinees a week.

Mandrell's showplace packs in a lot of visitors and gives those visitors their money's worth, boasting a large troupe of backup singers and dancers and an ensemble of gifted live musicians. During two-hour performances, Mandrell and company touch a lot of musical bases, incorporating not just country and bluegrass but gospel, patriotic, and big-band numbers as well. In November and

December she stages a separate Christmas show, complete with flying snowflakes, dancing snowmen, winter skating, and holiday songs.

Ms. Mandrell works musical magic on stage, quickly switching hats as she shows off on the fiddle, upright bass, accordion, and drums, just to name a few.

Several of the show's segments make it sparkle from a production standpoint as well. A patriotic tribute to the military, a hilarious send-up of Carmen Miranda, and a festive, high-energy finale are just a few examples of how Mandrell pulls out all the stops each and every night.

The Louise Mandrell Theater also hosts a number of nonmusical special events each year, including a charity run (see our Festivals and Annual Events chapter), the Mrs. International competition, and the annual Buckley Bash that benefits the Pigeon Forge K-9 unit.

In 2003 Mandrell welcomed the recently formed singing group Integrity to her theater as stars of a new morning show. Three of the quartet's members performed for many years as part of Dollywood's resident gospel group, the Kingdom Heirs. Now at the Louise Mandrell Theater, Integrity shares its Southern gospel harmonies with audiences beginning at 10:00 A.M. Tuesday through Saturday. The hour-and-a-half-long show also includes appearances by Mandrell.

Tickets to Louise Mandrell's show are $29.75 for adults 18 and older, $16.75 for ages 13 through 17, and $11.75 for ages 6 through 12. Tickets for the Integrity Quartet are $20.10 for ages 18 and older, $9.10 for ages 13 through 17, and free for ages 12 and younger.

Black Bear Jamboree
119 Music Road, Pigeon Forge
(865) 908-7469, (800) 985-5494
www.blackbearjamboree.com
This show debuted in 2002 in the Parkway theater previously occupied by a comedy/variety dinner theater. At today's Black Bear Jamboree, you'll still get a meal, but owners David Fee and Jim

Hedrick (co-owners of the Comedy Barn Theater in Pigeon Forge) have brought an entirely different kind of show to the stage of this unique theater space that accommodates up to 650 guests.

The premise is based on the "legend" of the Black Bear Jamboree, a secretive annual gathering of Smoky Mountain bears at which the beasts celebrate their bearhood with food, song, and dance. The show's cast members are "counselors" at Camp Black Bear and lead the audience on a musical journey in search of the mysterious bear jamboree. The plot thickens when the campers discover a couple of clans of bears, portrayed by larger-than-life animatronic figures. A papa, mama, and baby bear family turn the tables on the hikers and observe their behavior, while another rascally trio of bears plans to steal their backpacks. At first, the critters aren't happy to see their human guests, so to appease them the hikers entertain the bears with different varieties of music, including Broadway, oldies rock, country, and gospel. In November and December, the theater presents its Christmas show featuring lots of holiday music and a slightly different twist on the original plot.

Meals at Black Bear Jamboree consist of creamy soup and biscuits followed by Southern-style chicken, hickory pit barbecue, buttery corn on the cob, a vegetable medley, and seasoned potatoes. Hot apple cobbler and unlimited soft drinks, tea, or coffee round out the menu. Meals are served before the show begins, but background entertainment is provided by the live bluegrass band.

The theater is also the home of the legendary gospel group the Blackwoods, who present a breakfast show at 9:30 A.M. During the meal, which begins at 8:30 A.M., audiences watch a video that documents the history of the Blackwoods on the theater's two giant screens. Afterward, the Blackwood family members themselves take the stage.

The family's roots go back more than six decades, making the Blackwood name

If you want to get an autograph from your favorite performer or even pose for a photograph with them, they're usually very accessible and willing to oblige after a performance (sometimes during intermission). You can bring your own memorabilia for them to sign; however, if you're empty-handed, the theater gift shops will be happy to oblige by selling you a T-shirt or glossy photo.

very well known in the realm of gospel music. Over the course of its history, the group has won eight Grammy Awards and seven of gospel's Dove Awards, and they have sold more than 40 million records.

Today's incarnation of the group is fronted by Ron Blackwood, son of founding Blackwood Quartet member R. W. Blackwood. In addition to the group's soaring and inspiring harmonies, they deliver traditional country songs, including tributes to artists like Larry Gatlin and the Oak Ridge Boys. You'll even hear some oldies but goodies from the '50s added to help balance the repertoire. The show's comedian and musical director, Craig Hodges, keeps audiences chuckling between musical sets.

Each Blackwood show is a, high-energy vocal performance; the enthusiasm shown by the group is infectious and sweeps audiences away with its from-the-heart sincerity. The music is complmented by the playful sense of camaraderie shared by each performer.

The Black Bear Jamboree show runs year-round (on a more limited schedule in January), with shows at 5:00 and 8:00 P.M. nightly. One o'clock matinees are added as needed during peak season. Tickets are $38.45 for ages 12 and older, and senior citizens receive a $2.00 discount off that price.

The Blackwoods perform Thursday through Saturday mornings, March through December, and tickets are $21.90. Children 11 and younger get in free.

121

CLOSE-UP

Giving Back to Her Community

When Louise Mandrell opened her music theater in 1997, most people assumed that the multitalented entertainer would make a go of it in the highly competitive Smoky Mountain music theater business.

More than seven years later, however, Mandrell's Pigeon Forge showplace has done much more than simply hold its own in the market—it has become the home of the most highly attended show in the area.

The initial temptation might be to simply chalk this distinction up to the quality of the show and its star. And there are valid reasons to do so. With a dynamic singing voice, killer dance steps, boundless musical skills, and enough charm and energy to win over even the stodgiest of crowds, Mandrell is a magnetic force that draws and holds attention. And that doesn't take into account the fact that she surrounds herself with a corps of capable musicians, dancers, and singers and wraps everything up in a multimillion-dollar production.

But the secret to her success goes deeper than what people see on stage and under the lights each night. It's what Louise Mandrell does with her own time, when she's not on the clock, that perhaps has made the deepest and longest-lasting impact, not only on Pigeon Forge but on Sevier County as a whole. By donating not just her time but her talents, her financial resources, and even her theater to a wide variety of charities and organizations, Mandrell embodies the spirit of "giving back to the community."

Among the causes closest to her heart is Boy Scouts of America. To support scouting programs locally, Mandrell hosts a 5K run each spring in Pigeon Forge, an event that draws runners from all over the world. To date, the run has raised more than $150,000 for Boy Scouts since its debut.

Another event, created by Mandrell's daughter Nicole and named after one of the family dogs, is the annual Buckley Bash, which benefits the Sevier County Humane Society. The 2002 Bash, which was cohosted by actor Erik Estrada, helped raise money to buy two new police dogs for the Pigeon Forge Police Department's K-9 unit.

Mandrell and company even open the doors of their theater on Sunday mornings to host a nondenominational prayer and praise service. The service is targeted toward out-of-town visitors who might

Smoky Mountain Jubilee
2115 Parkway, Pigeon Forge
(865) 428-1836
www.smokymtnjubilee.com
Having opened its doors back in 1984, Smoky Mountain Jubilee is now the longest-running music show in Pigeon Forge and the second-oldest operating theater in the county. It's one of the smaller area auditoriums in size (seats about 900), but owner Elmer Dreyer has been packing in crowds by the busload for quite a stretch now. A longtime favorite with Smoky Mountain visitors, the

To show support for one of her favorite organizations, entertainer Louise Mandrell "camps out" with Boy Scouts in the lobby of her music theater. LOUISE MANDRELL THEATER

be looking for a place to worship while visiting the Smokies.

And these just scratch the surface. Mandrell, her family, and even her supporting cast members work hard within area communities to support a host of other local causes, from the United Way and the Fellowship of Christian Athletes to the March of Dimes and the Church of God Home for Children in Sevierville.

Some might say that Mandrell's success has led her, out of gratitude, to give back to the communities that have supported her so strongly. But one could even make the argument that her charitable spirit is one of the very reasons for that success in the first place.

Louise Mandrell is the golden rule in action, and she understands the fact that the entertainer-audience relationship is a two-way association. And she never takes for granted the importance of being a vital and active citizen in her adopted hometown.

Jubilee gets a lot of repeat business from fans who can't get enough of the theater's unadulterated blend of country, gospel, and bluegrass.

Smoky Mountain Jubilee is a family operation, an arrangement that seems to work well with the theater's philosophy of providing a wholesome family-oriented show. Dreyer is the emcee of the show and plays guitar as well. His daughter, Gayla, has been a featured vocalist with the show since day one, and you'll even find Dreyer's wife running the box office and working the phones.

On stage, Smoky Mountain Jubilee's cast includes an eight-piece band, a gospel quartet, featured female vocalists, and a resident clogging troupe, the Tennessee Mountain Sweethearts. From the show's first downbeat to the closing number, audiences soak in everything from blistering bluegrass fiddle and banjo to crooning country classics to perfectly jelled gospel harmonies. There's even a little bit of oldies rock 'n' roll thrown in for good measure.

Comic relief is provided by resident funnyman Highpockets, a hillbilly character who takes the stage several times during each performance wearing highwater overalls, a sleeveless flannel shirt, and a floppy felt hat. He plays an affable and sometimes dimwitted rube to Dreyer's straight man. Highpockets' Elvis send-up is always a show highlight.

The gang at Smoky Mountain Jubilee generally performs weekends only January through April, four nights a week in May, six nights a week during peak season, and about four nights a week in November and December. Curtain time is 8:00 P.M., and tickets are $21.95 each. Children 11 and younger are admitted free, and senior citizens receive a $1.00 discount off the full price.

Did you know that Billy Baker, star of Elwood Smooch's Ole Smoky Hoedown, got his start as a circus clown? In fact, Baker's funnyman roots were recognized in 2001 when he was inducted into the International Clown Hall of Fame. And we're not clowning around!

Elwood Smooch's Ole Smoky Hoedown
2135 Parkway, Pigeon Forge
(865) 428-5600, (888) 231-6444
www.olesmokyhoedown.com

For those craving a show with true Smoky Mountain flavor, Elwood Smooch's Ole Smoky Hoedown is a good choice. Who is Elwood Smooch, you ask? To put it simply, we'll say that he's just one of the

many comical characters presented by Hoedown front man Billy Baker. A more visual thumbnail sketch of Elwood would describe his baggy pants, crossed eyes, missing teeth, and sometimes spastic comic demeanor. Smooch is a quintessential lovable rube, and the man that brings him to life is able to contort his body and facial expressions in a manner that would make Jim Carrey envious.

With the help of his other characters, like Chlorine (a well-endowed, muumuu-clad woman), Uncle Mildew (who claims to be the world's oldest stand-up comedian), and Elwood Presley (which is self-explanatory), Baker brings guaranteed laughter and smiles to his audiences. In a show format that also includes a superb band, the Smoochers, and an assorted cast of comedians and featured vocalists, Ole Smoky Hoedown is two hours of hayseed hilarity interspersed with A-plus country and bluegrass music. Each performance also features Baker as he takes the stage sans his alter egos to sing a number of vocal standards in his richly pleasing baritone voice.

Billy Baker brings a full show business resume to his theater, including a longtime stint as a clown with Ringling Brothers and as a regular on *Hee Haw,* where his Elwood Smooch character gained a national following. Nowadays, he conjures up good ol' mountain humor in the barnlike atmosphere of the 450-seat theater. That hillbilly flavor is accentuated during the show by slide projections depicting scenes of the Smoky Mountains' natural beauty and rich history.

Elwood Smooch's Ole Smoky Hoedown is open three nights a week in March, four to five nights a week in April and May, and six to seven nights a week in peak season.

The theater presents a special Harvest Show from late September through mid-November, and after a short break, the action resumes in late November when the Christmas Show begins its run on a limited schedule through mid-December. The last week of the year is devoted to a Highlights Show, featuring the best elements of the Hoedown's three different shows. Admission prices are $29.00 for adults ages 20 and older, $26.50 for ages 50 and older, $18.00 for ages 13 through 19, and $11.00 for ages 6 through 12. Children younger than 6 are admitted free.

Memories Theatre
2141 Parkway, Pigeon Forge
(865) 428-7852, (800) 325-3078
www.memoriestheatre.com

Next door to Smoky Mountain Jubilee and Hillbilly Hoedown, you'll find Memories Theatre, home of another of the longer-running shows in Pigeon Forge. Since 1990, Memories has made its mark with the musical tribute, honoring a host of country, gospel, and rock 'n' roll greats through the songs that made them famous. The anchor of each Memories show, however, is the Elvis Presley tribute.

In late 2003 a brand-new Elvis entered the Memories building, replacing longtime headliner Lou Vuto, who ventured out with his own theater in Gatlinburg. Memphis native Bill Stiles officially took over the spotlight as Memories' brand-new King of Rock and Roll. Taking the stage in white studded jumpsuit reminiscent of Presley's Las Vegas years, Stiles bears an uncanny resemblance to the King, from his sideburns and raven-dark hair to his fluid stage movements and commanding presence. As he belts out hit after Presley hit, you have to constantly remind yourself that you're not watching the real thing.

Helping add authenticity to the Elvis tribute is the presence of Charlie Hodge, Elvis Presley's longtime friend, aide, and band member. Hodge makes his first appearance each night in the role of the raconteur, relating his personal experiences with Elvis to the audience in a casual, one-to-one manner. Later, he joins the band on stage, lending guitar and backing vocals to Stiles's tribute.

The Elvis portion of the show is only the second half of each Memories performance. The first half is devoted to other musical tributes to artists ranging from Roy Orbison and Kenny Rogers to Buddy Holly and Cher. The songs are handled by the seven-piece Memories Showband as well as the Three Inspirations, a female vocal trio. Overall, the cast has such a large repertoire to its credit that it frequently changes the show's makeup from night to night.

Memories Theatre is open weekends only in February and March, four days a week in April, November, and December, and five to six days a week May through October. Showtime is 8:15 nightly. Tickets are $24.50 for ages 20 through 54, $22.50 for ages 55 and older, $19.00 for ages 13 through 19, and $5.00 for ages 7 through 12. Ages 6 and younger are admitted free.

Country Tonite Theatre
129 Showplace Boulevard, Pigeon Forge
(865) 453-2003, (800) 792-4308
www.countrytonitepf.com

Since opening in Pigeon Forge in 1997, Country Tonite Theatre has presented its audiences with a fast-paced, high-energy show brimming with a broad spectrum of country music. With a beautiful, 1,500-seat auditorium as the setting, Country Tonite's cast of musicians, dancers, and featured vocalists all sizzle throughout the two-hour-plus salute to country music's legendary performers, both past and present.

In a sense, there really are no "stars" at Country Tonite, but rather a strong ensemble cast of talent that dishes out musical tributes to country artists ranging from Patsy Cline to Charlie Daniels. As a fresh twist, Country Tonite's featured singers include youth vocalists who always seem to win audiences over with their charm, and the crowds especially love Country Tonite's funnyman, Bubba, the Redneck Ranger. Bubba comes on frequently during each performance as a slow-witted park ranger who gets big yuks, typically using other cast members as straight men.

The original Country Tonite show opened in Las Vegas in 1992 and expanded to Branson, Missouri, in 1994. The Pigeon Forge production runs from late March through December, usually six days per week. Except for a few isolated dates, there are two shows daily at 3:00 and 8:00 P.M. Country Tonite's holiday show premiers annually in November, augmenting the regular show with strong influences of Christmas music and decoration.

In addition to the regularly scheduled Country Tonite performances, the theater hosts several special-event shows throughout the year. Highlights in previous years have included a tribute to Mayberry (starring cast members of *The Andy Griffith Show*), Merle Haggard in concert, and an evening with comedian Tim Conway.

Country Tonite Theatre is also home to a morning magic show, Terry Evanswood's Grand Illusion. At 10:00 A.M. three days a week, Evanswood brings everything from large-scale illusions to close-up sleight-of-hand to the Country Tonite stage. Consummate skill on the part of Evanswood, along with top-notch assistants, lighting, music, and smoke effects (not to mention four-and-a-half tons of props and equipment!), all combine to create a very enjoyable morning for all ages. By incorporating comedy, live animals, and even audience participation into his show, Evanswood has crafted a well-rounded morning of magic.

During the two-hour performance, guests witness Evanswood's variations on a number of classic feats of prestidigitation, such as levitation, sawing a person in half, disappearing in a box, and escaping from a trunk. In addition, there are plenty of other illusions that are probably unfamiliar to most audience members. And thanks to the use of a handheld camera and the theater's large overhead video screens, the audience can even try to follow Evanswood's skilled magician's hands as he astounds everyone with close-up favorites like the "cup and balls" routine as well as a number of card tricks. Speaking of cards, one of the most amazing segments of the show is the one in which Evanswood works with multiple decks of cards, seemingly producing them from thin air, fanning and manipulating them in ways that defy logic.

Evanswood, a Chicago native, has been studying magic since his parents gave him his first magic set at the age of 8. He started out performing at neighborhood birthday parties but has now appeared all over the world, including Las Vegas and the famed Magic Castle in Hollywood. At the age of 21, Evanswood became the youngest person ever to perform at the Magic Castle, which is also the headquarters for the Academy of the Magical Arts.

If you happen to be hanging out in the Country Tonite Theatre lobby, be sure to visit their Hall of Magic, a display of Evanswood's private collection of magic artifacts and memorabilia. Pieces include vintage magic sets, photos, autographs, publicity materials, and books related to magic's history as well as some of its most famous performers. There is no charge to tour the Hall of Magic.

Tickets to Country Tonite's afternoon and evening music shows are $25.75 for adults, $23.75 for seniors 50 and older, and $15.75 for children ages 13 through 17. Kids ages 12 and under are admitted free (two free per paid adult admission). Tickets to Terry Evanswood's morning magic show are $20.00 for ages 11 and older and $5.00 for ages 4 through 10. Kids 3 and younger are admitted free.

Oldies Showplace Dinner Theater
140 Showplace Boulevard, Pigeon Forge
(865) 453-0833, (888) 513-1403
www.oldiesdinnertheater.com
In the past few years, more and more shows have incorporated meals into their evenings of entertainment. Such is the case with Oldies Showplace Dinner Theater (formerly known—to those of you who go back a few years—as Eddie's Heart and Soul Cafe), which is located just past Country Tonite Theatre on Showplace Boulevard.

Your evening starts with a dinner of ribs, chicken breast, baked beans, coleslaw, potato wedges, corn on the cob, and roll with a hot apple turnover and all the water, tea, or soda you care to drink. The kids' meal, for ages 11 and younger, comes with chicken fingers, corn on the cob, potato wedges, and apple turnover.

The show itself is a revue of well-known songs from the '40s, '50s, and '60s in addition to pop, oldies, rock 'n' roll, country, gospel, patriotic, and comedy.

Oldies Showplace Dinner Theater is open April through December, from five to seven nights per week. Dinner/show-time is 7:00 P.M. The cafe's Christmas show runs in December only. Tickets are $30.00 for ages 12 and older and $13.00 for ages 5 through 11. Ages 4 and younger get in free.

Classic Country Theater
125 Music Mountain Drive, Pigeon Forge
(865) 774-7469, (866) 430-8422
www.classiccountrytheater.com
Here's another showplace that's located just off the Parkway, but it's not hard to find. Turn east at traffic light #2 in Pigeon Forge, and you'll soon see the theater just ahead on your left.

As its name suggests, the emphasis of this show is on the great country tunes of the '50s, '60s, and '70s—the classics, no less—songs made famous by the most legendary names in the long history of country music. Guests hear well-known hits by artists like Conway Twitty, George Jones, Patsy Cline, and Loretta Lynn. The show's singers are strong, faithfully capturing the vocal styles of the original artists, and along with the crisp accompaniment of the theater's band, they brew rich re-creations of the genre's best. The set list even includes songs from the worlds of gospel, bluegrass, and Elvis. Rounding out the cast are ventriloquist Alex Houston and his wooden pal, Elmer. The duo has more than 40 years of experience in the entertainment business, including television appearances and stints opening for some of the biggest names in country music.

Owner/producer Frank Auman is so sure you'll like his show that he offers a money-back guarantee if you don't have a good time. To date, he's the only theater operator in the area to make such a bold offer.

At Classic Country Theater, your music experience begins as soon as you walk though the doors. A museum located above the lobby showcases costumes and accessories worn on stage by some of classic country's greatest stars, such as Dolly Parton, Tammy Wynette, and Minnie Pearl. The free exhibit opens at 9:00 A.M. daily.

For a change of pace, the theater also presents the Back to the '50s Rock-N-Roll show at 2:30 P.M. Monday through Saturday. The show's five-piece band and cast of vocalists bring the '50s back to life through hits like "Johnnie B. Goode" and "At the Hop." The two-hour presentation is a lot of fun and even gets audience members dancing in the aisles.

The theater is open from late March through the end of the year. Generally, evening shows are scheduled Monday through Saturday at 8:00 P.M. Tickets for both the Classic Country and Back to the '50s shows are $26.96 for ages 18 and older and $15.50 for ages 7 through 17. Ages 6 and younger are admitted free.

Comedy Barn Theater
2775 Parkway, Pigeon Forge
(865) 428-5222, (800) 295-2844
www.comedybarn.com
You can't miss this place when you're driving down the Parkway in Pigeon Forge. It literally is a huge, metal, barnlike structure that towers high above most of the buildings around it. And once you've located this 1,000-seat theater, the show is certainly worth stopping in for. Since it opened in 1994, it's become one of the most attended shows in the area. In part, that's probably because it's been one of the few theaters in the area that places an emphasis on comedy. But at the Comedy Barn, you also get magic and some good ol' country music in addition to clean, family-friendly humor, making it one of the more popular tickets in town.

The theater's rural motif is as prominent on the inside as it is on the exterior; the stage's backdrop is a barn facade, and performers enter and exit through two barn doors. And while there is a bit of a country flavor to the show, that "twang" is more of an accent to the show than a traditional lampooning of Southern stereotypes. Each evening's entertainment is staged by an ensemble cast of talent consisting of jugglers, fire eaters, ventriloquists, magicians, and, of course, stand-up comedians who have credits ranging from *Hee Haw* to *Evening at the Improv.* It's interesting to note that everyone in the cast (even the owners) gets directly involved in running other operations of the theater—everything from selling concessions to parking cars!

The show's lineup is staggered with segments of country and bluegrass music courtesy of the Comedy Barn All-Star Band and its gifted pickers. The host for each performance is Grandpa Duffy, an animatronic hillbilly character perched in the window of his old country cabin. On closer inspection, however, you realize that Duffy is actually playing a real banjo! His mechanical head and body are combined with the real hands and voice of one of the Comedy Barn's cast members to provide an interesting "manimatronic" experience.

The Comedy Barn is open weekends in January, four nights a week in February, and daily for the remainder of the year. They even do shows on Thanksgiving and Christmas Day. Shows start at 8:15 P.M., and during peak season, there are almost always 5:00 P.M. matinees on the bill as well. Tickets to the Comedy Barn are $22.25 for adults and $20.00 for senior citizens. Each child 11 and younger (per paid adult) gets in free.

Dollywood Celebrity Theater
1020 Dollywood Lane, Pigeon Forge
(865) 428-9488, (800) 365-5996
www.dollywood.com
Located just inside the front turnstiles of the Pigeon Forge theme park, this large theater is the site of Dollywood's annual Showcase of Stars celebrity concert series. Each year, about 18 guest artists perform live, one-day engagements at the theater; past entertainers include the Oak Ridge Boys, Lorrie Morgan, Sawyer Brown, the Charlie Daniels Band, and Chubby Checker.

Celebrity concerts take place Sundays at 2:00 and 7:00 P.M. during peak season. Those attending the 2:00 P.M. show must pay park admission in addition to the show's ticket price. Park admission is not required for the 7:00 P.M. show. Concert ticket prices range from about $20 to $26, depending on the act. For details about theme park admission prices and general park information, see our Dollywood chapter.

Dixie Stampede
3849 Parkway, Pigeon Forge
(865) 453-4400, (800) 356-1676
www.dixiestampede.com
Saddle up, pardners, and get ready for a stampede at this unique Pigeon Forge dinner show that's owned by Dollywood. For more than a decade, Dixie Stampede has been one of the top theater draws in the Smokies. Each performance is a multifaceted event that includes trick riding, horseback competitions, music, magic, comedy, and a full, multicourse meal.

The premise of the Dixie Stampede show is a friendly, Civil War–style rivalry; the audience is divided into "North" and "South" sections that "battle" each other during the evening through a series of horse riding contests and other competitions. Most of the contests are staged by Stampede cast members who are dressed in appropriate blue and gray uniforms. Down in the arena's large, oval-shaped performance area, they saddle up their steeds and go head-to-head in feats of horse riding speed, skill, and dexterity. There are contests involving direct participation by some audience members while others require group efforts from both sides as a whole. Overall, there's a lot of whooping, cheering, and foot stomping!

Outside the framework of the competition, there's plenty to see, including high-speed trick riding, large-scale magic illusions, and hilarious comedy. There are a few impressive visuals as well. At one point, a large stage is lowered from the ceiling revealing Southern belles and gentlemen decked out in period costumes.

There are also state-of-the-art lighting effects plus a massive, shimmering American flag that are revealed during the show's finale, which joins North and South in a unifying patriotic salute to America.

Dixie Stampede does everything on a large scale and, being a dinner attraction, provides a meal that is no exception to that rule. Dinner consists of a whole rotisserie chicken, a slice of barbecued pork loin, creamy vegetable soup, a biscuit, corn on the cob, potatoes, a hot apple turnover, and a beverage. Each course is served en masse during the show by the waitstaff, which is actually considered part of the Stampede cast and is also decked out in Civil War regalia. By the way, if you're finicky about table manners, you can check your etiquette at the door. There's no silverware at Dixie Stampede—everything's eaten by hand!

Dixie Stampede is open six days a week in March, and starting in April, the theater is open seven days a week through October. In November and December, Dixie presents its Christmas show four to seven days a week through the end of the year. The regular show time throughout the year is 6:00 P.M., but during peak season and many off-season weekends there are two shows daily, at 6:00 and 8:30 P.M. When there's a demand, they'll even do a third matinee show. Admissions to Dixie Stampede are $39.59 for adults and $20.89 for ages 4 through 11. Children ages 3 and younger are admitted free if they sit in a parent's lap and share their meal.

Gatlinburg

Sweet Fanny Adams Theatre
461 Parkway, Gatlinburg
(865) 436–4039, (877) 388–5784
www.sweetfannyadams.com
The Smokies' oldest music variety theater has celebrated more than 25 seasons, featuring shows six nights a week April through September, seven nights in Octo-

ber, and a holiday show on weekends in November and December. Tickets are $20.75 for anyone 12 or older, $18.56 for seniors 55 and older, and $6.50 for kids 11 and younger. (See the next Close-up in this chapter for more information.)

NIGHTLIFE

Most of the establishments included below sell alcohol, but you should know that each city has different ordinances when it comes to selling by the drink. See our Restaurants chapter or Area Overview for the specifics, but we'll run down the basics here as well. In Sevierville and outside any city's limits (in the county), only beer can be sold by the drink, and only in some restaurants. Pigeon Forge prohibits alcohol by the drink altogether while in Gatlinburg, you can purchase wine, liquor, and beer in most restaurants and bars.

Reel Theatres Movies on the Parkway
713 Winfield Dunn Parkway, Sevierville
(865) 453–9055
www.reel-theatres-sevier.com
If you want to catch a flick while you're in Sevier County, there's only one game in town. Fortunately, it's a pretty good game, offering popular, first-run box office attractions seven days a week on six screens.

In addition to comfortable seating, each auditorium is equipped with Dolby Surround Sound and Digital Theater Sound to enhance the audio portion of its movies. There is also a video arcade and, of course, a well-stocked concession stand featuring all the standard movie theater favorites.

Throughout the year, Movies on the Parkway generally presents one matinee and two evening shows on each screen. During summer, there may be as many as three matinees per day as well as midnight screenings, depending on the movie.

Admission to Reel Theatres Movies on the Parkway is $7.00 for ages 13 and older and $4.75 for children ages 4 through 12

Madness in the Heart of Gatlinburg

"Unique" hardly begins to describe an evening at Sweet Fanny Adams Theatre. It's totally different from any other type of entertainment you'll see in the Smokies (or most other places, for that matter). In fact, the theater bills itself as the only area alternative to country music shows, presenting a two-hour extravaganza full of musical comedy that literally brings tears to the eyes (happy tears, not sad ones).

Your experience starts even before you enter the theater; the building's facade is reminiscent of a theater from the Old West or an English music hall. On the inside, that turn-of-the-twentieth-century look still dominates. The auditorium seats fewer than 200 and the stage is small, but once the lights go down, the comedy is dished out in huge portions. The humor is broad, full of slapstick and downright silly, but it's also undeniably hilarious. And one of the great things about the shows at Sweet Fanny Adams Theatre is that they're enjoyable for all ages.

The first half of each evening consists of a short musical comedy. Since opening in 1977, owners Don and Pat MacPherson have written/directed/produced nearly 40 different shows for their theater (each season features two new shows that play on alternating nights of the week). The titles of the shows themselves are usually a big hint as to what you're in for. Productions from previous years have included *Not Quite Snow White, Lucifer McRotten Strikes Again,* and *Everything You Wanted to Know about Davy Crockett but Were Afraid to Ask.* Are you starting to get the picture?

Bringing these comedy gems to the boards nightly is the Great Victorian Amusement Company, the theater's troupe of performers that includes the MacPhersons and about five other thespians, some of whom have been Fanny Adams mainstays for years. By the way, if you ask the MacPhersons to tell you about the origins of the "Great Victorian Amusement Company" or "Sweet Fanny Adams," you'll undoubtedly hear some sort of colorful and entertaining tale. You can be sure that it's probably nothing close to the truth, but you'll have a better time if you accept their answers for what they are!

After the intermission ("knock before entering the restrooms," you'll be reminded), the show forges ahead with an old-fashioned sing-along and a vaudeville-style revue of music and comedy sketches. During the revue, you may be fortunate enough to catch them on a night when they're doing the "paper dance"; and although we won't give away any secrets here, we will tell you that the

as well as anyone age 60 and older. Children younger than 4 are admitted free but may be required to sit in a parent's lap during sellout situations. During bargain matinees (movies that begin before 6:00 P.M.), tickets are $5.00 each for all ages. You can reach the theater's information line at the number above and receive specific show times, information on coming attractions, and directions to the theater.

The cast of Sweet Fanny Adams Theatre produces musical comedy, belly laughs, and guffaws.
SWEET FANNY ADAMS THEATRE

sing-along is always special for one "lucky" member of the audience. From beginning to end, the audience is very much a part of the show, and don't worry—it's never in a threatening way. The intimate feel of the room plus the fact that the actors have little regard for "the fourth wall" make for a night of interactive fun that just can't be captured in most area theaters.

Sweet Fanny Adams Theatre is truly a family affair. Pat's parents, Betty and Paddy O'Doherty, are box office manager and technical director, respectively. In past seasons, the MacPhersons' son, Chris, has been a featured performer at the theater (in addition to being a clown with the Ringling Brothers Circus). Both Pat and Don have extensive backgrounds in theater, having worked at one time or another as singers, dancers, actors, and directors throughout the United States and Europe. They settled in Gatlinburg in the '70s for the dual purpose of raising their children and finding a place where they could develop and produce their original shows. After just one night at Sweet Fanny Adams Theatre, we think you'll agree that what they've developed over the past two decades is, indeed, very original and a Smoky Mountain treasure in its own right.

Triple C Dance Barn
2659 Newport Highway, Sevierville
(865) 429–3311
Pull on your boots, put on your hat, and do-si-do over to the Triple C Dance Barn,

the area's number one hot spot for country dancing since 1999. Whether you're partial to line dancing, square dancing, or country swing dancing, Triple C gives you the opportunity to strut your stuff four

Looking for a place to worship while you're on vacation? Each Sunday from May through November, the Louise Mandrell theater hosts a prayer and praise service at 8:15 A.M. It is open to the public, free of charge, and guests are encouraged to "come as they are." The nondenominational service is full of music and testimony from special guests. And most Sundays, your greeter will be none other than Louise Mandrell herself.

nights a week. On Tuesday and Thursday, you can take dance lessons or come in later in the evening to dance to music provided by the DJ. Friday night is Teen Night, when younger boot-scooters can have a good time in a family-friendly environment. The big night is Saturday, when the Triple C's house band takes the stage and provides live accompaniment for the evening's dancing.

Triple C Dance Barn really is a suitable place for all ages, especially considering that no alcohol is served and smoking is not allowed. Snacks and beverages are available at the food concession, and an interesting selection of Western dancewear and accessories are for sale in the gift shop. Admission is $5.00 per person, although children 12 and younger are admitted free when accompanied by a paying adult. The doors open at 7:00 P.M. and close when the masses allow.

Big Mama's Karaoke Cafe
10605 Chapman Highway, Seymour
(865) 609-0208
www.karaokecafe.com

Are you one of those people who likes to sing in the shower or in the car on the way to work? Don't keep your vocal talents to yourself! Haul yourself over to Big Mama's Karaoke Cafe in Seymour, about 10 miles northwest of Sevierville on Chapman Highway. That's where you can lend your voice to your favorite songs and be the singer you always knew you could be. At least in your own mind.

Part of the appeal of doing karaoke at Big Mama's is, no doubt, its simplicity. You select your favorite song from their catalogue of more than 8,000 titles, and when your turn comes up, you take the stage, grab the mic, and wail to your heart's content. Best of all, it doesn't matter whether you're a talented singer or not. About 15 people per hour take the stage, and once the action starts for the day, it continues nonstop with no intermission.

While you're watching the singers (or waiting to go onstage yourself), you can order from Big Mama's full menu of appetizers, sandwiches, and entrees. House specialties include their Big Mama Burger and the "Love Me Tender" chicken tenders. Beer is also served for those who need to steady their nerves before taking the stage.

Big Mama's Karaoke Cafe is open Wednesday and Thursday from 11:00 A.M. to 10:00 P.M., Friday and Saturday from 11:00 A.M. to midnight, and Sunday from 11:00 A.M. to 10:00 P.M. After 4:00 P.M., there is a $5.00 minimum food and/or beverage purchase.

If you can't get enough of being at Big Mama's Karaoke Cafe, you can take the fun home with you. They offer karaoke systems and related products for both sale and rental, right on the premises.

Rocky River Brewery & Grille
1444 Hurley Drive, Sevierville
(865) 908-3686

Nighttime entertainment is slowly but surely making its way into Sevierville, thanks to places like this. Rocky River Brewery & Grille is a restaurant/microbrewery/sports bar located on the Little Pigeon River at Governor's Crossing. You can learn about its dining and beermaking aspects in the Restaurants chapter.

If you're interested in getting together for brews and appetizers and maybe a televised ball game, check out the sports bar adjacent to the main restaurant. There is a large-screen TV and a number of video monitors strategically placed throughout the bar for game-day viewing. For amusement, the sports bar has several video games as well as pool tables and dart boards; pool tournaments are held on selected weeknights. Schedules vary throughout the year, but live entertainment is usually presented Tuesday through Saturday and includes live bands or karaoke; guest performers are usually from the country and rock 'n' roll genres. Of course, whatever you do at the sports bar, you can enjoy it with any of the distinctive beers created at Rocky River's own microbrewery.

Onyx Restaurant and Night Club
458 Parkway, Gatlinburg
(865) 436-6033

Dance the night away in Gatlinburg at this club located on the top level of Carousel Mall, offering terrific views of downtown with the Smoky Mountains in the background. A DJ plays dance tunes six nights a week, and the atmosphere is enhanced by laser lights and fog effects. Onyx also serves dinner until 1:00 A.M. There is no cover charge for those 21 and older, but there is a nominal cover charge for guests ages 18 to 20. Plenty of parking is available across the street in one of the city's parking garages.

Blaine's Grill & Bar
812 Parkway, Gatlinburg
(865) 430-1978
ww.blainesgrillandbar.com

Every night the tables are cleared from Blaine's main floor, and the DJ cranks out dance music from 10:00 P.M. to 1:00 A.M. Many of the tunes are contemporary while some are modernized dance mixes of older rock 'n' roll favorites. The clientele is mostly in the 20-something age range, but those 30- and 40-something folks who like to get out on the floor and shake their stuff to a loud, pounding dance beat will love Blaine's, too. The big nights to go are Friday and Saturday, although there is a $3.00 cover charge on those nights. Blaine's also hosts a big New Year's Eve gala every year. For one package price, guests get dinner, a bottle of champagne, party favors, and a midnight buffet. Of

course, a DJ is still on hand to crank out the dance tunes.

Blaine's is a full-service restaurant and bar (formerly Ronnie Milsaps' Keyboard Cafe) located on the corner of Parkway and Historic Nature Trail (formerly Airport Road). From the outside, the three-story building is reminiscent of a Bourbon Street facade with its upper-level porches and iron railings. Inside, the main bar, dining areas, and dance floor are on the second level. There is a smaller bar area with limited seating on the third level. Although it is a restaurant, Blaine's stops serving food at 9:00 P.M., which is when the dancing starts. As such, you must be 21 to enter after that time.

Smoky Mountain Brewery
1004 Parkway, Gatlinburg
(865) 436-4200
www.calhouns.com/smb/index.htm

This restaurant and microbrewery is located at Calhoun's Village near the south end of Gatlinburg's Parkway. The village itself is unique in that it offers visitors plenty of free parking. The brewery is easily found just a few buildings back from the Parkway.

Smoky Mountain Brewery provides entertainment six nights a week. Typically, you'll find karaoke Monday and Tuesday (Tuesday's one of the big nights) and live bands Thursday through Sunday. The bands present varied styles ranging from light rock to bluegrass. The shows run from around 9:30 P.M. to 12:30 A.M., and except for one or two weeks out of the year, there is no cover charge. You don't

---

ℹ️

Although most area theaters offer free admission to younger children, always be sure to ask if any stipulations go along with that discount. For example, some theaters request that small children sit in their parents' laps to be admitted free while others will admit only one child free per paying adult.

have to be 21 to enter, but naturally, you must be to consume alcohol.

The main dining room, full-service bar, and entertainment section are upstairs. The heavily raftered room provides a simple and casual tavern-style atmosphere. There is a large-screen television, which is the center of attention during televised sporting events (especially Tennessee Volunteer football games). Those ordering from the menu will find a hearty selection of subs, sandwiches, and calzones as well as the restaurant's specialty—pizza. You can enjoy your meal in the main dining area or on the glassed-in porch.

Downstairs is where you'll find the microbrewery. The menu features as many as 13 different beers, although at any given time, anywhere from six to nine of

the labels are being served. Four of the house brands are always on tap: Cherokee Red Ale, Mountain Light, Black Bear Ale, and Old Thunder Road. In addition to these there are several brewmaster's specials and seasonal selections to complement the overall selection.

The Fox & Parrot Tavern—A British Pub
1065 Glades Road, Gatlinburg
(865) 435-0677

The Fox & Parrot is based on the design of any English pub built since man began walking upright. The naturally comfortable log interior is festooned with the national flags of every country in the British Isles and their patron saints. They serve lunch and dinner daily, and although the food is more than enough reason to warrant a visit, the awesome part of the Fox & Parrot is the beer menu; they've got more than 60 brands of foreign and domestic beers and ales available bottled or on tap. Because of a strong local following, including the Thursday night darts league, the Fox & Parrot has evening hours: Monday through Thursday from 11:00 A.M. to 8:00 P.M., Friday and Saturday until 10:00 P.M., and Sunday from noon to 5:00 P.M.

Be sure to check area hotels and restaurants for money-saving coupons to area shows. You'll typically receive a $1.00 or $2.00 discount. Also, don't forget to pick up those free tourist-oriented magazines that are usually rife with coupons as well (see the Media chapter).

ATTRACTIONS

L et's start with a hypothetical question. How many go-kart tracks does one town need? What would you think—four, five . . . seven? In Pigeon Forge alone there are 10 individual go-kart track operations, many of which have two or three tracks apiece. The majority of them are located within 2 miles of each other along the Parkway. Add Sevierville's and Gatlinburg's go-kart establishments to the mix and you've created heaven on earth for the speedster wanna-be.

When it comes to Smoky Mountain attractions, however, go-karts are just one slice of a very large pie. In fact, just about any business you encounter along the Smokies Corridor that's not a hotel, a restaurant, or a shop is likely to be an attraction of some sort. From the Sevierville fringes all the way to the national park entrance, you'll come across a little of everything—from museums and historical sites to a lot of things that are just out-and-out fun, like haunted houses, professional baseball, and even indoor skydiving.

One of the main things to keep in mind is that these attractions rely heavily on marketing themselves as "family" activities—those that can be enjoyed by all ages. For the most part, this is the case. Anyone who's ever drawn back the blade at a miniature golf course knows that the challenge of knocking a little colored ball into a dragon's mouth has universal appeal. Other attractions like museums and water parks also attract a wide age range.

But there are dividing lines when it comes to classifying activities according to their age appropriateness, which is why we've shared coverage of "what to do" between this chapter and Kidstuff. Between the two, you'll learn about most everything even loosely labeled as an attraction in the Smokies.

By the way, if you're looking for our coverage of Dollywood theme park, you won't find it in this chapter. Dollywood is such an expansive subject that we devoted a separate chapter to it. There, you'll learn just about anything you might want to know about Tennessee's most visited theme park.

What to Expect at Amusement Centers

Along the way, we've given many places write-ups in both Attractions and Kidstuff, and we've done a lot of cross-referencing, especially when it comes to what we call "amusement centers." These are the places that usually have some combination of go-kart racing, miniature golf, bumper boats, video arcades, and other pay-to-play games and amusements. It's not unusual to find things just for younger children side-by-side with activities just for the big people. In such cases, we've split our coverage. In this chapter we focus more on activities like the amusement centers' faster go-kart tracks and more "daredevilish" rides. In Kidstuff we emphasize the things in which younger children can participate, like miniature golf, bumper cars, and junior go-kart tracks. But Kidstuff has information for grown-up fun as well. After all, why should the kids have all the fun?

There are many universals you'll encounter from one amusement center to the next. First, think "safety." You play at your own risk on things like bungee towers and go-kart tracks; management prohibits deliberately bumping go-karts into each other and against track guardrails. Needless to say, pregnant women and people with heart and back conditions shouldn't participate in these activities.

Second, you can count on most go-kart rides lasting anywhere from three to six minutes. We've avoided comparing the speeds of the go-karts from one business to the next. If you were to ask each track manager who has the fastest karts in town, you'd hear an unqualified "We do!" from every one. Also, you'll notice that several go-kart tracks are referred to as "slick tracks." This means that the driving surface is smoother than normal surfaces. Speeds are a little slower, but drivers have fun spinning their wheels on the turns!

Finally, most amusement centers are open year-round. In season, you can count on businesses being open seven days a week from around 9:00 or 10:00 A.M. to as late as midnight or 1:00 A.M. in some cases; at night, facilities are appropriately lit. As for the off-season, you'll find that several establishments cut back to week-ends only or some other limited schedule. However, most of the managers with whom we spoke weren't willing to commit to definite autumn and winter schedules. Often, they choose to improvise and let factors such as the weather and holiday-related visitation determine when they're open. Your best bet for weekly and daily schedules in the off-season is to call ahead.

General Notes about Attractions

Most Smoky Mountain attractions provide adequate free parking, especially those in Sevierville and Pigeon Forge. In Gatlin-burg, there are places that don't have parking. Not to worry: In such cases, you can pay to park in a city lot or garage, or you can access your destination on foot or by trolley.

Except for a few spots that are off the main drag, we're presenting our attractions in the order they're found traveling south from Interstate 40's exit 407 to the national park entrance. Unless otherwise indicated, all prices include sales tax.

Whether you're young or young at heart, you'll surely find something to see, hear, drive, paddle, or jump off that will make your visit to the Smokies a little more memorable. Now it's time to go out and play!

SEVIERVILLE

Tennessee Smokies Baseball
3450 Line Drive, Kodak
(865) 637-9494, (888) 978-2288
www.smokiesbaseball.com
Since 2000, this AA minor league affiliate of the St. Louis Cardinals has played ball at Smokies Park in Sevierville, located just off I-40 at exit 407.

The facility features 6,000 fixed seats, grass berm seating for an additional 2,000 spectators on the hillside beyond the outfield, 18 private suites, and 2 patio areas. Ample restrooms and concession areas open directly onto the concourse that runs above and behind the stadium seating, ensuring that you don't miss any of the action when you have to leave your seat. There is a restaurant inside the sta-dium (overlooking the field) that's open year-round (see our Restaurants chapter), and visitors can also stop by an area wel-come center located on the 25-acre site.

The Southern League season runs from April through early September, and the Smokies play more than half of their 140 games at home. Special promotional nights are scheduled during home stands, and lots of prizes are given away during the games themselves. Between innings, there are usually contest events for kids taking place on the field. You might see the young ones playing musical chairs, throwing water balloons, or racing the Smokies mascot around the bases.

In 1999 the Smokies announced they would no longer play at Knoxville's Bill Meyer Stadium, the city's home of minor league baseball since the mid-1950s. After a strong show of support from Sevier County in terms of season ticket sales as well as an attractive bid on a new facility, the franchise made the decision to make the 18-mile move closer to the mountains.

Attendance during the team's first season in Sevierville was a vast improvement over previous years. More than a quarter-million fans passed through the turnstiles at Smokies Park in 2000, and the team received the Southern League Award of Excellence for posting a 114 percent increase in attendance compared to the 1999 season at Bill Meyer Stadium.

Ticket prices range from $5.00 to $9.00; there is also a $4.00 charge for on-site parking. Season tickets are available in different packages.

Scenic Helicopter Tours
1949 Winfield Dunn Parkway, Sevierville
(865) 453-6342
www.scenichelicopters.com
One of the most memorable ways to experience Smoky Mountain views is from high up in the air. This tour operator with more than 25 years' experience will take you on local helicopter flights that cover different areas between Douglas Lake and Pigeon Forge. These flights range from short introductory flights for $10 per person to 24-mile flights over the Pigeon Forge foothills for $45 per person. There are longer scenic mountain flights going as far as Gatlinburg and Wears Valley, ranging from 28 to 80 miles and costing between $65 and $210 per person. Riders on scenic flights are given headsets and hear in-flight narration. With both the local and the scenic flights, the exact flight times are flexible. If you're in town to get married, you might also consider Scenic's aerial weddings and honeymoon flights (inspires one's curiosity, doesn't it?).

Scenic Helicopter Tours is open year-round, but flights only run when weather permits. Children younger than two fly free, and the company accepts MasterCard, Visa, and American Express.

Great Smoky Mountain Helicopters
1101 Winfield Dunn Parkway, Sevierville
(865) 429-2426
This helicopter tour company flies a num-ber of local routes, starting with an introductory flight for $10 per person. There are a number of longer tours that range as far as flights over Dollywood that cover 24 miles and cost $55 per person. Smoky Mountain Helicopters also offers custom flights that provide more scenic mountain viewing. These charter flights cost a flat $700 for up to six people and are at least one hour in duration. MasterCard and Visa are accepted.

Great Smoky Mountain Helicopters is open seven days a week year-round, weather permitting. Tours begin at 9:00 A.M. in season and at 10:00 A.M. between Labor Day and Easter; tours end at sunset throughout the year.

Floyd Garrett's Muscle Car Museum
320 Winfield Dunn Parkway, Sevierville
(865) 908-0882
www.musclecarmuseum.com
If you're a "gear head," you'll feel like a kid in a candy store at this showplace of American custom and vintage performance cars. Open since the spring of 1996, the museum houses a collection of 90-plus "muscle cars" and occupies a massive 35,750 square feet of floor space. Most of the vehicles on display are owned by Floyd Garrett, and each has been reconditioned to virtual perfection. Automotive fans have enjoyed up-close inspections of cars like NASCAR star Richard Petty's 1977 STP Monte Carlo as well as speedsters driven by racers Bobby Allison and Dale Earnhardt. The collection is always evolving, so the lineup of cars may change from visit to visit. Visitors can also view walls lined with racing memorabilia, check out a display of rare racing engines, and browse the gift shop, which is stocked full of souvenirs for the NASCAR junkie. Floyd Garrett's Muscle Car Museum is open seven days a week throughout the year, except for Thanksgiving and Christmas. Admission is $8.95 for adults and $3.00 for children 8 through 12; children younger than 8 are admitted free. Prices do not include sales tax. Normal operating hours are 9:00 A.M. to 6:00 P.M. daily.

Sevier County Courthouse
Court Avenue, Sevierville
No general phone

After the Great Smoky Mountains, the towering 75-foot spire of this century-old structure is usually the second thing that grabs your attention when driving into the city of Sevierville. One of the most recognized and photographed courthouses in Tennessee, the building maintains a stately presence in an otherwise rapidly developing tourist market. In 1976 it became the first Tennessee courthouse to be placed on the National Register of Historic Places. The exterior is predominantly red brick with a foundation of large, locally quarried limestone blocks. The architecture is Victorian and features an imposing clock tower surrounded by a number of smaller domed structures on the rooftop. The clock is the same one that was installed in 1896 and to this day still faithfully chimes the hour and half-hour.

The present structure is the fifth to serve as county courthouse and was completed in 1896 at a total cost of just over $21,000. In 1971, plans to do away with the aging building were scrapped in favor of a complete renovation, which included gutting virtually all of the wood used in its interior. This was done to minimize the occurrence of fires that had devastated an earlier Sevier County courthouse. In the years that followed, two annexes were added to the original building—fortunately, these additions were made with considerations for both modern practicality as well as architectural compatibility.

Another popular subject for sightseers' cameras is the statue of Dolly Parton located on the east lawn of the courthouse. Sculpted by noted local artist Jim Gray, the life-size, cast bronze figure rests on a large rock base and depicts Sevier County's most famous offspring in her younger years, sitting with a guitar in her arms and a smile on her face. Because most of the courthouse's noteworthy attributes can be seen from the outside, a worthwhile visit there can be made any time of day, even if all you do is pull your car up to the curb and put your camera into action.

Sevier County Heritage Museum
167 East Bruce Street, Sevierville
(865) 453-4058
www.korrnet.org/schm

Take a trip back through time and see cherished relics and artifacts that tell the story of Sevier County's rich history. Inside, visitors can take a chronological tour that offers glimpses into the lives and times of the people who settled and developed the area. From the tools and arrowheads of early Indian inhabitants to an authentic telephone operator's switchboard of the mid-1900s, the museum's multiple displays and tributes bring treasured legends and memories to life.

All aspects of the lives of area pioneers and settlers are explored. Looking over preserved treasures like spinning wheels, butter churns, pantaloons, and corn shellers allows the visitor to conjure up images of a vanished era. See materials used in the construction of 18th- and 19th-century homes and marvel at the handcraftsmanship of muzzle-loading flintlock rifles. Other displays pay homage to Sevier Countians who served their country on the battlefield in the Civil War and World War II. Many of the items on hand, including photographs and newspapers, were donated by residents whose families had helped shape the events of their day. Those who wish to delve deeper into the past can peruse an extensive catalog of newsletters published by the Smoky Mountain Historical Society or purchase one of many different books on various facets of local history.

Located in downtown Sevierville, the building in which the museum is housed is historically significant itself. It was erected in 1940 and for years served as the city's post office. The museum originally opened in the summer of 1995 in conjunction with Tennessee's bicentennial celebration. Although admission is free, the museum also welcomes private donations. Its hours of operation are Monday, Tuesday, Thursday, and Friday from noon to 5:00 P.M. and Saturday from noon to 3:00 P.M. You can park for free anywhere along Bruce Street.

Tennessee Museum of Aviation
Tennessee Aviation Hall of Fame
**135 Air Museum Way, Sevierville
(865) 908-0171, (866) 286-8738
www.tnairmuseum.com**

Aviation and history fans alike will enjoy this 50,000-square-foot museum and hangar located near the Gatlinburg–Pigeon Forge Airport in Sevierville (yes, Sevierville). The Tennessee Museum of Aviation, which opened in December 2000, is home to a host of authentic memorabilia that tells the story of powered flight. Items such as photos, scale models, military flight suits, and aircraft paraphernalia bring the history of aviation to life through a series of professionally designed displays.

Although several of the sections showcase the role that aircraft played during times of war, one area taps more into the museum's theme, detailing the contributions that Tennesseans have made to aviation. Exhibits such as a large jet aircraft engine, a hands-on flight simulator, and a wall-size time line of national and statewide aviation milestones are captivating enough to draw in younger patrons.

The museum's main attraction, however, is the 10,000-square-foot Warbirds Hangar, where as many as 20 active, flying vintage aircraft are displayed on a rotating basis. If you visit at the right time, you might even be fortunate enough to watch the museum's owner, Neal Melton, as he takes one of the birds up for a fly-by.

The facility is also home to the Tennessee Aviation Hall of Fame, which celebrates the men and women from the Volunteer State who have made significant contributions to flying. In 2002 the museum inducted its inaugural slate of honorees, including Evelyn Bryan Johnson, a 92-year-old Morristown, Tennessee, resident who has racked up more flying time than any living human and still takes to the skies as a flight instructor. Please, no

jokes about her leaving her turn signal on.

The Tennessee Museum of Aviation and Hall of Fame are open year-round, except for Thanksgiving and Christmas days. Admission is $6.75 for ages 6 through 12, $9.75 for ages 60 and older, and $12.75 for those 13 and older. Veterans and military personnel pay $5.00.

Smoky Mountain Deer Farm and
Exotic Petting Zoo
**478 Happy Hollow Lane, Sevierville
(865) 428-3337
www.deerfarmzoo.com**

Visitors have been flocking to the Deer Farm and Petting Zoo for more than a decade to feed and get face-to-face (and often hand-to-mouth) with a live menagerie that includes camels and zebras, kangaroos and llamas, ferrets and reindeer. Although more than 70 percent of its visitors are adults, we've still included our detailed profile of the Deer Farm and Exotic Petting Zoo as a Close-up in the Kidstuff chapter. We felt that where children were concerned, this Smoky Mountain attraction is a great alternative to arcades and miniature golf courses. But as we mentioned, adults certainly love it too!

Admission to the Deer Farm and Exotic Petting Zoo is $7.50 for ages 13 and older and $4.00 for ages 3 to 12. Children ages 2 and younger are admitted for a shiny, new penny. Prices do not include sales tax. Discounted rates are available for groups of 15 or more. To feed the animals, use only the special feed provided, which comes in cups ranging from 12 ounces ($1.50) to 32 ounces ($3.50).

The facility is open year-round, seven days a week except for Thanksgiving and Christmas. Daily hours are from 10:00 A.M. to 5:30 P.M. Throughout the year, ticket sales stop one hour before closing. It's best to call ahead to verify hours during periods of bad weather. Owners Greg and Lynn Hoisington also operate Deer Farm Riding Stables, which is located on the same property. See our chapter on Parks and Recreation for more information on horseback riding opportunities.

Forbidden Caverns
455 Blowing Cave Road, Sevierville
(865) 453-5972
www.forbiddencavern.com

Although you won't exactly journey all the way to the center of the earth, you'll get a good feel for what it might be like in this large underground cave located approximately 20 miles east of downtown Sevierville. Stalactites, stalagmites, towering chimneys, and grottoes are among the many natural formations to be seen on your adventure. Interestingly, the natural temperature inside the caverns remains at a steady 58 degrees year-round. Enhanced by special lighting effects and a stereophonic sound presentation, your guided, 55-minute tour is chock full of memorable sights and will take you a half-mile into the heart of English Mountain. The trails are well lighted, and handrails have been provided where necessary. In addition to the rock structures, you'll also see a running stream that's believed to flow from a lake deep within the mountain. While you're there, you'll also learn about the people who carved out the cavern's colorful history, from the Eastern Woodland Indians who used the cave as shelter to the moonshiners of the 1920s and 1930s.

Forbidden Caverns' season starts April 1 and continues seven days a week through November 30. It is also open December 26 through January 1. Normal business hours are 10:00 A.M. to 6:00 P.M. Admission prices are $12.00 for adults and $6.00 for children ages 5 through 12. Souvenirs and refreshments are available, and there is free parking for cars and buses.

The Mine
1430 Hurley Drive, Sevierville
(865) 774-2031, (800) 345-6193
www.pigeonrivermine.com

Have you ever wanted to prospect for gems the way the old-timers did? Now you've got your chance! At the Mine, you can sift through bags of gem-rich North Carolina soil in search of naturally occurring precious stones. Located at Governor's Crossing, this 13,000-square-foot attraction is a newer, larger version of the now defunct Pigeon Forge Mine, a longtime fixture on that city's Parkway.

The activity is unique. You buy a bag of dirt and dump it into the prospector's sluice trough, located outside the main building under an open-air structure. You then sift the dirt away in the current of water. Resident miner Gem Dandy (hardy, har, har) is usually on hand to offer assistance until you get the hang of it. Any precious stones that happen to remain are yours to keep.

The dirt sold at the Mine comes from the gem-rich soil of North Carolina and costs $5.00 for one bag or $9.00 for two bags. They guarantee you'll find at least one stone in each bag; if not, you get another bag free. Among the precious and semiprecious stones that you might discover are rubies, sapphires, emeralds, topaz, amethyst, and garnet.

Once you've mined your gem(s), your options vary. First they'll give you a free appraisal in their "assay office." From there, you can either simply pocket the uncut gem and go home, or you can get quotes on cutting and mounting your stone, which does cost extra—sometimes substantially extra. You can even watch as the folks at the Mine cut gems and manufacture gold and silver jewelry settings on the premises. In most cases, you'll receive same-day service.

If you really want to be hands-on, you can design your own ring or join the Mine's Gem Cutters Club. For a one-time fee of $75, you get approximately four hours of one-on-one instruction from a professional gemologist, who will show you how to cut your own stone. Members also receive 10 percent discounts on merchandise on subsequent visits.

For those who aren't interested in prospecting at all, the Mine has cases full of finished jewelry pieces for sale (cha-ching) as well as novelty and gift items made from various gems and stones. Kids will like the cool rock and gem shop and the Mineral Museum. In fact, the entire main building is essentially a museum itself, telling the history of the mining industry and displaying many of the antiquities associated with the business.

Rainforest Adventures
NASCAR Drive, Sevierville
(865) 428-4091
www.rfadventures.com

This museum of reptiles and amphibians, located behind Governor's Palace Theatre at Sevierville's Governor's Crossing development, slithered into the Smokies in 2001. Throughout the facility's 15,000 square feet of exhibit space are snakes like cobras, mambas, pythons, and boa constrictors (sorry, Indiana Jones) as well as other interesting species like lizards, tarantulas, and scorpions. Habitats are designed to replicate each animal's natural surroundings and to create the feel of an Amazon rain forest. Live shows and demonstrations are scheduled every two hours throughout the day. Admission prices are $11.99 for adults, $9.99 for those over 55, and $6.99 for children ages 3 to 12. Prices do not include sales tax. Daily hours are 9:00 A.M. to 6:00 P.M. mid-August through mid-May and 9:00 A.M. to 8:00 P.M. during peak season (mid-May through mid-August).

NASCAR SpeedPark
1545 Parkway, Sevierville
(865) 908-5500
www.NASCARSpeedPark.com

Ladies and gentlemen—start your engines! With eight tracks spread out over 25 acres, NASCAR SpeedPark packs a lot of go-kart fun for speedsters young and old. The $15-million theme park opened in 1999, making it the county's third-largest attraction (after Dollywood and Ober Gatlinburg).

The tracks are all different and offer something for every driving preference and skill level. At one end of the spectrum is the Baby Bristol track for drivers who are at least 3 feet 4 inches tall. The small, single-loop circuit is just right for youngsters. At the other extreme is the quarter-mile Smoky Mountain Speedway track, which features ⅝-scale cars that go quite

Many of the prices you'll find quoted for area attractions don't include sales tax. For your information, state and local sales taxes combined are a whopping 9.5 percent in Gatlinburg and Pigeon Forge and 9.75 percent in Sevierville.

a bit faster than your average go-kart. You must be at least 5 feet 4 inches tall to drive on this track.

In between are other courses—the Qualifier, Young Champions, Slidewayz, the Intimidator, and the Competitor—that range from basic oval shapes to multiple-turn surfaces. Minimum height requirements for these tracks range from 3 feet 8 inches tall for the Qualifier to 5 feet 2 inches for the Competitor. The Family 500 track has double-seat karts so that adults and children can burn rubber together. Drivers must be at least 5 feet tall, and passengers must be at least 3 feet 6 inches tall.

If you're the competitive type, you'll probably enjoy NASCAR SpeedPark's timing and scoring system that measures lap times of each car down to thousandths of a second. The system is similar to the one used by NASCAR in its Nextel Cup, Busch Grand National, and Craftsman Truck series.

The number of tickets required to drive on the tracks ranges from three tickets for the Baby Bristol track to seven tickets for most of the bigger tracks. The quarter-mile Smoky Mountain Speedway takes 20 tickets. Tickets can be purchased at several locations throughout the park. Individual tickets sell for $1.00 each, or you can purchase one of several packages that offer larger numbers of tickets at discounted prices. Booklets come in denominations of up to 150 tickets. In addition to track admissions, tickets can also be used at SpeedPark's concessions areas.

One-day ride passes are also available. The Mini-Cup pass entitles any child 12 and younger to ride on any track where height requirements are met. The price is

$14.95. The Busch Series pass, $24.95, is available for those ages 13 and older and is good for every track except the Smoky Mountain Speedway. However, a $15.00 upgrade will get you two rides on that 0.25-mile track, provided you are at least 5 feet 4 inches tall and have a valid driver's license. SpeedPark's season pass costs $59.95 and entitles you to a Busch Series wristband every time you visit. But even with a season pass you must still pay an extra $15.00 and have a license to go screaming around the Smoky Mountain Speedway.

As a licensed activity of NASCAR, this attraction has a lot in store for fans of one of the fastest-growing spectator sports in the country. All 240 of the park's downsize race cars are custom-designed and built. Five actual NASCAR show vehicles are on display throughout the property as are more than 100 items of NASCAR memorabilia and hundreds of photos of NASCAR events and stars. Visits from more NASCAR drivers coincide with special events throughout the year, including each August, when the attraction hosts Sevierville's Food City Family Race Night event (see our Festivals and Annual Events chapter). Drivers appearing in 2002 included Tony Stewart, Rusty Wallace, and Dale Jarrett.

There's plenty to be found inside the main building, including the 28,000-square-foot Speed Dome arcade, featuring more than 60 racing games and driving simulators. You'll also find the Pit Stop Grill and souvenir shops full of SpeedPark memorabilia and apparel. All outdoor amusements include bumper boats, a climbing wall, and a miniature golf course.

NASCAR SpeedPark is open year-round. In summer, daily hours are from 10:00 A.M. until at least 10:00 P.M.; they may stay open until midnight if the masses allow. Once tourist visitation starts to slow down in Sevier County after August 1, the park is open from 11:00 A.M. to 8:00 P.M.

PIGEON FORGE

Mountain Valley Vineyards
2174 Parkway, Pigeon Forge
(865) 453-6334

This Pigeon Forge wine maker provides free guided and self-guided tours of its operation. From the grape-crushing machine to the massive steel fermenting tanks to the automated bottler, visitors can get a firsthand glimpse at a process that has produced national award-winning vintages. Those interested in tasting the finished product can sample, at no charge, any of Mountain Valley's 14 labels at their tasting bar.

Mountain Valley Vineyards is one of only 17 wineries in the state of Tennessee and primarily uses grapes from regional vineyards. Seven of the vineyards are located within a 60-mile radius of the winery itself. Because 85 percent of the grapes used are grown in-state, Tennessee agricultural laws allow Mountain Valley Vineyards to market its product in a city that otherwise is not permitted to sell wine. Forty different types of grapes and a variety of other fruits such as raspberries, blackberries, and strawberries are put through a fermenting process that can take anywhere from one to five years. The result: a menu of dry, semisweet, and dessert wines that has stood head to head with some of America's best. Mountain Valley Vineyards is open 365 days a year.

The Track
2575 Parkway, Pigeon Forge
(865) 453-4777
www.funatthetrack.com

Before you get behind the wheel or do anything else at this sprawling family amusement center, you'll need to buy tickets. Individual tickets are $2.50 each, or you can purchase discounted bundles, ranging from six tickets for $14.00 to 48 for $90.00. Also, before you head out to play you might grab one of the Track's handy maps that will help you navigate the many different areas, including the concessions facility, restrooms, and the arcade.

Although there's a lot to take on at the Track, the focus is on go-kart racing. There are two twisty, curvy, outdoor tracks on-site. The first, simply called the Track, utilizes one- and two-seat karts. One-seaters cost two tickets, and solo drivers must be at least 4 feet 6 inches tall. For two-seaters, drivers with passengers pay two tickets, and the driver must be at least 16 years old. Passengers in two-seaters must be at least 3 feet tall. Those between 3 feet and 4 feet 6 inches tall ride for free while passengers taller than 4 feet 6 inches must pay two tickets extra.

The other outdoor track, the Wild Woody, is a multitiered wooden track that goes through several humps and corkscrew twists. You must be at least 4 feet 10 inches tall to drive a single go-kart on the Wild Woody, which costs three tickets. Drivers with passengers pay three tickets, and the driver must be at least 16 years old. Two-seater passengers on the Wild Woody must be at least 3 feet tall. If you're between 3 feet and 4 feet 10 inches tall, you ride along for free. If you're more than 4 feet 10 inches tall, you pay an extra three tickets.

If you're in search of an even bigger adrenaline rush, fork over the six tickets required to bungee-jump from the Track's 60-foot tower. No experience is necessary. See Kidstuff for more information about other amusements the Track has to offer.

Elvis Museum
2638 Parkway, Pigeon Forge
(865) 428-2001
Elvis may have left the building, but he sure left a lot of stuff behind! Get an up-close peek at the largest privately owned collection of Elvis Presley memorabilia found outside the walls of Graceland—everything from clothes to cars, guns to guitars. The sounds of Elvis's music fills the air as you approach the front doors. Inside, you'll see plenty of authentic personal effects that belonged to the King, including stage costumes, backstage notes, sports gear, gifts from fans, jewelry, and sunglasses. There are several larger

If you're looking for a good deal on go-kart racing, try visiting the amusement centers before noon, when the majority of the tracks have some kind of two-for-one deal going. Plus, showing up in the morning is a good way to beat the intense heat of those Tennessee summers.

items in the collection as well, like the last limousine owned by Presley and living-room furniture from his Hollywood home. For those interested in adding to their own collection of Elvis trinkets, there is a souvenir shop on-site, carrying a healthy selection of music, videos, books, and other assorted knickknacks. In operation since 1982, Elvis Museum is open all year except for Thanksgiving and Christmas. In-season business hours (May through August and October) are 9:00 A.M. to 9:00 P.M.; off-season hours are 10:00 A.M. to 6:00 P.M. Admission prices are $12.99 for adults, $9.99 for any student older than 12, $6.99 for ages 6 to 12, and free for children younger than 6. Prices do not include sales tax.

Star Tracks
2757 Parkway, Pigeon Forge
(865) 908-1097
Star Tracks' lone Family Slick Track is open to drivers 4 feet 8 inches and taller. Admission is $7.00 per ride, or you can get three rides for $18.00 or 10 rides for $50.00 after noon. Two-seater karts cost $10.00 per ride, and drivers must be at least 16 years old.

Laserport
2782 Parkway, Pigeon Forge
(865) 453-0400
See our Kidstuff chapter for details on all the indoor laser tag fun that awaits you here. If you're in search of go-kart action, Laserport has an outdoor, single-loop track that costs $4.75 per ride or $12.00 for three rides. Drivers must be at least 4 feet 6 inches tall. Drivers of two-seat karts ($5.75 per ride) must be at least 16 years old.

Rockin' Raceway
2839 Parkway, Pigeon Forge
(865) 428-3392
This amusement center's Pro Track costs
$6.00, and drivers must be at least 14
years old and 4 feet 6 inches tall.

Rockin' Raceway offers more than go-
kart racing, however. The Hawk takes up
to 24 passengers at a time on a potentially nauseating pendulum ride that sends
them in complete multiple loops. The
Hawk costs $5.00 and requires that riders
be at least 4 feet tall. The Tornado takes
passengers on a dizzying, spinning ride
for $3.00. Inside the main building, you'll
find the SR2V simulator, in which "passengers" take a virtual high-speed trip around
a race course for only $3.00 per person.

Fast Tracks
2879 Parkway, Pigeon Forge
(865) 428-1988
Two of the three outdoor go-kart tracks at
this multifaceted family entertainment
center are designed for older kids and
adults (refer to Kidstuff for details about
the kids' track). On the multicurved Pro
Car Track, you must be at least 10 years
old and 4 feet 6 inches tall to drive alone.
To take a passenger, you must be at least
16, and your passenger must be at least 3
feet tall and 3 to 9 years old. The Pro Cars
cost $6.00 per ride, and passengers cost
$4.00 extra. On Fast Tracks' latest addi-
tion, the elevated track ($7.00 per ride),
you must be at least 5 feet 8 inches tall to
drive alone. Two-seaters cost $10.00 and
require at least a 16-year-old behind the
wheel. With both the Pro Cars and the
elevated track, you can buy four rides for
$20.00. Eleven bucks will get you a
combo ticket, entitling you to one Pro Car
ride and one ride on the elevated track.

For the more adventurous, there's the
Ejection Seat, a "reverse bungee" ride that
flings riders rapidly skyward to a height of
approximately 100 feet, followed by several up-and-down bounces on the springy
cords. The Ejection Seat costs $20.00 for
one person or $30.00 for two. Also look
for the Sky Scraper, a large pendulum-like

contraption that whirls occupants around
in vertical loops. This ride costs $20.00
per person or $30.00 per duo. Other Fast
Tracks offerings include a trampoline jump
and the VR Voyager (a simulator ride),
both of which cost $5.00 per person.

Adventure Raceway
2945 Parkway, Pigeon Forge
(865) 428-2971
Adventure Raceway features one outdoor
track—another of the many wooden go-
kart tracks that sprang up on the Parkway
in 1999. The curvy, multilevel wooden section was added to the existing figure-
eight, ground-level track. The cost is $7.00
per ride, and drivers must be at least 4
feet 8 inches tall. Children who are more
than 3 years old but who are still under
the minimum height requirement may ride
free as passengers on the go-karts. See
Kidstuff for more information about
Adventure Raceway and its sister attraction, Adventure Golf.

Smoky Mountain Car Museum
2970 Parkway, Pigeon Forge
(865) 453-3433
Since 1956, this showplace of rare and vintage cars has offered self-guided tours
through the history of the automobile. The
collection of more than 30 cars and trucks
features such notable vehicles as the silver
Aston-Martin driven by James Bond in the
films *Goldfinger* and *Thunderball*, Al
Capone's bulletproof Cadillac, Elvis Presley's 1971 Mercedes Benz, and the "Silver
Dollar" car owned by Hank Williams Jr. A
number of classic antiques are on display
as well: a 1930 Duesenberg, a 1909 Hup-
mobile, and a 1915 Ford Model T, just to
mention a few. All of the cars on display
have been reconditioned and are in running order.

What makes this museum truly unique
is that it's much more than just a "car
museum." Most of the wall space and virtually every spare nook and cranny are
packed with hoards of interesting
antiques and memorabilia. Many of the
relics are, of course, automobile-related:

newspaper clippings, photographs, model cars, antique gas pumps, and mechanic's tools. You'll also see items that would seem equally at home in any antique mall: old manual typewriters, nickelodeons, gumball machines, and even a display of different types of barbed wire! For the souvenir hunter, there is a gift shop on the premises, and auto enthusiasts are sure to find something to their liking in the museum's assortment of collectible books and magazines.

Admission to Smoky Mountain Car Museum is a reasonable $7.50 for adults and $2.00 for children ages 3 through 10. Children younger than 3 are admitted for free. The owners prefer to remain non-committal about their annual opening and closing dates, describing their season as running from "early spring through late fall." They also recommend calling ahead for specific hours of operation, although the museum generally is open from mid-morning to early evening.

Flyaway
3106 Parkway, Pigeon Forge
(865) 453-7777
www.bodyflight.net/flyaway
Have you ever wanted to go skydiving but chickened out because of your fears of heights and unopened parachutes? Now you have no more excuses. Flyaway is one of only two indoor skydiving simulation facilities in the United States (the other is in Las Vegas). It provides novices and seasoned skydivers alike the opportunity to experience the sensation of high-speed freefall in a safe, indoor environment. First-timers start off with a half-hour training session in which safety and body positioning techniques are discussed. After approximately 20 minutes of equipment preparation (flight suit and protective gear are provided), you're ready to soar in Flyaway's 21-foot-tall wind tunnel. A large airplane propeller, located under the mesh wire floor, generates wind speeds of up to 115 miles per hour and creates a column of air on which participants can learn the fundamentals and intricacies of free-fall

flight. Five "divers" enter the padded tunnel simultaneously and divide 15 minutes of flight time between them.

Flyaway is open all year but has limited hours during the off-season. They recommend calling in advance for a current schedule. Flights run on the hour and half-hour. The cost of the training and first flight (three minutes of personal air time) is $24.95, but you can tack on an additional flight for 15 bucks more. Spectators pay $2.00 each to watch the "dive" sessions. Group rates (11 or more), coaching packages, and five-ticket books are available. There is an additional cost if you would like a video of your adventure.

Participants at Flyaway are required to be in good physical condition and weigh at least 40 pounds. Maximum weight allowances are 220 pounds for those under 6 feet tall and 230 pounds for those over 6 feet. Children younger than 18 must be accompanied by a parent or guardian. Casual clothing with socks and sneakers is suggested.

Smoky Mountain Speedpark
3275 Parkway, Pigeon Forge
(865) 429-4639
This Parkway amusement operation has two single-loop go-kart tracks for drivers ages 12 and older (no height restrictions). On the original track, one-seat karts cost $6.00 per ride or five rides for $25.00; two-seaters cost $10.00. Speedpark's covered slick track costs $5.00 per person. For those of you who get your kicks in the air, look for the Sky Scraper. Riders are strapped into a cage that is swung over and over like a pendulum in 360-degree loops by a large mechanical arm. You must be at least 3 feet 6 inches tall (and slightly insane) to ride. The cost is $30 per person.

Bungee lovers have a choice of which direction to hurl themselves (and, possibly, their lunches). Those who prefer the trip down can leap off the regular bungee tower, while those who prefer high positive Gs can strap into the Sling Shot, a "reverse bungee" ride that flings passengers skyward before they start bouncing. Both bungee experiences cost $20 for one trip or $30 for two.

Other Speedpark activities include a rock-climbing wall, a mechanical bull, a multiaxis ride, and a trampoline jump, each of which costs $5.00.

Carbo's Police Museum
3311 Parkway, Pigeon Forge
(865) 453-1358
Calling all cars! Calling all cars! Be on the lookout for one of the most impressive private collections of police memorabilia in the nation. This Pigeon Forge attraction, which opened in 1976, is home to a 5,000-plus piece showcase of authentic police items, including guns, badges, uniforms, and handcuffs (just to name a few) from police departments all over the United States and around the world. Most of the items are displayed in glass cases and line the walls from floor to ceiling throughout Carbo's self-guided tour.

Among some of the more notable exhibits are gangster-related items, collections of illegal weapons, and drug paraphernalia confiscated in arrests as well as the prominently featured Buford Pusser display. The life of the McNairy County, Tennessee, sheriff of *Walking Tall* fame is told through newspaper clippings, videos, and even Pusser's own clothing and police equipment. The centerpiece of the Pusser exhibit is the 1974 Corvette in which Pusser was killed in a controversial and fiery crash in Adamsville, Tennessee, in 1974.

Carbo's Smoky Mountain Police Museum is open from 10:00 A.M. to 5:00 P.M. on a varying schedule throughout the

---

There are two new museum attractions on the Parkway in Pigeon Forge that are worth a look. The National Freedom Museum celebrates the contributions of our nation's armed forces while the adjacent Dinosaur Walk Museum provides a three-dimensional journey into the world of Tyrannosaurus rex *and friends.*

---

year. The museum is closed November through March, open Friday through Sunday in April, open every day but Thursday in May, September, and October, and open seven days a week from June through August. Admission is a reasonable $6.95 for ages 11 and older and $3.50 for ages 4 through 10.

Smoky Mountain Slick Track
3322 Parkway, Pigeon Forge
(865) 428-4955
This outdoor slick track runs along a bent, single-loop course and offers close-knit, competitive driving action. Solo drivers must be at least 4 feet 9 inches tall. Drivers with passengers must be at least 16 years old, and passengers must be at least 3 feet 4 inches tall. All single-seat go-karts cost $6.00 per ride, and two-seaters cost $10.00 per ride. Smoky Mountain Slick Track offers a discounted price of four rides for $20.00.

Speed Zone Fun Park
3315 South River Road, Pigeon Forge
(865) 908-7255
There are two outdoor go-kart tracks at the raceway's location just off the Parkway near the Old Mill neighborhood. The single-loop slick track is for drivers who are at least 4 feet 8 inches tall. Single karts cost $6.00, and two-seaters cost $10.00. You may also purchase three single-kart tickets for $15.00 or ten for $50.00. Sprint and Kiddie karts will set you back $5.00 per person. The Tennessee Twister is a wooden go-kart track with multiple levels and corkscrew turns. You must be at least 5 feet tall to drive. The Tennessee Twister costs $7.00 for one-seaters and $10.00 for two-seaters. Ten rides on the Twister cost $60.00. Drivers of all two-seat cars must be 16 years old, and passengers must be at least 3 years old. If you want to drive both tracks, you can do so for a discounted price of $11.00.

Riverside Raceway also has the Sling Swing, a multitowered setup that uses bungee cords to fling passengers up and down. The cost is $15.00.

The Old Mill
2944 Middle Creek Road, Pigeon Forge
(865) 453-4628

Just a block off the Parkway at traffic light #7 and across the river stands the Old Mill, a still-working grist mill built in 1830. It was the center of all activities in the old days and is still in the middle of the shopping area most long-term visitors remember. The mill is on the National Register of Historic buildings and still grinds corn into flour for sale in the general store. Guided tours of the mill are available in the summer and fall months. The scheduled 25-minute tours are conducted every half hour for the general public, and special tours are available for large groups. The cost of the tour is $3.00 for adults, $1.50 for children 6 through 12, and children 5 and younger are admitted free.

Movie Rider
3370 Parkway, Pigeon Forge
(865) 428-8511

At this movie attraction, you won't just be a passive spectator—you'll feel like you're part of the action. Viewers are strapped into chairs mounted on moving platforms that tilt, dip, and shift in synchronicity with the 70-millimeter film, which is displayed on a giant 40-foot by 30-foot screen. The 30-minute features are five-part presentations that put you safely in the seats of such thrilling settings as roller coaster rides or high-speed race cars. Films change throughout the season.

Movie Rider is open daily year-round between 5:00 P.M. and midnight. There is also a limited daytime schedule that varies throughout the year, so it's advisable to call ahead to verify matinee showings. Three rides (about 15 minutes) cost $9.98 for ages 11 and older and $12.21 for children 10 and under. Group rates are available. Most major credit cards are accepted. Participation by pregnant women, claustrophobic people, or anyone with back, head, or neck problems is discouraged. You must be 42 inches tall to participate.

Wild Wheels
3735 Parkway, Pigeon Forge
(865) 453-7942

The southernmost of Pigeon Forge's myriad amusements on the Parkway, Wild Wheels is a sparkling-clean layout featuring two go-kart tracks, a bumper boat pool, a big arcade, and a four-station bungee jump tower (no waiting!). Bungee jumping from the quad tower is priced at $20.00. The bumper boats have an age limit of 7 years for solo riders at $6.00 a head, which is also the going rate for a 12-minute trip on either of the two go-kart tracks. The junior track (7 years, minimum height 4 feet) has two kart configurations, as does the big track (age 10, height 54 inches). A special rate schedule permits a mix-and-match package of 10 rides on the go-karts and/or bumper boats for $37.50. The large arcade features a broad selection of electronic and interactive games.

GATLINBURG

Everything in Gatlinburg is convenient, and attractions are no exception. With the exception of five (three of which are on River Road a block off the Parkway), every attraction in Gatlinburg is contained in a 4-block section of town. As previously mentioned, some attractions that are geared specifically to the younger set are also included in the Kidstuff chapter, and most of those are also in or very near to the center of town.

Ripley's Davy Crockett Mini-Golf
188 North Parkway, Gatlinburg
(865) 430-8851
www.ripleys.com

Ripley's newest entry into the attractions field is a course that takes miniature golf to a new level of fun. Thirty-six holes of challenging putt-putt golf are complemented by the addition of new animated displays consisting of animals that pop up and offer golf advice and some other comments that have nothing at all to do with golf. The course features several holes with the tee on a different level from the green, making every putt a challenge. The 17th hole on the Fort Crockett course may be the longest in miniature golf history—it's about 40 yards from tee to green down a sluice filled with water. The Village course features a lot of curves and elevation changes. Wheelchair accessibility is provided for 18 full holes, 9 on each side. This course design, using interactive figures and hazards, is probably the future of miniature golf casting its shadow; say goodbye to the windmills and flat courses of the 20th century. Davy Crockett Mini-Golf is open 10:00 A.M. to midnight seven days a week, with plenty of free parking. Adult greens fees (age 12 and up) are $9.95 for 18 holes and $12.95 for 36. Kids 6 to 11 pay $6.95 and $8.75, respectively, and children under 5 years pay $4.95 for 18 or 36 holes, and receive a free souvenir golf set.

Hillbilly Golf
340 Parkway, Gatlinburg
(865) 436-7470

Another oldie with a really spectacular twist: You can't walk to the course. Hillbilly Golf's two 18-hole courses are on a mountaintop 300 feet above the Parkway, and the only way to get to them is to ride an incline railway. The ride is part of the admission, of course, and while you're waiting for the rail car, you can visit the arcade or get in a few strokes on the practice green. Once you get to the top, you'll play on your choice of courses (or both) set in the wilderness, with mountaineer hazards like stills and rock walls to make your shot selections a little more difficult.

The Historic Ogle Cabin
Parkway at Cherokee Orchard Road
Gatlinburg

Absolutely the oldest building in Gatlinburg, the Ogle cabin on the grounds of the Arrowmont School and the Arrowcraft Shop is the home that Billy Ogle cut and hewed the logs to build. His sons built the cabin in 1807 on a site about 300 yards back on Baskins Creek, and the cabin was occupied by various members of the fam-

ily until 1910. The walls and rafters of the original building were moved to the current site, and the present dwelling restoration was completed in 1969 as a cooperative effort of the city of Gatlinburg, Pi Beta Phi Fraternity, the Arrowmont School, and the Daughters of the American Revolution. Because of the volunteer nature of its docent staff, the cabin is open on an irregular schedule, but it's free and just takes a minute to look at if you happen to be in the neighborhood. It's also interesting to speculate on how Martha Jane Huskey Ogle cared for seven grown children and some of their 82 children in that kind of space.

Riverwalk
River Road, Gatlinburg

One of the most pleasant results of a massive ongoing urban beautification program begun in 1997, Riverwalk is an island of serenity on the northern edge of the downtown business district. The renewal project actually begins before traffic light #3, where the utilities have been buried to leave an uncluttered skyline, but our concern at the moment is the stretch that joins the river itself where River Road runs diagonally off the Parkway at traffic light #5. From that point to Maples Lane, about half a mile distant, Riverwalk is a pleasant stroll along the west prong of the Little Pigeon River at a reasonable enough remove from the downtown activity to make the noise and lights seem a million miles away.

The variegated sidewalk, sometimes brick and cobblestone, sometimes faux boardwalk, sometimes just plain cement, is flanked by old-fashioned globe streetlights, reminiscent of gaslights at the curb, and a wrought-iron fence along the riverbank. The fence is festooned with thousands of planters filled with homegrown flowers, courtesy of the Parks and Recreation Department's full-time horticultural staff. Early on, a footbridge across the river provides the main access to Ripley's Aquarium. That bridge and the sidewalk leading to Gatlinburg's Mysterious Mansion a few blocks down are the only two points where businesses are accessed directly from the Riverwalk; for the rest of the way, it's just you and the water and those millions of fresh flowers.

If you want to get a closer look at the river or go fishing in it (regulations are in our Parks and Recreation chapter), several stairways along the way lead to the river's edge, where the local duck population nests. And if strollin' and sittin' are more your style, several benches and gazebos have been provided. In a way, the Riverwalk is a reminder of what Gatlinburg used to be: a sleepy, friendly little town where you could just forget about your troubles for a while in nature's beauty. And you thought nobody listened when you asked whatever happened to that nice little town.

Ripley's Aquarium of the Smokies
88 River Road, Gatlinburg
(865) 430-8808
www.ripleysaquariumofthesmokies.com
This downtown Gatlinburg attraction has made a big splash since opening in late 2000. In its first full year of operation, Ripley's Aquarium of the Smokies pulled some two million visitors through its turnstiles, making it the most visited aquarium in the nation.

Where some attractions fail to live up to their own hype, this one succeeds, thanks to an impressive collection of aquatic life-forms that hail from all the world's oceans. The $70 million, 115,000-square-foot facility offers a multilevel, self-guided tour that fascinates from beginning to end. Even on repeat visits, Ripley's Aquarium loses little of its luster.

The tour is divided into major themed sections, such as Tropical Rainforest, Coral Reef, and Ocean Realm. In numerous display tanks are some of the earth's most interesting undersea creatures, including piranha, jawfish, and seahorses. One of the more unusual collections is in the Gallery of the Seas area, home to jellyfish, sea dragons, giant octopi, and the sprawling Japanese spider crab—the world's largest crustacean.

Several of the tanks are quite large. In the Coral Reef and Stingray Bay sections, schools of exotic, colorful reef fish and hordes of stingrays make their respective homes. In both tanks, resident divers interact with the fish during hourly dive shows. Spectators can watch the critters being fed and learn a lot about them in the process. At one point, near the end of the tour, guests themselves are allowed to pet the stingrays from topside.

The centerpiece of Ripley's Aquarium of the Smokies is Shark Lagoon, which alone holds nearly a million gallons of man-made seawater. Ten-foot sand tiger sharks, sandbar sharks, and nurse sharks as well as sawfish, eels, and a giant green sea turtle can easily be seen. What makes Shark Lagoon special, though, is that visitors are given the best view in the house, traveling through the tank in the world's longest underwater aquarium tunnel.

A 340-foot-long moving walkway snakes through the tunnel, which is built with 6-inch-thick acrylic that allows you to see fish all around you and directly overhead. The sharks appear close enough to touch!

One area not to be missed is the Discovery Center. This section is brimming with dozens of interactive exhibits that can be touched, felt, twisted, turned, and poked. There are places to crawl into as well as a "touch tank" where you can pet live horseshoe crabs.

Although it's designed primarily with kids in mind, adults almost always get in on the action, too. The Discovery Center also has rooms where staff educators deliver hourly multimedia presentations on a variety of sea life–related topics.

Although the most of what you see at Ripley's Aquarium of the Smokies is part of its permanent collection, some exhibits are displayed on a temporary basis. In 2002, for example, the aquarium opened "Titanic—Island of Life," a half-million-dollar exhibition constructed in the Changeable Display room. Its twofold theme depicted the cruise liner's ill-fated maiden voyage and offered a unique glimpse into the

A Quiet Company Makes a Big Noise

It's no secret in Gatlinburg that most of the major property owners and business operators in the city are members of the city's founding families. Although the names Ogle, Ownby, Trentham, McCarter, and Reagan are not as visible as they used to be, those families are still pretty much responsible for determining Gatlinburg's future. The fact is they're very much in evidence as landlords; most of them have leased their downtown properties to incoming businesses. Don't be completely fooled by the proliferation of new names; the old families are still calling most of the shots. It is notable, however, that one new name has popped up in town that is instantly recognized all over the world: Ripley's. And Ripley's Entertainment Inc. has quietly become a major player in Gatlinburg's business community.

The Ripley name first appeared in Gatlinburg in 1970 with the opening of Ripley's Believe It or Not! Museum, the company's first venture beyond the popular comic strip and radio show that have been around almost a century. Bob Masterson, currently the president of Ripley Entertainment, was the first manager of the Gatlinburg museum. By the mid-1980s, the Ripley family had shrunk to two brothers who didn't really have much expansionist blood in their veins, and the company lapsed into a comatose state. In 1985 the company was purchased by Jim Pattison, a Canadian multimillionaire with more dreams than you'll usually find in a hundred people. Famous for finding gifted executives, Pattison turned the Ripley company over to a group of savvy attractions types, who quickly built the company into the world's largest chain of museum-type entertainment venues in the world through acquisition (the Guinness Museum of World Records and Madame [now Louis] Tussaud's Wax Museum, to name a few) and innovation (Ripley's Moving Theater and Haunted Adventure, for starters). Based on the success of their ventures in Gatlinburg, Ripley Entertainment decided in 1998 to make their biggest ever investment (about $50 million) in a state-of-the-art aquarium right in the middle of the downtown business district. Ripley's Aquarium of the Smokies opened in late 2000, and to say it's been a success is the height (depth?) of understatement. Exceeding what appeared to be some pretty optimistic projections, the Ripley's Aquarium became the most-visited aquarium in the western hemisphere (that's the half of the world we live in) before its second birthday.

That's the business end of the story. Now we come to what's important to the folks in east Tennessee in general and the citizens of Gatlinburg and Sevier County in particular: This international outfit can come in here and spend a mountain of money and make themselves a mountain range of money, and that's all well and good, but what kind of a citizen are they? Do they, like the native business owners and local small businesses, contribute anything to the quality of life in the Smokies? And do they show proper respect for the environment that brings all those visitors here? The answer to these two questions is a quiet "Yes, they do, and they do a lot more than even the locals know."

Ripley's Aquarium of the Smokies is the most-visited aquarium in the United States, and the second-most-visited in the world, since opening in 2000. DICK McHUGH

The go-to guy for answers to the above questions is Karl Thomas, Ripley's sales and marketing director for all of the company's Gatlinburg attractions, and the first impression he conveys is that he, personally, is grateful to be here. Like so many new residents before him, Thomas is so happy to be living in Sevier County that he has no plans to move on. Ripley may have other plans for him, but right now Karl Thomas doesn't.

"We've learned a lot of positive things about Gatlinburg," Thomas says, "and none that are negative. The business climate here is perfect for what our company does; the tourist population is diverse enough to provide an audience for everything we have to offer, and the city administration is uniquely tuned in to the entertainment industry."

As a corporate citizen, Ripley's is a windfall. With six uniquely different attractions that are open year-round, Ripley's provides permanent employment for about 350 residents (275 in the aquarium alone). That's more than the city employs, and Gatlinburg's municipal workforce is based on the needs of a city 10 times its actual size. Added to that is the fact that the aquarium generated enough revenue to increase the *overall* figure by 20 percent, and the additional traffic generated by the opening of the aquarium was sufficient to move the city to build not one but two multilevel parking structures, both of which have placed millions of dollars directly into the city's coffers. But that still doesn't address the question about community citizenship, does it?

"We don't make a lot of noise about what we do," says Karl Thomas, himself a soft-spoken and apparently gentle man. "But we participate aggressively in most civic activities, and we have a couple of projects of our own. Our food drive to collect canned goods for the Sevier County Food Ministry's center generated twice as much tonnage as the rest of the participants combined, and our special programs for the area schoolchildren have brought in kids from all of the surrounding counties as well as Sevier to give them an experience they might not have otherwise." Based on figures provided, it appears that somewhere around 40 percent of the aquarium's visitors get in on a discounted or free pass during the peak season. In the winter months, when the parking deck looks like a school bus driver's convention is in town, that figure probably doubles.

"One thing we have gone public with," Thomas adds, "is our decision to become a major sponsor of the Friends of the Great Smoky Mountains National Park. Their work is so important to the protection and preservation of our park that we felt it was in everybody in the area's interest that they shouldn't have to spend most of their time in fund-raising activities. As a de facto protector of the environment it's created here, the aquarium is a natural partner for an organization like the Friends of the Smokies.

"While we try to be a good citizen everywhere we have businesses [like on every populated continent on the globe]," Thomas added, "there's nowhere that we're so deeply involved as Gatlinburg. The city's always been good to us, and our businesses here have thrived so well that we decided some time back that this is an excellent proving ground for new ideas. The Haunted Museum idea originated here, and it's been so successful that we opened one in Myrtle Beach last year, and we've got a bunch more on the drawing board. The Davy Crockett Mini-Golf was our first entry into that piece of the market, and it did more business in its first two months than we expected for the season. We'll probably be building more of those, too. And it looks like anything our people dream up in the future will probably show up in Gatlinburg first."

There is a school of thought in Gatlinburg that the opening of the aquarium was a watershed event that very well may have saved the city's economy. Although that is a debatable point, it has become abundantly clear to the local people that what Ripley has brought to town is more than they could have asked for, and any more will be additional icing on a cake that just tastes better all the time.

murky depths of the North Atlantic. In typical Ripley fashion, the *Titanic* show used photographs, models, re-creations, and lots of hands-on activities to tell the story of the ship, from construction to sinking. Along the way, visitors learned about the state of *Titanic* today and the various life-forms that make it their home.

Overall, allow several hours to do the aquarium justice and another hour if you plan to take in a temporary exhibition. The aquarium is laid out in roughly a one-way path, although it leaves you room to double back and see things twice, if you like. Along the way, you'll find the Feeding Frenzy snack shop; the Veranda, a lunchtime country buffet, and the Cargo Hold gift shop.

Ripley's Aquarium of the Smokies is open year-round from 9:00 A.M. to 9:00

P.M. Sunday through Thursday and 9:00 A.M. to 11:00 P.M. on Friday and Saturday. Admission prices are $17.95 for ages 12 and older, $9.95 for ages 6 through 11, and $3.95 for ages 2 through 5. Annual pass prices are $36.95, $21.95, and $11.95 for those respective age groups. These prices do not include sales tax. Stroller and locker rentals are available.

The Guinness World Records Museum
631 Parkway, Gatlinburg
(865) 436-9100

Take just about any adjective you can think of, add "est" to the end, and you'll find it at the Guinness Museum. From the moment you walk through the unusual whale's mouth and belly that forms the museum's opening, the Guinness folks will show you the biggest, smallest, baddest, longest, shortest, and richest of everything they've been able to uncover in more than 40 years of research. Since it's entertaining as well as educational, there's a little bit of the silliest thrown in as well.

Two jam-packed floors of superlatives in the worlds of art, sports, music, movies, television, and human nature will entertain you for as long as you want to stay and probably teach some things you didn't know about people you thought you knew pretty well. For instance, what has Oprah Winfrey got the world's biggest of at the moment? And how high do you come on the world's tallest man? Admission to the Guinness Museum is $9.95 for adults, $7.95 for senior citizens, and $5.95 for children 6 through 12. Children younger than 6 are admitted free. Special group rates are available on request. The Guinness World Records Museum is open seven days a week from 9:00 A.M. to 11:00 P.M., except Christmas. (And Oprah's got the world's biggest salary, by the way.)

World of Illusions
716 Parkway, Gatlinburg
(865) 436-9701

Just about nothing is real at World of Illusions—we think. These people do more with smoke, mirrors, and lighting than anyone around. Consider this: You can stand there and see an Imperial Warrior beam down from his starship, but you can't touch him, and you can turn the tables on Superman by spotting him with X-ray vision. Your friend can disappear while holding your hand, and a laser illusion will convince you that Elvis is alive. You can walk away from your shadow and watch Count Dracula turn into a flying bat, and Merlin, the world's best-known wizard, will appear before you and levitate. Watch carefully—you never know what will happen next—or seem to. World of Illusions is open from 10:00 A.M. to 10:00 P.M. daily. Admission is $6.99 for adults, $4.99 for kids 6 to 11, and children younger than 6 are admitted free with a paid admission.

The Gatlinburg Fun Center
716 Parkway, Gatlinburg
(865) 430-8985
www.smokymountainfun.com

Six different amusement venues (including on-site arcades with the latest in high-tech competition) stretch across the back of Reagan Square Mall in the heart of downtown Gatlinburg. Hours of enjoyment are available for the whole family in a close enough environment that nobody gets lost or separated by much distance. We'll present the attractions as they appear from left to right as you enter the complex. Prices vary depending on combinations of activities and group size. Groups of 15 or more can expect a 10 percent discount. The Gatlinburg Fun Center is open every day but Christmas from 10:00 A.M. until the last customer is served and goes away happy.

Old Gatlinburg Golf & Games
(865) 430-4653

Here are two unusual miniature golf courses laid out on the hillside that integrate old buildings into the play. Gatlinburg's Old Town Square Course delivers a local history lesson at every hole, including how the city got its name. The Smokies Old Mountain Trail Course describes the development of the Great Smoky

Mountains National Park in a peaceful setting reminiscent of the park itself. One hole plays through a replica of the old Elkmont post office. A single round of golf on one course is $8.95 for anybody older than five, while toddlers can play for $5.95. One of the best bargains in the area is the $12.95 golf pass that allows unlimited play for five consecutive days.

Fort Fun
(865) 436-2326

Fort Fun offers three family entertainment features under one roof. This big building at the back of the Family Fun Center contains a laser tag game with spectacular sound and light effects, a 3-D movie theater using special glasses and special effects that place you in the scene of your choice from a menu of five, and a bumper car track where the entire family can express their innermost feelings at the wheel of a bumper car. The separate venues vary in price from $7.00 to $9.00, with a variety of special package deals.

Bankshot Basketball
(865) 430-8985

This attraction is a fun-filled combination of miniature golf and basketball, where angled backboards put a special slant on every shot. Accuracy counts big in this contest of skill, and a little knowledge of plane geometry can't hurt. A trip through the Bankshot course is $4.95 with no time limit.

Hauntings
716 Parkway, Gatlinburg
(865) 436-4636, (865) 436-9701

A new slant in haunted houses: At Hauntings the house comes to you as you sit frozen in fascination in a room filled with things that go bump. And wiggle. And giggle. And scream their heads off. It's truly a terrifying collection of sights and sounds, complete with spooky lighting and otherworldly sounds (in stereo, yet) from the dark side. If it doesn't remind you of your worst-ever nightmare, it'll

probably provide you with a new one. A full serving of fright is available daily from 10:00 A.M. to 10:00 P.M. at $7.99 for adults and children ages 12 and up, and $5.99 for children under 12. Group rates are available for those who hate to shriek alone.

Gatlinburg Sky Lift
765 Parkway, Gatlinburg
(865) 436-4307

When it opened in 1954, the Sky Lift started from a point almost as sparsely settled at the bottom as it was at the top. Now leaving the Parkway in the center of downtown, it travels across River Road and 700 feet up the south face of Crockett Mountain. At the summit, the panoramic view of Gatlinburg and the surrounding Smokies is breathtaking. Safe, two-person lift chairs stay comfortably close to the ground during the ascent, and the automatic camera takes pictures as each chair approaches the top, providing a delightful souvenir. Other souvenirs and snacks are also available at the summit's rustic gift shop. The Sky Lift is most popular in autumn, as the fall colors take on whole new dimensions when viewed from the top of Crockett Mountain. Cameras are welcome on the Sky Lift, giving all riders the chance to take one-of-a-kind shots of downtown Gatlinburg and Mount LeConte together. Adult admission is $8.99, and children 11 and younger ride for $5.99. The Sky Lift is open daily from 9:00 A.M. to 9:00 P.M. in April, May, September, and October; from 9:00 A.M. to 11:00 P.M. June through August; and during posted hours November through March.

Ripley's Believe It or Not! Museum
800 Parkway, Gatlinburg
(865) 436-5096
www.ripleys.com

Robert Ripley (1893-1949) was a cartoonist by trade and an adventurer and world traveler by choice. Supported by his syndicated radio show, which was the first program ever broadcast simultaneously to a worldwide audience, and his world-famous comic strip, begun in 1918 and still running, Ripley traveled to 198 countries collecting unusual (some may say bizarre) facts, legends, and artifacts from places most people hadn't even heard of before Ripley went there. It's not stretching a point to call Ripley the father of trivia.

Believing It or Not (!) starts with a leap of faith at the entrance: Don't be concerned that the museum is going to collapse around you—the "interesting" architecture is just a warm-up for what you'll see during your self-guiding tour through three stories of exhibits in various forms, from the actual stuffed remains of a two-headed calf born in Gatlinburg to rare film footage shot in the early part of the 20th century. A lot of the exhibits are "hands on," allowing the visitor to experience such delights as actually touching a real shrunken head or playing a giant keyboard by dancing on it (remember the Tom Hanks movie *Big*?). The one-way layout erases concerns about families or groups getting separated, and everybody can go at their own pace until the end of the tour. The friendly attendants will tell you it's about a 45-minute tour, but plan on spending more time—this place, with more than 500 exhibits, is a real schedule-trasher. Ripley's Believe It or Not! Museum is open from 10:00 A.M. to 9:00 P.M. Sunday through Thursday, and 9:00 A.M. to midnight Friday and Saturday, every day but Christmas. Admission is $12.95 for adults and children 12 and older, $7.95 for children ages 6 to 11, and children younger than 5 are admitted free when accompanied by a paying customer.

Ripley's Moving Theater
904 Parkway, Gatlinburg
(865) 436-9763
www.ripleys.com

Two separate features assault your senses in this specially designed experience. Once you're strapped into your custom chair (minimum height requirement 43 inches), the 70mm screen comes alive and the six-channel digital sound system enters through every pore in your body.

A number of area rides and attractions have minimum height, weight, and age requirements. We've included most of that information in this chapter, but it's a good idea to call ahead before visiting these places, especially if you plan on taking children.

For the next five minutes, you will be buffeted in eight different directions (sometimes all at once) as your seat moves with the action on the screen. The first feature starts with a 3-D ride (special glasses are provided) across the surface of a glacier—if a glacier were built like a roller coaster. As you twist, turn, and plunge through the frozen tundra, you'll be drawn into a landscape, complete with snowstorms you'll actually feel, that you'd only visit on a movie screen. The second ride is through a haunted mine, complete with spectral "host," that'll make you as hot as the previous ride made you cold. The spectacular 3-D effects will bring you up close and practically personal with a lot of the spooky creatures that are known to inhabit places like mines. At the end of the experience, you'll be breathless, a little weak from the strain of the two rides, and thankful that white knuckles don't glow in the dark.

Ripley's Moving Theater is open from 10:00 A.M. to 9:00 P.M. Sunday through Thursday, and 9:00 A.M. to midnight Friday and Saturday. Admission is $11.95 for both shows in one sitting. A minimum height requirement of 43 inches applies.

Ripley's Haunted Adventure
908 Parkway, Gatlinburg
(865) 430-9991
www.ripleys.com

This is an interesting premise for those who truly enjoy getting scared stiff by real people offering to commit various unpleasant acts during a trip through an abandoned casket factory. From the time you enter the funicular rail car that takes you up to the second floor until you

Mountain Magic

You don't hear the words "skiing" and "Tennessee" used in the same sentence very often, and there's a reason for that. In the local vernacular, "They ain't but one ski resort in all of Tennessee, and we've got it!" And what started in 1962 as a sometimes (when there was snow) run down a mountain to a cinder block building has grown into a year-round resort that's a mainstay of Gatlinburg's tourist economy.

Ober Gatlinburg today is a sprawling year-round ski resort/amusement park tucked into a five-acre niche in Mount Harrison, 1,400 feet above downtown Gatlinburg. It's a 2-mile ride from the tram terminal on the Parkway (highly recommended) or 7 miles of two-lane mountain road (not recommended at all). In fact, Ski Mountain Road is frequently closed to all but local traffic (Ski Mountain is a large residential area) during the ski season. If you happen to be caught "topside" with your car when the road gets closed, you can always ride the tram down and then go back up some time later (maybe days later) to retrieve your vehicle. Please, please ride the tram. Round-trip fare is $7.00 for adults and $4.00 for children 7 to 11. If you're going skiing, show your tram ticket to the lift ticket seller; the price of the tram ride will be deducted from the lift ticket. Besides, they charge $2.00 for parking at the top, and on a busy day you could have a sizable hike after you park.

The aerial tramway is a wonder all by itself. Two counter-balanced tram cars run continuously, transporting up to 120 people and their equipment on each trip. At 10 minutes per trip at peak operating times, that's about 1,400 people an hour, and it's not an exaggeration to say the tram runs at peak capacity most of the time in the winter.

The tram cars are suspended on a complicated cable system designed to support more than 500,000 pounds per car. That's more than 10 times the weight of a car loaded to capacity. Leaving the docking stations at each end of the 10-minute journey, the tram glides 2 miles to its opposite terminal. The views alone are worth the cost of the ride ticket, and more photographs are taken from the Ober Gatlinburg tram cars than any other single known spot in the area.

Departing from the tram at the resort, you find yourself in an enormous indoor mall, and where you go from there depends a lot on the time of year. From this point we'll describe Ober Gatlinburg from the perspective of the calendar.

DAY BY DAY

The indoor section doesn't change a lot between seasons. As you leave the tram dock, the concession coupon booth is dead ahead. If you plan to do anything at all while you're on the mountain, buy a book of coupons. Eighteen dollars will buy a book of 10 coupons with a value of $2.00 each (you do the math), and the coupons are legal tender at most of the activities and ride-type attractions; not included in the coupon book are the bear habitat, ice-skating, the bungee tower, skiing, arcade games, gift shop merchandise, photos, lockers, parking, and food. The Municipal Black Bear Habitat is to your immediate left. Beyond the bear habitat, a line of souvenir shops and

The Alpine Slide is a family favorite at Ober Gatlinburg. OBER GATLINBURG

snack bars forms a ring around the skating rink, two floors below ground level. People-watchers sit at tables along the side or lean on the rail at the end of the rink. Across the rink from your vantage point, the indoor midway usually teems with kids of various sizes and ages engaged in all manner of physical activity. Completing the circle at your right, the arcade is alive with the strange mix of sounds and lights that can't be found anywhere else. Let's look at each of these areas in a little more detail.

The Municipal Black Bear Habitat is a privately funded zoo dedicated to behavioral research on the American black bear (*Ursus americanus*), the living symbol of the Great Smoky Mountains. A small population of nonreleasable bears is maintained at the habitat in as close to a natural state as possible, and yearling bears born as the result of the natural

mating process are released in bear sanctuaries managed by the Tennessee Wildlife Resources Agency. Medical care of the resident bears is provided by the University of Tennessee's College of Veterinary Medicine. The bears are observed by graduate students for digestive efficiency and sibling interaction. The current stars are a pair of female cubs born in captivity in 2000. They'll be released into the wild in the winter of 2004–2005, when they've reached maturity. An admission fee of $1.50 helps support the bear habitat. A museum exhibit outside the habitat provides interesting background information on black bears, including graphic displays of what happens when people make the mistake of treating wild bears like house pets.

Several gift and specialty shops line the wall along the side of the ice rink, offering a variety of local handcrafts and souvenirs. A couple of snack bars provide a chance to grab a drink or a meal and sit rinkside, watching the skaters while resting your feet.

The indoor ice rink is a spacious sheet of ice, more than 10,000 square feet in area—that's huge for a salon rink, which this is, but a bit undersized for hockey. With more than 400 pairs of rental skates available in almost every size, the rink gives interested spectators a chance to experience the joys of an activity seldom seen this far south. The $8.00 fee includes skate rental and up to three hours of continuous ice time.

Spread throughout the rest of the mall are a variety of midway-type attractions, most of which run one or two coupons. A special kiddie section has several rides for the toddler set. Games of skill and chance are usually good for a laugh, especially the spider web, a giant velcro-covered air cushion into which kids in padded suits hurl themselves, and the bungee run, where two participants test their strength against each other and a bungee cord. The cord always wins, but so does the person who can run farthest down a 35-foot alley before being snapped back into the air cushion by the cord around their waist. A batting cage provides virtual pitchers from little league to major league ability that release pitches up to 60 mph.

Out of sight of the tram terminal, the restaurant and lounge are on the mountain side of the building on the second floor, offering a great view of the ski slopes.

Outside the mall, a bunch of outdoor activities operate year-round, weather permitting. Dominating the scene is every mother's nightmare: The Air Boingo double bungee tower. Sixty feet high, the bungee tower provides a platform for otherwise perfectly sensible people to wrap a high-strength elastic cord around themselves and jump into space. Coupons are not usable for the bungee jump, which costs $15 per leap, or $40 if it takes three leaps to satisfy your selfdestructive urges. Beside the tower is the Trampoline Thing, where a bungee setup allows jumpers to attain ridiculous heights without having to jump off anything. Two coupons will buy three minutes on the trampoline.

At the other end of the outside area, convenient to the customer-service and first-aid stations, the longest scenic chairlift in the South goes to the summit of Mount Harrison. It's a relaxing 15-minute ride with lots of photo-quality scenery, and a bluegrass band at the top will entertain you while you enjoy the view. About halfway down on the return trip, you may choose to get off the sedately paced chairlift and finish the trip down in true white-knuckle fashion at the control of the Alpine Slide, a dry track simulated bobsled run. The manually controlled sled lets you set your own speed through the woods and curves as you drop 200 feet in an 1,800-foot ride. Speeds range from scary to horrifying. Round-trip fare for the chairlift is two coupons, and two more will buy a ride on the Alpine Slide.

THE GOOD OL' SUMMER TIME

When snow is out of the question, the foot of the ski slopes is taken over by three interesting water raft rides. The Blue Cyclone Rapids features an inflated bobsled with handles that carries up to two people twisting, turning, and usually screaming at the top of their lungs, more than 600 feet through a closed tube on a cushion of water. The Lightnin' Raft Ride and the Shoot-the-Chute are basically identical, each sending a raft down a 240-foot course with a vertical drop of 40 feet. The Lightnin' River Raft is open all the way, and the Shoot-the-Chute is covered for most of its distance. The Blue Cyclone is a two-coupon ride, and the other two go for one coupon each.

Kiddie Land moves outside in the summer with additional playground equipment. Kids 3 to 11 years old can enjoy the down-size slides, ladders, crawling nets, and swinging bridges, or ride on the carousel, cars, snowmobiles, or the Rio Grande train. Kiddie Land admission is two coupons good for all-day riding.

BABY, IT'S COLD OUTSIDE

When the weather turns cold (usually around December 1 at 2,700 feet) and Gatlinburg goes into Winterfest mode, Ober rocks. It's skiing time in Tennessee, and this is the only game around. With eight slopes, three full lifts, the most efficient snowmaking equipment available, and a kaleidoscope of plans to fit any budget, Ober Gatlinburg is at its absolute best. With all the different programs available for age groups, family or larger groups, and special sessions, the best thing to do here is contact the lodge when you arrive. They'll tailor the best plan for your circumstances. However, here's an idea of what a family of four could expect to spend if they appeared at the tramway terminal in street clothes:

Tram tickets—$26. Lift tickets (all day Saturday, the highest rate)—$104, including tram rebate. Complete equipment rental—$60. Ski school—$40. The total is $230 for a full day of activity for a family of four. Compared to what you'd pay for the same family to see a college football

Ober Gatlinburg is Tennessee's only ski resort.
OBER GATLINBURG

game, it's pretty reasonable—compared to a professional football game, it's dirt cheap.

First, let's talk about snow. Ober Gatlinburg's snowmaking system is capable of laying down enough snow overnight to provide ample powder when Mother Nature doesn't cooperate. Man-made snow is softer, fluffier, and longer-lasting than natural, and it provides an excellent foundation when a natural snowfall occurs. Snow is made by snow guns, which are placed at strategic points on the slopes and turned on. Mogul Ridge, one of the favorite advanced runs, has permanently placed guns. The point here is that Ober doesn't need snow to provide skiing; they need cold weather, and that's usually not a problem.

All of the indoor activities and a few of the hardier outdoor ones previously mentioned go on as usual during the ski season, but the emphasis is on getting you on the slopes, and it starts the minute you debark from the tram. Skiers who don't already have their lift tickets are guided to the booths to get them (remember, they'll deduct the cost of your tram ticket, but you have to show it to them). Next, for those who need it, is the equipment rental area. You name it, they got it. You can get off the tram in street clothes and be totally outfitted to ski in about 10 minutes, at a cost that will range from $15 to $35, depending on the type of stuff you rent. Breakage insurance is included in the rental fee. In addition to regular and shaped skis, snowboards are also available for rent at about $35, with a deposit required.

First-time skiers and snowboarders are required to attend ski school before going on the slopes. The instructors are professionally trained to get rookies on the hill as quickly and confidently as possible, and classes are usually broken down into ability and age levels. Group classes run about an hour. A $10 fee is charged for beginner group lessons, and private lessons are available for individuals ($25 per hour) or groups of no more than three ($15 per additional pupil). Snowboarding lessons are taught by group only, and run $15 for a 1½-hour session.

On to the slopes! Under full operational conditions, Ober Gatlinburg's two quad and one double lift can move 6,000 people up the slopes per hour, so there's seldom any waiting. Skiers at every level of expertise will be challenged by the eight slopes. Ober Chute, an intermediate run of 4,400 feet with a vertical drop of 556 feet, is a favorite because of its length; Mogul Ridge, a 300-foot washboard with a near-vertical 235-foot drop, will test the best. Cub Way, the beginner run, is a gentle slope with enough length to build confidence to tackle the tougher slopes.

Ski sessions are scheduled according to projections for attendance. The best time for avid skiers to hit the slopes is Monday through Thursday, when the resort is open from noon to 10:00 P.M., with two scheduled sessions, the combo (all hours) and the night session (6:00 to 10:00 P.M.). All trails except Grizzly, the appropriately named run through the woods, are lighted for night skiing. Non-holiday Fridays have three scheduled sessions: day (8:30 A.M. to 4:00 P.M.), twilight (3:00 P.M. to 10:00 P.M.), and night (6:00 to 10:00 P.M.). On Friday and Saturday in the holiday period (just before Christmas through New Year's), day (8:30 A.M. to 4:00 P.M.) and twilight (3:00 to 10:00 P.M.) sessions operate. All Sundays have a single day session from 8:30 A.M. to 5:00 P.M. Some twilight sessions are scheduled on Sundays by local option; ask if you're interested.

If you weren't aware of Ober Gatlinburg's existence before, you should check it out the next time you're in the Smokies. With enough variety to please just about any visitor, Ober Gatlinburg is a pretty good destination for the family that's looking for some close-in fun that will appeal to everybody.

scramble out of the elevator that delivers you back to the safety of the Parkway, the Haunted Adventure is an intense journey through a netherworld that wouldn't be nearly as creepy if some of the exhibits didn't keep joining your group. And we don't even want to talk about the spiders. Or the rats. In fact, they're not nearly as scary as the escaped prisoner who only wants to "play" with you, or the butler who shows up at some of the least opportune times. And when you finally get in the elevator to return to sanity, don't be too quick to breathe a sigh of relief; like the man says, "It ain't over 'til it's over."

Ripley's Haunted Adventure is open from 10:00 A.M. to 9:00 P.M. Sunday through Thursday, and 9:00 A.M. to midnight Friday and Saturday, every day except Christmas. Admission is $11.95 for adults and $7.95 for children 8 to 11. Because of the intense nature of this attraction, Ripley's asks that children younger than age 6 not be taken along.

Star Cars
914 Parkway, Gatlinburg
(865) 430-7900
www.starcarstn.com

When it comes to way-out designs for special cars, nobody does it better than George Barris. Starting back in the 1960s with the customized Pontiac GTO used by the Monkees and the first Batmobile, George Barris has been in constant demand to design cars that not only set the live characters that used them apart from the crowd but that also became stars themselves. The self-guiding three-story tour of specialty cars only begins with George Barris designs—also on display are cars actually owned by such luminaries as Elvis Presley and Frank Sinatra, and a special NASCAR exhibit features video highlights of the careers of several drivers. Each car is in its own setting with scenes from its movie or television show and accompanying soundtrack. TV and movie buffs will get their memories jogged thoroughly as they pass by the cars that became stars. Admission is

$9.95 for adults and $4.95 for children ages 7 through 12. Kids 6 and younger are admitted free in the company of an adult.

Christus Gardens
510 River Road, Gatlinburg
(865) 436-5155
www.christusgardens.com

A mainstay in Gatlinburg for almost 40 years now, Christus Gardens is a Christ-centered attraction of exceptional beauty. The beautifully planted and manicured exterior sets Christus Gardens apart from the moment you enter the parking lot alongside the Little Pigeon River. The mood throughout is one of reverence. When you enter the building, a circular exhibit of early American and European bibles and artifacts provides a diversion while you wait to start the 20-minute tour of dioramas. A short slide presentation describes the inspiration and construction of the facility, followed by a walking tour through 10 separate dioramas depicting significant events in the life of Jesus Christ. From the Nativity to his ascension into heaven, Jesus is shown surrounded by people whose lives he affected and who affected his. The figures are life-size and extremely lifelike, all dressed in authentic period costumes.

The tour concludes in the atrium featuring the six-ton block of marble with the face of Jesus carved in bas-relief. The face, which never lets you out of its sight, seems to actually turn as you pass by it. It's reputed to be the single most frequently photographed item in Gatlinburg. Beside the atrium is the Place of Parables, a circular exhibit of life-size paintings in old masters style depicting the Parables of Jesus. Also in the Place of Parables is a display of coinage used in Biblical times, including the Shekel of Tyre, reputedly the type of coin paid to Judas.

The grounds of Christus Gardens are an attraction by themselves. Planted and maintained with seasonal flowers, the grounds come alive during the Christmas season with special lighting effects that routinely stop traffic. Christus Gardens is completely wheelchair accessible and has plenty of parking for both cars and buses. Christus Gardens is open daily from 8:00 A.M. to 9:00 P.M. April through October, and 9:00 A.M. to 5:00 P.M. November through March. Admission is $9.95 for adults, $3.95 for children 7 through 12, and free for children 6 and younger. Special rates and tours are available to groups with advance reservations.

Ober Gatlinburg
1001 Parkway, Gatlinburg
(865) 436–5423, (800) 251–9202 ski line
www.obergatlinburg.com
What started as Gatlinburg Ski Resort in 1969 and consisted of a single slope running down to a cinder block building (when there was enough snow to open it) has grown over the years into one of the largest ski resorts in the Southeast. It's also a year-round attraction that's challenging that Parton girl's theme park in Pigeon Forge for overall entertainment supremacy in the Smokies. Ober Gatlinburg is happening! Seven miles from downtown at the top end of Ski Mountain Road, Ober is a five-acre amusement park in the nonski season and a several hundred-acre amusement park/ski resort with eight slopes in the winter.

Access to the resort is best attained by riding the aerial tramway out of the middle of downtown to the resort mall. The tram ride is an attraction in its own right, covering 2 miles on its 1,400-foot ascent. It's faster, much safer, and more environmentally sensible to ride the tram than to negotiate the 7 twisting miles of Ski Mountain Road. A huge variety of year-round amusement venues in the covered mall is enough to make a family trip worthwhile at any time of year. There's no admission charge to the mall itself, and the cost of most of the amusements is payable in coupons purchased from a central ticket office adjacent to the tram dock. The amusements themselves and the cost breakdown are covered in-depth in the Close-up in this chapter. Ober Gatlinburg is open daily year-round from 9:00 A.M. to 10:00 P.M.

DOLLYWOOD

One hundred and eighteen acres of rides, attractions, music shows, and mountain crafts make Dollywood the cornerstone of all-around fun in the Smoky Mountains. Open since 1986, Dollywood is the namesake of Dolly Parton, renowned country music star and Sevier County's most notable native. She is also a part owner who remains very active in the continued development of the park. The operational theme is one of a mountain community ripped from the pages of history.

Abundant greenery and beautiful flower gardens enhance the ambience of the park's numerous rustic wooden structures. Dollywood was built around a previously existing amusement park that had been in place for many years, operating most recently as Silver Dollar City theme park in the late '70s and early '80s. Since taking over, however, Dolly and company have continually added on to the complex—new features are introduced to the public every year. Since the closing of Opryland in Nashville, Dollywood is now the largest and most visited theme park in the state and hosts upwards of two million visitors each year. It has also been quite beneficial to the local economy, as evidenced by the fact that the various businesses that make up Dollywood Entertainment have become Sevier County's largest single seasonal employer.

Dollywood is open April through December. The park is open daily throughout the summer and runs on a more limited schedule during the other months. Hours of operation vary, depending on the time of year. Generally the park's open from 9:00 A.M. to 8:00 P.M. during summer and 10:00 A.M. to 6:00 P.M. during spring and fall. The winter schedule generally runs Thursday through Sunday from 2:00 to 9:00 P.M. with extended hours on weekends. The park is closed Thanksgiving and Christmas days. Dollywood also hosts a celebrity concert series featuring many of the nation's top country music artists. These concerts are presented more or less once a week in season.

The following prices are the most current available but are, of course, subject to change in the future. From April through October, one-day admission prices to the park are $42.40 for ages 12 and older, $32.35 for ages 4 through 11, and $39.00 for seniors ages 60 and older or who are AARP members. Prices include sales tax.

Tickets for Dollywood's Showcase of Stars celebrity concert series range from $19 to $25, depending on the act. Prices for other special music shows vary, again, depending on the show. We recommend consulting Dollywood's Web site for the most current price and schedule information. It's important to know that with all these special concert events, both matinee and evening shows are usually scheduled. Expect to pay Dollywood's regular admission prices as well if you plan on going to any ticketed concert before 6:00 P.M.

A number of discounts and price breaks are offered to enhance the value of your visit. Children 3 and younger are admitted free, and discounted prices are offered during Dollywood's Smoky Mountain Christmas in November and December. Group rates and season passes are available as well. In fact, if you purchase a one-day ticket and like what you see, you can apply the full value of your ticket toward a season pass that same day. And you're more than halfway there: A season

---

Dollywood's address is 1020 Dollywood Lane, Pigeon Forge. For information on the park and its programs, call (865) 428-9488 or (800) 365-5996. Or you can check out the park online at www.dollywood.com.

pass actually costs less than the price of two one-day tickets.

If you plan on attending both Dollywood and Dolly's Splash Country (see write-up at the end of this chapter), you can purchase Splash & Play tickets that allow three-day access to both parks for one discounted price. Or you can look into buying a Super Pass, a megaseason pass of sorts that gets you into both parks for the whole season. They are sold at varying price levels according to age and privilege options, but they usually include park admission and free parking as well as discounts on merchandise, concert tickets, and other regional attractions.

Another way to stretch your dollar at Dollywood is to arrive after 3:00 P.M., in which case your admission on the next operating day is free. This works especially well on hot summer days when you can take advantage of the cooler evening temperatures and the park's 9:00 P.M. closing time.

Admission prices include unlimited access to all regular shows, rides, attractions, craft showcases, and special events. As such, you can squeeze a lot of activity into one day (or two) without parting with too much more cash. But to park, eat, shop, and play games, you'll need to bring a good reserve of spending money. It costs $5.00 to park ($8.00 for RVs and oversize vehicles), and trams will take you from your parking area to the main entrance (or you can take either of the Dollywood trolleys operated by the cities of Pigeon Forge and Gatlinburg; see our Getting Here, Getting Around chapter for details). Generally, expect to pay inflated prices at the theme park's restaurants and other food concessions. The best way to approach this is to realize that this is simply a standard practice of theme parks and tourist destinations as a whole. The point is, be prepared and just have fun.

Frankly, Dollywood's days and hours of operation change throughout the year, and their detailed pricing structure can be quite complex when you factor in all the different age groups, discounts, and

passes. So for the most detailed information on schedules and prices, call their information office. Or you can find current information online at www.dollywood.com.

GETTING THERE

There are two ways to get to Dollywood. One is to take Dollywood Lane from traffic light #8 on the Parkway in Pigeon Forge to the park's main entrance, which is clearly marked by signs. The other is to follow Middle Creek Road south out of Sevierville or northeast out of Pigeon Forge until you see signs.

This second route is what locals usually call "the back entrance," and although that may be true for Dollywood, it's actually the main entrance to Dolly's Splash Country. No matter where you enter, an attendant is stationed to take your parking fee. You're on your own as far as finding a parking space, but once you do, note the lot number. You'll need to remember it when the tram takes you back to the parking areas later in the day.

NAVIGATING THE PARK

Dollywood is divided into several major sections that revolve around different themes and reflect various aspects of the Smokies and Americana. Within the boundaries of each area are a variety of rides, attractions, shows, restaurants, and shops related to that zone's theme.

Showstreet Palace is the site of Dollywood Celebrity Theatre and the Southern Gospel Music Hall of Fame. Adventures in Imagination is a newer section featuring the Smoky Mountain Wilderness Adventure movie ride and the Chasing Rainbows museum. Jukebox Junction takes you through a time warp back to the good ol' 1950s, complete with a neato diner. Rivertown Junction features several shops as well as Smoky Mountain Rampage, a white-water rafting ride. You'll have trouble dragging your children away from the Country Fair area. With carnival midway rides, games, and a log flume ride all in one compact location, the young ones could linger in this section alone for hours. In the Village, you'll discover the depot for the Dollywood Express and an antique carousel. Dreamland Forest is where you'll find the Mountain Slidewinder ride in addition to many of the children's activities. The arts-and-crafts hound will feel right at home in Craftsmen's Valley, the place where you'll find demonstrations of most of the old-time mountain arts. This is also where Dollywood's two roller coasters and its bald-eagle preserve are found.

WHAT TO DO AT DOLLYWOOD

Now that we've given you an overview of the park and pointed out the way there, it's time for some detail on many of the interesting aspects that make Dollywood special.

One of the best things about Dollywood is that it embodies in one (albeit expansive) location much of what people want out of a trip to the Great Smoky Mountains. Yes, it's a theme park with plenty of fun rides and attractions, but those thrills represent just one facet of your experience there. In contrast to places like Six Flags, where rides are the staple, Dollywood also offers its visitors a broad canvas of options, all presented professionally and in a first-class manner. The setting represents an old mountain community of yesteryear. It serves a slice of Appalachian life, telling many a homespun tale via mountain music, crafts, and awesome wonders of nature. Although we can only scratch the surface of what's to be found there, we will point out some of the highlights and hopefully give you a good feel for what's in store.

Take Me for a Ride

Inside the park, you'll discover rides that go both fast and slow, many rides that get you wet, and some that are designed just for the little ones.

Of course, there are rides of a more sedate nature. Amusement park mainstays like the Wonder Wheel (a classic Ferris wheel) and the Dollywood Express (an authentic steam-driven train) provide a pleasant means of taking a load off your feet. Watch out, though—the Dollywood Express inevitably gets "robbed" by outlaws!

Another of Dollywood's newer additions is a contender in the ongoing game of theme park one-upmanship. Daredevil Falls, which premiered in 1998, is currently the highest and fastest log flume ride in the country. What starts out as a tranquil drift with the currents culminates in a drop-off that sends you and your fellow riders plummeting at 50 miles per hour to a splashy welcome below. Another of our personal favorite water rides is the Mountain Slidewinder. This minimally wet ride is akin to a water slide, but its multiple riders occupy large foam rafts during their winding, rocking, speedy journey to the bottom.

An Interactive Experience

Dollywood's attractions offer something for all ages. For the 2002 season, the park debuted a new section called Adventures in Imagination, located in what was formerly the Dollywood Boulevard area. The $10 million development is highlighted by Smoky Mountain Wilderness Adventure—a new "movie ride" attraction that takes passengers on a rollicking journey with Dolly by land, sea, and air—and Chasing Rainbows, an interactive museum/attraction that displays behind-the-scenes collections, stories, and memorabilia that relate to Dolly's life and career. See yourself on video as you share the stage with Dolly and Porter Waggoner or see what you look like in one of Dolly's wigs—if you dare!

Try visiting Dollywood during the off-season. The crowds are smaller, you'll spend less time waiting in line for rides, and you can take advantage of the park's seasonal festivals like Harvest Celebration and Festival of Nations.

One longtime favorite attraction is Eagle Mountain Sanctuary, the nation's largest preserve of nonreleasable bald eagles. Presented in cooperation with the National Foundation to Protect America's Eagles, this 1.5-million-cubic-foot aviary re-creates the natural habitat of our national symbol and is used for the purposes of education, rehabilitation, and breeding. This safe haven is also the site of the Wings of America—Birds of Prey demonstration. Viewers can get up close and personal with some of nature's most interesting flying specimens, such as bald eagles that swoop down gracefully over the heads of the audience. Of course, this is all done under the supervision of specially trained handlers.

In 1999 Dollywood introduced the Southern Gospel Music Hall of Fame and Museum. Located next to Showstreet Palace Theatre, this facility utilizes a variety of memorabilia and artifacts that pay tribute to the Southern gospel artists who have shaped and influenced their genre of music. The attraction also features a "living museum," which uses numerous exhibits to examine the past, present, and future of Southern gospel music.

Dreamland Forest is anchored by what Dollywood bills as "America's largest interactive treehouse"—two large three-story structures that contain dozens of fun activities for kids ranging in age from toddlers to teens. Treetop games and gadgets include a birdhouse village, "grapevine gossip phones," and a magic looking glass. Further into the attraction, children will discover a three-level "beehive area" where they can shoot foam balls at targets (and each other) from air guns. Don't worry, the kids won't shoot their eyes out,

and even parents can get in on the fun helping gather balls on the lower level with their special collection devices. The Bullfrog Creek section of Dreamland Forest is where the younger ones can get wet with squirt guns, water blasters, fountains, and more. Nonparticipating parents will find plenty of benches nearby for safe and relaxed viewing. Truth is, however, you usually see the grown-ups having just as good a time as the kids when it comes to shooting it out with the foam balls and water devices!

Music, Music, Music

Music is a given at Dollywood, and that's to be expected considering that music is Dolly's original claim to fame. There is a definite emphasis placed on country and gospel music, although one of the shows journeys back in time with the songs and dances of the 1950s. Much of what you'll see on the stages of Dollywood are straight-ahead, live music performances: In all, about a dozen occupy a variety of indoor and outdoor venues. One features longtime favorite James Rogers while two others showcase members of Dolly's family, including her brother, Randy.

Another popular show, Heartsong, takes viewers on a musically enhanced journey through the Great Smoky Mountains with a large-screen motion picture presentation that is enhanced with multisensory extras. Um, let's just say you might get a little misty —and not from crying.

In addition to its regular daily musical fare, Dollywood presents a number of special concert events throughout the season.

Showcase of Stars, for example, is Dollywood's celebrity concert series that brings some of country music's biggest acts to Pigeon Forge. Stars like Pam Tillis, the Charlie Daniels Band, Loretta Lynn, and Ronnie Milsap are just some of the entertainers who have appeared on the stage of Dollywood Celebrity Theatre. Dolly herself also performs in benefit concerts in support of the Dollywood Foundation, an organization devoted to improving education in Sevier County (see the Close-up in our Education and Child Care chapter for more).

The Southern Gospel Jubilee is a month of old-fashioned, roof-raising gospel, featuring nearly 30 different acts.

Craftwork

One of the factors in the Dollywood equation that lends itself so well to the park's mountain home theme is the abundance of craftspeople that populate the complex. Craftwork has long been a staple of the mountain lifestyle in the Smokies, so it's only natural that those skills would be on display here. Masters of time-honored art forms like glassblowing, pottery throwing, candle making, and blacksmithing can be found conducting impressive demonstrations of their skills.

ANNUAL FESTIVALS

Although the regular season is usually the busiest time of year at Dollywood, more and more people are discovering the change of pace offered by the different seasonal festivals that are staged there throughout the year. The park looks different, and the entertainment is often different to boot. In addition to the write-ups below, we've covered two of the following events in our Festivals and Annual Events chapter.

Festival of Nations

Since 2001, Dollywood has gotten each season rolling with its Festival of Nations, a monthlong celebration that practically delivers the world to the heart of the Great Smoky Mountains. Some 400 performers from a dozen different countries do their acts throughout the park's many

To maximize your time and avoid heavy foot traffic, try getting to Dollywood when the gates open. Start your tour of the park in either Craftsmen's Valley or Country Fair and work your way toward the front entrance.

venues. In addition to the international guests, Dollywood's regular performers are scheduled as well, sharing the stage time at the park's various theaters. In previous years, Dollywood's Celebrity Theatre hosted the Irish dance troupe Rhythm Dance, and at Showstreet Palace Theatre the Russian Cossack Dance Troupe took the stage. Other acts hailed from Trinidad, Kenya, Italy, and Ecuador.

If you're not up for traipsing all over the park to get that global experience, you can hang out at Celebration Hall (formerly Imagination Station) in the Country Fair section. That's where countless food merchants, merchandise vendors, and entertainers can be found in one 7,000-square- foot location.

Dollywood's Festival of Nations isn't all music. Guests can get that Epcot feeling as they watch acrobatics and juggling on the streets of the park. At the international bazaar, street vendors have gifts and souvenirs for sale, and the cuisine of different countries is served by Dollywood's restaurants and food vendors. At the end of each day, all the international performers gather for a parade through the park, ending at the Butterfly Emporium. There, the entire cast joins together for a musical "world jam."

The park's schedule for the festival is 10:00 A.M. to 7:00 P.M. five days a week and 9:00 A.M. to 8:00 P.M. on Saturday. And remember that Dollywood's regular attractions, rides, and shows are all up and running during the festival.

Incidentally, the start of each new season at Dollywood is officially marked by Dolly's annual parade, which features Ms. Parton—and often many of her celebrity friends—traveling down the Parkway in

Pigeon Forge amidst floats and marching bands. The next day the park's gates open and the Festival of Nations commences.

Harvest Celebration

There are plenty of craftspeople working in the Smokies year-round, but during the annual Harvest Celebration in October and early November, skilled artisans from across the country converge on Dollywood for the Smokies' only outdoor crafts festival. Typically, some two dozen guest crafters are on hand, in addition to the resident artisans featured in the Craftsmen's Valley section of the park.

During Harvest Celebration, Dollywood is made over for fall with thousands of hay bales, pumpkins, cornstalks, and chrysanthemums. And the smells of traditional autumn foods, like deep-fried turkey legs and homemade sorghum, waft through the air, tempting guests as soon as they walk through the gates. The park also presents the joyful noises of the Southern Gospel Jubilee, featuring dozens of old-time gospel acts performing at different venues over the course of the festival. Best of all, the gospel shows are included in the price of admission.

Operating hours during Harvest Celebration are 10:00 A.M. to 6:00 P.M. daily, except Thursday, when the park is closed.

Worried about keeping up with your young'uns at Dolly's Splash Country? For an extra $2.00 per person, you can rent wristbands that work with the park's SafeTzone tracking system. Just swipe the waterproof band under the nearest scanner, and the locations of your other party members will light up on the park map display. Neat, huh?

A Smoky Mountain Christmas

The arrival of winter doesn't necessarily put a chill on the fun at Dollywood. During its Smoky Mountain Christmas festival, which runs from mid-November until the end of the year, the park takes on a whole new identity. It's really one of the single best seasonal celebrations in the county.

In terms of appearance alone, Dollywood is a spectacle, as more than two million holiday lights twinkle throughout the park. You'll also want to look for Carol of the Trees, an attraction that incorporates synchronized music and special lighting effects, and Tinker the Talking Tree. Tinker is a Christmas tree that looks like one of the fanciful characters from the old Sid and Marty Krofft TV shows. Tinker is quite interactive as he actually jokes with guests and answers their questions. Meanwhile, the many music shows at Dollywood adapt holiday themes. Christmas in the Smokies, the park's signature wintertime production, is a large-scale affair staged in the Celebrity Theatre, and Hometown Holidays is a nostalgic trip to the '50s. The spirit of the season is best captured with the gospel music of the Kingdom Heirs and Dollywood's live, outdoor nativity pageant, O Holy Night. Holiday foods and special concerts help round out the festival, and if that weren't enough, you can still ride the Tennessee Tornado in the middle of winter—a December roller coaster ride will certainly add new meaning to "chills and thrills."

SLIP SLIDING AWAY

The Dollywood empire got a lot bigger in 2001 with the addition of a 35-acre water park, Dolly's Splash Country. Located next to the original Dollywood theme park, Splash Country is a $20-million addition featuring a wave pool, a variety of single- and double-tube slides, and a family raft ride. More adventurous water lovers can try the corkscrew tunnels and multiple drops of the Mountain Scream Slides. Kids might prefer Little Creek Falls, the children's play pool area with its own water slides and activity pool. All ages can kick back on the "lazy river" that meanders the expanse of the water park or bob along in Mountain Waves, a 25,000-square-foot wave pool. The attractions are surrounded by scenery that was created with a Smoky Mountains theme in mind. Waterfalls, mountain streams, and natural-looking terrain help create the overall look. Other amenities include a shop for last-minute swimwear and sunscreen needs, a self-service restaurant, and a snack shop. By the way, you won't have to pay extra for the use of rafts or inner tubes. Those are free with park admission.

Dolly's Splash Country is open Memorial Day weekend through Labor Day, and the gates open at 10:00 A.M. Admission prices are $32.35 for ages 12 and older, $30.10 for seniors, and $26.75 for kids 4 through 11. Season passes range from $47 to $87, depending on age. As mentioned in the theme park section above, guests can purchase Splash & Play tickets or Super Passes that allow access to both Dollywood theme park and Splash Country water park for a discounted price. And just like at Dollywood, if you arrive after 3:00 P.M., you can splash the next day for free.

Carry your small electronics and other valuables in plastic zipper bags. This will help ensure that they stay dry when you're riding any of the park's numerous wet rides.

KIDSTUFF

Although you might be coming to the Smokies for hikes or craft shopping or music shows, you can't always count on your children enjoying those same activities. What's a parent to do? Plenty, if you keep your eyes open. If you just take a cruise down the Parkway in Sevierville, Pigeon Forge, or Gatlinburg, there's a good chance your kids will constantly point out the window, begging, "Can we stop here?" Welcome to the Midway.

In this chapter, you'll find all kinds of ways for kids to have fun, including traditional amusements like miniature golf, bumper boats, go-karts, and arcades. But purveyors of fun in the Smokies haven't limited themselves to these. There's laser tag, public library programs, museums, a water park, and more. So let's get going!

A Few Words about Amusement Centers

We've done a lot of cross-referencing between Kidstuff and our Attractions chapter. Quite a few of the businesses you'll read about in this chapter are what we refer to as "amusement centers" (featuring go-karts, miniature golf, arcades, bumper boats, and other activities where you pay as you go). Bear in mind that some of these activities aren't suitable for all youngsters, especially those younger than 10. Most go-kart tracks, for example, have specific age and height minimums when it comes to operating the karts.

What we've done in such cases is split our coverage of many amusement centers between Kidstuff and Attractions. Since it's a safe bet that most children will be accompanied by adults, this chapter gives comprehensive descriptions of what the centers have to offer all ages. That way,

the grown-ups can play right along with the kids. Information about things like the faster go-kart tracks, bungee towers, and other "grown-up" stuff are also covered in Attractions.

There are a few universals you'll encounter from one amusement center to the next. First, think "safety." Go-kart track managers prohibit deliberately bumping karts into each other and against track guardrails. Needless to say, pregnant women and people with heart and back conditions shouldn't participate in these activities. Second, you can count on most go-kart and bumper boat rides lasting anywhere from three to six minutes.

We also won't be going into any details on the arcades. For those of you who, for some strange reason, have never been in one, we'll be considerate and tell you to look for some combination of the following: video games, video simulators, pinball machines, air hockey tables, pool tables, and coin-operated kiddie rides. In some places you'll also see carnival-type games like ski ball and basketball shooting. Many of the arcades have games that award tickets, which can then be redeemed for prizes (those worthless trinkets that kids find fascinating!). Naturally, change machines are always on hand to convert your bills into quarters or tokens.

Finally, assume that most go-kart tracks, miniature golf courses, and arcades provide adequate free parking. In Gatlinburg there are places that don't have parking. You can pay to park in a city lot or garage, or you can access your destination on foot or by trolley. Most amusements are also open year-round. During the in-season (May through August), you can count on them being open seven days a week from around 9:00 or 10:00 A.M. to as late as midnight or 1:00 A.M. in some cases.

As for the off-season, you'll find that several establishments cut back to weekends only during winter months. However, most of the managers with whom we spoke weren't willing to commit to definite autumn and winter schedules. Often they choose to improvise and let factors such as the weather and holiday-related visitation determine when they open. Your best bet for weekly and daily schedules in the off-season is to call ahead.

Assume that the prices we've quoted in our write-ups include sales tax unless we note otherwise.

Child's Play

What all the listings in this chapter have in common are ways for the young ones to enjoy themselves. As in Attractions, we'll start in Sevierville, then putt, bungee, and go-kart ourselves all the way down through Gatlinburg. And hey! If you old fogies aren't careful, you might just find yourself having a pretty good time as well.

SEVIERVILLE

Sevier County Public Library
321 Court Avenue, Sevierville
(865) 453-3532

Every Thursday is story day at the library! Story hour starts at 10:30 A.M. and provides a free and entertaining experience for preschool children and their parents. During the session, volunteers read aloud to the children from age-appropriate books. Participation by preschool and day-care groups is especially high during these school-year months.

In addition to the normal morning story, the children can also listen to guest speakers from the community, such as firemen, veterinarians, and even clowns! These folks will use their time to tell the children about their occupations. The kids especially enjoy going outside to check out the real squad cars when a local policeman is part of the program.

The library itself has a separate section for children's books and has hundreds of children's videos on its shelves. Sevier County residents can easily obtain a library card, of course, but out-of-county residents can also check out materials with either proof of local property ownership or a $10 deposit.

Smoky Mountain Deer Farm
and Exotic Petting Zoo
478 Happy Hollow Lane, Sevierville
(865) 428-3337
www.deerfarmzoo.com

You won't find lions and tigers and bears (oh my!) at this unique animal exhibit, but you will encounter quite a few species of animals that can be just as interesting. Children and grown-ups alike have been flocking to the Deer Farm and Exotic Petting Zoo for more than a decade to feed and get face-to-face (and sometimes hand-to-mouth) with a menagerie that boasts quite a unique bunch of residents, including camels and zebras, kangaroos and llamas, and ferrets and reindeer. They even have pony rides for the little ones. Intrigued? See the Close-up in this chapter for more information on how to "talk to the animals."

Admission to the Deer Farm and Exotic Petting Zoo is $7.50 for ages 13 and older and $4.00 for ages 3 to 12. Children ages 2 and younger are admitted for a shiny, new penny. Prices do not include sales tax. Discounted rates are available for groups of 15 or more. Understandably, area school and day-care groups are frequent visitors to this place. To feed the animals, use only the special feed provided, which comes in cups ranging from

Remember to put hats and sunscreen on the little ones—and the not so little! And bring along extra water—or their favorite cups to fill—to keep the family hydrated, so the hot sun doesn't spoil the family fun time.

12 ounces ($1.50) to 32 ounces ($3.50). Pony rides cost $3.75 each.

The facility is open year-round seven days a week except for Thanksgiving and Christmas. Daily hours are from 10:00 A.M. to 5:30 P.M. Throughout the year, ticket sales stop one hour before closing. Pony rides are available from 10:30 A.M. through 5:00 P.M. April through November only, and the availability of pony rides depends on the weather. The owners also advise calling ahead to verify hours during periods of bad weather.

The same folks also operate Deer Farm Riding Stables, located on the adjacent property. See our chapter on the Parks and Recreation for more information on their horseback-riding opportunities.

Rainforest Adventures
NASCAR Drive, Sevierville
(865) 428-4091
www.rfadventures.com
Kids will squeal (and maybe shriek!) with delight at this museum of reptiles and amphibians. Rainforest Adventures' authentic habitats house deadly cobras, mambas, and vipers as well as snakes that will put the squeeze on you—anacondas and pythons. Also look for scorpions, giant tortoises, alligators, frogs, and turtles. You want to be sure to hang around long enough to catch one of Rainforest Adventures's live demonstrations, which take place every couple of hours. It's fun to watch the museum handlers get interactive with the residents, and you'll probably learn a thing or two about these exotic creatures while you're at it. Admission prices are $11.99 for adults, $9.99 for those over 55, and $6.99 for children. Prices do not include sales tax. Daily hours are 9:00 A.M. to 6:00 P.M. mid-August through mid-May and 9:00 A.M. to 8:00 P.M. during peak season (mid-May through mid-August).

NASCAR SpeedPark
1545 Parkway, Sevierville
(865) 908-5500
www.NASCARSpeedPark.com

For a complete rundown of what this megasize go-kart park has to offer, see our write-up in Attractions. Here, however, we'll tell you what's in store for kids.

The Baby Bristol track is for drivers who are at least 3 feet 4 inches tall. The small, single-loop circuit is just right for younger speed demons. The Qualifier track has a couple of extra bends in it but is still fairly short. You must be 3 feet 8 inches to drive on the Qualifier. The Young Champions track is longer and has a lot of twists and turns along the way. Those who are at least 4 feet tall will be busy with their steering wheel on this track.

SpeedPark also has the Family 500 track, where double-seat karts allow adults and children to tear up the track side by side. Drivers must be at least 5 feet tall, and passengers must be at least 3 feet 6 inches tall.

The number of tickets required to drive on the tracks varies. Baby Bristol costs three tickets, the Qualifier costs four tickets, and both Young Champions and Family 500 cost five tickets apiece.

Individual tickets sell for $1.00 each, or you can purchase one of several packages that offer larger numbers of tickets at discounted prices. Booklets come in denominations of up to 150 tickets. In addition to track admissions, tickets can also be used at SpeedPark's concessions areas.

One-day ride passes are also available. The Mini-Cup pass entitles any child 12 and younger to ride on any track where height requirements are met. The price is $14.95. The Busch Series pass, $24.95, is available for ages 13 and older and is good for every track except the Smoky Mountain Speedway. However, a $15.00 upgrade will get you two rides on that quarter-mile track, provided you are at least 5 feet 4 inches tall and have a valid driver's license. SpeedPark's season pass costs $59.95 and entitles you to a Busch Series wristband every time you visit. But even with a season pass, you must still pay an extra $15.00 and have a license to go screaming around the Smoky Mountain Speedway.

Besides the go-karts, kids will also love the huge Speed Dome arcade, featuring more than 60 racing video games and driving simulators. Recent kid-friendly additions include an indoor playground and kiddie rides. Other outdoor amusements include bumper boats, a climbing wall, and a miniature golf course.

NASCAR SpeedPark is open year-round. In summer, daily hours are from 10:00 A.M. until at least 10:00 P.M., although they may stay open until midnight if the masses allow. Once tourist visitation starts to slow down in Sevier County after August 1, the park is open from 11:00 A.M. to 8:00 P.M.

PIGEON FORGE

The Track
2575 Parkway, Pigeon Forge
(865) 453-4777
www.funatthetrack.com

We're not really sure how to classify this place. Is it a small amusement park or a huge amusement center? Considering that miniature golf and go-kart racing are the anchor activities here, we'll go with the latter. Before you turn the kids loose, you'll want to purchase tickets. Individual tickets are $2.50 each; you can purchase discounted bundles ranging from 6 for $14.00 to 48 for $90.00. To help you navigate the Track's layout, a handy, colorful map is provided, which indicates all of the different areas, including the concessions facility, restrooms, and the arcade.

There are two twisty, curvy, outdoor tracks on-site. The first, simply called the Track, utilizes one- and two-seat karts. One-seaters cost two tickets, and solo drivers must be at least 4 feet 6 inches tall. For two-seaters, drivers with passengers pay two tickets, and the driver must be at least 16 years old. Passengers in two-seaters must be at least 3 feet tall. Those between 3 feet and 4 feet 6 inches tall ride for free, while passengers more than 4 feet 6 inches must pay two tickets extra.

The other outdoor track, the Wild Woody, was a new feature in 1999 and helped usher in the advent of wooden go-kart tracks in the Smoky Mountains. The driving surface is actually a hybrid combination of the original, ground-level, concrete track and a newer, add-on section—a multitiered wooden track that goes through several humps and corkscrew twists. The driving is a little slower than on the run-of-the-mill go-kart track, but like wooden roller coasters, the wooden tracks give kartsters a ride you can really feel.

You must be at least 4 feet 10 inches tall to drive a single go-kart on the Wild Woody; the cost is three tickets. Drivers with passengers pay three tickets, and the driver must be at least 16 years old. Two-seater passengers on the Wild Woody must be at least 3 feet tall. If you're between 3 feet and 4 feet 10 inches tall, you ride along for free; if you're 4 feet 10 inches tall or more, you pay an extra three tickets.

For golfing action, you can try out the two 18-hole putt-putt courses of Gator Golf. Both courses have various animal and wildlife figures adorning the landscape. The cost is two tickets per person per 18-hole round for ages 13 and older. Ages 6 to 12 can golf for one ticket, and kids 5 and younger can tag along for free with a paid adult.

Daredevils might want to fork over the six tickets required to bungee-jump from the Track's 60-foot tower. For those who want to remain closer to the ground, bumper cars are available to anyone taller than 4 feet 2 inches. You can drive them for two tickets per trip. If you want to get wet on a hot summer day, you might be interested in the bumper boats. You must be 4 feet 2 inches tall and pay two tickets to operate the bumper boats, but those who are shorter can ride with an adult operating.

The younger children in tow might particularly enjoy the Track's Kid's Country. This area features a number of carnival-style rides on a pint-size scale that cost one ticket each. Rides include miniature

CLOSE-UP

All the Deer That's Fit to Feed

You're fairly warned when you enter! The llamas will spit if you invade their space! Even when they do, you can't help but laugh. It's all part of the one-to-one experience at the hands-on Smoky Mountain Deer Farm and Exotic Petting Zoo, located on a 140-acre Smoky Mountain farm. Once you've paid your admission (which is very reasonable when you consider that six bucks won't buy much more than a couple of soft drinks in some parts of the country), you're free to roam the grounds at your own pace and spend as much time as you like looking at and reading about different species of animals. Some of them, like the kangaroos and wallabies, are a long way from home.

There are two pens where you can actually go inside to pet and feed the animals. When you enter the pens of the pygmy goats and the fallow deer, make sure to quickly close the gate behind you! Once inside, feel free to pet these friendly beasts. Be aware, however, that if you're

carrying feed (only use feed provided by the petting zoo!), you'll soon become very popular with the animals. If you have smaller children in tow, keep a hand on them or else they may be a little overwhelmed. If you prefer, you can have the little ones feed the goats and deer from outside the fence.

You can also feed the various breeds of donkeys, zebras, and miniature horses that you'll see. When feeding any of the "horse-like" animals, make sure you feed them with a flat, open palm. There's even a stand where you can purchase apples to feed the live reindeer that live on the premises. There are animals, however, that you definitely must not feed—kangaroos and wallabies. They must consume a special diet provided by the owners.

As the name implies, there are many varieties of deer that you can visit, including the sika deer, mule deer, and the reindeer. Along the way you'll see many more types of animals like ferrets, pot-bellied pigs, prairie dogs, exotic cattle, emu,

versions of a train ride, swings, and a Ferris wheel; there's even a Kiddie Kart Raceway where the smaller ones can burn rubber on their own track. Drivers of the Kiddie Karts must be at least 4 years old and 3 feet 6 inches tall, and drivers of the Rookie Karts must be at least 4 feet 2 inches tall. Both karts cost two tickets. Kid's Country is closed during most of January and February, even when the rest of the Track is open.

Star Tracks
2757 Parkway, Pigeon Forge
(865) 429-5580
In addition to a fairly large indoor arcade, this amusement center features a single-loop go-kart track. The Family Slick Track is a covered track open to drivers 4 feet 8 inches and taller. Admission is $7.00 per ride, or you can get three rides for $18.00 or 10 rides for $50.00 after noon. Two-seater karts cost $10.00 per ride, and drivers must be at least 16 years old.

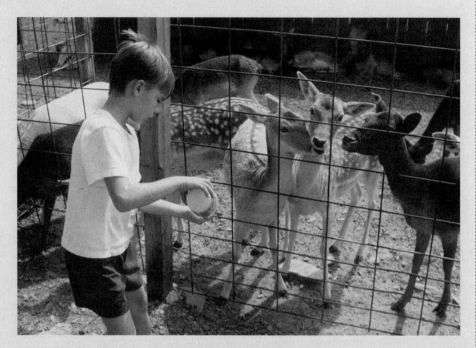

Dinner time at a deer farm. SMOKY MOUNTAIN DEER FARM AND EXOTIC PETTING ZOO

doves, and sheep! You can be sure that the animals are always well treated and well cared for by owners Greg and Lynn Hoisington. The facility is USDA inspected and approved. Once you've been to Smoky Mountain Deer Farm and Exotic Petting Zoo, you'll probably give it your own seal of approval as well.

Laserport
2782 Parkway, Pigeon Forge
(865) 453-0400
Welcome to high-tech laser tag fun! The laser games take place inside a large labyrinth interior with ultraviolet lighting. Combatants are divided into two teams, red and green, with up to 20 players per team. After a few minutes of briefing on how to play the game and use the equipment, players are suited up and let loose to blast away the opponent. Games last for 10 minutes; the team with the most points at the end wins. Afterward, players are given a computer printout of their shooting efficiency, including data on the numbers of successful shots made and hits taken. At Laserport, players are given infinite lives and shots, eliminating the need to reload laser guns.

Players as young as five or six years old can participate, depending on their size. The cost is $7.75 per game or $18.00 for three games. During summer months, you can buy one game and get one free between 9:00 and 10:30 A.M. In the off-season, the same deal applies between 10:00 and 11:30 A.M. Laserport also offers annual memberships where you pay a one-time $20.00 fee, receive your first game free, and then pay $3.00 per game afterwards. Each membership can only be used by the person in whose name it is purchased.

In addition to laser tag, Laserport has an outdoor, single-loop go-kart track that costs $4.75 per ride or $12.00 for three rides. Drivers must be at least 4 feet 6 inches tall. Drivers of two-seat karts must be at least 16 years old, and passengers must be able to sit upright and remain buckled into the safety harness. Two-seaters cost $5.75 per ride. You'll also find a massive indoor arcade at Laserport that is open year-round.

Rockin' Raceway
2839 Parkway, Pigeon Forge
(865) 428-3392

This amusement center's Pro Track costs $6.00, and drivers must be at least 14 years old and 4 feet 6 inches tall. There is also a junior go-kart track for ages 4 to 7 that costs $4.00 per ride.

Rockin' Raceway offers more than just go-karts. On the Hawk, up to 24 passengers at a time take a potentially nauseating pendulum ride, which sends them in complete multiple loops. The Hawk costs $5.00 and requires that riders be at least 4 feet tall. The Tornado takes passengers on a dizzying, spinning ride for $3.00. For the younger ones, Rockin' Raceway also has several carnival-type kiddie rides (miniature Ferris wheel, etc.), which only cost $2.00 each, or you can purchase seven tickets for $10.00. There is also a kiddie roller coaster for ages 2 and older that costs $3.00 to ride.

Inside the main building, you'll find the SR2V simulator, in which "passengers" take a virtual high-speed trip around a racecourse for only $3.00 per person. There is also, of course, a very large, well-equipped video arcade.

Fast Tracks
2879 Parkway, Pigeon Forge
(865) 428-1988

Here's another multifaceted entertainment center with fun for kids of all ages. The centerpieces of the facility, naturally, are the three outdoor go-kart tracks. On the multicurved Pro Car Track, you must be at least 10 years old and 4 feet 6 inches tall to drive alone. To take a passenger, you must be at least 16, and your passenger must be at least 3 feet tall and 3 to 9 years old. The Pro Cars cost $6.00 per ride and $4.00 for a passenger. On Fast Tracks' latest addition, the elevated track ($7.00 per ride), you must be at least 4 feet 10 inches tall to drive alone. Two-seaters cost $10.00 and require at least a 16-year-old behind the wheel. With both the Pro Cars and the elevated track, you can buy four rides for $20.00. Eleven bucks will get you a combo ticket, entitling you to one Pro Car ride and one ride on the elevated track. On the Junior Track, drivers ages 4 through 9 can zip around a small, single-loop track for $5.00 each.

The strong of heart may want to try out the Ejection Seat, a "reverse bungee" ride on which one or two people are strapped into a seating cage at ground level as bungee cords are pulled tight from high above. The cage is then released and riders are hurled rapidly skyward to a height of approximately 100 feet; from there they enjoy several up-and-down bounces on the springy cords. The Ejection Seat costs $20 for one person or $30 for two people. The Sky Scraper is a large pendulum-like contraption that whirls occupants around in vertical loops, and you pay $20 for the privilege.

Other Fast Tracks offerings include a trampoline jump and the VR Voyager simulator ride, which costs $5.00. Younger children will probably prefer the many kiddie rides that cost $2.50 each or six for $10.00. All the kids will have a blast in Fast Tracks' indoor arcade.

**Adventure Golf and Adventure Raceway
2925 Parkway, Pigeon Forge
(865) 453-9233**

**2945 Parkway, Pigeon Forge
(865) 428-2971**
Let's start with the go-karts! Adventure Raceway features one outdoor track—another of the several wooden go-kart tracks that sprang up on the Parkway in 1999. The curvy, multilevel wooden section was added to the existing figure-eight, ground-level track. The cost is $7.00 per ride, and drivers must be at least 4 feet 8 inches tall. Adventure Raceway also has bumper boats that cost $5.00 per ride. You must be 3 feet 6 inches tall to operate the boats. Children who are more than 3 years old but who are still under the minimum height requirements may ride free as passengers on both the go-kart track and the bumper boats.

At Adventure Golf, you'll find one of the more attractive and interesting miniature golf courses in the area. In fact, owners claim that it's the oldest commercial miniature golf course in Pigeon Forge. The figures and statues found on the site are mammoth versions of a dinosaur, a shark, an octopus, and more; large shipwreck and castle scenes add to the landscaping. Adventure Golf has two 18-hole courses that cost $6.50 each, and you can play a second round for only $3.00 more. There is also an indoor arcade for gaming fun.

**Professor Hacker's Lost Treasure Golf
3010 Parkway, Pigeon Forge
(865) 453-0307**
Although this newer attraction is devoted exclusively to miniature golf, there's not very much that's "miniature" about it. Its features easily grab your eye as you motor down the Parkway. An Aztec pyramid, a volcano, and a twin prop plane reminiscent of the Indiana Jones films are among the life-size props that tower above street level and enhance your putting experience.

The twin 18-hole courses are built around a theme of exploration and adven-

ture. According to course "legend," Professor Ephraim A. Hacker discovered an abandoned mining train that had been built by the Germans during World War I for the purpose of helping finance their war effort. Once you've selected your putter and ball, a train takes you and your fellow golfers up an inclined railway to the top of the park. From there, you can choose either the Gold course, which takes you under a large waterfall, or the Diamond course, which takes you through the pyramid.

Lost Treasure Golf costs $7.50 per course for ages 13 and older and $6.00 for ages 5 through 12. Children 4 and younger play for $3.50. It costs $3.50 for any age to play a second course.

**Ultrazone
3053 Parkway, Pigeon Forge
(865) 428-2444**
At Ultrazone, laser tag gamers can hunt each other down in a 3,800-square-foot play area designed to resemble a destroyed city. The layout also features three sniper areas from which shooters can pick off their opponents from aerial vantage points.

After a 10-minute period of equipment briefing and suiting up, players enter the game area and compete in a three-team system with up to 10 players on each team. After each 25-minute game, players get computer readouts detailing how many hits they made and how many times they were hit. At Ultrazone, anyone age 7 or older can play for $8.75. With groups of 10 or more, the price goes down to $6.75 per person.

**Fantasy Golf
3263 Parkway, Pigeon Forge
(865) 453-4183**
This is actually the address and phone number for Ogle's Gift Outlet, located next door to the golf course. That's where you must purchase your tickets to Fantasy Golf's two 18-hole courses, which, from a purely financial perspective, is one of the

better miniature golf values in town. You'll find some pretty interesting residents at this facility, such as a giant praying mantis, unicorn, and dragon. Ages six and older can play 18 holes for $8.00 or all 36 holes for only $6.00. Children five and younger play for free.

Smoky Mountain Speedpark
3275 Parkway, Pigeon Forge
(865) 429-4639 (track)
(865) 429-8600 (Sky Scraper)
This Parkway amusement operation has two single-loop go-kart tracks for drivers ages 12 and older (no height restrictions). On the original track, one-seat karts cost $6.00 per ride or five rides for $25.00; two-seaters cost $10.00. Speedpark's covered slick track costs $5.00 per person. For those of you who get your kicks in the air, look for the Sky Scraper. Riders are strapped into a cage that is swung over and over like a pendulum in 360-degree loops by a large mechanical arm. You must be at least 3 feet 6 inches tall to ride. The cost is $30.00 per person.

Bungee lovers have a choice of which direction to hurl themselves (and, possibly, their lunches). Those who prefer the trip down can leap off the regular bungee tower, while those who prefer high positive Gs can strap into the Sling Shot, a "reverse bungee" ride that flings passengers skyward before they start bouncing. Both bungee experiences cost $20 for one trip or $30 for two.

Other Speedpark activities include a rock climbing wall, a mechanical bull, a multiaxis ride, and a trampoline jump, each of which costs $5.00. Also look for a large, indoor video game center.

Smoky Mountain Slick Track
3322 Parkway, Pigeon Forge
(865) 428-4955
This outdoor slick track runs along a bent, single-loop course and offers close-knit, competitive driving action. Solo drivers must be at least 4 feet 9 inches tall. Drivers of passengers must be at least 16 years old, and passengers must be at least

3 feet 4 inches tall. All single-seat go-karts cost $6.00 per ride, and two-seaters cost $10.00 per ride. Smoky Mountain Slick Track has a discounted price of four rides for $20.00. If you're not on the track, you can still keep yourself entertained in their indoor arcade.

Speed Zone Fun Park
3315 South River Road, Pigeon Forge
(865) 908-7255
This amusement center is less than 1 block off the Parkway near the Old Mill area of Pigeon Forge. There are two outdoor go-kart tracks. The single-loop slick track is for drivers who are at least 4 feet 8 inches tall. Single karts cost $6.00, and two-seaters cost $10.00. You may also purchase three single-kart tickets for $15.00 or 10 for $50.00. Sprint and Kiddie karts cost $5.00 each. The Tennessee Twister is a wooden go-kart track with multiple levels and corkscrew turns. You must be at least 5 feet tall to drive. The Tennessee Twister costs $7.00 for one-seaters and $10.00 for two-seaters. Ten rides on the Twister cost $60.00. Drivers of all two-seat cars must be 16 years old, and passengers must be at least 3 years old. If you want to drive both tracks, you can do so for a discounted price of $11.00.

Riverside Raceway also has the Sling Swing, a multitowered setup that uses bungee cords to fling passengers either up and down, side to side, or both! It costs $15 to ride. If you don't care to be hurled through the air, you may just want to take it easy in the raceway's small indoor arcade.

Treehouse Golf & Games
3535 Parkway, Pigeon Forge
(865) 429-8008
It's like suddenly walking into a forest right in the middle of town. Treehouse is actually two 18-hole miniature courses side by side, but it's tough to tell one from the other until you get into them. With tall trees, thick bushes, and running water all around, Treehouse offers an island of serenity in the bustle that exemplifies

Pigeon Forge. A single round is $7.50 for adults, and kids 5 to 12 pay $6.00. An additional game is $3.00. Considering the prices and the peaceful environment, the $13.00 all-day ticket (kids $12.00) seems like a bargain. A good-size arcade beside the course has a wide variety of games for those not into sylvan golf.

Wild Wheels
3735 Parkway, Pigeon Forge
(865) 453-7942
The southernmost of Pigeon Forge's myriad amusements on the Parkway, Wild Wheels is a sparkling-clean layout featuring two go-kart tracks, a laser tag center, a big arcade, and a four-station bungee jump tower (no waiting!). Bungee jumping from the quad tower is priced at $20. Seven dollars a head is the going rate for a 12-minute trip on either of the two go-kart tracks. The junior track (7 years old, minimum height 4 feet) has two kart configurations, as does the big track (10 years, height 54 inches). The large arcade features a broad selection of electronic and interactive games.

GATLINBURG

The scene here isn't as frantic as it is in Pigeon Forge because amusement-type activities had to shoehorn themselves in among the shops that gave Gatlinburg its original reputation as a tourism center. Some of the older attractions hark back to the days when Mom and Dad first came to the Smokies, and the newer ones are striving to achieve the state-of-the-art condition found in the two cities to the north.

Hillbilly Golf
340 Parkway, Gatlinburg
(865) 436-7470
Another oldie with a really spectacular twist: You can't walk to the course. Hillbilly Golf's two 18-hole courses are on a mountaintop 300 feet above the Parkway, and the only way to get to them is to ride an incline railway. The ride is part of the admission, of course, and while you're waiting for the rail car, you can visit the arcade or get in a few strokes on the practice green. Once you get to the top, you'll play on your choice of courses (or both) set in the wilderness, with mountaineer hazards like stills and rock walls to make your shot selections a little more difficult.

Camp Thunder
514 Parkway, Gatlinburg
(865) 430-7223
www.smokymountainfun.com
Weather is not a factor when you're burning it up at Camp Thunder—it's indoors. Driving indoors feels a little strange at first, but once you get used to the slick track, it's just like driving outdoors but not as cold, hot, windy, or wet. It's climate-controlled and comfortable, and everybody in the family that's over 10 years old and over 54 inches tall (that's 4 feet 6 inches) can give it a ride. A full-speed ride runs 35 to 40 laps, depending on skill, and double cars are available for those who need a little help navigating. After a race, you've got a couple of choices: You can go upstairs to the 18-hole Great Smoky Mountains miniature golf course for a round of putt-putt golf on holes laid out to simulate the mountain trails in the national park, or take a seat on the motion simulator rides to keep the thrill of racing alive while you just watch. Camp Thunder is open seven days a week year-round (except Christmas). A dizzying variety of package deals is available, starting at $7.95 for a single experience at most venues. "Twofers" and combinations of three or more activities will save you money and keep you out of the weather longer.

Anna Porter Public Library
207 Cherokee Orchard Road, Gatlinburg
(865) 436-5588
Historically dedicated to children's education through reading and practical application, Anna Porter has operated programs at the preschool and in-school

level for as long as anyone in Gatlinburg can remember. The summer reading program for school-age children every Wednesday is so popular that groups are broken up by age, and volunteer help is necessary to keep order. The volunteers are usually mothers who were in the program when they were younger. During the school year, the Wednesday program shifts to preschoolers, with age-appropriate stories and games. Another popular feature is the Dial-a-Story program, which permits callers to hear a 3-to-5-minute story by dialing (865) 430-5026. The Gatlinburg Kiwanis Club underwrites the cost of this program. With all this encouragement to go into the library at such an early age, it's no surprise that Gatlinburg's splendid little library is a popular gathering place for the elementary school crowd when classes end every day.

Treasure Quest Golf
653 Parkway, Gatlinburg
(865) 436-3972

Here's a great rainy-day activity: It's indoors! Treasure Quest is a unique take on a theme that's everywhere you look in the Smokies: A miniature golf course that's under cover and that's clean enough to eat off the floor. Eighteen holes of fun miniature golf are set in a motif that features pirates and other treasure-hunters, with rock 'n' roll background music. Admission is $7.99 for ages 12 and up, $5.99 for children 6 to 11, and children 5 and younger are free with a paid adult admission.

Earthquake—The Ride
653 Parkway, Gatlinburg
(865) 436-9765

Shake-and-bake on the Parkway. A simulated subway car gets caught smack in the middle of an earthquake, and you're right in the center. Motion and electronic wizardry combine to provide a gut-wrenching eight-minute ride that'll leave you gasping for air and wondering if you want to do it again right now, or maybe wait a little while 'til all the body parts get

back where they belong. Earthquake admission is $7.99 if you're 12 or older, $5.99 for younger riders.

Fannie Farkle's Amusement Emporium
656 Parkway, Gatlinburg
(865) 436-4057

One of Gatlinburg's original arcades, Fannie Farkle's is distinguished by the fact that the premiums offered to the game winners include high-quality collectibles like porcelain figurines and crystal accessories. A couple of games also pay off in Beanie Babies. In business since 1980, Fannie Farkle's is the only stand-alone arcade we're including in this section; you shouldn't be afraid to send your children in alone. The "Ogle Dog," available at the snack bar, is a local favorite for a quick lunch.

The Gatlinburg Fun Center
716 Parkway, Gatlinburg
(865) 430-8985
www.smokymountainfun.com

Six different amusement venues (including on-site arcades with the latest in high-tech competition) stretch across the back of Reagan Square Mall in the heart of downtown Gatlinburg. Hours of enjoyment are available for the whole family in a close enough environment that nobody gets lost or separated by much distance. We'll present the attractions as they appear from left to right as you enter the complex. Prices vary depending on combinations of activities and group size. Groups of 10 to 15 who play together will save $1.00 a head for each venue; 16 or more in a group can expect a $2.00 discount. The Gatlinburg Fun Center is open every day but Christmas from 10:00 A.M. until the last customer is served and goes away happy.

Old Gatlinburg Golf & Games
(865) 430-4653

Here are two unusual miniature golf courses, laid out on the hillside, that integrate old buildings into the play. Gatlinburg's Old Town Square Course delivers a local history lesson at every hole, including how the city got its name. The Smokies Old Mountain Trail Course describes the development of the Great Smoky Mountains National Park in a peaceful setting reminiscent of the park itself. One hole plays through a replica of the old Elkmont post office. A single round of golf on one course is $6.95 for anybody over five years old; toddlers can play for $3.95. One of the best bargains in the area is the $9.95 golf pass that allows unlimited play for five consecutive days.

Fort Fun
(865) 436-2326

Fort Fun offers three different options for family entertainment under one roof. This big building at the back of the Family Fun Center contains a laser tag game with spectacular sound and light effects; a 3-D movie theater that uses special glasses and special effects to place you in the scene of your choice from a menu of five; and a bumper car track where the entire family can drive bumper cars. The separate venues vary in price from $7.00 to $9.00, with a variety of special package deals.

Bankshot Basketball
(865) 430-8985

A fun-filled combination of miniature golf and basketball, where angled backboards put a special slant on every shot. Accuracy counts big in this contest of skill, and a little knowledge of plane geometry can't hurt. A trip through the Bankshot course is $4.99 with no time limit.

Mysterious Mansion
425 River Road, Gatlinburg
(865) 436-7007

Things go bump in the Mysterious Mansion at all hours of the day and night. It's easy to find the mansion: Just go over to River Road and look for the only place with a big black hearse parked at the front door. Things get a little creepier when you get inside. Creepy things want to make you their "best friend," there's all kinds of awful noise going on, and the floor keeps acting like it's going to give way. And then there are the rooms with no way in or out, but somehow you got in, and . . . but we could go on like this all night—you really should be there. Getting in costs $7.95 for ages 13 and older, $5.95 for kids 7 to 12, and children 6 and younger are free. Getting out may cost you a piece of your soul if the residents take a liking to you.

FESTIVALS AND ANNUAL EVENTS

As if you didn't already have a million and one reasons to come to the Smoky Mountains, here we present you with 50 more. In our cities you'll find commemorations of seasons and holidays as well as festivals for arts and crafts, nature, and mountain ways of life. We celebrate automobiles, romance, and the performing arts. And along the way, look out for plenty of great music, delicious food, and festive decorations.

Although the events included here are by no means a complete representation of all the events that take place in the Smokies each year, we have tried to steer you toward the more popular ones and those with the most longevity. We've sidestepped many events sponsored by retailers that are basically nothing more than gimmicks to enhance business. Another category that we've given selective coverage to is the charity fund-raiser. Several of the events detailed below do raise money for specific organizations and causes, but we've only included those that might be of practical interest to the out-of-towner, i.e., music concerts, craft fairs, food tastings, etc. Other activities, like charity golf tournaments and walk/run events, rely almost exclusively on local or selective participation, and we've chosen to omit these.

You also won't find individual write-ups about any of the numerous custom auto shows that draw so many car buffs to the Smokies, especially during peak season. Usually, they generate more interest among show participants than with the typical tourist. But whether you like custom cars or not, you have no choice but to get an eyeful of them as you drive down the Parkway in Pigeon Forge!

In some cases, you'll find that we've outlined larger festivals as well as many of the specific events that take place within them. For example, Winterfest is a county-

More Information

Many of our inclusions are sponsored by the different cities in the county, so if you would like more information, contact:

Sevierville Chamber of Commerce
(865) 453-6411
(800) 255-6411
www.seviervillechamber.com

Pigeon Forge Department of Tourism
Office of Special Events
(865) 429-7350
(800) 251-9100
www.mypigeonforge.com

Gatlinburg Department of Tourism
Office of Special Events
(865) 436-0500
(800) 343-1475
www.gatlinburg-tennessee.com

wide celebration that lasts from mid-November through February. Obviously, there are quite a few Winterfest-related happenings going on during this period, and we've included many of the more notable ones.

We've departed from our usual north-to-south presentation in this chapter, choosing to instead list the events chronologically. Since most Smoky Mountains events take place on different dates each year, we've stated the general time of each month that they occur. Phone numbers that appear with listings sometimes correspond with the event sites, but in other cases we've given you the number of the event coordinators when we felt that would be more helpful. We have also given you specific prices, but these are also subject to change from year to year.

JANUARY

Many of the events in January and February are part of Winterfest, which begins in November and runs through February. (Refer to the November section of this chapter for a general overview of the Winterfest celebration.) Also in January, the cities of Pigeon Forge and Gatlinburg are continuing the trolley tours of their respective city's Winterfest lights displays. You'll find all the specifics about those trolley tours in the November section as well.

Wilderness Wildlife Week
Music Road Hotel and
Convention Center
303 Henderson Chapel Road
Pigeon Forge
(865) 429-7350
Although the events that take place throughout the week occur in different parts of the county, the Heartlander Resort in Pigeon Forge is headquarters for what has become one of the area's most popular annual events. Wilderness Wildlife Week is nine days of nature hikes and walks as well as seminars, displays, and workshops dealing with the study of

Smoky Mountain flora and fauna. And you can't beat the fact that the whole thing costs absolutely nothing. The hikes and other programs are led by approximately 90 scientists and other experts in the fields of wildlife, nature, and conservation. This all-volunteer staff converges from around the region to lend its expertise on subjects ranging from native black bears to wildflowers.

Generally, the different Wildlife Week events each have a limited number of spots available for participants. Registration takes place at the Heartlander and is done on a first-come, first-served basis. Registration for any of the week's 40 to 50 hikes takes place the day before the hike. As for the hikes themselves, transportation is provided to various points in the national park for the expeditions that range from short, casual nature strolls to overnight stays on top of mighty Mount LeConte. Most of the week's lecture-oriented programs take place at the Heartlander. The week typically closes out with a slide presentation at the Heartlander, narrated by guest speaker Bill Landry, host of WBIR TV's *Heartland Series* (refer to the Close-up in our Media chapter).

When Wilderness Wildlife Week was in its infancy, the turnout was pretty low, and the number of programs was limited. These days, thousands of people from all over the country journey to the Smokies specifically for this event, which usually takes place during the second full week of the month.

FEBRUARY

Special Olympics Winter Games
Ober Gatlinburg Ski Resort
1339 Ski Mountain Road, Gatlinburg
(865) 436-5423
Each year, scores of physically and mentally challenged youths go for the gold in the snow-covered mountains of Gatlinburg. Athletes as young as 11 compete in alpine skiing and ice-skating events during the first weekend in February. The

Once you know the specific dates you'll be visiting the Smokies, you might want to check with area departments of tourism beforehand to see if any parades or road races (5K or 10K runs) are scheduled for that time. During event such as these, sections of the Parkway and other side roads are often closed to automobile traffic. Knowing about them ahead of time will allow you to adjust your travel plans for the day of a particular event.

first day of the Olympics is usually reserved for coaching and training. During the next day, specific competitions take place between 8:30 A.M. and 4:00 P.M. Gold, silver, and bronze medals are given to the top three finishers in each event, and ribbons are awarded to all remaining participants. Closing ceremonies take place during the afternoon of the final day of competition.

There is no admission charge for spectators, but if you opt to take the aerial tramway up to the resort, the trip will cost $9.00 for ages 12 and older and $6.00 for ages 7 through 11. Children 6 and younger ride free with an accompanying adult. While you're at Ober Gatlinburg, all the usual attractions and activities are available at their regular prices (see our Attractions chapter). Note that while these Special Olympics normally take place in February, there have been years in the past when the dates were moved up to late January.

Saddle Up!
Various venues, Pigeon Forge
(865) 429-7350
This event, which debuted in 2001, has caught on right-quick-like and built up as much momentum as a cattle stampede. If you're a cowboy (or cowgirl) or have ever just fantasized about being

one, Pigeon Forge is the place to be in early February during this four-day immersion into all things Western. Among the daily activities featured are Western memorabilia shows, a chuck wagon supper show, and songwriting seminars and country dance classes at the Pigeon Forge Community Center. Friday and Saturday nights are capped off with Saddle Up! concerts at Country Tonite Theatre, featuring musical acts steeped in the classic sounds of the American West. Most of the events are free except for the chuck wagon show and the Saddle Up! concerts. Tickets for those run in the $20 range.

Smoky Mountains Storytelling Festival
Various venues, Pigeon Forge
(865) 429-7350
The mountain art of storytelling gets into high gear with a weekend of fun taking place at several different Pigeon Forge music theaters. Specific venues may change from year to year. Regardless of which events or sites you choose, get ready to be mesmerized by noted local storytellers from the Smoky Mountains and the rest of the nation. Admission to the festival events is free except where noted below.

Thursday through Saturday are highlighted by yarn spinning and storytelling workshops, both of which are scheduled from late morning until evening.

If you really want to add a chill to your winter nights, you might brave a ride on one of the "Haunts and Haints" trolley rides, which run on Friday and Saturday nights. For $3.00 per person, audience members can board trolleys taking them from Patriot Park to different locations around Pigeon Forge, where professional storytellers are waiting to spin their yarns. "Scary Stories for the Family" (suitable for all ages) begins at 9:30 P.M., and "Scary Stories for Grown-ups" gets underway at 10:30 P.M.

MARCH

A Mountain Quiltfest
Smoky Mountain Convention Center
4010 Parkway, Pigeon Forge
(865) 429-7350

At this free show you'll find exhibits of another time-honored form of mountain arts and crafts. Aficionados will recognize patterns like Double Wedding Ring, Log Cabin, and Dresden Plate. Quilters from all across the region will have between 150 and 200 quilts on display and for sale, and there are instructors on hand with classes and lectures to help quilters develop their skills. A Mountain Quiltfest takes place over a five-day period in mid-March. Hours are 9:00 A.M. to 7:00 P.M. Wednesday and Thursday, 9:00 A.M. to 5:30 P.M. on Friday, 9:00 A.M. to 7:00 P.M. on Saturday, and 9:00 A.M. to 4:30 P.M. on Sunday.

APRIL

Great Smoky Arts and Crafts Show
Gatlinburg Convention Center
234 Historic Nature Trail, Gatlinburg
(865) 436-0506
www.artsandcraftscommunity.com

Every Easter weekend approximately 10,000 visitors flock to the convention center to see artists from Gatlinburg's renowned Great Smoky Arts and Crafts Community (see our Mountain Crafts chapter) exhibit their talents and offer handcrafted treasures for sale. Craft products include baskets, candles, dolls, jewelry, pottery, quilts, toys, and much more. Representatives from nearly all of the community's 80-plus studios, galleries, and shops are present for the four-day event (which takes place in March when Easter falls in that month).

Admission to this arts-and-crafts show is free. The doors open at 10:00 A.M. daily, and closing times vary, depending on the day of the week. This is just the first of several shows that the Arts and Crafts Community sponsors throughout the year; others take place during the Thanksgiving and Christmas holidays (see the November and December sections of this chapter).

Dolly's Parade
Parkway, Pigeon Forge
(865) 429-7350

Everyone knows it's time for a new season at Dollywood when Sevier County's most famous offspring comes home to kick things off with her annual parade in Pigeon Forge. In mid-April the bands strike up and the floats start rolling down the Parkway as crowds line the streets, waiting to catch a glimpse of Dolly Parton. In past parades Ms. Parton has brought some of her friends along to help celebrate—stars like Burt Reynolds and Lily Tomlin. Around 6:00 P.M., the caravan starts on River Road, makes its way north along the Parkway, and winds up at the Wears Valley Road intersection.

Smoky Mountain Spring
Trout Tournament
Little Pigeon River in Gatlinburg,
Pigeon Forge, and Sevierville
(865) 429-3474
www.rockytopoutfitter.com

After a long winter without restocking, more than 5,000 trout are released into the Little Pigeon River running from the national park boundary in Gatlinburg all the way to Sevierville. Participants are allowed to keep what they catch, plus more than $10,000 in prizes is up for grabs as well. Prizes include $500 cash awards for the largest (and smallest) trout, gift certificates, trophies, fishing gear, and more.

The two-day event takes place the first weekend of April, and fishing hours are from sunrise to 4:00 P.M. on Saturday and sunrise to 2:00 P.M. on Sunday. The competition is open to anglers of all ages, although entrants are separated into "tourist" and "local" divisions and then subdivided into "adult" and "juvenile" groups. And tournament organizers say that no matter how they fare, all kids who enter walk away with a prize.

The $30 entry fee covers both days of the event, but a Tennessee fishing license and a trout permit in Gatlinburg are also required to participate (see the Parks and Recreation chapter for information on obtaining a license). In addition to the spring event, there is also a fall tournament that takes place the last week of September.

Smoky Mountain Music Festival
Gatlinburg Convention Center
234 Historic Nature Trail, Gatlinburg
(865) 436-0500

This competition features a variety of school bands, orchestras, and choirs from around the country performing in almost every conceivable style of music. On Friday the groups compete in the convention center, and on Saturday morning the outdoor portion of the event is held at Gatlinburg–Pittman High School's football field on U.S. Highway 321 from 9:00 A.M. to noon. Smoky Mountain Music Festival starts in the mid to latter part of April and runs for four consecutive weekends into May. There is no charge to attend.

Spring Wildflower Pilgrimage
Gatlinburg Convention Center
234 Historic Nature Trail, Gatlinburg
(865) 436-7318
www.springwildflowerpilgrimage.com

Every April, near the end of the month,

nature enthusiasts from near and far gather in Gatlinburg and the national park to experience the annual arrival of Mother Nature's blossoming beauty. Although most of the actual wildlife viewing takes place in Great Smoky Mountains National Park, the event is headquartered at W. L. Mills Auditorium in the Gatlinburg Convention Center.

For seven days some 90 different programs are conducted by more than 80 professional tour leaders selected from universities and colleges across the United States. Included in this staff are botanists, photographers, and hikers who are eager to share their expertise and experiences with their groups. Programs include half-day and daylong field trips, excursions that range from moderate scenic strolls to overnight trips to Mount LeConte. Meanwhile, at Mills Auditorium, visitors can view a collection of more than 200 flower and plant species native to the area.

The Wildflower Pilgrimage has deep roots that date back more than 50 years, when the University of Tennessee Botany Department conducted annual field trips in the Smoky Mountains. In 1951 the pilgrimage was officially established in cooperation with the Gatlinburg Chamber of Commerce, the national park, and the Gatlinburg Garden Club. That first year, approximately 400 "posie pilgrims" took part in 11 tours over two days.

Today, per-day registration fees are $15.00 for adults and $5.00 for high school and college students. Children ages 12 and younger are admitted free. Mills Auditorium is open for exhibition Tuesday from noon to 7:00 P.M., and Wednesday through Friday from 9:00 A.M. to 7:00 P.M.

MAY

Ramp Festival
Kineauvista Hill 321, Cosby

We're going to send you a few miles out of your way for this one, but we think

During Gatlinburg's annual Flower Fest, late April through late June, the city's parks department adorns the streets and utility fixtures with thousands of blooms and bulbs, adding splashes of color and bouquets of fragrance to the downtown area.

you'll agree it's in a category by itself. First, you're probably wondering what a "ramp festival" is. No, it's not a day to celebrate motorcycle stunt paraphernalia or interstate access points. Ramps are a cross between onions and garlic, and believe it or not, thousands of people travel from all over the country to sample and celebrate this pungent plant. Taking place the first Sunday in May, the festival's activities include country, folk, and bluegrass music and the always popular Maid of Ramps pageant, a beauty competition for young ladies ages 16 through 21.

Naturally, with a gathering devoted to an edible plant, there's bound to be food involved. Indeed, in addition to barbecued chicken and pig, a variety of ramp dishes are served up. A couple of the more popular ones are ramps with scrambled eggs and ramps served with hoe cake, a type of skillet-fried corn bread. You might want to know that ramps are five times stronger than onions when uncooked. In fact, it's rumored that enough ramp consumption will cause an odor to be released through the pores of the body. We can't validate that, but we do guarantee that if you show up to the Ramp Festival, you will hear plenty of home remedies for getting rid of "ramp breath."

The history behind the festival dates back more than 50 years ago to when a visiting *Knoxville News-Sentinel* columnist suggested to some of the Cosby locals that they start a festival in honor of the ramp. Several of the local men proceeded to form a club for just such a purpose, and the rest is history. Today, the event is sponsored by the Cosby Ruritan Club, whose members dig up 50 to 60 bushels of ramps in preparation for the festival. Festival hours are 9:30 A.M. to 4:30 P.M., and it takes place at Kineauvista Hill, a scenic area just off US 321 in Cosby. Admission is $5.00 for adults and $3.00 for children ages 11 through 18. Children ages 10 and younger get in free.

If you're an admirer of customized cars, you might want to plan your Smokies visit to coincide with any of the area's many custom auto shows—better known locally as "rod runs." Held mainly during the summer and in Pigeon Forge, these events showcase everything from modified vintage classics to Volkswagon Beetles. Be forewarned, however, that traffic slows to a snail's pace on the Parkway during most rod runs. In traffic the custom-car drivers like to move very slowly; when parked the cars themselves draw lots of stares from rubbernecking motorists. Our advice: Take an aspirin and learn a local shortcut (see Getting Here, Getting Around)!

Gatlinburg Scottish Festival and Games
Downtown and Mills Park, Gatlinburg
(865) 436-0500
www.gsfg.org
When the Smoky Mountains were settled about 200 years ago, many of the newcomers who settled were Scottish. Today, quite a few descendants of those pioneers still reside in our mountains (Gatlinburg's high school sports teams are even nicknamed the Highlanders). Since the early 1980s, Scots from all across the country (and even Scot wanna-bes) have gathered in Gatlinburg to celebrate that country's heritage. During the third weekend of each May, members of more than 60 clans drink deep from the well of their culture.

Things get kicked off on Friday with a parade through downtown Gatlinburg featuring kilted men and bagpipe bands. On Saturday and Sunday, the events move to Mills Park off US 321. Admission is $15.00 for either Saturday or Sunday or $20.00 for both days. One-day tickets for children 5 through 12 are $5.00. The festivities include band competitions, dance contests, and sheepdog demonstrations.

The different clans have tents set up where visitors can learn about each clan's history and colors. Authentic Scottish cuisine is available for the tasting—hot dishes such as meat pies and baked goods such as scones.

The Scottish athletic events are always popular with the spectators. Women especially enjoy the men showing their legs in the bonniest knees competition, and the caber throw (a telephone pole–like log) is a test of raw strength and skill. Then there's the haggis hurl! In case you're not familiar with haggis, it's a traditional Scottish dish prepared by taking the organs of a sheep or calf, mincing them with a few more palatable ingredients, and boiling them in the animal's stomach. It's not hard to imagine why people want to hurl them!

JULY

4th of July Midnight Parade
Parkway, Gatlinburg
(865) 436-0500
This event has the distinction of being the nation's first Independence Day parade each year. Just after the stroke of midnight on the 4th, the long procession of floats and marching bands winds its way down the Parkway. Naturally, there's no charge for watching.

Patriot Festival
Patriot Park, Old Mill Avenue
Pigeon Forge
(865) 429-7350
Join nearly 30,000 revelers to observe Independence Day. Things get under way at 1:00 P.M. with an arts-and-crafts exhibition. Children's games and live entertainment begin at 3:00 P.M. and continue until 7:30 P.M., when the headline music act takes the stage. Headliners in recent years have included acts as well known as the Charlie Daniels Band. At 9:30 P.M., get ready for a spectacle of fireworks that lights up the night sky in explosive color. The event is free, but due to the limited

amount of on-site parking, spectators are asked to park elsewhere and take a trolley to Patriot Park (see Getting Here, Getting Around).

Gatlinburg Craftsmen's Fair
Gatlinburg Convention Center
234 Historic Nature Trail, Gatlinburg
(865) 436-7479
www.craftsmenfair.com
This 10-day event in late July is the first of two Gatlinburg Craftsmen's Fairs held between July and October. Visitors can see time-honored mountain crafts and other traditional art forms created before their eyes. More than 150 artisans from across the country are on hand, demonstrating their skills in areas such as folk art, wood turning, and ceramic making. Finished products include works in all kinds of media, from leather to oil painting to sculpture.

The Gatlinburg Craftsmen's Fair was created in 1975 when the Southern Highlands Craft Guild left Gatlinburg. In the nearly quarter-plus century since, the event has grown into one of the most notable crafts happenings, not just in the Smokies but in the entire southeastern United States. The show's quality is maintained through a jury system, which is used to evaluate potential entries. Although there are new participants each year, roughly 80 percent of fair exhibitors are regulars. Some have been displaying their skills and wares since the fair originated.

In addition to arts and crafts, live bluegrass, gospel, and country music performances keep things hopping. The July fair is open from 10:00 A.M. to 7:00 P.M. Monday through Saturday and 10:00 A.M. to 5:00 P.M. on Sunday. Admission to the event is $5.00 for adults and free for children ages 12 and younger. See our October listings for the particulars of the second fair.

Smoky Mountain Run for Boy Scouts
Louise Mandrell Theater
2046 Parkway, Pigeon Forge
(865) 453-3534
We have traditionally shied away from including competitive runs in this chapter,

mainly because such events are primarily participatory and have a fairly narrow appeal. But we've made an exception in this case for two reasons: 1) The proceeds of this run go to a worthy cause; and 2) the event is hosted by music theater star Louise Mandrell.

Mandrell has been heavily involved in local charities since moving to the Smokies in 1997. This annual 5K walk/run, which takes place in late July, raises money for Boy Scouts, a cause that has always been near and dear to Mandrell's heart. In fact, the run has generated approximately $30,000 for scouting programs each year since its inception.

Runners must pay a $15 entry fee before vying for $10,000 in cash and prizes. Mandrell herself is on hand to start the race off, and she personally awards the prizes to the winning runners at the finish line. Typically, some 1,500 runners participate in the semi-hilly 5K run, which begins at the Louise Mandrell Theater and takes the competitors up and down the Parkway before returning to the starting point. The event also includes a 100-yard scuttle for children in attendance.

AUGUST

Drums Across America
Sevier County High School
1200 Dolly Parton Parkway, Sevierville
(865) 453-4026, (800) 495-7469
www.dci.org
First coming to Sevierville in 1975, Drums Across America is a drum and bugle corps competition that draws competing corps (don't ever call them bands) together for an evening of music and precision choreography that leaves most of the spectators slack-jawed and breathless for the better part of three hours. The competition is arranged and conducted by Drum Corps International and is the oldest continuing competition in the South. The number of competing corps varies, but a minimum of six is a pretty good bet each year. The 2003 competition included

teams from Wisconsin, New Jersey, and Ohio and featured performances by several national and world champion groups. In addition to the stirring music and precision routines, Drums Across America demonstrates graphically that there's still a significant amount of "Heartland America" spirit in a lot of today's youth. Admission is $24, and tickets are available in advance by calling the toll-free number listed above.

Celebrate Freedom!
Various venues, Pigeon Forge
(865) 429-7350
For one week in August, the city of Pigeon Forge delivers a big-time salute to the American veteran. Beginning the second weekend of the month, Celebrate Freedom! honors the men and women who served America in the armed services, and it does so with a well-balanced schedule that manages to weave together times of serious reflection and light-hearted fun. To learn more about this special patriotic event, see the Close-up in this chapter.

Food City Family Race Night
NASCAR SpeedPark, Sevierville
(865) 453-6411
NASCAR SpeedPark is the site of this extremely popular event where NASCAR fans get a chance to meet their favorite drivers and see their favorite cars up close. The Sevierville edition of Race Night is one of four such events held annually in different cities throughout the region. Race Nights traditionally take place prior to NASCAR Nextel Cup and Busch Series races held at Bristol Motor Speedway in Bristol, Tennessee, about 100 miles northeast of here. In previous years, the Family Race Night in Sevierville has taken place prior to the Food City 250, the Goracing.com 500, and the Goody's Headache Powders 500 races.

Beginning at 3:00 P.M. on this one-day event in late August, fans can meet, greet, and get autographs from a who's who of NASCAR Nextel Cup and Busch Series

CLOSE-UP

Celebration and Remembrance

Featuring everything from lectures. workshops, and speeches to parades, dances, and historical exhibits, Celebrate Freedom! is a true red, white, and blue salute to the men and women who have served our nation in the armed forces.

Even just after its inception in 2000, it was already evident that this one-week tribute to American veterans was going to become one of the most notable special events in the area. It seemed to tap into a sense of patriotism that shows up strongly in the demographics of those who usually find their way to the Smokies. And this was well before the events of September 11, 2001.

Coproduced by the city of Pigeon Forge and the University of Tennessee, Celebrate Freedom! is too large an event to contain in one space. It typically takes place at a variety of venues in Pigeon Forge, including the Louise Mandrell Theater, the Smoky Mountain Convention

Center, and the Music Road Hotel Convention Center. The Holiday Inn Resort, which serves as event headquarters, houses historical exhibits, photography displays, and a map room where veterans can identify their places of service.

Since its beginning, Celebrate Freedom! has revolved around a different war each year. The first three events focused mainly on World War II, the Korean War, and the Vietnam war, respectively. However, each edition's scope is usually broader than a single conflict and helps raise awareness of the need to celebrate all veterans from all eras.

Added to Celebrate Freedom! in 2002 was the Vietnam Moving Wall, a replica of the Vietnam Memorial in Washington, D.C. The full-scale wall was on display in Patriot Park and was one of the many focal points of that year's event.

Throughout the eight days of Celebrate Freedom!, guests can choose from

---

drivers. In 1999, the first year the event was held in Sevierville, Rusty Wallace, Kyle Petty, and Jimmy Spencer were among the NASCAR drivers making appearances. In addition, cars driven by Ricky Rudd, Rusty Wallace, and others were on display.

Besides the cars and drivers, those turning out for this NASCAR feeding frenzy can climb behind the wheel of a driving simulator, take part in an actual pit stop exercise, dig into free food, and enjoy live entertainment going on throughout the event.

Advance tickets to Food City's Family Race Night can be purchased for $5.00 each at any area Food City supermarket

location or any Sevierville welcome center. Tickets also cost $5.00 on the day of the event, and children younger than 12 are admitted free. Proceeds from the event benefit the United Way of Sevier County.

World Premiere Gospel Concert
Grand Resort Convention Center
3171 Parkway, Pigeon Forge
(865) 453-1000
www.gmtn.com
This three-day event, which takes place in late August, features some 60 different gospel groups representing more than

a full calendar of other special events and activities.

The past is remembered thanks to a series of symposiums entitled *Journey to Freedom: War Stories*. Former POWs are invited to share their tales and remembrances of wartime in an open microphone setting. A number of Freedom Forums are also staged, featuring notable veterans, authors, and historical experts, all discussing their military experiences. Forum topics have included "American Ex-Prisoners of War" and "America's Other Asian Wars."

One of the highlights of each year's Celebrate Freedom! is the keynote address, which is usually delivered by a notable figure. Previous speakers have included Bob Dole, Alexander Haig, and former NFL great Rocky Bleier.

Other activities include daily military book fairs, at which authors and veterans are available for book signings and discussions.

Celebrate Freedom! is also designed to entertain. Several canteen dances take place at the Music Road Hotel Convention Center and the Smoky Mountain Convention Center, each featuring live big-band style orchestras. Other musical events include a Glenn Miller and Andrews Sisters tribute as Country Tonite Theatre and *Celebrate Freedom!, the Musical* at Louise Mandrell Theater.

Celebrate Freedom! wraps up with the Operation Liberty Salute to Veterans Parade. Beginning at 8:00 A.M. on the Pigeon Forge Parkway, a host of military vehicles will roll in convoy along the parade route. Following the parade is a picnic at Patriot Park and the Young Patriots Parade, where kids decorate their trikes, bikes, and wagons in patriotic fashion.

Interestingly, the city of Pigeon Forge conceived Celebrate Freedom! as a way of observing the new millennium by looking back at the veterans of the 20th century and appreciating how they helped contribute to the American way of life.

400 individual artists. The 3,000-seat convention center hosts two shows daily, from 1:00 to 5:00 P.M. and from 7:00 to 11:00 P.M. Among the heavenly host of gospel greats that appeared in 2004 were Aaron Wilburn, the Crabb Family, Integrity Quartet, and Michael Combs, just to name a few.

The concerts are sponsored by Gospel Music Television Network, which is based in Pigeon Forge and is North America's only all-gospel channel, broadcasting inspirational acts 24 hours a day, seven days a week. GMTN broadcasts the World Premiere concerts worldwide via satellite and cable, reaching an audience of millions in the U.S. and Canada.

Other activities related to the concert include morning devotional services and a lecture series. Vendors of religiously themed merchandise are on hand throughout the three days of gospel, and the performers themselves have product tables set up where fans can buy CDs and T-shirts and even get handshakes and autographs from their favorite acts. There is also a cafeteria set up in one area of the convention center where attendees can not only eat with the stars but also meet and greet them as well.

One-day tickets for the event start at $29.95, and multiday packages that include lodgings, meals, and show tickets are available for upwards of several hundred dollars.

Gatlinburg's Heritage Festival
Great Smoky Arts and Crafts
Community, Gatlinburg
(865) 436-0506

The first of the myriad "festival" events to kick off the fall season, Gatlinburg's Heritage Festival celebrates the city's arts and crafts tradition with a two-week schedule of special events in the Great Smoky Arts & Crafts Community, beginning on the weekend preceding Labor Day. In addition to special demonstrations and other events at the individual artisans' galleries and shops, several special venues are set up throughout the Arts & Crafts Community east of downtown Gatlinburg, where guest artists and craftspeople exhibit their talents. Among the guest artists are most of the local professional, semiprofessional, and amateur musical groups, who are competing for cash prizes every time they perform. Audiences at each musical performance are asked to cast ballots for their favorite musical group during performances. Concession stands and special attractions are set up along the 8-mile loop that describes the community. From downtown Gatlinburg, take East Parkway (US 321N) out about 2 miles to Glades Road (traffic light #3A); the festival information booth is usually located at the Wood Whittlers complex. Event schedules are also printed daily in the *Mountain Press* during the festival.

Old-Fashioned Hayrides
Downtown Gatlinburg
(865) 436-3897

From late August through the end of the year, you can climb onboard a hay-filled flatbed and take an old-fashioned ride through the streets of Gatlinburg. The departure point is traffic light #6 at Mountain Mall. The rides run Sunday through Thursday (excluding Thanksgiving and Christmas). Daily hours are 6:00 to 10:00 P.M. in August and September, 6:00 to 9:00 P.M. in October and November, and 5:30 to 10:00 P.M. in December. The cost is only $2.00 per ride. During Winterfest (see November), the hayrides are a great way to see the city's many downtown lighting displays. And here's a bit of semantics to help you avoid confusion: The Old-Fashioned Hayrides are suddenly called Christmas Hayrides in December only. The rides themselves are the same as before.

SEPTEMBER

Boomsday
Downtown Knoxville

Boomsday is a daylong annual celebration on the first Monday of September, observed nationally as Labor Day. All kinds of carnival-style events take place throughout the day, but we're concentrating our attention on the way they wind it up, which is really hard to describe on a printed page. We'll tell you right off that what they do is blow off in 20-odd minutes about four tons of fireworks that take almost 48 hours to set up on Knoxville's longest bridge across the Tennessee River. This is not a truckload of fireworks we're talking about; it's a trainload. For the statistically inclined, more than 60 miles of wire are used to connect the computers that produce more than 12,000 pyrotechnic effects. The musical accompaniment broadcast by a local FM station (104.5 on your dial) is a nice throw-in.

Think about it: 12,000 explosions in about 20 minutes works out to 20 minutes of a sky filled with fire at a rate that will render most people slack-jawed. The fireworks, some of which you will never see anywhere else, are so spectacular for so long that you could discover a whole new capacity for staring without breathing. The display begins with what most local exhibits would die for as a grand finale and just keeps getting better until it reaches a climax that assaults the senses of viewers half a mile away (200,000 is a conservative crowd estimate).

If you're staying anywhere in Sevier County, plan to be on Chapman Highway (U.S. Highway 441N) no later than 7:30 P.M. Follow Chapman into Knoxville until you are required to turn away from the Henley Street Bridge, where the fireworks are set up. Turn in either direction, go anywhere from a few blocks to a mile to get a good view of the bridge, and find a place to park. Get as close to the river as you can (you won't be alone) by 9:00 P.M., and enjoy. Take snacks and drinks with you if you want them—at 15 years old, this event is still uncluttered by vendors. Enjoy the display, try to remember when you've ever seen anything like it, and go home happy in a traffic situation no worse than any rush hour.

Sevier County Fair
Sevier County Fairgrounds
754 Old Knoxville Highway, Sevierville
(865) 453-0770

There's nothing like a good old-fashioned county fair. This week of food, rides, games, and exhibits gets started each Labor Day and continues through Saturday night. The fairgrounds, which flank the Little Pigeon River in Sevierville, are the site for the festivities, which include midway rides and games, home-baked pies and preserves, and exhibits of prize-winning livestock, fruits, and vegetables.

Several events are annual favorites, like the tractor pull and the watermelon seed spitting contest. Another highlight of the week is the beauty competition in which young ladies from across the county vie for the title of Fairest of the Fair and the right to wear the crown. Admission to the Sevier County Fair is $3.50 for adults, and children ages 12 and younger get in free. Once on the grounds, you can buy individual ride tickets or pay $15.00 for an armband that gets you unlimited ride access. Daily hours are 5:00 to 10:30 P.M.

Smoky Mountain Fall Trout Tournament
Little Pigeon River in Gatlinburg, Pigeon Forge, and Sevierville
(865) 429-3474
www.rockytopoutfitter.com

This is the fall edition of a popular trout-fishing event that brings anglers of all ages to the shores of the Little Pigeon River. The September tourney takes place the third weekend of the month. See the write-up in the April section of this chapter for a more comprehensive overview.

Smoky Mountain Harvest Festival
Sevierville, Gatlinburg, and Pigeon Forge

This countywide festival more or less evolved from events already taking place among the three main cities. While late September and October have traditionally been a period of heavy tourism (primarily because of the turning of the leaves in the mountains), local governments found that most activity was taking place on weekends, and they wanted to find a way to increase midweek visitation. Thus, Harvest Festival was created as a sort of umbrella under which existing special events could be gathered. The festival has also spawned new events in keeping with the theme.

Smoky Mountain Harvest Festival begins in mid-September and runs into early November. During this period, you'll see a number of craft fairs and music festivals throughout the county. The centerpiece that ties all the cities together during Harvest Festival is the countywide decorating contest in which area businesses, governments, and civic organiza-

Major special events in Gatlinburg, such as the Fourth of July Midnight Parade or the Christmas Parade, can have equally major effects on traffic. It's not unusual to see traffic into the north end of the city backed up for miles on US 441 (The Spur). Entering Gatlinburg via US 321 may be a quicker alternative during these celebrations.

tions adorn their buildings and grounds with traditional harvest decorations like hay, pumpkins, cornstalks, and gourds. Awards are given to winners in a number of different categories.

All of the events included in this chapter for the remainder of September and October are considered to be official Harvest Festival Events by their respective host cities.

Bite of Sevier County
Boys & Girls Club of the Smoky Mountains, 209 McMahan Avenue, Sevierville
(865) 453-6411

Sample the best cuisine of local eateries at this event that takes place toward the end of the month. Participating restaurants in years past have included Damon's Ribs and the Park Grill. Because of limited seating, tickets must be purchased in advance at a cost of $25. All proceeds benefit the Boys & Girls Club of the Smoky Mountains. There is also a charity auction benefiting Sevierville Primary School. For tickets, contact the Sevierville Chamber of Commerce Office of Special Events at the number above.

"I Love Sevierville" Luncheon
Sevier County Courthouse
Court Avenue, Sevierville
(865) 453-6411

On the Friday following Bite of Sevier County (see the above listing), everyone is invited downtown to find a comfortable spot on the east grounds of Sevier County Courthouse for this casual lunch gathering. A box lunch can be purchased for $6.00, and while you're eating, you can enjoy live music performances from the courthouse veranda.

A Taste of Autumn
Gatlinburg Convention Center
234 Historic Nature Trail, Gatlinburg
(865) 436-0500

Late in the month, you can get your fill of great food prepared by local eateries. At this one-day event, you can sample items from the menus of participating restau-

rants beginning at 5:30 P.M. for a cost of $20. Tickets can be purchased in advance from Gatlinburg City Hall or either Gatlinburg welcome center. Along with the food tasting, the event features a charity auction benefiting United Way of Sevier County.

Smoky Mountain Wine Festival
Smokies Park
3450 Line Drive, Kodak
(865) 428-4416

Instead of hosting the Boys of Summer, the Tennessee Smokies baseball stadium plays home to the wines of autumn for this one-day event in late September. For $15, you'll get a souvenir wine glass that you may then use to sample the vintages of 11 different local and regional wineries. Live music, crafts, and specialty food vendors round out the day. More than 50 award-winning wines are available for the tasting at this event hosted by Mountain Valley Vineyards.

OCTOBER

Great Smoky Arts & Crafts
Community Fall Celebration
Great Smoky Arts & Crafts Community
Gatlinburg
(865) 436-4315
www.artsandcraftscommunity.com

The 8-mile loop that makes up the Smokies' most respected bastion of native craftsmen becomes one big outdoor crafts festival through the entire month of October. Weather permitting, the artisans of the Arts & Crafts Community are outside their shops selling their goods and demonstrating their crafts for the public.

Rotary Club Crafts Festival
Patriot Park
Old Mill Avenue, Pigeon Forge
(865) 429-7350

For more than two decades, this arts-and-crafts event in Pigeon Forge has featured dozens of local crafters as well as those from the Midwest and Southeast, displaying such skills as glassblowing, wood carving, and basket making. The festival takes place under a 200-foot tent at Patriot Park and runs for most of the month. Admission is free, but donations made during the festival benefit the many community projects sponsored by the Pigeon Forge Rotary Club throughout the year. Daily hours are 10:00 A.M. to 6:00 P.M.

Dollywood's Harvest Celebration
Dollywood Entertainment Park
1020 Dollywood Lane, Pigeon Forge
(865) 428-9488, (800) 365-5996
www.dollywood.com

Colorful autumn decorations abound throughout the park during Dollywood's Harvest Celebration, combining music, crafts, fall food, and fun throughout the month of October. Featured is the Smokies' only outdoor crafts festival with scores of visiting craftspeople from across the nation, showcasing and demonstrating their talents. Also, witness the country's largest Southern gospel music event, the Southern Gospel Jubilee.

One-day tickets to Dollywood range from $25 plus tax for ages 4 through 11 to $34 plus tax for ages 12 and older. Park hours during Harvest Celebration are 10:00 A.M. to 6:00 P.M. daily and 9:00 A.M. to 7:00 P.M. on Saturday; Dollywood is closed on Thursdays in October. See our Dollywood chapter for a complete profile, including more detailed admission and schedule information.

Gatlinburg Craftsmen's Fair
Gatlinburg Convention Center
234 Historic Nature Trail, Gatlinburg
(865) 436-7479

For nearly three full weeks beginning in early October, the Gatlinburg Convention Center hosts tens of thousands of people who come to see live craft demonstrations by artisans from all over the country. See the listing for the summer fair in late July for information on what can be found at both Gatlinburg Craftsmen's Fairs. Admission to the October fair is $4.00 for adults and free for children ages 12 and younger.

Pig Roast
St. Joseph the Carpenter Episcopal
Church, 345 Hardin Lane, Sevierville
(865) 453-0943

Everyone's invited to this annual one-day barbecue bonanza in the middle of the month. From noon until 5:00 P.M., enjoy live music, kids' activities and games, a craft bazaar, silent auction, and a whole lot of great barbecue. The $6.00 admission covers the cost of the meal, although there is also a child's hot dog plate available for $3.00. It's a great way to spend a Saturday afternoon and get to know some really nice people.

NOVEMBER

Winterfest
Sevierville, Pigeon Forge, and
Gatlinburg

Originally developed as a means of drawing more tourists to the Smokies during the winter, this nearly four-month-long festival has taken its place as the big kahuna of annual area festivals. Beginning in early November, the county's three main cities each host their own respective kickoff celebrations on different nights to launch an entire season's worth of music, parades, decorations, shopping bargains, and millions of holiday lights.

In Sevierville you can enjoy live music performances, a lighting festival, and decorations from 5:00 to 7:00 P.M. at the Community Center on Gary Wade Boulevard. Pigeon Forge's kickoff ceremonies take place at Patriot Park from 5:30 to 8:30 P.M. and include the turning on of the city's light displays, fireworks, live entertainment, food vendors, and free trolley tours of the holiday lights. In Gatlinburg the kickoff takes place at Ripley's Aquarium of the Smokies. There, you can taste the different entries in the chili cookoff beginning at 5:00 P.M. and watch city officials "flip the switch" on millions of spectacular lights. Live bands are also on hand.

Most of the events we have listed for the months of November and December

How many individual lights shine in Sevier County during Winterfest? Would you believe there are nearly 10 million lights in city-operated displays alone? Area departments of tourism estimate the following totals by city: Sevierville—more than 500,000; Pigeon Forge—4 million; Dollywood—2.25 million; Gatlinburg—2.5 million. And these figures don't even take into account lights that are displayed by businesses and residents.

are part of the official Winterfest celebration. For more, refer back to the January and February sections of this chapter.

Winterfest Trolley Tours of Light
Pigeon Forge
(865) 453-6444, (865) 429-7350

Starting on the Friday after Winterfest gets under way, you can see the lights of Pigeon Forge without the hassle of driving. Tours run through February and are offered to all who want to enjoy the city's four million lights. Heated buses and informed hosts will guide you through the history of the displays. The cost of each trolley ride is $3.00 per person. The tours run Monday through Friday evenings until New Year's Day and then Monday and Friday only through February. Tours depart the trolley office beginning at 6:30 P.M. Reservations are encouraged and can be made by calling the trolley office at the number listed above. Tickets may be purchased beginning at noon on the day of your tour. For more specifics about the Pigeon Forge trolley system, see Getting Here, Getting Around.

Winterfest Trolley Rides of Light
Gatlinburg
(865) 436-3897

From early November until the end of January, these sight-seeing trolleys offer spectacular views of Gatlinburg's Winterfest light displays. Tours depart from the downtown visitor information center at traffic light #3 and cost $4.00 per person.

In November and December, they run nightly at 6:30, 7:30, and 8:30 P.M. In January they run Saturday only. However, since tours don't run on Thanksgiving, Christmas, and a few other selected days, the city advises calling to verify specific times and dates. See our Getting Here, Getting Around chapter for more information about Gatlinburg trolleys.

Dollywood's Smoky Mountain Christmas
Dollywood Entertainment Park
1020 Dollywood Lane, Pigeon Forge
(865) 428-9488, (800) 365-5996
www.dollywood.com

Dolly's theme park is once again the setting for a large-scale seasonal celebration, beginning just after the Winterfest kick-off and running through the end of the year. During this time, Dollywood takes on a whole new character. The first thing you notice is all the lights—2.25 million to be more precise—arranged on buildings, trees, shrubberies, and attractions.

As during the rest of its season, music is a staple of Dollywood's Christmasfest. Besides its usual stock of holiday-oriented shows—productions such as Hometown Holidays, Christmas in the Smokies, and O Holy Night—the park also stages special musical events. In 1999, for example, the world-famous Vienna Boys' Choir performed at Dollywood's Celebrity Theatre in its first East Tennessee appearance.

Although many of Dollywood's regular-season attractions are closed for winter (water rides don't sound so fun in 40-degree temperatures, do they?), others appear only for the holiday season. Kids will love Peppermint Valley, a Christmas village filled with rides that also serves as home to Santa Claus, Mrs. Claus, and merry elves. Plus, all ages will love Carol of the Trees, an impressive synchronized lighting and music display. And if you still want your thrill rides, you won't be disappointed on that score. The park's Tennessee Tornado roller coaster keeps zipping along right through the end of the year, adding new meaning to the term "chills and thrills." On top of all the lights, shows, and attractions, Smoky Mountain Christmas still offers plenty of shopping opportunities and holiday foods as well (see our Dollywood chapter).

Dollywood is open Thursday through Sunday only from mid-November through December (except for Thanksgiving Day, Christmas Eve, and Christmas Day). Call first to verify specific operating hours. Admission to Dollywood's Christmasfest is $30 for adults and $10 for children ages 4 through 11. Children 3 and younger get in free. Prices do not include sales tax.

Tellabration
Pigeon Forge Community Center
170 Community Center Drive
Pigeon Forge
(865) 429-7350
On a Saturday in mid- to late November, some of the country's top storytellers take part in this international event along with those in more than 370 other locations worldwide. The show starts at 7:00 P.M. and features all kinds of tales and folklore. The $5.00 admission price benefits the Smoky Mountains Storytellers Association.

Community Chorus Holiday Concert
Smoky Mountain Jubilee
2115 Parkway, Pigeon Forge
(865) 428-1836, (865) 429-7350
Join the Pigeon Forge Community Chorus for this annual concert on a Sunday in the middle to latter part of the month. Singers use their voices to help usher in the holidays with a program of Christmas music and other seasonal favorites. The event starts at 2:00 P.M. and is free, although guests are asked to make a charitable donation of a nonperishable food item.

Great Smoky Arts and Crafts Show
Gatlinburg Convention Center
234 Historic Nature Trail, Gatlinburg
(865) 436-0506
www.artsandcraftscommunity.com
For more than a week surrounding Thanksgiving, this crafts event features the work of artisans from Gatlinburg's Great Smoky Arts & Crafts Community. It's

a great way to get a start on holiday shopping. The doors open at 10:00 A.M. daily, and closing times vary depending on the day of the week. Admission is free. See the write-up in the April section of this chapter for more details on what's to be found at all three of the Arts & Crafts Community's annual shows. Also see the listing below for scheduling information on their Christmas show.

DECEMBER

Great Smoky Arts and Crafts Show
Gatlinburg Convention Center
234 Historic Nature Trail, Gatlinburg
(865) 436-0506
www.artsandcraftscommunity.com
This is the final crafts event of the year for the Great Smoky Arts & Crafts Community. The show gets under way early in the month and runs for approximately 10 days. The doors usually open around 10:00 A.M., and closing times vary depending on the day of the week. Admission to the show is free. See the write-ups in the April and November sections of this chapter to learn about the Easter and Thanksgiving Great Smoky Arts and Crafts Shows.

Gatlinburg's Fantasy of Lights
Christmas Parade
Downtown Gatlinburg
(865) 436-0500
Lighted floats, marching bands, giant helium balloons, and of course, Santa Claus trek along the Parkway, basking in the glow of the city's numerous Smoky Mountain Lights displays. The mile-and-a-half-long parade, which takes place the first Friday of the month, starts rolling at 7:30 P.M.

Christmas Parade of Toys
Downtown Sevierville
(865) 453-6411
For more than 35 years, this Christmas parade has made its way along the Parkway and surrounding streets located in and around downtown Sevierville. You'll see marching bands, twirlers, decorative

floats, and of course, ol' Saint Nick himself. Parade spectators are invited to bring new, unwrapped toys that are taken up by Santa and his helpers as they make their way along the parade route. Donations go to Toys for Tots. The procession begins at noon.

Live Nativity
Evergreen Presbyterian Church
661 Parkway, Sevierville
(865) 428-3001

This depiction of the events surrounding the birth of Christ has become one of the most unique and moving holiday events to be found in the area. Taking place over a three-day, midmonth weekend, the large-scale, outdoor exhibit depicts seven different live scenes, beginning with Mary being told by an angel that she will give birth and ending with the mother and Christ child in a peaceful manger scene.

What gives the Live Nativity its authenticity is the fact that real people, along with authentic sets and costumes, are used to tell the story of Jesus' birth. Visitors view these reverent tableaus by walking along a lighted trail that leads from one scene to the next. All the while, spiritual songs of the season fill the air, and if you're lucky, the weather will be cooperative and provide a brilliant star-filled sky. At the end, hot chocolate and cookies await. There is no charge to view the nativity, which is open from 7:00 to 9:00 P.M. on each of the three nights.

Living Christmas Tree
Gatlinburg Convention Center
234 Historic Nature Trail, Gatlinburg
(865) 436-4990

The Gatlinburg Community Chorale closes out the year with this midmonth performance event. The chorale's members are positioned in a large, vertical Christmas tree. Appropriately colored costumes, bows, and garland complete the effect. The music presented is an all-encompassing selection of Christmas music, ranging from spiritual classics like "Joy to the World" to more contemporary holiday favorites like "Winter Wonderland." Admission to the concert is free, and show times are Thursday, Saturday, and Monday at 8:00 P.M.

Children's Hayride with Santa
Sevierville Community Center
200 Gary R. Wade Boulevard, Sevierville
(865) 453-6411

Let the kids hitch a ride with Saint Nick on a horse-drawn hay wagon while you enjoy live music and refreshments at the community center. Or you may be interested in hopping onboard yourself for the trip that travels the length of Bruce Street and tours the downtown area before returning to the loading zone. The hayrides are free and last for about 20 minutes, running continuously between 4:00 and 6:00 P.M. This event lasts for one evening only and takes place on a Thursday in the middle of the month.

New Year's Eve Ball Drop and Pyrotechnic Show
Space Needle
115 Historic Nature Trail, Gatlinburg
(865) 436-0500

It may not be Times Square in the Big Apple, but standing shoulder to shoulder with 25,000 other New Year's Eve revelers under the Space Needle isn't too bad for downtown Gatlinburg. Beginning around 11:30 P.M., the festivities start, leading up to the lowering of a lighted ball from the top of the Needle. When midnight strikes, the attraction becomes a towering inferno of sorts as it sparkles from top to bottom in a seven-minute display of pyrotechnics—about $10,000 worth, to be specific.

SHOPPING

S uffice it to say that this is an immense chapter—but it's not nearly as big as it could have been. Our aim is to introduce you to the kaleidoscope of shopping opportunities available in the Smokies. It would take a much larger space than we've allocated to just list all the businesses in the corridor (do you really need to know the details of more than a hundred T-shirt shops, and maybe double that number selling genuine "Made in Wherever" souvenirs?), so we're going to stick to the businesses that survived several cuts. We will break the shops and malls into workable categories by city, so you can narrow your search for specific items down a bit. Because of the rich heritage they represent and their importance to the region, mountain crafts are given their own chapter in this book. Likewise, the factory outlet stores that have helped make the Smokies an even more popular shopping destination earned their own chapter. And we encourage you to look through our chapter on Annual Events, as a number of these offer distinct Smokies items to the discerning shopper.

All of the shops, malls, and galleries listed in this chapter are interspersed with the attractions, restaurants, motels, and outlet malls throughout the Smokies Corridor. Understanding that they're here because they feel there's a buck or two to be made by accommodating the visitor population, it's logical to conclude that these businesses will operate primarily on the same schedule as their commercial neighbors. From Easter through Thanksgiving weekend, the vast majority of businesses that made the cut in this chapter will be open every single day from about 9:00 A.M. to at least 9:00 P.M. (many are open later).

Because the term "off-season" is rapidly becoming an anachronism in the Smokies, you can expect enough shops to be open year-round that you can shop any time you're here, although a lot of businesses are closed after 6:00 P.M. from January through March. The only day when a majority of businesses are closed is Christmas, and even then you can find open stores in most shopping malls. Note that our area includes a number of the popular chain department and discount stores, including a Kmart, a Big Lots, and a Wal-Mart Supercenter at which you could do almost all of your day-to-day shopping. Because we assume most of you have been in a Wal-Mart, we haven't written these places up, choosing instead to devote our limited space to the unique shopping opportunities found here.

Once again, we work from north to south, traveling from exit 407 on Interstate 40 to the national park entrance at the south end of Gatlinburg. We'll close with a separate section on shopping for food for those of you relocating to the area or if you're staying in a condo or cabin and need to stock the kitchen for the week.

So, knowing full well you're going to drop several times, let's go shopping.

SEVIERVILLE

Shopping Malls and Villages

Maplewood
2510 Winfield Dunn Parkway, Kodak
(865) 932-7637
www.maplewoodstores.com
If you're beginning your venture into the Smokies Corridor at exit 407 off I-40, it won't be long until you reach this unique collective of shops in the Riverbluff Landing development. A visit to Maplewood is a trip down Memory Lane—the relics and memorabilia placed throughout this

---

Blazing-hot summer sun notwithstanding, Tennessee law requires that shirts and shoes be worn in all places where the public congregates.

---

indoor shopping village are reminiscent of simpler times. You'll be intrigued by the 19th-century post office setup, the street clock, and the many authentic vehicles from yesteryear, such as a 1930s delivery truck, a Conestoga wagon, and an old horse-drawn taxi.

The individual shops found within also play into the intended nostalgia theme. At the farmers' market, you can buy fresh produce grown by local farmers. They have a generous stock of pantry items as well that will make cooking and eating a pleasure.

The Country Peddler and Country Elegance shops are both fashioned after old-time general stores and sport a wide selection of gift and collectible merchandise, from the everyday to the exquisite. Look for names like Boyd's Bears, Yankee candles, and Heritage lace. At Country Elegance Quilts (a separate store from the Country Elegance gift shop), you can choose from a large selection of handmade quilts in a variety of styles and colors. Kady's Korner Ladies' Boutique houses stylish accessories for women, as well as Belle Pointe Sweaters and several lines of crystal.

If you're in the mood for Santas and sleighs, visit Tennessee Christmas, a year-round shopping extravaganza where the season of magic can be experienced among countless varieties of Yuletide ornaments and other decorations. The kids will especially enjoy the working model train that snakes its way through the store and continues its journey on an elevated track outside the building.

You surely won't go hungry at Maplewood. There's an on-site bakery that makes fresh breads and pastries each morning. For meals, you can order from the full menu, which features a selection of steaks, chops, and omelets made to order. For dessert, they have hand-dipped ice cream and fresh baked goods like pies, cookies, and brownies. For even more sugary goodies, visit Hanna's Sweet Tooth, which bakes homemade fudge daily and carries different varieties of hard candies. Tucked away in one corner of Hanna's is their Kid's Korner, stocked with all kinds of toys and games.

The showpiece of Maplewood is McIntosh Mill, an authentic gristmill that was operational more than 100 years ago. The mill was disassembled at its original site in West Virginia, moved to the Smokies, and put back together by a restoration team. Today, the refurbished mill works once again with most of its original parts. With the help of an on-staff miller, McIntosh Mill grinds locally grown corn into a variety of products, including meals, flours, and even popping corn. In fact, many products from the gristmill are used in the Maplewood bakery to make delicious corn bread and other baked goods.

Art lovers might be interested in visiting the mill building's main floor, which is now used as gallery space for the noted area wildlife photographer Ken Jenkins.

Bookstores

The Master's Touch
532 Winfield Dunn Parkway, Sevierville
(865) 428-0231

In addition to shelves full of Christian-oriented reading, this bookstore carries many different versions and translations of the Holy Bible. You'll also find other merchandise like music CDs and cassettes, video tapes, gifts, greeting cards, jewelry, and T-shirts. One corner of the store is devoted to children, complete with all kinds of books, games, and activities.

Books-A-Million
190 Collier Lane, Sevierville
(865) 908-8994
www.booksamillion.com

At the end of Governor's Crossing outlet mall closest to the Parkway, Books-A-Million is probably the largest bookstore in the Smokies. More than 10,000 square feet of space are filled by books, from best-sellers to a variety of volumes on just about any subject you'd want to name. There's a whole wall of magazines and out-of-town newspapers, and a childrens' section (Kids-A-Million) as big as a lot of entire stores. Subjects are well laid out and clearly labeled (the Travel and Local Interest sections contain a great selection of *Insiders' Guides*). There's a good-size display of Hallmark greeting cards, and another section contains a lot of local literature and photography. If you want to take a long look at something, you're welcome to take it into the Joe Muggs Coffee Shop in the corner and browse before buying. The Smoky Mountain Scrabble Club meets at Books-A-Million on Thursday evenings.

Bible Factory Outlet
1645 Parkway, Sevierville
(865) 774-9005
www.bibleoutlet.com
Located in Tanger Five Oaks mall, the Bible Factory Outlet features a selection of books that deal with most aspects of everyday life (fiction, lifestyles, philosophy, and religion) from a Christian perspective. Greeting cards, calendars, and toys along the same lines are available, along with audio and video tapes. This company has another store in Belz Factory Outlet World in Pigeon Forge.

Clothing

Goody's Family Clothing
1408 Parkway, Sevierville
(865) 453-0552
This chain of stores started out in Knoxville and has developed over the years into one of the region's best sources for name-brand clothing for men, women, and children. Everything from casual sportswear to suits and dresses can be found on the racks at Goody's. The clothing tends to be of a more conservative nature, but it is of good quality and still offers a broad range of style.

The men's half of the store has clothing for adults and a boy's department for the "younger men." The women's half of the store is subdivided into ladies, misses, junior, and girls departments. There are also sections for plus sizes and petites. The ladies' shoe department carries brand names like Brook Hollow, Adidas, Keds, and Amanda Scott. Both sides have denim sections that feature a tremendous selection of Lee and Levi's jeans and shorts. Teens may be glad to know that Goody's isn't just for their parents. The store does a pretty good job of keeping up with the latest in adolescent fashion trends.

Antiques and Collectibles

S & G Comics & Collectibles
464 Forks of the River Parkway
Sevierville
(865) 908-8346
Kids and adults alike will have no trouble losing themselves in any number of fantasy worlds after stepping inside this place. Comic books, both new and used,

Attention, antiques hounds. The 8-mile stretch of Winfield Dunn Parkway (Tennessee Highway 66) between I-40 and downtown Sevierville is a veritable antiques and flea market heaven. You could literally spend a full day browsing the seemingly endless rows of booths and stalls at the eight different businesses catering to the collector and/or acquirer of the hard-to-find. What you will find ranges from legitimate antiquities to junk, but even if you're not out to buy, these places are still a lot of fun to visit!

CLOSE-UP

Apples to the Core

What do Adam and Eve, Johnny Apple-seed, Sir Isaac Newton, and William Tell all have in common? Well, each might have at least had a passing interest in spending a day at Applewood Farms in Sevierville.

If you're a lover of apples, you will truly be in your element. If you don't particularly care for apples, you'll probably enjoy yourself anyway. And like most interesting places in the Smokies, you can easily spend a lot of time there and wonder where the day went.

The place is easy to find, about a half-mile off the Parkway at the Sevierville-Pigeon Forge border on Apple Valley Road. The complex, which is open year-round, is nestled along the banks of the Little Pigeon River. The hillside apple orchards and whitewashed buildings are the giveaway that you've reached your destination.

The complex is made up of different shops and eateries all set against the backdrop of a working apple farm. You can stroll the property and see where 14 different varieties of apples are harvested from more than 4,000 trees. (By the way, want to know why the trunks of the apple trees are painted white? The paint reflects heat during spring and fall to keep the trunks cooler. It also has a repellent to discourage nibbling by rabbits and field mice.)

What happens to all those apples once they're harvested is where your options begin at Applewood Farms. The Apple Barn General Store was one of the first commercial ventures to appear on the property, in 1981. It was constructed inside the old barn that had stood on the property when the current owners purchased the farm in 1977. The General Store was first created as a place to market the apples from the orchard.

The General Store still carries bushel baskets full of fresh apples to be sure, but also much, much more. You can buy apple butter and apple jellies made next door in the Apple Butter Kitchen. Other sections of the store display cheeses, smoked hams, bacon, dried fruits, and popcorns. There are areas featuring gift items and an upstairs craft-and-basket loft.

Around the same time the General Store opened, the owners also cranked up the Cider Mill, so customers could see the apples being processed into apple cider. Nowadays, you can still see the mill at work, and in the Cider Bar, visitors can purchase fresh apple cider along with fried pies made in the neighboring Apple Pie Kitchen. (Another tidbit: Apple cider is a perishable product that will ferment if not refrigerated. Apple juice, on the other hand, is pasteurized and can be stored at room temperature.)

are the staple product, but sports card collectors will find a fair amount of merchandise as well. Many of S & G's display cases are filled with baseball, football, and basketball cards ranging from the common to the rare and valuable. Sports collectors will also take interest in the poseable action figures and other athletic

The Apple Barn General Store in Sevierville sells apples in more shapes and forms than you can shake a stick at. MITCH MOORE

Since the early 1980s, the Applewood Farms complex has been fruitful and multiplied. At the Candy Apple and Chocolate Factory, you can watch workers make candied and caramel apples as well as homemade fudge, taffy, stick candy, and lots more. Experienced candy makers use all natural ingredients in their old-fashioned recipes. If you visit the Creamery next door, you'll find homemade ice cream sundaes, sodas, and shakes and even fresh-baked apple breads (you were expecting bananas?).

Wine connoisseurs will definitely want to stop by the Apple Barn Winery. Since it opened in 1995, many of the winery's labels have won numerous awards at national and international wine competitions. You can stop by the winery's tasting bar and sample from their menu of 10 different wines, most of which are made from apples. Their most popular vintage is the Apple Blush, a semisweet wine made from an apple-grape blend.

There are two different dining establishments found at Applewood Farms. The first, the Applewood Farmhouse Restaurant, was converted from the actual farmhouse that had originally stood on the farm since 1921. Just a few years ago, the Applewood Farmhouse Grill opened for business. We go into more depth on both of these places in our Restaurants chapter.

memorabilia for sale, some of which is autographed.

Sci-fi collectors will want to check out all the different *Star Trek* and *Star Wars* collectibles, including trading cards, figures, and models. Many of the shop's collectible figures are current hot items from the worlds of film, television, and music.

Naturally, trading cards like Pokemon and Dragonball Z are quite popular as well.

"Surely," you're thinking, "that must be all." Wrong, laser breath! S & G Comics & Collectibles has books, figurines, dice, cards, and other supplies for all kinds of role playing games like Dungeons and Dragons. It's time to beam down!

Miscellaneous

Home Accents Direct
Two Rivers Boulevard, Sevierville
(865) 774-2007
www.homeaccentsdirect.net
With more than a million items in stock, Home Accents Direct Superstore Outlet Center offers lots of choices for anyone in the market for home decor. You'll find everything from lamps, pottery, art, iron works, and fountains to upholstered furniture, case goods, crystal, antiques, and more at factory-direct prices.

More than 100 different manufacturers are represented throughout Home Accents' 75,000 square feet of floor space. Look for names such as Textile Studio, Decorator's Reserve, Next Dimensions, Capel Rugs, White Rock Trading Co., and Dan River Factory Store, showcasing unique selections of factory-direct merchandise. Merchandise from both individual artists and national companies is on display, so you're sure to find something to suit your taste.

Smoky Mountain Knife Works
2320 Winfield Dunn Parkway, Sevierville
(865) 453-5871, (800) 251-9306
www.eknifeworks.com
It bills itself as "The World's Largest Knife Showplace." Once you've strolled through its three levels and 40,000 square feet of sales and display floor space, you probably won't dispute the claim. On the main level, you'll find display case after display case filled with just about anything that cuts—pocket knives, hunting and fishing knives, and hatchets. Look for brand

names like Case, Buck, Gerber, and Remington. Another area is devoted to out-of-the-ordinary weaponry like machetes, swords, Ninja gear, blowguns, and even paintball equipment.

On the lower level you'll find sections containing kitchen cutlery, jewelry, toys, T-shirts, gift items, and a knife sharpening service. There are also several displays that will make your visit even more visually interesting. Look for the life-size diorama scenes depicting an African watering hole, an American Indian with his canoe, and a Civil War soldier with cannon. The kids will be entertained by the Bubba Bear Band, a singing animatronic attraction.

The centerpiece of the lower level is the working grist mill apparatus. Complete with original gears and pulleys, this water-powered wheel works just like it did in the olden days.

The upper level is practically a museum, with many display cases filled with collections of rare and antique knives and related memorabilia. Many of the collections are arranged thematically, including those devoted to film and TV Westerns, weapons of Native American tribes, and Civil War weaponry (there are similar such displays on the main level near the front entrance as well). Although most of these collections are for display purposes only, Smoky Mountain Knife Works does have other cases filled with antique and collectible knives that are for sale.

Although you're upstairs, you'll also want to check out Trophy Mountain, a display that the store claims is the Smokies' largest indoor mountain and waterfall. Like other parts of the store, Trophy Mountain is home to a veritable zoo made up of stuffed game and mounted game trophies. Before you leave Smoky Mountain Knife Works, be sure to visit the gift and collectibles area and the sweet shop. They also publish several catalogs annually through which you can place orders over the phone by calling the toll-free number.

Everything Natural
209 Forks of the River Parkway
Sevierville
(865) 453-6112

Although there are quite a few health-food stores to be found in Sevier County, this Sevierville store has been around just about longer than any, since 1985, and has an experienced, knowledgeable staff on hand to help you with your shopping.

Naturally (no pun intended), they carry several lines of vitamin, mineral, and herbal supplements. In the back room, they also have a selection of loosely ground herbs which can be purchased in nonpill form, helpful for use in food or drink preparation. You'll also find sections of the store devoted to homeopathy, aromatherapy, and healthy pet food products.

Those who are into healthful cooking can pick from fresh, organically grown foods as well as prepackaged and frozen items. There is also a good selection of healthy snacks and hiking foods. Not just limited to food consumption, the store offers natural cosmetic items like shampoos and soaps, as well as informative books and magazines.

PIGEON FORGE

Shopping Malls and Villages

Bell Tower Square
2470 Parkway, Pigeon Forge

Since opening in 1986, this 43,000-square-foot Bavarian-style shopping village has grown into one of the top 10 Christmas and collectible destinations in the United States. It's located on the west side of Parkway, just north of the Wears Valley Road intersection. The anchor of Bell Tower Square is Christmas Place, where the trees and stockings are never taken down. When you walk through the doors, you enter a year-round Christmas fantasy-land filled with thousands of Yuletide decorations. Although an all-Christmas store could easily be presented in a tacky or junky fashion, Christmas Place is first-class all the way.

Dozens of lighted and decorated tree displays fill the main showroom, along with plenty of figurines, decorations, and gift items. In the North Pole Village area, you'll find a wide selection of artificial trees, ornaments, and lights. Look for collectible names like Department 56, Lee Middleton, Fontanini, and more. Other areas of Christmas Place contain miniature village scenes, and they even have an in-house floral department. At the east end of the store, keep an eye out for the large stained-glass window that looks down on a peaceful nativity scene. Thanks to a 13,000-square-foot expansion completed in 2000, Christmas Place offers more merchandise than ever before. To learn more about the store, visit their Web site at www.christmasplace.com.

Also at Bell Tower Square, you'll find the Collectible Gallery, featuring high-quality merchandise by respected names in the collectibles field. You'll see numerous displays containing Armani porcelain, Swarovski crystal, Fenton glass, Tom Clark gnomes, Thomas Kinkade lithographs, and plates from the Bradford Exchange.

Another shop that girls of all ages will enjoy is the Doll Shoppe. Inside, dolls and accessories by Madame Alexander, Lee Middleton, Ashton-Drake, and more are waiting for both novice and experienced collectors. Next on your visit to Bell Tower Square, you might step into Second Nature, featuring collectibles, jewelry, clothing accessories, and wall art, all centered around a "nature" theme.

We can't stress this enough: The summer afternoons around here can get fiercely hot. Dress comfortably, rest frequently, and carry liquids with you. The number of heat exhaustion cases in the area on a daily basis is staggering, and there are just not enough emergency personnel to handle it.

If you've got kids with you, you will have no choice but to stop by Toys and Trains. They have all sorts of model train kits in addition to toys and games that will really help spark the imagination and creativity of your child (that's right, creativity—they don't sell video games). Bell Tower Square also provides a respite for the empty stomach. At Mrs. Claus' Candy Kitchen and Sweet Shop, you can order from a deli-style menu of hot and cold sandwiches, and for dessert, you can try their selection of fresh-baked goods such as fudges and brownies.

Any visit to Bell Tower Square is enhanced by the Bavarian village setting in which the shops are set. The buildings themselves are of old-world architecture and are surrounded by cobbled brick walkways, wildflowers, and greenery. If you wish, you can sit on one of the park benches or at the shaded tables to enjoy your lunch from Mrs. Claus's Candy Kitchen and Sweet Shop or just take a load off. In the center of the courtyard, a large model train setup features cars winding their way through a village scene and running waterfall.

Pine Mountain Village
3152 Parkway, Pigeon Forge
You'll find this strip mall on the west side of the Parkway, just north of the Pine Mountain Road intersection. At Winner's Circle, NASCAR fans will find collectibles and sportswear galore, all with a stock car-racing theme. You'll find crafts and collectibles at Pigeon Hollow Crafts, and Good Shepherd Christian Bookstore carries bibles, books, music, and other Christian-based merchandise.

At the Dugout, sports fans will find trading cards and collectibles in their favorite sports. You can pamper your hands and nails at T Nails, and at the Small's World, parents of younger children will find a nice selection of boys' and girls' clothing in addition to toys that can be collected or played with. New to Pine Mountain Village is Country Music U.S.A., which has a large selection of country CDs and tapes as well as other country music-related merchandise.

Although it doesn't necessarily fall under our "shopping" umbrella, there is also a UPS Store at Pine Mountain Village that is handy for packaging and mailing home some of your Smoky Mountain loot. This might especially be useful for those who travel to the Smokies by plane or bus. Also at Pine Mountain Village, you'll find Pine Mountain Realty as well as places to eat, including Papa John's Pizza and the Sugar Shack.

Old Mill Village
Occupying several blocks east of the Parkway (on or near Old Mill Avenue), this collective of more than 25 specialty shops includes gift stores, art galleries, craft studios, and more. The neighborhood is generally clustered around the historic Old Mill, an active gristmill that was built in 1830 on the banks of the Little Pigeon River (see our Attractions chapter).

Old Mill Village doesn't occupy so large an area that you can't see it all on foot. Most of the shops offer free parking, and there's plenty of free parking at nearby Patriot Park. Or you can take the trolley to the Pigeon Forge Fun Time Trolley office, which is smack in the middle of the village. From there, you can find most of what's available within a block or two. There are also public restrooms at the trolley station.

The atmosphere in Old Mill Village is laid-back and leisurely, and the shopkeepers are always happy to visit with you. The shops listed here are all members of the Old Mill Village Merchants Association. While these businesses represent the vast majority of shops found in the neighborhood, you'll find a few others as well that we haven't included here. Because of the many merchants located in Old Mill Village, we'll simply be listing them by name along with a brief elaboration on their merchandise where needed. In some cases (and we'll indicate so), you'll find individual write-ups on some of these shops in our Mountain Crafts chapter.

Starting with the Old Mill as a reference point, we'll take you east in a counterclockwise direction: the Old Mill and Restaurant, Pigeon Forge Craft Center, Kitchen Kupboard, Beauty & Faith, Rachel's Christian Store, Miss Dee's Old-Fashioned Photos, the Finishing Touch (unique ladies boutique), and the Pattern Hutch.

Traveling 1 block east on Old Mill Avenue to Butler Street will deliver you to Dixie Darlin (needle art and decorative painting), and Helix Pewter & Copper. Back on Old Mill Avenue are several newer shops operated by the Old Mill's owners, including the Old Mill Toy Bin, Old Mill Gift & Basket Co., Old Mill Creamery, Old Mill Candy Kitchen, Old Mill Potting Shed, and the Old Mill Bakery Cafe. Also look for Pigeon River Pottery, a studio and shop doing business in the same facility as its longtime predecessor, Pigeon Forge Pottery.

Along Old Mill Street you'll find the Twisted Vessel Gallery, Smoky Mountain Dog House (everything for the dog lover), Candles by Donna, Smoky Mountain Cat House (what, you don't like dogs?!), Peggy's Dolls, the Diamond House, Randall Ogle Gallery, Pigeon River String Instruments, Amanda Jayne's (unique gifts and collectibles), Gourmet Coffee Shop, the Upper Room (Christian merchandise), Something Special by Sue (folk art, crafts, clothing, and more in a country flavor), and Jim Gray Gallery (see our Mountain Crafts chapter).

Log Cabin Shops
3509 Parkway, Pigeon Forge
(865) 453-6485

Very similar in appearance to the "hodge-podge" collections of merchants that used to dot the landscape, Log Cabin Shops is a fluid mix of commercial and handcrafted items in nine shops that offer current fad-type collectibles and made-to-order leather goods. Visiting craftspeople and musical groups keep the place interesting most of the time. Vending machines and an ice cream shop provide refreshments, which can be enjoyed at picnic benches while enjoying another favorite pastime: people watching.

Bookstores

Foozle's
2655 Teaster Lane, Pigeon Forge
(865) 429-1682

At the extreme northwest corner of Belz Factory Outlet World, Foozle's is chock-full of discounted and reduced-price books in a bright, airy setting. The selection is excellent, and the prices on titles that may be a little out-of-date approach 80 percent off retail. Foozle's appears to be operated by a bunch of teachers; they lean very heavily on educational material, particularly for the beginning reader. They also encourage their customers to be especially nice to teachers, which can't be an all bad thought. The selection of humorous material is outstanding.

Bible Factory Outlet
2725 Teaster Lane, Pigeon Forge
(865) 429-8170
www.bibleoutlet.com

This shop is almost identical to the one at Tanger Five Oaks mall described earlier, right down to the tile on the floor. It's near the eastern end of Annex #1 in Belz Factory Outlet World.

Book Warehouse
3127 Parkway, Pigeon Forge
(865) 428-5708

Here, you'll find over 200,000 new books at discounted prices. Although the deals are usually pretty good, we will tell you that the titles aren't necessarily hot off the presses. Nevertheless, depending on your

Pick up copies of Smoky Mountain tourist-oriented magazines to find discount coupons on merchandise at many of the county's most popular shopping destinations. Some of the publications include the What-to-Do Magazine, Tennessee Smokies Visitors Guide, Best Read Guide, *and* Sevier County Shopping Guide *(see our Media chapter).*

needs, this is still a great place to go book shopping. There are fiction and nonfiction books in almost every genre, just as in other bookstores. Categories include *New York Times* best-sellers and a large selection of inspirational books.

Besides books, you'll also find audio and video tapes, teachers' aids and materials, and locally made crafts. Book Warehouse has two other Smoky Mountain locations: a smaller version in the Pigeon Forge Factory Outlet Mall across the Parkway, and Mountain Mall in Gatlinburg (see the Gatlinburg section of this chapter).

Clothing

Stages West
2765 Parkway, Pigeon Forge
(865) 453-8086
Saddle on up, pardners, and head to Stages West, the Smokies' largest Western store, with more than 100,000 items in stock at discount prices. There are more than 5,000 pairs of boots in stock by manufacturers like Durango, Tony Lama, and Acme-Dingo. For kids, there are more than 1,000 pairs of boots from which to choose. The selection of leather continues with handcrafted purses, wallets, belts, and moccasins. If you like to do-si-do, you'll definitely want to visit Stages West; they specialize in Western wear and square-dance apparel.

Lid'l Dolly's Country Store
2828 Parkway, Pigeon Forge
(865) 428-2365, (800) 468-2365
Whether the "dolly" in question happens to be a toy or your own child, you'll find beautiful ways to get her gussied up at this dress manufacturer and retailer. Colorful and frilly is the best way to describe these handcrafted dresses made primarily for younger children. Made of a polyester-cotton blend, the dresses are machine washable and are appropriate for weddings, beauty pageants, or any situation where the little lady needs to look her

most adorable. Lid'l Dolly's has a limited selection of dress-up apparel for the young lad as well.

The shop got its start at Dollywood (naturally) and has since expanded to its current facility on the Parkway in Pigeon Forge. Although most of the inventory is made up of dresses for "real" girls, there is a section of the store devoted to collectible dolls and doll dresses. You'll also find a large selection of quilts, and in the front section of the store you can browse through their displays of homemade fudge, jellies, and preserves. Even if you're not in the area, you can still make purchases from Lid'l Dolly's by calling their toll-free number. They'll send you current dress and price information, and you can place your order over the phone.

Circle E Factory Boot Outlet
2746 Parkway, Pigeon Forge
(865) 453-1749
When Circle E opened its doors in the '60s, it was about the only building at the south end of Pigeon Forge. Now it's surrounded by motels and restaurants. Circle E is also reputed to be the first business in Pigeon Forge that used the word "outlet" in its title. Circle E features an impressive selection of boots from utility (Dan Post and Dingo) to full-dress (Tony Lama and Justin) at competitive prices, along with work shoes, Stetson hats, and one of the most complete lines of square-dance apparel in the Southeast.

Antiques and Collectibles

China and Gift Mart
2680 Parkway, Pigeon Forge
(865) 453-5679
More than 300 different patterns of china are available at discounts of up to 70 percent at this Pigeon Forge shop that's been in business since the mid-'80s. They stock more than a dozen name brands, including Noritake, Royal Worcester, Wedge-

wood, Nikko, Lenox, Royal Doulton, and Muirfield. The selection is all first-quality and includes complete place settings and accessories.

In addition to china, China and Gift Mart carries flatware by Oneida, Retroneu, and Towle Silversmith as well as collectibles by Precious Moments, Cherished Teddies, and Emmett Kelly Jr. Another section of the store, called Christmas and Collectibles, offers 15,000 square feet of gorgeous Christmas decorations, fine collectibles, dolls, and more.

The Barn Owl
3629 Parkway, Pigeon Forge
(865) 428-0846
A collector's must-see, the Barn Owl carries Hallmark and Precious Moments items (some that go back a few years) and high-class figurines and sculpture. They also carry an excellent selection of expert-level jigsaw puzzles from Milton Bradley, Springbok, and Ravensberger.

Miscellaneous

Cat's Compact Discs and Cassettes
1977 Parkway, Pigeon Forge
(865) 429-4600
In 1998 this regional chain of music shops brought its wide selection and low prices to the Smokies. The store carries CDs (mostly) and cassettes in all genres of music, but most of the store's inventory is centered around rock/pop and country. For more eclectic tastes, however, there's also rap, reggae, jazz, classical, comedy, and movie soundtracks.

Besides a generous inventory of new CDs, Cat's also has racks full of used compact discs at discounted prices in its Dog Pound. You can also trade in your own CDs for store credit. One neat, customer-friendly service that the store offers is access to the Cat's Listening Posts (instead of scratching posts—get it?). At three different stations, you can put on headphones and listen to selected new

Several of the merchants' associations in the Smokies publish coupon books that provide discounts and premiums. Check the local welcome centers, lodging places, and brochure racks everywhere for some hidden bonuses.

releases before you purchase a disc (and face it, we've all bought clunker albums based on one great song!).

Rocky Top Outfitters
2721 Parkway, Pigeon Forge
(865) 429-3474
You'll not only find supplies for fishing and camping at Rocky Top, but you can also receive instruction and guide services from this licensed outfitter. As for equipment, most of their stock is for anglers. They have fly rods, spin rods, reels, and all kinds of flies, baits, and lures. Look for rod-and-reel brand names like Redington, Shimano, and Hoffman. They also carry a large selection of Ultimate Poppers and single-hook rooster tail spinners. Although the emphasis is on fishing gear, there is a limited selection of camping equipment as well.

Rocky Top Outfitters brings more than 17 years of guiding experience to its customers, having conducted trips on 11 lakes and on more than 3,000 miles of rivers and streams. They do lead some hunting trips, but most of their guide business is fishing-related. They conduct about 200 guided trips annually.

In addition to guiding, the Rocky Top staff offers fly-fishing instruction, handmade jigs and flies, and award-winning taxidermy services.

Smoky Mountain Candy Makers
2880 Parkway, Pigeon Forge
(865) 453-9213
There weren't too many businesses on the Parkway in Pigeon Forge 30 years ago, but this candy shop was one of them. Since 1973, this family-owned confectioner has been turning out delectable treats like

taffy, fudge, candy apples, suckers, and hand-dipped chocolate and nut clusters. About 90 percent of the goodies in stock are made on the premises. In fact, if you visit at the right time, you'll be able to see the staff of candy makers turning out their products before your eyes. If you're lucky, you might even get to see the taffy machines pull, roll, and wrap!

GATLINBURG

When you go shopping in Gatlinburg, you're in one of the most retail-intensive areas in the eastern United States. Gatlinburg has crammed 14 shopping malls and more than 100 free-standing retail shops of dizzying variety into less than a half-mile of nonstop browsing space, and that only tells about half the story. You can walk the full length of the Parkway from traffic light #3 to #10 in about 15 minutes—if you're wearing blinders. A knowledgeable shopper will take an evening (anywhere from three to six hours) to do one side, and save the other side for another time.

A popular alternative is to use the half-and-half approach. Starting at about the Village shopping plaza (Reagan Terrace is also a popular starting point), walk east (toward the Ferris wheel at Fun Mountain); stay on the Parkway by crossing East Parkway at traffic light #3, and browse the shops at Carousel Mall and along the Parkway to the Atrium restaurant. At this point, cross the Parkway (use the crosswalk—you have the right-of-way, but be careful) and walk back to the Mountain Mall; if you still have time and strength on your side, go on to Baskins Square or Market Place. For the second half, head west (toward the park entrance) to traffic light #8 (the Space Needle). Cross the Parkway and return to the previous finishing point. Each of these routes will use up a few hours without losing sight of the start/finish point.

There are additional shops and malls at both ends of this route, but they're more

spread out. The best way to get to them is to drive to a parking lot near the end and work the same way as before: Hit one side of the street, cross, and return on the other. It's just not feasible to list every shop in town, but we'll give an overview of all the malls and shopping villages on the Parkway, and some detail on a representative sampling of the more established businesses. We'll also give some space to those shops that struck us as more interesting or fun than the norm. Remember, we always go from north to south, running in the same order as the traffic lights. Wear comfortable shoes.

Shopping Malls and Villages

Carousel Mall
458 Parkway, Gatlinburg
(865) 436-7625
Standing at the intersection of the Parkway and East Parkway, Carousel Mall is built into a hillside so steep that ground level on the East Parkway is three stories above ground level on the Parkway less than 100 feet away. Either way you enter, short stairways and a central elevator take you through several levels devoted mostly to art and collectibles galleries. Local artist Jim Gray has a ground-floor (Parkway side) gallery here (see our Mountain Crafts chapter for more information), and the Neumann Gallery on the top level specializes in Civil War art and artifacts. The Rampant Lion offers gifts with a Southwestern flavor, and Earth's Treasures features unusual geodes and sculptures of stone and metal.

Riverbend Mall
511 Parkway, Gatlinburg
(865) 436-3063
Two levels of convenient shopping include fine giftware at Barbara's Elegants, a long-time Gatlinburg mainstay, along with Miss Kitty's old-time photos, camping and fishing supplies at Old Smoky Outfitters, and Thomas Kinkade artworks at Things

Unique. Novelty machines line one wall of the ground floor for the amusement of family members who'd prefer not to shop. And if you get the hungries, Olympic Gyro and Souvlaki has a menu of authentic Greek dishes for a snack or a meal.

Mountain Mall
611 Parkway, Gatlinburg
(865) 436-5935
www.mtnmall.com
The largest retail concentration in town, Mountain Mall is a six-level structure containing 40 shops of various description. The split-level design makes stair climbing more negotiable, and the elevator stops at all levels. There's also an interesting little escalator that only goes up. From fast food at three different locations to top-of-the-line collectibles and the world's hottest sauces, the Mountain Mall is worth an extended stay indoors. A three-story wooden fountain at the west end sends water plummeting through a fascinating series of weight-activated ducts. Among the original tenants when the mall opened in 1978 are the Rhythm Section, the city's first record business; the Gatlinburlier, the only shop in town that's dedicated entirely to the smoker; and Aunt Mahalia's Candy, the first local sweet shop to open a satellite location. The newer shops include Buckboard Too, an old shop in a new location; Pepper Palace, where you can choose your poison if inner heat is your thing; emagictricks.com, an illusory treat; and the Book Warehouse, covered in its specific section of this chapter.

Baskins Square Mall
631 Parkway, Gatlinburg
(865) 430-2104
Running away from the Parkway toward River Road, Baskins Square has eight shops and three restaurants stuffed into a deceptively small area surrounding a brick courtyard. The Mountain Woodcarvers is a local mainstay of more than 20 years, as are Duffy's Tavern and the Funnel Cake Shop. The Terri Waters Gallery is covered in the Mountain Crafts chapter. The Little

Sparrow shop and the White Wolf Gallery specialize in Native American products.

The Village—A Shopping Place
634 Parkway, Gatlinburg
(865) 436-3995
www.thevillageshops.com
In the heart of downtown Gatlinburg, a group of shops is truly a slice of the Old World. The Village, which has pedestrian entrances on the Parkway and Baskins Creek Road, is a collective of 27 shops and eateries that offer something a little beyond the everyday.

The Village's true charm, however, lies in its architecture and surroundings. Its idyllic backdrop includes rock gardens, wildflowers, water fountains, and interesting relics like a British phone booth. Local wildlife are no strangers to the Village—squirrels, hummingbirds, and even the occasional bear have been known to pay visits to the courtyards.

The shops themselves generally convey an old-world look through an eclectic mix of architectural styles and designs, with moss and vine thriving on their facades. A great many of the furnishings and fixtures that go into the makeup of each shop are either unusual, antique, rare, or some combination of the three. For example, the front porch of one particular shop was obtained from the old parsonage of Knoxville's Second Baptist Church.

Other shops use pieces like beveled glass, wormy chestnut wood, and antique staircases to flesh out the old-world effect. Even the archway that forms the main entrance to the Village is historically significant. The bricks are believed to have been made by area slaves around 1843. Supposedly, they were used to construct the first brick building in Sevier County around that same time.

The 27 tenants occupying the Village offer shoppers merchandise ranging from unique and hard-to-find gifts to fine art to gourmet coffees and desserts. We've listed all of them below, along with brief parenthetical descriptions for those whose names aren't necessarily self-explanatory.

Business as Usual in Gatlinburg

If you spend enough time in Gatlinburg and dig in the right corners, you'll learn that a lot of the property in the downtown commercial district is owned by two families, the Ogles (surprise!) and the Reagans (surprise again). That situation probably won't change in the near future because the leaderships of the two families share a pretty hard-nosed attitude about selling land: Don't. What's different between the two families is how they came by their holdings and how they manage them.

The Ogle family is large and robust and given to long lives. They're also one of the oldest English-speaking families on the planet, with an unbroken line of succession that goes back 30 generations to 11th-century England, when people didn't have last names. Until her death in 2002, the matriarch of the local Ogle clan was the estimable Hattie Maples Ogle McGiffin, born February 24, 1898. Of Hattie's many descendants (40-plus and counting) from her marriage to Charles Austin Ogle (1893–1945), only two have died— her eldest son, Charles Earl, 80, and daughter, Lib Whaley, 78, both of whom died in the last week of December 1998. Most of the others are active in the family businesses in varying degrees.

Charlie Ogle died remarkably young considering his family's track record. Remembered fondly as "Uncle Charlie," he was one of the most beloved people in Gatlinburg's history. He inherited from his father the family grocery store started by his grandfather Noah (1833–97) on the present site of the Mountain Mall, which is now managed by Charlie's grandson, Charles Earl Ogle Jr., a stripling of 65 years. In the tradition of their forebears (William and Martha Jane Ogle, the original white settlers, had seven children who produced the astonishing total of 82 [!] children among them), the Ogle family has kept the management of their empire in the family. Counting children and three generations of grandchildren, HMO, Inc., the Ogle's land management corporation, has more than 20 family members involved in various aspects of property management.

The property ownership philosophy is simple: A family as big as theirs needed a lot of land just to grow enough food to feed them. As their fields became more valuable for development than for agriculture, the Ogles either developed it themselves or leased it to developers. That's

Hattie Ogle McGiffin, 1898–2002. HMO, INC.

Brownlee Reagan (left) and Charles Earl Ogle Jr.: These two industrious men help keep Sevier County running. DICK McHUGH

how Granny Hattie established herself as one of the finest business minds anywhere in the United States. Finding herself in possession of large tracts of downtown property, some of which she had inherited from her own Maples family, Hattie made or influenced every decision on how the land could best serve her growing family.

The result is an impressive array of family-operated and leased businesses in the downtown area that includes the outright ownership of three shopping malls, several motels, a couple of office/retail buildings, two downtown markets, and long-term land leases on the sites of several large motels. HMO is currently in the hands of the aforementioned Charles Earl Ogle Jr., who still likes to go down to one of the markets at 5:00 A.M. to unload produce (once a grocer, always a grocer). With four generations currently involved in running the businesses established by Granny Hattie, and the acquisitive nature and inherent business acumen continuing in her great- and great-great-grandchildren, the Ogle family's benevolent stewardship of the

Gatlinburg business community appears to be firmly settled in the right set of hands.

The Reagan story has the same result with a completely different approach. Brownlee Reagan was born in Gatlinburg on August 30, 1926. His great-great-grandfather, Daniel Wesley Reagan (1802–92), a native of Sevier County before the establishment of White Oak Flats, married Nancy Ogle, one of the 14 children of Thomas, and one of the eighty-two grandchildren of Billy and Martha Jane Ogle. Daniel and Nancy Ogle Reagan were the great-grandparents of both of Brownlee's parents.

The Reagans are an industrious lot, known for their hard work and community service. Their land holdings were modest compared to those of the Ogles, but their needs were also not quite as great. Brownlee Reagan appeared to be headed down the family's established path as a police officer and eventually police chief, but he combined his public service with an unusual perception of Gatlinburg's future. He began accumulating land before the tourist boom of the '70s by buying whatever land he could afford that came on the market, and building motels. The current figure is "somewhere between 7 and 10" downtown motels, and an indeterminate number of lodging places in other parts of the nation. He also kept an eye open to the availability of other commercial properties, and in the process has acquired a couple of shopping malls, and a restaurant or two. Not blessed with a large family, Brownlee Reagan has pretty much handled it all by himself, with some of the load being picked up by sons Lee and John, who seem to be unfazed at the size of the company they're gradually learning to control.

The Ogle and Reagan families have controlled their holdings and their destinies by maintaining active interests in the community: Hattie Ogle McGiffin lent her name and considerable talents to a variety of civic and charitable causes. Both families are deeply involved in local politics—Charles Earl Ogle Jr. and Brownlee Reagan have both served the city as commissioners, mayors, chamber of commerce presidents, and civic philanthropists.

In the cosmic scheme of things, Gatlinburg is still a young and growing city. Less than 200 years old, it has considerable growth potential in the undeveloped land to the east. When that potential is tapped, the local feeling that it's an Ogle/Reagan empire will probably dissipate. What won't go away for a while is the wondering what would have happened if the control had stayed in these capable hands.

The Day Hiker, the Honey Pot (glassware, pottery, and clay gift items), Verbenas (body, bath, and home delicacies), the Taylor Girls (two ladies' boutique shops), the Silver Tree (for the silver lover), Desserts & More Cafe, the Christmas Tree, the Treasure Nook (gifts and collectibles), Candle Cottage, L.C.'s Intimate Apparel & Fine Gifts, Cartoons & Toys, Coffee & Company, Hofbrauhaus Restaurant & Cheese Cupboard, the Donut Friar, the Jelly Jar (jellies, jams, preserves, etc.), Whiff-n-Pouff (ladies' fashions and accessories), Garden Gate (wind socks, bird feeders, chimes, etc.), the Hayloft (fine leathers and Western wear), the Art of Glynda Turley & More, Another Me Clothier (missy and plus fashions), Hills Creek Collection (Mark Hopkins bronze works), Thomas Kinkade at the Village (the art of Thomas Kinkade), God's Corner (Christian music, books, bibles, etc.), and, finally!, Celtic Heritage (Scots-Irish merchandise).

The Market Place
651 Parkway, Gatlinburg
(865) 436-3251
Built in 1980, the Market Place features imposing Georgian-style architecture and beautiful landscaping, with a waterfall and fountain at the River Road end. A full line of Christmas merchandise is available year-round at Lindz's, and the Civil War memorabilia at Armour House is impressive. Be sure to check out Del Sol—it has an amazing selection of products that are sun-powered. Fast food is available at Mama Bear's Kitchen.

Riverside Mini-Mall
715 Parkway, Gatlinburg
(865) 436-4460
While it doesn't look like an honest-to-goodness shopping mall, the 14 Riverside shops and booths stretched along the Parkway in front of the Riverside Motor Lodge comprise the oldest collection of retail

shops under one roof in the downtown area. Rustic Redwood Signs has been at the same location since 1971, and the Silver Express opened in 1975. The Funnel Cake booth, opened in 1987, is a relative new-comer to this interesting array of merchants.

Reagan Terrace Mall
716 Parkway, Gatlinburg
(865) 436-7781

Built around a courtyard on the Parkway, Reagan Terrace's 12 shops include Gatlin-burg Elegants, an upscale gift shop with other locations in town; STC Sports, an eclectic collection of handcrafts and cus-tom embroidery; Fantasy Fotos Empo-rium; a NASCAR theme shop; and several food shops. Reagan Terrace sits in front of the Gatlinburg Fun Center, described in our Attractions and Kidstuff chapters.

Downtown Traders
805 Parkway, Gatlinburg
(865) 436-4692

This one is different in that it's entirely below the sidewalk. A pretty little brick walk leads to a courtyard with a rock gar-den grotto that's a nice photo opportu-nity. The Buckboard is the anchor shop here, taking up about half of the mall with its collection of Tom Clark gnomes, local crafts, and Western-themed goods. Cac-tus Jack's restaurant features a marvelous choice of sandwiches. Mountain Leather & Co. has offered locally handcrafted leather items since 1980, and Smoky Mountain Collectibles has a broad line of NASCAR merchandise.

Elks Plaza
968 Parkway, Gatlinburg
(865) 436-7550

As you might guess from the name, this is the home of Gatlinburg's BPOE Lodge 1925, which takes up the second story. Included in the mall below are the Best Italian Restaurant; the Hillbilly Gift Shop; Aromatherapy; and Woodware, a longtime Gatlinburg craft business described in the Mountain Crafts chapter.

Tramway Mall
1001 Parkway, Gatlinburg
(865) 436-5423

The jumping-off point for the aerial tramway to Ober Gatlinburg (see our Attractions chapter), the Tramway Mall has goodies at the Kandy Kitchen, gifts at the Silver Galleon and Shelley's Baskets (sometimes Shelley's out in front paint-ing), and the Ober souvenir-and-clothing shop. If you're on your way up the moun-tain, film and camera supplies are avail-able at the Camera Shop.

Calhoun's Village
1004 Parkway, Gatlinburg
(865) 436-6004

A recent entry, Calhoun's Village is anchored by Smoky Mountain Brewery and Pizza, Gatlinburg's only minibrewery. This small group of shops and galleries ranges from the fine art of Earth to Old City and the Native American–oriented Bampton-Greene Gallery to the fantasy world of electric trains at Whistle Stop Junction.

River Oaks Mall
825 River Road, Gatlinburg
(865) 436-9551

River Oaks is primarily a "local service" location. It's notable for the fact that it contains the city's only downtown liquor store. A large chalet rental office and a hair salon fill out the slate at River Oaks.

Bookstores

Beneath the Smoke
467 Parkway, Gatlinburg
(865) 436-3460

This shop is dedicated to Mother Nature in all her splendor and could be included in any category in this chapter. We chose to list it as a bookstore because the variety of literature is so great. Art, sculpture, and camping products all exalt the great outdoors, and the selection of handbooks and guidebooks to the flora and fauna of the Southeast is outstand-

We haven't mentioned tattooing and body-piercing parlors because the local business communities would rather such establishments weren't here. The city of Gatlinburg is trying to enact legislation strong enough to prohibit these businesses. Be all of that as it may, it's your right to know that there are three tattoo parlors in Sevierville and three on the Parkway in Gatlinburg between traffic lights #1 and #3.

ing. The variety of bird guides is the best we found in the area.

Book Warehouse
611 Parkway, Gatlinburg
(865) 430-5972
Constituting practically the entire "E" level of the Mountain Mall, this Book Warehouse location has 1,200 square feet of space laid out to accommodate a full spectrum of fiction and nonfiction, with an outstanding selection of local guide books for bird-watchers and hikers.

A Little Bit of Heaven
734 Parkway, Gatlinburg
(865) 436-5433
www.alittlebitofheavenonline.com
Specializing in Christian publications and recordings, A Little Bit of Heaven is Gatlinburg's oldest bookstore. Small gifts and souvenirs with a Christian theme are complemented by an exceptional selection of religious and secular greeting cards for all occasions.

Clothing

The Hemp Store
411 Parkway, Gatlinburg
(865) 436-8300
Here's a kicky little shop featuring clothing and accessories from natural fibers.

Tie-dyed clothing and New Age jewelry items are also available, along with a selection of in-your-face environmental bumper stickers, pins, and posters. And if you have any need for hemp rope, this is one of the few places where you'll find it sold in bulk.

Jonathan's
733 Parkway, Gatlinburg
(865) 436-7148
A downtown mainstay since the late '70s, Jonathan's features an extensive line of upscale name-brand sportswear and accessories, and a broad line of camping supplies and literature. In the Gatlinburg tradition, Jonathan's clings to the belief that service and attention to detail are still important to its customers.

King's Designer Name Brand Outlet
978 Parkway, Gatlinburg
(865) 436-7805
One of the larger shops in the downtown area, King's offers designer labels at competitive prices. The spacious display area is arranged by clothing type to allow each family member to compare clothing by several designers without searching through a bunch of displays.

Antiques and Collectibles

Morton's Antiques & Baseball Cards
409 Parkway, Gatlinburg
(865) 436-5504
Doing business at the same location since 1949, Morton's is noted for its art glass and porcelain antiques and for its spectacular line of Italian inlaid wood furniture. A small selection of very rare (and very pricey) baseball cards and old coins is available for serious collectors. At our last look, Morton's had vintage Babe Ruth, Honus Wagner, Willie Mays, and Mickey Mantle trading cards, some of which bore five-digit price tags.

Gazebo Gifts
529 Parkway, Gatlinburg
(865) 436-4064
Predating the 1975 tourism boomlet, the Gazebo features specialty bottles and a gorgeous array of glass vases and bowls. Their collection of ANRI wood carvings (Hummel-like carved wood figures) is one of the largest in the eastern United States. Your children are welcome, but hang on to them.

Miscellaneous

Lloyd's of Gatlinburg
465 Parkway, Gatlinburg
(865) 436-7997
A popular gift shop since 1972, Lloyd's carries a mixed bag of big and little goods. Pine furniture and stained glass share space with an eclectic array of knick-knacks. Lloyd's selection of small brass bells is one of the best around. The gallery of Southwestern furniture and sculpture adjoins the original shop. And don't worry about getting your big furniture items home—Lloyd's has its own delivery service.

The Great Wall
604 Parkway, Gatlinburg
(865) 430-4498
www.thegreatwall.com
In a radical departure from the queasiness we normally feel when we see a label reading "Made in China/Hong Kong/Formosa, etc.," the feeling in the Great Wall is a sense of awe at the mastery that produced the pottery, ceramic figures, and knives in this gallery of upscale merchandise from an ancient culture. To be sure, there are some of the more definitive Oriental souvenirs, but they take a backseat in this shop devoted more to a culture than to an economy.

Clock Peddler of Gatlinburg
608 Parkway, Gatlinburg
(865) 436-5605
It's all about time at the Clock Peddler. If it

It only shows if you're really looking for it, but the Parkway in Gatlinburg runs steadily uphill toward the national park entrance. Consider that when planning your assault on the downtown shopping district.

tells time, they've got it or can get it. From bedside and kitchen novelty clocks to grandfather models with everything short of a symphony orchestra, and movements from wind-up and pull chain to the latest quartz model, the Clock Peddler has it all. And don't worry about getting your grandparent clock home in the family sedan—the Clock Peddler will arrange shipping for any large purchase.

Ranger Bob's Trading Post
624 Parkway, Gatlinburg
(865) 436-8551
Ranger Bob has apparently led an interesting life. His trading post runs the gamut from animal pelts you can wear to blacklight lamps and posters. A wide array of puzzles (jigsaw and brain-bender) could keep a puzzle nut of any stripe occupied for days, especially if they're worked under a blacklight lamp. The kids' backpacks in the form of woodland creatures are interesting enough to make Bob's worth a look.

Creations by Carole
644 Parkway, Gatlinburg
(865) 436-9203
www.creationsbycarole.com
Carole's has been a Parkway mainstay since the early 1970s (maybe earlier in a different incarnation). From its origins as a candle shop, whenever such occurrence may have taken place, Carole's has expanded to include an impressive collection of handmade local goods, including some incredible soft sculpture animals and the always popular mountain trolls. Carole's is one of the few shops on the Parkway that evokes memories of Gatlinburg that most of us wish were still realities.

Ola Kate's Candy Kitchen
645 Parkway, Gatlinburg
(865) 436-3720

Homemade candy is one of the oldest businesses in Gatlinburg, and Ola Kate's is one of the oldest candy makers. For a take-home souvenir to give you a sweet memory of your trip, or something to munch while walking the Parkway, Ola Kate's candy is always fresh because the small staff never seems to be able to get ahead of the demand.

The Karmelkorn Shop
647 Parkway, Gatlinburg
(865) 436-4373

Rick Berrier is as established a Parkway fixture as the weekend traffic. He's been up to his elbows in the wonderful things he does with popcorn for as long as anyone can remember, and he still looks like a kid. Get to the Karmelkorn Shop early in your stay—Rick's deals on refillable boxes will keep your fingers sticky for your whole trip at remarkably low cost.

The Acorn Shop
648 Parkway, Gatlinburg
(865) 436-5073

The original tenant in the Ogle Building since 1964, the Acorn Shop carries a line of quality souvenirs and the largest selection of knives in Gatlinburg. Every knife maker you can think of, and a few you'll discover, are represented in the Acorn's selections. The Acorn is also a favorite of local seamstresses and quilters looking for that special pair of scissors they can't function without.

Old Tyme Portraits by Treadway
702 Parkway, Gatlinburg
(865) 436-0458

Gatlinburg has an ordinance that bans the wearing of masks or face coverings in the downtown shopping area. The city makes an exception for Halloween, but only for kids.

Gatlinburg's oldest "dress-up" photo shop has more interesting and amusing get-ups that allow you to express your personality in graphic new ways than any other photo shop in Gatlinburg. The Treadway brothers have been in the novelty photo business longer than anyone else in town, and it shows in the imaginative way they approach their craft.

Aunt Mahalia's Candies
708 Parkway/952 Parkway/Mountain Mall, Gatlinburg
(865) 436-7792

The first candy shop in town to open multiple locations, Aunt Mahalia's has been threatening the dental health of three generations of visitors to the Smokies. It's hard to imagine the Parkway without the distinctive red-and-white striped Aunt Mahalia's stores beckoning to your sweet tooth from just about anywhere on the Parkway.

Glassblowers of Gatlinburg
729 Parkway/Mountain Mall, Gatlinburg
(865) 436-9114

Bob Myrick and his family started out in the early '70s with a small storefront operation on the present site of their three-story shop. With the addition of their Mountain Mall location in 1979, the Myricks solidified their reputation as one of Gatlinburg's leading merchant and philanthropic families. The Glassblower shops carry an impressive array of high-class glass and ceramic sculpture and a huge selection of souvenir jewelry. Personalizing of glass items is available while you wait.

Magnet-O-World
738 Parkway, Gatlinburg
(865) 430-9022

If it sticks to metal, it's here. More than 100,000 magnets are displayed in this fun house that passes for a retail store. There's enough variety of amusing, amazing, and appealing magnetic note holders in this place to make you go home and buy a bigger refrigerator.

Ole Smoky Candy Kitchen
744 Parkway, Gatlinburg
(865) 436-4886

Back when Gatlinburg was a lot smaller, the Candy Kitchen provided some of the town's most popular entertainment. Tourists came by the score to sit on the benches out front and watch the candy makers work their magic in the big picture window. Then they went inside and bought everything they saw being made, and usually more. The news is all good: Despite the fact that new forms of entertainment have thinned the crowd a bit, the benches are still there, and so are the candy makers in the window. Shops like this one are the reason Gatlinburg still enchants a large number of visitors looking for a simpler, gentler way of life.

One Hour Photo
754 Parkway, Gatlinburg
(865) 436-7556

The typical visitor to the Smokies takes a lot of pictures. One Hour Photo gives that visitor a chance to see the pictures they took while there's still time to do it over if something went wrong. They'll also tell you what (if anything) went wrong, how to fix it, and where to go to find more photo opportunities. And they've got whatever supplies you need to ensure that you get all the pictures you want to take.

Wacky Bear Factory
815-3 Parkway, Gatlinburg
(865) 436-0001

Here's a fun way for the younger set to create their own souvenir of the Smokies. Choosing from a variety of bear skins, kids of all ages can inject stuffing to whatever degree of firmness they want. Their bear will be finished by a resident seamstress, and an adoption certificate will be issued, for $14. From that point on, the sky's the limit as the proud new "parent" can choose from a dizzying variety of clothing, footwear, and accessories—there's even a name tag available if you didn't go completely wacky in christening your bear.

Nature's Kingdom
916 Parkway, Gatlinburg
(865) 436-5510

Wildlife forms are represented here in every fashion imaginable. Rugs, wall hangings, soft and cast toys, sculpture, and fine art all honor the beauty and dignity of wild animals in their natural habitats.

The Rock Shop
958 Parkway, Gatlinburg
(865) 436-5106

Established in the '60s, the Rock Shop carries anything that started out as a piece of some kind of stone. Arrowheads, custom jewelry, sculpture, and geodes all have their place in this quiet haven devoted to the beauty that only nature can provide.

The Gatlinburg Shop
963 Parkway, Gatlinburg
(865) 436-3454

Local headquarters for Department 56 collectibles, the Gatlinburg Shop also carries a fabulous line of hand-painted blown glass Christmas ornaments from world-famous artists. The selection of lifelike cast resin animals is among the best around.

SHOPPING FOR FOOD

If you're vacationing in the Smokies, you'll probably do your fair share of eating out in restaurants. Bon appetit! However, for those who may be watching their pocketbooks a little more closely, those who are staying in a cabin or condo and need to stock the pantry for the week, or those who might be relocating to the area, we thought we'd point you in the direction of some area supermarkets.

All but one belong to regional or national chains, and in most cases, you'll find the usual variety of grocery departments (bakery, deli, etc.). In Sevierville there is a Food Lion on Main Street, just 1 block west of the Parkway, and in 2002, a new Kroger store opened on Winfield

SHOPPING

Dunn Parkway, about a half-mile north of downtown. As you continue on the Parkway toward Pigeon Forge, you'll come across a Food City and later a Wal-Mart Supercenter that features a complete selection of groceries.

As much of Sevierville's residential growth has taken place on the east end of town, there has been a similarly growing demand for a major supermarket in that area. Traditionally, city residents had to drive into the thick of tourist traffic to shop for food. The dreams of many an East Sevierville resident came

true in 2003 when a Food City supermarket on Dolly Parton Parkway opened for business.

In Pigeon Forge, there's a Kroger store just off the Parkway on Wears Valley Road (traffic light #3). Further along the Parkway, toward the southern end of the strip, there's another Food City. Gatlinburg has a fourth (and counting) Food City on East Parkway, about a mile east of traffic light #3, and Save-A-Lot Market, about half a mile further out, at the intersection with Glades Road.

220

OUTLET SHOPPING

Shopping has replaced crafts as the second biggest reason families come to the Smokies on vacation (Great Smoky Mountains National Park is still number one). Most of the reason for that fact is that a couple of Pigeon Forge entrepreneurs made a decision in 1983 that changed that city's fortunes dramatically and quite permanently.

When Pigeon Forge was awakening after the Knoxville World's Fair, somebody took notice of a new national shopping trend where clothing manufacturers were opening their own stores in malls commonly referred to as "factory outlets." Since Pigeon Forge was suddenly attracting scores of thousands of new people who weren't just passing through anymore, why not see how this latest craze would fare? And so the Factory Merchants Mall (now the Pigeon Forge Factory Outlet Mall) was built at the northwest end of the Parkway, next to (then) the only music theater in town, which is now an independent outlet store. Now it's in the middle of town, and what was a strip mall with about 10 shops is actually two separate malls in a multilevel complex of several buildings with more than 80 outlet shops and concessions.

The success of Pigeon Forge Factory Outlet and the adjoining Z Buda Outlet Mall was significant enough that ears pricked up all over the place, and suddenly Pigeon Forge was a mecca for bargain-minded shoppers everywhere east of the Mississippi. It's frankly kind of appalling for an old-timer here to find out how many of these people have never even heard of the Great Smoky Mountains National Park and have no intention of going there.

A word or two about outlet shopping: *Caveat emptor* (let the buyer beware). The idea of manufacturers franchising outlet stores to sell more merchandise is a good one, and a huge majority of the outlets in

all of the malls have honest-to-goodness bargains available in every product line you can think of. Most of this merchandise is first-quality or clearly marked (particularly in the case of electronic devices and power tools) as "reconditioned," which usually means that the case is not in its first generation, but the components are new. Our experience while "shopping" most of the outlet stores indicates that it's a good idea to do a little homework before venturing onto the outlet scene. If you know what you're looking for, you should also have a pretty good idea of what you'd consider a bargain price. The good news is that the worst you'll do is pay retail for some things in stores that call themselves "outlets" but are not actually franchised by a company. To be sure you're getting the real thing, the best thing to do is restrict your shopping to names you know.

It appears that outlet malls are not a fad. The speed with which they've sprung up, and the names hanging out their shingles at the outlets, indicate that this is the coming thing in shopping. Pigeon Forge is at the forefront of the whole movement, with Sevierville coming up fast. To illustrate this point, Pigeon Forge's outlet malls were the city's leading revenue producer from 1997 through 2003; the total reported revenue from outlet shopping from those years averaged nearly 30 percent of the city's total and was almost twice the total of lodging revenues, the next highest source. And it's a long way from over; current planning indicates a total of at least two new malls in Sevierville will be operating by 2006, and those are only the ones we know about in an area that's full of surprises.

Here's a list of the outlet malls currently operating in Sevierville and Pigeon Forge (Gatlinburg is still on the "coming soon" list), along with their locations, and a rundown of each mall's shops. Store listings are arranged by category wherever possible. Significant characteristics are noted in the listings wherever clarity dictates, as well as brief descriptions where the names of shops are not widely known or don't obviously indicate the nature of the business. Just about every outlet mall has at least one bookstore; we'll name the bookstores in each mall in this section and describe them in detail in their own section in the Shopping chapter. As usual, we'll move from north to south. To get all of the information available in one place, there's a separate section of outlet mall literature at the Pigeon Forge welcome center on the Parkway, just south of traffic light #2.

SEVIERVILLE

Governor's Crossing Outlet Center
212 Collier Drive, Sevierville
(865) 429-2320

You'll be seeing this name a lot. Governor's Crossing is a full-fledged resort complex that opened in the spring of 1998 with plans for several restaurants, motels, and theaters that'll all be covered in their own chapters. The 25 outlet shops at Governor's Crossing take up a small corner of the total development, which only proves how big the development is. The mall's posted business hours are from 9:00 A.M. to 9:00 P.M. Monday through Saturday, and 9:00 A.M. to 6:00 P.M. on Sunday, but some stores stay open later.

Governor's Crossing currently includes Angel's Touch Dolls, Bon Worth (clothing), Books-A-Million, Capacity (clothing), Cato (clothing), Claire's Accessories, Country Clutter (crafts and souvenirs), Fairfield Smoky Mountains (condo sales), Fairfield Welcome Center (resort information and tickets to local shows), Farberware (housewares), GNC General Nutrition Center, Golf Depot, Ham 'n' Goodys (delicatessen), Hound Dogs (clothing), Kitchen & Candles, Myrick's Jewelry, the Olive Branch (clothing), Oneida, Quizno's Subs, Shoe Carnival, the Sunglass Superstore,

the Tool Zone, VF Factory Outlet (clothing), and Your Scrapbook Superstore.

Tanger Outler Center at Five Oaks
1645 Parkway, Sevierville
(865) 453-1053, (800) 408-8377
www.tangeroutlet.com

The entrance to this outlet mall (commonly called Five Oaks) is on the Parkway about a half-mile south of Governor's Crossing. At the rate they're building, you'll soon be able to walk from one to the other in less time than it takes to drive. With nearly 90 shops currently operating and more being built, Five Oaks is now the largest outlet mall in the area. How big is it? Well, it's big enough to have its own free trolley shuttling passengers around the acreage, and they're trying to figure out how to add to the 12 existing buildings without going underground.

Its immense size notwithstanding, Five Oaks is toward the upscale side, featuring labels associated with some of the more exclusive clothiers, and also has as strong a mix of merchandise as you'll find. The mall's posted business hours are seasonal. In January and February, the posted hours are 10:00 A.M. to 6:00 P.M. Sunday through Thursday, and 10:00 A.M. to 9:00 P.M. Friday and Saturday. The hours for the rest of the year are 9:00 A.M. to 9:00 P.M. Monday through Saturday, and 9:00 A.M. to 6:00 P.M. Sunday. Please note that these are minimum operating hours; businesses wishing to open earlier and close later are permitted to do so.

Clotheshorses can drop long before they're finished shopping at Five Oaks. Togs of every description can be found at Allen Edmonds, American Outpost, Banana Republic, Big Dog Sportswear, Brooks Brothers, Carter's, the Children's Place, Clothestime, Coach, Dress Barn, Eddie Bauer, Fossil, GAP Outlet, Haggar Clothing Co., Izod, Johnston & Murphy, Kasper, Koret, Levi's/Dockers, Liz Claiborne Outlet Store, Motherhood Maternity, Nautica, New York New York, Old Navy, Oshkosh, Pacific Sunwear, Peaches 'N' Cream, Polo/Ralph Lauren Factory Store,

Reebok Factory Direct, Rockport Factory Direct, Strasburg Children, Tommy Hilfiger, and the Woolrich Company Store.

For shoes and hosiery, check out Bass, Dexter Shoe Factory Outlet, Hush Puppies, Johnston & Murphy, L'eggs Hanes, Bali Express, Liz Claiborne Shoes, Nine West, Socks Galore & More, SAS Shoes, Van Heusen, and Wilson Leather.

The mall features home furnishings at Croscill Home Fashions, Lenox Factory Outlet, Villeroy & Boch, and Waterford/Wedgwood. For housewares, stop by Corning-Revere, the Hoover Company Store, Kitchen Collection, or Le Gourmet Chef. Electronics and sound equipment are available at Bose.

Five Oaks features prepared foods as well, from stores like Country Ritz Cafe, Fudgery, Harry & David, Mountain Edge Grill, and Pepperidge Farms. When you get tired of shopping and need some nourishment, you can stop at Connor's, the Chop House, or Hickory Hams Cafe & Deli.

Finally, the mall includes several specialty retailers, like Bath & Body Works, Black & Decker, the Bible Factory Outlet, Cosmetics Company Store, Disney, Kirkland's, Le Sportsac, Maidenform, Music for a Song, Paper Factory, Perfumania, Sunglass Outlet, Tool Warehouse, Totes, Ultra Jewelry, and Zales Jewelry Outlet.

PIGEON FORGE

As we continue into Pigeon Forge, we'll look first at the two Parkway malls in the center of town, and then double back to the Teaster Lane malls. The best way to get into the Pigeon Forge Factory Outlet and Z Buda malls is to turn right at the driveway at traffic light #4 and follow it to the upper level. If parking is available to your right at the top, take it—it's your best chance to see both malls without getting too far from your vehicle.

**Pigeon Forge Factory Outlet Mall
2850 Parkway, Pigeon Forge
(865) 428-2828**

This is the area's original outlet mall, located on the west side of the Parkway, identified by sloping orange metal roofs. It includes about 50 shops in eight buildings on two levels. Most parking is on the upper level, with access and egress available on Florence Street at the back. The Factory Outlet Mall abuts on two sides with the Z Buda mall. Hours for both malls are seasonal: Off-season (January through mid-March) hours are 10:00 A.M. to 6:00 P.M. Sunday through Thursday, and 10:00 A.M. to 9:00 P.M. Friday and Saturday. In-season hours are 9:00 A.M. to 9:00 P.M. Monday through Saturday, and 10:00 A.M. to 7:00 P.M. Sunday. Individual store hours may vary, but all stores in Pigeon Forge Factory Outlet and Z Buda Outlet malls are expected to be open during posted hours.

For clothing fans, the Factory Outlet Mall features Bon Worth, Capacity, Carter's Childrenswear, Claire's, New York New York, Oshkosh B'Gosh, Rue 21, Shadowline, and Van Heusen.

Shoe and hosiery stores include a Banister/Easy Spirit Shoe Outlet, Bass Factory Outlet, and Rack Room Shoes.

For housewares, check out the Black & Decker Outlet, Corningware/Corelle, Kitchen Collection, Mikasa Factory Store, Oneida Factory Store, Pfaltzgraff Factory Store, Tools & More, and Welcome Home (home accessories and giftware).

You can eat or buy prepared foods at the Fudgery.

Finally, amongst its specialty shops, the Factory Outlet offers Book Warehouse, Buxton (leather), Discount Christian Books, Jewelry & Handbag, K-B Toy Outlet, L'eggs/Hanes/Bali/Playtex, Samsonite Company Store, Tote's/Isotoner/Sunglass World, and Wallet Works.

Z Buda Mall

Directly behind and beside Pigeon Forge Factory Outlet (you'll think you're in the same mall), Z Buda shares the upper level parking lot. Built shortly after Pigeon Forge Factory Outlet, the Z Buda Mall has about 25 shops, half a dozen or so restaurant/fast-food properties, and an arcade. Unlike most of the other outlet malls, Z Buda is not loaded with national brands. This mall is as close as you'll come to the "flea market" (no offense intended) appearance of the very early outlet malls. It's a fun place to prowl because unexpected bargains pop up in the least likely places. Because of the unusual nature of this mall, we'll list all of the properties in a single list, with brief descriptions where the name of the business doesn't tell you what it sells.

At the Z Buda Mall, you'll find Booneway Farms (jellies), Bumbershoot Books, Christmas & Dolls (unusual glass Christmas ornaments and porcelain dolls), Country Cabin Crafts (mostly wood handcrafts), Game Room (arcade), Gift Gallery (jewelry and souvenirs), Gordon Garments (swimwear), Handbag Heaven, Handbags & Belts, Ice Cream Shop, Jewelry Sample Shop, Leather & More, Maggie's Deli, Moon Craft (women's clothing), Mountain Man (military surplus, camping gear), Owens Leather, Peddler Gift Shop, Pen & Ink Calligraphy, Prestige Fragrance & Cosmetics, Redwood Signs & Airbrush, Robears Excellent Yogurt, Shades of Mexico (house fixtures), Silver & Shades (jewelry and sunglasses), Slots-O-Fun Speedway (slot track auto racing), Smoky Mountain Gold & Diamonds, Snack Shack, Sock World, Sunglass Shack, Team Sports (licensed clothing), Tees 'N' Togs (T-shirts), and Yosemite's Sandwiches.

The Teaster Lane Outlets

This is a concentration of outlet malls in a single area that's currently about 20 percent as long as the Parkway, with the potential to be longer and more densely developed. Although the casual observer would probably guess the number of malls to be anywhere from three to seven, the actual number is four, with the biggest taking up space on both sides of Teaster Lane. Coming from the north, turn left at

traffic light #2 (Teaster Lane) or #3 (East Wears Valley Road). From the south, turn right at traffic light #5 (Jake Thomas Drive), then left at Teaster Lane.

Tanger Outlet Center
175 East Wears Valley Road
Pigeon Forge
(865) 428-7002, (800) 408-5775
www.tangeroutlet.com

This is a medium-size strip mall, kitty-corner from Belz Mall. It offers about 30 shops (and growing) in a compact two-level setting with convenient parking. Posted hours are 10:00 A.M. to 6:00 P.M. Monday through Thursday, and 10:00 A.M. to 9:00 P.M. Friday and Saturday in January and February, and 9:00 A.M. to 9:00 P.M. Monday through Saturday, 10:00 A.M. to 7:00 P.M. Sunday, March through December.

The wide array of clothing stores at Tanger includes a Coach Factory Store, Eddie Bauer Outlet Store, J. Crew, Liz Claiborne Outlet Store, Nautica, New York New York, Oshkosh B'Gosh, Reebok and Rockport Factory Direct, S & K Menswear, and Tommy Hilfiger.

Shoes and hosiery can be found at Easy Spirit and L'eggs/Hanes/Bali Express. For housewares and home furnishings, check out Farberware Inc. or the Springmaid-Wamsutta Factory Store. You can stop for a bite to eat at the Deli Factory/TCBY. Specialty shops here include Harry & David, Samsonite, and Totes.

Belz Factory Outlet World
2655 Teaster Lane, Pigeon Forge
(865) 453-3503, (865) 453-7316
www.belz.com

Boasting the biggest parking lot of the bunch, the Belz mall consists of two large malls with a freestanding anchor outlet on the north side of Teaster Lane (building #1 is the only truly enclosed mall in the area) and a strip annex with its own parking lot on the south side. The current numbers are about 66 shops in the north side malls and another 15 in the strip annex. One of the kiosks in the enclosed mall is the only known place where you can buy discounted tickets to most of the music theaters in Pigeon Forge. On days when the parking lots aren't jammed, the usual practice is to drive from the main mall to the strip annex—it saves a lot of walking.

Quickest access to Belz from the Parkway is to turn at East Wears Valley Road (traffic light #3, directly across from Wears Valley Road) and go up to the traffic light at Teaster Lane. If you're coming from Sevierville, turn left on Teaster Lane (traffic light #2) and follow it around. Mall hours during January and February are 10:00 A.M. to 6:00 P.M. Sunday through Thursday and 10:00 A.M. to 9:00 P.M. Friday and Saturday. For the balance of the year, the mall hours are 9:00 A.M. to 9:00 P.M. Monday through Saturday and 9:00 A.M. to 7:00 P.M. on Sunday. Old Time Pottery, the 90,000-square-foot specialty store that anchors the main structure, observes the latter hours year-round.

The main mall building boasts a number of clothing stores, including American Outpost, Bass Company Store, Big & Tall, Bon Worth, Burlington Brands, Buster Brown, Capers, Carters, Dickies, Dress Barn, Full Size Fashions, Geoffrey Beene, Izod, Jaymar/Sansabelt, Jockey Factory Store, Koret, Maidenform, Petite Sophisticates, and Van Heusen.

The rundown of shoe stores is no less impressive—Bass Company Store, Famous Footwear, General Shoe Factory, Hush Puppies Factory Direct, and Naturalizer. Housewares are covered at Royal Doulton.

There's as much food to choose from at Belz as at any mall in the area: Chick'n Lick'n Broasted Chicken, Geno's Italian Eatery, Great American Cookie Company, New Deli, Scoops, Smoky Mountain Express (soups, sandwiches, etc.), Subway, Sweet Shoppe, and TCBY Yogurt.

For specialty shops, the mall building offers American Tourister (luggage and accessories), Angel's Dolls & Gifts, Camp Coleman (camping supplies), Claire's (gifts), Craftworks, Diamond & Eelskin Factory Outlet, Fairfield Smoky Mountain Ticket Outlet, Foozle's Books, Fossil, Fuller

Most of the Pigeon Forge outlet malls are served by the Pigeon Forge trolley system. This is a convenient way to see the outlets but could be a problem if you have to ride the trolley back to your lodging place with a good-size load of packages.

Brush Factory Outlet, Jewelry Outlet, Mad Hatter, Music 4 Less, the Paper Factory, Perfumania, Smoky Mountain Fruit & Nut, Totes/Isotoner/Sunglass World, Toy Liquidators, and Vitamin World.

For clothing at annex #1, check out Capacity, Duck Head, or Levi's Outlet by Design. Shoes are available at the Boot Factory. Annex #1's specialty shops include the Bible Factory Outlet and Old Time Pottery (general merchandise).

There's more of everything in Annex #2 (across Teaster Lane), including clothing at Big Dogs Sportswear, Caribbean Traders, Casual Corner, Rue 21, Westport, Ltd., and Westport Woman. Annex #2 shoe options are Banister/Easy Spirit Shoe Studio, Etienne Aigner, Nike Factory Outlet, and Rack Room Shoes. For specialty shops and accessories, Annex #2 offers Fragrance Outlet and Game Depot U.S.A.

RiverView and RiverVista Factory Stores
2684 Teaster Lane, Pigeon Forge

The newest entries for now, RiverView and RiverVista are adjacent strip malls in distinctive pink brick buildings that appear to be extensions of the Belz annex on Teaster Lane. They are locally owned, and expansion plans exist in a form still not solid enough that the developers will make any firm statements beyond the fact that there's a half-mile of empty land between RiverVista and the next road, and they own or have options on all of it. RiverView and RiverVista are operated by one management company and keep the same hours as Belz Factory Outlet World, which has them surrounded on two sides; the Little Pigeon River is at their back. Because neither mall has more than 12 stores, we'll list them in alphabetical order without classification.

Shopping options at RiverView include Deep Discount Art & Framing, Little River Grille & Deli, Log Furniture, Quilts International, Sunglass Superstore, and Tool Factory Outlet.

RiverVista offers another handful of stores, including Angel's Dolls, Toys, & Gifts, Brass Crafters, Dalton Rugs, Delta Workshop Tools, Handbags, Etc., the Pro Shoppe (golf equipment), and the RCA Store (electronics).

You could cram several days absolutely full of mall crawling and see nowhere near half of the outlet stores in the Smokies Corridor, and it'd probably take another two or three days to recover. The seasoned outlet shopper who is determined to see all of the shops in all of the malls will probably require some form of residence in the Smokies area. Outlet malls are apparently here to stay, and the jumpstart Pigeon Forge got in the 1980s appears to have positioned the Smokies area at the forefront of the industry. For as long as this particular type of shopping remains popular, look for this area to maintain and probably increase its international leadership in the field.

MOUNTAIN CRAFTS

Before the outlet malls, water slides, amusement parks, and myriad other attractions brought tourists to this valley, even before the Great Smoky Mountains National Park was anything more than a gleam in the eye of a group of conservationists around the region, Gatlinburg was nationally known for the variety and enduring quality of the handcrafted merchandise being produced in practically every home and marketed nationally by the Pi Beta Phi women's fraternity. The term "Gatlinburg" is used advisedly here—it was the center of the industry, which flourished in the mountainous areas where farming wasn't practical, and craftspeople from Pigeon Forge and eastern areas of the county brought their crafts into Gatlinburg to sell.

This chapter is dedicated to the small number of native and immigrant craftspeople who are trying to keep the heritage of handcraft alive in the Smokies. It will also expose one of the area's best-kept secrets, one that has been known to extend some trips to the Smokies for a few days. To keep things on a fairly level plane here, a few ground rules will have to be observed: First, the term "handcraft" is narrowly defined. To qualify, any goods offered for sale must be produced either by guiding material through a stationary tool (like cutting on a band saw or weaving on a loom) or by guiding the hands or a handheld tool over moving or stationary material (like throwing on a potter's wheel or whittling a piece of wood). Additionally, the artisan must begin working with unfinished raw material, like wooden or composition boards, bolt cloth, hides, or tubes of paint.

The development of the handcraft industry was the result of a great deal of bush-beating by the Pi Beta Phi teachers when they arrived in 1912. They provided a market for the local artisans without requiring the locals to do anything more than they'd been doing all along, and everybody was happy with the arrangement. The trailblazers who subsequently opened businesses to increase their merchandising possibilities gave the large cottage industry a more localized group of outlets without significantly reducing Pi Phi's slice of the pie. The local businesses gave the home-based craftspeople a chance to produce more merchandise without really straining themselves and encouraged the idea of crafts as a family trade. The craftspeople who migrated to the area brought new crafts with them, which had no adverse effect on the existing home-based producers.

Although the number of craft businesses has increased steadily, Gatlinburg still has a lot of people who work at home. These are the "invisible craftsmen," and we're not going to expose them beyond noting the fact that they're still out there. These artisans are content to work in privacy and to sell their production to area shops, which then sell them to the public. The number of cottage businesses is probably larger than ever before, for a couple of reasons: First, there are more sales outlets available to the artisans; second, the life cycle of craftspeople usually finds them retiring from the public view into the cottage end. The financial rewards are smaller because they're selling at wholesale prices instead of retail, but the general feeling is that the freedom to work at their own pace is adequate compensation.

Today's invisible craftsperson is most likely a woodworker, a basketmaker, a weaver, or a quilter. In addition to being native crafts, the time required for most of them to be done properly almost dictates that the work be done without distraction. The number of cottage woodworkers is very large (it's well over half the total of active craftspeople) because woodworking, as one of the oldest and more popular crafts, is in more demand than the public artisans can hope to supply. The common bond of the invisible craftspeople seems to be the desire to work in solitude. Whatever their reasons, these craftspeople have chosen the reclusive lifestyle that is frequently accredited to all artisans, and their counterpart shops respect that choice. As it was in the beginning, the cottage craft industry of the Smokies remains an integral part of the heritage and attractiveness of the mountains, perpetuating the deep-seated conviction of the Appalachian people that they alone will choose the terms that define their lives.

Now that we understand what we're talking about here, we'll start with a few Sevierville and Pigeon Forge institutions. Then we'll move down the road to Gatlinburg, where Pi Beta Phi's large footprint is still clearly visible. Special pains will be taken to point out the shops where you can expect to watch craftspeople actually plying their trades. One final disclaimer: These businesses are for the most part small, family-operated enterprises, with no more than a few employees. Expect hours of operation to be limited to daylight hours, with at least one day a week off, usually Sunday. A lot of the craftspeople don't post their hours because they live basically from day to day, so we haven't even bothered trying to list when these places are open. Our best advice would be to call ahead on the day you want to visit to make sure the shop's open.

There's just one other little consideration before we start this tour, and that is what you can expect to pay for handcrafted goods and art. Pricing, like most everything else the craftspeople and artists do, is a very personal matter, and it leads to some interesting variations. As a rule (to the extent that rules apply to craftspeople), you can expect to find prices that are surprisingly low when you consider what you're getting. The best way to put it into perspective is to think

what you pay for a skilled tradesman like a plumber, an electrician, or an auto mechanic for an hour's work, and compare it to the price of a broom that took a few hours to make or a fine carving that may have taken several days. The best way to approach craft shopping is to consider that, in most cases, your purchase is worth what you pay for it. And the current craze in collectibles notwithstanding, handmade craft items have great potential for being upgraded to heirlooms in the histories of most families.

SEVIERVILLE

Pickings in Sevierville are pretty slim because the city has always been the center of government and local commerce. The ongoing entry into the tourism market has brought Sevierville into the overall picture in a big way, but handcrafts and art were never a part of the city's picture. The two artisans listed here, however, are among the most important artists in the area.

The Robert A. Tino Gallery
812 Old Douglas Dam Road, Sevierville
(865) 453-6315
www.roberttinogallery.com
The Robert Tino Gallery is located in a family-owned farmhouse clearly visible and accessible from Winfield Dunn Parkway (Tennessee Highway 66), about a mile north of Dolly Parton Parkway. Robert Tino, one of the younger artists in the area, has built an admirable reputation within the local artists' community. His sensitivity to the natural beauty of the world around him is translated to canvas in whatever medium Tino chooses. A Sevier County native, Tino has benefited from the tutelage of several artists in the area, and has returned the favor by assisting several promising young artists in starting their own careers. Tino's work, and that of his protégés, is displayed in a century-old farmhouse that's been in his family since it was built.

Ottolini Studios
116 Parkway, Sevierville
(865) 453-1563
www.ottolinistudios.com
Chuck Ottolini is the area's most accomplished stained-glass artist, with several commissioned works in local churches and civic centers. His imaginative approach to the use of glass and natural materials for decorative stained-glass work and distinctive signage have made Ottolini a local favorite of individuals and organizations looking for a truly distinctive way to express their personalities and beliefs in a monumental way.

PIGEON FORGE

Pigeon Forge's move toward a family-centered commercial base took a toll on that city's craftspeople by covering them up with a lot of noise and neon lights. A few stubborn souls have survived the onslaught, and they've pretty much concentrated themselves in the Old Mill area, clustered around the oldest continuing craft business in the city. To get to the area, turn east off the Parkway at traffic light #7 (Old Mill Avenue), cross the river, and look for a place to park. Every shop listed here, and many of the others that are described in the Shopping chapter, is within walking distance.

Jim Gray Gallery
3331 South River Road, Pigeon Forge
(865) 428-2202
www.jimgraygallery.com
Jim Gray is one of the better known of the Smokies' large group of superb artists. In addition to his flair with paint and canvas, Gray is a sculptor of considerable talent. His most visible local work is the Dolly Parton statue on the courthouse lawn in Sevierville (see Attractions). This Pigeon Forge gallery, set on the west bank of the Little Pigeon River, is a sampling of Gray's talents in various artists' media. Established in the area since the early 1970s, Gray is a prime benefactor of the Great

There are a lot of craft shows going on in the area throughout the year, particularly in October and November. This is a good way for the visitor to see a bigger selection of crafts, but if your interest is in local crafts, be careful. The visiting artisans who come here to do shows are pretty good or they wouldn't be here, but they leave when you do. If you have a problem with an item you bought at a craft show, it's sometimes hard to find the craftsperson; you won't have that problem if you buy it from a local establishment.

Smoky Mountains National Park; he's created several original paintings for the park's benefit. He was also an early resident of the Great Smoky Arts & Crafts Community and has three galleries in the area. The other two are in Gatlinburg: one on the Parkway and one in a converted church in the Arts & Crafts Community.

Pigeon River Pottery
175 Old Mill Avenue, Pigeon Forge
(865) 453-1104, (888) 453-5455
www.old-mill.com
Located in the heart of the Old Mill area, Pigeon River Pottery is just about what you'd expect from local craftspeople. An impressive collection of useful and decorative pottery items in blue and earth tones is complemented by a whimsical collection of black bears created by artist-in-residence Thomas Bullen, a third-generation native artisan. Many of the potters in Pigeon River's on-site workshop have been in the business in Pigeon Forge since the 1950s and '60s. All of the pottery produced at Pigeon River is protected with lead-free glazes and is microwave and dishwasher safe. The idea here is that you're buying pottery for its intended use before mass-produced dinnerware came along.

Randall Ogle Gallery
3300 Old Mill Street, Pigeon Forge
(865) 428-2839

A self-taught native artist, Randall Ogle is well known for his portrayals of Cades Cove historic buildings and pastoral scenes. New interest in old times is being generated by Ogle's nostalgic collection of Sevier County farm scenes and community landmarks, as well as by his wonderfully detailed reproductions of vintage cars.

Pigeon River String Instruments
3300 Old Mill Street, Pigeon Forge
(865) 453-3789

Bob Lazenby is one of the very few practicing luthiers (makers of stringed instruments) left in the nation. His Appalachian plucked and hammer dulcimers are becoming collector's items because of the rarity of handmade instruments. The shop also features a wide collection of banjoes, guitars, and other music makers, and Bob will be glad to step out from behind his workbench and demonstrate them.

GATLINBURG

Still the area leader, Gatlinburg's craft heritage is going through the same growing pains as the rest of the city. It's not easy to find actual craftspeople downtown, but locally made handcrafts and art are available if you know where to look. We'll start with the downtown area, then move out East Parkway to point out some real treasures on our way to the biggest concentration of independent artisans in North America.

Downtown

Jim Gray Gallery
458 Parkway, Gatlinburg
(865) 436-5262
www.jimgraygallery.com

Jim Gray's talents are described in the Pigeon Forge listings. This gallery is in the Carousel Mall. Another Jim Gray property is located in the Great Smoky Arts & Crafts Community.

Arrowcraft
576 Parkway, Gatlinburg
(865) 436-4604

Built in 1926 by Pi Beta Phi as a local outlet for Gatlinburg's artisans, Arrowcraft was purchased in 1993 by the Southern Highlands Craft Guild. As a regional outlet for one of the nation's largest craft associations, Arrowcraft is an outstanding gallery of traditional Appalachian crafts of all kinds, produced by the best of several hundred regional artisans. The nicest part of visiting Arrowcraft is the knowledge that everything displayed in the museum-like setting is a handmade item you can take home with you. Arrowcraft is located adjacent to the Arrowmont School campus (see our Arts and Education chapters). Also on the grounds of the shop is the reconstructed cabin originally built from the logs William Ogle cut for the home he never saw, but which housed his widow Martha Jane and those of her family who were the first white settlers of the area that became Gatlinburg. There's more on the cabin in our Attractions chapter.

Terri Waters Gallery
631 Parkway, Gatlinburg
(865) 436-5647

Terri Waters is a Gatlinburg native and one of a family of distinguished artists—she'll tell you which family. Her stunning triptych "Mt. LeConte Dawn" would be a crowning achievement for any artist, but Terri's best known for her Smokies Wildflowers watercolor series. The Terri Waters gallery is located in Baskins Square shopping mall.

The Woodware Co.
968 Parkway, Gatlinburg
(865) 436-5232
www.woodwareandmooreart.com

Darrell and Jean Moore came off the craft show trail several years ago to establish this unusual shop where you can watch Jean display her artistic talent on canvas and wood. A selection of Darrell's handmade wood items is complemented by the work of several local craftspeople. The Woodware Company showroom is located in the Elks Plaza shopping mall.

East Parkway

Heading out of downtown Gatlinburg on East Parkway (U.S. Highway 321N) toward the Great Smoky Arts & Crafts Community, a few notable shops and two of Gatlinburg's oldest craft businesses make worthwhile stops.

A Touch of Tiffany
1003 East Parkway, Gatlinburg
(865) 435-8425, (865) 436-9456
What Dorothy and Herb Jones do with stained and beveled glass is a sight to behold. From simple (and simply beautiful) night-lights and suncatchers to stained-glass lamps and windows, the Jones' artistry with glass is so pretty you'll have trouble deciding what to take home.

E. L. Reagan Furniture Shop
149 Poplar Lane, Gatlinburg
(865) 436-5289
Established in 1922, Reagan's Furniture Shop is Gatlinburg's oldest business under continuous management by the same family. In this case, it's Harlan Reagan, E. L.'s son, and Harlan's son-in-law Lester Flynn. Originally powered by a water wheel and belt-driven tools, Reagan's was the primary provider of furniture to the fledgling hotel industry in the '20s and '30s, and continues to build custom furniture and other fine woodwork at their original location. Poplar Lane is 3 blocks east of the Parkway; turn left at the sign, and follow the road across the river.

Kear's Broom Shop
659 Cartertown Road, Gatlinburg
(865) 436-4343
Kear's Broom Shop is well worth the side trip required to get there. Turn left at the light at Ridge Road (#2A), then take the first right (Cartertown Road) about a mile

to the broom shop on the left—it's easy to spot. Elmer Kear started tying brooms for Pi Beta Phi in 1928. His great-grandsons David Kear and Monie Parton are operating the business today, supplying durable and attractive brooms to several shops as well as their own. Several testimonies to the durability of Kear's brooms are found in the shop, including one that was used daily for more than 25 years. The shop also produces a wide selection of canes and walking sticks from wood they collect themselves in the mountains.

THE GREAT SMOKY ARTS & CRAFTS COMMUNITY

The Great Smoky Arts & Crafts Community has altered the lifestyles of several tourists over the years by turning them into residents. Three miles east on East Parkway (US 321) from traffic light #3 in downtown Gatlinburg, the Great Smoky Arts & Crafts Community begins at the intersection with Glades Road at traffic light #3A. If you don't already have a brochure, get one at the first stop, which is the parking lot to the right as you approach the intersection.

The term "The Great Smoky Arts & Crafts Community" can be taken in two contexts: First, it's a recognized geographic area bounded by the loop formed by Glades Road, Buckhorn/Bird's Creek Road, and East Parkway. With the exception of the Bird's Creek corridor, the area is totally contained within the city limits of Gatlinburg. Second, it's an organization of artists and craftspeople who own and operate businesses within the loop. The organization prints and distributes the excellent brochure that describes the area and lists the member businesses, and is

Don't be afraid to ask pointed questions in craft shops. A working craftsman has very few secrets as far as what he does and how.

the best guide through the neighborhood. Whether an individual shop belongs to the organization is of very little consequence to the visitor, but without their efforts (and ours), you'd be flying blind on a country road.

Here's a quick geography lesson: We're using traffic light #3 in Gatlinburg as a jumping-off point in keeping with our earlier promise, and Glades Road is the starting point if you come east out of town. There are two other ways you can approach the community:

1. If you're coming in from Sevierville or Pigeon Forge on Bird's Creek Road, you'll see a sign that says "Now Entering the Great Smoky Arts & Crafts Community" on your right about 4 miles from Caton's Chapel school. If you don't have a brochure, stop at John Cowden Woodcarvers, just beyond the sign on the right. They'll give you a brochure and tell you how to make the complete loop and leave the way you came in (or any other way you choose).

2. If you're coming from the east on US 321, turn right at Buckhorn Road a mile after you cross the Little Pigeon River on the Conley Huskey bridge—look for the sign on the left as you approach Buckhorn. Stop at the first complex of shops on the right for information. It's less than a half-mile in.

The Great Smoky Arts & Crafts Community got started in 1937 when Carl Huskey opened the Village Craft Shop in Whippoorwill Hollow. Carl's son Charles Ray keeps the family business alive as a cottage industry provider to several shops in the area. The area was pretty sedentary until it zoomed from a dozen or so shops in 1970 to 25 in 1975. The organization was formally chartered in 1978 with 28 charter member businesses, of which almost half are still operated by their founders or a succeeding generation. By the end of the '80s the secret was out among artisans, and the area has bloomed into a major commercial district (albeit a sprawling one, covering an 8-mile loop) with more than 100 businesses of various types.

The community is laid out along the corridor described earlier, with a few side trips to shops a little more remote, but all the roads are hard-surfaced. The area is laced with signage that keeps you from getting terribly lost, and there is ample parking at every shop in the community. Soft drinks and food are readily available from vending machines and several small eateries, which will be pointed out.

Once you're safely into the bosom of the community, you're in a mostly rural area populated by the shops and galleries of the local artisans. These people are preserving Gatlinburg's original industry by keeping alive the local heritage of handwork and fine art. Some of the shops are operated by second and third generations of local families who've been engaged in their crafts for nearly a century. Others are professional artisans who came here to practice their crafts because the area is one of the few in this country where craftspeople can still make a living on their own terms. The combination of native and immigrant craftspeople and artists makes this the largest concentration of independent artisans in North America, and no other area is even close. The operative word here is "independent": For the most part these people depend on their own talents for their income, with no known subsidies.

Because of its size, it's difficult to see the entire Great Smoky Arts & Crafts Community in a single day. You can either accept this notion and plan your trip by studying the brochure and deciding what shops appeal to your particular interests, or you can slice the trip into a couple of days. One other suggestion: The city operates a trolley route through the Glades that's designed for tourism. You can board the yellow route trolley at the Gatlinburg City Hall parking lot on East Parkway (parking is free). For a dollar, you can ride the yellow trolley through the Great Smoky Arts & Crafts Community, get on and off as often as you like, and see most of the community. The trolley stops at most of the shop complexes along the way and takes about 30 minutes to make a complete loop. It's a great way to map a trip if you're a detail freak; you can ride around without getting off, decide where you want to go once you get back to your car, and then drive through at your leisure with a more informed perspective.

The listings that follow include names and descriptions of shops within the Great Smoky Arts & Crafts Community's geographic boundaries that are known to produce a significant percentage of the merchandise they sell, and where you may expect to see craftspeople working without regard to whether these shops are members of the organization. We'll begin at the Wood Whittlers complex at the intersection of East Parkway and Glades Road. For consistency's sake, our travels through the community will follow the clockwise route of the organization's brochure.

Village Candles
1400 East Parkway, Gatlinburg
(865) 436-4299
This is Gatlinburg's original candle maker. Stephanie Lang casts more than 1,000 different designs from her own molds and finishes them in a fashion so attractive that you wonder if anyone would actually burn them.

Lucite by Louise
1400 East Parkway, Gatlinburg
(865) 436-8849
Harry Maloney uses new technology to create his handcrafted masterpieces. Using tools designed primarily for woodworking, Harry cuts intricate designs into clear Plexiglass. Keychains, desk accessories, and one-of-a-kind lamps and plaques can be personalized while you wait. And get Harry to talk to you while you're there; you'll figure out quickly that he's not from around here.

The Leather Works
1400 East Parkway, Gatlinburg
(865) 436-4014
Founded by Al Shirley in the early '80s, the Leather Works produces a variety of custom articles and represents the works of several area craftspeople. Their selection of leather handbags is the biggest in Gatlinburg.

Don Ringstrom Gallery
1400 East Parkway, Gatlinburg
(865) 436-9226
Don and Sylvia Ringstrom don't look like they've been in business since 1974. They don't look like they've been out of high school for 25 years, but they have. An accomplished artist in several media, Don Ringstrom has been painting scenes of the Smokies for as long as anyone in the area and is recognized as one of the best. Custom framing is available for your choice of prints.

The Betty Jane Posey Gallery
1402 East Parkway, Gatlinburg
(865) 430-7874
Betty Posey is a rarity among artists—she sells many originals without ever making prints of them. Working across media lines and capturing everything she sees in her mind's eye as well as her own, Betty's imaginative approach to painting is the envy of her peers. Custom matting and framing set off Betty's originals. Prints of some of Betty's works are available as note cards and stationery.

Buie Pottery
1402 East Parkway, Gatlinburg
(865) 436-3504
A fine arts graduate of the University of Tennessee, Buie Hancock creates a colorful variety of useful and decorative pottery from start to finish. From bathroom items to oil lamps, every product at Buie Pottery is one-of-a-kind.

Scrimshaw, Knives, Silversmithing
1402 East Parkway, Gatlinburg
(865) 430-3496
The influence of the southwestern Indians is clearly visible in the silver work of Paul Stewart. Sterling silver and semiprecious

gemstones dominate Stewart's handiwork in this shop, which also features knives and scrimshaw by Newman and Peggy Smith. Jewelry repairs are available.

Licklog Hollow Baskets
1402 East Parkway, Gatlinburg
(865) 436-3823
Billie and Lisa Canfield (Billie's the mother) augment their own excellent basket-making talents with those of several area wicker workers. An interesting array of ironwork and folk art complement the basketry.

Glades Homemade Candies
1402 East Parkway, Gatlinburg
(865) 436-3238
Here's another Gatlinburg tradition practiced by another native family. Connie and Ronnie Bohanan whip up daily batches of fudge, brittle, taffy, and hand-dipped chocolates to satisfy the most demanding sweet tooth. Helped when necessary by Connie's parents, Billy Ray and Helen Moore, Glades also produces a full line of sugar-free dietetic candies.

The Wood Whittlers
1402 East Parkway, Gatlinburg
(865) 436-7187
Owned and operated by the Compton family since 1944, the Wood Whittlers is a leading producer of fine woodwork and carvings using both local and exotic woods. The workshop alone at the Wood Whittlers is bigger than most of the shops in the community, and the showroom is a woodworker's heaven. Anything having to do with wood is available, from rough wood to finished masterpieces, including a complete selection of how-to books and woodworking tools. Every woodworker in the Gatlinburg area is emotionally or directly attached to the Wood Whittlers. Shirl Compton, the company's founder, was a principal employer and teacher in the industry from the end of World War II until his death in 1977, and the company still finds ways to help struggling new

craftspeople. The idea for organizing the craftspeople came to life at the Wood Whittlers in 1978.

Lorelei Candles
335 Glades Road, Gatlinburg
(865) 436-9214
www.loreleicandles.com
When Lori Tierney was a college student in 1979 (she still looks like one), her father's candle factory in Sevierville was destroyed by a fire. Lori dropped out of school, bought a building on Glades Road, and sifted the ashes of her father's business until she had reclaimed enough molds to start her own factory. Some of those resurrected molds are probably still in use among the several thousand novelty candles produced daily at Lorelei, along with a line of original art candles that's constantly being updated and expanded.

Gemstone Custom Jewelry
337 Glades Road, Gatlinburg
(865) 436-4448
www.jewelrybygemstone.com
Malcolm (Mac) and Susie MacDonell stopped off in Gatlinburg in 1976 on their way to their planned retirement home in Costa Rica. The visit was extended when Mac rented a shop to store his jewelry-making equipment and set it up to give himself something to do. Gemstone Custom Jewelry was an instant hit with the locals, who know a good thing when they see it, and became a landmark business in the Great Smoky Arts & Crafts Community because of the excellent work and outgoing personalities of its owners. Costa Rica will have to wait: Gemstone Custom Jewelry, a charter member of the Great Smoky Arts & Crafts Community, will probably go on producing fine jewelry from precious metals and stones for a long, long time.

Gary McCoy-Craftsman in Leather
513 Glades Road, Gatlinburg
(865) 436-6890
www.leathertherealmccoy.com

You'll know Gary's in his shop if you see his motorcycle parked outside. "Free spirit" is an appropriate description of this longtime resident, but the quality and beauty of his belts and leather accessories are solid testimony to his ability. His work ethic is really outstanding, for good reason: He has to work long hours year-round to keep his inventory presentable.

Morning Mist Galleries
601 Glades Road, Gatlinburg

Morning Mist is a large shopping mall—in excess of 20 shops with a high turnover. Among the regulars are a couple of food service facilities, several gift shops that come and go on a regular basis, and the following four shops where craftspeople produce and sell their wares.

Henry Parker's Lighthouse Gallery
601 Glades Road, #1, Gatlinburg
(865) 430-9449

Nobody can quite figure out why an artist with a national reputation for painting lighthouses and other maritime subjects lives in the mountains, but then Henry's not the easiest guy in the world to get a handle on. Henry delights his visitors with an off-the-wall sense of humor that makes his artwork make perfect sense. A visit to Henry Parker's gallery is worth the trip just to meet an artisan with a completely unique point of view.

Smoky Mountain Gold
601 Glades Road, #8, Gatlinburg
(865) 436-6805

There's a lot of fun with gold going on in this shop that makes the proprietor look like a mad scientist. John DeSanto produces a line of natural items dipped in gold while Carolyn Mikles' specialty is rose petal jewelry. John DeSanto Jr. creates his own brand of custom jewelry nature art. There's always something interesting going on at Smoky Mountain Gold.

Beech Branch Crafts & Signs
601 Glades Road, #3, Gatlinburg
(865) 436-9065

Gatlinburg natives Teddy and Sandy Osborne personalize their own slate signs, brick buildings, and fireplace screens. They're also one of the last places in the Arts & Crafts Community where you can get a totally personalized routed redwood sign.

Candles by Dick and Marie
601 Glades Road, #15, Gatlinburg
(865) 430-9148, (866) 837-3193

Dick and Marie Pinner have taken an entirely new slant to the ancient craft of candle making. Using a modern casting material instead of paraffin, the Pinners create crystal-clear candles that would be gorgeous if they were just left alone. But that's just the beginning; the clarity of the material lets this talented couple then create artworks by adding natural and artificial materials, making every candle a work of art. And if that's not enough, they're also scented. Sacrificing nothing for the sake of art, the Pinners' candles will burn as long or longer than wax candles, and they smell good, too. Because they do all their work on-site, a visit to the Pinners' candle shop is as educational as it is fun.

First Impressions Pottery and More
612 Glades Road, Gatlinburg
(865) 436-3642

The first impression you get in this shop is that a lot of real talented people are contributing some real nice handcrafts to it. The reality is that it's all being done by Jim Coffelt, a multitalented Sevier County native who can work magic with whatever tool he picks up. Coffelt started out as a wood-carver in high school, worked as a potter's apprentice for a while, and dabbled in art and serious woodworking during a few winters. Now he spends his winter as a guest instructor in woodworking at the Arrowmont School of Crafts (see our Education and Child Care chapter).

Alewine Pottery
623 Glades Road, Gatlinburg
(865) 430-7828
www.alewinepottery.com

Function and form come together in Robert Alewine's beautiful and useful pottery items. From kitchen utensils to bathroom accessories to oil lamps, Alewine's attention to detail and special painting and glazing techniques set his work apart from any other. Alewine is the only potter in the area who is known to "foot" every piece he produces to ensure that all his pieces sit evenly without rocking.

Spinning Wheel Crafts
711 Valley Road, Gatlinburg
(865) 436-7793

Bea Bakley is a third-generation native weaver who's been doing her rag rugs, place mats, and table runners forever. Husband Elmer keeps just enough space cleared on his workbench to produce a complete line of traditional folk toys and intricate wind-driven whirligigs that will dress up any yard or patio needing a truly unusual decoration.

Cliff Dwellers
668 Glades Road, Gatlinburg
(865) 436-6921

This historic building was previously the oldest craft shop in downtown Gatlinburg and was moved into the Glades and reconstructed. It's now a fine art and craft gallery featuring the works of several contemporary and traditional artisans, one or

The local craftspeople are merchants who take a lot of pride in what they do, and what they do is usually their principal source of income. One of the things that bugs them more than anything else is being treated like a flea market exhibitor. You may try to bargain with these people if you feel like it, but don't be surprised if their normally cheerful attitude chills quickly.

more of whom demonstrate their craft on-site regularly.

Church Mouse Gallery
670 Glades Road, Gatlinburg
(865) 436-8988
www.jimgraygallery.com

The largest of Jim Gray's three locations in the Smokies, this one's in a restored church building that's more than 100 years old (the new church is a few blocks up the road). A complete collection of Gray prints and sculpture is available, along with the works of several regional artisans. A special feature, available only in the Church Mouse Gallery, is the amazing stone sculpture and bronze castings of noted Canadian Mohawk artist Thomas Maracle.

Cosby Hill People Crafts
676 Glades Road, Gatlinburg
(865) 430-4675

From useful to whimsical to just nice to look at, the products of Carl and Libby Fogliani remind us of the way the hill people used to live. Simple hand toys of wood and cloth, bird feeders, pinecone wreaths, and quilts and quilting supplies (including hard-to-find quilt frames) all flow from the hands of these versatile craftspeople.

The Smiths
676 Glades Road, Gatlinburg
(865) 436-3322
www.thesmithsshop.com

Scrimshaw by Cherokee artisan Peggy Smith and custom knives and silver work by her husband, Newman, stand out in this shop featuring local and regional Native American artifacts and handcrafts. Newman Smith's custom knives are nationally known for their originality and durability.

A Troll in the Park
676 Glades Road, Gatlinburg
(865) 436-0091
www.trolls.com

Smoky Mountain Trolls have been part of the area's folklore for more than 30 years.

The Arensbak family produces the trolls and their individual histories, along with an unusual line of accessory items.

Ownby's Woodcrafts
684 Glades Road, Gatlinburg
(865) 436-5254

One of the area's oldest working craftspeople, James "Lum" Ownby and wife, Jan, produce a broad line of wood products from native materials, assisted by daughter and son-in-law David and Jody Penny. Lum Ownby is one of the few craftsmen still active who started out whittling at a card table in downtown Gatlinburg. Ownby's Woodcrafts is located in the former home of the late Lee M. Ogle, one of the progenitors of Gatlinburg's craft industry.

Ogle's Broom Shop
688 Glades Road, Gatlinburg
(865) 430-4402, (800) 443-4575
www.oglebrooms.tripod.com

Located in a log cabin that was moved out of the national park around 1940, Ogle's Broom Shop is a name that's been around almost a century. David Ogle, the current proprietor with his wife, Tammie, is a fourth-generation broommaking Ogle; his father Wayne was a nephew of the aforementioned Lee M. "Pop" Ogle, credited by many as the father of the broom industry in Gatlinburg. (Lee Ogle was also related to Elmer Kear, the founder of Kear's Broom Shop in the Cartertown settlement.) David and Tammie employ the same techniques that the Ogles have used since the beginning—advances in technology are helpful to the cosmetic appearance, but a broom tied by Tammie Ogle in 1999 is in no way different from one tied by Lee Ogle or Elmer Kear in 1925.

Concrete Statuary Designs
701 Glades Road, Gatlinburg
(865) 436-3524

If Dale Teague hadn't already been a world-class weightlifter when he went into this business more than a decade back, he would have become one just by showing up for work. Dale and Kathi (also an accomplished weightlifter) pour mixed concrete in molds all day, making birdbaths, flower pots, fountains, and indoor and outdoor ornaments. Don't worry about the weight of your purchase; there's always someone on hand to load it for you or to arrange shipping.

Wholesale terms are available for volume buyers.

Smoky Mountain Pottery
744 Powdermill Road, Gatlinburg
(865) 436-4575

A true production pottery, Smoky Mountain Pottery is a constant beehive of activity. Dennis and Gay Ann McEvoy seem to be everywhere at once, throwing pottery on their own wheels or supervising the pouring of clay into molds for the hundreds of wall plaques and other accents and ornaments, small to large. Smoky Mountain Pottery will be happy to pack and ship your purchase, and they always welcome wholesale inquiries.

Whaley Handcrafts
804 Glades Road, Gatlinburg
(865) 436-9708

Opened in 1954 by Frank and Augusta Whaley as a weaving business, the shop is now operated by son Randy, a woodcarver of the highest order. Randy Whaley has earned a reputation as a master carver with his large renditions of animals, birds, and fish. Lathe turnings and carvings by other members of the large Whaley family find their way into the shop, and Frank shows up now and then with some of his exquisite woven place mats. Whaley Handcrafts is a charter member of the Great Smoky Arts & Crafts Community.

The Chair Shop
830 Cantrell Circle, Gatlinburg
(865) 436-7413

Randy Ogle is the fourth generation of his family who believes the only way to produce quality furniture is to use solid American hardwoods and methods that have passed every test time can devise.

It's not really a cash-and-carry operation; your custom order will probably take the Chair Shop a while to build and deliver, but you and your great-grandchildren will have the rest of your lives to enjoy it.

Gatlinburg Ceramics
805 Glades Road, Gatlinburg
(865) 436-4315
The ceramicists' profession is proud to have Judy Bailey as a member since 1973. A nationally recognized producer and teacher, Judy does the job from start to finish. She pours her own molds (several of which she makes herself) and hand-paints and fires a dazzling selection of useful pitchers, bowls, and decorative holiday items. Reproductions of antique oil and electric lamps are also a crowd favorite. Judy is a charter member of the Great Smoky Arts & Crafts Community and has been a board member and president of the organization almost continuously since the organization was formed in 1978.

Tothill Pottery
813 Glades Road, Gatlinburg
Mary Tuttle is a vivacious, charming, one-woman show with more than a decade of experience in pottery design. All of her work is done on-site and is safe for food dishes, microwave, and dishwasher. Mary's special touch in stoneware pottery is complemented by her unique use of glazing techniques.

Mullikin Antique Clock Restorations
944 Glades Road, Gatlinburg
(865) 436-6717
Old-world craftsmanship is the standard at Mullikin's. Carl and Judy Mullikin depend on a lot of their friends all over the country to find antique clocks for them to restore to complete working order. This craft requires an encyclopedic knowledge of clockworks dating back to the 18th century and the ability to make parts that are needed for their restoration. After that, a cabinetmaker's skills are required to make the clock case (usually wooden) look brand-new. The Mullikins have all of this knowledge, and their efforts make it possible for the visitor to own an authentic antique clock in perfect working order. Complete use and care instructions are included with every clock.

Baxter's Stained Glass
1069 Ogle Hills Road, Gatlinburg
(865) 436-5998
Visitors are always welcome at Baxter's, and they'll find themselves right in the middle of whatever John and Donna have going on—there's really no point where the workshop ends and the showroom begins. The Baxters have been making their suncatchers, candle holders, nightlights, and windows since 1984 in the shop that adjoins their home, a short drive back into the woods off Glades Road.

John Cowden Woodcarvers
4242 Bird's Creek Road, Gatlinburg
(865) 436-3629
John Cowden is a third-generation whittler who learned cabinetmaking from Shirl Compton after World War II. Following in his father's and grandfather's footsteps, John carved animals on the front porch of Hattie Ogle's Bearskin Shop in the '40s until he opened his own shop in the Glades in 1954. A charter member and original director of the Great Smoky Arts & Crafts Community, John is arguably the oldest remaining active wood-carver in the Smokies today.

G. Webb Gallery
795 Buckhorn Road, Gatlinburg
(865) 436-3935
www.gwebbgallery.com
Located in a 1910 homestead at the corner of Glades and Buckhorn Roads, the G. Webb Gallery has a garden so rich in wildflowers and other natural wonders that the artist needs only to walk out the front door for a lot of his inspiration. Custom matting and framing to provide the perfect complement to your selection are available while you wait.

Smokies' Edge
540 Buckhorn Road, Gatlinburg
(865) 436-3988

Don Getty was one of the first tenants of the Mountain Arts complex when it was built in 1985. His distinctive style in original leather handbags, wallets, and decorative accessories has been expanded to include a line of beautiful lathe turnings he started producing after attending winter classes at the Arrowmont School a few years back. Maybe it's something in leather, but Don's another free-spirited type who uses a motorcycle as basic transportation. It's not unusual for him to load up his equipment and head west in the dead of winter to indulge his passion for skiing in the mountains of Colorado.

Otto Preske—Artist in Wood
535 Buckhorn Road, Gatlinburg
(865) 436-5339
www.opartistinwood.com

When Otto Preske built his two-story log cabin home and showroom in 1976, it was the only shop on his side of the road for 2 miles. He has persevered to the point where he's now in the middle of several buildings. Otto's skill as a wood sculptor is unmatched in the area, and his large commissioned sculptures of sacred objects are in churches throughout the midwestern and southern United States. How good is Otto Preske? Give him your picture and enough time to do the job and Otto will carve your likeness.

Smoky Mountain Baked Bears and More
522 Buckhorn Road, Gatlinburg

You have to see this one—Dennis Mansell bakes bears. Not real bears, of course; Dennis molds his distinctive Teddy-type animals and bakes them to provide a realistic finish to a truly unusual craft item. Bears are baked daily and placed in original settings. You can't eat 'em, but you'll have a lot of fun explaining to the folks at home how you came to own a Smoky Mountain Baked Bear.

Vern Hippensteal Gallery
480 Buckhorn Road, Gatlinburg
(865) 436-4372, (800) 537-8110

Possibly Gatlinburg's most successful native artist, Vern Hippensteal came to prominence when he built this imposing gallery in 1982. His reputation has grown steadily since as his watercolor depictions of the mountains he's always called home have increased in popularity. His work is also available at Hippensteal's Mountain View Inn (Bed-and-Breakfasts and Country Inns chapter).

Turtle Hollow Gallery
248 Buckhorn Road, Gatlinburg
(865) 436-6188

Woodturnings and original basketry are the hallmarks of this gallery that features the work of several regional artisans. Proprietor Ross Markley is also a guest lecturer and instructor at the Arrowmont School of Arts & Crafts.

GREAT SMOKY MOUNTAINS NATIONAL PARK

The Great Smoky Mountains National Park is an international treasure. One of the most ancient undeveloped pieces of real estate on Earth, the park has been molded and softened by eons of natural forces into a user-friendly visitor's paradise, with just enough manual development to provide limited access to most of its wonders.

Now recognized as an International Biosphere Reserve, Great Smoky Mountains National Park (GSMNP) has an excellent chance of surviving man's attempts to screw it up by "limited" development and "strategic" deforestation by the real estate and lumber industries. One of the biggest concerns of local management is that America's most-visited national park will be "loved to death" by the upwards of 10 million well-intentioned visitors who pass through each year.

The park is the prime reason this area is a principal tourism destination. Everything else is locally regarded as eyewash that owes its existence to the park. Every survey taken in the area—and there are enough that survey-taking is an industry by itself—reveals that an overwhelming percentage (currently about 37 percent) of the area's visitors are here to see the park first. The other attractions get their fair share of attention, but less than 10 percent of all survey respondents rate other attractions as the primary reason they're here. Number two? Shopping—and that subject takes up more pages in this book than any other.

Great Smoky Mountains National Park is unique among federally operated American facilities because the government didn't originally own it. The land was in private hands in the early part of the 20th century, largely owned by various lumber companies, and 80 percent of it was cut. The area along the Tennessee–North Carolina border was purchased through an organized effort by people in both states and donated to the government to be preserved as a national park. Most of the work of actually creating the park (roads, bridges, etc.) was done by the Civilian Conservation Corps (CCC), one of the myriad federal programs designed to help end the Great Depression of the '30s. Because it was privately owned, certain strings were attached to the donation to the government, one being that the park must never charge an admission fee. The government has thus far held up its end of the agreement.

The other side of the coin is that funding for improvements in Great Smoky Mountains National Park is hard to come by in times when the Department of the Interior's budget isn't real flush. To that end, two nonprofit organizations provide fund-raising projects and volunteer support. The Great Smoky Mountains Association, established in 1953, produces most of the printed material offered in the park and funds projects that don't fit into the normal budget process, like wildlife management programs and educational exhibits.

Friends of the Great Smoky Mountains National Park, organized in 1995, helps provide funding for larger-scale projects and facilities and assists in lobbying state and federal agencies for additional funding. One of the Friends' most visible activities is the creation of vanity license plates in Tennessee and North Carolina to provide a continuing revenue stream. As status symbols go, this one is very big in the counties surrounding the park in both states. Friends of the GSMNP has also placed collection boxes at strategic points to raise funds that stay in the park to provide upkeep services. All help is appreciated.

These two organizations have put their considerable influence and talents behind the most ambitious project ever undertaken by the National Park Service or any other research organization on the planet: a complete inventory of plant and animal life in the park that's under way as you read this page. The All Taxa Biodiversity Inventory (ATBI) is the biggest long-term scientific program ever undertaken in the history of the world and is expected to take a team of several hundred (perhaps thousands) knowledgeable scientists and support staff 10 to 15 years to complete.

That's what those people you might see with clipboards, laptop computers, and calculators are doing. They're even using global positioning satellite technology to document the exact location of everything they find. In 1999 the planning process began to build a laboratory to provide on-site space to study the results of the program.

When the ATBI is completed sometime in the second decade of the 21st century, it's anticipated that the number of known species within the park will increase tenfold. For example, when a small group of scientists came into the park for a three-day weekend to study algae and diatoms (this is deep scientific stuff—diatoms are single-cell algae), 85 percent of what they found was previously undiscovered. This estimated surge in knowledge, where the currently documented number of 9,800 species of flora and fauna is expected to exceed 100,000, will change the way our

Warning

Your first close-up encounter with some of the resident wildlife could very well occur at Sugarlands, where deer and a variety of smaller furry creatures graze on the lawn and occasionally try to mooch a treat from the visitors roaming the grounds.

Which brings us to the park's most important rule: Don't approach any wild animal—anywhere! The animals appear to be friendly, which will probably cost them their lives someday, but they're just hungry, which could cost you or someone close to you a body part you probably had other plans for. First, none of the forest animals know where the food ends and your fingers, hands, or even your arm begins. Further, the preservation of the

wildlife in the park depends on their being required to find their own food. If they depend on humans to feed them, they will either starve to death when there aren't any humans around, or they'll be put to death because they become dangerous and aggressive beggars when they lose their self-reliance, or they'll be slaughtered by poachers who will take advantage of an adult black bear's dependence and will kill it for its claws alone.

You're going to hear this a lot in the park, and everybody here knows it's tough to resist the temptation to feed an animal that will come to you for a handout, but you must resist. If it's a truly hungry animal, it may take your hand as part of its handout.

children and generations to follow them learn the natural sciences. The increase in knowledge is expected to engender a re-classification of a lot of known species of plants.

Although the great majority of new dis-coveries will probably remain obscure or unnoticed outside of the scientific com-munity, new species of butterflies and fish could attract public attention. The discov-ery of two new flies and one turtle never before seen on the planet occurred in the planning stages of the inventory, while the whole idea was still being considered, and two new salamanders and a toad that have never been seen before popped up in Cades Cove! Discover Life in America, a national nonprofit research agency, is coordinating the project. Because the researchers will study areas most people bypass, this inventory may also be the greatest thing going on in the park that you never saw.

Great Smoky Mountains National Park has the fortunate characteristic of being situated in one of the world's few moun-tain ranges that runs predominantly north and south. During the most recent ice age (about 10,000 years ago—you probably missed it), the Smokies became home to many northern species of plants and ani-mals that migrated south ahead of gla-ciers moving down North America from Canada. These species then moved up to the mountain peaks as the glaciers retreated. As a result, the Smokies now contain more tree species (130 known) than all of Europe and more flowering plants, ferns, fungi, mosses, and lichens than any other spot on earth. All totaled, there are more than 3,000 different vege-tative plant species (not including trees) in the park's 800 square miles.

The park is one of the best-preserved temperate deciduous (leaf-bearing) woodlands in the world, and the 100,000 acres of virgin timber within its bound-aries make up the largest pristine forest-land east of the Mississippi. A three-hour hike from 1,500 feet to the range crest above 6,500 feet contains as much

diverse forest growth as you could see in a three-day drive-and-hike marathon from Georgia to Newfoundland. With the proper timing, you can see enough differ-ent flowering plants bloom over a 90-day stretch to make you wonder if the Smok-ies have a perpetual spring season.

The story on animal diversity is equally impressive: Great Smoky Mountains National Park is home to more than 50 mammals, 200 birds, 70 fish, and 80 rep-tiles and amphibians. The latter group includes 29 species of salamander alone, the largest collection in the United States. The red-cheeked salamander is a local phenomenon found nowhere else on the planet. This is all great information to take home with you, and it may come in handy when conversations turn in the direction of things natural, but the learning experi-ence is enhanced by actually visiting some of the places where these facts can be seen and felt. And when the All Taxa Bio-diversity Inventory reaches its conclusion, you can come back and learn again what treasures this wilderness contains.

What follows is a description of the wonders available to visitors who enter this paradise on a short-term basis. For those planning to stay longer and really get back to nature, contact the park headquarters at (865) 436–1200 for detailed information. Better yet, stop in at the Sugarlands Visitor Center to inform them of your intentions.

INTO THE WOODS!

We'll start by recommending a visit to the Sugarlands Visitor Center, a few minutes into the park from the Gatlinburg/Park bypass end. From anywhere in Gatlinburg, just head for traffic light #10 and don't turn; from Pigeon Forge, come down the Parkway Spur about 4 miles to the park bypass on the right (just past the visitor information center) and take it around Gatlinburg. Remember the great photo opportunities at the two scenic overlooks. When either route brings you to the intersection of U.S. Highway 441 and Little River Road, turn right on Little River and immediately right into the visitor center parking lot.

If the park service had its way, every visitor would be required to spend some time at one of the visitor centers before going into the park proper. Sugarlands is an attraction all by itself, with museum-type exhibits of flora and fauna, an out-standing 20-minute film in its own ultramodern theater, an excellent book-store featuring many local authors, and a host group of highly trained, friendly per-sonnel to tell you anything you want to know about the park. Schedules are prominently posted showing the times and locations of "Ranger Walks and Talks," an informal program where park rangers meet with visitors in the park. Guided walks on some of the shorter trails, evening campground talks, and hayrides in Cades Cove help bring the park staff and the public closer together to improve the public's appreciation of the value of this natural resource.

Sugarlands is the best single place to pick up reams of literature on every developed attraction within the park. You can also become acquainted with the rules of conduct in the park. The rules may seem a bit restrictive, but think about what your backyard would look like if 10 million people came into it over the course of a year, and each one of them picked one blade of grass and left one plastic soft drink bottle. A visit to the Sugarlands Visitor Center is a great way to temporarily restore your faith in gov-ernment; it's an uplifting demonstration of your tax dollars at work.

Once you've decided what your day in the park will involve, it's time to move on. When you leave the Sugarlands Center, you'll come out on Little River Road, and it's time to make your first big choice: Turn right if you're headed for Elkmont, Metcalf Bottoms, the Sinks, Tremont, or Cades Cove. (We'll deal with each of these individually below in the order you'll encounter them.)

If your goal is the Chimneys, Alum Cave, Morton Overlook, Newfound Gap, or anything in North Carolina, turn left on Little River Road, go back to US 441 (about 100 yards), and hang a right.

Now, a few specifics depending on which way you turned:

If You Turned Right Leaving the Visitor Center

You're on Little River Road, and it'll be more than 20 miles before you see another building or neon sign. Little River Road is flat and serpentine and was almost totally destroyed by the devastat-ing flood of 1994. Rebuilding took two years to complete, so you're on one of the better roads in the park. Little River Road is closed to commercial vehicles except tour buses. Along with some spectacular scenery, here's what Little River Road has to offer:

About 5 miles from Sugarlands, the Laurel Falls trail goes off to the right. It's paved, and for the 1-mile stroll back through the pine-oak forest to Laurel Falls, it's as level as you're going to find in the park. The falls themselves are quite lovely, and the trail passes directly across them.

Another 2 miles up the road, the Elk-mont campground road goes off to the left. The campground was the site of the original Wonderland Hotel and several cabins belonging to a select few influen-tial citizens. Both are now deserted and receiving minimal maintenance while the park service and local preservation groups decide their fate. Because they're

There are 25 species of snakes in the park, of which only two are poisonous: the timber rattler and the copperhead. Snakes like warm spots and sunlight. Be careful when climbing on rocks.

old and falling down, public entry is prohibited. Elkmont campground is a favorite jumping-off place for some of the more challenging hiking trails in the western sector of the park.

Continuing west, the next point of interest is Metcalf Bottoms picnic area, about 4 miles up. The picnic area stretches for about a half-mile along the Little River, with plenty of tables, charcoal grills, and fire pits. The river is shallow (and very cold), excellent for swimming, and one of the most popular places in the park to begin a tubing adventure.

A short drive across the river, the entrance road goes onto an unpaved trail. Turn right on the trail, and a short distance up is the parking area for the Little Greenbrier School, an original one-room schoolhouse. Little Greenbrier was an actual school, and a "teacher" is in attendance during the summer to conduct lessons the old-fashioned way. It's a fun little half-hour diversion. Warning: If you miss the trail, or turn right instead of left coming back out, you're headed for Wears Valley and you're on your own. If you wind up at Wears Valley Road, turn right; you'll be in Pigeon Forge presently.

Little River runs right alongside the road from Metcalf Bottoms for a couple miles to the Sinks, so tubers can be escorted without losing sight of them. Tubers: Get out of the river before you get to the Sinks. There's room along the river as soon as the bridge comes into view. ·

One of the truly awesome works of nature in the park, the Sinks is a sinkhole of undetermined depth that causes the Little River to roar and swirl madly in a maelstrom that's every kid's dream and every mother's nightmare. The sight of young people diving into the river from the tops of cliffs at heights that should be illegal is enough to make most parents shriek with horror. The Sinks is fascinating and beautiful. And dangerous. No kidding—a couple of young people die here every year trying to do something stupid. Enjoy it from your car, or stand a respectful distance back along the edge, and move on.

A mile or so further, Meigs Creek joins Little River. If you look up the creek to the left, you'll see Meigs Falls, one of the prettiest waterfalls in the park. Meigs Creek is one of the places where river otters were reintroduced to the park a few years ago in a highly successful program that's become very popular with the visitor population. There is no more delightful creature anywhere than the otter at play, which is how it spends most of its life, and if you really get lucky, you'll see one here.

The next several miles of Little River Road follow the river on the right with sheer metamorphic sandstone crags coming down the left side. At the intersection of Tennessee Highway 73, you can go off to the right for gas, food, snacks, or a meal in Townsend, if you're so inclined. If you keep going on Little River Road, the entrance road to the Great Smoky Mountains Institute at Tremont is about 0.1 mile up on the left (see below for more on Tremont), and you'll be in Cades Cove in about 5 more miles of wilderness driving. If you go into the cove, do yourself a favor: Spring for whatever it costs nowadays for the self-guiding brochure. It's a great little guide, and the park can use the money.

To do the trip justice, figure on a minimum of two hours in Cades Cove—an hour or so of driving around the full 11-mile loop and at least an hour's combined time spent at the several home sites and churches. Be prepared: Gridlock happens. Traffic can get tied up for hours and there's no other way out. If you brought a

Hunting is absolutely forbidden in the park. Fishing is okay with state licenses (see our Parks and Recreation chapter for details—no federal stamps are necessary), but the taking of brook trout is illegal. The brookie is a protected species. Live bait is prohibited—you may fish only with a single hook and artificial flies or lures. If you're not sure of what's on your hook, let it go.

picnic with you, you're welcome to pull over and enjoy it anywhere along the loop road where there's space to pull completely off the road. Animal sightings along the road usually bring traffic to a stop, but it tends to clear quickly. And watch the meadow closely when you see clusters of animals: They're not cattle. Cades Cove is your best chance to see wild turkeys and the reclusive red fox. Various mammals—raccoons, rabbits, and relatively harmless (if left alone) skunks— hang around the parking lot at Cable Mill and the Oliver homestead. The campground (see our Campgrounds and RV Parks chapter) and picnic area are near the end of the loop road. Refreshments and a small line of sundries are available at the campground store.

TREMONT—CONNECTING PEOPLE AND NATURE

Great Smoky Mountains Institute at Tremont
9275 Tremont Road, Townsend
(865) 448-6709
www.gsmit.org

About 20 miles west of the Sugarlands Visitor Center, Great Smoky Mountains Institute at Tremont conducts a series of educational programs designed to provide hands-on training to nature lovers of all ages. The Great Smoky Mountains Association, in cooperation with the National Park Service, conducts institute programs. Using the national park as a classroom, the institute's educational programs for all ages are internationally renowned for their leadership in the field of residential environmental education.

A wide variety of three- and five-day courses bring natural and cultural education to groups of elementary and high school students, with specific lessons selected by their teachers. Students are housed in a dormitory that holds up to 125 people, fed family-style in a dining hall, and taught in an environment that has several indoor classrooms and one huge outdoor laboratory. Course fees are

remarkably low considering what's involved—they range from about $90 to $120, depending on course content, with discounts available for early registration.

The summer months are loaded with age-sensitive adventure camps. Weeklong camps in June, July, and August give kids a wilderness adventure they'll never forget as they actually hike the trails, swim in the cold rivers, sing around the campfire, and choose their own schedules from a fascinating menu, all under the watchful care of environmental educators. The Discovery Camp (ages 9 to 12) and Wilderness Adventure Camp (ages 13 to 17) sessions run Monday through Saturday each week and cost between $225 and $275. For the truly adventurous child, the National Wildlife Federation Partnership (NWFP) offers three intensive 12-day camping programs that will give kids in the same age groups enough fun and training that they'll be able to live on a diet of nuts and water for the rest of their lives. The NWFP camps start on Monday morning and end on the second Thursday following. All-inclusive costs are $650 for the 9 to 12 and 13 to 14 age groups, and $680 for those 15 through 17.

It's not like the adults are being ignored here, either. Several adult courses are offered throughout the year, ranging from hiking adventures to wilderness first aid to photography workshops to elderhostels. Weeklong and weekend courses are available on a schedule that's not quite as structured as the academic courses. For up-to-date adult scheduling and any other information, contact the institute or visit the Web site.

Whatever your destination when you left Sugarlands, bear in mind that on your return you're going back over the same road you traveled. If it's late afternoon, the traffic sharing Little River Road with you is going to increase a bunch when you get to US 441. Be prepared to move slowly toward Gatlinburg, and consider taking the bypass toward Pigeon Forge. Even if you're heading for Gatlinburg, taking the bypass and doubling back on the Parkway is an option.

If You Went Back to US 441 (Newfound Gap Road) and Turned Right

You'll be going south and uphill for the next 16 miles, after which you'll be going down for another 17. There are a lot of curves that some might call dangerous, so be careful. It's a good road; it's just not straight or level. As a matter of information, Newfound Gap Road is the highest thoroughfare in the eastern United States. It's also usually self-governing because the volume of traffic makes it hard to drive too fast.

There are several short nature trails, also referred to as quiet walkways, on Newfound Gap Road. They're usually no more than a quarter-mile into the woods, and they're a nice opportunity to stretch your legs and learn a little about the natural history of the park. The cutting of paths to create quiet walkways is an ongoing project in the park. Because the location of walkways is in a state of flux, it's tough to tell you exactly where to look for quiet walkways; keep your eyes open. One clue to keep in mind is that there's usually a "turnout" cleared where you can pull off the road and park.

The first landmark on the right is the Chimneys picnic area about 5 miles from the Sugarlands Visitor Center. Situated along a particularly noisy and rocky stretch of the West Prong of the Little Pigeon River about 2 miles below its source, Chimneys is a big local favorite. It cleanses the soul to grab a bucket of chicken or some other fast food and run up there at the end of a busy day and sit on a rock. Or to take along the fixings for a cookout on one of the many grills the park service has provided. Daylong parties are commonplace at Chimneys, and your chance of seeing wildlife is excellent. At dusk, a few bears will appear looking for supper, and they've been known to invite themselves right onto a particularly appealing picnic table. If it happens to

you, don't reward the bear for aggressive behavior; scream, yell, wave your arms, and run it off. The bear will leave if you're very clear that it's not welcome.

Continuing up (literally) Newfound Gap Road, the over-and-under loop is a creative approach to road-building in an area not designed for such things. To avoid tunneling through the mountain, the CCC road builders constructed a 360-degree loop where the road travels up the mountainside in a constant spiral and passes over itself, all in less than half a mile.

A few miles further on, the popular Alum Cave trailhead is on the left (along with its large parking lot). The Alum Cave trail runs about 5 miles to LeConte Lodge, where it meets the Boulevard Trail, which leads to the Appalachian Trail, (a wonderful way to travel from Maine to Georgia if you really enjoy hiking). Many dedicated hikers walk the Appalachian Trail in several stages over a period of time, and hundreds will take it on as a summerlong project. Pigeon Forge resident Morgan Briggs, a locally renowned "ridge runner," walked the entire 2,150-plus miles in the summer of 1998.

Alum Cave is one of the popular trails in the park in its own right and leads to caves where the Confederate army mined alum to make gunpowder during the Civil War. It's a 5-mile round-trip with a 1,400-foot elevation gain, rated as moderately strenuous by the National Park Service. If you're headed for LeConte Lodge, you can leave your vehicle at the Alum Cave lot; be sure you don't leave any valuables. The "medium" rating assumes that you're properly attired for hiking (good, strong hiking-style shoes are highly recommended) and that you have appropriate survival equipment (water, first-aid kit, food, rain gear—check with the rangers) with you.

A few more miles will bring you to Morton Overlook on the right. This is one of the more popular scenic stops, providing a panoramic view of totally unspoiled wilderness. It's worth a few minutes. Panhandling bears frequent this area in the late afternoon.

The Newfound Gap parking area is the next stop, after a couple of miles of extreme turns on a fairly steep grade. Remember this part going up; it's even more fun coming down. Just stay cool.

At Newfound Gap, elevation 5,048 feet, a tablet marks the spot where President Franklin Roosevelt dedicated the park to the American people in 1940. The parking area has been enlarged and improved in the time since FDR was there, but the view you're seeing is exactly what he saw in 1940.

Proceeding south, the Tennessee–North Carolina border and Clingmans Dome Road come up almost simultaneously. Clingmans Dome Road goes off to the right and leads to the Clingmans Dome observation tower 7 miles away. The tower, about a half-mile up a strenuous trail from the parking lot, is reputed to be, at 6,643 feet, the highest point in Tennessee. There are some people around who will present a persuasive argument (like any accurate map) that Clingmans Dome is in North Carolina, but the park service and the two states say otherwise.

Clingmans Dome Road is "trailhead central," with five locations along the road and at the overlook parking lot. The trails along Clingmans Dome Road are rated from medium to strenuous, and all are long and mostly downhill from the road, which means you'll be coming uphill to get back. The Spruce–Fir Nature Trail, about midway between Newfound Gap and the Dome, is a short, nearly level walk through a high-elevation forest. It's the only one of the five on Clingmans Dome Road that's recommended for nonserious hikers.

Back to Newfound Gap: The road you've followed up out of Gatlinburg for what seems to be a lot longer than 16 miles is now over the top, and you're going to descend steadily for about 17 miles to the Oconaluftee Visitor Center at the south end of the park. Along the way you'll have several opportunities to pull over and enjoy the scenery, which is little different than north of the gap. The

Smokemont Campground on the left as you descend is a few miles short of Oconaluftee, and Mingus Mill is just ahead on the right. At the end of a short walking trail, Mingus Mill is a working gristmill, grinding corn into meal with an enclosed water turbine. Products from the mill are available for sale. It's an interesting place, completely devoid of any commercial gimmickry, and the only place in the park other than the visitor centers and the campground stores where you'll find merchandise for sale. It would be a shame to come this far and not spend a few minutes there. And your brakes could use some cooling-off time.

One more mile takes you into the pioneer farmstead at the Oconaluftee Visitor Center. This is a real-life exhibit of how the settlers of Appalachia lived in times past, and it's worth your time to check it out. Dead ahead is Cherokee, North Carolina. It's covered in detail in our chapter of the same name.

It probably would be a good idea to head back toward Gatlinburg in time to be off Newfound Gap Road in daylight. In the summer this would mean leaving Cherokee by 6:00 P.M. and leaving Newfound Gap no later than 7:00 P.M. If those curves just short of Newfound Gap impressed you going up, they're even more impressive coming down in daylight. Coming down after dark? Make up your own adjectives.

This section has covered the two most popular excursions in Great Smoky Mountains National Park, and each of them will pretty well use up a day because of the distances they cover. Also, because you

In cold-weather seasons, be particularly careful to avoid hypothermia, the lowering of the body's core temperature. Hypothermia kills one or two people a year in the park, even in the summer, because they didn't have warm clothing handy after they went wading in a cold stream and came out into a sudden rainstorm.

CLOSE-UP

LeConte Lodge

In the late 1960s, astronaut Wally Schirra once joked from his orbiting spacecraft, "We're coming to you live from the Apollo Room, high atop everything." Such a greeting could be appropriately revised and used by the folks who run LeConte Lodge, a mountain retreat perched atop the third-highest peak in the entire Smokies range. At 6,500 feet above sea level and 1 vertical mile above Gatlinburg, LeConte Lodge is an overnight haven for the ambitious hiker in search of a satisfying meal, rustic accommodations, good company, and unparalleled views.

For those wary of long, strenuous hikes, this journey may not be your cup of tea. There's only one means of getting to the top of Mount LeConte and that's by foot. Several hiking trails lead to the lodge from different starting points in the national park. On Newfound Gap Road you'll find trailheads for Alum Cave Trail (4.9 miles) and the Boulevard Trail (8 miles, the first 2.7 of which are actually the Appalachian Trail). From Roaring Fork Motor Nature Trail, which is accessible by car from downtown Gatlinburg, you'll find the origins of three LeConte-bound routes. Trillium Gap Trail is 8 miles long, Bull Head Trail is 6.4 miles long (the first half-mile of which is the Old Sugarlands Trail), and Rainbow Falls Trail runs for 6 miles before intersecting with Bull Head Trail for the last half-mile to the lodge.

LeConte Lodge, the highest-elevated guest lodge in the eastern United States, was built in 1924 and today serves up to 50 guests nightly between late March and mid-November. Advance reservations are required and should be made about a year prior to visiting. The cost is $80 per person per night, and what you get for your money is pure simplicity. There is no electricity, telephone service, or running water. Light is provided by kerosene lamp; heat, by stove. Because there is no road to the top of the mountain, supplies are airlifted up to the retreat each spring. The rest of the season, llamas are utilized to bring up fresh supplies like food and clean linens three times a week. The native South American beasts ferry dirty linens and garbage on their trips down.

The outpost is laid out like a compact little village, a collective of primitive cabins anchored by an office, a dining hall, and common bathrooms. The cabins vary in size, sleeping anywhere from two to six people. The larger ones are older, of log and mortar construction, with bunk beds and woodstoves inside. The smaller ones have outer shells of wooden boards. Scattered about the grounds are picnic tables and old-fashioned water pumps for drinking, hand washing, or tooth brushing.

know where they are, you might choose to devote some more time to picnicking at Metcalf Bottoms or Chimneys, or to a tubing excursion with an extended visit to contemplate the wonder of the dreaded Sinks.

The next section covers a couple of lesser-known but wonderfully satisfying side trips that don't require using the

LeConte Lodge offers a top-of-the-world view. MITCH MOORE

Guests of the lodge get two meals during their stay. Dinner is usually a traditional "meat and potatoes" affair with roast beef, mashed potatoes, green beans, and corn bread. Wine is served with dinner. Breakfast consists of eggs, Canadian bacon, hot cakes, grits, biscuits, and coffee. Between meals, overnighters are on their own as far as keeping themselves entertained. In colder weather, many huddle in the warmth of their cabins, passing the time by reading, making music, playing games, or engaging in pleasant conversation with new friends. On temperate days, you're more likely to find guests outside enjoying the views of surrounding mountain peaks or Gatlinburg in the valley far below.

The lodge itself doesn't really provide the best views from LeConte, however. You can hike a half-mile to Myrtle Point, which is an excellent spot to view sunrises, or you can climb two-tenths of a mile to Cliff Top, which has 180-degree western exposure for remarkable sunsets.

park's main roads but afford a wilderness experience without ever getting more than a few miles from civilization. It is commonly held among the locals that any visit to the Smokies isn't complete without spending some time in Great Smoky Mountains National Park. Even if your only real purpose in coming here is to shop the outlets (an honorable pursuit), you should at least get a look at the beauty of the park. You wouldn't go to Myrtle Beach and not look at the ocean, would you? Of course not.

The Cherokee Orchard–Roaring Fork Motor Nature Trail

The trip we're describing here is tailor-made for those who feel obligated to see the park because they're here anyway, and it just happens to be one of the most beautiful ways you'll ever spend a couple of carefree hours. What we're talking about is another local favorite, the Cherokee Orchard–Roaring Fork Motor Nature Trail. It's a one-way drive on the northern slope of Mount LeConte, and you leave downtown Gatlinburg to start it. The Motor Nature Trail (local parlance) is about 10 miles long from start to finish, and you can make it in an hour or spend a day. Most people (nonhikers) spend up to three to four hours on the Motor Nature Trail, including a stop somewhere along the way for a picnic lunch, if you happen to have one with you.

For starters, you want to be on Historic Nature Trail heading out of downtown Gatlinburg. You can get there by going through town to traffic light #8. Just stay on Historic Nature Trail past

---

To help you plan your day a little better, here's a mileage chart of distances from the Sugarlands Visitor Center to some of the more popular destinations: Chimneys picnic area: 5 miles; Newfound Gap: 16 miles; Clingmans Dome: 23 miles; Cherokee, North Carolina: 34 miles; Elkmont picnic area: 7 miles; Metcalf Bottoms picnic area: 12 miles; Cades Cove: 27 miles; Greenbrier Cove: 5 miles; Cosby Campground: 22 miles.

Mynatt Park (another nice picnic site with charcoal grills—see our Parks and Recreation chapter) and into the woods. About a mile up is the Noah Ogle Homestead at Junglebrook, the first of several home sites the park service has preserved along the trail. Take a few minutes and tour this farm and mill settled by the son of Martha Jane Huskey Ogle, Gatlinburg's first white settler. There's a pamphlet available that explains it.

Continuing away from town, you'll see a turnout or two if you're interested (they're trailheads for the Rainbow Falls and Bull Head trails—serious stuff) and maybe some wildlife. You might notice that the trees on the left are in more orderly rows than usual; that's the remnant of Cherokee Orchard, one of the last settled areas of the park.

Approaching the Motor Nature Trail, you'll see that the road you're on continues. It loops around the orchard and returns to Gatlinburg. You want to turn right onto the Motor Nature Trail (it's clearly marked), and it's highly recommended that you buy the self-guiding brochure at the entrance. If you're not already sold on the value of these little pamphlets, this one should do the trick. It's $1.00 on the honor system. We'll let the pamphlet be your guide around the Motor Nature Trail, and we'll supplement it slightly with a little advice based on a lot of personal experience.

Pine Tops, an early landmark, offers an interesting view of Gatlinburg and a nice picnic site. It's also known as a hangout for hungry bears, so be vigilant. If a bear joins your picnic, excuse yourself, take your food, and go sit in your car until the bear leaves. You're on its turf, and the bear is neither a gracious host nor a grateful guest. Because they're so used to having people around, bears in the Smokies don't fear people the way they should. Don't, under any circumstances, try to pet or feed a bear. Regardless of how cute you find them these are wild animals, and should be treated with respect and given a wide berth whenever you encounter them. Be especially cautious if you see a mother bear and a cub; the mothers are terribly protective and won't think twice about attacking if they feel their youngsters are threatened.

Heavy traffic could slow you down at the Trillium Gap Trail parking lot. Unless you want to hike to Grotto Falls on the Trillium Gap Trail (moderate to difficult, 2.8 miles), get through this area as quickly as possible. This is the point where you stop going up and start going down.

You'll find a couple of neat things at the turnoff by the old cemetery, a short distance from the Trillium Gap Trail parking lot. First, across the road is a good-size confluence of three streams. A short scramble down the bank (stay on the path for better traction) will give you a view of some real busy water at a decibel level you won't believe. Back across the road, if you take the path past the cemetery (very short), take your camera; there's a meadow where the sight of young animals playing is fairly common. This isn't well known or documented—if you're treated to a Bambi moment, enjoy it and kind of keep it to yourself. And you're welcome. Shortly after the cemetery, the Baskins Creek Bridle Trail crosses the road. Be alert for riders on horseback—they have the right-of-way.

The Ephraim Bales place is very popular among picnickers. It's the largest open space on the trail and has a great stream with large rocks you can relax on. The Bales place is also a fascinating look at how the original settlers lived. The living quarters will make you wonder how the high birth rate in the mountains was possible. You should stop here for a few minutes to let your brakes cool.

Now you're really going downhill. You're also going to encounter a few fairly sharp turns and a narrow bridge or two. Stay alert. As you near the end of the trail, the Reagan tub mill and farmhouse is an interesting departure from the rest of the architecture in the park—the house was ordered precut from a Sears catalog. The last stop on the trail is

the Thousand Drips, and it's worth a look; it's not often you see a waterfall coming right down on the road.

When you exit the Motor Nature Trail you'll be on Roaring Fork Road. A short drive through a residential/condo neighborhood will bring you to traffic light #1A at East Parkway (US Highway 321), less than a mile from the Parkway at traffic light #3. Turn left to go back to downtown Gatlinburg. You've just completed a journey of about 15 miles through an enchanting area packed with local history and marvelous scenery, and you never really left Gatlinburg.

Greenbrier

There's one more picnic/wildlife area that's nice to visit because of its isolation, and that's the Greenbrier picnic area about 5 miles east of Gatlinburg on East Parkway (US 321). The road goes off US 321 to the right and runs along the Little Pigeon River, another usually busy stretch of water. After you've passed Buckhorn Road at the bottom of the long, steep grade on US 321, look for the sign about a mile further on that says "Greenbrier." If you miss it, you'll cross the river immediately. Just turn around and go back.

The Greenbrier road is about 5 miles long, quite narrow, and mostly unpaved. Since it runs alongside the river, the number of parked cars can make it practically a one-way road at some points. As a matter of local custom, the cars coming out

Thunderstorms can gather very quickly and dump a lot of precipitation on the park in very short order. If you get caught in a thunderstorm, stay low to avoid lightning strikes and seek shelter immediately. The storms don't last long, and they're the reason everything around you is that lovely shade of green.

have the right of way. Be alert for pedestrians and bicyclists.

There are several points along the road where small parking areas have been carved out of the woods for people to get out and walk down to the river. The Middle Prong is moderately deep and fairly wide with a strong current, and it's a favorite swimming site because of the large rocks that serve as jumping and sunbathing platforms. Tubing is also popular here. The river turns away from the road about 5 miles in from the highway, providing a beautiful picnic area with tables, charcoal pits, and restrooms. Another great local favorite because of its accessibility and privacy, the Greenbrier picnic ground is also visited frequently by deer who will roam through without paying much attention to the human population, as long as said population returns the favor.

About a mile past the picnic grounds, a bridge across the river leads to the Ramsey Cascades Trail (not for novices). The remnants of several residence fence lines are visible in the area around the parking lot. Greenbrier Cove was once a bustling community, populated mostly by Whaleys, and a few of them are still around.

Beyond the bridge, there's a picnic pavilion with tables and a concrete floor. And outhouses. This is a really nice spot for family or small-group gatherings, and the pavilion is very handy if a sudden summer rain should come along. The road ends in a loop at the Porter's Creek Trail, an easy 2-mile walk beside a stream with a lot of pretty cascades. There's an original cantilever barn at the end of the

Porter's Creek Trail. The cantilever barn is an architectural style unique to East Tennessee and disappearing quickly. This barn, and one in Cades Cove that the park service built in the 1960s, may soon be the only ones left in the area.

Greenbrier is an area that has the park service a little concerned. It's there because the Greenbrier Cove settlers created the road before the park was established, and it made sense to keep it open without a lot of preservation or construction necessary. It's a leading candidate for what the park refers to as "overuse," where the number of people tramping through an area will destroy its natural ecology. Public incursion into the Greenbrier area hasn't threatened it yet, and probably won't as long as the public continues to obey the park maxim, "Take nothing but pictures; leave nothing but footprints."

A Camping We Will Go

Here's another amazing statistic: According to figures developed by the park's public affairs office, less than 10 percent of the 10 million people who visit Great Smoky Mountains National Park every year ever get off the pavement. That means there's more than 795 square miles of backcountry out there that are seldom seen and never felt. This is good news to the park service folks, who are trying to keep the wilderness serene, and it's even better news to those visitors who come here seeking solitude and oneness with nature.

It's out there if you want to go enjoy it up close and personal. There are two ways to approach "roughing it" in Great Smoky Mountains National Park. You can stay in a developed campground in your RV, trailer, or tent, like civilized campers. Or you can go out into the wild and live like Tarzan. Both choices are easy on the pocketbook, especially the Tarzan route—it's free. We'll deal with each choice, starting with the developed campgrounds.

Our Campgrounds and RV Parks chapter describes four developed campgrounds in the park that are close enough to the Smokies Corridor to be considered part of it and explains the rules for usage. Listed here are the remaining six, four of which are in North Carolina. We'll list the two Tennessee sites first, followed by the North Carolina campgrounds listed from east to west. Remember, we're listing these campgrounds only because they're in the national park—the closest one is more than 50 miles from Gatlinburg. To reserve spaces in national park campgrounds, call (865) 436-1266 for Tennessee and (828) 497-1930 for North Carolina.

TENNESSEE

Look Rock Campground
Foothills Parkway

The Foothills Parkway runs outside of the western border of Great Smoky Mountains National Park; the section where Look Rock Campground is located is accessible only off TN 73, about 10 miles west of Townsend. At an elevation of 2,600 feet, the Look Rock Campground is the highest in the Tennessee side of the park. Look Rock is open late May to November 1 and has 92 sites. Site rental is $14, and RV length is restricted to 35 feet.

Abrams Creek Campground
Happy Valley Road, somewhere in East Tennessee

Remember the old line, "You can't get there from here?" Well, here it is. Abrams Creek Campground is on the extreme western edge of Great Smoky Mountains National Park, convenient to nowhere and accessible only by taking Happy Valley Road off U.S. Highway 129, some 30 miles south of Maryville, which is about 15 miles west of Townsend. The campground is open from mid-March to November 1 and has 16 campsites. Site rental is $12 per night, and RV length is restricted to 12 feet.

NORTH CAROLINA

Big Creek Campground
Waterville

The Big Creek area is about 6 miles south of exit 451 on Interstate 40, right at the Tennessee–North Carolina border. The campground is in a valley surrounded by woods. No RVs are allowed in this 12-site enclave, which is open from mid-March to November. Campsite rental is $12 a night.

Cataloochee Campground

Way deep in the woods and way up in the mountains, Cataloochee Campground really requires a map to find. Really. The *Great Smoky Mountains Trail Map* ($1.00 at any visitor center) will show the unnamed roads that lead to the Cataloochee Campground at location D-11. Cataloochee is 2,610 feet up in the mountains, with 27 available campsites. Open from mid-March to November 1, campsites at Cataloochee are $12. RV length is restricted to 31 feet.

Balsam Mountain Campground

If you like the idea of going to Cataloochee, you'll love Balsam Mountain. There are two ways to get to Balsam Mountain—we're only going to show you one because the other one could require pack animals. Balsam Mountain campground is at 5,310 feet elevation and is easily the highest campground accessible to vehicles in the park. The 46 campsites are open from late May to late September, and RV length is restricted to 30 feet. Campsite rental is $14 a night. To get

Don't be surprised if you feel a little short-winded while you're in the park. You're probably not used to the higher elevations. If you're going to be in the woods for an extended time, take plenty of water with you and drink it. Dehydration is a by-product of oxygen deprivation at high altitudes.

there, take the Blue Ridge Parkway north from Newfound Gap Road (US 441) about 12 miles to Heintooga Ridge Road on the left. Don't worry about missing Heintooga Ridge Road—it's the first road you'll come to. Turn left and follow the road into Balsam Mountain, about 8 miles.

Deep Creek Campground

This one's also pretty remote from the Tennessee side, but it's convenient to the Fontana resort area. The best way to get there is off U.S. Highway 19, about 3 miles east of Bryson City or 20 miles west of Cherokee. Deep Creek has 108 campsites, 42 of which are for tent camping only. Deep Creek is open from early April until October 31 and has a 26-foot trailer length limit. All campsites are $14 a night and reservations are recommended.

Camping au Naturel

It would be nice to say you're welcome to just go lose yourself in the forest for whatever time you'd like, but you can't. The park service is a branch of government after all, and although they have no problem with your wandering in the wilderness for an indefinite period, they want to know you're out there. They'd also like to know approximately where you are during your stay, so they're quite insistent that you register for a backcountry permit at any ranger station, campground, or visitor center. Registration is totally free and requires only that you fill out a simple form and drop it in a box at the station.

All camping in the park requires planning. All shelters and the more accessible

Leave as small a footprint as you can. This area will remain virginal as long as everybody makes an effort to remove all traces of human presence in the Great Smoky Mountains National Park.

campsites are rationed due to space limitations. To stay at these sites, you will have to contact the park service. On the other hand, you'll have to hike a greater distance to reach the 70-plus nonrationed sites. To start your planning, spend a buck for the *Great Smoky Mountains Trail Map*, which will identify all 88 of the backcountry campsites and all 16 of the trail shelters in the park. The map and any park personnel will answer all of your questions, but we'll list a few of the more important points here just to give you an idea of what you're getting into.

1. It's very strongly recommended that you stay on the trails at all times (not unreasonable—there are more than 850 miles of trails in the park).

2. Maximum party size is eight.

3. You can spend no more than three consecutive nights at a campsite and no more than one night in the same trail shelter.

4. You must stay each night in a designated site and follow your identified itinerary.

5. Horses are permitted in the park on marked trails, and horse parties may only stay at campsites designated for horse use on the map—50 such campsites are so designated, of which 9 are rationed.

6. All food for horses must be packed in—grazing is prohibited.

7. Horses are not permitted within 100 feet of trail shelters or in cooking areas of campsites.

8. When not being consumed or transported, all food and trash must be suspended at least 10 feet off the ground and at least 4 feet from any tree branch to keep it out of the reach of bears (all campsites have cable and pulley systems to facilitate pack suspension).

9. All plants, wildlife, and historic features are protected by law. Do not cut, carve, or deface any trees or shrubs.

10. Polluting park waters is prohibited—do not wash dishes or bathe with soap in any stream.

11. Firearms and hunting are prohibited.

Anyone arrested by park rangers for violation of any rule is subject to trial in a federal court. The maximum fine for any conviction is $500 and/or six months in jail for each violation.

Take a Hike!

We've outlined several of the more convenient hiking trails in the park at the points where they begin and given brief descriptions concerning length and degree of difficulty. We recommend you stick to these trails and the quiet walkways the park service has provided. Most of the 850 miles that cross the park like a giant spider web are intended to connect primitive campgrounds and trail shelters so any hiker can see the park without having to strike into uncharted forest. It's difficult to argue with the folks who believe the park should be a deeply tactile experience and can only be truly appreciated if you go out and get semi-lost in it, but the fact is that the park is there for what you want it to be. If that involves walking around in it, wonderful. If not, that's OK, too. But if you do plan to hike anywhere in the park beyond a short stroll, talk to the park service people at the Sugarlands, Cades Cove, or Oconaluftee visitor centers, and get whatever literature you can to make your hiking experience safe and memorable. In addition to the invaluable *Great Smoky Mountains Trail Map*, there's a huge selection of books on the subject by park service and civilian experts.

PARKS AND RECREATION

When you distill any Smoky Mountains experience down to its essence, you're left with one irrefutable fact—people come here to have fun. Whether you're an adult or a kid, play is an essential part of life—especially when you're on vacation, but just as much so once you're comfortably settled into a community's lifestyle. Those that live and visit here find that the area's trademark backdrop of mountains, woodlands, and waters make the Smokies a natural when it comes to outdoor recreation. And various city governments and businesses have also done their part to see to it that ample indoor recreational activities are available as well for all who choose to take advantage.

What you'll find among the following pages are plenty of ways to enjoy the beauty of the Smokies and, at the same time, have a little fun and maybe even get some exercise. There's really no better combination of activities we can think of. We do have a few specific notes about what you will and will not find in this chapter. For example, Great Smoky Mountains National Park is such an exhaustive subject in its own right that we've given it its own chapter. There you'll find plenty of information on the park's more popular outdoor endeavors like camping, hiking, and fishing.

Even on its own, camping in the Smoky Mountains is such a broad subject that we've covered it in several other areas of the book as well. In this chapter, you can refer to the section on Douglas Dam Park, or you can check the Campgrounds and RV Parks chapter for more comprehensive opportunities for roughing it. Fishing is another subject that gets multiple coverage. Again, we've addressed it in the

National Park chapter, but in this chapter, refer to our write-up on Douglas Dam Park as well as the section on Gatlinburg.

Then there are several popular forms of recreation that you won't find in this chapter at all—rather, we've felt it more appropriate to place them elsewhere. Information on ice-skating and snow skiing are found in Attractions. And don't worry—we haven't forgotten about golf! It has its own chapter as well.

Finally, a few remarks about the structure of this chapter. We start out with a profile of Douglas Dam Park in northern Sevier County. Next are sections on the facilities and recreational programs offered by each of Sevier County's three primary cities. Following that is a host of noncivic recreational activities that we've grouped by category. We then close with a separate section on youth sports opportunities, which include both civic and independently organized programs.

PARKS

Douglas Dam Park
Tennessee Highway 338 or
Tennessee Highway 139

In 1942 the Tennessee Valley Authority (TVA) constructed Douglas Dam on the French Broad River, primarily to help provide the surrounding area with much-needed electricity. The man-made reservoir that resulted was appropriately named Douglas Lake. One of the more pleasant outcomes of the TVA's actions was the development of a recreational area surrounding the dam itself. Today, visitors can access both the waters above and below the dam at little to no cost. What they get in return are gorgeous summertime views and a variety of warm-weather activities like fishing, boating, swimming, and camping.

From Tennessee Highway 66 (Winfield Dunn Parkway) you can access the area via TN 139, although the more logical and direct approach is to go east on TN 338 (both routes are known as Douglas Dam Road—see our Getting Here, Getting Around chapter for clarification). No matter which route you choose, you'll encounter small markets along the way that sell food and fishing and camping supplies. If you haven't already stocked up before leaving on your outing, these convenience stores might be your last best chance for provisions. Once you get into the TVA area, the pickings are slim (more on that below).

On arriving at the park, signs will give you a choice of heading toward the "head-waters" or the "tailwaters." Headwaters are the lake waters above the dam, and tailwaters refer to the continuing French Broad River below the dam. We'll start with the headwaters. To help you avoid any confusion, we'll point out a commercial venture that you'll find as you near the headwaters area, which is not affiliated with TVA. Douglas Dam Marina and Campground offers gasoline and permanent boat docking and is described fully in the Campgrounds and RV Parks chapter.

The TVA headwater facilities include a free boat-launch ramp, restrooms, and picnic areas. There is also a designated swimming area, complete with sand. The best time to swim there is during the peak summer months, when lake levels are at their highest. Regardless of the time of year, however, you swim at your own risk—there are no lifeguards on duty.

Most of the headwaters area is devoted to camping spots, some of which include RV hookups. Primitive camping is allowed as well. Most sites include a parking spot, picnic table, and a barbecue grill. Rates are $20 per night for sites. Payments are deposited on the premises on the honor system. For more information on amenities and payment procedures at Douglas

Anglers who venture out to Douglas Lake find it is a bountiful source of many different types of fish. The best time to drop lines in the headwaters is in spring, when you're likely to be more successful catching crappie or large-mouth bass. In summer, try trolling for bass, but keep your bait in the top 25 feet of water where there's more oxygen. In late summer and autumn, you might try for both largemouth and white bass, and in winter, try using minnows as bait for crappie. Fishing in the tailwaters is also best in spring. Depending on your bait, you're likely to catch more types of fish in the river than in the lake. The main thing you'll need to watch out for is the surge in waters that occurs when the dam's generators are running.

Dam Park, see our chapter on Campgrounds and RV Parks.

Once you get out onto the lake itself, you've got 30,600 acres of waters before you, not to mention 550 miles of shoreline. The waters are ideal for boating, waterskiing, or use of a personal watercraft. For the safety of yourself and your fellow boaters, please be sure to observe all TVA water regulations, which are posted at the boat launch.

If you choose to go to the tailwaters area on the other side of the dam, you'll be faced with a few more forks in the road and more destination choices as you approach. Don't worry—there is plenty of adequate signage to point you toward the location you're seeking. Just above the tailwaters you'll find two overlook areas, both of which provide stunning views of Douglas Dam itself (in case you're curious, it's 705 feet long and 202 feet high). The upper overlook has restrooms, free picnic sites and a covered picnic pavilion, which can be reserved for $50 a day by calling (866) 494-7186.

A campground and a boat launch are located further below, right on the French Broad River. As with the headwaters area, use of the ramp is free, and the same rules and regulations apply to the campground (see our Campgrounds and RV Parks chapter). As you near the ramp and the camping area, you'll see Douglas Lake Canteen, a small store where you can purchase a fishing license, bait, and snacks. As we hinted earlier, the store's selection is fairly narrow, but it will do in a pinch. For more details on requirements for purchasing a Tennessee fishing license, refer to the Gatlinburg section of this chapter.

Sevierville

One of the best things about living in or even visiting Sevierville is the number of programs offered through the city's department of parks and recreation. What's even better is that much of what's available is either free or very reasonably priced, and it's accessible to anyone, even vacationers. On top of all that, you'll find that most of these activities have two centralized locations, the Sevierville Community Center, which opened in 1982, and Sevierville City Park, established in 1974. To reach either by phone, call (865) 453-5441.

Sevierville Community Center
200 Gary R. Wade Boulevard, Sevierville
Conveniently located near downtown, just 1 block off Dolly Parton Parkway, the community center provides many diverse forms of recreation, mostly in a climate-controlled, indoor environment (outside, there's a walking/jogging trail and a playground for the kids).

The center is open seven days a week year-round except for the months of June, July, and August, when it's closed on Sunday. Normal hours of operation are 8:00 A.M. to 9:00 P.M. Monday through Friday, 9:00 A.M. to 4:00 P.M. on Saturday, and 1:00 to 6:00 P.M. on Sunday (September through May). While it wouldn't be practical to completely cover all of the center's specific schedules and fees here, we will provide you with a good starting point

from which you can explore on your own.

One of the center's more popular offerings is the 25-meter, six-lane swimming pool. Open year-round, the pool's daily schedule is generally divided between lap swimming, exercise classes, and open swimming (just for fun). There is a diving board in the deep end, and a certified lifeguard is always on duty. Several instructional programs are available, including swimming lessons and water exercise classes. They'll also teach you how to be a water safety instructor or a lifeguard.

The base fees for pool access are $2.50 for adults, $2.00 for children, and $1.25 for spectators. Booklets of 25 tickets as well as four-month and yearly passes are available at discounted prices. Group rates are available for birthday parties and other private groups, but reservations must be made in advance. At all times, children 7 and younger must be accompanied by someone age 18 or older, and normal pool schedules are subject to change due to swim meets.

Of course, what would a rec center be without a gymnasium? The space can be used as a full-size basketball court or divided into two volleyball courts. If you want to just show up and shoot hoops with whomever else happens to be there, there's no charge, but the cost to rent part or all of the space costs $25.00 per hour or more. If a game of volleyball is what you're interested in, the same rental fees apply. There are two racquetball/wallyball courts on the premises that cost $3.00 per person per hour before 4:00 P.M. After 4:00 P.M. and on weekends, the rates are $4.50. With all of the above sports, you can bring your own stuff or rent balls and other equipment from the office.

The gymnasium is also a great place to get an aerobic workout. Instructors utilize step aerobics, interval aerobics, cardio kickboxing, and body design programs (using hand weights) to work with anyone from beginner to advanced at both low and high impact levels. Classes are offered Monday through Saturday, generally in the early morning and/or late afternoon. Daily fees are $3.25 for adults and $3.00 for seniors. Twelve-class passes are available at a discounted price.

At the Sevierville Community Center, they'll also pump (clap) you up! The fitness center includes multistation weight machines, free weights, rowing machines, stair climbers, and stationary bikes to help you in your strength and/or cardiovascular training. If you're interested in combining both types of exercise, the center offers aerobic weight-training classes Monday through Thursday in the early morning and/or middle evening.

Fees for regular use of the fitness center are $2.25 daily for adults and $1.75 daily for senior citizens. Discounted rates are offered for four-month and yearly passes. Note that the center requires you to attend a one-time orientation program before allowing you to use the fitness center. Aerobic weight-training classes cost $3.50 per individual class session or $46.00 for a three-month session.

Bowling offers a good way to have fun, socialize, and maybe even work a few muscles along the way. The center's bowling center has 10 air-conditioned lanes, which were totally refurbished in 2002. The facility was all but gutted and outfitted with brand-new synthetic lanes and state-of-the-art pin replacement and scorekeeping equipment.

Operating hours are Monday through Thursday from 11:30 A.M. to 10:00 P.M., Friday and Saturday from 11:30 A.M. to midnight, and Sunday from 1:00 to 6:00 P.M. (closed Sunday, June through August). On Friday and Saturday, it's time for Cosmic Bowling: The lights go down, the music cranks up, and the pins glow in the dark! Cosmic bowling costs $9.95 on Friday, and on Saturday, $17.95 gets you two lanes; the cost includes shoe rental. Regular bowling fees range from as low as $2.35 per game for kids' and seniors' open bowling before 5:00 P.M. to as high as $2.95 per game for open adult bowling after 5:00 P.M. The shoe rental fee is $1.87.

In addition to open play, the center hosts several monthly tournaments and bowling leagues; the latter generally run September through May.

Speaking of league play, the Sevierville Community Center has organized adult leagues in sports other than bowling. Options include three-on-three basketball, volleyball, wallyball, and racquetball. Most of these leagues play in fall and winter, and registration fees can range from $42 per person to $110 per team.

If you have children, the whole family will appreciate the many kid-oriented recreational programs made available at the community center. These programs are fun-filled, educational, and affordable and allow the kids to participate in activities like swimming, arts and crafts, games, and bowling. There is an ongoing after-school program as well as Christmas, spring break, and summer camps (see our Education and Child Care chapter). You'll also find youth athletic programs like a seventh-and-eighth-grade basketball league and the Youth American Bowling League (see the Youth Sports section of this chapter). Annual events include a kids' dog show and a track and field meet.

Sevierville City Park
1005 Park Road, Sevierville

Especially during the summer months, Sevierville City Park becomes a beehive of activity. The sense of community belonging is strong as you see softball teams going head-to-head out on the diamond, family reunions taking place in the covered pavilions, and friends enjoying strolls around the walking trail at sunset.

The favorite park hangout from late May through Labor Day weekend is the outdoor pool and food concession area. Pool hours are Monday through Friday from

In addition to its main park, Sevierville operates several smaller neighborhood parks throughout the city, including the McMahan Addition and J. B. Waters–Love Addition parks and Northview Optimist Park in northern Sevier County.

11:00 A.M. to 6:00 P.M., Saturday from 10:00 A.M. to 6:00 P.M., and Sunday from 1:00 to 6:00 P.M. The main pool is quite large, with shallow and deep waters as well as a diving area. Smaller wading pools accommodate younger children, and two certified lifeguards are on duty at all times. The main building houses showers and restrooms. Fees for swimming at the park are the same as those for the community center pool. As with the community center pool, this pool can also be reserved at group rates for private functions, but these events must be held after regular pool hours and by reservation only.

Outdoor playing surfaces include a four-goal basketball court, a regulation soccer field, two junior-size soccer fields, and eight tennis courts, four of which are lighted for night play. There are also four lighted baseball/softball fields that are used for Little League programs as well as adult league play. Men's and women's softball leagues play during spring and summer, and a coed league goes into action in the fall. Entry fees are $375 and $235 per team, respectively.

One section of the park is located along the banks of the west prong of the Little Pigeon River. This area is dominated by large shade trees and features a number of picnic tables and barbecue grills. Several covered picnic pavilions are onsite as well. These can be used at no cost, but because demand for them is high (especially in summer), it's best to make reservations in advance through the parks department.

Circling the majority of the City Park complex is a half-mile-long walking/jogging trail. Near the west side of the park, you'll find an entrance to another trail, the Memorial River Trail Greenway. This 8-foot-wide path runs for 2 miles, starting at City Park and running alongside the west prong of the Little Pigeon River. The trail crosses the Parkway and continues north to Main Street. The trail is well landscaped and has plenty of lighting and park benches. There's also a gazebo where you can rest in the shade and look out over the river.

Pigeon Forge

Pigeon Forge Community Center
170 Community Center Drive
Pigeon Forge
(865) 429-7373
When it comes to civic recreational facilities, Pigeon Forge now finds itself on more-than-equal footing with its fellow Sevier County cities. This 86,000-square-foot, $13-million complex opened in late 2000, giving both locals and visitors access to year-round opportunities for fun and conditioning. The center is open weekdays from 6:00 A.M. to 9:00 P.M., Saturday from 8:00 A.M. to 6:00 P.M., and Sunday from 1:00 to 6:00 P.M.

The daily usage fee for the center is $5.00 per person; weekly passes ($20.00), and monthly passes ($70.00) are available. Annual memberships can be purchased, offering even more value. They range from $50.00 per year per adult for Pigeon Forge residents to $75.00 per year for Pigeon Forge area workers to $120.00 per year for nonresidents. Student, senior citizen, and family memberships offer even better savings, although they're still set up under the same resident/worker/nonresident structure. These fees and memberships allow access to and use of most of the center's facilities, with two exceptions that we'll note below.

We'll start our tour of the Pigeon Forge Community Center on the first floor with the 10-lane bowling center, featuring state-of-the-art pin placement and scoring equipment. Just off the entrance to the bowling center are a video arcade and vending areas. New bowlers can take advantage of lessons, and those of all experience levels can get involved in league play. The center also hosts Cosmic Bowling nights on Friday and Saturday, featuring special music, lights, and late-night hours.

The bowling center operates on its own schedule: Monday through Friday from 11:00 A.M. to 10:00 P.M., Saturday from 1:00 to 10:00 P.M., and Sunday from 1:00 to 6:00 P.M. Of course, the cost of bowling is not covered by standard usage or membership fees. Day rates range from $1.90 per game for members to $2.45 per game for non-members. Evening rates are 35 cents higher, and shoes will set you back $1.50 a pair. Cosmic Bowling costs $8.25 per two-hour session. Bowling classes are $2.00 per session. Other recent additions to the bowling program include a pro shop and league play for adults.

The gymnasium occupies 22,000 square feet of the two-acre community center building. Curtains can be drawn to separate the three full basketball/volley-ball courts or to subdivide one of the courts into two half-courts. Just off the main floor are two racquetball/handball courts. Although all these facilities have times scheduled for open play, they are also utilized for adult basketball, volleyball, wallyball, and racquetball leagues that play throughout the year. Rates range from $40 per team for the Winter Rac-quetball League to $100 per team for Coed Adult Winter Volleyball. Portions or all of the gym can be rented for private use as well, as long as it doesn't conflict with league schedules.

The third major component of the ground floor is a six-lane, 25-yard indoor pool. The pool's schedule is divided throughout the week, with times slotted for lap swimming, open swimming, exercise classes, swim lessons, and swim meets. Although the indoor pool is open year-round, it's primarily utilized as an instructional facility during summer. Operational hours are Monday, Wednesday, and Friday from 9:00 A.M. to 8:00 P.M., Tuesday and Thursday from 6:30 A.M. to 8:00 P.M., Saturday from 10:00 A.M. to 5:30 P.M., and Sunday from 1:00 to 5:30 P.M.

The outdoor pool, open generally from late May through early September, is identical to the indoor pool, except that it has a water slide and diving board. Outside swimmers will also find a concession stand and shower facilities. The outdoor pool operates on the same schedule as the indoor pool, but its use is not covered by community center fees.

Rounding out the first level are a subdivisible, multipurpose conference room that can accommodate 300, a food preparation area that serves the conference area, and a child-care center that takes potty-trained kids ages two through eight. Child-care rates are $2.00 per child per visit with a maximum of two hours per day.

Now, let's move upstairs. The highlight of the community center's upper level is the Fort Sanders Fitness Center, filled with more than $100,000 worth of cardio and weight-training equipment. The center's staff is able to offer health and conditioning assessments, equipment orientation, personal training, and weight-loss programs. Fitness classes are taught in aerobics, indoor group cycling, kickboxing, yoga, senior exercise, circuit training, and group weight training. Classes cost $3.00 each or $32.00 for 16 classes.

The fitness center opens directly onto a walking/running track that circles the perimeter of the gymnasium, at second-floor level. Nine circuits equal 1 mile. Administrative offices are also located on the second floor.

The community center hosts a variety of general interest classes for both adults and children. Adults might be interested in offerings such as art, crafts, karate, CPR/first aid, and ballroom dancing. Kids can try out activities like cheerleading, tumbling, dance, and karate. Most classes cost around $30 to $50 per month.

The center also has after-school sports camps for ages 6 to 11 as well as summer camp programs.

Currently, two city parks serve the folks of Pigeon Forge well with free, easily accessible facilities. For more information on both parks as well as any of the city's recreation and athletic programs, you can contact Pigeon Forge's Department of Parks and Recreation at (865) 429-7373.

Pigeon Forge City Park
2446 McGill Street, Pigeon Forge
This park is handily located just off Wears Valley Road, only a couple of blocks from the Parkway. The site centers around five

lighted baseball/softball fields, two out-door basketball courts, six lighted tennis courts, a lighted volleyball court, a horse-shoe pit, and a playground. A 1.25-mile walking/jogging trail surrounds most of the area, and there are also two covered picnic pavilions. Although there is no cost to use the pavilion, city officials do recom-mend making reservations since it is fre-quently in use.

Patriot Park
Old Mill Avenue, Pigeon Forge

Patriot Park is located just 1 block off the Parkway in the heart of Pigeon Forge's Old Mill Community. And as the site of the city's main trolley office (see our Getting Here, Getting Around chapter) as well as many of its special events (see our Festivals and Annual Events chapter), the park is fre-quented by locals and vacationers alike.

Three soccer fields (two regulation, one smaller) dominate most of Patriot Park's acreage. At the southwest corner of the park, a charming gazebo has even been used for private wedding ceremonies. At the northwest corner is a covered picnic pavilion, which, like the one at the city park, can be used at no cost (again, reser-vations are encouraged). Surrounding the soccer fields is a half-mile walking/jogging trail.

Before the city educational/recreation complex on Wears Valley Road was com-pleted, this was Pigeon Forge's only pub-lic park, and it didn't have an official name. When the new city park opened in 1990, during the Persian Gulf War, Patriot Park was christened. On display in a glass enclosure near the park entrance is a Patriot missile (we presume it's unarmed) identical to the ones used by U.S. forces during the Persian Gulf War. The missile battery was donated by the Raytheon

Corporation, the manufacturer of Patriot missiles. It's one of only four on display in the United States. Also on the premises, at the far east end of the grounds, is a 32-foot-high and 28-foot-wide replica of the Liberty Bell, which is constructed of an aluminum frame with a shell made of woven metal lace. Both displays help play up the park's patriotic theme.

Patriot Park is the site of a number of city-sponsored special events held each year in Pigeon Forge. Among them are traditional holiday events like the annual Patriot Festival on the 4th of July and the city's official Winterfest Kickoff celebrations.

Gatlinburg

The gateway city's matriarchal attitude is heavily indicated in the way it treats its residents. Long a leader in entertaining visitors, Gatlinburg takes excellent care of her own as well, with a wide variety of recreation programs designed to provide cradle-to-grave diversion for whatever interests may develop. Although these programs are designed primarily for local use, the need of visitors to the Smokies to get involved with local activities is accom-modated by special considerations in most activities.

One of the more interesting and fun diversions for fishermen in Gatlinburg is the trout-fishing program, which allows game fishing right in the middle of town. We'll deal with the downtown fishing details once we dispose of the obligatory info: the types of licenses required.

You need three items to fish in town: a federal stamp, a state license, and a municipal permit. A special federal stamp is required for trout fishing in Tennessee. It costs $12.00 a year and can be pur-chased with a Tennessee fishing license. The state fishing license availability chart looks like a train schedule, but the essence is this: Any child under 13 can fish in Tennessee without a license. Adult

The Sevierville Parks and Recreation Department also operates Eagles Land-ing Golf Course in Sevierville. Refer to our Golf chapter for the details.

licenses are based on resident and non-resident status—an annual fishing license costs $21.00 for a resident and includes hunting privileges, while a nonresident annual fishing license (no hunting allowed) is $26.00. A one-day fishing license is available to residents only, for $2.50. Nonresidents may buy a three-day fishing license for $10.50 or a 10-day license for $15.50. Tennessee or North Carolina fishing licenses are required to fish in the Great Smoky Mountains National Park, and each is honored at all locations inside the park, regardless of which state you might be in at the time. Other licenses (handicapped, veterans, senior citizens) can be purchased at Tennessee Wildlife Resources Agency field offices—call the East Tennessee Regional Office at (800) 332-0900 for details.

The Gatlinburg Recreation Department raises trout from fingerling to adult size in feeding pens at Herbert Holt Park and releases them into the city's streams on a weekly schedule through the tourist season. The local trout program has a creel limit of five fish per day during the April through November catch-and-keep season, and possession of more than 10 fish at any one time is prohibited. From December through March, all fish caught must be released unharmed, and possession of trout during that season is prohibited. Fishing is permitted daily except Thursday (the day the streams are stocked) from a half-hour before sunrise until 30 minutes after sunset.

A single rod and single hook are required year-round. There are no bait restrictions or minimum length requirements during the catch-and-keep season, but artificial lures are required during the catch-and-release season. Two areas are designated as "children's streams," where only children 12 and under can fish, with a daily creel limit of two fish. The designated children's streams are Dudley Creek and the Little Pigeon River at Herbert Holt Park, and LeConte Creek in the Mynatt Park area. Local police are authorized to act as game wardens within the city limits.

A regular state fishing license and a federal trout stamp are required before the special municipal permit can be purchased for $2.50 per day. This is a great way to teach a kid how to fish without ever leaving civilization, and the stocking program almost guarantees a good-size trophy sometime during the season. The two most popular adult fishing spots in the city are both on the west prong of the Little Pigeon River, right in the middle of town. The area along River Road between Christus Gardens and the bridge at Greystone Heights Road is easily accessible from the Riverwalk (see our Attractions chapter) and is usually well stocked. The stretch that runs parallel to the Parkway heading north from behind Applebee's restaurant to the bridge at traffic light #2 is a little more private, with motels and a few businesses hiding the river from the street traffic. Details of the program are available at City Hall, the Gatlinburg welcome centers, Ace Hardware on East Parkway (U.S. Highway 321N) between downtown and City Hall, and Proffitt's Woodcrafts on East Parkway, about 5 miles east of town.

Gatlinburg operates three beautiful municipal parks, each with its own special attraction. All three have covered pavilions with picnic tables and cooking facilities, which are available for group use at no cost. Reservations may be made by calling the Gatlinburg Recreation Department at (865) 436–4990.

Herbert Holt Park
Pigeon River Road, Gatlinburg

This award-winning facility is on the site of the old sewer plant at the north end of the city and is only visible from the Spur. The road into the park is north of traffic light #1 (turn right coming toward town, left going out). Herbert Holt Park's picnic pavilion has a huge barbecue grill for sheltered cooking. Picnic tables with individual cooking grills along the stream are convenient to the playground and horseshoe pits. A short hiking trail above the restrooms provides a nice way to walk off a meal or build a prefeast appetite. The city's trout-rearing facility lies beside the pavilion at Herbert Holt Park in what used to be the sewage plant settling beds. Trout of various sizes are visible to the public, along with special provisions made to foil the flock of blue herons that moved into the park the day after the first trout fingerlings were brought in. They haven't figured out a way short of killing to get rid of the fat, *very* happy otter that took up residence in the summer of 2000, and killing is out of the question. If you're there at the right time, he's a treat to watch.

Mynatt Park
Asbury Lane, Gatlinburg

The biggest, oldest, and most complete municipal recreational site in the city, Mynatt Park is about 6 blocks from traffic light #8. An absolute jewel, Mynatt Park pretty much has it all, including picnic tables and charcoal grills in a shaded section alongside a busy stream, a large pavilion for group use (call 865-436-4990 for reservations), a lighted basketball court, six tennis courts, horseshoe pits, playground equipment at two sites, a baseball diamond, and plenty of open land for free-form play. There's even a gazebo convenient to the pavilion that's become a popular spot for alfresco weddings. Mynatt Park is a great favorite with the local population, who turn out in force to walk their pets and watch Little League baseball. A word to the wise: The Mynatt Park pavilion is the most-requested facility in the city. If you're planning anything that includes this particular site, call as far in advance as possible.

Mills Park
Mills Park Road, Gatlinburg

Adjacent to the community center and Gatlinburg-Pittman High School, Mills Park is primarily an athletic venue. Lighted softball and football fields are in almost constant use by high school and youth organizations, and the high school uses the quarter-mile track as its home oval. The only concession stand in the munici-

pal park system is convenient to the football and softball fields and sits right in front of the two lighted tennis courts (also a home site for the high school team). At the other end of the park, a pavilion with picnic tables is close to the playground and jogging trail. Mills Park Road runs off East Parkway (US 321N) about 5 miles from downtown. Two parking lots are convenient to whatever type of activity you've planned, and the high school and community center parking lots handle the overflow for large events like the Scottish Games each spring (see our Festivals and Annual Events chapter).

Gatlinburg Community Center
Mills Park Road, Gatlinburg
(865) 436-4990
www.ci.gatlinburg.tn.us/parksrec/parks.htm

The Gatlinburg Community Center is a wonderful fallback solution if your plans have been disrupted. The community center is a 50,000-plus-square-foot indoor facility that's jam-packed with things to do. To get there, take East Parkway (US 321N) about 5 miles out from traffic light #3 in Gatlinburg to Mills Park Road. Turn left and go about a half-mile until you see the big sign, and turn left again. The parking lot is at the top of the hill. Usage fees are moderate to dirt-cheap, and the center is open seven days a week. Our tour begins with the swimming pool, goes up progressively for two levels to the multi-purpose area and gymnasium, then returns to the ground floor to visit the racquetball courts and bowling center/game room complex.

The 25-meter swimming pool is available for open swimming any time there's not a swim meet or a group activity (adult lap swimming is OK during afternoon and evening water exercise classes). Pool admission is $2.00 a session for those age 13 to 65, $1.50 for children 4 to 12 and adults 65 and over, and free to children younger than 4. Frequent swimmers can buy extended-use passes to the pool—a pass good for 25 visits is $30.00 for adults and $22.50 for children and senior citizens. For the truly addicted aquaphile, an unlimited-use six-month pass is available at $72.00 and $54.00, respectively, by age group. Water exercise classes are conducted Monday, Wednesday, and Friday from 11:00 A.M. to noon, and Tuesday and Thursday evenings from 7:00 to 8:00 P.M. The cost is 25 cents plus the pool admission fee. Certified lifeguards are on duty at all times the pool is open.

On the second floor, a patio area with tables and chairs provides a bird's-eye view of the pool. Snacks and soft drinks are available at vending machines nearby. The multipurpose room next to the upstairs patio is big enough to accommodate a meeting of 300 people or can be divided for two smaller events. The hourly rental rate includes use of the fully equipped kitchen. The multipurpose room is the meeting place for the Gatlinburg Garden Club, the Gatlinburg Retired Citizens Club, and the Gatlinburg Community Chorale. It's also used for specialty classes that occur through the year in subjects as varied as line dancing and CPR–first aid.

The central hallway that runs the length of the building looks down into the racquetball courts. The double gymnasium has several basketball goals, including junior-height models. Equipment usage is free during open play, but some form of collateral is required (car keys and driver's licenses are the usual adult fare; kids can leave textbooks, wallets, etc.). During fall and winter, the gym is booked pretty solid on weekday evenings for adult basketball and volleyball leagues. Aerobex classes are conducted in the gym on Monday, Wednesday, and Friday mornings from 9:00 to 10:00 A.M. and in the exercise area above the gym on Tuesday and Thursday evenings from 5:30 to 6:30 P.M. Daily admission to Aerobex is $3.00, a 12-ticket booklet is available for $25.00, and a yearly membership is $270.00.

The Tone Zone, an exercise area with weight machines and other torture devices, provides a complete fitness center with qualified supervision available for counseling. A one-hour orientation session is required on your first visit. Pick your price: Admission to the Tone Zone costs $4.00 a day, $10.00 a month, $50.00 for a six-month pass, or $100.00 a year. For a price comparison, check out any health club in the world.

Back downstairs, the four racquetball courts that line the central hallway are very popular with the locals and have spawned several champions at the local and regional level. Racquetball courts are rented on an hourly basis. An hour's use is $2.75 per person Monday through Friday before 5:00 P.M. and on evenings and weekends the rate is $3.75 per player. Racquets are available for rental at $1.25 per hour, and racquetballs are sold for $3.50 a can. A 15-hour racquetball card can be used in either prime or nonprime time for $34.00. Wallyball, a singular twist on volleyball, is a popular game for groups. Rental of a racquetball court for wallyball is $8.00 an hour, including the net and ball.

Large locker and shower rooms are convenient to all perspiration-inducing activities, with direct entry to the swimming pool. If you want a locker for storage while using the facilities, that'll set you back anywhere from a quarter to 75 cents per day, depending on locker size. Long-term locker rental rates are available.

The bowling center and game room are on the first floor, with separate entrances that also open to the rest of the building. The bowling center has eight synthetic lanes. Local leagues take up most of the lanes through the week from October through March, but open bowling is available every day and most weekend nights. Open bowling before 6:00 P.M. is $1.75 per game. After 6:00, the price jumps to $2.00 for adults 19 to 65, while junior and senior citizen rates don't change. Shoe rental (you must use bowling shoes— either yours or theirs) costs $1.25 a pair. To prevent gutter balls, channel bumpers can be installed in the lanes for 50 cents a game extra. Open bowling discount cards provide 25 games at a 40 percent savings: The adult card is $30.00, and juniors and senior citizens can buy a discount card for $26.25. Specialty tournaments (moonlight bowling, no-tap, Scotch doubles, etc.) are conducted most Saturday nights during the bowling season.

Adjacent to the bowling center and its refreshment area is the game room, containing two professional billiard tables, two world-class Ping-Pong tables, and an air hockey table. Thirty minutes of billiards costs $1.00. Ping-Pong is free, but you need your own ball. They're available at the bowling counter for a quarter if you don't have one with you. Air hockey costs 50 cents a game—first player to seven goals, or the leader after seven minutes of play, wins.

CANOEING, TUBING, AND RAFTING

Shirley's Texaco Service
1141 Parkway, Gatlinburg
(865) 436-4109
Located at traffic light #10, right at the park entrance, Shirley's maintains a large stock of truck tubes for sale only, at about $10 apiece.

McKinney's Market
819 East Parkway, Gatlinburg
(865) 436-2272
About a mile east of traffic light #3, McKinney's rents tubes for $5.00 a day, with a $10.00 deposit. You'll get your $5.00 back when you return the tube in good condition.

Maples Brothers Gas & Grocery
1674 East Parkway, Gatlinburg
(865) 430-3766
East of town and near the popular middle prong of the Little Pigeon River in the Greenbrier area of the park, Maples Brothers tube rentals run about $6.00 a day, with a cash deposit required.

Rafting in the Smokies
2470 East Parkway, Gatlinburg
(865) 436-5008, (800) 776-7238
www.raftinginthesmokies.com

White-water rafting has come into its own as a Smokies trip experience, and that's as it should be. There's no better way to enjoy the unmatched scenery of the Smokies than from the middle of a river, and there's no better way to gain an appreciation for the awesome power of nature than to plunk down in the middle of it for some hair-raising, white-knuckle excitement in a totally safe environment. No experience is necessary (they've got professional guides with remarkable credentials), and children ages eight and up and weighing at least 60 pounds can join in the fun. Rafting in the Smokies provides four different ways to enjoy rafting in the mountains, and they all start at the headquarters on East Parkway, about 6 miles east of traffic light #3 in downtown Gatlinburg, or the Pigeon Forge office at 3249 River Road. The Gatlinburg headquarters is actually in the mountain town of Pittman Center, a well-kept secret that would like to stay that way. The headquarters staff will provide tickets and directions to the appropriate outpost for the planned trip. (Note: This can get a little confusing. If you've made telephone reservations and already have received your tickets and directions in the mail, you can just go directly to the outpost.) All rafting trips go as planned, regardless of weather conditions—if there's any question about what you're facing, pack a bathing suit, a complete change of clothes, and a towel. That'll do in warm weather; if it's cool or worse, wool socks and sweaters are recommended. And be sure of this: You are going to get wet, probably to your skin. Showers and changing rooms at the outpost will let you depart as warm and dry as when you arrived.

So now you're headed for the outpost. If the trip planned is on the Big Pigeon River, it's about an hour's drive along the eastern edge of the Great Smoky Mountains National Park to the outpost—the directions given are excellent. If Nantahala is your destination, the drive is a little longer and will take you into North Carolina through the park and Cherokee. The

Ocoee River adventures require a longer drive into Polk County on the western edge of the national park. At the outpost, here's what to expect:

Big Pigeon River: Two trips are available on the Big Pigeon, and they're as different as night and day. The Big Pigeon run is rated as one of the most exciting white-water raft rides in Tennessee. Starting just below the Waterville Electric Plant, the Big Pigeon River is a maelstrom of roaring water, and your raft is right in the middle of it. Flanked by the National Park on one side and Pisgah National Forest on the other, the Big Pigeon run drops sharply through 5 miles of almost continuous rapids in a fast-moving hour and a half. Listen to your guide, and enjoy the trip. The power company has guaranteed that they'll release water from the dam on Tuesday, Thursday, and Saturday through the rafting season: Keep those days in mind for the hottest rafting. For those not quite into fear and loathing on the water but who like getting wet, the lower Pigeon float trip is just the ticket. Leaving from the outpost, the float trip rides the swift, gentle current for 3 miles through one of the most beautiful stretches of forest in North America. Rafters are allowed at some points to get in the river and swim along. The float trip takes about an hour and a half, and the shuttle is waiting to return everybody to the outpost. The Big Pigeon white-water raft run costs $39.95 plus a $2.00 county user fee per boater; the float trip is $16.95 a head, plus the same user fee.

If Nantahala is your choice, you're in store for an 8-mile plunge through the gorge of the same name. The spectacular beauty of the Nantahala National Forest surrounds you for the entirety of the trip, which takes less than two hours. It's a tiny bit tamer than the Big Pigeon, but you've got a little better chance to enjoy the breathtaking scenery. The Nantahala rafting adventure costs $29.95 per adventurer.

The mighty Ocoee River was the site of all of the white-water events in the 1996

When renting an inner tube for a river float, try to avoid the old-fashioned, black rubber tire tubes of yesteryear. They soak up the sun quickly and can get very hot to the touch. Most outfitters these days provide tubes with handles and skin-friendly materials that are specially designed for tubing and other water sports.

Olympics and is considered the most exciting white-water river in the Southeast. Each of the one-hour trips through the Cherokee National Forest is a breathtaking ride through a stunningly beautiful river gorge—if you've got the nerve to look at the scenery. The middle course is 5 miles long (it can seem longer), rips through more than 20 world-class rapids, and has an overall vertical drop of 260 feet. The upper course, the actual Olympic competition site, is another 5-mile hairraiser through a narrower, faster gorge designed for the more experienced rafter. If you've never rafted a white-water river, the aforementioned caveat isn't really a warning—it's just to let you know you're starting out at a really serious level if you've chosen the middle Ocoee. The Ocoee River ride costs $35.00 per rider for your choice of levels. A $4.00 user fee applies for the upper course only.

Rafting is still regarded to be a coming sport, and its popularity is growing. Most first-time rafters plan their vacations around the times when the water is the best. Rafting in the Smokies is open every day, March through October.

HORSEBACK RIDING

A cautionary note: Horseback stables will invariably require you to sign a release form before you ride in which you agree not to hold the business responsible if you happen to take a nasty spill. In other words, you ride at your own risk.

A Llovely Way to Spend a Day
(or more)

The use of llamas as pack animals in the mountains is not really a new concept. The "South American camel" has been a familiar sight (once the shock passes) on several trails, packing supplies up to LeConte Lodge. The use of these interesting and somewhat comical animals to pack sundry items and lunch for hikers is a new idea hatched by a striking immigrant from the wilds of Miami Beach.

Sandy Sgrillo was born in Connecticut and as a young adult moved to Miami, where she spent several years as a limousine driver. Looking for a lifestyle of more serenity, she visited a lot of places before settling in the Smokies. A chance encounter with the only llama-hike operator in the Smokies area led to the eventual purchase of the business and a few llamas (joined by few more later, for a current total of six), and Sandy Sgrillo found what she had been looking for.

Lesson number one when you meet Sandy and her herd is that llamas are as gentle and friendly as they look—if they're treated with respect. "They're a lot like house pets," Sandy says. "Big house pets. They're intelligent and respond to the treatment you give them. Since I love my guys and demonstrate it, they love me right back. And after they are introduced to other people, they're very easy to get along with."

That's good to know; when you go out on the trail with Sandy and her "guys," chances are you'll be leading one of them on a tether long enough for

them to try to exercise a little independence from time to time. A firm hand keeps them in line without any real problems, but they do like to nibble on certain grasses and flowers, and a little bit of forbearance will make the whole trip smoother. Because certain plants (most notably rhododendron) are poisonous, Sandy will tell you which ones the animals can't eat.

But we're getting ahead of ourselves. Let's back up for a minute and get you headed for the trail before we set you on it. Because the National Park Service does not allow commercial operators to use the park (except for certain concessionaires that don't include llama owners), Sandy's trips are pretty well confined to the slopes of Bluff Mountain and Chilhowee Mountain, a few miles southwest of downtown Sevierville. When you make your reservation, Sandy will give you excellent directions to the trailhead, where she and her beasts will be waiting. The number of llamas depends on your individual situation; the type and length of your trip tells Sandy what she'll need to feed and shelter you, and each person will usually need one llama for their personal effects. That one llama will be your personal companion for your hike.

The current local schedule includes a choice of three hikes: a one-hour hike along a scenic wooded trail with time for picture-taking, soft drinks and water provided ($25 per person); the half-day trip, three to four hours of moderate hiking

Sandy Sgrillo discusses a trip with Domino while JJ Bird listens in. DICK McHUGH

with frequent stops for refreshments and pictures, featuring a gourmet lunch ($45 a head); and a full day of hiking up and down trails and through creeks, with several rest stops and photo-ops, for $65 per person. The all-day hike includes a lunch you'd die for in any restaurant. Specialty trips include an opulent overnight hike with a decadent meal at the end of the trail, a sleeping tent with a queen-size air mattress and linen bedding, and the music of the woods to lull you to sleep. You'll wake to find the llamas have gone back to the trailhead to pick up coffee and muffins, which will be steaming and delicious. The overnight excursion is limited to two people at $225 per person.

Because all of her trips originate at the trailhead you've decided to use, Sandy doesn't operate an office like most businesses. You can contact her at Smoky Mountain Llama Treks, LLC, 2590 Bluff Mountain Road, Sevierville, TN 37863; call her at (865) 428–4606; or visit her Web site: www.smokymountain llamatreks.com.

Your choice of trips to take with Sandy and her pals will probably depend on what kind of time you can give to this activity. Whatever you decide, the combination of this charming guide, her affable and amusing companions, and the beauty of the mountains will make you wish you'd signed on for a longer trip.

Sevierville

Douglas Lake View Stables
1650 Providence Road, Sevierville
(865) 428-3587
www.douglaslakestables.com
These riding stables are located among scenic rolling hills near Douglas Lake, just a few miles off TN 66. They've been providing guided horseback tours for more than 10 years and offer approximately 35 different horses and 12 miles of trails for riders of all levels of experience. The stables are open year-round.

It costs $29.95 per hour to ride, although you pay half price if you pay up front 90 days in advance. Discounted rates are extended to groups, and kids three to six years old can ride in the saddle with an adult for $5.00 each.

Typically, tours last from a half hour to five hours. Trip options include lakeshore rides (ask about the old Indian burial ground), sunset rides, and moonlight rides which cost $35.00 (prepaid) and are for adults only. You can take riding lessons for $40.00 per hour or take a Friday evening hayride ($15.00 per adult, $5.00 per child). The property also features a free petting zoo for customers that's home to everything from goats, emus, and llamas to rabbits, geese, and chickens. For those who are romantically inclined, owner Jim Chambers, a chaplain, will perform wedding ceremonies and vow renewals for couples on horseback at a variety of rustic sites. Weddings range from $199 to $239.

Deer Farm Riding Stables
478 Happy Hollow Lane, Sevierville
(865) 429-2276
www.deerfarmzoo.com
You'll find these stables in the scenic hills east of Sevierville off U.S. Highway 411. They're owned by the same family that operates the Smoky Mountain Deer Farm and Exotic Petting Zoo, which is located on the same property (see the Close-up in our Kidstuff chapter). Gentle horses are available for anyone age five or older, with the maximum weight for riders at 250

pounds. It costs $14.95 to ride for half an hour, $19.95 for a full hour, and $39.95 for two hours (off-season only). Group rates are available for 15 or more people.

The well-maintained trails are a comfortable 8 feet wide and are shaded by trees for approximately 80 percent of the route. Deer Farm also provides riding instruction, mounting stands, padded equipment, and guides who will tow your younger riders if you wish. Speaking of young riders, pony rides are also available near the stables for $4.00 each. Deer Farm Riding Stables are open year-round from 10:00 A.M. to 5:30 P.M. Reservations are recommended.

Five Oaks Stables
1650 Parkway, Pigeon Forge
(865) 453-8644
Although their address technically places them in Pigeon Forge, you'll actually find the entrance to the stables on the Parkway in Sevierville, just shy of the Pigeon Forge border. As such, it's one of the more conveniently located riding establishments in the area. Like at Cedar Ridge, you can ride for a half hour for $16.50 or one hour for $22.00. There are no age or weight limits.

The stables have more than 50 gentle horses from which to choose for your scenic trip through nearby rolling and wooded hills. At Five Oaks, only guided tours are provided, and guides are experienced. They're open year-round and run tours daily from 9:00 A.M. to 6:00 P.M., weather permitting.

Pigeon Forge

Walden Creek Riding Stables
2709 Waldens Creek Road
Pigeon Forge
(865) 429-0443
www.waldencreekstables.com
You'll find horseback riding and a whole lot more at these stables located just a few miles outside Pigeon Forge off Wears

Valley Road. A scenic 500-acre ranch is the setting for guided day rides that last anywhere from 40 minutes to eight hours. There are approximately 100 horses on the premises from which to choose. Well-maintained trails take riders through valleys, over foothills, and across mountain streams. Undeveloped trails lead to nearby mountain tops. And the adventures aren't limited to daytime hours. Evening rides and overnight excursions to primitive campsites add a whole new element to traveling on horseback.

In summer and fall there are bonfire hayrides two nights a week (free to horseback customers). These trips are highlighted by singing cowboys and rowdy "bandits." At the bonfire, customers enjoy dinner as well as a show featuring rope tricks, horse races, and trick riding. And yes, they perform wedding ceremonies on horseback as well.

Middle Creek Riding Stables
2909 Millers Way, Sevierville
(865) 428-8363

Okay, here's another address that requires explanation. For all intents and purposes, the stables are located in Pigeon Forge, just past Dollywood off Upper Middle Creek Road. But because they are outside city limits, they are in "the county" and are given a Sevierville address (just remember that the stables are near Dollywood).

Middle Creek Riding Stables charge $12.95 for half-hour rides, $18.95 for 45-minute rides, and $22.95 for one-hour rides. However, they have coupons that knock three bucks off all those prices. Kids ages five and younger ride for free if they share a horse with an adult (using a provided custom saddle). About 35 horses are on hand to take riders on guided and unguided tours along hilly, wooded trails. The stables are open year-round, from 9:00 A.M. to 6:00 P.M. in the summer and 10:00 A.M. to 5:00 P.M. in the off-season.

Lil' Ponderosa Riding Stables
909 Little Cove Road, Pigeon Forge
(865) 453-5278

Although most horseback-riding stables list specific closing times, it's important to note that the last ride of each day usually departs up to an hour before that closing time. In other words, you can't show up five minutes before closing and expect to ride the horses.

Located on the grounds of Lil' Ponderosa Campground and RV Park (see our Campgrounds and RV Parks chapter), this stable offers the novelty of boarding services for campground customers (the usual health certificates are required). They've got some big horses, so the weight limit at Lil' Ponderosa is 250 pounds. A one-hour ride on a multi-elevation trail is $18.00 ($15.00 for campground guests), and group tours are available. The stables are open year-round.

Gatlinburg

There is one riding stable convenient to Gatlinburg, and it's operated as a concession within the boundaries of the Great Smoky Mountains National Park.

Smoky Mountain Stables
East Parkway, Gatlinburg
(865) 436-5634

About 4 miles east of downtown Gatlinburg on US 321N, Smoky Mountain Stables is owned and operated by Kenny Kear, a Gatlinburg native with an impressive string of credentials as a trainer of champion show horses. Open from early March through November, Smoky Mountain Stables welcomes children five and older and enforces a weight limit for riders of 225 pounds. Several mountain-savvy guides are on hand to ensure that the ride through the mountains will be as safe and pleasant as possible. It's important to consider that you're riding in an untamed wilderness. The experience and local knowledge of the guides here is best proven by the fact that the stable has never had a customer injured seriously enough that medical assistance was required to remove the rider from the park.

FITNESS CENTERS

National Fitness Center
950 Dolly Parton Parkway, Sevierville
(865) 429-2400

This 42,000-square-foot fitness center (which debuted in 1999) is one of the largest in East Tennessee. Facilities and programs are available for men and women of all ages. The upstairs half of the building contains an aerobics studio, a massive area of free weight and circuit training equipment, an indoor track, and more than 60 pieces of cardiovascular equipment such as stair steppers, tread-mills, and stationary bikes. While you're working out on the cardio equipment, you can plug into one of 14 overhead television monitors. Downstairs areas include a junior Olympic-size pool, juice-and-snack-bar, sauna, hot tub, locker rooms, ladies' work-out room, and day care center.

National Fitness Center offers an incredible variety of fun and healthy classes with certified instructors. Among the subjects available are karate, yoga, dance, and aerobics. Also, a hiking club meets each Saturday in the summer to take on scenic trails in the national park. Although the center provides a free child-care facility, there are also special pro-grams just for kids, including swim lessons, dance, karate, and even summer camps with an emphasis, naturally, on fitness.

Health education and disease preven-tion are stressed. You can attend work-shops on nutrition, blood pressure, cholesterol, back pain, smoking cessation, and more. The center's staff also includes certified trainers to help you design your own personalized workout program based on the results of your initial fitness test.

The club offers a wide range of pay-ment plans, ranging from daily rates to monthly and yearly membership packages.

The center is open Monday through Friday from 5:00 A.M. to midnight. Saturday hours are 8:00 A.M. to 8:00 P.M., and on Sunday it's open from noon to 6:00 P.M.

Everything for Fitness
446 East Parkway, Gatlinburg
(865) 436-8945

Located at the back of Winery Square shopping mall, Everything for Fitness is everything the name implies. Although the most visible feature is the usual workout equipment and juice bar, the services offered by Frederic Leyd and his team of experts are concentrated on whole-life wellness rather than on rock-hard abs. Per-sonal health and nutritional consultations form the foundation for long- and short-term programs intended to achieve well-ness through exercise and dietary programs tailored to individual needs. Dietary supplements and an on-site herbal pharmacy head the list of available take-home materials, which also includes work-out clothing, commercial and residential weights, and exercise machinery. There are no "memberships" at Everything for Fit-ness; limited-length user passes are offered in a variety of configurations depending on the needs and status of the individual. In addition to a strong local base, Everything for Fitness offers a unique set of visitors' programs, including several that offer lodg-ing, transportation, meals, and even enter-tainment. The center is open Monday through Saturday. Although walk-in traffic is welcome, appointments are recom-mended to assure personal attention.

MARTIAL ARTS

Sevierville Ishinryu Karate Club
(865) 428-1894

Chief instructor Bill Marshall operates this karate school at Sevierville Intermediate School, located at 416 High Street. Classes meet every Monday and Wednesday from 6:30 to 8:30 P.M. The club is open to males and females ages seven and older. It costs $25 a month to participate.

Sessions usually start out with warm-ups and exercises by all students, then break up into individual instruction groups that are divided by levels of experience. Marshall himself is a sixth degree black belt with more than 25 years of experience. Assisting him are any of his group's black belt students. Although Marshall encourages his students to take part in area karate tournaments, he doesn't put too much emphasis on them in terms of advancement. Rather, his approach is to stress the fundamentals of karate in order to move up to the next belt.

YOUTH SPORTS

Baseball and Softball

Greater Sevierville Little League
(865) 908-7063
Since 1996, this league has given area boys and girls ages 5 through 18 the opportunity to participate in America's pastime. As with Little League baseball nationwide, Sevierville's teams are built on the principles of having fun while learning the skill of the sport. Each child is guaranteed to play at least two innings of each six-inning game. Sevierville Little League is open to any child regardless of physical or mental ability.

Teams are grouped by age. Five- and six-year-olds play T-ball, while seven- and eight-year-olds play coach-pitch ball. Ages 9 through 18 are divided into two-year age groupings. Registration for the regular season takes place in February, and the games are played from April through June. There is also a fall league in play during August and September. In the fall, the emphasis is on training and development, and actual games are played in the older divisions only.

The cost to play in the Greater Sevierville Little League starts at $35 per season. However, fees are dependent on the parents' ability to pay. If a particular family isn't able to afford the fee, they are not required to pay for their child to participate. The league furnishes all equipment except for baseball cleats and gloves.

Sevier County Baseball Association
(865) 428-0171
The key distinction between the Sevier County Baseball Association and the Sevierville organization is that the former primarily draws its players from Pigeon Forge, Gatlinburg, and Sevier County at large. The league is open to boys and girls ages 5 through 15, and the players are grouped in two-year spans. Five- and six-year-olds play T-ball, and seven- and eight-year-olds are in the coach-pitch division. The older teams are subdivided by age groupings and have their own pitchers.

The season begins in April and consists of 60 to 70 games, culminating in tournament play in mid-July. Players are guaranteed a minimum playing time per game of six defensive outs and one turn at bat. All games are played at Pigeon Forge City Park. Registration begins prior to the start of the season and costs $11 per player. Team sponsors and parents are responsible for providing uniforms and equipment.

Football

Sevierville Little League
(865) 429-5366
In this organized football league, kids have been strapping on the pads and tearing up the gridiron for nearly 40 years. The league is open to both boys and girls, although the girls are somewhat of a rarity. Children must be between 5 years old (and in kindergarten) and 11 years old to play. There are four divisions altogether, with several teams in each division. Two divisions of "grasscutters" are for ages 5 through 8, and two divisions of "pee wees" are for kids between 9 and 11. Each year, registration begins the third Saturday in July and runs for several days. The cost is $40 per child, but the league provides all playing equipment except for cleats.

The season begins in early August and, after a nine-game schedule, wraps up with a "Super Bowl" game in late October.

Basketball

7th and 8th Grade Basketball League
200 Gary R. Wade Boulevard, Sevierville
(865) 453-5441

Sponsored by the Sevierville Department of Parks and Recreation, this youth basketball program plays at the Sevierville Community Center. It is designed for seventh- and eighth-grade youngsters who are not playing on school-sponsored teams. The league helps the kids develop their hoop skills in a fun and competitive manner. The league plays mid-October through late January, and the fee is only $3.15. Registration takes place at the start of the season.

Soccer

American Youth Soccer Organization (AYSO)
P.O. Box 5588, Sevierville 37864-5588
(865) 429-2976
www.teamdiscovery.com/aysoregion440

Soccer has really caught on with youngsters in the United States over the last 10 years or so. Local Sevier County children are fortunate to be able to participate in AYSO, a program that stresses positive coaching, balanced teams, and good sportsmanship. Best of all, each child is guaranteed to play at least half of every game.

All of these factors add up to a truly fun league that manages to avoid the cutthroat spirit of heated competition so prevalent in many youth sports leagues these days. At AYSO games, you never hear venomous parents yelling at referees as they try to live vicariously through their children. The kids are taught that having fun is more important than winning. As a result, a lot of children that would ordinarily slip through the cracks of organized sports get a fair chance to participate and develop their skills.

Sevier County is included in AYSO Region 440, with teams located in Sevierville, Pigeon Forge, and Gatlinburg in addition to Caton's Chapel, New Center, Kodak, and Pittman Center. The smaller communities usually just have one or two teams per age division. Cities like Sevierville that have larger permanent populations may have as many as 10 teams per division, especially among the younger ages.

AYSO is open to any boy or girl from age 5 to 18. In this range are seven different divisions of two-year age groupings. Among the younger kids (U6 and U8), the teams can be coed. When the kids get up to U10, the boys and girls are usually split into separate leagues. AYSO offers both fall and spring seasons. In spring, the teams in U10 and higher go head-to-head at the end of the regular season and compete in a countywide tournament. All children who participate get some sort of trophy or medal for their efforts.

Registration takes place several times annually. The best time to sign up is during the spring tournament, but if you miss that, there's another big push in fall when school starts. It costs $35 per child to play in either the spring or fall seasons and $40 to play in both, and there are discounts for registering more than one child per family. The costs of equipment and uniforms are extra.

Bowling

Young American Bowling Association (YABA)
200 Gary R. Wade Boulevard, Sevierville
(865) 453-5441

This kids' bowling league is sponsored by Sevierville's Department of Parks and Recreation and plays at the community center's bowling lanes. The program is open to kids ages 6 through 18, and the fun takes place each Saturday morning at 9:00 A.M. beginning in mid-September. The cost is a one-time fee of $12.00 plus a weekly fee of $6.00.

GOLF 🏌

Compared to other vacation spots in the South, like Myrtle Beach, South Carolina, or the Pinehurst area of North Carolina, the Smokies aren't huge as a golf destination. The landscape doesn't lend itself to multiple course layouts, and the mountain lifestyle that's been in place here since, well, forever, isn't one that leads to a lot of golf.

That doesn't mean, however, that you should leave your clubs at home. There are four beautiful golf courses spread about Sevier County, and all but one is within 5 miles of the Smokies Corridor. Two are less than 10 years old. Two are municipally owned, and top-flight course architects designed all four. Greens fees vary slightly from course to course, and most have in-season and off-season rate schedules—all rates quoted here are in-season. Because the local temperatures remain moderate through December, it's not unusual to see golfers out on most of the area courses year-round, but the idea of coming to the Smokies to play golf in January and February isn't really a good one.

Reserved tee times are recommended from spring through fall, and some form of golf/lodging packages are available at most courses. They're described here from north to south, starting with the newest.

Eagles Landing Golf Club
1556 Old Knoxville Highway, Sevierville
(865) 429-4223
www.eagleslandinggolf.com

Laid out along Tennessee Highway 66 between Interstate 40 and Dolly Parton Parkway, Eagle's Landing opened in 1994. The course is owned by the City of Sevierville. From downtown Sevierville, go west on Dolly Parton Parkway (U.S. Highway 411/441) less than a mile from the TN 66 intersection to the next traffic light at Old Knoxville Highway. Turn right and go about 2½ miles. You'll see the course on

the right before you see the driveway. If you're somewhere on 66, take Boyd's Creek Road (Tennessee Highway 338—there's a traffic light) west about 1.2 miles to Old Knoxville Highway and turn left. The course entrance is a little more than a mile on the left.

The course is essentially flat, wide open for now (that'll change as the trees planted along the fairways mature), and very forgiving. The par 72 layout runs from 6,900 yards at the championship tees to an almost pitch-and-putt 4,600 from the ladies' tees. Rough that isn't a real hazard borders wide Bermuda grass fairways. The Little Pigeon River wanders through the course, providing more scenery than anything else, but it can jump up and bite you if you're not paying attention.

Information on course layout approaches the overload stage, with five tee levels to shoot from. Pin placements are changed daily according to a zone diagram, and all pins are placed in the same zone every day. The scorecard shows the zoning for each green, and they'll tell you before you tee off which zones to shoot for.

Eagles Landing breaks the day into three parts, with fees sliding to match the time of day. Regular fees (opening until 2:00 P.M.) are $41 weekdays and $51 weekends. From 2:00 to 4:00 P.M., fees are $36 and $46, respectively, and the twilight rate of $26 kicks in at 4:00 P.M. every day. Carts are required, and all fees include carts. Eagles Landing is a member course of the National Audubon Cooperative Sanctuary Program, a national organization dedicated to preserving wildlife on golf courses. Non-play areas of the course are maintained as wildlife refuges, and sightings of deer, otters, beavers, several duck species, Canada geese, and even wild turkeys lend a grace note to playing the course. American bald eagles have been seen over the course as well. Eagles Landing has golf package tie-ins with several area lodging facilities and has detailed information available on the Internet. Advance tee times are recommended during the summer to avoid long waits once you arrive.

River Islands Golf Club
9610 Kodak Road, Mascot
(865) 933-0100, (800) 347-4737
www.riverislandsgolf.com
Let's just get this out of the way and be done with it: River Islands is a spectacular golf course. Laid out alongside and in the middle of the French Broad River, River Islands is visually as pleasing as any course you'll play anywhere. Getting there requires a little more attention to the road than the other three area courses, but it's worth it.

Coming out of Sevierville on Winfield Dunn Parkway (TN 66), turn left at the traffic light at Tennessee Highway 139 (Kodak Road). It's the first traffic light after you cross the river on 66. Look for the blue and white signs. About 3 miles in on TN 139, look for the Northview fire hall on the right, and take the next left (it's a four-way stop). Less than a mile later, turn right at Kodak Road, and follow it about 3 miles to the course entrance on the left. You'll see most of the course before you get to the driveway.

River Islands is an Arthur Hill design, and it is the only course in the area rated by *Golf* magazine (four stars). It's a classic links-style layout, with five holes distributed among three natural islands in the French Broad River. Being laid out entirely along a river bottom, it's pretty level; it's also heavily forested. This course also has the interesting distinction of being located in two counties; from the tee at the par three third hole in Knox County, your drive crosses the river and the county line, (hopefully) coming down 175 yards later on the green in Sevier County. Tee layouts make River Islands whatever you want it to be: The forward tees neutralize the ever-present river, and the back tees will test your club selection skills. The fairways are

a particularly lush Zoysia grass that feels almost spongy but sets a ball up nicely. Of the four courses, this is the one that can bring you to your knees the quickest and for the longest time. Played from the championship tees, River Islands is a test of every shot-making skill in the game. From the two intermediate tees, it's a constant challenge, and from the ladies' tees it's not really a pussycat but it's a lot drier.

Greens fees are $55 Monday through Friday and $59 Saturday and Sunday until 11:00 A.M. Fees drop to $45 and $49, respectively, from 11:00 A.M. until 3:00 P.M. when the twilight fee of $29 becomes effective every day. This is an arduous course despite its relative flatness, and carts and spikeless shoes are required. Due to its extreme popularity, River Islands requires reserved tee times during the tourist season.

Gatlinburg Country Club
520 Dollywood Lane, Pigeon Forge
(865) 453-3912, (800) 568-4748
www.ci.gatlinburg.tn.os
The Gatlinburg Golf Course is the oldest and most mountainous of the bunch. Established in Pigeon Forge in 1955—because that's where the land was available—the club was closed for an entire year in 1993 and completely renovated. To get there, turn off the Parkway at traffic light #8 (the Dollywood light) in Pigeon Forge. You'll see the course on the right long before you get to the clubhouse driveway.

Gatlinburg is the only course of the four in the area that's landlocked, and the only water at all is two artificial lakes that play with your head on the 18th hole. The layout stretches about 6,300 yards and par 71 from the longest tees, 4,710 yards and par 72 from the ladies' tees, and it's like playing two completely different courses. The front nine is reasonably level and sandy, with three long par fives. Fairways are broad and most of them run downhill to the greens. Indian guides are no longer required on the back nine, but you may feel the urge to yodel from time to time. The 12th hole, aptly named "Sky

Hi," is internationally known for its 200-foot drop from tee to green, making the 195-yard length look like a greenside chip shot. Play it long—there's nothing between the tee and the green but deep wilderness and the occasional cloud. There are very few sidehill lies on the back nine; most of the fairways look like canyons. Gatlinburg is a lot of fun to play if you really enjoy variety. Approaching 50 years old, the course lets its natural growth provide most of the challenge and scenery. Carts are required on this course, and you'll appreciate that fact after a round. Regular greens fees are $47 Sunday through Thursday and $57 on Friday and Saturday. Twilight fees of $38 and $48, respectively, start at 2:00 P.M. A hundred memberships are available at $750 a year, but don't reach for your checkbook just yet. The waiting list for memberships is just slightly shorter than the one for annual tickets to the Masters tournament.

Bent Creek Golf Village
3919 East Parkway, Gatlinburg
(865) 436-3947, (800) 251-9336
www.bentcreekgolfvillage.com

The farthest course from the Smokies Corridor, Bent Creek lies along the foot of Webb's Mountain about 10 miles east of Gatlinburg on U.S. Highway 321. A word of warning: Bent Creek is situated on a large resort property named Sunterra Resort. Don't be confused by the presence of signs bearing both names as you approach the course.

The course is a Gary Player design, running from a fairly flat front nine to a couple of mountain goat specials on the back. At 6,200 yards from the championship tees to 5,100 for the ladies', the course is medium length par 73, with generous fairways and forgiving rough. Most of the greens are moderately sloped with practically no bunkers in front. There's a lot of water on the course, but it only comes into serious play on a couple of holes. Bent Creek is a very playable course for the intermediate golfer. For the fanatic who's only coming here to play golf, the resort has several combination golf/lodging packages available. Regular greens fees are $52 Sunday through Thursday and $57 on Friday and Saturday. Twilight fees are $30 and $34, respectively, starting at 3:00 P.M. Carts are required. Bent Creek's easy accessibility and long-term reputation make it a local favorite, and tee times are at a premium during the season.

The national move to spikeless golf shoes has finally made its way to the Smokies. Most of the courses in the area "strongly recommend" spikeless shoes—Gatlinburg Golf Club and River Islands require them. Don't be surprised if you're turned away for spiked shoes, especially when the greens have been dried by the summer sun.

WEDDINGS 🔘

How serious is the wedding business in the Smokies? More than 21,000 couples tie the knot here each year—exponentially more than the entire population of Sevier County. As a possible spin-off of the area's reputation as a premier honeymoon and romantic getaway destination, the Smokies have become a favorite spot for both weddings and marriage renewals.

Not too many years ago, you could count the number of wedding chapels in the county on one hand; these days you need both hands—about four times. As the scenic backdrop of the Great Smoky Mountains became a natural honeymoon destination, the wedding chapel industry slowly took root. Some say that the chapels were meeting an already existing need. Others contend that the Smokies became the "Wedding Capital of the South" because of the proliferation of chapels. In actuality, there's probably a little bit of truth to both schools of thought.

The Preliminaries

Tennessee's fairly liberal marriage laws probably have a lot to do with the wedding boom. There's no blood test required, no waiting period, and a duly-empowered official is as near as the telephone.

First, you don't even have to be a Tennessee resident to get a license here, and if you're a Tennessean from outside Sevier County, chapels will honor a license you purchased in your home county, provided your ceremony takes place within 30 days of its issue.

If you can provide proof of age with a valid ID, you can get a marriage license at age 18 without parental consent, or at 16 with on-site parental consent. (That means all parents involved—if there's a single parent, the other parent's absence must be documented by death certificate, custody agreement, etc., and be presented with the license application.) In extreme circumstances, a court order can be requested for people as young as 14, with the same parental stipulations.

As for marriage license fees, that's where Tennessee has made it a little harder to say "I do" these days. In an effort to lower the state's high divorce rate, the laws were changed to encourage couples to take advantage of premarital counseling. The upshot is if you are a Tennessee resident, you'll pay $38.50 (cash only, please) for a license in Sevier County, provided you and yours receive four hours of premarital counseling from an approved institution (church, family therapist, etc.). Otherwise, you'll pay $98.50 for the privilege of rushing blindly into matrimony. So far, the majority of couples seem to be skipping the advice and paying more money for the sake of convenience. If you're from out of state, however, don't worry. None of this applies to you. You'll simply pay the $38.50.

You can get your marriage license from the Sevier County Court Clerk. The main office is at the courthouse in Sevierville, (865) 453-5502. Office hours are Monday through Thursday, 8:00 A.M. to 4:30 P.M. and Friday from 8:00 A.M. to 6:00 P.M. There are two branch offices as well. In Gatlinburg, go to the Shilling Center office building, about 2 blocks off the Parkway on Reagan Drive. The phone number is (865) 430-3404, and office hours are Monday and Friday from 8:00 A.M. to 4:00 P.M., Wednesday from 8:30 A.M. to noon and Saturday from 9:00 A.M. to 3:00 P.M. In Pigeon Forge, visit City Hall on Pine Mountain Road, (865) 908-6613. This branch is open Saturday only from 9:00 A.M. to 5:00 P.M.

Goin' to the Chapel

The option of a chapel wedding can be attractive to prospective married couples for a number of reasons. For one, they are often less expensive than large church weddings, and they can be planned more easily in a shorter period of time. Wedding chapels can offer unique alternatives to the traditional wedding, including multidenominational services and out-of-the-ordinary locations. One of the most appealing aspects of the chapel wedding is the fact that all of the elements of the event can be coordinated centrally in a cooperative effort between the couple and the chapel's staff.

Admittedly, when one hears the term "wedding chapel," images of the cheesy glitz of Las Vegas may come to mind. We definitely don't want to leave you with the impression that any of our chapels are the quickie-marriage type of operation where you'll be hitched in less than 10 minutes by an Elvis clone who hands out casino chips as a gift. Yes, you can get married in a relatively short period of time, but the chapels we've included are established, reputable businesses with tasteful, attractive facilities.

And you won't have to worry about someday finding out that your marriage wasn't legal. Each of the chapels we've listed (and most likely many of those we haven't) use ordained ministers to perform the ceremonies, most of whom have backgrounds in various Protestant denominations. Although all chapels offer nondenominational, Protestant-based ceremonies, there are those (which we'll mention) that are also able to provide marriage rites in other religious faiths. Just to be on the safe side, however, always ask about your minister's credentials, no matter where you choose to wed.

What to Expect from a Chapel

The chapels we've chosen will present you with a fairly wide range in terms of price and available services. Just about every chapel offers its own preset wedding packages, and you'll also find those that are willing to work with you to put together the kinds of services and amenities that you'd like.

What you get boils down to how much you're willing to spend. You can get a basic, straightforward ceremony for as little as $60 in some places. On the other hand, you can still spend thousands of dollars, just like you would in a larger church wedding. In between the extremes is where you have to decide what you want out of your wedding—a simple exchange of vows in a chapel or a more elaborate ceremony in a unique setting like a gazebo, waterfall, or scenic garden. Some chapels can even arrange for you to be married on horseback or in a helicopter!

The chapels we've profiled provide most of the traditional tokens that are associated with wedding ceremonies themselves. Depending on the specific package, your wedding can include music (live or recorded), flowers, a garter, a cake, candles, mints and nuts, a wedding album, and more. All of the wedding providers with whom we spoke can either directly supply or make arrangements with other businesses for related services like photography, videography, limo transportation, and honeymoon lodgings, as well as receptions and catering. In some

If you're planning a chapel wedding in the Smokies, consider making your wedding arrangements before making your honeymoon lodging reservations. You may get a better accommodations deal as part of your wedding package than if it had been purchased separately.

instances, a chapel might offer wedding packages that include honeymoon vacation activities like horseback riding, snow skiing, white-water rafting, or music theater shows.

For payment, you'll find that most major credit cards and cash are accepted. If you are reserving a chapel for a specific date, you will likely have to post a deposit of some sort; the deposit may vary depending on the total price of the wedding and the length of time between reservation and wedding. In most cases, deposits can be paid with either credit card or cash.

Most chapels will take walk-ins, but whether you will be accommodated depends on if the chapel has already been booked and if a minister is available. If you drop by on a Saturday in summer or in February (Valentine's Day fever!), you're not likely to have much success. You'll probably have better luck with a walk-in wedding on a weekday morning in the off-season. Your safest option: Call ahead of time and schedule your wedding.

Finally, bear in mind that the addresses we've included with the chapels below are primarily for the companies' business offices. In some cases, the chapel itself is not located at that address, and you'll need to start your inquiry by either calling or stopping by the business office first.

You can make the assumption that our wedding chapels are open year-round, although some are closed on major holidays.

For this chapter, we've divided our listings by city, then listed the chapels alphabetically within each.

SEVIERVILLE

A Perfect Moment Wedding Chapel
110 Echota Way, Sevierville
(865) 428-6312, (888) 741-5683
www.aperfectmomentweddingchapel .com
Although it's only been joining couples in matrimony since 1997, this chapel offers a variety of wedding packages in a scenic resort setting. Located just off Winfield Dunn Parkway (Tennessee Highway 66) at Echota Resort in Sevierville (see our Vacation Rentals chapter), the chapel itself is a spacious log structure with a "woodsy" interior look. With its cathedral ceilings and stacked-stone fireplace, the room conveys a mountain lodge atmosphere. The chapel accommodates up to 90 people, and reception facilities are available on premises.

A Perfect Moment Wedding Chapel offers several wedding ceremony options. With one of their more popular packages, couples can get married in their Echota Resort cabin. This wedding services provider has a staff of four, in addition to having three ministers on call.

Smoky Mountain Wedding Chapel
158 Court Avenue, Sevierville
(865) 428-4741, (800) 922-2052
www.smokymtnweddingchapels.com
Couples have been saying "I do" at this downtown Sevierville chapel for more than a decade.

Because it's located across from the Sevier County Courthouse, there is short ground to cover between getting your marriage license and walking across the street to the chapel. Reverend Robert Parsons, a retired Methodist minister, conducts the ceremonies in the chapel, which features an altar surrounded by white lattice, colorful flowers, and greenery. The facility accommodates up to 25 people.

Smoky Mountain Wedding Chapel can make arrangements for weddings in other locations. Previous ceremonies have taken place at sites like the Cades Cove area of the national park and the Old Mill in Pigeon Forge. In addition to the Sevierville chapel, Reverend Parsons also has wedding chapels in Pigeon Forge that operate under the same business name.

PIGEON FORGE

Back Home Wedding Chapel
2202 Ridge Road, Pigeon Forge
(865) 428-8074, (800) 269-7799
www.backhomeweddingchapel.com
A variety of unique ceremonial settings is available through this wedding chapel, which has been in operation since 1996. Couples-to-be can choose from packages that range from traditional candlelight ceremonies in the chapel itself to outdoor weddings by a gazebo, bridge, or waterfall. Other packages include horse-and-carriage weddings and even helicopter ceremonies!

The chapel, which is separate from the business office, is located on Chapel Ridge Road in Pigeon Forge. Its cedar structure conveys what the owners call a "rustic elegance." Inside, candelabra, cedar pews, a golden chandelier, and burgundy carpet highlight the interior, which will seat as many as 45. Back Home Wedding Chapel has two ministers available and a regular staff of six to assist you with your options.

Golden Valley Chapel
4152 Dellinger Hollow Road
Pigeon Forge
(865) 436-3700, (800) 408-8577
www.goldenvalleyweddings.com
Since 1996, Golden Valley Chapel has offered new couples a picturesque, country setting in which to say their vows. Located approximately 3 miles from the Parkway in Pigeon Forge, the chapel is an attractive wood structure that overlooks a peaceful mountain lake.

The spacious chapel seats up to 75 guests and offers an eclectic look that includes a prominence of wood with accents of burgundy and green. Candles, flower arrangements, and antiques help adorn the interior. In addition to the chapel, wedding services can also be held at the outdoor gazebo where up to 15 guests can be seated. Other packages include lakeside and honeymoon cabin weddings.

In the Smokies Wedding Chapel
2225 Parkway, Pigeon Forge
(865) 429-1440, (800) 893-7274
www.smokyweddings.com
This wedding business actually runs two chapels, both of which are separate from the Parkway business office. The Smokey Ridge Chapel, located on a panoramic mountaintop, seats up to 40 guests within its cedar walls. The Mountain Mist Chapel seats as many as 80 and also is located in a secluded country setting.

In the Smokies has been conducting weddings since the early 1990s. They have access to five church-ordained ministers and employ a staff of 12 wedding coordinators. They provide a number of different wedding packages, some of which include gazebo weddings, on-site receptions, and honeymoon accommodations through their Mountain Mist Cabin Rentals.

Mountain Valley Wedding Chapel
2256 Parkway, Pigeon Forge
(865) 453-6343, (800) 729-4365
www.mvchapel.com
Their office is right on the Parkway in Pigeon Forge, but the chapel itself is on a scenic hilltop (they call it a mountaintop, but that's a bit of a stretch) just off Wears Valley Road—only a couple of miles off the Parkway.

The chapel's rustic cedar and glass exterior and classically decorated interior make for a charming juxtaposition of styles. The hilltop location offers some pretty decent views and creates a general feeling of seclusion; ceremonial settings include a gazebo and a waterfall. Inside, the tastefully decorated, candlelit chapel can handle up to 100 guests.

Mountain Valley steers away from pre-set wedding packages, opting for custom-tailored ceremonies, dependent on the couple's specific needs. Receptions, photography, and in-house videography are among the services provided.

GATLINBURG

Chalet Mountain Wedding Chapel
890 Holly Branch Drive, Gatlinburg
(865) 430-5568, (888) 686-5683
www.chaletmountain.com
This place is truly in the mountains. On Mount Harrison, near Chalet Village, you'll find this sparkling white Victorian-style chapel, which seats 25 to 30 and was opened in 1997. You'll find a predominance of white on the inside as well, along with wooden pews, burgundy carpeting, and a 6-foot-tall stained-glass angel. Other Chalet Mountain wedding settings include a gazebo and a 25-foot waterfall.

The chapel offers a full slate of wedding package amenities, including fully catered wedding receptions in the on-site banquet facility that accommodates 60 people. The company also has a rental and realty office that offers approximately 60 chalets for honeymoon lodging.

Chapel at the Park
175 Parkway, Gatlinburg
(865) 430-3372, (800) 693-6479
www.chapelatthepark.com
The business office for Chapel at the Park is one of the first you'll encounter coming into Gatlinburg from the north. The chapel itself, as its name implies, partially borders the national park on U.S. Highway 321. Owner and minister Lee Bennett prefers that physical separation between the main office and the chapel because it affords more privacy for the ceremonies themselves. Bennett also schedules no more than one wedding per hour so that back-to-back groups don't overlap.

The chapel is placed in a quiet, wooded setting, surrounded by native dogwoods and seasonal flowers. The building exudes elegance with a mountain theme. Outside, the traditional Appalachian-style exterior features white wood, a green tin roof, bell tower, and lots of windows. Inside, 50 guests can be seated in a plush room that boasts a large chandelier and candlelit pews.

Other amenities include separate dressing rooms for bride and groom and a state-of-the-art, three-camera video taping and editing system. In addition to the chapel, ceremonies can be performed in front of the outdoor gazebo or waterfall.

Chapel in the Glen
412 Glades Road, Gatlinburg
(865) 436-5356, (800) 537-1505
www.chapelwedding.com
A beautiful hilltop in the Great Smoky Arts & Crafts Community is the setting for this wedding chapel, in operation since 1995. The white pine chapel (complete with bell tower) and award-winning landscaping welcome couples into an interior decor replete with "woodsiness." A teal runner down the main aisle leads toward the altar, which is highlighted by a stacked-stone wall and candelabra. The chapel seats 40 comfortably.

There are outdoor ceremonial settings as well, including a gazebo, a reflecting pond, and a waterfall. Chapel in the Glen provides a full-time staff of six to help couples with wedding preparations. They do perform walk-in ceremonies but caution that they will not join couples who have just met and are looking for a speedy wedding.

Cupid's Chapel of Love
706 East Parkway, Gatlinburg
(865) 430-3851, (800) 642-8743
www.cupidschapeloflove.com

We're just going to throw this one out there so you'll know. The Hard Rock Cafe in Gatlinburg is the only member of that national chain that has a wedding chapel on the premises.

Owner Rose Fisher opened her chapel in 1995, and in the years since has built up her business to the point that at times, she has bookings as far as two years ahead. That doesn't mean she's booked solid for the next two years, but it does mean that her available spots for walk-ins are few and far between.

The quaint chapel is built of white-washed, hand-hewn logs. Inside, the pew cushions and carpeting are shades of burgundy, and the walls are lined with colorful stained-glass windows. Seating is available for up to 65 guests. Near the altar is a trellis with a climbing vine and magnolias. Outdoor settings include a bridge over a stone waterfall and a gazebo.

Cupid's Chapel has several wedding packages available, including the '50s Nostalgia package complete with oldies music. They can also arrange weddings on horseback for outdoor types. Some packages include lodging at Cupid's Love Nest, their own honeymoon accommodations.

The chapel uses 4 ministers and a regular staff of 16, most of whom have been with Fisher since day one. In addition to traditional, nondenominational ceremonies, Cupid's can also make arrangements to perform weddings of other religious faiths. They are open 365 days a year.

Gatlinburg's Little Log Wedding Chapel
1350 East Parkway, Gatlinburg
(865) 436-8979, (800) 554-1451
www.tennweb.com/logchapel
This chapel is located near the entrance to the Great Smoky Arts & Crafts Community on US 321. As the name states, the building itself is of log construction and offers a combined decor of rustic log and refined elements like stained-glass windows, flowers, and candelabra. It seats 30 people. Outside the chapel, a gazebo that's used for ceremonies can seat four to six guests.

Little Log Wedding Chapel has been in business since 1992. Their staff of ministers and coordinators will provide wedding services seven days a week.

Victorian Gardens Wedding Chapel
571 East Parkway, Gatlinburg
(865) 430-8667, (800) 597-1371
www.victorianweddingchapel.com
As you're driving away from downtown Gatlinburg on East Parkway (US 321), you can't help but notice this grand, Victorian-style chapel—with a seating capacity of 80, it's one of the largest ones in the area. The interior's colors are white with burgundies and mauves as accents. Two-story stained-glass windows and large chandeliers add to the elegance found inside.

Although most of their ceremonies are nondenominational ones performed by an ordained Southern Baptist minister, Victorian Gardens has arranged for non-Christian weddings in the past. Since 1997, they have offered a broad range of options in their wedding packages and have featured on-site receptions in their solarium. Victorian Gardens maintains a staff of 8 to 10 people to assist couples-to-be.

If you are a Tennessee resident and planning on purchasing a marriage license in Sevier County, remember that it will set you back $98.50 unless you can manage to squeeze in four hours of premarital counseling before tying the knot. The Sevier County Court Clerk's office, (865) 453-5502, can even steer you in the direction of a qualified counselor if you're interested.

THE ARTS 🖼

There's just something about a snowcapped mountain peak, a misty waterfall, or a still country meadow that can't help but inspire artistic expression. Whether that inspiration ultimately translates into a painting of wispy watercolor, a multitextured wood carving, or a classic mountain tale, there's no denying that the Smoky Mountains have long been fertile ground for those who transform thoughts and feelings into what we loosely call "art."

If you ask those who live around here to name specific examples of "art," you're likely to get different answers. Some will quickly point to the hand-produced wares of mountain craftspeople. Others might name their favorite music theater show. Others still might cite the work of their favorite local painter. Of course, all would be correct. However, in discussing the artistic and cultural landscape of the Smokies, we've divided this vast territory into two general camps. We've labeled one category as art that caters largely to the tourist and vacation markets. This includes the wide world of Smoky Mountain arts and crafts studios, including individual painters and their galleries. You'll find an in-depth discussion of these types of creative art in our Mountain Crafts chapter.

Similarly, we are also lumping the many music theaters of the Smokies under a more commercial umbrella. These shows feature talented musicians, singers, comedians, and dancers who hail from all across the country (not to mention our own backyard). Refer to our Music Theaters and Nightlife chapter for a more detailed look at Sevier County's community of performance venues.

In this chapter, however, we'll be looking at a different brand of the creative and performing arts—the less financially motivated offerings that, for the most part, promote participation as much as they do patronage. Several of our inclusions are nonprofit organizations with volunteer members who simply enjoy "art for art's sake." But in these cases, being "amateur" from a financial standpoint doesn't necessarily translate to "amateurish" work. On the contrary, Sevier County boasts theater and choral groups whose work rivals that of some of their professional counterparts.

The bad news is that because Sevier County has long been a haven for professional craftsmen and performers (who generate revenue), the other types of arts haven't always enjoyed that same favored status within local communities. The good news is that as resident populations have increased in recent years, the demand has likewise grown for accessible creative outlets. Hopefully, as interest in the arts flourishes at the grassroots level, support, recognition, and respect will follow in kind from the local governments and the citizens in general.

The best news of all is that for a county with a relatively small permanent population, there is no shortage of means by which one can leap headlong into artistic endeavors. So let that serve as a cattle call of sorts for all you actors, painters, writers, dancers, singers, musicians, and craftspeople. And if you're the nonparticipatory type who simply wants to sit back and enjoy the fruits of someone else's artistic labors—we're here to tell you that the fruit is ripe for the picking.

East Tennessee Writers Guild
P.O. Box 504, Kodak 37764
(865) 436-2078
Devoted to the enjoyment and promotion of the art of writing, this group meets monthly to read and critique the works of its members. Both fiction and nonfiction

writing are explored. The writers also hold workshops that explore various aspects of the writing and publishing industries, covering such topics as how to obtain copyrights and watching out for unscrupulous publishers. The guild is open to anyone interested in improving their knowledge of writing and getting published; annual dues of $26 are required of regular members. East Tennessee Writers Guild meets the third Thursday of each month from 6:30 to 8:30 P.M. at the Sevierville Community Center on Gary Wade Boulevard.

Elizabeth Williams School of Dance
126 Kilby Street, Sevierville
(865) 453-9702

Since 1985, this dance academy has taught classical ballet, pointe, jazz dancing, and tumbling to aspiring dancers ages three to adult. Instruction is available for dancers at all levels of experience. Although the length of any student's overall participation is open-ended, the school's regular sessions run concurrent with the school year. Summer sessions and a summer dance camp are available to students as well. Each spring, Williams' school presents its annual recital, where all students get the chance to show off their steps. The school also holds annual tryouts for five different performing companies that participate in numerous local, regional, and national events throughout the year. In past years, students have appeared in venues at Disney World and Six Flags over Georgia.

Gatlinburg Community Chorale
P.O. Box 5, Gatlinburg 37738
(865) 436-4990

Offered as a nonathletic activity by the Gatlinburg Department of Recreation, this choral group is open to anyone age 16 or older. Founded in 1981, the Gatlinburg Community Chorale averages about 50 members throughout the year, and except for the director and the accompanist, all members are volunteers and no auditions or interviews are required to join.

Many of the area's nonprofit guilds and associations publish periodic newsletters that keep members and other interested parties up-to-date on group activities. Most will be happy to put you on their mailing lists.

Each year, the chorale puts on two major shows (three performances each) at the Gatlinburg Convention Center. The spring concert, which is usually presented in early June, is a showcase of diverse musical styles, including show tunes and patriotic songs. The Living Tree, which is staged each December, is a presentation of religious and secular music that celebrates the holiday season.

The "Living" moniker comes from the fact that the chorale's members are actually arranged on stage in the form of a vertical Christmas tree, complete with garlands and bows. No admission is charged for either of the annual concerts, and the City of Gatlinburg provides free parking for attendees.

Knoxville Museum of Art
1050 World's Fair Park Drive, Knoxville
(865) 525-6101
www.knoxart.org

Located in downtown Knoxville overlooking World's Fair Park, this art museum has in recent years featured exhibits by such noted artists as Rodin, Ansel Adams, Red Grooms, Andy Warhol, and M. C. Escher. Other exhibits throughout the year explore all types of art media, including painting, sculpture, and photography. Even the artworks of ancient civilizations have made their way into KMA's galleries. Although it's located well outside the bounds of our familiar Smokies Corridor, we felt it's good enough to be included in this chapter. The Knoxville Museum of Art is explored in more detail in the Knoxville section of the Day Trips chapter. If you happen to make a Knoxville excursion part of your East Tennessee experience, this museum's worth a look-see.

Pigeon Forge Community Chorus
P.O. Box 1390, Pigeon Forge 37868
(865) 453-8574

This chorus has been an entity of the City of Pigeon Forge since its formation in the early 1990s. Its steady average membership of 50 encompasses vocalists of all ages and backgrounds. The group has no requirements for membership other than a desire to sing and to have a good time. That philosophy is revealed in the chorus's motto, "We don't sing because we're happy—we're happy because we sing." Pigeon Forge Community Chorus puts together two annual presentations, an outdoor Fourth of July show at Patriot Park and an indoor Winterfest program held at the Smoky Mountain Jubilee music theater (see our Festivals and Annual Events chapter). The musical styles performed attempt to appeal to a wide audience and include patriotic tunes, music from the '50s and '60s, show tunes, and Christmas music.

Sandra J. Blaine Galleries
556 Parkway, Gatlinburg
(865) 436-5860

This 1,800-square-foot facility is located on the second floor of the main educational building of Arrowmont School of Arts and Crafts (see our Mountain Crafts chapter). Since its construction in 1970, the galleries have regularly featured works of fine art in all imaginable media; on the average, exhibits are displayed for six to eight weeks at a time.

Throughout the year, the galleries provide numerous opportunities for amateur and professional artists alike to show their work. During its annual faculty invitationals, Arrowmont's resident instructors are able to display their creations, while smaller sections of the facility are devoted to the finished work of students. The school also hosts a number of juried shows throughout the year that spotlight the talents of locally, regionally, and nationally known artists. Several times each year, Arrowmont sponsors conferences devoted to a particular artistic medium. During these conferences, the main gallery's exhibition space becomes a showplace for works done in that medium.

Sandra J. Blaine Galleries are open Monday through Saturday from 8:00 A.M. to 4:30 P.M. Tours are self-guided. Admission to the gallery is free; many of the pieces you'll see on display, however, are for sale.

Sevier County Choral Society
P.O. Box 4189, Sevierville 37864-4189
(865) 429-0252

This group was founded in 1998 for the purpose of advancing the appreciation of choral music in Sevier County and East Tennessee. According to its mission statement, the society's focus is "presenting musical masterworks in an excellent, enjoyable, and enthusiastic manner for the purpose of enhancing musical expertise in both performing and listening." The Sevier County Choral Society is an independent, secular, not-for-profit organization open to anyone who loves music and is willing to seriously commit to group projects.

Through the work of composers like Bach, Mozart, Schubert, and Handel, the group brings the classical genre of music to audiences via two recital events—one in spring and the other, a Christmas show, in December. The society also stages two performances of Handel's *Messiah* each Christmas. The public is invited to participate in the *Messiah* singings, which are backed up by an orchestra. Concerts take place at a variety of venues throughout the county, including the Sevierville Civic Center and larger area churches. You can learn about specific performance dates by contacting the society.

Sevier County Heritage Museum
167 East Bruce Street, Sevierville
(865) 453-4058

A free self-guided tour of this museum brings the history of Sevier County to life with exhibits that date from ancient Indian civilizations to the 20th century. Housed in the building that once served as Sevierville's post office, the museum showcases artifacts like Indian pottery and tools, relics from the homesteads of early pioneer settlers, like butter churns, spinning wheels, farm implements, and guns. In addition to the actual physical evidence of the past, the museum makes good use out of newspapers and photographs to chronicle the accounts of the people, places, and events that shaped local history.

Although admission to Sevier County Heritage Museum is free, donations are welcome. Its hours of operation are Monday, Tuesday, Thursday, and Friday from noon to 5:00 P.M. and Saturday from noon to 3:00 P.M. You can park free anywhere along Bruce Street in historic downtown Sevierville. See the Attractions chapter for more specific information about what the museum has in store for its visitors.

Sevier County Theatre Guild
P.O. Box 5461, Sevierville 37864
(865) 428-9067

Although this not-for-profit community theater group has been in existence for decades, it's only been in the past five years or so that the guild has sustained a steady level of participation and presented shows on a regular basis. Recent productions include diverse works such as The Crucible, The Odd Couple, Godspell, Bus Stop, Twelve Angry Men, Hedda Gabler, and The Wizard of Oz.

The only factor that's been a hindrance to the guild has been its lack of a permanent home. Leading a nomadic existence reminiscent of theater's infancy, SCTG has migrated from venue to venue. Currently, the group stages most of its productions at the Sevierville Civic Center.

Their season consists of four productions, one of which is a variety night showcasing the individual talents of the members.

SCTG is a member of the Knoxville Area Theatre Coalition, a regional theater association that has recognized the guild with several awards at its past annual awards ceremonies. Accolades have

included top honors in the acting, costuming, and sound categories. Sevier County Theatre Guild also stages its own awards banquet each winter, recognizing the previous season's efforts.

Smoky Mountains Storytellers Association
P.O. Box 23054, Knoxville 37933
(865) 428-6701
www.smokymountaintellers.org

Storytelling in the Smoky Mountains is a big deal, and you'll find plenty of people who not only consider it a passion but are able to supplement their income with it as well. Whether it's a humorous story, a mountain fable passed down through generations, or one of many "Jack Tales" (Jack, of beanstalk fame), storytelling in these parts is pretty much an art form in itself and helps to preserve and perpetuate the culture of the Smokies.

The Smoky Mountains Storytellers Association evolved from a group of people who had periodically gathered to tell stories in the Cades Cove area of the national park, beginning in the late 1980s. Realizing that they could function better as an organized collective, they became a chartered, not-for-profit group in 1994. Since then, they have maintained a steady membership of about 30 people, most of whom are storytellers. Some members function primarily as listeners (otherwise, why tell a story?), and some are involved in the more promotional and administrative aspects of the organization.

Each year, the group participates in a number of local and regional storytelling events and festivals, including Tellabration and the Smoky Mountain Storytelling Festival in Pigeon Forge. Smoky Mountains Storytellers Association meets the third Sunday of each month at the Graystone Presbyterian Church in Knoxville. Meetings start with a two-hour "story swap" at 2:00 P.M. and are followed by a half-hour business meeting. The group requires annual membership dues of $15.

CHEROKEE, NORTH CAROLINA

A journey from the Tennessee side of the Smokies to North Carolina's side is a little like traveling to a parallel dimension. Both places are similar but, at the same time, a little different in important ways. Both are growing tourist centers that border opposite sides of Great Smoky Mountains National Park. However, the character of each destination is distinct from that of its counterpart. The area we've described in this chapter, the Cherokee Indian Reservation, has its fair share of shopping, attractions, and entertainment opportunities, but most of them are very much flavored by the character and the culture of the people who inhabit the region. There's a lot to do, see, and learn while you're in Cherokee. In fact, there's much more than you could possibly take on in one day.

The 56,000-acre Cherokee Indian Reservation, known by the people who live there as the Qualla Boundary, borders Great Smoky Mountains National Park on the south and also includes the southern terminus of the Blue Ridge Parkway. At one time the Cherokee culture was prevalent throughout the Carolinas. Its influence can still be seen today in the names of many towns and other geographic features in this area (Nantahala National Forest, Tuckasegee River) as well as in the foods that are staples in western North Carolina. The 11,000 members of the Eastern Band of Cherokee (as opposed to the Western Band, similarly relegated to Oklahoma) have done their part to keep the culture alive. For much more on the history and background of the Cherokee, we encourage you to pick up a copy of the *Insiders' Guide to North Carolina's Mountains.*

Like Sevierville, Pigeon Forge, and Gatlinburg, Cherokee's tourism season generally runs from May through October. From November through April, some area businesses are closed, although lately many are finding it easier to stay open all year as larger numbers of tourists discover everything Cherokee has to offer. When planning a visit to Cherokee during the off-season, be sure to check ahead of time to make sure that your intended lodgings, attractions, restaurants, and other places to visit will be open when you're there. We've included seasonal schedules for many of the attractions outlined below.

Speaking of lodging, the Cherokee Indian Reservation contains some 50 motels, nearly 200 rental cabins, and approximately 25 campgrounds from which to choose, many of which are easily accessible from the heart of the reservation. Other locations offer scenic riverside and mountainside settings. Most of the hotels and motels are independent mom-and-pop establishments, but there are several nationally known franchises to be found.

Understandably, craft and gift shops abound on the reservation, dealing in everything from tourist souvenirs to art, jewelry, and clothing. If you're interested in narrowing your search for shopping finds to authentic products made by Native American craftsmen, you might want to start with this list endorsed by the reservation (look for more information on some of these below): Bear Meat's Indian Den, Bigmeat Pottery & Museum, Cherokee Heritage Museum & Gallery, Eagle's Nest Gift Shop, Happy Hunting Ground Crafts, Medicine Man Crafts, Museum of the Cherokee Indian, Native American Craft Shop, Qualla Arts and Crafts, Talking Leaves Bookstore, Trail of Tears Gallery, and Traditional Hands Gallery.

GETTING THERE

The simplest way (although not always the quickest) to get to Cherokee from Sevier County is to take U.S. Highway 441 from Gatlinburg into the national park and simply follow it all the way into Cherokee. As the crow flies, it's about 35 miles from Gatlinburg, but the road is curvy and often steep. Especially during peak-season periods, traffic consists of large numbers of sightseers, so you'll be lucky to ever do more than 40 miles per hour. Count on a good one-hour drive from Gatlinburg. During the winter, US 441 is sometimes closed because of snow, ice, or landslides. Always be sure to contact the national park's information line if you're in doubt about road conditions.

The drive along US 441 is worth it, however. You'll see vast, towering mountainsides and deep valleys that stretch toward the horizon. In October, when the leaves are changing, the foliage becomes a patchwork quilt of fiery color blanketing the landscape. Along the way, there are a good number of pull-offs and parking areas where you can stop and relax while you take in the views or put your camera to work. See our national park chapter for more information about what you'll encounter along the way.

Once you get to Cherokee, you'll find that things are laid out pretty simply. US 441 merges with U.S. Highway 19 (which runs perpendicular to US 441), forming a T. Most of what you'll be interested in lies on or just off these two roads within a radius of only a few miles. There are a lot of signs, and with the aid of a map, you shouldn't have much trouble finding what you're looking for.

CHEROKEE ATTRACTIONS

An exploration of the Cherokee Indian Reservation reveals a wealth of Native American cultural activities that are both educational and entertaining. We've outlined a few.

Oconaluftee Indian Village
Drama Road, off US 441
Cherokee, NC
(828) 497-2315
www.oconalufteevillage.com
Oconaluftee Indian Village is a re-creation of a Cherokee village of around the mid- to late 1700s. Cherokee guides lead visitors on tours depicting history through craft exhibits, replicas of early homes, and a seven-sided Council House as well as demonstrations of beadwork, canoe and pottery making, blow guns, and more. The presentation is done in a forested outdoor setting and gives visitors an authentic glimpse into traditional Cherokee ways of life.

While you're there, you'll also see indigenous plant life in the Cherokee Botanical Garden located along the village's nature trail. The Oconaluftee Indian Village is open 9:00 A.M. to 5:30 p.m. from mid-May through late October. Prices are $13.00 for adults and $6.00 for ages 6 through 13; group rates are available.

The Museum of the Cherokee Indian
US 441 at Drama Road
Cherokee, NC
(828) 497-3481
www.cherokeemuseum.org
The Museum of the Cherokee Indian underwent a $3.5 million renovation several years ago and now utilizes state-of-the-art technology to tell the story of the tribe's history. The museum is an interactive attraction in which visitors are able to

If you're traveling to Cherokee mainly to visit Harrah's Casino, consider taking a shuttle. Rocky Top Tours, (865) 429-8687, runs buses that depart from Pigeon Forge and Gatlinburg Tuesday and Thursday mornings and Sunday afternoons, pulling up to the casino about an hour and a half after departure. The cost is $20 per person and entitles each rider to $20 worth of tokens from the casino on arrival.

learn about the Cherokee past by walking through "time zones" representing specific periods and events, from prehistory through modern times, including the infamous Trail of Tears. Along the way, computer-generated images, lasers, lights, and sound effects enhance the rituals and history that have long been kept alive by Cherokee "myth keepers." There's also a terrific gift shop. The museum opens daily at 9:00 A.M. year-round except for Thanksgiving Day, Christmas Day, and New Year's Day. Admission is $8.00 for adults and $5.00 for children ages 6 through 12; group rates are available as are AAA and AARP discounts.

Unto These Hills Outdoor Drama
Drama Road and US 441
Cherokee, NC
(828) 497-2111
www.untothesehills.com

You can absorb more Cherokee history at this acclaimed outdoor drama, *Unto These Hills.* The show is presented evenings at Mountainside Theatre, a 2,800-seat outdoor amphitheater. The show was created in 1950 and has since been viewed by more than six million people. The story begins with the arrival of Hernando de Soto and closes with the Cherokee migration along the Trail of Tears. The cast and technical crew of more than 130 people, many of whom are descendants of the characters depicted, bring the Cherokee story to life through drama, traditional dances, costumes, and a strong musical score. *Unto These Hills* is performed nightly (except Sunday) between mid-June and late August. Reserved tickets are $18.00 for all ages, and general admissions are $16.00 for ages 14 and older and $8.00 for ages 6 through 13.

Cherokee Heritage Museum and Gallery
Saunooke Village, US 441
Cherokee, NC
(828) 497-3211

In addition to showing a new exhibit each month, this museum is a great place to shop for authentic Cherokee items like masks and crystals. There's also a selection of educational taped tours, books, and craft demonstrations. The museum is open year-round, and admission is $2.50 for ages 11 and older, $1.50 for ages 6 through 10, and free for ages 5 and younger.

Qualla Arts and Crafts Mutual
US 441 and Drama Road
Cherokee, NC
(828) 497-3103

This craft cooperative displays the works of some 350 Cherokee artisans, in addition to offering crafts from other American Indian craftspeople from across the country. The store has a fine selection of historical baskets, masks, pottery, fingerweaving, and wood carving. It's open year-round at 8:00 A.M. daily although closing times vary throughout the year. There is no admission charge.

OTHER ATTRACTIONS

Harrah's Cherokee Casino and Hotel
777 Casino Drive, Cherokee, NC
(828) 497-7777, (800) HARRAHS
www.harrahs.com

This legal gambling establishment, operated by the Eastern Band of Cherokee Indians, did for Cherokee what Dollywood did for Tennessee's Smokies—that is, helped it start the transition from a seasonal destination to a year-round one. Since 1997, Harrah's has provided gaming action and live entertainment 24 hours a day, seven days a week. It's very much like what you'd find in Las Vegas or Atlantic City, with a few exceptions that we'll address shortly.

If you arrive at Harrah's in your car, you can either park free in one of the many parking areas or pull up to the main building and have your car valet parked for $6.00. If you park in the lots, you can either walk to the casino or take Harrah's free shuttle to the front doors. As of 2002, the casino also has on-site accommodations for its guests in the form of a new luxury hotel. The 15-story facility features two restaurants, a conference center, gift shop, indoor swimming pool, fitness room, and much more. The 252-room hotel is enhanced with Native American crafts and artwork on each floor.

A few rules before entering the casino: You must be 21 or older to set foot inside, and although alcohol is not permitted on the premises, smoking is. Videotaping is not allowed, but flash photography is welcome.

Inside, you'll find more than 2,700 video gaming machines spread out over nearly 80,000 square feet of casino floor space. Sixty thousand used to be the maximum square footage allowed by law, but a revised compact between the tribe and the state allowed for unlimited expansion of the actual gaming area.

All of the gambling at this Harrah's is done on video machines, although you will find live dealers assisting on the video blackjack games. And you'll still find video versions of all the typical casino games like poker, keno, craps, and Lock 'n' Roll, Harrah's own version of the basic slot machine. The games have minimum costs ranging from 25 cents to $1.00. The maximum house payout on many of the games is unlimited thanks again to changes in state law. In addition to quarters, machines also take small and large denomination bills.

Near the main entrance is the Games Master area, where staff members will help you learn how to play the different games. Although the games are all played on machines, they're very user-friendly once you figure out what you're doing. There are no buttons to push or levers to pull. All actions are conducted by simply touching a finger to the appropriate spot on the video screen. When you're ready to start pumping quarters, you'll find three cashier areas along the perimeter of the main floor. After that, you're on your own. If you need assistance with a particular game, you can call for an attendant by

Once upon a time, Harrah's Cherokee Casino offered extensive on-site child care services. Now things aren't so kid-friendly, considering you have to be 21 just to walk through the doors. And that rule applies even if you're just looking for a bite from one of the restaurants. The only kids' activity now is a video arcade located in its own facility, separate from the casino. You can leave children ages 13 and older unattended, but for younger ones, you're obliged to supervise. Our advice: Leave the kids at home while you're at Harrah's trying to double their college fund.

pushing a button on your machine. You'll also find plenty of servers on the floor distributing free nonalcoholic beverages.

There is more to Harrah's than just gaming, however. Harrah's Cherokee Pavilion is a large auditorium adjacent to the casino that accommodates up to 1,500 people for concert performances, show revues, and even boxing matches. Performers that have appeared on the pavilion stage include B. B. King, Bill Cosby, and Wayne Newton. Tickets to these shows range anywhere from $35 to $100, depending on the performer, and can be purchased at the box office in the casino. During peak season, there are shows nightly at 8:00 P.M., with occasional 2:00 P.M. matinees. Performances are scheduled sporadically during the off-season.

Harrah's Cherokee Casino has five eating establishments on the main premises and two more in the hotel. In the casino itself you'll find the Fresh Market Square, serving lunch and dinner in an all-you-care-to-eat buffet format. For one price, you can choose from a wide selection of international and traditional dishes. The Fresh Market Express offers 24-hour counter service if you're looking for something quick and light—sandwiches, pastries, ice creams, and coffees. For full sit-down dining service, step into the Seven Sisters restaurant, where the menu features steaks, seafood, pasta, desserts, and more.

In the hotel are the Selu Garden Cafe, which serves a well-rounded menu for breakfast, lunch, and dinner, and Club Cappuccino, a great place to go for all kinds of coffee drinks, not to mention pastries, desserts, and fresh fruits. Other amenities found at Harrah's include a kids' arcade, a coat-check facility, a passenger lounge area for those awaiting bus transportation, plenty of restrooms, and the Jackpot Gift Shop.

Tribal Bingo
U.S. Highway 19 Cherokee, NC
(828) 497-4320, (800) 410-1254

At Tribal Bingo, which is also operated by the Eastern Band of Cherokee Indians, you can play one of the South's favorite games of chance for $5,000 as well as progressive jackpots, and all prizes are awarded in cash. The facility accommodates up to 1,000 players and is open Wednesday through Sunday year-round.

Santa's Land Family Fun Park and Zoo
US 19, Cherokee, NC
(828) 497-9191
www.santaslandnc.com

From early May through the end of October, the entire family can have vacation fun with a Christmas theme at Santa's Land Family Fun Park and Zoo. You can ride the Rudi-Coaster or the Ferris wheel, take a train ride, cruise on the paddleboats, or enjoy many other activities. The kids will get a kick out of visiting with Santa and his elves while the adults visit the park's many shops. There are also live shows, restaurants, and the Santa's Land Zoo, where you can pet and feed a variety of domestic and exotic animals. The park is open daily from 9:00 A.M. to 5:00 P.M., and the single admission price of $16.59 (children two and younger get in free) allows visitors access to all activities.

Cherokee Fun Park
US 441, Cherokee, NC
(828) 497-5877
www.cherokeefunpark.com

At Cherokee Fun Park you'll find two miniature golf courses, a go-kart track, a game room, bumper boats, and kiddie rides for the little ones. This attraction is open April through October from 10:00 A.M. to 10:00 P.M., with more limited daily hours during the off-season months. Prices vary according to the ride.

Oconaluftee Islands Park

Naturally, being in such a beautiful, mountainous setting, you'll also find yourself face to face with a host of outdoor activities that allow you to capture the essence of any Smoky Mountain experience.

Oconaluftee Islands Park is a recreational facility located on a patch of acreage in the middle of the Oconaluftee River. Wheelchair accessible by footbridge, the park has picnic tables, grills, a covered pavilion, and a walking trail. Along the trail, you'll encounter nine different audio stations that are part of the park's Talking Trees project. At the stations, visitors learn about the use of the different trees present at the site as well as their value to the Cherokee culture. There is no charge for use of park facilities.

Oconaluftee River Trail
US 441 at national park entrance
Cherokee, NC

Oconaluftee River Trail is a 1-mile trail (one-way) that runs from the national park entrance sign on US 441 to the Oconaluftee Park visitor center. The trail is flat and well maintained and takes visitors on a peaceful trek through a wooded setting accented by the sounds of the Oconaluftee River.

If you'd like to take a more active role in Cherokee's great outdoors, there are many other activities for the partaking, including mountain biking, tubing, white-water rafting, trout fishing, and horseback riding.

DAY TRIPS 🚗

Frankly, it's hard for us to imagine anyone finding themselves at a loss for something to do in the Smokies. There are enough activities here to fill up weeks and weeks of hard-earned vacation time. However, if you're still itching to get out and explore the surrounding region during your stay, we aim to oblige.

Remember that the Smoky Mountains are centrally located within a one-day drive of two-thirds of the country's population. When it comes to searching for a brief excursion away from the mountains, that same centrality works in your favor. A host of great day trips lies within only an hour's drive or so from the Smokies, and these short hops are the ones we've included.

Because Knoxville is only a half-hour's drive from Sevier County, we've given it more extensive coverage than our other selections. Beyond that, get ready for road trips to Asheville, North Carolina, and maybe some places you might not have even heard of. We'll show you attractions, shopping, and a lot of rich Southern history. When you're done, just don't forget that our Smoky Mountains are waiting for your return.

KNOXVILLE

Getting to Knoxville from the Smokies is a simple proposition. You have two choices, both of which require starting near downtown Sevierville, where U.S. Highway 441, U.S. Highway 411, and Tennessee Highway 66 all converge. From there, one option is to head north on TN 66 until you get to Interstate 40. Then follow I-40 west for about 20 miles, at which point you start encountering Knoxville exits.

The other choice is shorter as the crow flies, but because of numerous stoplights near Knoxville, the driving time is roughly the same as if you take the interstate.

That route involves heading west from Sevierville on Main Street (aka US 411, aka Chapman Highway). Follow this road all the way through Seymour and you'll find yourself angling north toward the southern fringes of Knox County. Eventually, the road takes you into the heart of downtown Knoxville itself.

And since we're downtown already, why not start our Knoxville day trip here?

World's Fair Park and Surrounding Areas

Sometimes, a physical structure becomes so closely associated with a city that it becomes an icon of sorts. New York City has the Statue of Liberty, St. Louis has its Gateway Arch, and Knoxville has the Sunsphere. You've surely seen pictures of it. It looks like a giant, reflective copper-colored golf ball perched high atop a steel girdered "tee."

Once the proud centerpiece of the 1982 World's Fair, the 266-foot Sunsphere now stands unused in an area that is still officially called World's Fair Park. The space inside the golden orb has been used for everything from meeting rooms to a restaurant, but nothing ever really caught on with the public.

Regardless, visit the World's Fair Park neighborhood, wedged between Henley Street and Cumberland Avenue on the west side of downtown. The Sunsphere is still an impressive object to view, and there are plenty of places to shop as well as things to do and see in the surrounding area, much of the latter at little to no cost.

A good place to start is the historic Candy Factory building on World's Fair Park Drive. It was constructed in 1919 by Littlefield and Steere Candy Company, a confectioner whose candies were prominent in the South during the early decades of the 20th century. The building was renovated for the World's Fair and today is the operational site of the South's Finest Chocolate Factory, (865) 522-2049, one of the only full-line chocolatiers in Tennessee. In fact, members of the families who owned Littlefield and Steere help manage the existing chocolate factory. In case you're wondering—yes, there's a candy shop full of goodies on-site.

The other floors of the Candy Factory building are occupied by art galleries, gift shops, and craft centers. The Arts Council of Greater Knoxville, (865) 523-7543, has its offices there, and the Knoxville Museum of Art, (865) 525-6101, operates a gift gallery on the main floor. Also on the main floor is an information center that provides a wealth of free literature on Knoxville area hotels, restaurants, and attractions.

Speaking of the Knoxville Museum of Art, the gallery facility itself is located next door to the Candy Factory building on World's Fair Park Drive. Constructed in 1990, KMA houses multiple galleries that have held a diverse range of traveling exhibits over the years. Featured have been works by classic artists like the sculptor Rodin, as well as more contemporary artists like Ansel Adams, M. C. Escher, and Red Grooms. KMA has displayed everything from the treasures of ancient Peru to modern art made from trash. The museum also has an eclectic and admirable permanent collection of more than 1,000 objects in all media.

In addition to the exhibits, visitors can browse the gift shop or attend hands-on workshops, lectures, and theatrical performances. Throughout the year, KMA's award-winning jazz concert series, Alive After Five, draws big crowds each Friday evening in the museum's Great Hall. Alive After Five costs $6.00 for non-KMA members and $3.00 for University of Tennessee (UT) students. A buffet is available for around $5.00 plus tax, but the exact cost depends on the caterer being used. Guests who enjoy their jazz on the rocks will also find a cash bar.

Museum admission is free for KMA members and children younger than 12 and $5.00 for ages 12 and older; for school tours, it's $2.00 per person. The museum is open Tuesday and Wednesday from noon to 8:00 P.M., Thursday and Friday from noon to 9:00 P.M., and Saturday and Sunday from 11:00 A.M. to 5:00 P.M. It's closed on Mondays and some major holidays. You can keep up with the museum's latest exhibits and special events by visiting them on the Web at www.knoxart.org.

Directly across the street from the Knoxville Museum of Art is Fort Kid, a free playground for ages 2 through 12. There are all kinds of things to climb over, slide down, crawl under, shimmy through, and hang from. Just about all of the equipment is made of wood or tires, and it's designed to help spark the kids' imaginations as they play. Nearby are restrooms and a snack shop. Standing tall with historic grace overlooking Fort Kid is a short row of Victorian houses that were also renovated for the World's Fair. These days, the pastel-colored buildings are home to galleries, shops, and the Knoxville Performing Arts Institute.

Everything we've described in this neighborhood is located on the west side of the waterway at World's Fair Park. You can cross to the other side on foot by bridge. There, you'll find the Sunsphere and the newly completed Knoxville Convention Center, which has more shops and restaurants.

The University of Tennessee, Knoxville

Immediately south of World's Fair Park, the campus of one of the nation's leading universities stretches for more than a mile along Fort Loudon Lake. Justly famous for its nationally ranked athletic programs and facilities, UTK is consistently cited as one of the nation's top 25 educational values among all colleges and universities. An average student population of 26,000 includes students from every state and more than 100 countries, pursuing studies in 15 colleges and schools. The main campus is isolated enough to provide an intimacy not usually found in a "downtown" school but convenient to downtown Knoxville and several shopping malls. Cumberland Avenue, the northern boundary of 90 percent of the campus, is a main Knoxville traffic artery. The campus proper is laid out so that resident students live in easy walking distance to their classrooms and athletic facilities, and "Fraternity Row" is almost exactly centered in the campus. A drive (or even a stroll) through the campus is an interesting diversion if you're downtown and looking for a way to kill some time in pleasant surroundings. For general campus information, call (865) 974-1000.

Knoxville Zoological Gardens

Welcome to an amazing world of wildlife, displaying animals both familiar and exotic. More commonly known as the Knoxville Zoo, this 54-acre park was opened in 1948, and today it hosts more than 400,000 visitors annually. The simplest way to get to the zoo from any direction is to take exit 392 off I-40 at Rutledge Pike. From there, just follow the signs to the zoo, which is adjacent to the Knox County Fairgrounds. Plenty of parking is available for zoo visitors at a cost of $3.00.

The Knoxville Zoo, (865) 637-5331, has undergone substantial renovations and rearranging in the last few years. The entrance was moved from one end of the zoo's linear layout to a point that now lies roughly in the middle. As such, to take the self-directed tour, you must explore one side, make your way back to the center, and then take in the other side. Future restructuring at the zoo calls for creating a layout that takes guests along a more circular path. No matter which way you go in the meantime, however, you'll see a lot of animals you've heard of and quite a few that may be totally new to you. Near

History buffs can choose from several different historic tours in Knoxville, many of which are in the downtown area. Look for the Frank McClung Museum, James White's Fort, the Mabry–Hazen House, and Marble Springs, the home of Sevier County namesake John Sevier.

the new entrance, visitors are introduced to the look and feel of the Smoky Mountains, thanks to rustic-looking structures, native foliage, and an exhibit that opened in 2000—Black Bear Falls. If you stay to the left on your tour, you'll see animals like the unique red panda—which actually resembles a large fox—and a stretch of large habitats that are home to elephants and white rhinos. Toward the far left is an extensive collection of reptiles and amphibians.

Back near the entrance, at Penguin Rock, you'll enjoy watching those lovable, waddling creatures as they play in their splashy habitat. At the Kids' Zoo, the children will really enjoy crawling through Prairie Dog Pass, a series of tunnels that let the kids pop up into special Plexiglass domes, allowing them to go nose-to-nose with the zoo's prairie dog population. Nearby are a children's petting zoo and camel rides.

Birds are prominently displayed at the Knoxville Zoo. One exhibit takes you on an authentic outdoor tour through a Central American rain forest that puts you in the same enclosed area as several exotic species of flying creatures. There is also an amphitheater where demonstrations of free-flying birds are staged three times daily (except Monday) during peak season. Featured are birds of prey, along with talking parrots, penguins, and other winged wonders.

The animals of Africa are well represented on the other side of the Knoxville Zoo. In one of the largest outdoor animal habitats at the zoo, you'll see zebras, giraffes, and Marabou storks living in har-

While you're in downtown Knoxville, consider visiting the Women's Basketball Hall of Fame located on (appropriately enough) Hall of Fame Drive. Inside are 30,000 square feet of exhibits and hands-on experiences celebrating women's basketball at the collegiate and professional levels. The building is easy to spot from a distance—outside, a 30-foot-wide, 20,000-pound basketball sits suspended over a giant hoop. Admissions are $7.95 for ages 16 to 61, $5.95 for senior citizens and ages 6 to 15, and kids 5 and younger get in free. Call (865) 633-9000 for more information.

mony. In the African Forest, look for the simian inhabitants of Chimp Ridge and Gorilla Valley. At Grasslands Africa, you'll see adult lions roaming their territory. If you're lucky, you'll get some close-up views of the baby lions playing near one of the glass walls separating man from beast. Along the way, you'll find other ferocious felines like tigers, leopards, and cheetahs as well as a few unsavory characters such as the vulture, the hyena, and the African wild dog.

Many of the exhibits throughout the zoo are equipped with Story Boxes. These boxes provide informative audio narration that give visitors a little more background on the animals than is provided on the exhibits' placards. However, to activate the boxes, you must use a special "key" given only to zoo members. Also throughout the park there are ample numbers of restrooms, refreshment vendors, and gift shops. During the summer, there are even hoses that spray mists of water to help keep you cool in the heat.

At the main entrance you'll find the Zoo Shop, the main gift store, where you can pick up a map of the zoo and rent strollers ($6.00 for a single, $8.00 for a double) and wheelchairs ($5.00). By the way, all of the zoo's exhibits are wheelchair accessible. The Knoxville Zoo is open every day except for Christmas. Hours are 9:30 A.M. to 6:00 P.M. in summer. The zoo closes at 4:30 P.M. on weekdays during the off-season. Admission is $10.95 for adults, $8.95 for seniors ages 62 and older, and $6.95 for children ages 3 through 12. Children 2 and younger are admitted free. Discounted rates are available for groups of 20 or more, and the zoo accepts major credit cards as payment. Learn more about the Knoxville Zoo at their Web site: www.knoxville-zoo.org.

Ijam's Nature Center

The Knoxville Zoo isn't the city's only haven for nature lovers. Ijam's (pronounced *eye*-ums) Nature Center, (865) 577-4717, is a nonprofit, environmental, and education center on the Tennessee River, where visitors can get close to dozens of species of native animals, plants, trees, and flowers. From downtown Knoxville, cross the Tennessee River via the Henley Street Bridge, take a left on Blount Avenue, and follow the signs. Ijam's is located on Island Home Avenue, about 2 miles from your starting point.

The 80-acre nature reserve offers different and interesting areas to explore—a forest, meadows, sinkholes, a spring-fed pond, and gardens. Living among these environs are animals like opossum, muskrats, rabbits, snakes, turtles, and frogs as well as breeds of birds like ducks, owls, and herons. Among the native vegetation are native grasses, trees, and wildflower species like toothwort, trillium, trout lily, and bloodroot.

Visitors can view the park by taking any of the 3 miles of mulched and paved trails (some are wheelchair accessible) that meander about the acreage. A map is provided to help you navigate your way around the refuge and show you what types of wildlife to look out for in its different sections. One of the more scenic routes is the River Trail, which actually runs out over the Tennessee River via a boardwalk.

At the heart of Ijam's Nature Center is the education center surrounded by a paved plaza, waterfall pond, pavilion, and gardens. Inside the center, visitors can browse the gift shop or view the center's many educational exhibits. Of particular interest is the giant cross-section of a 353-year-old tree that was cut down in the 1940s.

In keeping with its mission statement to "increase knowledge, understanding, and appreciation of the natural world," Ijam's offers multiple environmental and scientific education opportunities in addition to the self-guided nature trail tours. The center features entertaining programs like Owl Prowls and Bat Walks as well as canoe trips, summer day camps, and group tours. Visitors can even take part in the many special events, like the Fall Festival and Plant Sale and Symphony in the Dark, that are held at Ijam's annually.

Kids especially love exploring the natural world around them. Needless to say, Ijam's is a popular school-field-trip destination, and they'll even host kids' birthday parties with themes like Reptiles and Amphibians or Insects and Spiders! Older kids can take advantage of Ijam's Junior Naturalist program, and younger children can participate in the Wee Ones Series, where they learn about animals and plants through activities, songs, crafts, and live animal presentations.

The trails at Ijam's Nature Center are free and open daily from 8:00 A.M. until dusk. The Nature Center and the Museum Store are open Monday through Friday from 9:00 A.M. to 5:00 P.M., Saturday from noon to 4:00 P.M., and Sunday from 1:00 to 5:00 P.M.

TOWNSEND, TENNESSEE

For years, this small burg—located about 20 miles west of Gatlinburg in Blount County—has made a name for itself as "the peaceful side of the Smokies." That billing is based on the fact that although Townsend and its surrounding environs

To learn about any special events that may be taking place while you're in Townsend, Tennessee, contact the visitor center there at (865) 448-6134.

are every bit as scenically fetching as what you'll find in neighboring Sevier County, the city has managed to escape many of the pitfalls that go hand in hand with high-traffic tourism.

In other words, Townsend offers much of what Smokies purists desire from a trip to the mountains without all the inconveniences and hassles. Visitors get quick, handy access to the national park, exposure to mountain crafts and culture, and views and scenery galore, but they are spared going shoulder to shoulder with teeming throngs of fellow visitors and miles and miles of bumper-to-bumper traffic.

As usual, let's start with the driving directions. If you're leaving from Gatlinburg, go to the national park's Sugarlands Visitor Center and head west on Little River Road (Tennessee Highway 73) as if you were going to Cades Cove. Instead of diverting to the cove, however, stay on TN 73 all the way to Townsend, which will be about 20 miles from your starting point. From Pigeon Forge, take U.S. Highway 321 (Wears Valley Road) and follow it for a little more than 15 miles until you hit a stoplight. Bingo, you're in Townsend. Both routes are generally curvy and scenic. Traffic runs slowly on these roads in peak season, so don't get in a hurry.

Townsend is laid out in a long, narrow strip that stretches for several miles, running on its west end along US 321. At the traffic light, US 321 heads northeast toward Pigeon Forge, and the primary route through Townsend continues eastward along TN 73. Sticking to this main drag gives you access to the majority of what Townsend offers. Some businesses, such as cabin rental offices, are often located within a few miles on smaller county roads. But since this is just a day trip, who needs cabin rentals anyway?

Knoxville's Old City

East of World's Fair Park, on the other side of downtown Knoxville, is a little neighborhood known as the Old City. Bordered by Central Avenue, Jackson Avenue, Gay Street, and Summit Hill Drive, it is now regarded as one of the more colorful sections of Knoxville. However, its present character is nothing compared to that of its lively and often notorious past. So, before we tell you what you can find in the Old City today, let us take you back about 100 years, to the days when gunslingers, gangsters, prostitutes, and bootleggers made this section of downtown Knoxville their stomping grounds.

From the late 1800s through the early 1900s, there were quite a few characters, famous and infamous, who found themselves woven into Old City history. One night, Buffalo Bill and some Native Americans from his Wild West Show got drunk and decided to shoot holes into the walls and ceilings of one of the saloons. On that same street in 1901, Kid Curry, a member of Butch Cassidy's Hole-in-the-Wall Gang, shot two local deputies and escaped on horseback across the Gay Street Bridge. During Prohibition, Knoxville was known as a clearinghouse for alcohol, and gangster Al Capone was often rumored to be in town.

In general, the area was considered to be less than savory. A newspaper article from 1900 regarded Central Avenue as being where "nine-tenths of the criminal element congregate." The article went on to describe all-night saloons, cheap lodging houses, and prostitutes in abundance. Over the years, the neighborhood was the site of a race riot, a

For outdoor recreation, you can take advantage of horseback riding, hiking or—perhaps Townsend's favorite summertime activity—inner tubing on the Little River. River Rat Tubing and Kayaking, (865) 448-8888, is a good place to go for shuttle service to put-in points. Or you can rent a tube and head out on your own to the Y (as in fork, not YMCA) in the Little River, located a few miles east of town on TN 73. In fact, if you drive into Townsend from Gatlinburg, you'll pass right by this longtime favorite tubing and swimming hole.

If fishing is your sport, the Little River is good for that, too. Stop by Little River Outfitters, (865) 448-9459, to stock up on gear essentials as well as to get a little advice about where to fish and with what bait. Golfers might want to tee it up at Laurel Valley Golf Club, (865) 448-6690.

For shoppers, Townsend has its share of antiques and craft shops, where you'll find everything from handmade wood carvings and stringed musical instruments to baskets and patchwork quilts. Look for establishments like Nawger Nob, (865) 448-0860; Wood-N-Strings, (865) 448-6647; and Antiques & Uniques, (865) 448-1033.

For fun dining, be sure to stop by Deadbeat Pete's, (865) 448-0900, serving hearty Tex-Mex lunches and dinners throughout the week as well as live music hanging, a train wreck, and a hiding place for runaway slaves on the Underground Railroad.

Today, things are decidedly different. The structures are still there, their turn-of-the-20th-century architecture reminiscent of the Old City of yesteryear. However, the buildings are now filled with new and vibrant businesses that appeal to all demographics. The streets are lined with restaurants, nightclubs, and coffeehouses where aspiring musicians and poets often get the chance to present their fledgling works. There are unique shops, boutiques, and antiques galleries, many of which house treasures straight out of the Old City's past.

On the cultural front, local artists display their works in the various restaurants and shops, and theatergoers attend shows at a performance space shared by many of the region's acting companies. Once a year, the Knoxville Area Theatre Coalition holds its Spotlight Festival in the Old City. During this two-day event, the Coalition's member theater companies stage plays at different venues around the neighborhood. Attendees get to see as many as six plays over the course of a day.

Throughout the year, there are other special events and happenings in the Old City, such as the Folk Music Festival and many others that are tied into holiday celebrations on Halloween, New Year's Eve, Mardi Gras, and St. Patrick's Day.

About ten years or so ago, the Old City was enjoying the height of its modern popularity. Unfortunately, a few isolated incidents of crime have tarnished the neighborhood's strengthening reputation. Despite the setbacks, Old City promoters and business owners are working as hard as ever to rehabilitate the area's image. In the meantime, we recommend that you check it out and hopefully do your part to make the Old City, once again, a neat place to be.

Wednesday through Sunday nights. You'll love the laid-back atmosphere, particularly the graffiti-covered one-dollar bills stapled to nearly every square inch of wall space. Other restaurants to keep in mind are the Back Porch, (865) 448-6333; Tuckaleechee Trout Farm Restaurant (865) 448-2290; and Trailhead Steakhouse (865) 448-0166.

Townsend hosts a number of special events each year, most notably the fall and spring editions of its Heritage Festival. That's where locals and visitors alike gather to celebrate the area's history and culture. The event showcases crafts, barbecue, storytelling, and live country and bluegrass music performances. The festival is also a good opportunity to meet descendants of the families who once lived in the areas now occupied by the national park. Many of those displaced families make their homes in Townsend today.

Lest we present Townsend as a perfectly idyllic mountain hamlet (and in many ways, it is), we'll let you know that you will see a few tell-tale signs of tourist-targeted influence there. US 321 is now a spacious four-lane highway as it runs through town, new cabins and rental homes are springing up like mushrooms, and yes, you'll even find tacky souvenir shops and a go-kart track.

But overall, a day in Townsend is a day well spent, and compared to much of

Sevier County, it aptly embodies its moniker, "the peaceful side of the Smokies."

THE BACKBONE OF TENNESSEE

The Great Smokies area of Tennessee is a programmed tourist destination where myriad activities can keep a family busy for untold periods of time. But you already know that. What escapes the notice of a huge number of visitors seeking a true "wilderness" experience is that that experience is also in the neighborhood. But because what we're talking about here is wild and woolly country, it's not immediately accessible on four-lane highways or visible from your hot tub. What we're talking about is the northern half of Tennessee's central spine, the Cumberland Mountains, and the river gorges that provide scenic views from 500-foot cliffs, all within two hours of the Smokies Corridor. A day trip to any of these places can be experienced entirely in daylight hours during summer and early fall, and the scenery is well worth the time and effort.

Big South Fork National River and Recreational Area

The Big South Fork of the Cumberland River and its tributaries wind through 90 miles of scenic gorges and valleys in the Big South Fork National River and Recreational Area, an unimproved wilderness that straddles the Kentucky–Tennessee border. Call (423) 569-9778 for information. The southern end begins at the Bandy Creek Visitor Center, about 15 miles west of Oneida, Tennessee, on Tennessee Highway 297. From I-40 westbound, exit 347 (Harriman/Rockwood) is U.S. Highway 27; go north about 60 miles to Oneida, and take TN 297 west into the

park (about 15 miles). From Interstate 75 northbound, use exit 144 and follow Tennessee Highway 63 west about 20 miles to TN´297, and then through Oneida into the park. If your plans include riding the Big South Fork Scenic Railway (highly recommended and dealt with separately later on), your target is Stearns, Kentucky, about 20 miles north of Oneida on US 27 and Kentucky Highway 92.

You can get your bearings and a lot of local information at both visitor centers. The Bandy Creek (Tennessee) center, (931) 879-3625, is open daily year-round except Christmas. Hours are from 8:00 A.M. to 6:00 P.M. June through October, and 8:00 A.M. to 4:30 P.M. November through May. The Kentucky Visitor Center, (606) 376-5073, is open daily May through October from 9:00 A.M. to 5:30 P.M. Hours may vary November through April. The park is open year-round, and there are no entrance fees. Once you park your car at either visitor center, you're in a wilderness area dominated by the rivers. There are very few amenities, even in the camping areas. As a "deep" wilderness, Big South Fork is a bird-watchers paradise, with sightings recorded of more than 160 resident and migratory species. Commercial licensees provide white-water rafting, canoe rentals, and horseback-riding excursions. Five campgrounds within the park provide facilities ranging from primitive to prehistoric for nominal fees, and backcountry camping is permissible anywhere you want to throw down a bedroll. Keep the term "wilderness" uppermost in your mind at all times; although you're not totally isolated from civilization, this is not a trip for people unaccustomed to a fairly uncompromising lifestyle.

ASHEVILLE, NORTH CAROLINA

Asheville has always played a prominent role in the development of western North Carolina, especially gaining vibrancy around the turn of the 20th century. At that time, Asheville built its reputation as a place where those of poor health could retreat and recuperate in a cool mountain climate. When the city became connected to surrounding regions by the railroad, it began to truly stake its claim as a tourist destination. For much more information on Asheville and the surrounding mountain counties of North Carolina, pick up a copy of the *Insiders' Guide to North Carolina's Mountains*.

GETTING THERE

From downtown Sevierville, take US 411N and follow it for approximately 25 miles east (yes, US 411N heads east) to Newport, Tennessee. At Newport, take I-40 eastbound and follow the signs to Asheville. Once you near Asheville, you can either stay on I-40 (more convenient to Biltmore Estate) or take Interstate 240, which routes you more through the heart of Asheville and is more accessible to downtown.

If your point of origin is downtown Gatlinburg, take US 321 North to Foothills Parkway, which will take you directly to I-40. From there, you'll take the interstate the rest of the way to Asheville as in the directions from Sevierville.

From Pigeon Forge, there is no direct route to I-40 without having to follow one of the above routes. If you want to keep it simple, make your way to downtown Sevierville or Gatlinburg and follow the directions above. In either case, there's a little bit of backtracking involved. Base your decision on which city you're closer to as well as other factors like the heaviness of incoming and outgoing traffic.

If you're starting from Pigeon Forge and you're a shortcut-taking kind of person, consider following Dollywood Lane out of town until it dead ends about 10 miles to the east. Take a left on Bird's Creek Road, and within a mile you'll see a sign for a right turnoff onto Pittman Center Road. Follow Pittman Center Road all the way to US 321N and take a left. From there, continue to Foothills Parkway as in

the directions from Gatlinburg.

Once you're on I-40, however, you're in for a wondrous, scenic drive that winds you to the crest of the Smokies range at the North Carolina border and then back down through beautiful vistas until you reach Asheville. Because the roads are hilly and curvy and the speed limits generally don't top 60, count on anywhere from an hour and a half to two hours to make the drive.

Speaking of scenic drives, consider going into North Carolina through Cherokee and then taking the Blue Ridge Parkway to Asheville. Overall, the parkway is a 469-mile stretch of road running from Tennessee to Virginia that offers the motorist some of the most spectacular views of the Appalachian range. The drive combines nature's beauty with historical sites, mountain wildlife, and numerous camping and picnic sites. At its extreme ends are Great Smoky Mountains National Park and Shenandoah National Park.

Biltmore Estate

Sited on 8,000 forested acres, this 250-room French Renaissance chateau was the private residence of the millionaire George Vanderbilt and his wife, Edith, at the turn of the 20th century. In 1930, the Vanderbilts' daughter and son-in-law opened up the estate to the public, charging an admission to help add a boost to the local economy during the Great Depression. Today, Biltmore Estate hosts more than 800,000 visitors annually. It stands as a monument to the opulent heights reached by one successful American family.

When visiting the Biltmore home, you can rent audiocassette players that enhance the self-guided tour with useful information.

The 127 Yard Sale—Only in America

This article could appear in any one of a dozen or more Insiders' Guides, in the Midwest, central plains, or southeastern United States. In fact, it might be in one your authors haven't read yet. It's a phenomenon that only an American mindset could conceive and only an American neighborhood that extends about 450 miles through four states could pull off on one mind-bending weekend. Trust us on this one: The Highway 127 Yard Sale is something that you'll not see anywhere else in the world.

Conceived in the early 1990s by the Jamestown, Tennessee, Chamber of Commerce as a local fund-raising activity for an otherwise dull August weekend, the 127 Yard Sale has grown in a decade into a national event that involves a cooperative effort of tens of thousands of people and hundreds (maybe thousands) of organizations from Cincinnati, Ohio, to Gadsden, Alabama. The people directly involved will probably never meet; they're all busy at their local levels making this improbable event happen. The event is usually planned for late August, officially beginning on a Thursday and running for eleven days. Enough exhibitors set up in our day-trip area to make a Wednesday trip worthwhile, when the early-bird exhibitors are setting up, but most of the food vendors don't fire up until Thursday or Friday. Our recommendation for this excursion is that you plan it for a Thursday or Friday, when everything's up and running and relatively uncrowded, or Saturday if you enjoy masses of bargain-hunting people. If you're interested in shopping at the local churches and organizations, wait until the second week. To provide a selection of alternatives, our intrepid team of researchers spent the entire weekend (and a lot more money than they were budgeted) developing three "trip packages" that don't involve overnight accommodations—there's nothing available within 30 miles of U.S. Highway 127 anyway, unless you have reservations at least a month in advance. Our quest for treasure begins at exit 317 on I-40, in Crossville, 90 miles west of Sevierville. FYI, you're in the central time zone, where it's one hour earlier than in the Smokies Corridor. Downtown Crossville (population about 7,500) is about 2 miles south of the exit. The first of our three individual days is centered on Crossville; the other two use exit 317 as a start/finish point.

TRIP #1—TAKING THE MIDDLE GROUND

This is the only one of the three trips described that uses I-40 as its center, and it's the shortest in miles because of the high density of exhibitors. Turning right (north off the interstate), it looks like you're heading for a lot of nowhere. Persist—as soon as you clear the motels and fast-food restaurants that surround most interstate exits, you'll find yourself in a principally rural area that quickly becomes an almost nonstop line of hastily assembled roadside stands. Let the looting and pillaging begin! Most of the action in the first mile or so is on the left side of the road, and the traffic is probably already a hassle, so concentrate on the right side; you can catch the other side coming back. This is probably the best way to operate at all times unless

There's no apparent limit to what can be found at the Highway 127 Yard Sale. GORDON BRUGMAN

something really grabs your attention across the road. About 5 miles out, it's obvious you've left a metropolitan area, and the number of individual sites has dwindled. You've also probably spent more than an hour looking at several small exhibits, mostly in front yards along the highway. If you've reached Tollett's Chapel Methodist Church on the right, it's a good place to grab a drink and maybe a homemade fried pie snack, and look at what they have to offer—there's usually a lot of games and Christian-themed books and records, and one of our collectors found a rare Pez dispenser. Then go back to the highway and head back (left) toward Crossville. After several homes on the way back have tempted you, the first big organized area awaits. It's a huge open-air sale area that fronts a campground/trailer park. This will be your first encounter with a combi-

nation of commercial and private operators, and it's easy to tell the difference. The commercial exhibitors make no pretense to be anything but what they are, and bargains are available in their booths. The primary difference between the commercial (or "professional," if you prefer) exhibitors and private sellers is that the pros do this kind of thing for a living, and they know where the action is this weekend. The pros are usually selling new or reconditioned goods or genuine antiques and collectibles. The private sellers are usually offering used goods like you'd expect to find at any garage or yard sale. One of the highlights of this particular area is the booth operated by the residents of Fairfield Glade, the largest retirement resort in the area. These folks have learned one of the hardest truths about retired living the hard way, and their collection of suddenly unnecessary stuff is amazing. Bicycles, electronics, kitchen appliances, and housewares abound at prices bordering on outright theft. If you're not interested in driving a lot of miles on pure speculation, this place can eat up as much time as you want to give it. But let's press on. Crossing back over the interstate, the highway is lined with exhibitors set up in front of a variety of businesses until the downtown area interrupts for about a mile. Shortly thereafter, the Crossville Senior Citizens Center presents the first opportunity to shop and rest since leaving Tollett's Chapel. They serve an excellent breakfast and lunch menu during the sale; you can eat pretty well for less than $5.00. Continuing south along US 127, another mile will bring you to a large open area on both sides of the road that's covered with goods of every description. One of our Insiders bought an antique golf club from a dealer who knew what he was selling, and one from an individual who didn't. The upshot here was two articles with a combined value of about $100 that were bought for a total of $36. Whatever the opposite of caveat emptor is, it worked this time. Our photographer/computer geek scored big here—he found a Microsoft Intellimouse (the optical version) in the original package for $12. This item is still being sold in the stores for 50 to 60 bucks. His wife got a bargain across the street, picking up a brass coatrack for a song. By the time this field has been mined, it's OK if you feel "shopped out." There's not much left in the next few miles traveling south, so a return to the interstate is suggested. Between the downtown area and I–40, there are a lot of places to do some last-minute shopping, and our most knowledgeable "collector" made a major score at one of them: She bought two eminently collectible pottery pitchers for a

buck apiece. The catalog value of the smaller one is $85; the bigger one is appraised at $100. It was probably an act of charity that she didn't try to haggle with the unfortunate guy who sold them to her. This completes our slice of the middle, which is also pretty close to the geographic center of the whole shebang, and the total amount of miles traveled is less than 20. The next two described trips involve more miles and more scenery, and each has a rewarding experience at its turnaround point.

TRIP #2—NORTH TO THE BIRTHPLACE

This trip begins with a right turn at exit 317 and will continue north on US 127 for about 30 miles to Jamestown, the place where this entire project had its birth. Traveling north through the previously described area, there's a profusion of small, single-family layouts along the way, including a large farmhouse on the left with a huge display that's reputedly collected from a subdivision not visible from the highway. Whatever the truth, it's about the biggest nonprofessional exhibit in the area, and it's worth a look. We found a lot of video and computer games there. About 15 miles up, shortly after entering Fentress County, the small community of Clarkrange goes all out for the sale with a huge mixed exhibit area right in the center of town. It's a shopper's paradise with a huge variety of merchandise and some interesting food booths. If you want a little more conventional setting for lunch, Darryl's Restaurant right across the highway has a full and generous menu and a hustling staff who will attend to your needs promptly and cheerfully. Our staff ate at Darryl's and were overfed with home cooking for about $10 a piece. Depending on the time, you could choose lunch or an early dinner before pressing on to Jamestown or stop for dinner on your way back. Our pottery collector bagged another pitcher in Clarkrange for less than 10 percent of its catalog value and a good-size selection of a popular dinnerware pattern for about a third of its value. There's not a lot in the 20 or so miles from Clarkrange to Jamestown except new highway construction (which bodes well for future yard sales), but Jamestown is heavily lined with what appear to be pretty slapdash setups. The area just south of downtown is thick with sales areas containing amateur and professional exhibitors. We found an unusually high number of auto parts in Jamestown, and the biggest professional exhibit featured an amazing variety of collectible glassware. Our collector had to be physically escorted out of the booth. Twice. There's very little activity north of Jamestown to the Tennessee–Kentucky border, so our recommendation is that you head back toward Crossville. Your experience by now has pretty well told you what stops you can make on the return trip. This round-trip from I-40 exit 317 to Jamestown and back is about 60 miles. With the number of stops you decide to make, this trip can take anywhere from four to eight hours.

TRIP #3—THE SOUTHERN ROUTE

Traveling south from exit 317 into the scenic Sequatchie valley, the southern route involves more sustained driving than the northern trip, with a much larger concentration of sales sites at the end. After clearing the large sites at the southern end of Crossville, the number of sites is pretty small for the next 25 miles.

There's a lovely subdivision just south of town with several sale sites spread across a lot of spacious yards, where the usual "garage sale" stuff prevails. Several small sites dot the next 15 to 20 miles until you reach Pikeville, but what you'll find in this hamlet of less than 2,000 will be well worth the drive. First, as you enter Pikeville, note the Pikeville Family Restaurant on the left. Lunch for two (two-hand hamburgers, a mountain of fries, and drinks) set us back about $7.00. Then brace yourself. It appears that Pikeville was once (and may still be) a prosperous place—the highway is occupied on one side by about a mile of stately old homes in lovely condition and on the other by several churches, the county courthouse, and the county high school. Every unoccupied square inch of ground on both sides of the highway is covered with sale merchandise, most of it offered by individuals. Although the presence of local church and charitable organizations is obvious, there are very few professional exhibitors in Pikeville. If you ever wondered what a truly "hometown" affair looks like, where everybody gets out and participates, Pikeville will show you. Our shoppers found more honest-to-goodness bargains in Pikeville than in any other concentrated area we visited. Our pottery collector rang up a couple of impressive finds, and the frustrated athlete bought a mixed bag of golf clubs for $5.00 that contained an amazing collection of old and new equipment. A selection of old 78 RPM records at one place included hits by Bing Crosby, Perry Como, Doris Day, and several other World War II musical stars. The First Southern Baptist Church provided an oasis for weary shoppers, offering the use of their restrooms and fellowship hall, where complimentary drinks and cookies were served. Their pastor worked the crowd outdoors, handing out fans to help ward off the heat. Pikeville was not an easy place to leave.

It's difficult to say what the future holds for the 127 Yard Sale. It's been growing constantly since its inception, and conventional wisdom suggests that it will continue to grow for the next decade or so. It may even spawn rival versions along other highways; Americans are very adept at copying things that work well. Whatever happens, this event is so unique in nature that anybody living within reasonable driving distance of US 127 anywhere between Ohio and Alabama should take a look at it. As frothy as an undertaking of this type may seem to be, it's refreshing from time to time to see what Americans working together can accomplish.

It was as much a showplace 100 years ago as it is today, featuring then state-of-the-art luxuries that were only afforded by the wealthiest of people. Over the course of the two- to three-hour self-guided tour, visitors can marvel at technology that was ahead of its day—amenities like central heat, electric lights and appliances, and indoor plumbing. Overall, allow yourself the better part of a day to take in everything the whole estate has to offer.

Biltmore Estate is most easily reached by taking exit 50 off I-40. From there, signs will guide you to the main entrance, which is flanked by a gift shop and a group sales office. The main driveway takes you to the Reception and Ticket Center where you can purchase your tickets. You'll be given a free guidebook to assist you in your tour, but more in-depth literature is available for purchase as well. There's also a scaled-down replica of the entire estate on display inside, which will help you get your bearings as you plan your visit.

From the Ticket Center, it's a 3-mile drive to the main house. Along the way, you'll pass through some gorgeous countryside. The trees and shrubberies are all carefully orchestrated plantings, originally designed by the Vanderbilts' landscape architect, Frederick Law Olmsted. As you approach the house, you will be guided into one of several free parking lots. You're then left with only a short walk to the house. From the outside, the Biltmore home is truly palatial in appearance. Designed by architect Richard Morris Hunt, its limestone facade and four acres of ground area lend to its stately presence among the immaculately maintained lawns and surrounding gardens.

Once you enter, the tour starts on the main floor and allows partial to full entry of many of the rooms that the Vanderbilts used for entertaining and dining. Typical of almost all of the mansion's rooms, the salon, billiard room, banquet hall, music room, tapestry gallery, and library are liberally and ornately adorned with fine furnishings, fixtures, and artwork. Featured are many of the treasures collected by George Vanderbilt in his travels, such as 16th-century tapestries and a chess set once owned by Napoleon Bonaparte.

The grand staircase spirals its way between all levels of the home and guides visitors to the upstairs levels. There, guests get an inside glimpse at some of the private living areas of the Vanderbilt family, including Mr. and Mrs. Vanderbilt's separate bedrooms as well as a host of guest rooms and sitting rooms.

Perhaps the most interesting area of the home, the basement is not only where the Vanderbilts' guests enjoyed several indoor recreations but also where the servants lived and performed many of their daily tasks. The indoor bowling alley is one of the oldest in existence, and the indoor pool still boasts its original underwater lighting. Family and guests stayed fit in the gymnasium with its once-cutting-edge exercise equipment. Visitors can also view the many kitchens, pantries, and laundry facilities utilized by the Vanderbilts' house staff of 80-plus. Staff members lived in small individual rooms in the basement and had their own common dining room and sitting room for relaxation.

The tour concludes back on the main floor with a pass through the Bachelor's Wing of the house and quick peeks into the smoking room and gun room. On exiting, guests are pointed to an adjacent courtyard and set of buildings once used as stables. Today, the structures house several gift shops and eateries, including a bakery, ice cream parlor, confectionery, and the Stable Cafe, a full-service restaurant. For convenience, restrooms and an ATM machine are available in the Stable Courtyard area.

No visit to the Biltmore Estate is complete without a walking tour of the massive and colorful gardens. Your guidebook indicates the different walking trails that crisscross the grounds, leading past tour highlights such as the Italian Garden and its three formal pools, the four-acre Walled Garden (half of which is planted with just roses), and the Bass Pond. The latter is located a half-mile from the house and features a boathouse and waterfall.

Among the many beautiful and fragrant flowers that bloom throughout the year are tulips, dogwoods, azaleas, roses, and chrysanthemums. Flowering shrubs and many varieties of wildflowers also color the landscape, and in autumn the estate's thousands of acres go through their annual kaleidoscopic metamorphosis.

Of course, what we've described only scratches the surface of the Biltmore experience. A casual drive along the estate's many miles of paved roads reveals acres and acres of farmland, all part of George Vanderbilt's vision of a self-sufficient estate. Situated in the middle of the acreage, about 3 miles from the house, you'll find the Deerpark Restaurant, one of three full-service restaurants located on the property.

Five miles from the house is the Biltmore winery, open since 1985. The 96,500-square-foot facility is located in one of the buildings originally used in the estate's dairy operations. Tours of the winery take visitors through the entire winemaking process. A tasting room, wine shop, and the Bistro restaurant complement the experience.

In spring 2001 a 213-room deluxe inn opened on the Biltmore property. Inn on Biltmore Estate (as it's officially known) is a $31 million project and the only lodgings located on the Biltmore grounds themselves. It's located on a hill above the Biltmore Estate Winery and affords terrific mountain vistas from porches, balconies, and guest areas. In keeping with the estate's general atmosphere of opulence, the inn also offers a regal slate of amenities, including fine dining, a fitness room, pool, library, and outdoor programs. Reservations can be made by calling (800) 624-1575.

Biltmore Estate is open year-round except for Thanksgiving and Christmas (incidentally, the home achieves new levels of visual splendor during the holidays with all its candles, poinsettias, wreaths, 35-plus Christmas trees, and thousands of feet of garland!). The house is open from 9:00 A.M. to 5:30 P.M. seven days a week. The rest of the estate and the Reception and Ticket Center are also open throughout the week from 9:00 A.M. to 4:00 P.M. January through March and 8:30 A.M. to 5:00 P.M. the rest of the year.

The winery is open seven days a week from 11:00 A.M. to 6:00 P.M. January through March and from 11:00 A.M. to 7:00

For more information about what to do in Asheville, contact the chamber of commerce at (800) 257-1300 or visit their Web site at www.ashevillechamber.org.

P.M. April through December. Throughout the year, the winery opens at noon on Sunday. All of the Biltmore's restaurants and eateries are open year-round, except for Deerpark Restaurant, which is closed January through March. The full-service restaurants begin serving at 11:00 A.M. Most Biltmore shops are open year-round, opening between 9:30 and 10:00 A.M. (depending on the shop) and closing at 6:00 P.M.

Smoking is not permitted in any of the restaurants or in the Biltmore house itself. Also forbidden in the house are pets, photography, videotaping, sketching, and any food or drink. Except for some sections of the house and gardens, most areas are wheelchair accessible. Hosts are stationed throughout the house to help answer your questions, and optional Behind-the-Scenes and Rooftop Tours are available for an additional charge.

Regular admission to the Biltmore Estate is $39.00 for adults and $19.50 for ages 6 through 16. In November and December, the prices are slightly higher. Children ages 5 and younger are admitted free year-round with a paying adult. To learn more about Biltmore or find out about specific annual events taking place there, call (800) 624-1575 or visit the estate on the Internet at www.biltmore.com.

Other Attractions and Points of Interest

If you're looking for more to do in Asheville, you won't be disappointed. A visit to the city's historic downtown district could, in and of itself, take up the better part of a day. Many of the buildings you'll find there managed to escape the urban renewal process that has compromised the downtowns of so many other American cities. With a prominence of art deco architecture, much of Asheville's historical charms are still intact. Thanks to the efforts of various preservation-minded groups in the 1970s and a more recent renaissance of sorts in the 1990s, this section of town still has quite a strong pulse.

Today, visitors will discover an abundance of shops, boutiques, galleries, and restaurants as well as a strong antique district and even condominiums. Whether you're looking for a unique eatery or special gift to remember your visit, there's something to be found for every budget among the businesses of downtown Asheville. One structured way of seeing the area is to follow Asheville's Urban Trail, a self-guided walking tour that highlights significant architectural and historical points. Maps can be obtained from the visitor center at the Asheville's Area Chamber of Commerce on Haywood Street.

The life and times of one of the century's most influential writers can be relived at the Thomas Wolfe Memorial on Market Street. At the visitor center, you'll find exhibits and audiovisual programs that highlight the life of the Asheville native. Also displayed are works of art based on quotes from Wolfe's works. Normally, the memorial includes a tour of the Victorian-style boarding house run by Wolfe's mother, where the author spent a good part of his boyhood. Although much of the structure was destroyed by fire in 1998 and is in the process of being refurbished, the visitor center alone is well worth the stop. This attraction is open year-round but runs on a slightly more limited schedule from November through March. Admission prices are only $1.00 for adults and 50 cents for students.

Asheville, like the rest of western North Carolina and Tennessee's Smokies as well, is a haven for mountain craftspeople. You'll see the work of some of its best representatives at the Folk Art Center, located on Blue Ridge Parkway at Milepost 382. The center is also the corporate headquarters for the Southern Highland Craft Guild. The guild has an active juried membership of more than 700 craftsmen, and only their works are displayed in the various guild-owned shops found across the region, including the Arrowcraft Shop in Gatlinburg (see our Mountain Crafts chapter for details).

The main gallery of the Folk Art Center hosts a wide range of exhibitions throughout the year, including the annual Members' Exhibition, which showcases works in all craft media from the traditional to the contemporary. The center is also home to a permanent collection of craft objects dating back to the turn of the 20th century. Adjacent to the main gallery is the Robert W. Gray Library Collection, one of the region's most notable resources of craft publications and books on Southern Appalachian history.

Visitors to the Folk Art Center are likely to show up on any of its special event days that take place throughout the year, such as Fiber Day, Clay Day, and Wood Day; these events often provide hands-on opportunities for guests. Craft demonstrations can also be seen from April through December, showcasing the talents of artists working with brooms, corn shucks, wood, and more. The Folk Art Center is open year-round except for Thanksgiving, Christmas, and New Year's days. The doors open at 9:00 A.M., and admission is free (although donations are welcome).

One of the Southern Highland Guild's craft shops can be found on site at the Folk Art Center. The Allanstand Craft Shop is generally regarded as the nation's first craft shop, having been founded in 1895. It was in downtown Asheville until 1980, when it moved to its current home. Currently, it houses works of pottery, wood, glass, fiber, metal, and jewelry made by members of the Southern Highland Guild. Another guild shop, Guild Crafts, is also located in the Asheville area, at 930 Tunnel Road (U.S. Highway 70).

Pack Place Education, Arts & Science Center is a multifaceted complex located in downtown Asheville consisting of five different museums and cultural attractions. The Asheville Museum of Art, western North Carolina's only art museum, displays 20th-century American art in a variety of media. The museum's permanent collection and special exhibits showcase the work of artists from around the region and the nation.

At the Health Adventure, kids of all ages can learn about the human body, challenge their minds, and stimulate their imaginations in the attraction's 11 different galleries. Kids eight years old and younger can also enjoy their own world of fun in the Health Adventure's Creative PlaySpace. Pack Place is also home to the Diana Wortham Theatre, a 500-seat multiuse facility that is the setting for a diverse range of performing arts, including music concerts and theatrical performances.

Pack Place's Colburn Gem And Mineral Museum has been dubbed "a mini Smithsonian of gems" by the *Washington Post*. An appropriate attraction, given the abundance of gems and minerals found in North Carolina's soil, this museum has numerous displays and hands-on exhibits devoted to stones from around the world. Finally, don't forget about the YMI Cultural Center. Commissioned as the Young Men's Institute by George Vanderbilt in 1893, this refurbished cultural center contains various galleries that host exhibitions, classes, and performances presenting African-American art, culture, and history.

Metropolitan areas like Atlanta and Nashville are also within an easy half-day's drive of the Great Smokies. If you're interested in visiting either of those markets, check out the two Insiders' Guide books devoted to those cities.

NEIGHBORHOODS AND REAL ESTATE

If you browse through Smoky Mountain area real estate listings, you'll frequently come across the headline "Views, Views, Views!" It's no wonder. Though abundant, views of the majestic Great Smoky Mountains are a treasured commodity around here. You could argue that views are what it's all about when it comes to the local real estate market. Those mountains are what brought tourism here in the first place, and time has proven that many who find the Smokies "a nice place to visit" do, indeed, want to settle among them as well. Then, consider all the people who have migrated to Sevier County to work in the businesses and industries that service the vacationer. The result has been long-term growth in all areas of real estate—not just in the sheer numbers of properties being developed, bought, and sold, but in the very nature of the industry itself.

While the nation's economy has slumped in the first few years of the millennium, the Smoky Mountains real estate market has enjoyed a corresponding boom. The war for real estate dollars has been won on two fronts. The commercial and investment property markets have grown, fed by buyers shifting their money out of the seemingly riskier stock market and into real estate. And of course, the sagging economy has spurred cut after cut in interest rates, resulting in historic, low prime rates and making it practically a buyer's market for those shopping for home mortgages. More good news for home owners and buyers is that thanks to the large amount of revenue generated by tourism, property tax rates in Sevier County are among the lowest in Tennessee.

Those who are seriously considering relocating to the area should be given a few general notes up front about what to expect when it comes to the housing situation. If your idea of a "dream house" is a historically significant structure on a quaint, tree-lined street, you're going to find slim pickings. With certain exceptions, the communities of the county are characterized by neighborhoods and subdivisions that have generally been around fewer than 35 years, much of that being developed just within the last 15 years. There are pockets of homes in the central areas of Gatlinburg and Sevierville that have longer histories, but basically, you're looking at a fairly new market. In the more isolated, rural areas outside the main communities, you'll find mixes of both newer and older homes; it's not uncommon to find an old, fixer-upper farmhouse situated within a mile of a new, sprawling, cedar and stone home perched atop multiple grassy acres.

You'll also find that Sevier County is an architectural patchwork quilt in which the styles and types of homes vary from community to community, depending on the prevalence of tourist activity in that area. Part of one town might have a generous supply of ranch-style homes. Another section of another town might be saturated with chalets built into steep hillsides. Yet another area might provide a steady landscape of newly constructed log cabins. Condos are becoming increasingly popular countywide, and in both the cities and the rural areas, there are numerous sites to place mobile homes. In the northern half of the county, variations on the standard ranch-style house are typical, while southern Sevier County has more cottages, cabins, condos, and chalets. What you ultimately choose depends on your aesthetic preferences, your price range, and, to some degree, your motives for moving here in the first place.

NEIGHBORHOODS

To shed further light on the gradations in the Smokies' real estate marketplace, we'll take you through the area's primary population centers and give you some of the basic information about what you'll find and how much it will cost. We've divided this section according to Sevier County's three primary towns, but throughout each, we'll cut a wide swath of territory, incorporating several smaller, outlying communities. Because it's the primary residential center of the county with a year-round population of about 12,000, Sevierville and its outlying areas will receive a little more attention than the smaller cities of Pigeon Forge and Gatlinburg.

Sevierville

One of the more rapidly expanding areas, both commercially and residentially, is the Tennessee Highway 66 corridor that runs for about 8 miles from Interstate 40 to Sevierville and also encompasses the small, unincorporated community of Kodak. This whole area, residentially speaking, is an especially popular location among couples in which one partner might work in Sevier County and the other may commute to a neighboring market like Knoxville or Jefferson County. Kodak's proximity to a number of surrounding job markets and its relatively light traffic make it a favorite site to put down roots. Northview Elementary School is also located there. Overall, home resale values are generally considered to be good.

Anyone who's home shopping in this territory can use some advance information about the utility services available. First, note that the city of Sevierville has annexed the narrow strip of land bordering both sides of TN 66, from I-40 all the way in to the main part of the city. The homes

and businesses that are so annexed receive all city utilities, except for sewer service, which stops a little north of the French Broad River. Most of the residential locations along TN 66, however, lie outside the annexation boundaries. Some of those still receive city services but at higher rates. In the other cases, utilities are either provided by companies that service surrounding areas, or septic and well water systems are utilized. When looking at a home that borders TN 66, be sure to ask your real estate agent about its sources of electricity, water, and sewer.

There are a number of subdivisions in the Kodak/TN 66 area, some of which are worthy of mention here. Bentwood, which started development in 1990, had several of its speculative homes featured in the local Parade of Homes showcase during its first year of existence. With more than 50 houses now completed there, prices in Bentwood start around \$200,000 and go up. Another subdivision in this region is Grandview. It was first developed as an exclusively upscale neighborhood, but after years of subsequent phases, many of its initial restrictions have been relaxed. As a result, less expensive homes are more prevalent further back into Grandview's newer additions. You'll find homes ranging from around \$135,000 up to \$370,000. The Royal Heights neighborhood lies within Sevierville city boundaries. Consisting of more upscale homes, you'll find prices generally starting at about \$170,000 and peaking in the \$500,000 range. Union Hill, located off Allensville Road, is a newer development popular with first-time home buyers. New homes can be purchased in the \$100,000 to \$110,000 range.

On our next stop, we're going to take a slight detour and briefly leave Sevierville altogether. The Seymour/Boyds Creek area is similar to Kodak in that it offers a convenient location for the couple that has careers split between Sevier and Knox Counties. Seymour is a small community about 12 miles from Sevierville that lies in the extreme northwest end of the county, right along the Knox County border. Although it is regarded a "hot" area in terms of commercial development, Seymour is primarily a residential suburb of Knoxville with three public schools, one private school, and handy access to the rest of Sevier County via Chapman Highway. Boyds Creek Highway connects Seymour to TN 66 with a 12-mile stretch of road. On this scenic drive, you'll find a mixture of older, historical homes and newer construction of subdivisions like Valley View Farms. This area serves its residents well with distant but unobstructed views of the Great Smoky Mountains.

The real estate agents with whom we spoke quoted price ranges of about $110,000 to $300,000 for newer homes in the Seymour area. Taking into account homes of all ages, the average selling price of a house was $133,550, according to 2003 MLS statistics. Although there was agreement that buyers can usually get more bang for their real estate buck compared to other communities in the market, the downside is that these properties don't appreciate as quickly as in places like Pigeon Forge or Gatlinburg. For that reason, Seymour is a better buy for someone who plans on staying put for a while. Again, many new residents are choosing to buy in newer subdivisions. Some of the popular developments are Van Gilder, Van Haven, Double D, Sharps Vista, and Clydesdale.

Back in Sevierville, you'll find several major pockets of residential concentration that offer homes with a more diverse range of prices and ages. If you're driving in to Sevierville on Chapman Highway from Seymour, you'll come across the Hardin Lane neighborhood just as you near downtown. As you turn off onto

---

In 2003, the average selling price of a home in Sevierville was $158,691. However, statistics have indicated that home prices there are rising more slowly than in neighboring Pigeon Forge and Gatlinburg.

Hardin Lane, you'll encounter several apartment complexes (see apartment section later in this chapter), but further back, you'll enter a nice, established neighborhood where the homes date back to the 1970s. The streets are quiet and the yards are green and wooded—this could explain, in part, why these homes appear on the market infrequently. Prices here hover in the $125,000 to $150,000 range, although there are several homes in the neighborhood that are more upscale and more expensive. In the past several years, there has also been a lot of new construction activity in nearby developments like Paine Lake, Steeplechase, and Saddleback Ridge. There, you'll find homes in an assortment of scenic settings including the banks of the Little Pigeon River and a nearby hillside. Prices are in the $185,000 to $400,000 range.

Downtown Sevierville is home to many of the older two-story homes with wooden exteriors. Some of these date back to the early 1900s and have historical value. This section of town is noteworthy for its proximity to retail businesses and schools as well as county and city government offices. However, the same families have occupied a lot of these homes for years, and they don't appear very frequently on the market.

One of the fastest-growing regions of Sevierville is the area east of Middle Creek Road. Commercially, land bordering Dolly Parton Parkway has been very active of late with frequent construction of offices, retail space, and restaurants. Much of this came in response to the rapid residential growth in that part of town. The area in general has thrived because of a migration of local residents away from the more central, tourist-trafficked areas of Sevierville. As for housing, there are quite a few neighborhoods, both new and old, that border key streets and roads like Dolly Parton Parkway, Earnest McMahan Road, and Pullen Road. Broadly speaking, this area features rolling countryside with awesome Smoky Mountain views. As with the Kodak area, be sure to check with your real estate agent about utility services for these homes; some lie within city limits and some do not.

Among the more well established areas are upscale neighborhoods like Birchwood and Blalock Woods. These both date back to the 1970s and are marked by large, handsome homes that are fairly well separated from each other and sit on wooded tracts. Birchwood homes start around $140,000. In Blalock Woods, values are higher, with homes starting around $200,000.

Rivergate is a popular area that offers housing in the $135,000 to $175,000 range with the benefit of city utilities. Since lots were first auctioned off there in 1996, homes have sprung up like dandelions. Somerset Downs falls somewhere in between the old and new classifications. It also has large, attractive homes in a more sprawling setting but utilizes water wells and septic tanks. Prices there start around $190,000.

Near Somerset Downs are the newer Sunrise Estates and Snappwood, where nice, modern homes started going up in the early 1990s. They start as low as $180,000 with a few going into the $300,000 and $400,000 range.

Other names to look for include Shaconage, which is located off Pittman Center Road, and Victoria Landing, a hilltop condominium development with units starting at around $93,000. One of the best-known subdivisions in this neck of the woods is Belle Meadows. The homes there are relatively new, large, and attractive, but because it does receive city utilities, the lots are somewhat small and the houses are situated pretty close to each other. Nevertheless, it's a very popular neighborhood for families with children. Prices start around $200,000.

If you travel even further east on Dolly Parton Parkway (U.S. Highway 411, which eventually becomes Newport Highway) and turn south onto Long Springs Road, you'll be on your way to two towns that are favorites among those who desire sce-

Property taxes in Sevier County are among the lowest in the state of Tennessee at $1.45 per $100 of assessed value. City rates are 38 cents in Sevierville, 12 cents in Pigeon Forge, 18 cents in Gatlinburg, and 77 cents in Pittman Center.

nic, remote settings. New Center and Jones Cove, both of which are unincorporated, are 10- and 20-minute drives from downtown Sevierville, respectively. Although these communities offer little commercially, each has its own elementary school. In addition to the more idyllic atmospheres found there, the property values of these two hamlets can sometimes be more competitive compared to their neighboring markets. The average selling price of a home in New Center was $129,847 in 2003; for Jones Cove the corresponding figure was only $108,530. These figures are in line with a general assumption to be made about real estate prices in Sevier County: You'll usually find better prices on houses and land located in the more rural undeveloped areas.

Another section of Sevierville that offers nice homes in varying price ranges is the residential area that lies just west of the Parkway and runs from Forks of the River Parkway south to Lynn Road near the Governor's Crossing development. A conglomeration of different subdivisions, this area is sometimes generally referred to as Marshall Woods, which is actually the name of just one of its more popular neighborhoods. Within its streets, you'll find a little bit of everything, from large, split-level homes on quiet, shaded streets to houses that are more of the cookie-cutter variety but still make for good values in this popular family setting. This area hasn't seen a lot of recent construction. Most of the building activity there took place from the 1960s through the 1980s.

Pigeon Forge

Pigeon Forge has probably experienced more commercial growth than any city in the county within the past 10 years, but it accounts for the second-smallest population among Sevier County's three main towns.

Upon seeing nothing but tourist-oriented businesses along the Parkway, vacationers to Pigeon Forge have often asked, "Where do people around here live?" One only needs to travel a block or two in either direction off the Parkway. Although the main strip consists of one commercial venture after another, there are bands of residential areas that run parallel to the Parkway on both sides, from one end to the other. When you drive into these neighborhoods, it's like entering a whole new world. The often chaotic atmosphere of amusement rides, attractions, and traffic is immediately supplanted by tranquil environs consisting of ranch-style homes and cabins on quiet streets. At the same time, however, you're never far away from all the shopping and recreation.

There are also residential areas along the arteries that feed into Pigeon Forge's city limits from the county. Side roads like Henderson Chapel Road, Wears Valley Road, Mill Creek Road, Dollywood Lane, and Middle Creek Road all contain quite a mix of homes in terms of age, style, and price. Speaking in general terms, the residential construction in Pigeon Forge has gradually evolved over the decades. The real estate picture is one of old frame farmhouses, brick ranchers, and cabins often mixed together in a random fashion, with few clearly defined "neighborhoods." In 2003, the average home in Pigeon Forge sold for $190,824.

Much of Pigeon Forge's more recent construction is geared to the vacation and overnight rental markets and usually consists of cabins, cottages, and condos (see our Vacation Rentals chapter). These types of properties can be found on or near the secondary roads mentioned above.

A heavy concentration of cabins and log homes can also be found in the community of Wears Valley. About 8 miles southwest of Pigeon Forge, this unincorporated town has become a heavy contender in its own right in the second-home market. A popular location with retired people as well as vacation/investment home buyers, Wears Valley is very much of the same nature as Gatlinburg when it comes to real estate. For one, property values are a little higher than those in other parts of the county. Undeveloped house lots can go for as much as $75,000, and the average sale price of a home in 2003 was $209,959. But on the plus side, property values seem to appreciate well. What makes this area so popular is its setting. Nestled in a peaceful valley at the foot of Cove Mountain, Wears Valley provides its residents with tremendous views in a laid-back country setting. The community also has its own back entrance to Great Smoky Mountains National Park via Lyon Springs Road.

Another community that's easily accessible from Pigeon Forge is Caton's Chapel. Traveling approximately 10 miles out Dollywood Lane will take you to this unincorporated town, the location of which makes for handy back-road access to Pigeon Forge, Sevierville, and Gatlinburg. In addition to convenience, Caton's Chapel also retains a tranquil country setting. Outside of a few small stores and an elementary school, there's not a lot of activity. The growth that has taken place out there has been a blend of permanent residency and investment in second homes and rental property.

Gatlinburg

Like Pigeon Forge, its neighbor to the north, Gatlinburg has a daily population of more than 30,000 people during the peak season, most of whom are tourists. Only about 4,000 people call Gatlinburg "home" on a year-round basis. Because the city is surrounded by the national park on three sides, it is somewhat limited when it comes to finding new areas into which this permanent population base can expand. Gatlinburg is also topographically confined by its location, tucked in the narrow valleys among the Smoky Mountain foothills. There are a lot of businesses and homes packed and wedged into the compact dimensions of central Gatlinburg. The surrounding hills and mountainsides are also liberally dotted with chalets, cabins, and condos. The only release valve that has been able to allow for physical expansion has been the area surrounding U.S. Highway 321 (East Parkway), heading north and east away from downtown Gatlinburg.

Also, as with Pigeon Forge, the makeup of Gatlinburg's residential communities is a jigsaw puzzle of development that has evolved over the years. Locals live in a hodgepodge of commingled house styles, including cabins, chalets, cottages, condominium developments, and even some traditional ranch-style homes. Many of these homes are found along the numerous side roads that feed into US 321. Near that highway, you'll find Quail Run, where homes can be found in the $200,000 range. One of the more recent subdivisions on the scene is Brent Hills, also located off US 321 in the neighborhood of Mills Park and Gatlinburg-Pittman High School. There are also several established residential pockets found fairly close to central Gatlinburg. These include the Roaring Fork area, the Baskins Creek neighborhood, the McClain addition off River Road, and the neighborhood near Gatlinburg's Mynatt Park. Outside Gatlinburg city limits, there seems to be an endless network of intertwining country back roads, along which you'll find random scatterings of homes which can include cabins and older farmhouses.

Because of its proximity to the national park, Gatlinburg real estate prices tend to be higher than those in other markets in the county. Although the selling prices of homes there averaged $177,408 in 2003,

there are more affordable permanent homes to be had. You can find prices in the $90,000 ballpark, and of course, the diligent home shopper should always keep his or her eyes open for the occasional "steals" that pop up from time to time.

Another section of Gatlinburg deserves to be treated as an entirely different animal when it comes to real estate—the area generally referred to as "Ski Mountain." This unique section of town, which began developing in 1968, is spread along the east face of Mount Harrison and occupies more than 1,000 gorgeous, wooded acres. Driving just a couple of miles up Ski Mountain Road from downtown Gatlinburg, you'll reach Chalet Village, a realm where the chalet indeed reigns supreme. There are also quite a few condominium developments further up the mountain as you near the top (by the way, the ski resort of Ober Gatlinburg is located at the summit of this mountain; see our Attractions chapter for more). Overall, chalets and condos account for approximately 75 percent of the homes found in this region. Although we deal with condos in more detail in the Vacation Rentals chapter, there are several names worth mentioning here, including the Summit, Edelweiss, High Alpine, and High Chalet.

In the Ski Mountain area, the terrain is hilly and sometimes downright steep, but the setting is unsurpassed with its abundant woodland growth, rugged complexion, and the always present native black bear. Those fortunate enough to live there year-round never grow tired of viewing the nearby mountains that dominate their picture windows.

The trade-off is that this is some of the most expensive property in the entire county. In 2003 the average selling price of a chalet was close to $190,378. Properties in the $200,000 and $300,000 range are common. Condominiums can be found in a wide range of prices, starting as low as $39,000 for a one-bedroom unit to as high as $430,000 for a two- or three-bedroom unit. Prices often depend on the condo's location as well as its amenities.

As for the demographics of Chalet Village home owners, most are permanent residents, many of those being retirees. Understandably, however, there are a lot of homes that were purchased as vacation homes or investment properties; commonly, in these cases, the owners are absent and the properties are put on rental programs.

Another part of the county that's attracted both permanent residents and investment is the corridor of land along US 321 between Gatlinburg and the community of Cosby in neighboring Cocke County. Along this stretch of real estate, you'll find resort communities like Cobbly Nob, Acadia, and Deer Ridge where houses and condos can be purchased for both permanent or vacation residence. All of the properties mentioned offer outstanding mountain views in a remote country setting as well as numerous amenities and convenient access to Bent Creek Golf Course. Homes in this area run, on average, from $138,000 to $430,000. Condos cost as little as $40,000 and as much as $160,000.

APARTMENTS

Just 10 years ago, apartments were in woefully short supply in the Smokies. Back then, the modern, sprawling megacomplexes typical of suburban America were virtually nonexistent here. The few developments that did exist contained only a handful of units and had few on-site amenities. As the tourism industry began to snowball in the late 1980s and early 1990s, more and more people heeded the siren song of the Smokies and ventured

---

Although one-year leases are standard in Sevier County apartments, some complexes offer six-month leases for those looking for shorter-term stays. The trade-off for this convenience, however, is usually a higher monthly rent.

---

here in search of business and employment opportunities. Accordingly, the demand for apartments and other long-term rentals grew. In response, developers began meeting those needs. Today, the situation has improved markedly, although there is still a somewhat narrow selection available when it comes to sizes and styles of apartment. Even today, one- and three-bedroom units are overwhelmingly outnumbered by two-bedroom setups.

Fortunately, finding vacant apartments in general is much easier than it used to be. Only a few years ago, when apartments were scarce, your best bet was to grab the local newspaper first thing in the morning and start making calls. The good ones were rarely available and when they were, they were snatched up quickly. Now that more complexes have been built, there is a little more competition, and you see more advertisements for apartments in area newspapers and magazines.

In 2003 the average rent for a two-bedroom apartment was $511, according to East Tennessee Development District statistics. One-bedrooms averaged $482 per month, and efficiencies were $461.

One of the main contributing factors to this dilemma is land value. Newer complexes must charge higher rents to compensate for the costs of land acquisition. High-dollar investments are also what prevent the building of more three-bedroom apartments. Larger units usually require more parking areas and playground space for children, thus increasing the amount of capital needed by developers.

The vast majority of apartment complexes are in Sevierville. Gatlinburg and Pigeon Forge are better known for scatterings of long-term rentals (more often in the form of single-family homes and duplexes) rather than centralized apartment developments. As such, the complexes mentioned below are all in Sevierville, and even though it's not a totally comprehensive review of what's available in that city, it does represent most of the larger developments with the greatest number of units.

Off Dolly Parton Parkway, places like the Meadows, River Country Apartments, and Riverwalk Apartments all offer attractive, modern two-bedroom units in good neighborhoods, close to schools. All three of these developments have swimming pools on the premises. Rents among these properties range from $500 to $665 per month, and year-long leases are required.

Another area of Sevierville that offers a high number of units is the Hardin Lane neighborhood, just off Chapman Highway near the Little Pigeon River. There, you'll find three complexes within a short distance of each other, all requiring one-year leases. One and two-bedroom units are available at Mountain View Apartments in the $300 to $600 range, but the rate is dependent on your income. At Raeco Apartments, all units have two bedrooms and range from $400 to $450 per month. Nearby Woodland Park Apartments offers one-bedroom units exclusively and limits its clientele to senior citizens age 62 and older (see our Senior Scene chapter).

On the opposite side of Chapman Highway, on Old Knoxville Highway, are Riverpark Apartments, with one-, two-, and three-bedroom units ranging from $350 to $525 per month. Just off the Parkway in Sevierville is Cross Creek Village Apartments, with two-bedroom layouts in single level units and town houses ranging from $430 to $550 per month.

FINDING REAL ESTATE LISTINGS

A useful resource for the Smoky Mountains property seeker is *Homes & Land of the Smokies.* This publication is part of the largest real estate publishing network in the country, which, as a whole, distributes millions of magazines annually throughout thousands of real estate markets nationwide.

The Smoky Mountains edition of *Homes & Land* has been in print for more than 15 years and is generally regarded to be the area's primary printed source for

real estate listings. *Homes & Land of the Smokies* turns out 12 slick, full-color issues per year distributed in typical high-traffic areas throughout Sevier County. The magazine is also accessible via the Internet at www.homeandland.com. In 1998 this site was recognized by the *Wall Street Journal* as being one of the best real estate Web pages in the nation. Those wishing to subscribe to *Homes & Land* by mail can do so at a cost of $60 for 12 issues or $30 for six issues.

Another resource for listings is the *Mountain Press,* the county's daily newspaper (see our Media chapter). Properties for sale and lease are found in the paper's classified section each day, and on Sunday, the *Mountain Press* features a separate real estate section with both classified ads and display ads for local real estate companies. Of course, accessing a real estate company's Web site is an excellent means of viewing its most current inventory. We've included Internet addresses, where available, in our company profiles below.

REAL ESTATE COMPANIES

The growth of real estate as a service industry spread like kudzu through this area in the 1990s. In Sevier County alone, there are approximately 143 real estate firms with affiliated agents totaling 1,398 (including resort and time-share agents). By comparison, only a little more than 100 real estate companies and a few hundred agents served the Smokies in 1993. Succumbing to the corny temptation to call the local real estate business a "cottage" industry, we can say with certainty that its lifeblood has been a direct transfusion from the popularity of the Smokies as a tourist destination.

In this section, we've included a representative sampling of real estate companies found in Tennessee's Great Smoky Mountains. Although each firm we've mentioned is found within Sevier County borders, we have included a geographic

When choosing a real estate company in the Smokies, you can do a fair amount of research by visiting a prospective firm's Web site. You'll usually find links to the company's inventory of properties as well as background information on its agents. In some cases, you can even get access to all the properties currently listed in the local MLS system.

mix with offices found in some of the county's outlying areas in addition to the primary cities of Sevierville, Pigeon Forge, and Gatlinburg. These companies represent diverse shares of the local market and generally offer a wide variety of real estate services. Some have in-house or affiliated property management companies, and some do not. Those that do typically operate some sort of short-term rental program through which a client's investment properties or second homes are leased out when not being occupied by the owner.

Because this section of the chapter focuses on the buying and selling of real estate, we've made only passing references to overnight rentals here. For more details on that subject, refer to the Vacation Rentals chapter in this book. There, you will find listings for many other companies that will manage your own investment property or through which you can lease someone else's on a short-term basis.

Those who might be looking to buy real estate in the Smokies should be aware of the practice of "buyer's agency." Following a growing trend in real estate nationwide, Tennessee passed legislation that allows real estate agents to break away from the traditional practice of representing only property sellers and instead enter into similar fiduciary relationships with buyers. Such compacts ensure that the real estate agent works in the buyer's best interests when trying to purchase a home, business, or piece of land. The

terms of such relationships are spelled out in contracts, and of course, a real estate agent cannot act as a buyer's agent and a seller's agent within the same transaction.

Finally, a bit of semantics. The name "Realtor" is a trademark name signifying a member of the National Association of Realtors (NAR). Although not all real estate businesses are members of that association, each of the companies we've listed below is a member of NAR through either the Great Smoky Mountains Association of Realtors or the Knoxville Association of Realtors. One reason we've done so is that more than half of the real estate companies and agents in the area are Realtor members anyway, and because these associations require continuing education and adherence to a strict code of ethics by their members, we feel that steering you in that direction is a wise course of action. Realtors also serve their clients and customers through exclusive access to the area's multiple listing system, a direct-access line of information on all Realtor listings currently on the market.

Overall, the Great Smoky Mountains Association of Realtors represents 83 realty companies and approximately 410 real estate agents. They can be reached at (865) 453-1248.

Century 21 A+ Realty Group
239 East Parkway, Gatlinburg
(865) 436-2100, (877) 436-2100
www.c21aplusrealtygroup.com

This locally owned Century 21 company has been doing business under a new franchise name these past few years, but many of its agents are well established, having served Gatlinburg's residential and investment markets for decades. The staff of more than 10 Realtors handles primary residences, condo units, and chalets in the Gatlinburg area as well as residential properties in Pittman Center, Wears Valley, and Pigeon Forge. The firm's location on East Parkway makes it handy to both downtown and US 321 traffic.

Colonial Real Estate
953 Dolly Parton Parkway, Sevierville
(865) 453-3333, (800) 336-1899
www.colonialproperties.com
One of this company's greatest strengths is its lineup of 20 agents, a solid, experienced core who have been onboard since owner/broker Steve Lane opened for business in 1985. Many of Colonial's affiliate brokers are consistent million-dollar producers and rank among the top selling agents in the area. Colonial Real Estate is a full-service agency, listing and selling all types of property from residential to commercial to lots and acreage. A good percentage of their inventory is made up of primary residence homes located throughout the county. The company was voted "Best Real Estate Company in Sevier County" by readers of the *Mountain Press* in 1998.

First Choice Realtors
1338 Parkway, Suite 9, Sevierville
(865) 286-0257, (800) 982-1647
In addition to the usual mix of primary residential, commercial, and acreage, First Choice Realtors specializes in chalet sales in both Gatlinburg and Pigeon Forge and is also involved in developing a number of new area subdivisions. Owner/broker Roy Helton, who opened First Choice in 1986, also does consulting work with several companies that do high-volume investment in area rental properties.

Greenbrier Valley Resorts and Real Estate
3629 East Parkway, Gatlinburg
(865) 436-2015, (888) 546-1144
www.cobblynob.com
Although this agency has been in existence since 1986, broker Laurie Contois and agents have taken their business to new levels since taking over the company's operations several years ago. The majority of this company's listings are located along the corridor from Gatlinburg to the resort community of Cobbly Nob, about 15 miles away. Most of the properties represented are residential, but one of Greenbrier's agents is a commercial specialist. The company is also involved in long-term management, with 42 properties currently in its rental program.

McCarter Real Estate & Auction Company
3140 Newport Highway, Sevierville
(865) 453-1600, (877) 282-8467
www.mccarterauction.com
Over the years, this company has slowly evolved from a full-service real estate company to one that is exclusively an auction house. Owner and auctioneer Scott McCarter started the business in 1983, successfully tapping into the demand for auction sales, a property selling method that has become increasingly popular in the area. The company almost exclusively utilizes "absolute" auctions, by which properties are sold on the day of the auction, regardless of the final high bid. Including McCarter, there are a total of three auctioneers on staff, all of whom are members of the National Auctioneer's Association. Conducting approximately 25 auctions annually, McCarter Real Estate works primarily in home sales but also with vacant lots, farms, estates, and commercial properties.

Pioneer Realty
436 Winfield Dunn Parkway, Sevierville
(865) 453-0502, (877) 746-6410
www.pioneerrealestate.com
Pioneer has had a presence in the Smokies for quite a few years, and it remains strong today with a staff of 10 affiliate brokers. Much of their business involves new construction in areas of northern Sevier County such as Kodak and the Boyd's Creek area as well as Dandridge in Jefferson County. They also list a fair number of lots and commercial properties in the Kodak/TN 66 areas in addition to established residential properties throughout Sevier County.

Realty Executives Smoky Mountains
113 Sugarfoot Way, Suite 7
Pigeon Forge
(865) 774-4307, (888) 886-2230
This is a fairly new company to the area, but its 9 brokers, agents, and assistants represent a vibrant mix of both experienced and new, eager talent. One of the company's more successful agents was the area's top-selling residential agent in the county in both 2000 and 2001. As is typical with Pigeon Forge–based realty firms, Realty Executives Smoky Mountains offers properties scattered over a wide range of territory, from Douglas Lake in the northern part of the county to the chalets of Gatlinburg's resort areas.

Realty World Barnes Real Estate
2264 Parkway, Pigeon Forge
(865) 453-5181, (800) 222-0589
www.realtyworld-barnes.com
This Realty World franchise is the oldest real estate company in Pigeon Forge and one of the oldest in the entire county, having first opened its doors in 1969. Owner/broker Don Clayton's staff of 15 agents has decades of collective experience and makes up a company that can handle all types of properties and real estate transactions.

RE/MAX Adventure Realty
2703 Colonial Drive, Pigeon Forge
(865) 908-6000, (877) 446-7355
www.remaxadventurerealty.com
Open only a few years, this RE/MAX franchise includes a base of agents with many years of real estate experience in the Smokies. The company offers a wide range of properties spread out among Sevier and several neighboring counties. The inventory includes a balance of residential and resort properties as well as acreage, lots, and businesses. Adventure Realty and its staff of 10 Realtors and administrative assistants are also members of the Knoxville Association of Realtors, which gives even more exposure to their listings and agents.

RE/MAX All Pro, Realtors
815 East Parkway, Suite 1, Gatlinburg
(865) 436-0444, (800) 818-8133
www.gatlinburghomes.com
Owners Jeff and Karen Schoenfield, along with their 10 affiliate brokers, have been a part of the Gatlinburg real estate scene since 1998. They've built a successful agency thanks to a team of knowledgeable agents and a diverse inventory of residential and commercial properties all over the county. Many of their sales are in the overnight rental market, including the resort log home community of Black Bear Falls in Gatlinburg.

Sunset Cottage Rentals and Realty
3630 South River Road, Pigeon Forge
(865) 429-8478, (800) 211-4599
www.smokymtnrealty.com
With more than 10 years of experience in the real estate field, owner/broker Dayna Day started her own company in Pigeon Forge in 1995. Having initially focused on the overnight rental aspect of her business, Day has developed the listing side of her enterprise to a point of equal footing with her rentals. She currently has more than 150 properties on that overnight rental program and, along with her staff of affiliate brokers, deals in homes, commercial properties, and acreage all over the county.

Wears Valley Real Estate
2750 Wears Valley Road, Sevierville
(865) 428-3896, (800) 553-1425
www.wearsvalley.com
On the far west side of Sevier County in the scenic Wears Valley community, this company does a lot of business in the second-home market. Although most of their activity is in the Wears Valley area, Wears Valley Real Estate represents properties from buyers and sellers all over the county. The business has been in operation since 1989, and owner/broker Craig Reed has four agents on staff. They also have more than 20 properties on their rental program, most of which are cabins.

THE AUCTION ALTERNATIVE

Over the years, one alternative to listing and buying property through traditional real estate methods has emerged with an enthusiastic following—buying and selling property through auctions. The practice is especially strong in Sevier County, where auctions initially flourished and grew more popular through heavy regional advertising in newspapers, radio, and television. Auction companies themselves have traditionally thrived on strong word-of-mouth recommendations. Currently, approximately seven area real estate companies utilize auctions to a significant extent. The types of property that go up on the block are varied and include subdivision home sites, houses, farms, estates, and commercial properties.

Two of the more frequently used auction methods are absolute auctions and confirmation sales. In absolute auctions, the property is sold on the day of the auction to the highest bidder, regardless of the price. This obviously has advantages for the buyer, who may wind up getting a great deal. In a confirmation sale, the owner can exercise the option of accepting or rejecting the final high bid. Although this does provide a measure of protection to the seller in terms of guaranteeing a good sale price, this method tends to attract fewer bidders, which can actually reduce the chances of a higher sale price being offered.

Regardless of the method used, auctions in general have many benefits. The seller knows that his property will be moved on a specific date, on his terms and conditions. Buyers know, of course, that they can possibly get a good price. In the case of developed subdivision lots, prospective buyers have the convenience of inspecting the site before the sale and often selecting the "pick of the litter."

Those interested in using an auction service should learn as much as they can about the company and its reputation. Much of this can be done by checking references through the company's previous clients. Property owners might also check any professional affiliations that the firm might have, such as membership in the National Association of Auctioneers. When it comes to paying the auction company, sellers can often negotiate the terms, which usually involve some sort of commission. As for buyers, they are required to pay a deposit on the day of the auction and also sign a demand note that backs up the financial obligation. The buyer can then arrange financing through the institution of his choice; sometimes the auction company has its own financing program established through a local lender.

TO BUILD OR NOT TO BUILD?

Compared to other areas of the state and even the nation, the new-home construction business in the Smokies is in pretty good shape. One 1998 study, commissioned by the City of Gatlinburg, compared new construction growth in rural areas that adjoin national parks and other wilderness areas to rural areas that do not border such regions. The latter communities historically experienced only about a 4 percent growth rate in new construction while construction in the rural communities near national parks typically grew at a rate of 25 percent. The towns of Tennessee's Great Smoky Mountains are right in line with this trend, with the inherent beauty and grandeur of the area continuing to be influential factors in the expansion of that new-homes market. A booming economy and still-competitive interest rates have also encouraged housing starts. Although there are typical "off" times during periods of interest rate increases or higher materials costs, the construction business has grown steadily and is expected to remain strong for many years to come.

The builders with whom we spoke agreed on a number of trends when it came to construction in Sevier County. Many of the new homes built are used for retirement purposes. As the nation's ever-growing number of retirees seek more active lifestyles, the Smoky Mountains region is becoming a popular nesting ground for seniors who want to spend their leisure years near a variety of activities set in a healthy and scenic environment. Many of these people had vacationed here in earlier years and saw the Smokies as a natural choice for a retirement destination. A significant percentage of new homes are also going up as second homes and investment properties for both local and out-of-town owners who are playing into the vacation rental market.

As for the types of homes under construction, there are no cut-and-dried answers when it comes to size and style. The typical three-bedroom ranch home is still popular in the more primary residen-tial areas of the county like Sevierville. In areas with hilly terrain, split-level homes are in great abundance. Investment properties and vacation homes frequently tend to be log cabins or chalets, and can be found not only in the mountainous regions of Gatlinburg but also in other scenic settings like Wears Valley and the Douglas Lake area in the northern part of the county. Recently, the log-home industry has become an entity in itself, with its own selection of area companies that specialize in the sale and construction of those rustic dwellings. Condominium developments and planned communities are becoming more prevalent in all regions of Sevier County and are especially popular among retirees because of their on-site amenities and maintenance programs.

Construction prices also vary greatly, depending on location. Building in more mountainous terrain is usually more expensive because of the added costs of hillside excavation and extra foundation and basement materials. Beyond that, land costs are another crucial factor. Although actual construction costs are pretty much in line with those of neighboring Tennessee counties, land prices in Sevier County are higher (as we've mentioned), adding to the overall cost of building a home. Although you can get better land prices in the rural, undeveloped parts of the county where there are no city services, there is a trade-off in the form of additional costs for septic and well water systems.

ℹ️ *The Sevier County Home Builders Association is the local chapter of the National Home Builders Association. It has more than 110 home construction and remodeling firms as members, plus more than 120 affiliate member companies representing such industries as banking, insurance, and building supply. They can be reached by phone at (865) 453-4712 or on the Internet at www.seviercountyhba.com.*

MEDIA 📺

Whether you're talking about television, radio, or newspapers, the communities of Tennessee's Great Smoky Mountains are somewhat dependent on their proximity to Knoxville when it comes to major media influence. Sevier County does lay claim to a radio station, two locally published newspapers, and, naturally, a passel of magazines geared to serve the tourist. But as one surfs the television and radio dials or scans area newspaper and magazine racks, it becomes clear that these mountains' primary sources of information lie elsewhere.

This is a situation that gives locals a more proactive choice when it comes to the nature of information they desire and the means by which they choose to receive it. On one hand, there are those who must have their daily doses of *USA Today*, the *New York Times*, or CNN; those are all available here. On the other hand, there are still some around these parts who are content to sit back, put their feet up, and enjoy the more insular offerings of the local paper. As far as they're concerned, most of the nation may know what the Smokies have to offer, but they aren't necessarily interested in what the rest of the world has to offer them. So take your pick. No matter how involved or detached you care to be, you'll be well accommodated.

NEWSPAPERS

Sevier County is served by one daily newspaper and one weekly, both published in-county. Several papers from peripheral areas have also made their way into area newsstands, including the *Knoxville News Sentinel*, the *Knoxville Journal*, *Tri-County News*, and the *Seymour Times*. We'll give you thumbnail sketches of the two local publications as

well as the *Knoxville News Sentinel*, because these are the biggest players in the Smokies' newsprint medium.

The *Mountain Press*
119 Riverbend Drive, Sevierville
(865) 428-0746
www.themountainpress.com
The *Mountain Press* is a study in contrasts. Although it has remained very much a small-town newspaper with a conservative, local focus, it has managed to grow into a daily publication that currently operates out of a modern, 22,000-square-foot facility that opened in 1995. The paper's full-time staff of 50 generates a circulation of approximately 10,000 issues per day, reaching Sevier and surrounding counties. Subscriptions account for approximately 70 percent of this circulation; the remainder is available in racks and newsstands.

The *Mountain Press* has a long history of producing award-winning editorial and has been honored with numerous accolades from the Tennessee Press Association. In 2002 several staff writers were also honored by the Tennessee Commission on Children and Youth for stories that raised community awareness of a variety of different children's issues. Inside its pages, readers will find the typical array of hometown news, including everything from 4-H livestock contests, local politics, and high school sports to coverage of area crime and new commercial development. A number of regular departments, some of which have a distinct rural bent, focus on such topics as agriculture or veterans' affairs. There is even a daily feature called Personality, in which one local resident has his or her mug plastered on the front page of the *Mountain Press* in full color along with a minibio. It's surprising how often readers actually know the person being profiled! Suffice it to say that such a vehicle could only work in a small-town environment.

If you have trouble finding a copy of the Mountain Press *in store racks late in the day, try looking at Cresswell's Market on Dolly Parton Parkway or Layman's Market & Grill on Newport Highway. These popular local convenience stops are among the paper's biggest dealer distributors and usually have an abundant supply on hand.*

Beyond the reporting of community happenings, there is also limited coverage of events from around the region, the nation, and the world. Although the daily version of the *Mountain Press* can vary from one to two sections, the Sunday edition is fairly thick for an operation of its size. In addition to the standard fare, readers will also find expanded real estate coverage, an entertainment and TV listings section, Sunday comics, and the *USA Weekend* magazine insert. The *Mountain Press* also publishes a monthly insert, *Experienced Living,* that's especially geared toward senior citizens, as well as an annual newcomer's edition that's chock full of useful information for anyone relocating to the Smokies.

The *Mountain Press* can trace its history back to 1897, when it was originally known as the *Record-Republican.* Through the years, the paper went through various mergers and changes of ownership and name, for many years operating as *Montgomery's Vindicator.* In 1964 the publication was split into two versions, the *Gatlinburg Press* and the *Sevier County News-Record.* In 1984 the two were combined into the *Mountain Press* that area residents know today. In June 1995 ownership of the paper was taken over by Paxton Media, based in Paducah, Kentucky.

The cost of the *Mountain Press* is 50 cents daily and $1.00 on Sunday. Terms for in-county home delivery range from one month ($10.50) to one year ($210.00). There is also a discounted senior citizen rate of $105.00 for a year.

Tennessee Star Journal
2713 Parkway, Pigeon Forge
(865) 453-0626

The tagline under this weekly publication's nameplate says it all: "A Hometown Southern Newspaper." Serving Sevier County and neighboring Jefferson County, its focus is decidedly local in scope, presenting features and departments that capture the flavor of life in a small town. Being a weekly newspaper, there is less emphasis on time-critical events that could be considered "old news" six or seven days after the fact.

Generally, there is a positive slant on much of the reporting, and overall, the *Tennessee Star Journal* reflects the conservative nature and values of the communities it serves. This fact reveals itself through the regular features that appear in its pages. "Looking Back" is an award-winning column that offers in-depth examinations of area history, and "Viewpoints and Faith" addresses religious issues.

The *Tennessee Star Journal's* full-time staff of nine produces 10,000 copies that circulate each Thursday. In addition to rack distribution and subscriptions, a copy of the paper is placed in each of the rooms of a local motel chain.

The paper costs 50 cents per issue; one-year subscription rates are $20 per year for Tennessee residents and $24 for those living outside the state.

Knoxville News Sentinel
2332 News Sentinel Drive, Knoxville
(865) 523-3131
www.knoxnews.com

This daily has served Knoxville and surrounding areas since 1926 when the *Knoxville Sentinel* (founded 1886) merged with the *Knoxville News* (founded 1921). Today, the paper occupies a wide berth on the ideological spectrum. It can reflect the more liberal viewpoints of a medium-size university city while never straying too far from the Bible Belt population it serves. On a daily basis, the *News Sentinel* provides a good dose of world and national news coverage in addition to that of regional and local happenings. The multiple sections of the Sunday edition offer a full range of news, features, and other information including editorial, arts and entertainment, lifestyles, and automotive.

The *News Sentinel* is owned by the E. W. Scripps chain and employs a staff of more than 500 people, who work in the paper's $50 million facility off Western Avenue. Between 120,000 and 180,000 copies are circulated daily, depending on the day of the week. The paper has a strong presence in Sevier County through both rack distribution and home delivery. The Wednesday edition features a special section called "Community News" that is distributed in Sevier County and southern Knox County. This section has news of a more local flavor for residents of those areas.

The daily cost of the *Knoxville News Sentinel* is 50 cents, and the Sunday edition costs $2.00. Subscription rates are less expensive and are billed in 13-week periods. Costs for each three-month period average around $55.00 to receive the paper daily and $35.00 for weekends.

TOURISM PUBLICATIONS

Along with brochures and rack cards, tourist-oriented publications are on the front lines when it comes to providing vacationers with information on what the Great Smokies have to offer. They're found everywhere—welcome centers, chambers of commerce, shopping centers, convenience stores, supermarkets—anywhere that publishers suspect that large numbers of travelers may gather. Although sporadic perusal of magazine racks and displays always reveals new contenders in this stiff competition for visitor readership, we will be profiling three publications that have effectively proven themselves over the years to be the consistent leaders in both tourist readership and local advertising.

First, some generalizations about what most of these magazines have in common. They are all primarily advertising-centered,

Although tourism magazines are a great source of information and entertainment once you've arrived in the Smokies, they can also be used for pretrip planning. You can obtain copies of most of these publications through the mail, but a quicker and cheaper option is to visit the Web sites of those magazines. These include **Best Read Guide, Tennessee Smokies Visitors Guide,** *and the* **What-to-Do Magazine.**

with varying degrees of editorial content (we'll go into more detail in the write-ups). Much of the editorial you do find is more advertisement in nature; although the stories are usually positive promotions of that magazine's advertisers, they can be entertaining and informative, nonetheless. For the most part, advertisers consist of music theaters, arts and crafts shops, restaurants, attractions, hotels and motels, retail shops, and outlet centers (see related chapters for our favorite picks).

These publications almost always contain money-saving coupons in addition to area maps and handy charts that organize theater, restaurant, and hotel information into user-friendly formats. Many of the magazines also include calendars of events and useful information related to Great Smoky Mountains National Park (see our chapters on those subjects). Any of these publications would serve as a useful companion to your *Insiders' Guide,* and let's not forget the best part—they're all free in area racks (though in most cases you'll pay a few bucks for a subscription or to get a single copy sent in the mail).

Best Read Guide of the Smoky Mountains
1239 East Ridge Road, Sevierville
(865) 908-4368
**www.smokymountainsbestreadguide
.com**
This compact, digest-size magazine is presented monthly in full color. With nearly one million copies distributed each year,

Best Read Guide contains a healthy balance of advertising and editorial. In addition to the Smokies, *Best Read Guide* is also published in more than 25 other vacation markets throughout the country. Subscription rates are $20.00 per year in the United States, $30.00 per year in Canada, and $50.00 per year in other countries. Single copies cost $3.00 in the United States and Canada and $5.00 elsewhere.

Tennessee Smokies Visitors Guide
**1800 Country Meadows Drive
Sevierville
(800) 422-0742
www.vgnet.com**

This slick, full-color magazine packs a lot into each of its two annual issues. There is plenty of advertising, but the editorial content within is also abundant. Stories cover a diverse range of topics including entertainment, shopping, golf, the national park, and profiles of outlying communities like Cosby and Townsend. *Visitors Guide* is published by Vista Graphics in Virginia Beach, Virginia. This company has *Visitors Guides* in nine other markets, primarily throughout North Carolina and Virginia. The Tennessee Smokies edition of *Visitors Guide* has an annual distribution of 800,000. Individual copies can be ordered by phone and shipped at a cost of $5.00.

The welcome center at Smokies Park (the baseball stadium at exit 407, Interstate 40) is the first area chamber that you'll pass as you enter the Smokies Corridor. This is a good place to stop to pick up most of the area's free tourist publications. With them, you can utilize coupons, maps, and calendars of events to help you plan your stay. Of course, the Departments of Tourism in Pigeon Forge and Gatlinburg and the Sevierville Chamber of Commerce also operate visitor centers in their respective cities at which you'll find much of the same information.

In addition to its *Visitors Guide* publication, Vista Graphics also circulates 80,000 in-room menu guides.

What-to-Do Magazine of the Great Smoky Mountains
**P.O. Box 764, Pigeon Forge 37868-0764
(800) SUNNY DA
www.what-to-do.com**

In publication since 1993, this digest-size magazine has been one of the consistent area leaders in advertiser coupon redemption, making it popular with tourists and advertisers alike. There is a good balance between advertising and editorial, although most of the information contained in *What-to-Do* is related to Great Smoky Mountains National Park, including hiking charts, a park map, seasonal forecasts, and useful profiles of different sections of the park.

What-to-Do has a total circulation of 625,000. It is one of the few publications of its kind with exclusive distribution in area hotel rooms. Although the in-room magazine contains no hotel or motel advertising, an expanded edition of 200,000 copies is also printed, which is made available in the typical high-traffic distribution points and contains a special section of lodging advertisers. Publication of the *What-to-Do Magazine* was taken over by Sunny Day Guides of Virginia Beach, Virginia, in 1998. Sunny Day publishes similar magazines in 11 other travel markets stretching from the east coast to Lake Tahoe. They also produce a user-friendly Smokies area map, which has an annual circulation of 400,000, and a coupon book, 150,000 of which are printed each year. All of Sunny Day's Smoky Mountains publications begin distribution each spring.

TELEVISION

Nowadays, anyone still receiving television channels via the good old rooftop antenna is part of a rapidly vanishing breed. This is especially true in Sevier

County, where the hilly terrain and the 25-mile distance from Knoxville, the nearest source of network affiliates, don't always make for good broadcast reception. Although the area's two cable companies are responsible for bringing most viewers their programming, there are limits to the geographic range that they service, thus leaving some rural dwellers out in the cold. Those who live outside the reach of the giant spools of coaxial cable either rough it with antennae or purchase satellite systems.

Broadcast Stations

Tennessee's Smokies pick up affiliates of the three major networks as well as a Fox affiliate and a public television station. All of these broadcast stations are located in the Knoxville area, the 64th-largest television market in the country.

The three network affiliates have been on the air since the early to mid-1950s. Each remains active in community involvement through participation in and sponsorship of various public service projects and charitable causes. Of particular interest to the Smokies is the annual Friends Across the Mountains broadcast, produced each year by WBIR Channel 10, the local NBC affiliate. Proceeds from this charity event go to Friends of Great Smoky Mountains National Park, or "Friends of the Smokies," as they're more commonly known. Friends of the Smokies is a nonprofit organization that assists national park administration in preserving and improving the condition of the park (see our chapter on Great Smoky Mountains National Park).

WATE Channel 6 (ABC)
WBIR Channel 10 (NBC)
WKOP/WSJK Channel 15/Channel 2
(Public Television)
WTNZ Channel 43 (FOX)
WVLT Channel 8 (CBS)

Cable Television Companies

Charter Communications (865) 671-1100

This company provides service to homes and businesses within the city limits of Sevierville, Pigeon Forge, and Gatlinburg. Viewers can choose from a menu of nearly 70 channels, including several premium movie channels. Tourists might be interested in tuning in to any of the three visitor-oriented channels carried by Intermedia. Channel 5 and Channel 35 are advertising showcases for area retail shops, outlet centers, restaurants, and attractions. Channel 35 also airs a lot of programming on the shops of the Great Smoky Arts & Crafts Community. Many of these craft shops are profiled in detail with up-close interviews and on-site demonstrations. Debuting in 1998, the Visitors' Information Channel appears on Channel 54, providing similar profiles of area music and variety theaters as well as some crafts and attractions coverage. The show's hosts often take viewers inside music theater doors for interviews with the performers.

Comcast Communications (865) 637-5411

Formerly known as Greenbrier Cablevision, this company serves only limited areas of Sevier County. Comcast carries

Gatlinburg visitors will find a couple of cable television channels in the lineup that surfers won't come across anywhere else in the county. Channel 4 broadcasts information on upcoming city events and also features interviews with local luminaries. Channel 69 is devoted to advertising for Gatlinburg businesses, which may be of use if you're vacationing in or considering moving to the area.

CLOSE-UP

The Heartland Series

Since 1984, viewers of this series of abbreviated documentaries have been regularly introduced to what its producers call "a celebration of a people and their land." Produced and aired by WBIR Channel 10, each of *The Heartland Series'* five-minute segments explores some aspect of East Tennessee life, usually from a historical or environmental perspective. The series is part time capsule, part history lesson, and sometimes cautionary tale, all presented in a delightful and easily digestible format. Each weekday morning, noon, and evening, host and narrator Bill Landry takes audiences on captivating explorations of the people, places, and events that were and still are responsible for shaping the region into what it is today.

Some of the segments are character studies, such as the reflective conversation with Herb Clabo, a gentleman who had grown up in the Roaring Fork community before it was absorbed by the national park in the 1930s. Through the course of a casual stroll with Mr. Clabo, viewers get an inside glimpse into what it was like to live in the mountain communities of old.

Other episodes reveal facets of antiquated mountain lifestyles. One in particular deals with the rituals of doing laundry in the days before washing machines, dryers, and detergent. A woman who once lived in the Sugarlands area of the Smokies (before the creation of the national park) demonstrates the laborious routines of wash day, from the boiling of water and adding of homemade lye soap to the drying of the clothes on lines and the inevitable chore of ironing.

Another popular *Heartland Series* format is the reenactment, where true events and fables from the pages of regional history are re-created through visual portrayal by actors as well as narration. A viewer favorite from the first season was "The Cow Barn," a charming account from the life of Wiley Oakley, a Gatlinburg legend who was best known as a pioneering mountain guide of the early 1900s. Host Landry himself frequently winds up with principal roles in these tales, many of which are quite humorous.

Sometimes, you'll see things on *The Heartland Series* that make you wonder if they're pulling your leg. One segment details the honest-to-God practice of making wintergreen candy from birch trees by adding sugar to the strippings of a birch's sap layer. At other times, series producers are most definitely pulling your leg. Every April 1, they present what appears from the outset to be a typical *Heartland* installment. By the end, viewers realize they've been royally suckered into a hilarious April Fools' Day prank. An example is the episode where university scientists demonstrate how they have learned to generate electricity from trees. It all seems on the up-and-up until the researchers begin running wires from household appliances to tree trunks. As you watch them switch on a food mixer that's electrically connected to a tree, you slowly realize that you've been had.

All joking aside, much of the focus of *The Heartland Series* is on the preservation of the environment, particularly that of the Smoky Mountains. Going beyond its usual five-minute snapshot, the series has produced several half-hour-long documentaries on such topics as the health of Little River, the region's foresting industry, and the reintroduction of the red wolf into the national park. For its efforts, The Heartland Series received numerous awards in the area of environmental awareness and protection.

The Heartland Series was started by WBIR in 1984 as a six-month project to commemorate the 50th anniversary of the creation of Great Smoky Mountains National Park. After its initial half-year run, public opinion was so overwhelmingly in favor of extending the series that producers decided to continue the project for another six months. That six months turned into another six months, and 20 years later, *The Heartland Series* is still going like the Energizer Bunny.

Over the course of its run, close to 1,400 episodes have been produced. The best of the series have been compiled into more than 25 video volumes, with each tape containing approximately 30 of what producers consider to be the best episodes from a particular year. In addition, special videos that focus on Reelfoot Lake, Cades Cove, and Big South Fork have been put together that

Bill Landry hosts WBIR's The Heartland Series. WBIR-TV

present in-depth studies of each of these areas of Tennessee. *Heartland Series* videos can be purchased at select locations, including Heartland Antiques in Pigeon Forge, Wears Valley Antique Gallery in Wears Valley, and Borders in Knoxville. They are also available on loan through Anna Porter Public Library in Gatlinburg and Sevier County Public Library in Sevierville.

more than 63 channels, including several premium channels.

RADIO

WMIX (105.5 FM) and WSEV (930 AM), located in Sevierville, are the only radio stations broadcasting from the Smokies. Until February 2000, Mix 105.5 was owned by Dollywood and had the call letters WDLY. Referred to as "Dolly's Station," it played country music, while the sister AM station, WSEV, had more of a gospel emphasis. When Dollywood sold the two stations to East Tennessee Radio Group in early 2000, the new owners changed the name of the FM station to Mix 105.5 and replaced the country music with an adult contemporary format. WSEV is still primarily a gospel station.

The remainder of the stations we've included are located in the Knoxville area. Although we haven't listed all the Knoxville stations pertinent to the different categories, we have attempted to base selections on how strong a particular station's signal is received in Sevier County.

You might notice that we've listed only

one country music station. That wasn't an oversight on our part. Knoxville's WIVK is consistently rated as one of the top country stations in the nation and has traditionally dominated the country market in this region. Presumably, that level of influence has intimidated competitors from jumping into the game.

CHRISTIAN AND GOSPEL

WJBZ 96.3 FM
WRJZ 620 AM
WSEV 930 AM
WYLV 89.1 FM

CLASSICAL

National Public Radio 91.9 FM

COUNTRY

WIVK 107.7 FM

ROCK

WBON 104.5 FM (classic)
WIMZ 103.5 FM (classic)
WNFZ 94.3 FM (alternative)
WOKI 100.3 FM (new rock, blues, reggae)

TALK AND NEWS

WNOX 990 AM
WNOX 99.1 FM

TOP 40 AND POPULAR

WJXB 97.5 FM (soft rock)
WMIX 105.5 FM (adult contemporary)
WMYU 93.1 FM (oldies of the '60s and '70s)
WWST 102.1 FM (adult contemporary)

When visiting Great Smoky Mountains National Park, tune your radio into 1610 AM to receive information on park activities, events, and schedules.

EDUCATION AND CHILD CARE

We East Tennesseans are familiar with the jokes and stereotypes. We're well aware that there are those (especially our northern friends) who imagine that we run around all day in overalls and straw hats, without shoes, a stalk of wheat dangling from one corner of the mouth. Surely, we send our children off each morning to the ol' one-room schoolhouse where the teacher gives the little tykes a rudimentary dose of the Three Rs (that is, if they even attend school at all!).

Despite any preconceived ideas you may have about the state of education in these Tennessee hills, we're happy to say that Sevier County children and adults alike have access to a full slate of progressive educational programs on all levels, both public and private. To be sure, there are school systems throughout the region, especially those in more rural areas, that aren't so fortunate. But Sevier Countians have built an educational infrastructure that makes their children a treasured priority.

Fact is, the tourism industry isn't the only thing that's endured sweet growing pains. Thanks to a constantly expanding base of permanent residents, our local public school system has found itself in a perpetual state of development and metamorphosis. Although the very nature of our existence in the Smokies intertwines us with tourism, no one has lost sight of the fact that this is still a terrific place to raise children. Because education is an integral part of that upbringing process, great emphasis has been placed on the importance of having quality teachers and up-to-date facilities to prepare our children for their futures.

To use computer jargon as an analogy, the Sevier County school system has done quite a bit of upgrading in recent years, including both "hardware" and "software." As for the hardware, construction of new schools and additional classrooms has just barely managed to keep up with swelling enrollment. When it comes to the software, local schools have benefited from broad-minded approaches to curriculum and solid accreditation standards. Even the subject of year-round school was deliberated in recent years—it fell short of implementation, but there was still substantial interest in giving it a whirl, and the issue may rear its head again someday.

Regardless of whether a child attends public or private school, the state of Tennessee requires that he or she attend kindergarten. To register, the child must be five years old on or before October 1 of the year he or she plans to attend. The registration procedure requires parents to provide a certified copy of the child's birth certificate along with an up-to-date immunization record and medical examination forms signed by the child's physician or the Sevier County Department of Health. Such health records are considered valid if they are dated any time between the start of school and the previous January 1. The public school system has a prekindergarten screening process as well, and most private schools, of course, have their own individual application and interview processes.

This chapter begins with an overview of the Sevier County public school system, followed by a look at area private schools as well as the new frontier in local education—homeschooling. You'll also find profiles on the many adult education programs found in the county, including our local community college annex. The second half of the chapter

If you're interested in receiving informa-tion about child-care resources for low-income families, or if you'd like to check out the background of a particular child-care center, you can contact the Sevier County office of the Tennessee Department of Human Services at (865) 429-7005.

focuses on child-care and preschool opportunities as well as after-school pro-grams and other services that benefit the concerned parent.

PUBLIC SCHOOLS

Sevier County School District
226 Cedar Street, Sevierville
(865) 453-4671
www.sevier.org
Unlike many districts, Sevier County allows parents to send their children to any school within the system, regardless of residence. A family in Sevierville may enroll their teenager at Gatlinburg–Pittman High School, for example, or a younger child who lives in Seymour might attend Sevierville Primary.

As mentioned previously, one of the primary challenges the local school board has faced is how to accommodate the growing number of children who enter the school system each year. That number is currently over the 13,768 mark and rising.

The county's incorporated and unincor-porated communities include 11 elemen-tary or primary schools, 6 intermediate and middle schools, and 4 high schools. Also included in the public system are a vocational center (at Sevier County High School) as well as institutions that serve adults and special-needs children.

To stave off overcrowding, the school system implemented a three-year, $30 million construction and renovation pro-gram that touched most of the communi-ties in the county in one way or another. Many benefited from badly needed new

schools, classroom additions, and remod-eling projects. Pigeon Forge underwent an interesting shuffling process. In 1999 they launched the county's fourth high school, which now occupies the former Pigeon Forge Middle School. In turn, the middle school moved to the existing pri-mary school, and the primary school moved into a brand-new facility. Financial expenditures are another sure indicator of growth. Between the 2001–2002 and 2003–2004 school years, the county's total budget rose from $75 million to $87 million.

About 2,300 employees (roughly half teachers, half support personnel like cus-todians and cafeteria workers) are cur-rently employed by Sevier County schools, although this number is sure to increase as enrollment rises. Teacher salaries here are generally on an equal footing with those in other Tennessee districts. Begin-ning salaries range from the upper $20,000s to the low $30,000s, depending on whether the teacher has a bachelor's or master's degree. As of 2004, the aver-age salary was a little more than $37,000 per year. Teacher-student ratios are favor-able: by 2001, Tennessee was required to have maximum ratios of 1 to 20 for kinder-garten through third grade, 1 to 25 for fourth through sixth grades, and 1 to 30 for seventh and eighth grades.

Of course, modern buildings and an adequate teaching staff don't necessarily add up to a quality education. Sevier County schools pride themselves on their accreditation standards. Since 1991, every school in the system has been accredited by the Southern Association of Colleges and Schools. Its requirements for educa-tional standards and student-teacher ratios are tougher than the minimums set forth by the state.

Administrators have implemented a number of programs to help local stu-dents keep pace with their peers nation-wide, with particular recent emphasis on development in math and technology. The 21st Century program, for example, put computers into every fifth, sixth, and seventh grade classroom; current efforts are going into equipping eighth grade classrooms as well. Other programs focus on developing accelerated math skills for seventh and eighth graders and language and math skills at the primary level.

Incidentally, the county does not operate on a "track system" that separates classrooms according to student ability. Rather, classes contain children with a mix of ability levels.

On the secondary level, students have a fair amount of flexibility in selecting their educational path. In eighth grade, each student is asked to choose between a college preparatory or a vocational curriculum for his or her upcoming high school years, and approximately 60 percent of the county's high school students are on track for a college education. Despite the path chosen, all students must complete a basic core of credits, in addition to seven or eight electives dependent on the student's area of emphasis. High school students can also earn college credit through advance placement courses and the Dual Enrollment Program, the latter being in conjunction with Walters State Community College (see the section on "Adult Education" in this chapter).

When it comes to standardized test scores, the report card is mixed. In 2003–2004, the average composite ACT score was 22.6, which is higher than the statewide average of 20.4.

On average about 70 percent of graduates from high schools in Sevier County go on to college. Remember, though, that this number reflects the fact that roughly 70 percent of all high school students are on a college prep curriculum compared to the 30 percent who are on a vocational track. Overall, around 85 percent of Sevier County's high school graduates go on to some form of post-secondary education, including college and vocational schools.

In the area of special education, the Sevier County school system is well equipped to serve the educational needs of learning disabled and handicapped students ages 3 to 22. Every school in the

Since 2000, the transition for incoming freshmen at Sevier County High School has been made a lot easier thanks to the school's Freshmen Academy program. Highly rated teachers, a team approach to education, and age-segregated classrooms have all helped to slash the school's dropout rate among sophomores.

district has some sort of special education program. In some cases, special-needs children are integrated into regular classrooms; there are also self-contained classes for students with significant disabilities that can't be served in regular classrooms. Students that are more severely impaired can be enrolled in Parkway Academy, a facility adjacent to Sevierville Middle School that utilizes specially trained instructors and individualized curricula. The school system also offers outlets for exceptionally gifted students with its Children with Special Abilities program.

PRIVATE SCHOOLS

The small number of private schools in Sevier County might be evaluated from different perspectives. An argument could be made for the fact that the broad base of laborers in the tourist industry (who make between $5.00 and $7.00 per hour) simply can't afford private schools. Although there is some validity to that, it's also true that many residents are simply happy with the public school system.

On the flip side of the coin, some parents enroll their children in private schools because of dissatisfaction with the public system. One of the primary complaints received about public schools is that they lack the Christian emphasis that a growing number of parents desire for their children (the same rationale applies to homeschoolers). Two of the three private schools we've included here are church-affiliated institutions.

Covenant Christian Academy
1625 Old Newport Highway, Sevierville

3222 Chestnut Hill School Road
Dandridge
(865) 429-4324
www.mandateinc.org

This private school, a program of Christ Covenant Reformed Episcopal Church, started out with only six students in 1989. More than a decade later, the school boasts an overall enrollment of more than 400 (including homeschoolers). The student body ranges from three-year-olds to 12th graders and is split into two different facilities. The original Sevierville site serves 90 kids in preschool through third grade. In 2001 the school opened a second campus in Dandridge, Tennessee, which currently accommodates 100 students in 4th through 12th grades. The Dandridge campus is located on 10 acres and boasts an auditorium, running track, and soccer field.

The curriculum is a nondenominational Christian-based one, with all subjects being taught from a Christian perspective. Daily activities include a chapel service and prayer. Covenant Christian is a day school that runs on typical school day hours. Enrolled students can be picked up as late as 6:00 P.M.

Covenant Christian School also serves as a satellite facility for its homeschool program (see section on homeschooling in this chapter). Of the school's total enrollment of 420, nearly 220 are educated at home by their parents. Parents who wish to participate in the program must submit an application (and fee), and on approval pay an annual tuition as well

Reflective of the demographic makeup of the county's general population, the students in Sevier County schools are overwhelmingly white. Minorities make up less than 5 percent of the student population; 1 percent is African-American, 1 percent is Asian and 1.5 percent is Hispanic.

as the cost of the curriculum. The curriculum can be purchased through the school, but if it is obtained elsewhere, it must be approved by the school.

Kodak Montessori Academy
2941 Douglas Dam Road, Kodak
(865) 933-8751

Since 1990, this not-for-profit private school—formerly known as Riverside Academy—has utilized the Montessori philosophy to educate children age two through sixth grade (grades one through six are actually taught an integrated curriculum that includes Montessori). The school uses hands-on programs that center around the individual development of each child. Students' needs are met according to their different levels of development and paces of learning. Although only the kindergarten is accredited, students consistently test in the top one-fifth percentile on national achievement tests and, as a result, have not encountered difficulty in transferring educational credits to other schools.

The school's enrollment averages around 45 students per year and is distributed among three age groupings. The preschool is for ages two to five, and the kindergarten includes ages five and six; the student-teacher ratio at these levels is 10 to 1. The school-age level includes grades one through four, and the student-teacher ratio is 8 to 1. The entry process is nondiscriminatory. The primary concern of administrators is that a child's parents are supportive of the Montessori philosophy.

Although the school maintains typical school day hours, the building is open from 7:30 A.M. to 6:00 P.M. Monday through Friday. The tuition price includes after-school care up until closing time. Kodak Montessori Academy also has a summer education program that includes a Montessori curriculum in addition to fun warm-weather activities. Currently, the summer program is only available to the preschool levels, but plans are under way to extend it to the school-age levels and include activities like a computer camp.

King's Academy
202 Smothers Road, Seymour
(865) 573-8321
www.thekingsacademy.net

Founded in 1880, King's Academy is the oldest continuously run school in Sevier County. It provides a high-quality, college preparatory education, not only for local children but also for those from across the nation and as many as 50 different countries. Originally known as Harrison Chilhowee Baptist Academy, the school is run by a president and board of trustees appointed and approved by the Tennessee Baptist Convention. Accordingly, students study a well-rounded curriculum presented with a Christian-centered worldview.

The school, for kindergarten through 12th graders, operates as both a day and boarding facility; the boarding program is only available to 7th through 12th grades. To be accepted, children cannot have been expelled from another school, nor have had severe behavioral problems, and administrators look for previous exemplary behavior in the application process.

The school's recent enrollment was 350 students, the highest number since the community of Seymour built its own public high school in 1961. Contributing to that growth has been the school's elementary program, implemented in 1995. Of the students who graduate from King's Academy, approximately 95 percent go on to college, the highest such percentage among area secondary schools. With an average class size of 19, student-teacher ratios are well below the maximums allowed by the state.

The school boasts a state-of-the-art computer lab and offers special programs like the Experiential Curriculum for the Outdoors classroom (ECO). A required course in the upper-level grades, ECO takes students into the Smoky Mountains twice a year. The intent is to teach them skills like hiking, camping, rapelling, and canoeing while at the same time developing an appreciation of God's glory through the wonders of nature.

Extracurricular activities are well supported at King's Academy. It maintains a full sports program, fielding secondary-level teams in sports like football, basketball, and baseball. The campus also has an Olympic-size pool and gymnasium. Overall, the school is spread out over a 67-acre campus and exudes the feel of a small college. During the summer months, its retreat and conference center hosts activities like band clinics, athletic camps, and church retreats. Also in the summer, the school offers an English as Second Language program that is primarily designed to assist its Latin American and Asian students.

HOMESCHOOLING

For more and more families nationwide, the option of homeschooling has become a viable alternative to public schools. Nationwide, the number of home school families is estimated to be between 1 and 1.5 million while regionally, it's estimated that around 3,000 families in Knox County and surrounding counties teach their children at home. The reasons for such a choice vary and can range from dissatisfaction with public schools to assisting a learning-disabled child. Because the Smokies are locked firmly in the heart of the Bible Belt, one of the more common reasons cited is that homeschooling gives parents the freedom to incorporate their religious values into their children's education.

Generally, parents who educate their children at home operate through and are accountable to a "satellite" school. In some cases these schools can be part of a public school system, but in the vast majority of instances, satellite schools are private religious schools. Parents can create and administer their own curricula, and working under the umbrella of a religious school usually allows for fewer snarls with governmental regulation or interference.

Nevertheless, Tennessee has several laws to which homeschoolers must

The Dollywood Foundation

In 1988, hometown girl Dolly Parton and the Dollywood Corporation jointly established the Dollywood Foundation to develop and support educational programs in Sevier County. In its 15-plus years of existence, the foundation has raised millions of dollars; funds have come from individual and corporate donors as well as through celebrity benefit concerts staged by Ms. Parton herself.

Thus far, the proceeds have gone toward numerous programs within the local public school system, such as first-grade teaching assistants, guidance counselors, computer labs, and college scholarships. Outside the schools, an after-school tutoring program has been implemented at the Boys & Girls Clubs of the Smoky Mountains (see the write-up in this chapter).

One of the foundation's hallmark achievements has been the Imagination Library, which began development in 1995. The Imagination Library is designed to foster an interest in reading among preschool children and to help kindle their imaginations. Any child five or younger may register to receive a free, hardcover book in the mail once a month until he or she begins attending school. Children born at Fort Sanders Sevier Medical Center in Sevierville automatically receive their first book and registration form at birth. If a child begins collecting the library at birth, he or she will amass a total of 60 books by the time kindergarten rolls around.

As of the end of 2003, 260 communities in 35 states were participating in the program. The number of children receiving books each month had grown to more than 63,000—twice the number from the previous year. The total number of books distributed in 2003 had likewise doubled. Some 850,000 books were mailed out in 2002 and 2003 combined, and more than 1.2 million books were expected to be given away in 2004.

Interest in the program is sparked by the Imagination Library's "Imagineer,"

adhere. Children must attend class for at least four hours per day, 180 days out of the year. They must also take periodic standardized achievement tests. Although there are no particular curricular requirements at younger grade levels, children at the high school level must complete a certain number of credits in subjects like English, math, science, etc. If the child plans on attending college, parents will generally choose an educational plan geared toward helping him or her score well on college entrance exams.

Within the prescribed limits, parents may tailor the curriculum to suit the child's needs and abilities. Materials can be purchased through the various satellite schools or through any number of companies that specialize in homeschool curricula. Locally, parents interested in getting started in homeschooling may want to contact the Smoky Mountain Home Edu-

All aboard for Dollywood Foundation's Imagination Express. DOLLYWOOD

who regularly drives her specially made "train" to day-care centers, Head Start programs, and libraries throughout the county, reading to children and encouraging them to join the program. Throughout the year, the Imagineer makes three or four daily visits to area children.

cation Association on the Internet at wwww.smhea.org. They'll help you take those first steps and also refer you to one of several local support groups for home education families.

ADULT EDUCATION

Who says you can't teach an old dog new tricks? In Sevier County, educational opportunities for adults include classes within the public school system as well as on the private level. Whether you're going for your high school equivalency, interested in taking a computer class, or starting on a college degree, there are several options waiting for you here in the Smokies.

Adult Education Program
226 Cedar Street, Sevierville
(865) 453–4671

Funded and administered through the county's public school system, the Adult Education Program offers free classes on a variety of levels, serving hundreds of adults each year. Basic skills classes help adults improve in the areas of reading, writing, and math. Those pursuing a high school diploma can choose from two routes. They can attend classes at White's Adult High School in Sevierville or they can take any of the GED equivalency classes offered at various times and different locations throughout the county.

Tennessee Technology Center
109 Industry Drive, Sevierville
(865) 453-5644

This vocational school operates through 28 sites statewide, including the one in Sevierville. Accredited by the Council of Occupational Education, the Sevierville branch teaches courses in industrial electricity and computer electronics. Each course is worth 27 college credit hours, and upon completion, students may then seek certification in their field if they wish. Graduates are qualified to work in such occupational fields as residential and industrial wiring or computer, TV, VCR, and stereo repair.

The center maintains an average of 14 full-time students who attend class five days a week for six hours per day. There are usually about 28 part-time students at-tending either two or four nights per week. All students must have a high school or GED diploma to enroll. Registration takes place at the beginning and middle of each quarterly term.

Walters State Community College
1720 Old Newport Highway, Sevierville
(865) 774-5800
www.wscc.cc.tn.us

Calling itself "The Great Smoky Mountains Community College," Walters State is a two-year, nonresidential college serving more than 6,000 students among its different campuses. Sevierville's annex is one of three branches of the main campus, which is based in Morristown, Ten-

nessee (about a one-hour drive from Sevierville). Individual courses are taught in various facilities in more than 10 East Tennessee counties. The Sevierville site has an enrollment of around 1,100 students per semester. About 60 percent of day students are recent high school graduates while 60 percent of those who attend evening classes are older students seeking continuing education.

Accredited by the Southern Association of Colleges and Schools, Walters State offers associate of arts, associate of science, and associate of applied science degrees. The first two degrees are university parallel programs easily transferable to most four-year colleges; the majority of Walters State students pursue one of these degrees. The associate of applied science degree is a nontransferable, technical education path. For many years the Sevierville campus had not been equipped to teach science classes, so those requirements had been met at the Morristown campus in order to complete a degree. However, a $6.5 million, 68-acre campus opened just a few years ago in Sevierville, offering science courses and allowing for full satisfaction of most areas of study.

Dozens of courses are offered in Sevierville, including those in computer science, math, English, and history. Two of this campus's flagship programs are studies in culinary arts and in hospitality management. The first gives students real-world experience in food preparation by cooking and serving lunches and dinners that are available to the public (see our Restaurants chapter). Hospitality Management prepares students for careers in hotel and motel management, an appropriate field for such a tourist-oriented area. Beginning in 2001, classes in both areas of study were offered in Sevier County public schools, up to nine credit hours of which are transferable to Walters State.

Another unique program, Professional Entertainment, provides education and training for all aspects of show business, from acting, singing, and dancing to set design, television/record production, and management. The school even provides training for auditions at entertainment companies like Opryland Productions, Dollywood, and Busch Gardens.

To enroll, new students must provide proof of two doses of measles, mumps, and rubella immunization since their first birthday. They must also submit an application and corresponding fee, provide a high school transcript, have ACT or SAT scores sent to the admissions office, and of course, follow the appropriate class registration and fee payment procedures.

In addition to degree-related studies, Walters State offers a number of other programs designed to reach out to all segments of the population. Each semester, about 25 noncredit, "community-oriented" classes are taught in subjects ranging from art to business education; the majority are in the field of computer studies. For prospective college students, college credit courses are available to high school juniors and seniors with a B average. Students who have difficulty attending classes at the main campus might want to take advantage of the college's distance learning opportunities such as Interactive Television courses (which utilize closed-circuit TVs) and Internet courses, through which some or all of a course's work can be completed online.

CHILD CARE

We'll start by looking at the state of full-time day care for children younger than school age; later in this section is a subsection on after-school and summer programs for older kids.

Full-Time Programs

Although the local public school system has made admirable efforts to keep up with the county's swelling school-age population, the same hasn't always applied to the area's child-care industry. That isn't a commentary on the quality of

What's better than free college? Not much, especially if you plan on attending the local campus of Walters State Community College. Sevier County government pays full tuition for any student who graduates from a county high school with a minimum 2.7 GPA, scores well on the ACT test, and meets minimum residency requirements.

existing child care, necessarily, but on the amount of it. Many day-care facilities and preschools consistently find themselves at maximum capacity with a waiting list of names. It's not a hopeless situation, however. Sevier County's 41 licensed child-care centers are allowed a combined, maximum enrollment of 1,653 kids. Statistics for 2004 indicated that slightly more than 1,247 children were enrolled in this type of facility, so child care can be found if you do some digging. And it's never too early to begin the search process.

In your quest for child care, we'll help you do some sorting by first making a distinction in classification. You basically have a choice of going with an unlicensed caregiver or one that's licensed by the Tennessee Department of Human Services. The state requires anyone caring for more than four nonrelated children to be licensed, regardless of whether the setting is in the home or at a center. Maximum student-teacher ratios should range from 5 to 1 for infants between 6 weeks and 15 months of age to 25 to 1 for children age 6 and older. In 2004 there were more than 40 licensed child-care operations in Sevier County. Of that number, 15 were in-home facilities.

We would definitely advise steering clear of any unlicensed day care that cares for more than four nonrelated kids. But it's otherwise difficult and sometimes foolhardy to make generalizations when comparing unlicensed, in-home care (for four or fewer nonrelated children) to licensed child-care centers. Some licensed day-care facilities might be bad choices; by the same token, some small, unlicensed, in-home providers might provide a wonderful and safe environment. The latter type of care can usually be found by scanning classified ads in local papers or by watching supermarket and other types of community bulletin boards. Also note that although the state doesn't require an in-home day care with four or fewer children to be licensed, there are those that voluntarily register with the Department of Human Services and are subject to monitoring procedures.

The bottom line in any case is to do research. This involves more than just comparing rates. Parents should take their children to the facility in question and see how the kids react to the environment, the teachers, and the other children.

Ask the director about things like teachers' qualifications, student-teacher ratios, and discipline policies. Most importantly, get several references and follow up by actually checking on them. Trust your parental instincts; even if everything seems great on the surface, don't hesitate to continue your search if any particular child care leaves you with that "unsettling" feeling that parents sometimes get. As an added peace-of-mind measure, you might contact the Department of Human Services to see if the caregiver in question has received any negative reports. Their toll-free number is (800) 462–8261, and they have a Web site where you can find information on specific day-care facilities in the county; the address is www.state.tn.us/humanserv.

Another distinction you might want to consider is the difference between a day care and a preschool. You'll find that many area child-care centers include the word "preschool" in their name. A child-care provider isn't supposed to call itself a "preschool" unless it teaches a specific curriculum that helps prepare children for kindergarten and school. Because these teaching materials are an added expense for preschools, rates are usually a little higher. Your choice ultimately depends on what you want your child to get out of the experience.

Statistics from the Tennessee Department of Human Service indicate that the average weekly cost of day care for one child in Sevier County is $78. Broken down by type of facility, the prices don't vary much from group to group. If you look at average costs per age group, the costs of care for infants (up to 12 months old) and toddlers (12 months to 2 years old) average $91 and $86 per week, respectively. For two- to five-year-olds, weekly costs average from $74 to $84.

What you get for your money will vary from center to center, so always ask specific questions when doing your research. As we mentioned, some day-care providers teach a preschool curriculum while others simply offer structured play. Some places include meals in the price, while others provide snacks only. Other cost-related considerations include discounts for enrolling more than one child and fees for late pickups.

After-School and Summer Programs

Just because the kids are big enough to go to school doesn't mean that the issue of quality child-care ends. Many families with working parents and little extended family still must provide the children with a place to go after school and during the summer months. And as with any child-care situation, it's important to find a safe, fun, and educational environment in which the youngsters can thrive.

An obvious place to start is with some of the area's licensed day-care centers and preschools. Several have after-school and summer camp programs in addition to full-time care for preschoolers. In some cases, the center will even pick the kids up at school and transport them to the day care. Specific after-school activities may include playtime, craft projects, or homework periods. In summer, field trips to movie theaters, amusement centers, and swimming pools are popular with the kids. Naturally, rates will vary depending on the individual facility and the scope of its programs.

Outside the day-care environment, there are a few other resources that have proven themselves to be popular with local families when it comes to after-school and summer care.

Boys & Girls Clubs of the Smoky Mountains
209 McMahon Avenue, Sevierville
(865) 428–6550
www.bgcsmoky.com

This nationally known "Positive Place for Kids" opened in the Smokies in 1991. According to the club's mission statement, its purpose is to "serve the community by helping our youth build character, develop social skills, inspire dreams, and instill leadership qualities necessary to become successful, contributing citizens of Sevier County and beyond." The Boys & Girls Clubs are open to all children ages 6 through 18, regardless of race, religion, culture, or income.

After many years of hard work and a $1.5 million fund-raising campaign, the club moved into a brand-new facility in the summer of 1998. There is a well-equipped game room (no video games), a large, multipurpose gym, and an arts-and-crafts center where kids receive instruction in drawing, painting, clay work, and more. The Boys & Girls Clubs also provide several opportunities throughout the year to take part in outdoor activities like camping, hiking, and fishing. Its services and activities include homework assistance and tutoring, computer education classes, drug and alcohol prevention programs, and nutrition programs.

The annual enrollment fee of $100 per child covers all of his or her expenses during after-school care. There is also an 11-week day camp that runs during the summer. Registration for the summer camp begins in the spring, and the cost is $350 per child.

The club is usually at full enrollment, and the recent waiting list had about 30 names. At the end of each year, current members get the first opportunity to sign up for the following year; after that, names are taken from the waiting list. Anyone new to the area who is interested in joining is advised to get on the waiting list as soon as possible. Boys & Girls Club of the Smoky Mountains is open from 3:00 to 7:00 P.M., Monday through Friday during the school year. In summer, the hours are 7:00 A.M. to 6:00 P.M. The center is open from 8:00 A.M. to 5:00 P.M. on school holidays but is closed on major holidays.

Sevierville Community Center
200 Gary R. Wade Boulevard, Sevierville
(865) 453–5441

To learn about everything this community center has to offer, refer to our Parks and Recreation chapter. Fortunately, much of what's available is incorporated into the center's after-school and summer programs.

During the school year, children ages 6 through 11 can unwind after a hard day of hitting the books with educational and fitness-oriented activities like swimming, bowling, games, outdoor play, and crafts; an afternoon snack is also included. Both the community center and Sevierville City Park are used for educational and fitness-oriented fun. The after-school program runs throughout the academic year, ending daily at 5:30 P.M. The program is usually full, with even more kids on a waiting list, so early sign-ups are highly recommended.

The community center has other programs to serve children year-round. The center sponsors short camps during the Christmas and spring break vacation periods. When school's out for the year, the community center runs a summer camp that takes up to 60 children ages 6 to 11; registration begins in March. In addition to taking advantage of the community center facilities, the kids go on numerous field trips to places like the city park pool, local amusement centers, and movies. Summer hours are 7:45 A.M. to 3:30 P.M. weekdays; extended after-camp hours are 3:30 to 5:30 P.M.

Gatlinburg Community Center
Mills Park Road, Gatlinburg
(865) 436-4990

Although it doesn't operate an after-school program, this community center runs a series of weeklong day camps through the summer for ages 5 through 13. Each week is tailored to a different age group and features a specific theme. Activities range from arts and crafts projects to rock climbing, white-water rafting, and trips to the Knoxville Zoo. A maximum of 15 children get into each session, and sign-ups begin the first Monday in May. Weekly costs range from $50 to $75. Daily hours for the community center's day camps are from 8:30 A.M. to 3:30 P.M., except for the five- to seven-year-old group, which attends from 10:00 A.M. to 3:00 P.M.

Options for Low-Income Families

Head Start
(865) 453-8959

This federally funded program serves as many as 180 three-, four-, and five-year-olds in six different centers throughout Sevier County. Head Start was designed as a cognitive preschool program that works in the areas of education, health and social services, parent involvement, and literacy to help families and children become more self-sufficient and to prepare children for school. It primarily serves children from low-income families, but approximately 10 percent of enrollment is reserved for special-needs children, regardless of income. Special-needs children are integrated into the regular Head Start classrooms.

Countywide, Head Start has facilities in Wears Valley, Pigeon Forge, and Sevierville and three in the northern section of the county near Kodak. Five of the six centers are half-day programs that generally run from 9:00 A.M. to 2:00 P.M. The full-day center is open from 6:00 A.M. to 6:00 P.M. It is more geared toward working parents and parents involved in school or other vocational training.

There is no charge for the partial-day programs. The full-day center charges $55 per week, but families that can't afford the cost can apply for financial assistance through the Tennessee Department of Human Services and the state's Child Care Brokers program.

On a daily basis, children at Head Start centers are exposed to a comprehensive preschool program and more. Typical activities include working on letter and number skills, learning about health and nutrition, taking field trips, and developing social skills. Beyond the basics, all children are given speech and hearing tests, dental checkups, and psychological evaluation in the classroom within the first 45 days of the term, all of which are paid for by Head Start.

The Head Start program in Sevier County has traditionally worked closely with the public school system, and it's been successful in preparing young children for school. It's not an uncommon occurrence for kindergarten teachers in the local public schools to be able to pick out a Head Start kid from the rest of the class, based on that child's preparedness.

HEALTH CARE (H) AND WELLNESS

In what is probably a rare turn of events, the medical-care field has actually stayed ahead of the curve during the explosion of tourism and population in Sevier County over the past decade. Rescue services and medical care have stayed abreast of the increasing demand by training practically every city and county employee in first aid and CPR, and the combination of a constantly growing population and the still-rural charm of the area continues to attract medical professionals to the mountains.

The county's only hospital has also committed itself to medical excellence by attracting generous donations for building and service expansions. By joining a large regional medical system, Fort Sanders Sevier Medical Center has made available to its patients facilities and services far beyond the reach of a "rural" hospital. Mental health has also become a significant concern as the nation's atten-

tion has shifted from restorative to preventive care, and several area churches conduct ongoing family-centered "wellness" programs. The single public mental-care facility and the oldest retreat center in the city are listed.

The list of medical services and facilities that follows has been compiled to provide the visitor with a service provider convenient to wherever they might be when such service becomes necessary. The hospital and walk-in clinics are fully cognizant of the population makeup of the Smokies Corridor and tend to lean toward the idea of treating their patients as guests who've had a bad turn of luck. All of the facilities listed accept most insurance programs and national credit cards. If payment is a problem, they'll work something out. The clinics usually operate Monday through Friday from 8:00 or 9:00 A.M. to 4:30 or 5:00 P.M., but calls at all hours are answered.

Local Emergency Numbers

Any emergency—911
Medical Emergency Hot Line—(865) 453-7111
Tennessee Highway Patrol—(865) 693-7311
Sevier County Ambulance Authority—(865) 453-3200
Sevier County Sheriff's Department—(865) 453-4668
Sevierville Police Department—(865) 453-5507
Sevierville/Sevier County Fire Department—(865) 453-9276
Pigeon Forge Police Department—(865) 453-9063
Pigeon Forge Fire Department—(865) 453-4044
Gatlinburg Police Department—(865) 436-5181
Gatlinburg Fire Department—(865) 436-5112
Pittman Center Police/Fire Department—(865) 436-9684

HOSPITALS AND CONVALESCENT CARE CENTERS

Sevierville

Fort Sanders Sevier Medical Center
709 Middle Creek Road, Sevierville
(865) 429-6100
www.fssevier.com
What was a small, well-run, but very limited rural hospital as recently as 1990 has grown into one of Tennessee's recognized leaders in overall health care. Fort Sanders Sevier Medical Center, still locally referred to as "Sevier County Hospital," has expanded in every direction (including straight up and down) until the original building is no longer visible. The current emergency room is larger and has a bigger staff than the original hospital had, and the addition of special-care facilities like the state-of-the-art intensive-care unit and the six-bed Dolly Parton Birthing Center has raised its level of available service to that of most metropolitan hospitals.

The current configuration includes an acute-care facility with more than 80 beds in private rooms, and an on-site 54-bed nursing home providing intermediate and skilled long-term care. Complete in- and outpatient surgical services are provided in more than a dozen specialties. Therapeutic services are available in long- and short-term programs, and support group contacts are usually on hand. As the hospital has continued to grow in a largely unsettled area of the county, it has had the added benefit of becoming the geographic center for the construction of several professional centers offering medical service in every conceivable fashion, with most of the specialists having hospital certification.

Fort Sanders Sevier Nursing Home
709 Middle Creek Road, Sevierville
(865) 429-6694
www.fssevier.com
Adjacent to and operated as a satellite service of the Fort Sanders Sevier Medical Center, the Fort Sanders nursing home

provides 24-hour nursing care and service to residents at ICF Level I and skilled Level II. Various activities (exercise classes, craft classes, special holiday programs) are available for ambulatory residents.

Sevier County Health Care Center
Beal Road, Sevierville
(865) 453-4747
Dedicated to more serious care of the aging and terminally ill, the Sevier County Health Care Center has 149 beds and is certified in all phases of treatment, rehabilitation, and hospice services.

Pigeon Forge

Royal Care of Pigeon Forge
415 Cole Drive, Pigeon Forge
(865) 428-5454
Royal Care specializes in rehabilitation services intended to return injured and incapacitated patients to mainstream living through inpatient and outpatient programs designed to meet the individual needs of the patient. Physician involvement is one of Royal Care's keys to developing and implementing individual programs to suit the needs of the individual patient.

WALK-IN CLINICS

Sevierville

Rocky Top Medical Clinic
1105 Oak Cluster Drive, Sevierville
(865) 908-3636
One of the newer entries on the local health-care scene, Healthstar is a regional organization of walk-in clinics. The only one in the Smokies Corridor is staffed by an MD and two PA-Cs (certified physician's assistants), with a sizable administrative staff. Rocky Top provides a full range of services, including diagnostic and urgent care, with the latest technology available. The clinic is open Monday through Friday from 8:00 A.M. to 5:00 P.M.,

and Saturday from 9:00 A.M. to 1:00 P.M. Most insurance plans are accommodated, and the clinic accepts MasterCard, Visa, and Discover cards.

Pigeon Forge

Pigeon Forge Medical Clinic
3342 Parkway, Pigeon Forge
(865) 453-1924
Right in the center of Pigeon Forge, this clinic is at traffic light #7. One MD is assisted by a nurse practitioner. Full X-ray and diagnostic services are available. Treatment is available up to simple fractures, and prescriptions can be filled at the drugstore next door. The Medical Clinic is an independent clinic, open Monday through Friday from 8:30 A.M. to 5:30 P.M. and Saturday from 9:00 A.M. to noon. Most insurance programs are accepted, as are MasterCard and Visa.

Gatlinburg

First Med Family Medical Clinic
1015 East Parkway, Gatlinburg
(865) 436-7267
Gatlinburg's original walk-in clinic, First Med is operated by an MD during the week and a PA-C on Saturday. This independent clinic is equipped for urgent care and diagnostic services but doesn't apply casts. First Med is open Monday through Friday from 9:00 A.M. to 3:00 P.M., and Saturday from 9:00 A.M. to noon. Some insurance plans are accepted, along with MasterCard, Visa, and Discover cards.

CHIROPRACTIC CLINICS

Sevierville

Ratcliff Chiropractic Clinic
826 Middle Creek Road, Sevierville
(865) 453-1390
www.ratcliffchiro.com

The Doctors Ratcliff (there are two of them) apply the techniques of spinal manipulation to promote healing and better general health through nonsurgical means. Specializing in personal and sports injuries, the Ratcliff Clinic is one of the area's oldest practices in continuous operation. The clinic is open Monday, Wednesday, and Friday from 8:00 A.M. to 6:00 P.M., and Tuesday and Thursday from 8:00 A.M. to 4:00 P.M. Most insurance programs that cover chiropractic care are accommodated. MasterCard, Visa, and Discover cards are also accepted.

MENTAL CARE
Sevierville

Peninsula Health Care
124 North Henderson Avenue, Sevierville
(865) 970-9800
www.covhealth.com
Peninsula provides crisis intervention services and long- and short-term counseling. For emergency services, call the hot line at (865) 539-2409.

SELF-HELP AND ADVOCACY GROUPS
Sevierville

Nicotine Anonymous Support Group
709 Middle Creek Road, Sevierville
(865) 429-9052

If your situation requires ongoing attention, like a chronic disease or respiratory care, the person who handles check-in at your lodging place can usually provide you with a telephone number for specialized care; if not, call the emergency services number at Fort Sanders Sevier Medical Center: (865) 453-7111.

Available to all comers who are trying to kick any form of nicotine habit, Nicotine Anonymous meets on the first Monday of every month at 6:30 P.M. in the Fort Sanders Sevier Medical Center conference room.

Overeaters Anonymous
709 Middle Creek Road, Sevierville
(865) 428-6109
For those with problems pushing away from the table, Overeaters Anonymous meets at 1:30 P.M. every Thursday in the Fort Sanders Sevier Medical Center conference room.

SafeSpace
Sevierville
(800) 244-5968
A quick-response service for battered women, SafeSpace provides shelter and support services for women in Sevier County regardless of residency status. Legal and court assistance are available when needed, along with round-the-clock counseling, referrals, and emotional support. A support group is available weekly for residents, and child care can be arranged.

Note: In addition to the help groups listed above, the *Mountain Press* runs a listing called HelpLine once a week that includes information on other groups. The HelpLine column appears every Thursday on the comics page and includes listings of several self-help and support organizations, complete with meeting times and places.

VETERINARY SERVICES

It's not unusual for visitors to the Smokies to bring pets with them, and why not? We're dealing with families here, and a lot of American families have furry, finny, and feathered members. If your animal friend gets a case of the punies during your vacation, here's a list of veterinary clinics that provide complete services, including boarding and overnight hospital care.

Sevierville

Mountain Home Veterinary Hospital
302 Middle Creek Road, Sevierville
(865) 453-9346

Parkway Animal Hospital
104 South Boulevard Way, Sevierville
(865) 428-0190

Sevier County Animal Clinic
803 Mize Lane, Sevierville
(865) 453-1221

Gatlinburg

Mountain Home Veterinary Clinic
1661 East Parkway, Gatlinburg
(865) 436-3350

SENIOR SCENE 🏠

rominent among the many unusual aspects of living in the Smokies is the size and character of the senior population. Our central location and temperate climate combine to draw a great many visitors who are looking for a place to spend their "golden days," and the natural charm of this place convinces a healthy percentage (no pun intended) of the visitors to make the Smokies their home when they retire. Where the definitive retirees in the Smokies part company with their contemporaries in other parts of the country is what happens when they move to East Tennessee.

First, they'd better be in good shape—"retirement" in the Smokies means a lot more than a rocking chair and an occasional stroll down to the shuffleboard courts. There are very few traditional "retirement communities" in the area right now. Additionally, most of the Smokies seniors have chosen this place after careful consideration, have probably purchased property or even a home well in advance of moving here, and usually intend to become part of the mainstream community when they move. Those who choose not to work or even start a new business career when they move to the Smokies are able to stay active by performing volunteer work at local chambers of commerce, visitor information services, hospitals, and the Great Smoky Mountains National Park. The role of the senior citizen in the Smokies is so firmly entrenched in the community at large that, abundant services notwithstanding, the older members of the Smokies' permanent population are simply regarded as neighbors, and that's about as dignified a status as one can aspire to here.

Naturally, a host of services and organizations provide assistance where it's needed, but the city and county governments have been slow to recognize their retirees as a "special needs" group because the people in question have been reluctant to accept that status. As the population grows exponentially, and the number of retirees seeking a more conventional refuge for their ultimate homes increases, more attention is being given to the elder population's needs.

The recent formation of a citizens task force to address the issue head-on is spurring new approaches to promoting the Smokies as a retirement haven. To that end, more conventional retirement agencies are popping up and promoting local interest in the retired population as an organized group. It is estimated that by 2005, municipal retirement services and facilities in the Smokies will be at parity with services offered in any community of 100,000 permanent population, assuming that the permanent population doesn't actually achieve that figure. Updates of this book will pay close attention to those developments, but it's tough at the moment to tell a "retired" citizen in the Smokies from any other until you get to know them well. Then you learn the biggest difference: The retirees in the Smokies are usually busier, healthier, and generally happier than their counterparts who still work for a living.

The following list of services and organizations will help steer the potential retiree toward the answers to questions they may have about relocating to the Smokies area, beginning with the only true assisted-living facilities in the county dedicated to retired citizens.

RETIREMENT HOMES AND VILLAGES

Assisted Living

Mountain Brook Village
700 Markhill Drive, Sevierville
(865) 428-2445

Secluded from the traffic on the Parkway a block away, Mountain Brook Village is a community unto itself. Single-story dwelling units are laid out along the middle prong of the Little Pigeon River across from Sevierville City Park, ensuring that commercial incursion won't disturb the residents in the foreseeable future. The Mountain Brook system provides whatever level of care is desired by its residents, from complete freedom to the highest level of assisted care in a nonmedical facility. The Mountain Brook residents are generally considered no different from any other residents of Sevierville, except that they're more active than most. Monthly rentals are available.

Wellington Place
1020 Middle Creek Road, Sevierville
(865) 774-2221

Convenient to Fort Sanders Sevier Medical Center, Wellington Place is a new assisted-living facility that offers its residents a full menu of options. The facility is far enough from any commercial district to consider itself "rural" at the moment, and on a big enough piece of land that privacy will be ensured when commercial spread reaches the area south of Dolly Parton Parkway. Wellington Place has 60 units in various configurations. On-site services are pro-

vided by professional staff and visiting specialists, ranging from special dietary programs to weekly haircuts. Medical and health monitoring services are available on-site, as are housekeeping and laundry services. Transportation can be arranged for trips into Sevierville for shopping or recreation. The beautifully landscaped grounds and communal facilities provide an active social atmosphere for Wellington Place's permanent residents, and the variety of available services make living easy for those unable to travel too far from home.

Independent Living

Douglas–Cherokee Economic Authority
534 East First North Street
Morristown
(423) 587-4500

The Douglas–Cherokee Economic Authority is the local umbrella organization for most of the federal agencies responsible for government assistance programs. Among a huge number of facilities and programs in its portfolio, Douglas–Cherokee operates two small apartment complexes in Sevierville that are reserved for people aged 62 years and up who meet the federal (HUD) guidelines to qualify for low-income housing. The units are single-family dwellings in single-story apartment-style buildings. Income-based rental rates include standard utilities—cable television and telephone service are available at the tenants' discretion. The housing authority provides part-time maintenance and administration services. Availability of units is practically nonexistent now and for the foreseeable future—there's a long waiting list at both sites. The Woodland Park site has land available for further development if money can be found to build more units.

Gateway Village Apartments
120 West Paine Street, Sevierville
(865) 453-1729

Contained within the Gateway complex of low-income and wheelchair-accessible housing are 16 dwelling units reserved for senior residents. The Gateway complex is next to Sevierville City Park on the east side of the downtown business district, in one of the city's oldest residential neighborhoods. The administrative office is open from 8:00 A.M. to noon Monday through Friday.

Woodland Park Apartments
202 Hardin Lane, Sevierville
(865) 429-6896
With 55 units in operation and more being prayed for, Woodland Park looks like any other suburban apartment complex. The single-story units are laid out on a gently curved road across the Little Pigeon River from the downtown shopping area. The administration building includes a community room where residents can get together for social functions. The office is open Monday through Friday from 12:30 to 4:30 P.M.

SENIOR INFORMATION AND ASSISTANCE

Sevier County Senior Citizens Center
1220 West Main, Sevierville
(865) 453-8080
A full slate of activities and directory services are available Monday through Saturday at the center, where activities and meals are provided to drop-in guests. Helpful services (shuttles, tax preparation, and more) are also available by appointment.

Senior Citizens Home Assistance Services
109 Parkway, Sevierville
(865) 453-6853
Government and commercial services available to homebound seniors are coordinated by this office in cooperation with the Senior Citizens Center and local hospitals.

E-Z Access
(865) 453-8080
Originally established as a transportation system for older people unable to drive, E-Z Access has become a dependable public transportation service with no restrictions on age or means. The E-Z Access van will pick up any caller, deliver

him to any destination within the county, and return him home for a flat fee of $6.00. The program is administered by the Sevier County Council on Aging.

Tel-A-Tend
(865) 453-6271
Tel-A-Tend is a computerized system that provides services such as daily monitoring and reminders to take medicine. It raises an alarm if the subscriber doesn't answer the telephone or doesn't respond properly. The service costs $10 per year (waived in most cases). Monies collected are used to offset the cost of additional telephone lines. Tel-A-Tend requires that the subscriber have a touch-tone telephone and touch-tone service on the line, and a friend, neighbor, or relative who will agree to check on any subscriber who doesn't answer a scheduled call. If the secondary number doesn't answer, Tel-A-Tend will automatically call the E-911 service and request that a police unit be sent to the residence.

PUBLICATIONS

The *Mountain Press* publishes a tabloid-size supplement on the 15th of each month that's dedicated to providing information for citizens 50 years of age or older. *Experienced Living* usually runs about 24 pages in length and is primarily a compilation of relevant articles gleaned from other sources. Features on prominent local seniors are indicative of the "normal" expectations of senior citizens in the area. Schedules throughout the paper note regular and irregular events of particular interest, and a listing of emergency

---

Most of the local real estate firms keep sets of special listings to accommodate retirees. If you're looking for a one-bedroom home or rental property for the special needs of a retired person, be sure to let the Realtor know your needs as quickly as possible.

and assistance hot line numbers is always included. Unfortunately, the only easy way to get a copy of *Experienced Living* is to buy the *Mountain Press* on the 15th of any month. A free copy can be requested by writing *Experienced Living* c/o the *Mountain Press,* P.O. Box 4810, Sevierville, TN 37864, or sending an e-mail request to editor@themountainpress.com.

ORGANIZATIONS

American Association of Retired Persons (AARP)
Senior Citizens Center
Old Knoxville Highway, Sevierville
(865) 453-8080
The Sevier County chapter of AARP meets at noon on the first Wednesday of each month at the Senior Citizens Center. Meetings usually include lunch and guest speakers.

Retired Citizens of Gatlinburg
Gatlinburg Community Center
Mills Park Road, Gatlinburg
(865) 436-4990
This large, energetic group meets on the first Monday of every month at 1:00 P.M. for a light luncheon and to plan the activities for the month ahead. These usually include several hikes, a few get-togethers for domestic interests like knitting and sewing, and a field trip to a concert or athletic event. They also have their own informal bowling league that meets for all-comers competition on the Community Center lanes every second and fourth Thursday at 1:00 P.M.

Sevier County Senior Citizens
Senior Citizens Center
Old Knoxville Highway, Sevierville
(865) 453-8080
The best way for seniors to meet new people in Sevier County is to attend one or two monthly meetings of the Sevier County Senior Citizens. They meet at noon on the third Tuesday of every month for a covered-dish luncheon aimed at welcoming newcomers, and they hold a special party on the fourth Friday at 11:30 A.M. to celebrate birthdays and wedding anniversaries. The covered-dish luncheon is followed by a musical performance by the Good Time Band. Special holiday parties are also held throughout the year.

Assistance Hot Lines

Local

Ambulance, Fire, and Police	911
Sevier County Ambulance Authority:	
Emergency	(865) 453-3200
Business Office	(865) 453-3248
Sevier County Office on Aging	(865) 453-8080

National

Alzheimer's Association	(800) 621-0379
Arthritis Foundation	(800) 283-7800
Elder Hot Line	(800) 677-1116
Parkinson's Educational Program	(800) 344-7872
Security Fraud	(800) 863-9117

WORSHIP

East Tennessee is smack in the center of that portion of middle America that's referred to as the "Bible Belt." Overwhelmingly Christian in orientation, most Sevier County natives continue to practice the old-time religion of their forebears. Meanwhile, non-native residents who couldn't bring themselves to accept the deep fundamental religious attitudes they found here have brought their own more liberal brands of faith with them. When you think about it, you can understand the depth of religion in a place like the Smokies—it's difficult to look at the grandeur of these surroundings and question the existence and the awesome power of a supreme being.

Because the original settlers took their religion seriously, the church was the major center of social life. Church services were the only social activity that operated on a dependable schedule, and the mountain people of the southern end of the county moved quickly to establish chapels instead of hiking 15 or 20 miles to Sevierville or Wear's Fort, usually carrying their shoes. (This was an interesting conceit found among mountain people: They carried their shoes to church and to school so they wouldn't get scuffed and worn out on the dusty, rocky roads, and so they'd look their best during services and classes. It's kind of ironic that one of the few vanities actually practiced by these people was to surrender the protection of their feet so the covering would look good.)

Mostly Presbyterian on arrival, the settlers took to the Baptist faith early on when they found that seminary-trained ministers of other faiths were not exactly standing in line to move to the mountains and work for livestock instead of a salary. In contrast, any member of a Baptist congregation who "felt the calling" could preach if he was approved by the local church board. The Baptist system of homegrown preachers ministering to their own flocks is still in widespread use in East Tennessee, and its effectiveness is proved by the fact that Sevier County alone has a separate Baptist church for about every 75 residents.

The Baptists had another advantage in the early days. They were more tolerant than their Presbyterian and Methodist brethren of some of the mystical practices that bordered on voodoo in the deeper recesses of the mountains, particularly those involving the occasional sacrifice of poultry. The Baptists reasoned that most of these practices were harmless, and nearly all of them were used for medicinal purposes.

As the population of the area grew more by emigration than reproduction, other Protestant faiths took hold. The county today is still more Baptist than anything else, but just about every Protestant denomination currently in practice has a home in the Smokies. Roman Catholicism, unlike the pioneer trends of its missionaries elsewhere in the world, was a latecomer to the scene. The first established Catholic church opened in 1950 in Gatlinburg as a chapel extension of a Maryville church, and St. Mary's Catholic Church was consecrated there in

To accommodate as many people as possible in as many ways as possible, there are religious services offered in some pretty unconventional places. Several motels have services in their meeting facilities, and some of the music theaters offer nondenominational services on Sunday morning. There are also services available at Ober Gatlinburg, Dollywood, and at several locations within the park. Check with your host or desk clerk for more options.

CLOSE-UP

If You Can't Make It to Church . . .

One of the problems most vacationers face during their stays in strange places is finding a place of worship that fits both their emotional needs and their schedules. Despite the fact that Sunday services may be part of their schedules at home, a lot of folks figure they'll take a break from their routines and give up church just this once and then find themselves in a wrestling match with their consciences. If the information in this chapter has failed to match your needs with your schedule, there's an alternative in the Smokies that attempts to add a little convenience to your vacation schedule and satisfy your spiritual needs at the same time.

Smoky Mountain Resort Ministries is an outreach program of the Southern Baptist Convention that conducts religious services in a host of unconventional venues. If your schedule for Sunday involves a trip to Dollywood, a day on the slopes at Ober Gatlinburg, watching the sunrise at Le Conte Lodge, or just about anything else that pre-

cludes visiting a local church, Smoky Mountain Resort Ministries probably has something convenient that will ease your spirit. And don't be put off by the Southern Baptist part—the services are more nondenominational than you'd expect to find in a Baptist tabernacle. The emphasis in the SMRM's programs is on Christianity before any other consideration, and it's not unusual to see local ministers of all faiths helping out at special services that don't conflict with their own schedules.

Operated by a small administrative staff and a huge group of volunteers, Smoky Mountain Resort Ministries has been directed by the husband-and-wife team of Bill and Cindy Black, an extremely attractive and enormously popular Gatlinburg couple, since the program's inception in 1981. And the program appears to be a private fountain of youth for them; several people who have known both of the Blacks since they came to Gatlinburg in 1976 swear they haven't aged a day since they got here.

1953. Forty years later, a second Catholic church was built in Pigeon Forge, and it reaches out to the migrant worker population by celebrating the Mass in Spanish at a special service every Sunday.

There are more than 40 churches of various Christian denominations within 3 miles of the Smokies Corridor, most of them on or in sight of the Parkway. Sevierville's two biggest churches (Baptist

and United Methodist) are on the Parkway just south of Dolly Parton Parkway.

The same is true of Pigeon Forge, where the biggest Baptist church is on the Parkway just north of traffic light #7, and the Methodist church is on River Road just south of the same light.

Gatlinburg has six churches of varying denominations (including Catholic and Church of Christ) in a 4-block area of His-

Both are avid outdoor types who stay in shape by hiking and skiing a lot (Bill worked as a part-time ski instructor at Ober Gatlinburg for a lot of years), and both have sufficient other interests to keep them highly visible in the local community. Bill is a board member and supervising minister for the popular ministry program in the national park, which provides Sunday church services in the campgrounds and visitor centers, and serves on several local boards concerned with environment, education, and the future of the area. Cindy is a favorite choice when several of the local craftspeople need temporary help in their shops, and she is also recognized as one of the finest cooks in East Tennessee. Her cookbook, *All My Favorites,* is a local and regional favorite. Like Bill, Cindy's an expert skier and enjoys hiking.

The Blacks and their program become particularly visible during the busy fall season. With all the crowds in the area taking up most of the available space, Smoky Mountain Resort Ministries gets stretched to the breaking point (they haven't broken yet) by a long string of demands. The Gatlinburg Craftsmen's Fairs in July and October depend on ministry volunteers to provide relief for hundreds of craftspeople, and every service group in town is looking for someone to conduct worship services at hotels, motels, theme parks, shopping malls, and special events. During this time Bill and Cindy Black seem to be everywhere at once, making sure everything is going as it should (it is), and that the needs of the people present are being met (they are). An ordained minister, Bill also conducts services when he can schedule them. Cindy makes herself constantly available for prayer meetings and counseling. This rare couple and the services they oversee with amazing grace and no apparent effort provide a lot of spiritual comfort to a lot of folks who will probably never see them or hear their names. Smoky Mountain Resort Ministries can be reached at (865) 436-4076 or contacted through their Web site at www.smrm.org.

toric Nature Trail (formerly Airport Road) and Reagan Drive near the center of town. In keeping with the character of the area, the churches all welcome visitors.

The following list of denominations by city may be helpful in planning your visit to a place of worship: Sevierville has the only congregations of Assembly of God, Church of Jesus Christ of Latter-day Saints, Jehovah's Witnesses, Pentecostal, and Seventh Day Adventist. Pigeon Forge has the county's only Christian Science Society center. Among the rest of the represented faiths, the following numbers apply:

Baptist—12 churches—1 in Sevierville, 2 in Pigeon Forge, 4 in Gatlinburg

Christian Church—1 each in Sevierville and Pigeon Forge

Church of Christ—1 each in Sevierville, Pigeon Forge, and Gatlinburg

Church of God—2 in Sevierville, 1 each in Pigeon Forge and Gatlinburg

Episcopal—2 in Sevierville, 1 in Gatlinburg

Lutheran—1 each in Sevierville, Pigeon Forge, and Gatlinburg

Presbyterian—2 in Sevierville, 1 in Gatlinburg

Roman Catholic—1 each in Pigeon Forge and Gatlinburg

Also, there's an **AME Zion Church** in Strawberry Plains, less than 10 miles west of Sevierville–Goodes Temple. AME Zion church is at 476 Old Dandridge Pike, (865) 933-8099.

Several non-Christian faiths are accommodated in Knoxville, about 30 miles west of Severville. These include:

Baha'i World Faith, (865) 687-0444

Knoxville Jewish Federation, (865) 693-5837

Muslim Community of Knoxville, (865) 637-8172

This list doesn't include anywhere near all the churches in Sevier County, nor does it mention several Christian denominations whose affiliations are not readily understood by the layman. It does attempt to provide enough of a choice that the visitor can find a house of worship that is close enough to the center of their beliefs to be sufficient while they're away from home.

The only non-Christian religious organization in Sevier County is a Hindu ashram in Sevierville. The local telephone directory Yellow Pages contain a complete list of churches by denomination, and the Friday edition of the *Mountain Press* has a full page listing the locations and worship services of every church that provides the information.

INDEX

ABOUT THE AUTHORS

Dick McHugh

When "the smoke" got in Dick McHugh's eyes during a vacation in 1974, most of it was blown there by his wife, Joan. So in August 1975 the McHugh family uprooted and headed south to the sleepy city of Gatlinburg.

The massive growth of the area in general, and in the cities of Gatlinburg and Pigeon Forge in particular during the 1980s, was significant enough to Dick that he started keeping track of developments in a journal in 1981. That journal formed the foundation for his contribution to this book.

When the children were grown, the McHughs closed their business and sought other niches. Joan expanded her prodigious talents into several handcraft disciplines, and Dick pursued his love of writing and worked as a bowling center manager, motel desk clerk, and custodian to keep bread on the table. It seems both McHughs will do whatever it takes to stay in their adopted home, but that's a story you'll hear from anybody who lives in the Smokies but wasn't born there. And don't look for them to wipe their eyes while they're talking; they know the smoke won't come out.

Mitch Moore

Mitch Moore lived his first 18 years in the flat, rural farmlands of northeast Arkansas.

The journey to East Tennessee and its curvaceous terrain was a gradual one. Mitch attended Vanderbilt University in Nashville, where he wrote for the student newspaper and was also heavily involved in the theater department, appearing in a number of productions. In 1984 he received a BA in political science but promptly returned to the stage, pursuing a career in stand-up comedy. He spent the following seven years as a professional comedian, touring the nation and sharing the bill with such performers as Tim Allen, Drew Carey, and Jeff Foxworthy.

Today Mitch is a freelance writer for several Smoky Mountain area tourism publications as well as the *Knoxville News Sentinel*. He is also working on his first novel. He lives with his wife, Jennifer, and their sons, Paul (16) and Ian (10).

HELP US KEEP THIS GUIDE UP TO DATE

Every effort has been made by the authors and editors to make this guide as accurate and useful as possible. However, many things can change after a guide is published—phone numbers change, facilities come under new management, etc.

We would love to hear from you concerning your experiences with this guide and how you feel it could be improved and be kept up to date. While we may not be able to respond to all comments and suggestions, we'll take them to heart and we'll also make certain to share them with the authors. Please send your comments and suggestions to the following address:

The Globe Pequot Press
Reader Response/Editorial Department
P. O. Box 480
Guilford, CT 06437

Or you may e-mail us at:

editorial@GlobePequot.com

Thanks for your input, and happy travels!